JOHN R. WALKER, DBA, CHA, FMP

McKibbon Professor of Hotel and Restaurant Management
and Fulbright Senior Specialist,
University of South Florida
Sarasota-Manatee

The Restaurant

FROM CONCEPT TO OPERATION

Seventh Edition

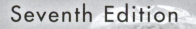

To Donald Lundberg, PhD,
my mentor, colleague, and friend.
Don was admired and respected
in the halls of academia
as a scholar and pioneer
of hospitality and tourism education.

And to you, the professors, students,
and future restaurant owners, wishing
you success and happiness.

Contents

Preface

I recently spoke with a former student, now the owner of a new independent restaurant venture in a large city full of delectable dining spots. This restaurant, over time, had established itself as a pillar of the community. This particular restaurateur had been in business for just over two years; and from day one, his seats were filled with eager and optimistic guests who had either heard the hype or already experienced the wonder this establishment was known to offer.

I asked him how he managed to continuously garner so much business in an area known for being a dining "mecca." Moreover, how had he managed to maintain relevance and peak interest in a city that both opens and closes more restaurants than anywhere else in the country? His response was simple, but it spoke wonders about what I have been trying to accomplish as a teacher and writer of restaurant books. He said: I went to school, I read your book, and I paid attention to the details.

Now in its *Seventh Edition, The Restaurant: From Concept to Operation* continues the success of previous editions, providing the skills and information needed to succeed in this highly competitive and rewarding industry.

The opportunity to be the leader of a highly efficient and enthusiastic team is appealing—the responsibility for the business rests on your shoulders. With *The Restaurant, Seventh Edition,* you will learn how to lead and empower a well-trained team to increase guest satisfaction, revenues, and return on investment. After all, isn't profit the goal? In today's competitive market, a well-thought-out concept and location are paramount to the success to the operation. Whether your concept is for a small town or large city, strip mall or free-standing operation, franchise or new concept, the basic rules outlined in *The Restaurant* will apply.

About This Book

FOR THE STUDENT

Opening a restaurant is a distinct challenge. It is also a thrill that gives one the opportunity for tremendous creative expression. Developing the menu, creating a new dish, designing the décor, attending to the level of service, and establishing an ambience—all of these factors contribute to exceeding guest expectations.

The Restaurant will help those who are interested in learning more about the restaurant industry. It will help students gain the knowledge they need to be successful in an easy-to-read style with several pedagogical features—such as sidebars, case studies, and profiles of successful restaurateurs—that impart the knowledge of experts for the benefit of students.

FOR THE INSTRUCTOR

The Restaurant is a comprehensive primer for restaurant management courses at the college and university level. It is used for a variety of restaurant courses and covers everything from the concept; types of ownership; types of restaurants; menus, planning, and equipping the kitchen; purchasing; bar and beverages; operations, budgeting and control; food production and sanitation; restaurant leadership and management; organization and staffing; training and development; service and guest relations; technology; business and marketing plans; financing and leasing; and legal and tax matters.

The Restaurant assumes no specific knowledge other than a general familiarity with restaurants. It can be used at any course level in a restaurant, hospitality, or culinary arts program. It is also suitable for seminars and continuing education courses.

Helping to meet continuing restaurant challenges is the oncoming wave of students who have studied culinary arts and restaurant management, and those who view the restaurant business as a career of choice. A restaurant can be fun to operate, and the profit margins can be substantial. It is interesting to learn that at least one billionaire, Tom Monaghan, made his fortune in the pizza business, and that dozens of millionaires have acquired fortunes in restaurants. Some of their stories are told in this book.

New To This Edition

For *The Restaurant, Seventh Edition,* revisions include:

- **New reorganization of the chapters:** This edition is condensed to 15 chapters, now better fitting a traditional semester schedule and consolidated for a more coherent read.
- **A Case Study has been added to each chapter:** These new case studies will help improve students' critical thinking skills. A shorter version of the Case Study is included at the end of each chapter, while an extended version is available on the Wiley Book Companion website (www.wiley.com/college/walker) for this new edition.
- **Information on pop-ups, food trucks, gluten-free cooking, and menu items** is now included
- Examples and discussions of **new restaurant concepts** and their founders are now included.
- **New sections on successful strategies in healthy eating, veganism, and vegetarianism,** and how they all relate to the restaurant business, are now included.
- **A new section on food allergy safety precautions** and properly training staff to handle allergy attacks is now included.
- An updated discussion on how it's easy being "green": The **themes of sustainability** and **sustainable restaurant management** have been updated throughout this new edition.
- An increased **focus toward the independent restaurateur** has been continued for this new edition.
- **An updated and extended section on purchasing meat** has been added to Chapter 6: Food Purchasing.
- **New sections** on **wine** have been added to Chapter 7: Bar and Beverages.
- **Additional emphasis on restaurant business plans, restaurant management, training,** and **restaurant operations** is included in this new edition.

Additionally, each chapter has been revised, updated, and enhanced with numerous industry examples, sidebars offering advice, charts, tables, and photographs. All these additions and changes enhance the contents, look, and usefulness of the book.

ORGANIZATION

The Restaurant, Seventh Edition is carefully structured for teaching and learning. Now consolidated into 15 chapters, *The Restaurant* is organized into five parts that take the reader step-by-step through the process of creating, opening, operating, and managing a restaurant:

Part One: Restaurants, Owners, Locations, and Concepts
Chapter 1. Introduction
Chapter 2. Restaurants and Their Owners
Chapter 3. Concept, Location, and Design

Part Two: Menus, Kitchens, and Purchasing
Chapter 4. The Menu
Chapter 5. Planning and Equipping the Kitchen
Chapter 6. Food Purchasing

Part Three: Restaurant Operations
Chapter 7. Bar and Beverages
Chapter 8. Operations, Budgeting, and Control
Chapter 9. Food Production and Sanitation

Part Four: Restaurant Management
Chapter 10. Restaurant Leadership and Management
Chapter 11. Organization, Recruiting, and Staffing
Chapter 12. Training, and Service
Chapter 13. Technology in the Restaurant Industry

Part Five: Business Plans, Financing, and Legal Matters
Chapter 14. Restaurant Business and Marketing Plans
Chapter 15. Financing and Leasing

LEARNING FEATURES

The writing in *The Restaurant, Seventh Edition,* is clear, engaging, and written in a conversational style using numerous industry examples for ease of understanding.

Following are pedagogical features found within each chapter:

- Clearly stated **Learning Objectives** help students and faculty monitor learning progress.
- Numerous **Industry Examples** are interspersed throughout to help students understand the topics and concepts being discussed.

- Interesting **Sidebars** engage students with highlighted facets of the restaurant industry.
- New **Photos** enliven the text, while updated **diagrams, flowcharts,** and **sample materials** provide examples and focal points for discussion.
- **Restaurant Profiles** are featured at the beginning of each of the five parts of the book. These profiles highlight a particular restaurant and detail all components of its organization.
- **Summary** sections are found at the end of each chapter, recapitulating the overall major points for students and instructors to reference.
- **Key Terms and Concepts** are highlighted in the text and described in the glossary. A list of these key terms is also provided at the end of every chapter.
- **Review Questions** help hone the students' skills and offer critical-thinking opportunities.
- A new **Case Study** feature with critical thinking questions has been added to each chapter.
- **Internet Exercises** provide opportunities to go beyond the book in search of information relating to each of the chapters. These exercises are available online on the Wiley Book Companion website (www.wiley.com/college/walker) for this edition.

Additional Resources

To aid students in retaining and mastering restaurant management concepts, there is a *Student Study Guide* (ISBN: 978-1-118-62960-4) that includes chapter objectives, chapter outlines, and practice quizzes with key term and concept review. Additionally, a comprehensive online *Instructor's Manual* with *Test Bank* accompanies this book and is available to instructors to help them effectively manage their time and to enhance student learning opportunities.

The *Test Bank* has been specifically formatted for *Respondus,* an easy-to-use software program for creating and managing exams that can be printed to paper or published directly to Blackboard, WebCT, Desire2Learn, eCollege, ANGEL, and other eLearning systems. Instructors who adopt this book can download the *Test Bank* for free.

A password-protected Wiley Instructor Book Companion website devoted entirely to this book (www.wiley.com/college/walker) provides access to the online *Instructor's Manual* and the text-specific teaching resources. The *Respondus Test Bank* and the *Lecture PowerPoints* are also available on the website for download.

John R. Walker, DBA, CHA, FMP
McKibbon Professor of Hotel and Restaurant Management
and Fulbright Senior Specialist,
University of South Florida Sarasota-Manatee

Acknowledgments

For their insightful suggestions on this and previous editions of the text, I thank James McManemon, University of South Florida Sarasota-Manatee, for his excellent work on the case studies; Joe Askren, University of South Florida Sarasota Manatee for his contribution to the menu chapter; Ed Norman, for his advice on the Planning and Equipping the Kitchen chapter; all the restaurants that allowed a case study to be written; all the restaurants that allowed photos to be used in the text; Ken Rubin, CPA; Dr. Cora Gatchalian, University of the Philippines; Volker Schmitz of California Cafe Restaurants; Dr. Jay Schrock of the University of South Florida; Dr. Greg Dunn of Metropolitan State University Denver and Dr. Katerina Annaraud of the University of South Florida Sarasota-Manatee; Karl Engstrom of Mesa College, San Diego; Brad Peters of Mesa College, San Diego; Dr. Andy Feinstein of California Polytechnic University, Pomona; Dr. Karl Titz, University of Houston; Anthony Battaglia, Glendale Community College; Dr. Paul G. VanLandingham, Johnson and Wales University; Dan Beard, Orange Coast College; Marco Adornetto, Muskingum Area Technical College; Thomas Rosenberger, College of Southern Nevada; C. Gus Katsigris, El Centro College; Karl V. Bins of the University of Maryland—Eastern Shore; Marcel R. Escoffier of Florida International University; H. G. Parsa of the University of Denver; and Chef John Bandman.

Thanks to the National Restaurant Association and to the restaurants that allowed me to include their menus or photos, and to these restaurant companies for their provision of resource information:

Burton M. Sack, Past President of the National Restaurant Association

Chris Sullivan

Bob Basham

Charlie Trotter

John Horne

Red Lobster Restaurants

Gary Harkness

T.G.I. Friday's

Stephen Ananicz

The Lettuce Entertain You Group

The Hard Rock Cafes

David Cohn and the Cohn Restaurant Group

Dick Rivera

Sean Murphy, The Beach Bistro

Jim Lynde, Senior Vice President People, Red Lobster

The Garcia Family

John C. Cini, President and CEO of Cini Little

U.S. Bank

The Childs Restaurant Group

Danny Meyer

Restaurant Magic

Outback Steakhouse, Inc.

Union Square Hospitality

NCR ALOHA Technologies

SYSCO Food Service

Aria Restaurant

B. Café

Niche

Panificio

21 Club

David Laxer, Bern's Restaurant

Richard Gonzmart, Columbia Restaurants

I am especially grateful to the reviewers of this text for their diligence and suggestions—the book is better because of your efforts.

Bill Burk, Mira Costa Community College

Elizabeth Dugan, The Art Institute of Pittsburgh, Online Division

Marcella Giannasio, Johnson & Wales University

Zaher "Zach" Hallab, California State University

Sotiris Hji-Avgoustis, Indiana Purdue University

And, finally, to the numerous restaurant operators who have graciously given their time and ideas, photographs, and menus, my sincere appreciation.

Restaurants, Owners, Locations, and Concepts

The Concept of B. Café

B. Café is a Belgian-themed bistro offering a wide variety of beer and a cuisine that is a Belgian and American fusion. B. Café has three owners, Skel Islamaj, John P. Rees, and Omer Ipek. Islamaj and Ipek are from Belgium, and Rees is American. The owners felt that there was a niche in New York for a restaurant with a Belgian theme. Out of all the restaurants in New York, only one or two offered this type of concept, and they were doing well. Since two of the owners grew up in Belgium, they were familiar and comfortable with both Belgian food and beer. Today B. Café offers over 25 Belgian brand beers, and the list is growing.

Courtesy of B. Café

LOCATION

B. Café is located on 75th Street in New York City. The owners looked for a location for two years before finding the right place. They came across the location after checking the area and finding a brand-new restaurant whose owner offered to sell. According to owner Islamaj, going with a building that held occupancy as a restaurant was "a good way to control cost." They did some renovations and adapted what already existed.

MENU

B. Café's third partner, John P. Rees (who is also the culinary director and executive chef) created the menu. The men wanted a menu that was a fusion of Belgian and American, but did not want to compromise their ethnic backgrounds. They created a menu with many options that was not too ethnic as to alienate people. By doing this they hoped to target the mainstream.

PERMITS AND LICENSES

The building where B. Café is located today was previously a restaurant. This made the obtaining of permits and licenses a bit easier than it would have been had the building not been a restaurant before. Some of the licenses were transferred over. The owners hired lawyers to obtain other permits and licenses needed to gain occupancy. B. Café is a limited liability corporation (LLC) with three owners. The owners of B. Café strongly recommend going with a preestablished site when opening a new restaurant.

MARKETING

The owners of B. Café were lucky to be well known in the food critic and journalism community. Their preopening marketing consisted of contacting old connections, which landed them an article in a newspaper. They recommend that anyone who is considering opening a restaurant should send out a one-time press release.

CHALLENGES

The first main challenge for the owners of B. Café was finding the right staff. They also found organizing vendors and purchasing products (such as their beer) in quantity to be challenging because when you first open, "you have to buy, buy, and buy" to be sure that you have enough, but you don't know what quantities you will need. You should also expect to go over budget. At minimum, you should take what your expected budget is and then add on 20 percent.

FINANCIAL INFORMATION

Annual sales at B. Café are expected to reach $1 million in the first year. They have about 540 guest covers a week. Guest checks average $38 per person. A breakdown of sales percentages follows.

- Percentage of sales that goes to rent: approximately 9 percent
- Percentage of food sales: 85 percent
- Percentage of beverage sales: 15 percent

- They cannot estimate their percentage of profit (it is 0 percent so far), as the Café opened three weeks prior to this interview.

WHAT TURNED OUT DIFFERENT FROM EXPECTED?

The sales the first week were as expected. Sales in the second week went down due to the holidays. This was not anticipated. Other than this, all went as planned.

MOST EMBARRASSING MOMENT

When I asked Skel Islamaj what his most embarrassing moment during opening was, he responded that on the day of opening, a customer ordered coffee. That is when "we realized that we forgot to order coffee!" There was none! All was okay though; a server went to a coffeehouse and purchased some to get them through.

ADVICE TO PROSPECTIVE ENTREPRENEURS FROM THE OWNERS OF B. CAFÉ

1. Understand the business before you get into it.
2. Location, location, location!
3. Believe in your business, never give up, and be persistent.

CHAPTER

1

Introduction

LEARNING OBJECTIVES

After reading and studying this chapter, you should be able to:

- Discuss reasons why some people open restaurants.

- List some challenges of restaurant operation.

- Outline the history of restaurants.

- Compare the advantages and disadvantages of buying, building, and franchising restaurants.

Courtesy of the Cohn Restaurant Group

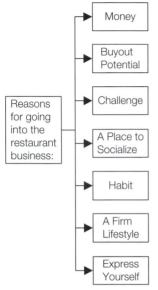

Money

Buyout Potential

Challenge

Reasons for going into the restaurant business:

A Place to Socialize

Habit

A Firm Lifestyle

Express Yourself

FIGURE 1.1 Reasons for going into the restaurant business.

Restaurants play a significant role in our lifestyles, and dining out is a popular social activity. Everyone needs to eat—so, to enjoy good food and perhaps wine in the company of friends and in pleasant surroundings is one of life's pleasures. Eating out has become a way of life for families. Today, more meals than ever are being eaten away from home.

The successful restaurant offers a reasonable return on investment. One restaurant, then two, then perhaps a small chain. Retire wealthy. To be a winner in today's economy requires considerable experience, planning, financial support, and energy. Luck also plays a part. This book takes you from day one—that time when you dream of a restaurant—through the opening and into operation. The kind of *restaurant concept* you select determines, to a large extent, the kind of talents required. Talent and temperament correlate with restaurant style. Managing a quick-service restaurant is quite different from being the proprietor of a luxury restaurant. Each choice makes its own demands and offers its own rewards to the operator.

This book shows the logical progression from dream to reality, from concept to finding a market gap to operating a restaurant. Along the way, it gives a comprehensive picture of the restaurant business.

Going into the restaurant business is not for the faint of heart. People contemplating opening a restaurant come from diverse backgrounds and bring with them a wealth of experience. However, there is no substitute for experience in the restaurant business—especially in the segment in which you are planning to operate.

So why go into the restaurant business? Here are some reasons others have done so, along with some of the liabilities involved. Figure 1.1 shows reasons for going into the restaurant business.

- *Money:* The restaurant is a potential money factory. According to the *National Restaurant Association (NRA)* the restaurant industry totals $632 billion in sales Successful restaurants can be highly profitable.[1] Even in a struggling economy the NRA predicts the restaurant-industry employs 12.9 million in 970,000 locations.[2] A restaurant with a million-dollar sales volume per year can generate $150,000 to $200,000 per year in profit before taxes. But a failing restaurant, one with a large investment and a large payroll, can lose thousands of dollars a month. Most restaurants are neither big winners nor big losers.
- *The potential for a buyout:* The successful restaurant owner is likely to be courted by a buyer. A number of large corporations have bought restaurants, especially small restaurant chains. The operator is often bought out for several million dollars, sometimes with the option of staying on as president of his or her own chain. The older independent owner can choose to sell out and retire.
- *A place to socialize:* The restaurant is a social exchange, satisfying the needs of people with a high need for socialization. Interaction is constant and varied. Personal relationships are a perpetual challenge. For many people there is too much social interplay, which can prove exhausting. On a typical day in America, more than 130 million individuals will be food service patrons.[3]
- *Love of a changing work environment:* A number of people go into the restaurant business simply because the work environment is always upbeat and

constantly changing. A workday or shift is never the same as the last. One day you're a manager and the next day you could be bartending, hosting, or serving. Are you bored of sitting behind a desk day after day? Then come and join us in the constantly evolving restaurant world!

- *Challenge:* Few businesses offer more challenge to the competitive person. There is always a new way to serve, new decor, a new dish, someone new to train, and new ways of marketing, promoting, and merchandising.
- *Habit:* Once someone has learned a particular skill or way of life, habit takes over. Habit, the great conditioner of life, tends to lock the person into a lifestyle. The young person learns to cook, feels comfortable doing so, enjoys the restaurant experience, and remains in the restaurant business without seriously considering other options.
- *A fun lifestyle:* People who are especially fond of food and drink may feel that the restaurant is "where it is," free for the taking, or at least available at reduced cost. Some are thrilled with food, its preparation, and its service and it can also be fun to be a continuous part of it.
- *Too much time on your hands:* A lot of people retire and decide to go into the business because they have too much time on their hands. Why a restaurant? Restaurants provide them with flexibility, social interaction, and fun!
- *Opportunity to express yourself:* Restaurant owners can be likened to theatrical producers. They write the script, cast the characters, devise the settings, and star in their own show. The show is acclaimed or fails according to the owner's talents and knowledge of the audience, the market at which the performance is aimed.

When restaurant owners were asked by the author and others what helped most "in getting where you are today," steady, hard work came out far ahead of any other factor. Next in line was "getting along with people." Then came the possession of a college degree. Close also was "being at the right place at the right time." Major concerns were low salaries, excessive stress, lack of room for advancement, and lack of long-term job security.

Opening and operating a restaurant takes dedication, high energy, ambition, persistence, and a few other ingredients discussed throughout this text. As Carl Karcher, founder of Carl's Jr., said, in America you can easily begin a restaurant as he did, on a cart outside Dodger Stadium selling hot dogs.

Early History of Eating Out[4]

Eating out has a long history. Taverns existed as early as 1700 B.C.E. The record of a public dining place in Ancient Egypt in 512 B.C.E. shows a limited menu— only one dish was served, consisting of cereal, wild fowl, and onion. Be that as it may, the ancient Egyptians had a fair selection of foods to choose from: peas, lentils, watermelons, artichokes, lettuce, endive, radishes, onions, garlic, leeks, fats (both vegetable and animal), beef, honey, dates, and dairy products, including milk, cheese, and butter.

The ancient Romans were great eaters out. Evidence can be seen even today in Herculaneum, a Roman town near Naples that in 70 A.D. was buried under some 65 feet of mud and lava by the eruption of Mt. Vesuvius.[5] Along its streets were a number of snack bars vending bread, cheese, wine, nuts, dates, figs, and hot foods. The counters were faced with marble fragments. Wine jugs were imbedded in them, kept fresh by the cold stone. Mulled and spiced wines were served, often sweetened with honey. A number of the snack bars were identical or nearly so giving the impression that they were part of a group under single ownership.

Bakeries were nearby, where grain was milled in the courtyard, the mill turned by blindfolded asses. Some bakeries specialized in cakes. One of them had 25 bronze baking pans of various sizes, from about 4 inches to about 1.5 feet in diameter.

After the fall of Rome, eating out usually took place in an inn or tavern, but by 1200 there were cooking houses in London, Paris, and elsewhere in Europe, where cooked food could be purchased but seating wasn't available. Medieval travelers dined at inns, taverns, hostelries, and monasteries.

The first café was established in then Constantinople in 1550. It was a coffeehouse, hence the word *café,* the French word for *coffee.*[6] (Both *café,* usually described as a small restaurant and bar, and *cafeteria,* find their roots here.) The coffeehouse, which appeared in Oxford in 1650 and seven years later in London, was a forerunner of the restaurant today. Coffee at the time was considered a cure-all. As one advertisement in 1657 had it: ". . . Coffee closes the orifices of the stomach, fortifies the heat within, and helpeth digesting. . . is good against eyesores, coughs, or colds* . . ." Lloyd's of London, the international insurance company, was founded as Lloyd's Coffee House. By the eighteenth century, there were about 3,000 coffeehouses in London. Coffeehouses were also popular in Colonial America. Boston had many of them, as did Virginia and New York.

In the eighteenth century, with the exception of inns that were primarily for travelers, food away from home could be purchased in places where alcoholic beverages were sold. Such places were equipped to serve simple, inexpensive dishes either cooked on the premises or ordered from a nearby inn or food shop. Tavern-restaurants existed in much of Europe, including France and Germany, which had Winestuben serving wine, *Delicatessen* (delicious food), sauerkraut, and cheese. In Spain bodegas served tapas. Greek taverns served various foods with olive oil.

French Culinary History

The first restaurant ever was called a "public dining room" and originated in France. Throughout history France has played a key role in the development of restaurants. The first restaurant that actually consisted of patrons sitting at a table and being served individual portions, which they selected from menus, was founded in 1782 by a man named Beauvilliers. It was called the Grand Taverne de Londres. However, this was not the beginning of the *restaurant concept.*

* http://restaurantmanagementandoperations.blogspot.com/2013/04/early-history-of-eating-out.html retrieved on April 30, 2013.

The first restaurant proprietor is believed to have been A. Boulanger, a soup vendor, who opened his business in Paris in 1765.[7] He sold soups at his all-night tavern on the Rue Bailleul. He called these soups *restorantes* (restoratives), which is the origin of the word *restaurant*. Boulanger believed that soup was the cure to all sorts of illnesses. However, he was not content to let his culinary repertoire rest with only a soup kitchen. By law at the time, only hotels could serve "food" (soup did not fit into this category). In 1767, he challenged the *traiteurs'* (hotel restaurateurs') monopoly and created a soup that consisted of sheeps' feet in a white sauce. The *traiteurs'* guild filed a lawsuit against Boulanger, and the case went before the French Parliament. Boulanger won the suit and soon opened his restaurant, Le Champ d'Oiseau.

In 1782, the Grand Tavern de Londres, a true restaurant, opened on the Rue de Richelieu; three years later, Aux Trois Frères Provençaux opened near the Palais-Royal. The French Revolution in 1794 literally caused heads to roll—so much so that the chefs to the former nobility suddenly had no work. Some stayed in France to open restaurants and some went to other parts of Europe; many crossed the Atlantic to America, especially to New Orleans.

Birth of Restaurants in America

The beginning of the American restaurant industry is usually said to be in 1634, when Samuel Coles opened an establishment in Boston that was named Coles Ordinary. It was a tavern—the first tavern of record in the American colonies. It was quite successful, lasting well over 125 years.[8]

Prior to the American Revolution, establishments selling food, beverages, and a place to sleep were called ordinaries, taverns, or inns. Rum and beer flowed freely. A favorite drink, called flip, was made from rum, beer, beaten eggs, and spices. The bartender plunged a hot iron with a ball on the end into the drink. Flips were considered both food and a drink. If customers had one too many flips, the ordinaries provided a place to sleep.

In America the innkeeper, unlike in Europe, was often the most respected member of the community and was certainly one of its substantial citizens. The innkeeper usually held some local elected office and sometimes rose much higher than that. John Adams, the second president of the United States, owned and managed his own tavern between 1783 and 1789.[9]

The oldest continually operating tavern in America is the Fraunces Tavern in New York City, dating from about 1762. It served as the Revolutionary headquarters of General George Washington, and was the place where he made his farewell address. It is still operating today.

The restaurant, as we know it today, is said to have been a byproduct of the French Revolution. The term *restaurant* came to the United States in 1794 via a French refugee from the guillotine, Jean-Baptiste Gilbert Paypalt. Paypalt set up what was likely the first French restaurant in this country, Julien's Restaurator, in Boston. There he served truffles, cheese fondues, and soups. The French influence on American cooking began early; both Washington and Jefferson were fond of French cuisine, and several French eating establishments were opened in Boston by Huguenots who fled France in the eighteenth century to escape religious persecution.

DELMONICO'S

Other early American restaurants include the Union Oyster House in Cambridge, Massachusetts, opened in 1826 by Atwood and Bacon and still operating,[10] and Delmonico's, located in New York City. Delmonico's opened its doors in 1827. The story of Delmonico's and its proprietors exemplifies much about family-operated restaurants in America. John Delmonico, the founder, was a Swiss sea captain who retired from ship life in 1825 and opened a tiny shop on the Battery in New York City. At first, he sold only French and Spanish wines, but in 1827 with his brother Peter, a confectioner, he opened an establishment that also served fancy cakes and ices that could be enjoyed on the spot. New Yorkers, apparently bored with plain food, approved of the *petits gateaux* (little cakes), chocolate, and bonbons served by the brothers Delmonico. Success led in 1832 to the opening of a restaurant on the building's second story, and brother Lorenzo joined the enterprise. Lorenzo proved to be the restaurant genius. New Yorkers were ready to change from a roast-and-boiled bill of fare to *la grande cuisine*—and Lorenzo was ready for New Yorkers.

A hard worker, the basic qualification for restaurant success, Lorenzo was up at 4:00 A.M. and on his way to the public markets. By 8:00 A.M. he appeared at the restaurant, drank a small cup of black coffee, and smoked the third or fourth of his daily 30 cigars. Then home to bed until the dinner hour, when he reappeared to direct the restaurant show. Guests were encouraged to be as profligate with food as they could afford. In the 1870s a yachtsman gave a banquet at Delmonico's that cost $400 a person, astronomical at the time.

Delmonico's pioneered the idea of printing a menu in both French and English. The menu was enormous—it offered 12 soups; 32 hors d'oeuvres; 28 different beef entrees, 46 of veal, 20 of mutton, 47 of poultry, 22 of game, 46 of fish, shellfish, turtle, and eels; 51 vegetable and egg dishes; 19 pastries and cakes; plus 28 additional desserts. Except for a few items temporarily unobtainable, any dish could be ordered at any time, and it would be served promptly, as a matter of routine. What restaurant today would or could offer 371 separate dishes to order?

Delmonico's expanded to four locations, each operated by one member of the family. Lorenzo did so well in handling large parties that he soon was called on to cater affairs all over town. Delmonico's was *the* restaurant. In 1881 Lorenzo died, leaving a $2 million estate. Charles, a nephew, took over, but in three years he suffered a

Courtesy of Delmonico's Restaurant
The famous Delmonico's Restaurant in New York City.

nervous breakdown, brought on, it was believed, by overindulgence in the stock market. Other members of the family stepped in and kept the good name of Delmonico's alive.

Delmonico's continued to prosper with new owners until the financial crash of 1987 forced it to close, and the magnificent old building sat boarded up for most of the 1990s. Delmonico's has since undergone renovations to restore the restaurant to its former brilliance. Restaurants bearing the Delmonico name once stood for what was best in the American French restaurant. Delmonico's served Swiss-French cuisine and was the focus of American gastronomy (the art of good eating). Delmonico's is also credited with the invention of the bilingual menu (until then French was the language of worldwide upscale restaurant menus, so diners could understand the menu in any part of the world and order their choice of dishes knowing what would be served), Baked Alaska, Chicken a la King, and Lobster Newberg. The Delmonico steak is named after the restaurant.

Few family restaurants last more than a generation. The Delmonico family was involved in nine restaurants from 1827 to 1923 (an early prohibition year), spanning four generations.[11] The family had gathered acclaim and fortune, but finally the drive for success and the talent for it were missing in the family line. As has happened with most family restaurants, the name and the restaurants faded into history. In the case of Delmonico's, however, the restaurant was resurrected due to its familiar name.

AMERICAN-STYLE RESTAURANTS

Although Delmonico's restaurant is to be admired for its subtlety, grace, and service, it will probably remain more of a novelty on the American scene than the norm. While it won the kudos of the day and was the scene of high-style entertaining, there were hundreds of more typical eating establishments transacting business. It has been so ever since. It should be pointed out that there is also an American style in restaurants; in fact, several American styles. There are coffee shops, quick-service restaurants, delis, cafeterias, family-style restaurants, casual dining restaurants, and dinner house restaurants, all now being copied around the world. They meet the taste, timetable, and pocketbook of the average American and increasingly that of others elsewhere.

The Americans used their special brand of ingenuity to create something for everyone. By 1848, a hierarchy of eating places existed in New York City. At the bottom was Sweeney's "sixpenny eating house" on Ann Street, whose proprietor, Daniel Sweeney, achieved the questionable fame as the father of the greasy spoon. Sweeney's less-than-appealing fare ("small plate sixpence, large plate shilling") was literally thrown or slid down a well-greased path to his hungry customers, who cared little for the social amenities of dining.[12] The next step up was Brown's, an establishment of little more gentility than Sweeney's, but boasting a bill of fare, with all the extras honestly marked off and priced in the margin.

In 1888, Katz's deli (a fancy word for sandwich shop) was opened by immigrants in the Lower East Side of New York City. Long before refrigeration, smoking, pickling, and other curing methods of prolonging the useful life of food had been perfected. The Lower East Side was teeming with millions of newly emigrated families and, given the lack of public and private transportation, a solid community of customers was readily available. Katz's reputation for serving the flavors of the Old World created a loyal following for many generations of residents and visitors to New York.[13]

More and more, eating places in the United States and abroad catered to the residents of a town or city and less to travelers. The custom of eating out for its own sake had arrived. Major cities all had hotels with fine restaurants that attracted the rich and famous.

The nineteenth century also saw the birth of the ice cream soda, and marble-topped soda fountains began to make their appearances in so-called ice cream parlors. This century brought about enormous changes in travel and eating habits. Tastes were refined and expanded in the twentieth century and it is interesting to note that 35 restaurants in New York City have celebrated their one-hundredth birthdays. One of them, P.J. Clark's, established in 1890, is a real restaurant-bar that has changed little in its hundred years of operation. On entering, one sees a large mahogany bar, its mirror tarnished by time, the original tin ceiling, and a tile mosaic floor. Memorabilia ranges from celebrity pictures to Jessie, the house fox terrier that guests had stuffed when she died and who now stands guard over the ladies' room door. Guests still write their own guest checks at lunchtime, on pads with their table number on them (this goes back to the days when some servers could not read or write and were struggling to memorize orders).[14]

The public restaurant business grew steadily, but even as late as 1919 there were still only 42,600 restaurants in this country. For the average family in small cities and towns, dining out was an occasion. The workman's restaurant was strictly meat and potatoes. In 1919, the Volstead Act prohibited the sale of alcoholic beverages and forced out of business many restaurants that depended on their liquor sales for profit. It also forced a new emphasis on food-cost control and accounting.

In 1921, Walter Anderson and Billy Ingram began the White Castle hamburger chain. The name White Castle was selected because white stood for purity and castle for strength. The eye-catching restaurants were nothing more than stucco building shells, a griddle, and a few chairs. People came in droves, and within 10 years White Castle had expanded to 115 units.[15]

Marriott's Hot Shoppe and root beer stand opened in 1927. About this time, the drive-in roadside and fast-food restaurants also began springing up across America. The expression *carhop* was coined because as an order-taker approached an automobile, he or she would hop onto the running board. The drive-in became an established part of Americana and a gathering place of the times. In 1925, another symbol of American eateries, Howard Johnson's original restaurant, opened in Wollaston, Massachusetts. Howard Johnson is credited with being the first restaurant to franchise. His first store was an ice cream parlor. In 1928, he had convinced a friend to build a restaurant and sell Howard Johnson's ice cream. Johnson's profit came from selling Howard Johnson's ice cream to the restaurant. By 1939 there were 107 Howard Johnson's restaurants operating in six states.

After the stock market crash of 1929 and the Great Depression, America rebounded with the elegance and deluxe dining of the 1930s à la Fred Astaire. The Rainbow Room opened in 1934. This art deco restaurant championed the reemergence of New York as a center of power and glamour.

Trader Vic's opened in 1937. Although the idea was borrowed from another restaurant known as the Beachcomber, Trader Vic's became successful by drawing the social elite to the Polynesian-themed restaurant where Vic concocted exotic cocktails including the mai-tai, which he invented.[16]

At the World's Fair in 1939, a restaurant called Le Pavillon de France was so successful that it later opened a nightclub in New York. By the end of the 1930s, every city had a deluxe supper club or nightclub.

The Four Seasons opened in 1959. The Four Seasons was the first elegant American restaurant that was not French in style. It expressed the total experience of dining, and everything from the scale of the space to the tabletop accessories was in harmony.[17] The Four Seasons was the first restaurant to offer seasonal menus—spring, summer, fall, and winter, with its modern architecture and art as a part of the theme. Joe Baum, the developer of this restaurant, understood why people go to restaurants—to be together and to connect with one another. It is very important that the restaurant reinforce why guests choose it in the first place. Restaurants exist to create pleasure, and how well a restaurant meets this expectation of pleasure is a measure of its success.[18]

RESPONSES TO CHANGING TIMES

The savvy restaurateur is adaptable. Being quick to respond to changing market conditions has always been the key to success in the restaurant business. An interesting example of this was demonstrated in the early 1900s by the operator of Delmonico's. As business declined during a recession in the 1930s, Delmonico's opened for breakfast, then began delivering breakfast, lunch, dinner, and other fare to Wall Street firms for late-evening meetings. Next, Delmonico turned his attention to the weekends when Wall Street was quiet. He built up a weekend catering business and developed a specialty of weddings. Later he connected with tour groups going to Ellis Island and encouraged them to stop off for meals.[19]

World War II was the watershed period that made eating away from home a habit to be enjoyed by millions of people and thought of as a necessity by other millions. Since World War II, a number of social and economic trends have favored the restaurant business. The most important has been the rise in family income, the principal source of which has been the working woman. The more disposable income available, the greater the likelihood of eating out. Lifestyle changes have also been important for restaurant sales. Millions at work or traveling eat away from home at restaurants out of necessity, forgoing a "brown bag." Despite economic cycles, many people perceive restaurant eating to be something deserved or even a different kind of necessity. The tremendous increase in divorce and the number of singles living alone, coupled with smaller living quarters, favors dining out as an escape.[20]

FAST-FOOD RESTAURANTS

Following World War II, North America took to the road. There was a rapid development of hotels and coffee shops. They sprang up at almost every highway intersection. The 1950s saw the emergence of a new phenomenon—*fast food*.[21] Perhaps one of the most colorful of the franchise stories involves the originator of Kentucky Fried

Chicken, "Colonel" Harland Sanders. He had been a farmhand, carriage painter, soldier, railroad fireman, blacksmith, streetcar conductor, justice of the peace, salesman, and service station operator. At the age of 65, he found himself operating his own Kentucky restaurant/motel with little business because a new interstate highway bypassed it by 7 miles. His only income was a social security check of $105 per month.[22] He had previously experimented with frying chicken in his restaurant and found that preparing it in a home-sized pressure cooker produced an especially tender product in seven minutes. He set off on a trip around the country to sell restaurant operators a franchise to produce and sell what he now called Kentucky Fried Chicken (KFC). He often slept in the back of his old car wrapped up in a blanket because he could not afford a motel room. Since it was a promotion package and procedure only for cooking chicken, the franchise could be used in an existing restaurant. The initial investment was low, only enough to buy a few needed pieces of cooking equipment. The franchisee would pay the Colonel 5 cents for every order served.[23] The Colonel's thoughts on marketing: "If you have something good, a certain number of people will beat a path to your doorstep; the rest you have to go and get."[24] A $5,000 investment in KFC in 1964 was worth $3.5 million five years later.

Of all the hospitality entrepreneurs, none have been more financially successful than Ray Kroc. Among the remarkable things about him was that it was not until the age of 52 that he even embarked on the road to fame and fortune. The accomplishment is all the more astounding because Kroc invented nothing new. In fact, the concept was leased from two brothers who had set up an octagonal-shaped, fast-food "hamburgatorium" in San Bernadino, California. Kroc was impressed with the property's golden arches, the McDonald's sign lighting up the sky at night, and the cleanliness and simplicity of the operation. Even more fascinating was the long waiting line of customers.[25]

Kroc's genius came in the way of organizational ability, perseverance sparked with enthusiasm, and an incredible talent for marketing. His talents extended to selecting equally dedicated close associates who added financial, analytical, and managerial skills to the enterprise. The McDonald's Corporation is the projected image of one man, entrepreneur par excellence, who believed with a passion that business means competition, dedication, and drive. The empire was built in good part as a result of his arch-competitiveness, best illustrated by his reply to this question: "Is the restaurant business a dog-eat-dog business?" His reply: "No, it's a rat-eat-rat business."

The 1960s and 1970s saw the introduction of new establishments like Taco Bell, Steak and Ale, T.G.I. Friday's (now Friday's) Houston's, Red Lobster, and others. Several new chains have emerged and are discussed in the subsequent chapters from time to time, and the "indy" (independent) restaurateur is also discussed throughout the text.

Challenges of Restaurant Operation

Long working hours are the norm in restaurants. Some people like this; others get burned out. Excessive fatigue can lead to general health problems and susceptibility to viral infections, such as colds and mononucleosis. Many restaurant operators have to work 50 hours or longer per week, too long for many people to operate effectively. Long hours mean a lack of quality time with family, particularly when children are young and of school age. Restaurant owners have little time for thinking—an activity required to make the enterprise grow.

In working for others, managers have little job security. A shift of owners, for example, can mean discharge. Although restaurant owners can work as long as the restaurant is successful, they often put in so many hours that they begin to feel incarcerated. Family life can suffer. The divorce rate is high among restaurant managers for several reasons. Stress comes from both the long hours of work and the many variables presented by the restaurant, some beyond a manager's control.

One big challenge for owners is the possibility of losing their investment and that of other investors, who may be friends or relatives. Too often, a restaurant failure endangers a family's financial security because collateral, such as a home, is also lost. Potential restaurateurs must consider whether their personality, temperament, and abilities fit the restaurant business. They must also factor the economy into the equation. New restaurants are always opening, even in a failing economy. New restaurant owners can count on the fact that, even in a bad economy, people still have to eat, even if they go out less often and spend less when they do.[26]

Consumers are carefully watching how they spend their hard-earned money, and restaurant dining is a part of discretionary income, meaning people will spend first on essentials and then on niceties like dining out. They may trade down and dine at quick-service or casual restaurants instead of using fine-dining restaurants. Even grocery stores are going head to head with restaurants, trying to lure budget-conscious and time-starved consumers away from eateries toward a variety of prepared foods.[27]

Christopher Muller, a restaurant professor at the Rosen College of Hospitality Management, says that it would not surprise him if around 10 percent of restaurants closed in this the most challenging times for restaurants in decades.[28]

A few years ago, the well-known and highly successful football coach Vince Lombardi described the perfect football player as "agile, mobile, and hostile." In a restaurant context, he or she is someone who enjoys serving people, can handle frustration easily, and is tireless. Lacking one or more of these traits, the would-be restaurant operator can consider a restaurant as an investor only and find someone else to operate the restaurant.

Operating a restaurant demands lots of energy and stamina. Successful restaurant operators almost always are energetic, persevering, and able to withstand pressure. Recruiters for chain restaurants look for the ambitious, outgoing person with a record of hard work. The trainee normally works no fewer than 10 hours a day, five days a week. Weekends, holidays, and evenings are usually the busiest periods, with weekends sometimes accounting for 40 percent or more of sales. The restaurant business is no place for those who want weekends off.

Knowledge of food is highly desirable—a must in a dinner house, of less importance in fast food. Business skills, especially cost controls and marketing, are also necessities in all foodservice businesses. Plenty of skilled chefs have gone broke without them. A personality restaurant needs a personality; if the personality leaves, then the restaurant changes character.

Whatever the true rate of business failure, it is clear that starting a restaurant involves high risk, but risks must be taken in order to achieve success. Restaurants may require a year or two, or longer, to become profitable and need capital or credit to survive. A landmark study by Dr. H. G. Parsa found the actual failure rate of restaurants in Columbus, Ohio, was 59 percent for a three-year period. The highest failure rate was during the first year, when 26 percent of the restaurants failed. In the second year, 19 percent failed, and in the third year, the failure rate dropped to only 14 percent.

Dr. Parsa's study is valid because it used data from the health department in determining when the restaurants opened; some studies obtain their data from other sources, including the Yellow Pages. Parsa adds that many restaurants close not because they did not succeed financially, but because of personal reasons involving the owner or owners.[29] If a restaurant survives for three years, its chances of continued operation are high. This suggests that in buying a restaurant, you should choose one that is more than three years old.

One reason family-owned restaurants survive the start-up period is that children and members of the extended family can pitch in when needed and work at low cost. Presumably, also, there is less danger of theft by family members than from employees who are not well known. Chain restaurant owners reduce the risk of start-up by calling on experienced and trusted personnel from existing units in the chain. Even restaurants started by families or chains, however, cannot be certain of a sufficient and sustainable market for success. When a new restaurant opens in a given area, it must share the market with existing restaurants unless the population or the per-capita income of the area is increasing fast enough to support it.

Many restaurants fail because of family problems. Too many hours are spent in the restaurant, and so much energy is exerted that there is none left for a balanced family life. These factors often cause dissatisfaction for the spouse and, eventually, divorce. In states such as California, where being married means having communal property, the divorce settlement can divide the couple's assets. If a divorcing spouse has no interest in the restaurant but demands half of the assets, a judgment of the cost can force a sale of the operation.

When a husband and wife operate a restaurant as a team, both must enjoy the business and be highly motivated to make it successful. These traits should be determined before the final decision is made to finance and enter the business.

Buy, Build, Franchise, or Manage?

A person considering the restaurant business has several career and investment options:

- To buy an existing restaurant, operate it as is, or change its concept
- To build a new restaurant and operate it
- To purchase a *franchise* and operate the franchise restaurant
- To manage a restaurant for someone else, either an individual or a chain

In comparing the advantages and disadvantages of buying, building, franchising, and working as a professional manager, individuals should assess their own temperament, ambitions, and ability to cope with frustrations as well as the different risks and potential rewards. On one hand, buying a restaurant may satisfy an aesthetic personal desire. If the restaurant is a success, the rewards can be high.

If it fails, the financial loss is also high, but usually not as high as it would have been if the investment were made in a new building. When buying an existing restaurant that has failed or is for sale for some other reason, the purchaser has information that a builder lacks. The buyer may know that the previous style of restaurant was not successful in that location or that a certain menu or style of management was unsuccessful. Such information cuts risks somewhat. On the other hand, the buyer may find it difficult to overcome a poor reputation acquired by the previous operator over a period of time. There are no quick fixes in overcoming a poor reputation or a poor location, but clearly, knowledge of these circumstances decreases risk. Figure 1.2 illustrates the restaurant career and investment options.

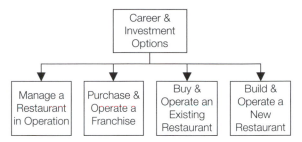

FIGURE 1.2 Restaurant career and investment options.

Without experience, the would-be restaurateur who builds from scratch is taking a great risk. Million-dollar investments in restaurants are fairly common. Finding investors who are ready to join in does not reduce that risk.

A 100-seat restaurant, fully equipped, costs anywhere from $6,000 to $10,000 or more per seat, or $600,000 to $1 million. In addition, a site must be bought or leased. Examples can be given of inexperienced people who have gone into the business, built a restaurant, and been successful from day one. Unfortunately, more examples can be given of those who have failed.

By contrast, a sandwich shop can usually be opened for less than $30,000. As one entrepreneur put it, "All you really need is a refrigerator, a microwave oven, and a sharp knife."

Franchising involves the least financial risk in that the restaurant format, including building design, menu, and marketing plans, already has been tested in the marketplace. Some franchises require less than $10,000 to start, including the franchise fee and other operational expenses.[30] Even so, franchises can and have failed.

The last option—being a professional manager working for an owner—involves the least financial risk. The psychological cost of failure, however, can be high.

Luckily, no one has to make all of the decisions in the abstract. Successful existing restaurants can be analyzed. Be a discriminating copycat. The advantages and disadvantages of the buy, build, franchise, or manage decision are shown in Figure 1.3.

	Original Investment Needed	Experience Needed	Potential Personal Stress	Psychological Cost of Failure	Financial Risk	Potential Reward
Buy	Medium	High	High	High	High	High
Build	Highest	High	High	Highest	Highest	High
Franchise (A) Ex. Subway	Low to medium	Low	Medium	Medium	Medium	Medium to high
Franchise (B) Ex. Applebee's	High	High	High	High	High	High
Manage	None	Medium to high	Medium	Medium	None	Medium

FIGURE 1.3 Buy, build, franchise, or manage—advantages and disadvantages.

Borrow the good points and practices; modify and improve them if possible. It is doubtful that any restaurant cannot be improved. Some of the most successful restaurants are surprisingly weak in certain areas. One of the best-known fast-food chains has mediocre coffee; another offers pie with a tough crust; yet another typically overcooks the vegetables. Still another highly successful chain could improve a number of its items by preparing them on the premises.

The restaurant business is a mixed bag of variables. The successful mix is the one that is better than the competition's. Few restaurants handle all variables well. Michelin has been in the business of evaluating and recommending restaurants and hotels for over a century.[31] For restaurants, Michelin stars are based on five criteria: quality of the products, mastery of flavor and cooking, "personality" of the cuisine, value for the money, and consistency between visits.[32] In all of France, only 18 to 20 restaurants are granted the Michelin three-star rating. In the United States, hundreds of restaurants do what they were conceived to do and do it well—serve a particular market, meeting that market's needs at a price acceptable to that market but they do not earn a Michelin three-star rating.

The person planning a new dinner house should know that even huge companies like General Mills can make big mistakes. Once owner of two profitable dinner house chains, Olive Garden and Red Lobster, General Mills bombed with Chinese, steak, and health-food restaurants.

The small operator lacks the purchasing power of the chain, which can save as much as 10 percent on food costs through mass purchasing. The new operator is usually unsophisticated in forecasting. Compare this with Red Lobster's system, which provides the manager with the number of each menu item to be prepared the next day. Each night, the manager uses a computer file on sales records to forecast the next day's sales. Based on what was served on the same day in the previous week and on the same day in the previous year, sales dollars for each menu item are forecast for the next day. Frozen items can be defrosted and preprepped items produced to meet the forecast. Wholesale purchasing and mass processing give the chain an additional advantage. The Red Lobster chain processes most of its shrimp in St. Petersburg, Florida. The shrimp are peeled, deveined, cooked, quick-frozen, and packaged for shipping daily to Red Lobster restaurants. Swordfish and other fish are sent to several warehouses, where they are inspected and flown fresh to wherever they are needed.

Quality control is critical; all managers should carry thermometers in their shirt pockets so they can check at any time that food is served at exactly the correct temperature. For example, clam chowder must be at least 150°F when served; coffee must be at least 170°F; and salads at 40°F or lower. Swordfish is grilled no more than four or

Courtesy of Sean Murphy
The Beach Bistro, Anna Maria Island, Sean Murphy's award-winning restaurant.

five minutes on a side with the grill set at 450°F. A 1-pound lobster is steamed for 10 minutes. In chains, illustrated diagrams tell cooks where to place a set number of parsley sprigs on the plate.

Individual operators can institute similar serving-temperature and cooking controls. They may be able to do a better job of plate presentation than chain unit managers can. Independent operators can develop a personal following and appeal to a niche market among customers who are bored with chain operators and menus. This puts individual owners at an advantage over chain competitors. Being on the job and having a distinct personality can really make the difference.

Courtesy of the San Diego Convention & Visitors Bureau
Dining at the popular La Jolla restaurant in California.

The restaurant business has both the element of production (food preparation) and of delivery (takeout). Food is a unique product because in order to experience the exact taste again, the customer must return to the same restaurant. The atmosphere is important to the patrons. Some would argue that restaurants are in the business of providing memorable experiences.

Starting from Scratch

Occasionally, a faculty colleague from another discipline (usually arts and sciences) says that he or she is thinking of opening up a restaurant and do I have any advice. My reply is: "Let me bring a few of my friends over to your house for dinner for the next month, and then after that we'll talk about it." So far, no takers. Joking apart, doing all it takes to prepare 100's of meals night in and night out is very different from having a few friends over for dinner because, for one thing, there are multiple choices on the menu.

Would-be restaurant operators may have already worked in their family's restaurant, perhaps starting at an early age. Hundreds of thousands of aspiring restaurant operators have tasted the restaurant business as employees of quick-service restaurants. For others, their first food business experience was in one of the 740 cooking school programs offered in vocational school or community college programs or at cooking institutes. Yet the industry still does not have nearly enough employees, and the turnover rate is high. The tens of thousands of young people who work in restaurants know that, but also welcome the experience and enjoy working with other young people who never consider the job as a career. One message comes through loud and clear: The restaurant business is highly competitive and requires inordinate energy, the ability to work long hours, and the willingness to accept a low salary. According to the National Restaurant Association, the restaurant industry is expected to add 1.3 million jobs by 2020, for total employment of 14.1 million in 2019.[33]

Following the European tradition, students who wish to become known as master chefs often seek jobs at the name restaurants in big cities. Many go abroad for the same reason, building their skills and rounding out personal resumes.

Restaurants as Roads to Riches

Probably the biggest reason thousands of people seek restaurant ownership is the possible financial rewards. With relatively few financial assets, it is possible to buy or lease a restaurant or to purchase a franchise. Names like Ray Kroc of McDonald's, Colonel Sanders of KFC, and Dave Thomas of Wendy's exemplify the potential success one can experience in the restaurant business.

Dozens of McDonald's franchise holders are multimillionaires, yet some McDonald's restaurants fail. Some owners and franchisees of KFC stores are also wealthy. A surprise billionaire is Tom Monaghan, the Domino's Pizza entrepreneur. Hundreds of lesser-known people are also making it big, some by building or buying restaurants, others by becoming franchisees.

Declining consumer confidence took a bite out of restaurants' sales and profits in 2007–2012, leading to bankruptcy filings at casual dining chains like Bennigan's and the closure of more than 600 Starbucks locations.[34] With the economy still struggling, all segments of the restaurant industry are feeling the effects. Consider all the effects of a weak economy. While prices of food and energy costs (heating, lighting, kitchen equipment, etc.) go up, sales slow down.

Here are some of the things this book will help you with:

■ *Ownership:* Sole proprietorship, partnership, company, or franchise.
■ *Development of a business plan:* A good business plan may take a while to develop, but you're not going to obtain financing without one.
■ *Marketing/sales:* You need to know who your guests will be and how many there are of them.
■ *Location:* Will your location be freestanding, in a mall or a city center, suburban, or something else?
■ *Who is on your team?* Your chef and staff, lawyer, accountant, insurance, sales, marketing, and public relations.
■ *Design/Ambience:* What design/ambience will you select?
■ *Menu:* What will your menu feature? How many appetizers, entrées, and desserts will you offer?
■ *Beverages:* Who will develop your beverage menu, and what will be on it?
■ *Legal:* What permits do you need?
■ *Budgets:* What will your budget look like?
■ *Control:* What kind of control system will you have, and how will it work?
■ *Service:* What style of service will you select, and how will it operate?
■ *Management:* How will your restaurant operate?
■ *Operations:* An overview of restaurant operations.

Global Issues

Many of the world's top restaurants have similar concerns and overall goals in regards to competing in today's hospitality industry:

- Innovative menu concept
- Successful marketing (price and promotion strategies)
- Site selection
- Remodeling/capital investments

Creating a unique menu that is noticed and appreciated by their guests is probably at the top of the list. Menu innovation needs to be ongoing in order to keep up with today's demanding diner. The restaurateur has realized that matching their culinary capabilities with their guest's greatest desires is the key to a successful menu. The successful restaurateur will have a menu that also supports their overall theme.

Just as hotels depend on a successful marketing department, so should today's restaurants. After the perfect product is created, the restaurant will need to decide on an overall pricing structure that is accepted by the customer. Finding unique ways to promote the restaurant has also changed drastically over the past decade. Restaurants are getting away from expensive advertising that mass market their business and are using more focused forms of promotion such as social media and public relations. Using social media gives the restaurant the ability to target specific groups of guests that may have certain noticeable buying behaviors. A public relations initiative, which can also be combined with the social media tool, has the powerful third party endorsement characteristic that positively affects the guest response. Even corporate chain restaurants are finding that getting in touch with the local community can be very powerful and often times more effective than expensive advertising.

Site selection, remodeling, and capital expenditures are also some global concerns that restaurants have. Today's technology has shrunk the playing field for most businesses. Corporate restaurants understand that continuous growth is important. However, trying to predict the success of future sites can be challenging. Many companies have found that conducting marketing tests and profitability studies will help answer the many questions when making these decisions. Outside consulting groups are available for tests and studies such as these. Optimizing their investments in remodeling and capital expenditures is the ultimate goal. For example, after remodeling, the restaurateur will expect their location to increase menu prices and/or capture more guests in the long-term.

Summary

The purpose of this book is to take the would-be restaurateur through the steps necessary to open a successful restaurant. Sitting in a busy restaurant can be a fascinating experience. Food servers move deftly up and down aisles and around booths, guests are greeted and seated, orders are placed and picked up, the cashier handles a steady stream of people paying their bills and leaving. The flow of customers, the warm colors, and the lighting create a feeling of comfort and style.

The fascinating history of eating out and the birth of restaurants in America is discussed with examples from leading restaurants and operators.

Food servers are usually young, enthusiastic, and happy; the broiler cooks tend to their grilling and sandwich making with a fierce concentration. Food orders are slipped onto a revolving spindle to be taken in succession or pop up on the electronic printer in the kitchen; the orders are prepared, plated, and placed on the pickup counter. A silent buzzer informs the food server that an order is ready. The entire operation could be likened to a basketball team in action, a ballet of movement.

Among the players, the restaurant personnel, the emotional level is high. This ensures that each player performs his or her assigned role, one player's actions meshing with those of the other players. The observer may perceive an elaborate choreography paced to the desires of the customer; the restaurant is orchestrated and led by a conductor, the floor manager. How intricate, how complex, how exciting, how pleasurable—perhaps.

When the characters are in their places, know their assigned roles, and perform with enthusiasm, the restaurant operates smoothly and efficiently. To keep it that way means attention to detail and to the product, its preparation, its service; the personnel, their training and morale; cooking equipment, its maintenance and proper use; cleanliness of people, the place—and don't forget the toilets. A hundred things can go wrong, any one of which can break the spell of a satisfying restaurant experience for the guest.

Few jobs have the degree of staff turnover found in a restaurant. Few jobs require the attention to detail, the constant training of staff, the action, the movement, the reaction to and the attempt to satisfy the multitude of personalities appearing as customers and staff, day after day, week after week, year after year. The variables that must be controlled to ensure a smoothly operating restaurant can be overwhelming; the restaurant can, indeed, become a multivariate nightmare. Good luck on your way to becoming a small-town or, perhaps, a large-town, dignitary!

Key Terms and Concepts

Franchise

National Restaurant Association

Quality control

Restaurant

Restaurant concept

Review Questions

1. Give three reasons why someone would want to own and operate a restaurant.
2. Success in any business requires effort, perseverance, self-discipline, and ability. What other personality traits are especially important in the restaurant business?
3. In entering the restaurant business as an owner/operator, the individual has a choice of buying, building, or franchising. Which would you choose for minimizing risks? For expressing your own personality? For maximizing return on investment?

4. How important do you think it is to have restaurant experience before entering the business as an owner/operator?
5. Give three reasons people patronize restaurants.
6. What can we learn from the history and development of restaurants?
7. Which comparisons can be made between the past and present of restaurant operations?

CASE STUDY: Castelli's Restaurant at 255

Four Generations of Castelli's

Castelli's Restaurant at 255 is a casual, family-owned restaurant serving traditional Italian-American comfort food made from secret recipes that have been handed down from generation to generation of the Castelli family. The restaurant is located in Alton, Illinois, a small farming community that sits just outside of St. Louis, Missouri. In approximately 75 years of existence, spanning four generations of rich family history, Castelli's has remained relevant by sticking to the basics with its menu items and ingredients, maintaining a family tradition of striving to provide excellent quality and service, and offering fair prices. However, like many long-running restaurants, Castelli's has had to overcome its share of difficulties throughout the years.

In the mid-2000s, Castelli's began experiencing financial difficulties, which continued to escalate when the economy began struggling. The fourth generation of the Castelli family, great-grandchildren Matt and Tracy, dropped what they were doing and moved back to Illinois to reassume control of their family's business and eventually purchase the building back from the bank.

Back to the Basics

After they assumed ownership of the restaurant, Matt and Tracy did not change a lot about the restaurant concept. They kept the original recipes and ingredients that have been in the family for generations. The reason was that their biggest customer base consists of the Alton, Illinois, locals. Many of these people are long-time patrons from an older generation, who are familiar with the concept and menu items and love it for what it is.

At Castelli's, the mentality has always been to give the customers whatever they want. This had been passed down from the beginning by the original owners, Alfonso and Theresa. Because of this mentality, Castelli's offers a large and impressive menu with over 75 items to choose from. It also offers carry-out party packs and carry-out combo meals to feed larger groups in need of a little comfort food. Castelli's is open on weekdays from 11 A.M. to 9 P.M., and on weekends from Friday 11 A.M. to 10 P.M. The restaurant is busiest on weekends and holidays, at times serving up to 800 guests on a Saturday night.

Success Moving Forward

Matt and Tracy's philosophy for success revolves around the idea that they need to be in the restaurant constantly, watching over their business. They believe it is important to establish relationships with customers to ensure they have a good time at the restaurant. And in return, Castelli's has done well for itself under new ownership. With that being said, Matt and Tracy are still faced with many challenges every day. It is a challenge to maintain consistency in both the front of house and back of house operations by getting everyone to work as a team and produce a smooth and steady flow of service every shift.

A few years ago Castelli's annual revenue was approaching $2 million. Recently, the restaurant has seen a gradual increase in annual revenue and business demand, which reached $2.5 million at the end of 2012. With that in mind, their food and beverage cost was 38 percent in 2012 and their labor cost was

25 percent. Matt and Tracy's goal is to increase revenue by 5 to 10 percent, lower their food and beverage cost to 30 to 35 percent and lower their labor cost to 22 percent in 2013. Ultimately, their long-term goal is to increase annual revenue to $3 million and eventually expand the business to a second location.

QUESTIONS

1. Chapter 1 discusses different challenges of restaurant operation. What are some of the challenges the Castelli family has faced operating the restaurant over the years?

2. Does the current concept have lasting longevity? Should the owners alter the concept in any way?

3. What are some things the owners could do to increase their annual revenue?
   a. How can they lower food and beverage cost?
   b. How can they lower labor cost?

4. What are some things the owners could do to generate more business demand with younger generations between the ages of 25 to 45?
   a. What can you do to give people a reason to travel to Alton, Illinois, and visit the restaurant?

Endnotes

1. National Restaurant Association. July, 27, 2012. Available at http://www.restaurant.org/aboutus/ and www.restaurant.org/research/ind_glance.cfm.
2. Ibid.
3. Ibid.
4. This section draws on Donald E. Lundberg, *The Hotel Restaurant Business*, 6th ed. (New York: Van Nostrand Reinhold, 1994, pp. 216–218).
5. Joseph J. Deiss, *Herculaneum, Italy's Buried Treasure* (New York: Thomas J. Crowell Co., 1969).
6. Peter Montagne, ed., Larousse Gastronomique, author, *Larousse Gastronomique* (London: Clarkson Potter, 2001), p. 194.
7. "A. Boulanger." *Encyclopedia Britannica*. 2009. Encyclopedia Britannica Online. www.britannica.com/EBchecked/topic/75484/A-Boulanger. June, 2009.
8. Paul R. Dittmer and Gerald G. Griffin, *Dimensions of the Hospitality Industry: An Introduction* (New York: Van Nostrand Reinhold, 1993), p. 60.
9. John R. Walker, *Introduction to Hospitality*, 6th ed. (Upper Saddle River, NJ: Prentice Hall, 2012), p. 11.
10. Donald E. Lundberg, *The Hotel Restaurant Business* 6th ed. (New York: Van Nostrand Reinhold, 1994), p. 217.
11. Thomas Lately, *Delmonico's a Century of Splendor* (Boston: Houghton Mifflin, 1967).
12. John R. Walker, *Introduction to Hospitality* 6th ed. (Upper Saddle River, NJ: Prentice Hall, 2012), p. 13.
13. www.katzdeli.com. Retrieved November 16, 2009.
14. Linda Glick Conway (ed.), *The Professional Chef*, 5th ed. (Hyde Park, NY: The Culinary Institute of America, 1991), p. 5.
15. John Mariani, *America Eats Out* (New York: William Morrow, 1991), pp. 122–124.
16. Ibid.
17. Martin E. Dorf, *Restaurants That Work* (New York: William Morrow, 1991), pp. 122–124.
18. Ibid.
19. Ibid.
20. Lundberg, p. 215.
21. Richard A. Wentzel, "Leaders of the Hospitality Industry or Hospitality Management," *An Introduction to the Hospitality Industry*, 6th ed. (Dubuque, IA: Kendall Hunt, 1991), p. 29.
22. Lundberg, p. 295.
23. Ibid.

24. Colonel Harland D. Sanders, *Finger Lickin' Good* (Carol Stream, IL: Creation House, 1974).
25. Lundberg, p. 299.
26. "Despite economic woes, new restaurants open." *Miami Herald*. www.miamiherald.com/457/story/782910.html (January 2009): p. A1.
27. Sandra Pedicini, "Slump will take toll on restaurants," *Orlando Sentinel* (January 12, 2009).
28. Ibid.
29. H. G. Parsa, presentation at the ICHRIE Conference 2003, Indian Wells, California, August 2003.
30. Seay, B. "How much money do I really need?" *Franchise Prospector*. franchiseprospector.com/money-financing/franchise-article-3.php. June, 2009.
31. *Michelin Guide*. www.michelinguide.com/us/guide.html. June 2009.
32. Ibid.
33. National Restaurant Association. http://www.restaurant.org/careers/. Retrieved on July 28, 2012.
34. http://seattletimes.com/html/businesstechnology/2008028854_starbucks02.html.

CHAPTER
2

Restaurants and Their Owners

LEARNING OBJECTIVES

After reading and studying this chapter, you should be able to:

- List and describe the various kinds and characteristics of restaurants.

- Compare and contrast chain, franchised, and independent restaurant operations.

- Describe the advantages and disadvantages of chef-owned restaurants.

- Identify several well-known celebrity chefs.

- Define what a centralized home-delivery restaurant is and what it offers.

Courtesy of Sysco

Kinds and Characteristics of Restaurants

Broadly speaking, restaurants can be segmented into a number of categories:

- *Chain or independent (indy) and franchise restaurants:* McDonald's, Union Square Cafe, or KFC
- *Quick service (QSR), sandwich:* Burgers, chicken, and so on; convenience store; pasta; pizza
- *Fast casual:* Panera Bread, Atlanta Bread Company, Au Bon Pain, and so on
- *Family:* Bob Evans, Perkins, Friendly's, Steak 'n Shake, Waffle House
- *Casual:* Applebee's, Hard Rock Cafe, Chili's, T.G.I. Friday's
- *Fine dining:* The French Laundry, Morton's The Steakhouse, Fleming's, The Palm, Four Seasons
- *Other:* Steakhouses, seafood, ethnic, dinner houses, celebrity, and so on

Of course, some restaurants fall into more than one category. For example, an Italian restaurant could be casual and ethnic. Leading restaurant concepts in terms of sales have been tracked for years by the magazine *Nation's Restaurant News and Restaurants & Institutions*. An extrapolation of segment chains by US sales is summarized in Figure 2.1.[1]

CHAIN OR INDEPENDENT

The impression that a few huge quick-service chains completely dominate the restaurant business is misleading. *Chain restaurants* have some advantages and some disadvantages over independent restaurants. The advantages include:

- Recognition in the marketplace
- Greater advertising clout
- Sophisticated systems development
- Discounted purchasing

When franchising, various kinds of assistance are available, which is discussed later in the chapter.

Ranking	Concept	Sales
1	Burgers	$102,132,100,000
2	Casual dining	$27,152,900,000
3	Sandwiches/bakery-cafe	$25,053,200,000
4	Coffee/tea/donuts	$19,835,600,000
5	Family dining	$14,797,200,000
6	Mexican: Limited service	$10,512,100,000
7	Seafood: Full service	$6,080,600,000
8	Mexican: Full service	$1,706,200,000

FIGURE 2.1 Top 400 segment ratings.

Independent restaurants are relatively easy to open. All you need is several thousand dollars, knowledge of restaurant operations, and a strong desire to succeed. The advantage for independent restaurateurs is that they can "do their own thing" in terms of concept development, menus, decor, and so on. Unless our habits and taste change drastically, there is plenty of room for independent restaurants in certain locations.

Restaurants come and go. Some independent restaurants will grow into small chains, and larger companies will buy out small chains. Once small chains display growth and popularity, they are likely to be bought out by a larger company or will be able to acquire financing for expansion.

A temptation for the beginning restaurateur is to observe large restaurants in big cities and to believe that their success can be duplicated in secondary cities. Reading the restaurant reviews in New York City, Las Vegas, Los Angeles, Chicago, Washington, DC, or San Francisco may give the impression that unusual restaurants can be replicated in Des Moines, Kansas City, or Main Town, USA. Because of demographics, however, these high-style or ethnic restaurants will not click in small cities and towns.

FRANCHISED RESTAURANTS

Franchising is a possible option for those who lack extensive restaurant experience and yet want to open up a restaurant with fewer risks than starting up their own restaurant from scratch. Or, if you're a go-getter, you can open up your own restaurant, then another, and begin franchising. Remember that franchisors (the company franchising the rights to you and others) want to be sure that you have what it takes to succeed. They will need to know if you:

- Share the values, mission, and ways of doing business of the franchisor
- Have been successful in any other business
- Possess the motivation to succeed
- Have enough money not only to purchase the rights but also to set up and operate the business
- Have the ability to spend lots of time on your franchise
- Will go for training from the bottom up and cover all areas of the restaurant's operation

Franchising involves the least financial risk in that the restaurant format, including building design, menu, and marketing plans, has already been tested in the marketplace.

Franchise restaurants are less likely to go belly-up than independent restaurants. The reason is that the concept is proven and the operating procedures are established with all (or most) of the kinks worked out. Training is provided, and marketing and management support are available. The increased likelihood of success does not come cheap, however. There is a franchising fee, a royalty fee, advertising royalty, and requirements of substantial personal net worth.

For those lacking substantial restaurant experience, franchising may be a way to get into the restaurant business—providing they are prepared to start at the bottom and take a crash training course. Restaurant franchisees are entrepreneurs who prefer to own, operate, develop, and extend an existing business concept through a form of contractual business arrangement called franchising. Several franchisees have ended up with multiple stores and made the big time. Naturally, most aspiring restaurateurs want to do their own thing—they have a concept in mind and can't wait to go for it.

Here are samples of the costs involved in franchising:

- A Miami Subs traditional restaurant for a single unit has a $30,000 fee, a royalty of 6 percent of monthly gross sales, a payment of 3 percent of monthly gross sales to the advertising fund, and a net worth of at least $300,000 with $150,000 of this minimum net worth in liquid assets.[2] Miami Subs has an Express Unit from 500 to 1,000 square feet for food courts, airports, universities and convenience stores which require and investment of $175,000.
- Chili's requires a minimum liquidity of $1,000,000 plus a monthly fee based on the restaurant's sales performance (currently a service fee of 4 percent of monthly sales) plus the greater of (a) monthly base rent or (b) percentage rent that is at least 8.5 percent of monthly sales.[3]
- McDonald's requires an initial down payment when you purchase a new restaurant (40 percent of the total cost) or an existing restaurant (25 percent of the total cost). The down payment must come from nonborrowed personal resources, which include cash on hand; securities, bonds, and debentures; vested profit sharing (net of taxes); and business or real estate equity, exclusive of your personal residence.

    A minimum of $750,000 of nonborrowed personal resources is required to be considered for a franchise. Individuals with additional funds may be better prepared for additional or multi-restaurant opportunities including a $45,000 initial fee, plus a monthly service fee based on the restaurant's sales performance (about 4 percent) and rent, which is a monthly base rent or a percentage of monthly sales plus equipment and preopening costs ranging from $905,200 to $1,746,000.[4]

- Pizza Factory Express units (200 to 999 square feet) require liquid capital of $65,000 and a $7,500 franchise fee, a royalty of 5 percent, and an advertising fee of 2 percent. Equipment costs range from $25,000 to $90,000, with miscellaneous costs of $3,200 to $3,900 and opening inventory of $6,000.[5]

What do you get for all this money? Franchisors will provide:

- Help with site selection and a review of any proposed sites
- Assistance with the design and building preparation

Courtesy of Columbia Restaurant
100th Anniversary of Columbia Restaurant, Tampa, Florida.

- Help with preparation for opening
- Training of managers and staff
- Planning and implementation of preopening marketing strategies
- Unit visits and ongoing operating advice

There are hundreds of restaurant franchise concepts, and they are not without risks. The restaurant owned or leased by a franchisee may fail even though it is part of a well-known chain that is highly successful. Franchisers also fail. A case in point is the highly touted Boston Market, which was based in Golden, Colorado. In 1993, when the company's stock was first offered to the public at $20 per share, it was eagerly bought, increasing the price to a high of $50 a share. In 1999, after the company declared bankruptcy, the share price sank to 75 cents. The contents of many of its stores were auctioned off at a fraction of their actual cost. At one point in time, McDonald's purchased Boston Market, only to sell it months later to Sun Capital Partners.[6] Fortunes were made and lost. One group that did not lose was the investment bankers who put together and sold the stock offering and received a sizable fee for services. The offering group also did well; they were able to sell their shares while the stocks were high.

A restaurant concept may do well in one region but not in another. The style of operation may be highly compatible with the personality of one operator and not another. Most franchised operations call for a lot of hard work and long hours, which many people perceive as drudgery. If the franchisee lacks sufficient capital and leases a building or land, there is the risk of paying more for the lease than the business can support.

Relations between franchisers and the franchisees are often strained, even in the largest companies. The goals of each usually differ; franchisors want maximum fees, while franchisees want maximum support in marketing and franchised service such as employee training. At times, franchise chains get involved in litigation with their franchisees.

As franchise companies have set up hundreds of franchises across America, some regions are saturated: More franchised units were built than the area can support. Current franchise holders complain that adding more franchises serves only to reduce sales of existing stores. Pizza Hut, for example, stopped selling franchises except to well-heeled buyers who can take on a number of units.

Overseas markets constitute a large source of the income of several quick-service chains. As might be expected, McDonald's has been the leader in overseas expansions, with units in 119 countries. With its roughly 33,500 restaurants serving some 50 million customers daily, 18,000 locations are outside the United States, accounting for about half of the company's profits.[7]

A number of other quick-service chains also have large numbers of franchised units abroad. While the beginning restaurateur quite rightly concentrates on being successful here and now, many bright, ambitious, and energetic restaurateurs think of future possibilities abroad.

Once a concept is established, the entrepreneur may sell out to a franchiser or, with a lot of guidance, take the format overseas via the franchise. (It is folly to build or buy in a foreign country without a partner who is financially secure and well versed in the local laws and culture.)

Reading the life stories of big franchise winners may suggest that once a franchise is well established, the way is clear sailing. Thomas Monaghan, founder of

Domino's Pizza, tells a different story. At one time, the chain had accumulated a debt of $500 million. Monaghan, a devout Catholic, said that he changed his life by renouncing his greatest sin, pride, and rededicating his life to "God, family, and pizza." A meeting with Pope John Paul II had changed his life and his feeling about good and evil as "personal and abiding." Fortunately, in Mr. Monaghan's case, the rededication worked well. There are more than 8,000 Domino's Pizza stores worldwide, with sales of about $3 billion a year in the United States.[8] Monaghan sold most of his interest in the company for a reported $1 billion and announced that he would use his fortune to further Catholic Church causes.

A suggestion for any would-be restaurateurs is to work in a restaurant you enjoy and perhaps would like to emulate in your own restaurant. If you have enough experience and money, you can strike out on your own. Better yet, work in a successful restaurant where a partnership or proprietorship might be possible or where the owner is thinking about retiring and, for tax or other reasons, may be willing to take payments over time (see Figure 2.2).

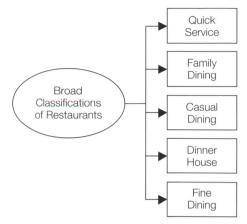

FIGURE 2.2 Broad classifications of restaurants.

Sandwich Shops

Sandwich and sub shops are comparatively simple to open and operate compared to a full-service restaurant. The menu consists of various kinds of hot and cold sandwiches made with a selection of bread/buns and toppings or fillings of different meats and vegetables/salad and pickle items. Little or no cooking is required. Hot and cold soups and pastries may also be offered along with a selection of hot and cold beverages.

A good example of a sandwich shop is Jimmy John's gourmet sandwich shop, which now franchises over 1,347 stores. Founded in 1983, with an investment of only $25,000 by then 19-year-old Jimmy John Liautaud, Jimmy John's sandwich shops have enjoyed impressive growth. Franchisers are required to make a total investment of $305,000 to $485,000, pay a franchise fee of $35,000, and pay ongoing royalty fees of 6 percent. The terms are for 10 years with a renewal option.[9] Part of the success is due to the irreverent attitude expressed by signs in the window that advertise "free smells" and "freakishly fast service," and employees are hired for their ability to "be real." The company is focused on fresh gourmet sandwiches—for example, turkey sandwiches are made with boneless turkey breasts, not pressed turkey, and name-brand ingredients are used.

Another interesting example is The Sandwich Shop in San Francisco, which offers the East Coast, piled high with the California freshness. Guests rave about the place and even say that if you're not into a "sammy," they have an incredible homemade teriyaki or Korean barbecue beef with kimchi.* In Seattle, the Baguette Box serves "multi-culti" subs like crispy drunken chicken, lemongrass steak, and grilled chorizo.**

*http://www.yelp.com/biz/the-sandwich-shop-san-francisco#query:sandwich%20shops.
**http://baguettebox.com/menu/menu.pdf

Sandwich shops require limited kitchen equipment and a much lower investment than a conventional restaurant. All that is required are a couple of stainless steel tables, service counters, a slicer, a can opener, and a few hotel pans to hold the sandwich ingredients. Add a few tables, chairs, and decor of choice and you're in business.

Quick-Service Restaurants

Americans in a hurry have often opted for *quick-service* food. The first known quick-service restaurant (QSR) dates back to the 1870s, when a New York City foodservice establishment called the Plate House served a quick lunch in about 10 minutes. Patrons then gave up their seats to those waiting. Today, many quick-service restaurants precook or partially cook food so that it can be finished off quickly.

Seconds count in quick-service establishments. The challenge for the quick-service operator is to have the staff and product ready to serve the maximum number of customers in the least amount of time.

The *QSR* segment drives the industry and includes all restaurants where the food is paid for before service. QSRs offer limited menus featuring burgers, chicken in many forms, tacos, burritos, hot dogs, fries, gyros, teriyaki bowls, and so on. Guests order at a brightly lighted counter over which are color photographs of menu items and prices. Guests may serve themselves drinks and seasonings from a nearby counter, then pick up their own food on trays.

(In order to cut costs, some QSRs now serve the sodas and hand out a couple of ketchup packets—when requested—along with napkins for each order.) QSRs are popular because they are conveniently located and offer good price and value.

POP-UP RESTAURANTS

Pop-ups are restaurants that appear only for a few days, generally with an upfront ticket price. Organizers must market them effectively—if they don't sell tickets, they can't pay for food. Social media play a role in filling seats. They're brief, but not easy—challenges include ordering the right amount of food, getting proper health department permits, finding competent staff, and even finding a location.[10]

The hot San Francisco pop-up's literally 'pop-up' for a few nights and are the latest food trend. Richie Nakano of Hapa Ramen has hot California-style organic soup at the Ferry Building farmer's market twice a week. The Hapa Ramen team also uses restaurants when they are closed to sell its food.

The pop-up concept began in London, England, and quickly spread around the world. Some pop-ups will take over a restaurant for a night, while others will go wherever they can find space. People who find one they like, may keep track of it using social media like Twitter or Facebook.[11]

FOOD TRUCKS

Food trucks are another interesting restaurant phenomenon. Food trucks, the next step up the evolutionary ladder from the traditional sidewalk food cart (trucks are generally larger, more tricked-out, and self-propelled), aren't exactly new. "Trucks serving pizza or halal chicken and rice have fed midtown office workers and outer-borough revelers for years. What is new is the elevation of the form—the quality, variety, and sheer number of the things have never been greater."[12]

"As food trucks have emerged on the area's dining scene, they've had to grapple with laws in cities and towns that in some cases prohibited them from operation. In St. Louis—the sweet spot in the food truck scene—lawmakers initially asked food trucks to stay clear of restaurants, who accused the trucks of poaching business. But, food truck operators have long argued that they enhance rather than detract from the city's food culture and that competition."[13]

Courtesy of Baja Boy's Grill

A Baja Boy's Mexican Grill food trailer/truck.

The city of Tampa mayor Bob Buckhorn has kicked off the inaugural mayor's Food Truck Fiesta, an event that will be held the first Wednesday of each month. The trucks have catchy names: Killer Samich, Taco Buns, Burger Culture, Fat Tortillas, Jerk Hut, Coconut Bo's and Gone Bananas. The mayor sees the rallies as a way to get people downtown. He added that he thinks downtown restaurants may benefit from the exposure. Well, some did and some didn't, as you might have guessed.[14]

In the Washington, DC, area, the Food Trucks Association is having a Truck-toctoberfest at Union Market. Cities across the country are in some cases making it easy for food trucks and others are not so welcoming. How is your city handling food trucks?

🍷 THE NORMAN BRINKER STORY

Norman Brinker, former chief executive officer (CEO) of Brinker International, climbed the corporate ladder with ambition and ability. President of the then-fledgling Jack in the Box burger chain, he started his own company, Steak and Ale, which was bought out by Pillsbury.

Brinker became the largest stockholder of that company, as well as executive vice president and board member. He went on to become CEO of Chili's and, finally, head of Brinker International, which now numbers more than 1,000 restaurants worldwide.

Brinker is credited with leading much of the growth of the casual dining sector of the restaurant business, including Steak and Ale, Bennigan's, Romano's Macaroni Grill, and Chili's. Similar casual dining restaurants opened in the 1980s, characterized by table service

(continued)

often provided by college students, bright cheerful decor, and moderate prices—a step above the fast-food level. Often there is something new in style. Bennigan's, for example, became known for the plants arranged around its bar. Brinker believed restaurants have a seven-year life cycle, after which they need a major change. The original concept, he says, gets tired. Upgrading, however, must be ongoing.

Brinker's type of casual dining restaurants lend themselves to rapid expansion via franchise, joint venture with financial partners,

or issuing new public stock with which to buy other restaurants.

Brinker, who was very athletic and an avid horseman, suffered a devastating polo accident in 1993. He was in a coma for two and a half weeks and suffered partial paralysis. With physical therapy and prodigious determination, he recovered completely.

Brinker's enduring advice is making life an adventure. Take risks, he said. "If you have fun at what you do, you'll never work a day in your life. Make work like play—and play like hell!"

Courtesy of Chili's Grill and Bar

Chili's is one of the successful concepts developed by Norman Brinker.

Quick Casual Restaurants

Filling a niche between quick service and casual dining, the defining traits of quick casual restaurants are: the use of high-quality ingredients; fresh, made-to-order menu items; healthful options; limited or self-serving formats; upscale decor; and carry-out meals. Fast casual restaurants are on the increase with new concepts continuously opening up. For instance, in the fresh Mex segment, there are a number of established chains and independents, like Chipotle, Rubio's Fresh Mexican Grill, Chevy's Fresh Mex, and La Salsa and relative newcomers like Pei Wei, and Texas-based Freebirds World Burrito. Other quick casual restaurants include Panera Bread and Raving Brands (which includes Moe's Southwest, Doc Green's Gourmet Salads, Flying Biscuit, and Monkey Joe's). Many more concepts continue to thrive and are increasing sales, mostly via take-out. Other established leaders in this segment are Atlanta Bread Company and Au Bon Pain, both bakery-cafés.

When does a bakery become a café? The thin dividing line is blurred when coffee, sandwiches, salads, and soups are on the bill of fare. The smell of fresh-baked bread and cookies triggers memories of home cooking. Many independent *bakery-cafés* and chains are expanding. Some are mainly take-out; others are sizable restaurants. The small ones are quick-service establishments distinguished by skilled bakers who start their work at 3 A.M. Many bakery-cafés mislead customers; they do not bake from scratch but bake goods prepared elsewhere, a practice that drastically reduces the need for highly skilled personnel on the premises. An in-between approach has the basic product being produced centrally, then delivered to the bakery-cafés where final proofing and bake-off is done.

Interestingly, Starbucks paid $100 million to buy the 19-unit chain of La Boulange bakeries in the San Francisco Bay area. This strategic move will enable Starbucks to boost and improve its bakery offerings along with juices and sometime alcohol.[15]

Panera Bread and Au Bon Pain, the largest of the chain bakery-cafés, bake bread throughout the day, and the company conducts training for bakers. Unit employees learn about breads and are able to suggest to customers which breads go best with which sandwiches. Other large bakery-café chains also use the central commissary system. For example, Corner Bakery, which is Chicago based, has a central commissary where bakers turn out 150 products from scratch.

Bakery-cafés offer a variety of settings and products. The La Madeleine chain, based in Dallas, Texas, presents a leisurely French country ambience, with wood-beam dining rooms and authentic French antiques. Some units have libraries; others, a wine cellar. The luncheon menu has, in addition to soups and sandwiches, such items as chicken *friand,* made with mushrooms and béchamel sauce placed between layers of pastry crust. A patisserie carries such items as chocolate éclairs, crème brulée, and napoleons. The dinner menu features beef bourguignonne and salmon in dill sauce. Between 4,500 and 5,000 square feet in size, each La Madeleine unit seats from 120 to 140 guests.

Carberry's, an independent bakery coffeehouse in Cambridge, has 72 seats and His shop produces 40 types of bread, including unusual sourdoughs such as sour cherry walnut and one with raisins, dates, figs, apricots, and sour cherries. Salads, sandwiches, and focaccias are offered. All baking is done from scratch.[16]

Bakery-cafés can start small, but the owners should expect long hours of work and a slow buildup of customers. As with most restaurants, the best way to start is to learn the ropes as an employee working for a successful operator and then, with a knowledge base and capital, try for a high-volume location or become a franchisee of a chain with a proven track record.

PDQ, short for People Dedicated to Quality, or as some say, "Pretty Darn Quick," is an interesting new concept in Tampa from Robert Basham, an original founder of Outback Steakhouse. The motif is of a rugged roadhouse that looks modern with plenty of glass and polished wood. The kitchen is open, similar to Chipotle, so guests can see their food prepared fresh. Everything is fresh but the menu is limited so associates can focus on doing everything perfectly. Each site will be about 3,200 square feet and Bob Basham said that PDQ will start the way Outback did: Build one, perfect the process, then build another and keep perfecting.[17]

Family Restaurants

Family restaurants grew out of the coffee shop–style restaurant. In this segment there are prominent chains like Bob Evans, Perkins, Marie Callender's, Cracker Barrel, Friendly's, Steak and Ale, and Waffle House, just to name a few. There are an even greater number of independent family-operated restaurants in this segment. Often, they are located in or within easy reach of the suburbs or Interstate roads. They are informal with a simple menu and service designed to appeal to families. Some offer wine and beer, but most do not serve alcoholic beverages.

Casual Restaurants

Casual dining is popular because it fits the societal trend of a more relaxed lifestyle.

Defining factors include signature food items, creative bar menus or enhanced wine service, and comfortable, homey decor. Among the recognizable chain operators in the casual segment are Applebee's, Outback Steakhouse, Chili's, T.G.I. Friday's, Hard Rock Cafe, and Ruby Tuesday. A new casual concept is Carmel Café and Wine Bar, developed by Chris Sullivan, founder of Outback Steakhouse. Carmel is a modern, Mediterranean-themed concept that offers tapas-like dishes for sharing or individual consumption. Carmel also uses tablets to place orders directly to the kitchen by scrolling through the available menu items and clicking on the ones selected. Guests can also pay their bills directly by using the same tablet.

Courtesy of Carmel Café

Carmel Café and Wine Bar have a warm, welcoming ambiance.

CHIPOTLE MEXICAN GRILL

Few restaurants move quickly into the success column. In 1993, Stephen Ells, a 32-year-old with a degree in art history from the University of Colorado, Boulder, and a degree from the Culinary Institute of America, opened a quick-service restaurant just off the campus of the University of Denver, called the Chipotle Mexican Grill. The restaurant, which has only 800 square feet of space, features burritos made with fresh lime juice and cilantro wrapped in a big flour tortilla. One of the salsa accompaniments is roasted chile and corn. The traditional guacamole and beans contain the best ingredients Ells can buy. A meal with a drink averages about $8 per person. The success of Chipotle is virtually unparalleled in the restaurant business. Using sustainably raised food and having respect for the animals, the environment, and the farmers make a strong impression on those who want food with integrity.

Blending and cooking the chicken, pork, or beef, grilled peppers, and onions draws on his food training skills and sense of flavor. His goal, Ells says, was to create a gourmet experience that could be enjoyed in 15 minutes—a big, hand-held burrito. The concept is not new; however, the way Mr. Ells does it and the setting for his restaurants make the difference. Chipotle does more than $2 billion a year in sales—and now there are 1,230 locations in 35 states.[18] The restaurant design fits the concept: stained floors, corrugated metal barn siding, steel pipe for table bases and foot rails. Plywood is used for the building's trim, part of a package that fits together well.

Courtesy of Chipotle

Chipotle serves food with integrity.

Fine-Dining Restaurants

Fine dining refers to the cuisine and service provided in restaurants where food, drink, and service are expensive and usually enjoyed leisurely. Turnover per table may be less than one an evening. Many of the customers are there for a special occasion, such as a wedding or birthday. Many customers bring business guests and write off the meal cost as a business expense. The guests are often invited because they can influence business and other decisions favorable to the host. Fine dining is usually found in enclaves of wealth and where business is conducted—cities such as New York, San Francisco, and Palm Beach. Las Vegas has several fine-dining restaurants catering to tourists and high-stakes gamblers. The restaurants are small, with fewer than 100 seats, and proprietor- or partner-owned.

The economics of fine dining differ from those of the average restaurant. Meal prices, especially for wine, are high. The average check runs $60 or more. Rents can be quite high. Large budgets for public relations are common. Because of the expertise and time required for many dishes and because highly trained chefs are well paid, labor costs can be high. Much of the profit comes from wine sales. Flair and panache in service are part of the dining experience. Tables, china, glassware, silverware, and napery are usually expensive, and the appointments can be costly, often including paintings and interesting architectural features.

The menus usually include expensive, imported items such as imported Scottish smoked salmon, caviar, and truffles. Only the most tender vegetables are served. Colorful garnishment is part of the presentation. Delectable and interesting flavors are incorporated into the food, and the entire dining event is calculated to titillate the guests' visual, auditory, and psychological experience. Expensive wines are always on hand, offered on an extensive wine list.

Food fashions change, and the high-style restaurant operators must keep abreast of the changes. Heavy sauces have given way to light ones, large portions to small. The restaurant must be kept in the public eye without seeming to be so.

If given a choice, the restaurant operator selects only those guests who will probably be welcomed by the other guests. Doing this helps to create an air of exclusivity. One way to do this is to park the most expensive autos near the entrance for all to see (Rolls-Royces do well). It also helps to have celebrities at prominent table locations.

Courtesy of Daniel Restaurant

Daniel Restaurant is an example of a fine-dining restaurant showcasing elegance in its cuisine, service, and ambience.

Hotel Restaurants

Luxury hotels, such as the Four Seasons and the Ritz-Carlton chains, can be counted on to have restaurants boasting a highly paid chef who understands French, Asian, and American food, who likely attended an American culinary school or trained at a prestige restaurant, and who has mastered French cuisine. Would-be restaurant operators should dine at a few of these restaurants, even though they are expensive, to learn the current meaning of elegance in decor, table setting, service, and food. (To avoid paying the highest prices, go for lunch and do not order wine.) Better yet, anyone planning a restaurant career should take a job in a luxury restaurant, at least for a while, to get the flavor of upscale food service—even if you have no desire to emulate what you see.

Several hotels across America have top-notch restaurants as a plus amenity for their guests. The French Room at the Adolphus hotel in Dallas; Clio at the Eliot Hotel in Boston; the Inn at Little Washington, Virginia; North Fork Table and Inn, Southold, New York, and Maialino at Gramercy Park Hotel, New York City, are good examples of hotels with outstanding restaurants. Las Vegas, being Vegas, attracts a number of top-flight chefs to operate restaurants in the casinos. Among them are: Aureole by Charlie Palmer, Joel's Robuchon, Piero Selvaggio's Valentino, Michael Mina's Nobhill Tavern, Andre's at the Monte Carlo by Andre Rochat, Alain Duchess's Mix on the 64th floor of THE Hotel, Chef Andre Rochat's Alize atop the Palm's Casino Resort, Nobu Matsuhisa's Nobu in the Hard Rock Hotel and Casino, and Pierre Gagnaire's Twist (which is the famed Michelin Three-Star chef's only restaurant in America).

Restaurants inside hotels have always tried to support a guest's desire for a needed meal, a cup of coffee, or just a cocktail. Taverns and Inns coming together to provide convenience for the guest is probably the root of a full service hotel. Today's hotel restaurants may also serve multiple locations on the hotel's property. For example, Nellie Cashman restaurant at the Westin Keirland Resort and Spa in Scottsdale provides food to the following areas on property: the general dining room area, two separate bars on property, room service, pool service, and the nearby Westin Villas Vacation Property. Most major hotels have a "three-meal" style restaurant. This means that the restaurant can serve breakfast, lunch, and dinner throughout the week. Many hotels will also have 24-hour room service where the "graveyard" cooks will serve room service at all hours of the night. A banquet facility inside a hotel may also be run directly out of the main restaurant kitchen. Hotels will have a separate banquet kitchen, however, if the banquet business warrants such a need.

The hotel restaurant, although berated in the past, has become a shining star in many hospitality operations. Most hotel restaurants in the past were seen as outlets that offered average to subpar cuisine, high prices, and poor service under the hotel's roof. Today, many restaurants residing on hotel grounds have become very successful and have even garnered national acclaim. Many hotel restaurants today have helped dispel the image of bland food and boring cuisine that most guests would associate with hotel food. Luxury hotels, for example, have used their popular restaurants to help market their hotel brand. The Bellagio Hotel in Las Vegas, for example, boasts such award winning restaurants as: Picasso, Prime Steakhouse, Le Cirque, and Michael Mina.

Another popular strategy for hotels is to outsource the restaurant operations to a professional restaurant brand/operator. Many experts believe this recent trend is due to the struggling economy. Hotels have to put all of their revenue producing departments under the microscope. Many hotels have come to the conclusion that it makes good business sense to let a professional restaurant company or chain control their food and beverage operations. The three most common deal structures for a hotel are: lease agreement, a franchise agreement, and a licensing arrangement.[19] Each one of these deal structures will have specific requirements for both parties. Choosing the best structure will depend on the objectives created by the hotel.

Steakhouses

Entry into the *steakhouse* category of restaurants is appealing to people who may wish to be part of a business that is simplified by a limited menu and that caters to a well-identified market: steak eaters. A number of steakhouse franchisers are looking for franchisees. All steakhouse concepts feature steak, but the range in service offered is wide—from walk-up to high-end service. The size of the steak served varies from a few ounces of a less expensive cut of beef to a 24-ounce porterhouse served on formal china on a white tablecloth.

Steakhouses present the operator with food and labor cost combinations that are found in few restaurants. It is common for food costs to be as high as 50 percent of gross sales, whereas the labor cost may be as low as 12 percent; compare this to full-service restaurants, with about 34 percent food cost and 24 to 28 percent labor costs. Another difference: A high percentage of steakhouse customers are men. They enjoy aged beef, in which the enzymes have broken down much of the connective tissue, yielding a distinctive flavor and tenderness.

The prototypical steak eater likes his steak slapped on a very hot grill or griddle so that the surface is seared and the next layer yields a cross-section of flavors.

Meat that has been wrapped in Cryovac, sealed, and refrigerated for several days is called wet aged. The meat is not dried out. Dry aging takes place under controlled temperature, humidity, and air flow, a process that causes weight loss of 15 percent or more. The two processes result in different flavors.

LORE OF STEAK

Steak lovers rhapsodize about their favorite form of steak and its preparation. Tenderloin steak is the most tender, cut from the strip of meat that runs along the animal's backbone and gets the least exercise. T-bone steaks are cut from the small end of the loin and contain a T-shaped bone. Porterhouse steaks, taken from the thick end of the short loin, have a T-bone and a sizable piece of tenderloin. (The Peter Luger Steakhouse in Brooklyn, New York, is known for serving a single steak dish—porterhouse, cut thick to serve two, three, or four people.) Peter Luger's has an interesting history

Courtesy of Sysco

The decor and ambiance of a restaurant should contribute to the dining experience.

that can be looked up on the Web—it has been voted best steakhouse in New York for 25 years in a row. Most steakhouses promote their rib-eye steak, top sirloin, tenderloin, and roasted prime rib.

The New York strip steak, served in hundreds of steakhouses around the country, is a compact, dense, boneless cut of meat. A Delmonico steak (or club steak) is a small, often boned steak taken from the front section of the short loin. Sirloin steaks come from just in front of the round, between the rump and the shank. The age of the meat and its treatment affect flavor, but the amount of marbling created by fat between the meat fibers affects flavor even more.

High-end operations feel that about a million people are needed as a customer base. They require considerable investment in building, fixtures, and equipment. They may not be in competition with the Outback, Lone Star, Steak and Ale, Stuart Anderson's Black Angus chain, and Longhorn Steakhouse, which compete with each other in another price bracket. Forty percent or more of the high-end operations serve well-aged beef and may have sales of more than $5 million a year. Low-end operations may do well with sales of $500,000 a year. High-end steakhouses expect to have a high percentage of wine and hard liquor sales. Mid-end steakhouses may stick with beer and moderately priced wine. The high end may stock Kobe beef, imported from Japan, which may sell for $100 a pound.

Before the recent recession, steakhouses were thriving and expanding. Now, due to the recession, chains like Ruth's Chris stock price have actually halved. The medical community generally has argued that red meat, particularly highly marbled red meat, is good for neither the waistline nor the vascular system. However, the popularity of low-carb diets (e.g., the Atkins diet) had many consumers trading their pasta bowls for porterhouses—and loving it. Steak connoisseurs say that the taste is exquisite.

OUTBACK STEAKHOUSE

One of the most successful concepts of all time is Outback Steakhouse. Who would have guessed that Outback founders Chris Sullivan and Robert Basham and Senior Vice President Tim Gannon's philosophy of "No rules, just right" would become so successful? When it opened in 1988, beef was not everyone's favorite dish. Now there are about 1,000 Outbacks. Chris Sullivan says,[20] "Our restaurants serve the freshest food possible, using our imported Parmesan cheese, grated fresh daily, and our imported virgin olive oil. Our fresh Midwestern grain-fed beef is the highest-quality choice beef available, and we serve only fresh, never frozen, chicken and fish. Almost everything is made fresh daily. We like to describe our menu as 'full flavored.' "[21]

In 1993, the Outback concept was growing so well that they decided to diversify into Italian food and purchased a 50 percent interest in Carrabba's Italian Grill. In 1995, Outback purchased the sole rights to develop the Carrabba's concept, which features a casual dinner in a warm, festive atmosphere with a variety of fresh, handmade Italian dishes cooked to order in the exhibition kitchen. Continued growth of all concepts came, in large part, from Outback's mission statement:

> We believe that if we take care of Our People, then the institution of Outback will take care of itself. We believe that people are driven to be a part of something they can be proud of, is fun, values them, and that they can call their own. We believe in the sanctity of the individual, the value of diversity, and in treating people with kindness, respect, and understanding. We believe that caring for people individually results in their emotional involvement in Outback. We believe in working as a team: having shared goals and a common purpose, serving one another, and supporting their Outbackers. We believe the most important function of the organization is to enable Partners and Managers to effectively run their restaurants and to support their Outbackers.

> Our purpose is to prepare Outbackers to exercise good judgment and live our principles and beliefs. This preparation will result in a company of restaurants that endures, prospers, and increases shareholder's value.[22]

Outback has five principles for success: hospitality, sharing, quality, fun, and courage. Hospitality is defined as giving for the sake of giving, rather than for the sake of gaining. Given these ingredients, it is not surprising that Outback continues to grow and acquire other concepts. In 1999, it purchased Fleming's Prime Steakhouse, an upscale contemporary steakhouse concept designed to be an ongoing celebration of the best in food, wine, and the company of friends and family. In addition to the finest prime beef and steaks, it sells more than 100 wines by the glass. In 2000, Outback opened the first Lee Roy Selmon's restaurant, featuring soul-satisfying Southern comfort cooking. (Lee Roy Selmon's no longer appears on the company Web page as it was sold to the Selman family and other investors). The next year it acquired Bonefish Grill, a very popular fresh seafood concept with a stylish decor and great ambience.

"What's next?" you ask. Outback has amassed an awesome collection of great restaurant concepts, and it all started with a "G'day mates, and have a Bonzer day!" approach to the business. Outback's parent company Bloomin' Brands, completed an initial public offering on August 8, 2012, and became a publicly traded company on NASDAQ (ticker symbol BLMN).

Courtesy of Red Lobster

Red Lobster, the largest seafood chain restaurant, gains about $2.8 billion worth of annual sales.

Seafood Restaurants

In Colonial America, seafood, plentiful along the East Coast, was a staple food in taverns. Oysters and other seafood were cheap and plentiful. In New England, cod was king, a basis for the trade among Boston, the Caribbean islands, and England. Dried cod was shipped to the Caribbean islands as a principal protein for the islanders. Sugar and rum made by the islanders were shipped to England, where manufactured goods were made and sold to the American colonies.

Seafood restaurants present another choice of operation for would-be restaurant operators, a choice that continues to gain in consumer favor with several thousand restaurants.

Many seafood restaurants are owned and operated by independent restaurant owners. Red Lobster, with about 700 restaurants, is the largest chain, with $2.7 billion in annual sales and average sales per restaurant of almost $3.8 million. Red Lobster serves almost 3 million guests a week, 145 million a year. In a good economy, customers do not hesitate to spend as much as $30 for a seafood meal; now they go for value and may spend $20 a head.[23]

At the low end of the menu price range is a chain like Captain D's, with an average check of $5.50. Seventy percent of sales are batter-dipped items, which reduces portion costs. (Batter is inexpensive compared to the fish itself.) Captain D's franchises its concept.

Farm-bred fish is changing the cost and kind of fish that are readily available. French-farmed salmon, grown in pens, outnumber wild salmon from the ocean by 50 to 1. Aquaculture has turned some marine biologists and many farmers into marine farmers, who are concerned with water temperature and fish breeding. Tilapia, grown in ponds in Mississippi and other southern states, is relatively inexpensive. Pollack, used widely in fish fingers, is also less expensive for the restaurant market. Other kinds of seafood, such as stingray and squid, are growing in popularity.

Seafood prices continue to rise but are in competition with shrimp grown in Mexico, India, and Bangladesh. Aquaculture is predicted to grow and may bring the price of seafood down dramatically.

Ethnic Restaurants

MEXICAN RESTAURANTS

The food of Mexico covers a wide range of choices, much greater than that found in the usual Mexican restaurant in the United States. The menu is built around tortillas, ground beef, cilantro, chiles, rice, and beans. In the past, the food was commonly fried in lard; a practice almost guaranteed to add to the waistline and frowned on by the American Heart Association. Today, some Mexican restaurants use vegetable oil in their recipes. Generally, Mexican-style food is relatively inexpensive because of the small percentage of meat used, which results in a food cost of less than 28 percent of sales. Labor costs are also low because many of the employees are first-generation Americans or recent immigrants willing to work at minimum wage.

Menus, decor, and music in Mexican restaurants are often colorful and exciting. Menus may include tasty seafood items and spicy sauces. Burritos—tasty ingredients wrapped in a flour tortilla—can be handheld meals in themselves. Before the day of the big-chain Mexican restaurants, there were mom-and-pop places, typically owned and operated by a Mexican family. These still abound in the Southwest and California.

ITALIAN RESTAURANTS

Of the hundreds of types of ethnic restaurants in the United States, Italian restaurants, including pizza chains, boast the largest number. They also offer an array of opportunities for would-be franchisees and entrepreneurs and the possibility of coming up with a concept modification.

Italian restaurants owe their origins largely to poor immigrants from southern Italy, entrepreneurs who started small grocery stores, bars, and restaurants in Italian neighborhoods in the Northeast. The restaurants began serving their ethnic neighbors robustly flavored, familiar foods in large portions at low prices. The foods were based on home cooking, including pasta, a paste or dough item made of wheat flour and water (plus eggs in northern Italy). Spaghetti, from the word *spago*, meaning "string," is a typical pasta. Macaroni pasta, is tubular in form. In the north of Italy, ravioli pasta is stuffed with cheese or meat; in the south, it may be served in a tomato sauce without meat. Pastas take various shapes, each with its own name.

Pizza is native to Naples, and it was there that many American soldiers, during World War II, learned to enjoy it. Pizza eventually made John Schnatter a millionaire; his Papa John's chain has made hundreds of small businesspeople wealthy.

Although independent Italian restaurant owners typify the Italian restaurant business, chain operators are spreading the pasta concept nationwide and selling franchises to those qualified by experience and credit rating. The range of Italian-style restaurants available for franchise is wide, from stand-in-line food service to high-style restaurants where the guest is greeted by a maître d'hôtel, seated in a plush chair, and served with polished silver. A Romano's Macaroni Grill costs between $2.25 and $4.99 Million to build, equip, and open.[24] As is true in upscale Roman restaurants, guests get to review fresh seafood, produce, and other menu items as they enter the restaurant. An extensive menu lists more than 30 items, including breads and pizza baked in a wood-burning oven.

The Olive Garden chain, with more than 750 units, 85,000 employees, and billions in annual sales, is by far the largest of the Italian restaurant chains.[25]

As might be guessed, many Italian-style restaurants feature pizza and might be properly called stepped-up pizzerias. Pasta House Co. sells a trademarked pizza called Pizza Luna in the shape of a half moon. An appetizer labeled Portobello Frito features mushrooms, as does the Portobello fettuccine. Spaghetti Warehouses are located in rehabilitated downtown warehouses and, more recently, in city suburbs.

Paul and Bill's (neither owner is Italian) sells antipasto, salads, and sandwiches for lunch, then changes the menu for dinner. The sandwiches are replaced by such items as veal scaloppini with artichokes and mushrooms in a Madeira sauce. Osso buco (veal shank) is another choice. Potato chips are homemade, and a wood-fired oven adds glamour to the baked breads and pizza.

Courtesy of Romano's Macaroni Grill

Romano's Macaroni Grill is an Italian-theme restaurant with plenty of atmosphere, moderately priced good food, and good service.

Fazoli's, a Lexington, Kentucky, chain, describes itself as fast casual dining. Guests place their orders at a counter, then seat themselves. A restaurant hostess strolls about offering unlimited complimentary bread sticks that have just been baked. The menu lists spaghetti and meatballs, lasagna, chicken Parmesan, shrimp and scallop fettuccini, and baked ziti (a medium-size tubular pasta). The sandwiches, called Submarinos, come in seven varieties. Thirty percent of sales come via a drive-through window. The chain franchise has some 280 units and is growing.

Italian restaurants based on northern Italian food are likely to offer green spinach noodles served with butter and grated Parmesan cheese. Gnocchi are dumplings made of semolina flour (a coarser grain of wheat). Saltimbocca ("jumps in the mouth") is made of thin slices of veal rolled with ham and fontina cheese and cooked in butter and Marsala wine. Mozzarella cheese is made from the milk of water buffalo. Risotto, which makes use of the rice grown around Milan, is cooked in butter and chicken stock and flavored with Parmesan cheese and saffron.

ASIAN RESTAURANTS

Though they represent a small percentage of all restaurants, Chinese restaurants find a home in most corners of North America, becoming part of the community and, in many towns and cities, staying for many years. Historically, they are owned by hardworking ethnic Chinese families who offer plentiful portions at reasonable prices.

The cooking revolves around the wok, a large metal pan with a rounded bottom. The shape concentrates the heat at the bottom. Gas-fired woks are capable of reaching the high temperatures required for quick cooking. Small pieces of food are cut into uniform, bite-size pieces and quickly cooked. Bamboo containers, perforated on the bottom and fitted with domed covers, are stacked in the wok to quickly steam some dishes.

China is divided into three culinary districts: Szechuan, Hunan, and Cantonese and northern style centered on Beijing. Cantonese food is best known in the United States and Canada for its dim sum (small bites), steamed or fried dumplings stuffed with meat or seafood. Szechuan food is distinguished by the use of hot peppers.

Chinese cooking styles reflect the places in China from which the chefs came. In the early 1850s, many Chinese joined the gold rush and opened restaurants in Western states.

These cooking styles have been blended in many Chinese restaurants. The typical Chinese dinner was an extended affair, with each guest choosing an entrée and passing it around to share with the others. New Chinese chain restaurants are appearing, some financed by public stock offerings.

P. F. Chang's China Bistro came on the culinary scene as Chinese chic. It has 207 restaurants and is opening more. The average check is about $28 per person, including entrée, appetizer, and beverage.[26]

China Bistro departs from the often dimly lit restaurant operated by a Chinese family and offers, instead, an exhibition kitchen. Guests can see the woks as they flame and sputter. A sister restaurant called Pei Wei Asian Diner offers a more casual dining experience with counter or take-out service at about 177 restaurants, where the entire menu offerings are under $10.[27]

Courtesy of Sysco
Panda Express is on a roll and looks to grow.

Panda Express has more than 1,500 units. Located mostly in malls and a few supermarkets, Panda Express is headed by an immigrant husband-wife team, the Cherngs. All entrées are prepared on-site using the freshest ingredients and recipes from Master Chef Ming-Tsai. The Panda Restaurant group now includes Hibachi-San and Panda Inn concepts.

Pei Wei Asian Diner (pronounced pay way) is a chain of quick-casual restaurants that serve freshly prepared, wok-seared, contemporary pan-Asian cuisine in a relaxed, warm environment with friendly, attentive counter service as well as the flexibility, speed, and convenience of take-away service. Pei Wei offers the same spirit of hospitality and commitment to providing fresh, high-quality Asian food at a great value that has made these Bistro restaurants successful.[28]

Theme Restaurants

Theme restaurants are built around an idea, usually emphasizing fun and fantasy, glamorizing or romanticizing an activity such as sports, travel, an era in time (the good old days), the Hollywood of yesterday—almost anything. Celebrities are central to many theme restaurants. Some celebrities are part owners and show up from time to time—for example, Justin Timberlake's Southern Hospitality BBQ in New York City, Bon Jovie's Sole Kitchen, Gavin De Graw's The National Underground on New York City's Lower East Side, Yao Ming's YOA Bar and Restaurant, Jay-Z's 40/40 Club in New York City, Ashton Kutcher and Wilmer Valderrama's Dolce Enoteca e Ristorante, Michael Jordan's Steakhouse in New York City, and Robert Redford's Zoom in Park City Utah.[29]

As early as 1937, a Trader Vic's restaurant in California became popular with its South Sea Island theme, which was licensed for operation in a few hotel dining rooms over the next several years. Jack Dempsey, world heavyweight boxing champion in the 1920s, was associated with a New York City restaurant called Jack Dempsey's.

Joseph Baum created several theme restaurants in New York City beginning in the 1950s. He was well-known for La Fonda del Sol (Inn of the Sun), a theme restaurant that featured foods from Latin America. Another of his early restaurants, The Forum of the Twelve Caesars, was built on a Roman theme; the food servers dressed in modified togas. Roman helmets were used as wine coolers.

Theme restaurants like Planet Hollywood, which for a time experienced huge popularity, have a comparatively short life cycle. They do well located just outside major tourist attractions. Local residents, however, soon tire of the hype and, as is often the case, the poor food. Much or most of the profit in many theme restaurants comes from the sale of high-priced merchandise.

Large theme restaurants involve large investments and employ consultants, such as architects, colorists, lighting, and sound experts. Color, fabrics, wall and floor treatments, furniture, and fixtures are blended to create excitement and drama. Theme restaurants of the kind found in Las Vegas and in large cities require large budgets and often fail because the food and food service are lost in the drama and high theater. Novelty wears thin after a time, and customers seek a more relaxing meal. In many theme restaurants, food is incidental to the razzmatazz.

The cost of most of the large theme restaurants is high, both in capital costs and in operations. The Rainforest Cafés, for example, spend large amounts on creating and operating the illusion that guests are in a rain forest. In addition to a regular full-time staff, each restaurant has a full-time curator with a staff of four: an aquatic engineer with an assistant and four bird handlers. The decor includes electronic animals (a 9-foot crocodile, live sharks, tropical fish, and butterflies). The concept, says its creator, Steven Schussler, won't work unless the restaurant has at least 200 seats.

Martin M. Pegler, a noted writer on retail and restaurant design, describes 60 successful theme restaurants in Europe and America in his book *Theme Restaurant Design*. He divides theme restaurants into six categories:

1. Hollywood and the movies
2. Sports and sporting events
3. Time—the good old days
4. Records, radio, and TV
5. Travel—trains, planes, and steamships
6. Ecology and the world around us[30]

Some theme restaurants appeal to an older generation and present a time for reflection and nostalgia. Flat Pennies in Denver presents a railroad theme. Steel railroad tracks hold up the bar canopies and are used as foot rails. Lampposts suggest telegraph poles that once bordered railroad tracks. A huge Santa Fe train front, a mural, seems to be heading directly into the restaurant.

Motown Café, New York City, was designed to reflect elements of music and American musical history. Nostalgia for the 1950s and the 1960s is part of the theme. A two-story merchandise shop accounts for much of the revenue. As in most high-style theme restaurants, vibrant primary colors are widely used.

The restaurant Dive in Las Vegas used to create the illusion of eating in a submarine. A team of architects, designers, and consultants using color, sound, and imagination assembled the place at considerable expense. The restaurant was so costly and unusual that it could be successful in only a few places where large numbers of people congregate for pleasure. Dive, like most unlikely theme restaurants, did not depend on repeat customers for profit. The featured food was a submarine sandwich, and prices were high enough to cover the large cost of planning and construction. Like so many theme restaurants, Dive was more about entertainment than food. Much of the income came from merchandise, which yields higher profits than food does. Dive unfortunately closed a few years ago as the novelty quickly wore off and the overpriced, lackluster food quality kept guests away.

Would-be restaurant owners can visit one of the Irish pubs of Fadó, the casual chain that offers a composite view of pubs in various stages of Irish history. Nearly all of the decor items are made in Ireland. They are clustered together into five sections within Fadó, each forming a little piece of Irish history with artifacts. The word *fadó* means "long ago" in Gaelic. Informality begins at the pub entrance with a sign reading "please seat yourself." As in Ireland, patrons are expected to become part of the atmosphere. Plenty of named draft brews—like Guinness Stout, Harp Lager, Bass Ale—stimulate the merriment, and alcohol accounts for about 70 percent of the revenue. Food and beverage servers are trained in the Irish serving tradition, which prizes individuality. Each Fadó pub has one or more Irish citizens on hand to impart the authentic accent and philosophy. Managers come either from Ireland or from the city where the pub is located.

Music is part of the entertainment mix and includes traditional jigs and live musicians for special occasions. Background music is played during lunch and dinner; after midnight, it is moved to the foreground. The music changes with the age of the customer—from mellow for older customers in the early evening, to more lively for a 23- to 40-year-old group as the evening goes on.

Both Irish mainstays and contemporary dishes are served. A potato pancake stuffed with fillings like corned beef and cabbage or salmon is popular. Cottage pie, which has chunks of chicken breast, mushrooms, carrots, and onions, is another favorite. According to the owners, "In the tradition of Pubs today and long ago, it's the Irish spirit that makes a Fadó." Currently, there are 14 Fadó locations in the United States.[31]

There is almost no end to what can be done with themes, some expensive, others much less so. As with any restaurant, there needs to be a market of people who will patronize the place, preferably as repeat customers. Would-be restaurant operators who have the time—and they should take time—can visit these restaurants to get ideas to use or adapt for their own plans.

The Benihana chain of Japanese-style restaurants can be considered theme restaurants. The razzle-dazzle of the highly skilled knife work of the chefs chopping

Courtesy of Charlie Trotter

Charlie Trotter's in Chicago has established itself as one of the finest restaurants in the world. Chef Trotter stresses the use of pristine seasonal and naturally raised foodstuffs.

and dicing at the separate table grills is memorable theater. Examples of other ethnic restaurants that border on being theme restaurants follow:

- The Evvia Estiatorio in Palo Alto, California, suggests a Greek tavern with a California aesthetic.
- Tapas Barcelona in Chicago features regional Spanish tapas (hors d'oeuvres) and *mariscos* (seafood).
- Cucina Paradiso in Oak Park, Illinois, features northern Italian cuisine. Vivid murals, ·exposed brickwork, and a stainless-steel pasta sculpture add to the atmosphere.

It can be argued that every ethnic restaurant that is well designed is a theme restaurant emblematic of the cookery, food, and decor of a national culture. The restaurant can be Mexican, Moroccan, Chinese, Korean, and so on, or a combination of cuisines—Thai–French, Italian–Middle Eastern, or Japanese–Chinese, for example. If the restaurant is exciting because it presents an exotic cuisine and features serving personnel in national costumes and furnishings using traditional ethnic colors and artifacts, it is a theme restaurant.

Coffee Shops

Coffeehouses or coffee shops have long been a part of our culture and history and can be a way into the restaurant business for those who may not want to mess with a full-service restaurant. Coffeehouses originally were created based on the model of Italian bars, which reflected the deeply rooted espresso tradition in Italy. Much of the same concept was re-created in North America, where this was a niche in the beverage industry that was yet to be acknowledged and filled. The original concept was modified, however, to include a much wider variety of beverages and styles of coffee to meet the tastes of consumers, who have a tendency to prefer a greater selection of products. Consequently, the typical espresso/cappuccino offered by Italian bars has been expanded in North America to include items such as a variety of teas, iced mocha, iced cappuccino, and light food items such as soups and sandwiches.[32]

Nearly all communities have a coffee shop, be it a chain or independent. Surprisingly, chains like Starbucks only began to spread after being sold to Howard

Schultz in 1987, although the original store dates back to 1971. Starbucks now serves about 7 million people a day—now that's some brew ha ha![33]

All one needs to open a coffee shop is a good name and location, permits (more about that in Chapter 3), a coffee machine and an espresso machine, limited kitchen equipment, a few tables and chairs, some decorations, and voilà! You're in business.

Chef-Owned Restaurants

Chefs who own restaurants have the advantage of having an experienced, highly motivated person in charge, often helped by a spouse or partner equally interested in the restaurant's success. However, hundreds of chefs are less knowledgeable about costs, marketing, and "the numbers" that are requisite for a restaurant's success. Many chef-owners learn the hard way that location and other factors are just as important for success as food preparation and presentation. Working in a name restaurant as an employee may bring a chef $100,000 or more a year in income, while owning and operating a restaurant entails considerable risks. Gaining acclaim as a chef-owner has made a few quite rich and has made others poor.

Chef-owners are part of the American tradition of family restaurants in which papa is the chef and mama is the hostess who watches over the operation from her post at the cash register. The family's children start work young and fill in where needed. Ethnic restaurants—Chinese, Greek, German, Mexican, and others—have flourished in this category since the days of the Colonial taverns.

Chef-owners seeking fame and fortune can consider contracting with publicists to get the restaurant's name in the press a certain number of times over an agreed-on period. The effective publicist knows a lot about restaurants as well as whom to court and how to devise interesting stories about the restaurant and the chef. Promotion-minded chef-owners and other restaurant owners are adept at gaining public attention by appearing on TV programs, doing charity work, and making sure that the press knows that a film or sport star who is an investor in the restaurant appears in person occasionally.

The first thing a chef-owner should do is get a good backup person to share in management, food preparation, and, it is hoped, marketing. This move anticipates periods of illness, family emergencies, and vacations, ensuring that an experienced hand remains at the wheel.

Consider the possibility of marital or partner dispute. Much of successful restaurant keeping is stressful—meeting meal hour deadlines and coping with delivery delays, plumbing breakdowns, and other unpredictable events. Co-owned restaurants can be beset by disagreements. Husband-and-wife teams are subject to divorce, often resulting in ugly litigation that is costly and stressful.

WOLFGANG PUCK AND BARBARA LAZAROFF

One of the best-known former husband-and-wife culinary teams was Wolfgang Puck and Barbara Lazaroff. Puck, a native of Austria, gained some prominence as the

Courtesy of The Beckwith Company

Spago Beverly Hills, one of Wolfgang Puck and Barbara Lazaroff's creations.

chef-partner at Ma Maison restaurant in Los Angeles (later closed), and then he and his former wife became well known for their restaurant Spago, also in Los Angeles. His open and friendly personality and his passion for restaurants are part of the reason for his success. Also responsible is his ability to work 16 hours a day in the kitchen when necessary. For example, his workday at Spago started at 8 A.M. and lasted until 1 A.M. the next morning. Lazaroff handled the marketing and much of the planning for new restaurants.

While at Spago, Puck went to the fish market in downtown Los Angeles five times a week because, he said, it is important to touch and feel the food you are about to cook.

Starting Spago in 1982 was a real trial for the couple. They had only $3,500 and could not have opened without a friend who cosigned a $60,000 loan. Later, they had to spend $800,000 to purchase land for more parking. Two other partners invested $30,000 each and $15,000 more was raised, and, finally, the remainder was raised from more than 20 other investors. Within a few years, Puck and Lazaroff were said to be worth more than $10 million.[34]

Puck's career speaks of the ups and downs of restaurant keeping and what can be achieved with determination, perseverance, a high energy level, good health, and goodwill. In partnership with his wife, who designs the properties, Puck enjoys widespread recognition as a chef-entrepreneur.

His cooking style has been imitated from Tokyo to Paris, and his Wolfgang Puck Food Company, which markets a line of frozen gourmet pizzas nationwide, is carried by a number of grocery chains. Mini vending areas in airports even carry Puck sandwiches. Puck and Lazaroff were known for their interest in and support of several charities and social issues.

Puck's advice to the new restaurateur: Work hard and be patient. Each of his restaurants, he says, has been a struggle. Success does not come easily. His history bears him out. He started as an apprentice at age 14 and worked for several years in France. In 1974, he became a partner at Ma Maison restaurant with Patrick Terrail, and also conducted the Ma Maison cooking school.

Since beginning Spago, they have gone on to open a number of restaurants. The Puck–Lazaroff partnership has done what few others have: designing and managing a number of different styles of restaurant. Each restaurant is headed by an executive chef and a sous chef. Each chef, said Barbara Lazaroff, adds his or her own accents and personality, and each is a star in his or her own right.[35]

The skills, talents, and perseverance required to become a chef are told in detail in *Becoming a Chef* by Andrew Dornenburg and Karen Page. The book is valuable reading for anyone wishing to know about the skills, the temperament, and the time required to undertake a chef training course.[36]

TOP TEN AMERICAN CHEF-OWNED RESTAURANTS

Here is the top ten list of American chef-owned restaurants as compiled on the advice of TripAdvisor editors and travelers:[37]

1. *Per Se, New York City, Chef Thomas Keller:* Inspired by Keller's popular restaurant, French Laundry, in Yountville, California.
2. *Daniel, New York City, Chef Daniel Boulud:* Critically acclaimed for seasonally inspired contemporary French cuisine.
3. *CUT, Palazzo Las Vegas, Las Vegas, Chef Wolfgang Puck:* A "gourmet heaven"; great steaks in a sleek, modern environment.
4. *Osteria Mozza, Los Angeles, Chefs Mario Batali and Nancy Silverton:* Authentic Italian cuisine, complete with a mozzarella bar.
5. *Morimoto, Philadelphia, Chef Masaharu Morimoto:* "Splurge-worthy Japanese cuisine" served in a trendy setting, spectacular décor, and creative menu draw patrons back.
6. *Mesa Grill, Caesars Palace, Las Vegas, Chef Bobby Flay:* Known for amazing margaritas and flavorful Southwestern entrees.
7. *Hamersley's Bistro, Boston, Chef Gordon Hamersley:* Local, seasonal ingredients in high-quality, rustic dishes have been a staple at Hamersley's Bistro for the past 20 years.
8. *NOLA Restaurant, New Orleans, Chef Emeril Lagasse:* Southern hospitality and comfort food are the hallmark of this French Quarters restaurant.
9. *Craftsteak, Las Vegas, Chef Tom Colicchio:* Craftsteak favors high quality, fresh ingredients, including organic choices.
10. *Olives, Las Vegas, Chef Todd English:* "Unobtrusive service, elegant atmosphere, and romantic patio" draw travelers visiting Las Vegas.[38]

WOMEN CHEFS AS RESTAURANT OWNERS

There are numerous examples of women chefs who are partners and do well as restaurateurs. Susan Feniger and Mary Sue Milliken, co-owners of the award-winning Border Grill in Santa Monica, California, illustrate what can be done when trained chefs with food knowledge and a flair for showmanship become partners. It is often said that restaurants are at least 50 percent theater. In many restaurants, including the Border Grill, that's true.

Trained at American culinary schools, the partners met in 1978 while working at Le Perroquet in Chicago. Later, they both made the food pilgrimage to France often made by Americans who want hands-on experience in French cuisine. Feniger worked at Oasis on the Riviera, Milliken at Restaurant d'Olympe. Upon returning to the United States, they became partners and opened the tiny City Café in Los Angeles.

Before opening the Border Grill in Santa Monica, they traveled extensively and added the City Restaurant in La Brea, California, to their responsibilities. Ebullient and fun loving, and with seemingly unlimited energy, the partners have become food and restaurant celebrities and written five cookbooks. They also have a TV series called *Too Hot Tamales*. Feniger and Milliken bring a casual yet highly informed knowledge of food to the television screen and to the radio. Both enjoy teaching classes and mingling with customers.

In 1999, they opened a sister Border Grill in Las Vegas, offering appetizers such as green corn tamales and seviche (raw fish and seafood marinated in lime juice with tomatoes, onions, and cilantro) and luncheon items such as turkey tostada and a variety of tacos, including those made with fish, lamb, and *carnitas* (small pieces of cooked meat). A full bar offers more than 20 premium tequilas. At the entrance to the restaurant, they placed the Taqueria, where a variety of tacos are served (thin disks of unleavened bread made from cornmeal or wheat flour rolled around beans, ground meat, or cheese). More about this restaurant can be seen at the website www.bordergrill.com. The color, vivacity, and menu of their latest restaurant, Ciudad, can be seen at www.ciudad-la.com.

Of course, few restaurant owners or franchisees have the zest or special talents of Feniger and Milliken. Be sure to get people like them on the staff—people who enjoy fun and are full of life lift the spirits of both employees and patrons. Professional public relations people can also put a fun spin on a restaurant's image. The restaurant business is democratic; its practitioners come from a variety of social, educational, and ethnic backgrounds. A number of women have made it big in the restaurant business as heads of chains. For example, Ruth Fertel, founder of Ruth's Chris Steak House, led the nation's largest upscale restaurant chain.

Auntie Anne's Anne Beiler introduced her rolled soft pretzels in 1988 at an Amish farmers' market in Gap, Pennsylvania. The pretzels were hand-rolled in front of the customers and served fresh from the oven. Today sales from 890 stores are $250 million a year. Beiler had the marketing smarts to come up with pretzel glazes like whole wheat, jalapeño, and raisin. The pretzel lover also has a choice of dips like chocolate, cream cheese, caramel, and marinara.[39]

Some African Americans have made it big as franchisees of large fast-food companies working in inner-city locations. Valerie Daniels-Carter is one example. As president and CEO of V & J Holdings, she is the largest minority owner of Burger King and Pizza Hut franchises in the United States. Daniels, who is in business with her brother, is a self-described workaholic—as, she says, was her father. In 1984, she bought her first franchise; by 1999, she had 98 stores in Wisconsin, Michigan, and New York. Many of the company's units are in poor inner-city locations. As for her view of employee relations: "When I hire people, I look for a moral stance, work experience, drive, and initiative." When buying an additional unit, she says, "It must make economic sense for everyone and, most importantly, offer opportunity for all of us, whether it's the manager or the dishwasher."[40] Reflecting her concern for employees, she negotiated with Burger King to allow some stores to schedule shorter evening working hours so that workers and employees would feel safer.

Is it possible that the typical restaurant manager of the future will be a woman? Yes! Even though women with families sacrifice some of their personal life and time to managing a restaurant, those with stamina and ambition may be better suited for management than are men with similar backgrounds. Women, it is agreed, are more concerned with details, sanitation, and appearance. Plus, they are likely to be more sensitive to and empathetic with customers than are men. Two national organizations—Les Dames d'Escoffier and the Round Table for Women in Foodservice—are both excellent networks for female professionals in the restaurant industry.

Celebrity Chefs

Celebrity chefs are bigger today than ever before in history. Long ago are the days of Julia Child, when she was the only celebrity chef one could think of. Even Emeril Lagasse is surprised at the extent to which things have changed for celebrity chefs over the past 10 years. Lagasse said, "Chefs weren't really respected other than being in the kitchen. . . . You rarely saw them in the dining room interacting with people. . . . Now all of a sudden, people have started looking at chefs and saying, 'Wow! That person really is a craftsman, is really a business person, they can do publicity."[41] Not only are the celebrity chefs becoming a household name, so are their brands! From Emerilware (Emeril cookware) to Rachael Ray's "EVOO" (extra virgin olive oil), celebrity chefs are creating their very own empires. Not to mention the cookbooks, television shows, and restaurants! In the next sections we will discuss just a few of the top celebrity chefs. Daniel Boulud is featured in a profile at the opening of Part Two.

SUZANNE GOIN

Chef Suzanne Goin, a graduate of Brown University, was born and raised in Los Angeles, California. Throughout her career, Goin has worked in several successful restaurants, including Alice Water's Chez Panisse, Ma Maison in Los Angeles, and Paris's acclaimed restaurants Pain and L'Arpège. Today she is the owner of the following restaurants:

- Lucques, located on Melrose Avenue in Los Angeles, California (co-owner and chef)
- A.O.C., located in Los Angeles, California
- The Hungry Cat, located in both Los Angeles and Santa Barbara

Goin also has an impressive list of awards:

- Six James Beard Award nominations
- James Beard Award for "Best Chef: California"
- Three stars in *The New York Times* for her restaurant Lucques
- *Food & Wine* magazine's "Best New Chefs of 1999"
- Three stars in *The New York Times* for her restaurant A.O.C.
- James Beard Foundation's Award for "Best Cookbook from a Professional Viewpoint" for her cookbook *Sunday Suppers at Lucque's*

In addition, her restaurants have been praised by *Gourmet* magazine, *Bon Appétit* magazine, *Los Angeles Times Magazine,* and *Food & Wine* magazine. On a more personal note, Alice Waters, godmother of the good-food, good-earth connection, rates Goin as one of the most eco-conscious chefs in the country.[42] She uses organic ingredients for about 80 percent of her dishes and is a regular at the local farmers' market. Goin also has her own cookbook, *Sunday Suppers at Lucques: Seasonal Recipes from Market to Table*.

ALICE WATERS, THE IDEALIST IN THE KITCHEN—CHEZ PANISSE

Outspoken, yet speaking softly, Alice Waters has a mission: to awaken our thinking about food selection and its relationship to the planet. She might be called a kitchen philosopher whose writing reemphasizes the importance of using only the freshest locally grown organic and seasonal produce and animals that have been raised in a humane, wholesome manner.

Her degree from the University of California, Berkeley, was in French cultural studies. Waters says that the goal of education is not the mastery of a discipline but the mastery of the self and responsibility to the planet.

Waters had financial problems upon her entry into the restaurant business. Her father mortgaged his house to help get her started. In 1971, when Chez Panisse opened, it was overstaffed; she had 50 employees who received $5 an hour. It took little time before the restaurant was $40,000 in debt. A woman who ran a cookware shop loved the restaurant so much that she picked up all the charges and paid the bills, but she soon became disenchanted

with Alice's lack of monetary motivation. Other business partners bought out the Good Samaritan, but it was eight years before the restaurant showed a profit.

Waters never gave up her requirements for "the perfect little lettuces and the most exquisite goat cheese." The restaurant now operates on a budget and some of the staff own stock in the restaurant—and the place is a moneymaker. To ensure that the "best and freshest" foods are selected, Waters employs a "forager" to search out and get the best from about 60 farmers and ranches in the area.[43]

Both her restaurants and her publications have brought Waters national attention and won her numerous honors. Not only do steady patrons come to her two restaurants, Chez Panisse Café and Chez Panisse Restaurant, but chefs, food writers, and others come great distances to eat there. Chez Panisse prints its menu seven days in advance; its diversity proclaims the place's virtuosity. The café menu changes twice daily, at lunch and at dinner.

To spread the gospel of ecology and the need to eat only fresh, organic food, Waters has fostered the Edible Schoolyard project, in which gardens are part of children's school curriculum. She is also involved as an adviser to the horticultural project in the San Francisco County Jail and its related Garden Project. In 1997, she was named Humanitarian of the Year by the James Beard Foundation.

Courtesy of Alice Waters

Alice Waters is a pioneer of California cuisine.

MARC VETRI

Trained in Bergamo, Italy, by some of the region's most noted chefs, Marc Vetri brings a bold, contemporary sensibility to classic Italian cooking.[44] Throughout his career Vetri has worked in several restaurants including Wolfgang Puck's Granita, Coco Pazzo, and Bella Blu. Today, Vetri is the chef and owner of two award winning restaurants:

- Vetri Ristorante, located in the heart of Center City Philadelphia, Pennsylvania
- Osteria, also located in Philadelphia on Broad Street (co-owner and chef)

In 2010, he opened his third Philadelphia restaurant, Amis.

Under his direction as executive chef, Bella Blu was named "Best New Restaurant" by *New York* magazine. Vetri himself, Vetri Ristorante, and Osteria have won the praise of *Gourmet* magazine, *Wine Spectator, Restaurant Hospitality, Food & Wine* magazine, *The New York Times, Philadelphia Inquirer, Philadelphia* magazine, *Bon Appétit,* and *Philadelphia Weekly*. Vetri's impressive portfolio includes the following awards:

- *Food & Wine*'s "Ten New Best Chefs"
- James Beard Award for "Best Chef Mid-Atlantic"
- *Philadelphia Inquirer*'s highest restaurant ranking
- *Philadelphia Magazine*'s "50 Best Restaurants" for Osteria
- Referred to as a "culinary genius" by the Zagat Survey

Vetri takes pride in his ownership of both restaurants. According to *The New York Times,* he spends half of every night at Vetri, half at Osteria, because he can't just let either of them be! In addition to his restaurants, he also has his own cookbook, *Il Viaggio Di Vetri: A Culinary Journey*.

BARBARA LYNCH

James Beard Award–winner Barbara Lynch is regarded as one of Boston's, and the country's, leading chefs and restaurateurs.[45] Lynch has built a company of nine culinary businesses with 250 employees and $19 million in annual sales.[46] While growing up in South Boston, Barbara, at the age of 13, got her first kitchen job cooking at a local rectory. But it was a high school home economics teacher and a job working with Chef Mario Binello at Boston's esteemed St. Botolph Club piqued her interest in one day becoming a professional chef.[47]

During her early twenties, Barbara worked under some of Boston's greatest culinary talents, including Chef Todd English, first at Michaela's then at Olives and later Figs. After working with Todd for several years, Barbara went to Italy to learn about Italian cuisine. On her return to Boston she became the executive chef at Galleria Italiana, bringing national acclaim to the tiny trattoria when she captured *Food & Wine*'s "Ten Best New Chefs in America" award.[48]

Always wanting her own restaurant, Barbara opened No. 9 Park, in Boston's Beacon Hill neighborhood in 1998. The restaurant immediately received rave reviews from publications around the country and was named one of the "Top 25 New Restaurants in America" by *Bon Appétit* and "Best New Restaurant" by *Food & Wine*.[49]

Barbara has also opened two restaurants in the South End in 2003: B&G Oysters, serving exquisitely fresh seafood, and The Butcher Shop, a wine bar and full-service butcher shop. In 2005, Barbara began catering with the opening of Niche Catour. Barbara opened Plum Produce in September 2006, and next door, in August 2007, Stir, a demonstration kitchen and cookbook store. Barbara has also launched two other concepts in Boston's Fort Point neighborhood. Drink, which is a bar dedicated to the craft of the cocktail and Sportello (Italian for counter), Barbara's modern interpretation of a diner. Barbara also opened Menton, Boston's first and only Relais & Châteaux property.[50]

Barbara has won numerous awards including, *Travel & Leisure* proclaimed No. 9 Park one of the "Top 50 Restaurants in America." For two consecutive years, No. 9 Park was named "Best Restaurant, General Excellence" by *Boston* magazine, and *Gourmet* included it as one of "America's Top 50 Restaurants" in 2006. In 2007, *Boston Magazine* named Barbara "Best Chef." In 2009, Barbara was honored to receive the Crittenton Women's Union's Amelia Earhart Award. Past recipients include Doris Kearns Goodwin and Julia Child. Barbara's first cookbook *Stir: Mix it up in the Italian Tradition* was published by Houghton Mifflin and won a Gourmand award for "Best Chef Cookbook" for the United States.[51]

Centralized Home Delivery Restaurants

Meals are being ordered and delivered via the Internet in the same way as fresh flowers. Existing food courts lend themselves to being changed into order and preparation centers where four or five popular food items, such as pizza and Mexican, Italian, and Chinese foods, can be prepared and delivered within a local area by car, motorcycle, or bicycle. The center can be where a bank of phone operators and clerks take orders via the Internet or by telephone. The home delivery centers verify and process credit card information and use computers to perform the accounting.

Home delivery has been well established by individual pizza parlors and pizza chains. Much of the delivery cost is shifted from the pizza producer to the delivery person, whose income comes partly from customer tips.

Centralization reduces the costs of order taking, food preparation, and accounting. Marketing costs, however, may not decrease. Competition will continue to force most players to advertise heavily. Economies of scale (efficiency resulting from high volume, automation, staffing efficiency, buying power, and specialized equipment) can reduce food, labor, and overhead costs.

In theory, the order taking and accounting can be done at any location connected to the Internet, locally or internationally. The system does not even require that operators know what the customer has ordered; they simply transmit the order to a delivery person.

An order for pizza, theoretically, can be processed in China and prepared and delivered in California or New York. The Internet is inexpensive to use, faceless, formless, and global. The real question is whether the food can be delivered hot, tasty, and ready to eat.

Home delivery is being offered for upscale dining as well. Steak-Out Franchising, an Atlanta company, offers steak dinners for home delivery. Its home-delivered steak dinner comes with baked potato, tossed salad, dinner roll, beverage, and dessert for about $14.

To promote home delivery in affluent communities, meals are delivered in special boxes or baskets. For example, a Japanese meal may be packed in a partitioned lacquered box called a bento box.

A variation on the home delivery theme is found in Chicago, where some hotels distribute the menus from 12 selected restaurants to their patrons for room service. The guest can call room service, which faxes or e-mails the order to the restaurant of choice. The hotel picks up the meal in 25 or 30 minutes and adds on charges of $6 to $8 for delivery.

Several chains are contemplating home delivery for more complicated, more expensive meals. The concept has worked for years via Meals on Wheels, a service provided for people who have difficulty getting out of their apartments or homes. The meals are nutritionally balanced and are delivered mostly by volunteers. An entrepreneur could learn home delivery by participating in the program.

Take-out meals have been available for many years. The old corned beef and cabbage meal available in several Northeastern cities was essentially take-out. In cities, take-out meals are delivered to the address in minimal time. In cases where customers do their own pickup, requests for meals can be phoned in or faxed to restaurants, cutting wait time at the restaurant.

Summary

This chapter describes the kinds and characteristics of restaurants and their owners. Restaurant categories have not been universally agreed on and, from time to time, new segments are conceived in the literature. A comparison of corporate-owned, independent, and franchised restaurants is made. Chef-owner restaurateurs, notable female restaurateurs, celebrity chefs, and centralized home delivery restaurants are also discussed.

Key Terms and Concepts

Bakery-café

Casual restaurant

Centralization

Chain restaurant

Chef-owned restaurant

Ethnic restaurant

Family restaurant

Fine-dining restaurant

Independent restaurant

Quick casual restaurant

Quick-service restaurant

Steakhouse restaurant

Theme restaurant

Review Questions

1. Briefly describe the kinds and characteristics of restaurants.
2. What kind of restaurant would you be most interested to work in? Why?
3. What kind of restaurant would you most like to own? Why?
4. What are the highlights of Mexican restaurant menus?
5. Name elements that make for fine dining.
6. Name three women chefs who are restaurant partners and describe their activities.

CASE STUDY: EVOS

Origins

EVOS was started in Tampa, Florida, in 1994 by Alkis Crassas, Michael Jeffers, and Dino Lambridis, three friends from different backgrounds who enjoyed eating the classic all-American meal of burgers, fries, and shakes, but were tired of feeling guilty after consuming food that was unhealthy and contained so many calories. After determining that a niche for healthy fast-food was nowhere to be found in the market, they decided to start a new restaurant concept based on that notion. The end result was EVOS, a fast-casual restaurant offering the typical fast-food items that people love to eat, but re-creating them with better ingredients and healthier preparation techniques. Originally, the restaurant was more similar to an independent café, but over the years, EVOS has evolved into a well-developed concept franchised at multiple locations throughout the southeast. Currently, there are six EVOS locations—including four in South Florida, one in Atlanta, Georgia, one in Chapel Hill, North Carolina—and several in development.

Recipe for Success

At EVOS, menu items are "air-baked" instead of deep-fried with oil, which significantly cuts down on excess fat. EVOS supports sustainable farming whenever possible, and many of its fresh products and ingredients are sourced from local family farms. The best-selling item on the menu is the Original Steakburger, made with naturally raised grass fed beef, which is both hormone and antibiotic-free. Other favorites include "airbaked" chicken strips made with hormone-free white meat chicken, fresh salads made with locally grown organic field greens, homemade milkshakes made with organic milk and sugar, and real fruitshakes made with natural fruit juices. Because the food is fresh, high in quality, and unique, EVOS runs on a significantly higher food cost than many of their fast-food competitors, as approximately 31 percent.

The owners' philosophy for success is built from a three-piece recipe. First and foremost, food is the star in a restaurant business, and you have to get that right before moving forward. Once you have the right food, you need to hire and retain the right people. At EVOS, the philosophy from day one has been a coaching mentality instead of a managing mentality. This means that managers should focus on coaching and developing their employees in an environment that cultivates participation and gives employees empowerment to make important decisions. Finally, it is important to build restaurants that are comfortable and inviting, while maintaining the focus on eco-friendly initiatives.

Environment

EVOS is a company dedicated to eco-friendly and sustainable business practices. The name EVOS means "fast food evolved," which epitomizes both their revolutionary outlook on fast-food taken to new heights and their environmentally conscious mentality. EVOS has made numerous commitments to the implementation of clean renewable energy by purchasing commercial restaurant equipment from Energy Star, using compact fluorescent lighting, which produces less energy, and using energy conserving light switches in the bathrooms, which turn off automatically when they are not being used. Furthermore, the owners use a variety of sustainable materials when building EVOS establishments, such as eco-friendly paints and adhesives, recycled wood supplies, and eco-friendly flooring panes. The paper products used in the restaurant are printed on recycled paper with soy- and vegetable-based inks, and the plastic cups and bags are biodegradable. According to the owners, the use of recycled paper and biodegradable products can amount to more than 5 percent of a restaurant's operational costs.

Challenges and Goals

The owners of EVOS have faced many challenges from the beginning, including start-up and operational issues. Healthy fast-food did not exist when the original restaurant was conceptualized, and everything was new territory for the owners. Creating a menu was difficult because there were not many places you could use as a reference. In the beginning, they offered items such as tomato basil soup, traditional turkey and cheese sandwich, or tabouleh and hummus, all of which were made fresh from scratch. Additionally, only one of the three owners had previous restaurant experience before starting EVOS. When the restaurant opened, business took off from the beginning, which required all three owners to perform the daily operations, while learning the ins and outs of running a restaurant business on-the-go.

EVOS has many goals moving forward as a company. The most general goal is bringing healthy fast food to America in as many communities as possible. One of the most important goals that EVOS owners have established is maintaining the culture they have created within the organization. This involves running a company that the owners are proud of, and would want to work for if they were outsiders looking in, as well as a company they and their employees continuously want to work for as insiders looking out. The owners believe that this is extremely important to their success because the food and the look of the restaurant is something that can be copied, and probably has been to a certain extent, but the culture and the people are harder to copy, which has made EVOS unique in the long-term.

QUESTIONS

1. What type of restaurant would you classify EVOS as (quick-service, fast/quick-casual, casual, theme)? Why?
2. What other restaurant concepts is EVOS most similar to?
3. Who are EVOS's competitors, and what are some ways that they differentiate themselves from their competitors?
4. What are the advantages and disadvantages of placing such a heavy focus on eco-friendly and sustainable business practices?
5. Why do you think the EVOS concept has had such a modest growth over the last 18 years? What should their goal be for expansion over the next 5 or 10 years?

Endnotes

1. Selected extrapolation from *Nation's Restaurant News*, June 25, 2012.
2. Miami Subs website. http://miamisubs.com/financial-info July 30, 2012.
3. Chili's/Brinker International website. http://www.franchise.org/franchisordetailsview.aspx?id= 26768. Retrieved on July 30, 2012.
4. McDonald's website. www.mcdonalds.com/corp/franchise/purchasingYourFranchise/newRestaurants .html. July 2009, and http://www.aboutmcdonalds.com/mcd/franchising/us_franchising/aquiring_a_ franchise.html Retrieved on July 30, 2012.

5. Pizza Factory Express website. www.pizzafactory.com/express.html June, 2009 and http://www .franchisehelp.com/franchises/pizza-factory. July 30, 2012.

6. "McDonald's Is Lovin' Its Sale of Boston Market." *Forbes.* www.forbes.com/2007/08/06/mcdonalds-boston-market-markets-equity-cx_cg_0806markets44.html. July 2009.

7. "Our History." http://www.mcdonalds.com/us/en/our_story/our_history.html Retrieved on July 30, 2012.

8. "Domino's 101: Basic Facts." Domino's Pizza website. www.dominosbiz.com/Biz-Public-EN/ Site+Content/Secondary/About+Dominos/Fun+Facts/. Retrieved on July 2009.

9. "Jimmy John's Gourmet Sandwich Shops," *Entrepreneur.* Available at http://www.entrepreneur. com/franchises/jimmyjohnsgourmetsandwichshops/282480-0.html. Retrieved on July 30, 2012.

10. Brenna Halwey, "Pop-up Restaurants Become Elusive Trend in Kansas City," *Kansas City Business Journal* (June 22, 2012). Available at www.bizjournals.com/kansascity/blog/2012/06/pop-up-restaurants-become-elusive.html. Retrieved July 30, 2012.

11. Ken Miguel, "Latest San Francisco Food Trend: Pop-up Restaurants," *KGO-TV* (May 11, 2012). Available at http://abclocal.go.com/kgo/story?section=news/assignment_7&id=8658755. Retrieved July 30, 2012.

12. Aileen Gallagher, Daniel Maurer, and Helen Rosner, "Trucks on a Roll," New York Restaurants (July 11, 2010). Available at http://nymag.com/restaurants/cheapeats/2010/67139/. Retrieved on September 13, 2012.

13. Georgina Gustin, "Food Trucks Are Still on a Roll," *St. Louis Post Dispatch* (July 29, 20120). Available at http://www.stltoday.com/business/local/food-trucks-are-still-on-a-roll/article_b4d903fa-d830-11e1-bec9-0019bb30f31a.html. Retrieved on September 10, 2012.

14. "Food Trucks Roll More Variety into Downtown Tampa Lunch Scene," *Tampa Bay Times.* http:// www.tampabay.com/news/humaninterest/food-trucks-roll-more-variety-into-downtown-tampa-lunch-scene/1199764. Retrieved on October 10, 2012.

15. Tiffany Hsu, "Starbucks Adds Artisan Pastries with La Boulange Bakery Purchase, *Los Angeles Times* (June 4, 2012). Available at http://articles.latimes.com/2012/jun/04/business/la-fi-mo-starbucks-la-boulange-bakery-20120604. Retrieved December 18, 2012.

16. http://www.10best.com/destinations/massachusetts/boston/cambridge/restaurants/carberrys-bakery-coffee-house/ retrieved on May3, 2013.

17. Richard Mullins, "First PDQ Chicken Restaurant Going up in Tampa," Tampa Tribune (September 22, 2011). Available at first-pdq-chicken-restaurant-going-up-in-tampa-ar-259464 retrieved July 30, 2012.

18. Eliabeth Olson, "An Animated Ad with a Plot Line and a Moral," The New York Times (February 9, 2012), http://www.nytimes.com/2012/02/10/business/media/chipotle-ad-promotes-sustainable-farming.html. Retrieved May 20, 2013.

19. David Mansbach and Jeffrey Kolton, "Hotel Restaurant Solutions—Turning a Headache into an Opportunity," Hoteliers (April 30, 2010). Available at http://www.4hoteliers.com/4hots_fshw .php?mwi=5034. Retrieved July 2012.

20. Personal conversation with Chris Sullivan, March 26, 2013.

21. Ibid.

22. Courtesy of Chris Sullivan and Bloomin Brands.

23. Darden 2012 Annual Report, http://investor.darden.com/files/doc_financials/darden_2012ar% 5B1%5D.pdf.

24. "Romano's Macaroni Grill," Francise Direct, http://www.franchisedirect.com/foodfranchises/ Romanos-Macaroni-Grill-07418/ufoc/ retrieved on May 6, 2013.

25. "Darden Restaurants Reports Third Quarter Diluted Net Earnings Per Share of $1.02; Declares a Quarterly Dividend of 50 Cents per Share," Darden news release (March 22, 2013). http://investor. darden.com/investors/news-releases/press-release-details/2013/Darden-Restaurants-Reports-Third-Quarter-Diluted-Net-Earnings-Per-Share-of-102-Declares-a-Quarterly-Dividend-of-50-Cents-Per-Share/default.aspx. Retrieved May 6, 2013.

26. Personal conversation with PF Chang's Corporate office, September 19, 2012.

27. Ibid.

28. P.F. Chang's China Bistro, Inc. "Our Restaurants." Available at http://www.pfcb.com/restaurants. html retrieved on December 18, 2012.

29. Meredith Galante, "The Ultimate List of Restaurants Owned by Celebrities," Business Insider (November 21, 2011), http://www.businessinsider.com/restaurants-owned-by-celebrities-2011-11?op=1. Retrieved on May 6, 2013.

30. Martin Pegler, *Theme Restaurants Design—Entertainment and Fun in Dining* (New York: Reporting Corporation, 1997), p. 11.

31. Fadó Irish Pub website. http://www.fadoirishpub.com/washington/about-fado#. Retrieved on April 23, 2013.

32. John R. Walker, *Introduction to Hospitality*, 5th ed. (Upper Saddle River, NJ: Pearson, 2009), pp. 337–338.

33. Ibid.

34. Personal conversation with Donald E. Lundberg March 26, 2000.

35. Martin E. Dorf, *Restaurants That Work: Case Studies of the Best in the Industry* (New York: Whitney Library of Design, 1992).

36. Andrew Dornenburg and Karen Page, *Becoming a Chef* (Hoboken, NJ: John Wiley & Sons, Inc., 2003).

37. Belinda Goldsmith, ed., "World Chefs: Top 10 Celebrity Chef-Owned Restaurants in the U.S." Reuters (April 17, 2010). Available at http://www.reuters.com/article/2010/08/17/us-chefs-celebrity-idUSTRE67G1M720100817. Retrieved on September 19, 2012.

38. Ibid.

39. Auntie Anne's website. www.auntieannes.com. July 2009.

40. "Another View," *QSR*, http://www2.qsrmagazine.com/articles/interview/90/Daniels-Carter-1.phtml retrieved on May 7, 2013.

41. Ari Shapiro. "Americans' Insatiable Hunger for Celebrity Chefs." National Public Radio. www.npr.org/templates/story/story.php?storyId=4522975. Retrieved on July 2009.

42. *Food and Wine* Magazine. Accessed through Lucques press section. www.lucques.com/press/green-goddess.html. Retrieved on July 2009.

43. Alace Waters address to the National Restaurant Association May 18, 2001.

44. Vetri Ristorante website. "The Restaurant." Available at http://www.vetriristorante.com/index.php/aboutvetri/. www.vetriristorante.com/index.php?a=biography. Retrieved on April 23, 2013.

45. http://barbaralynch.com/about/ retrieved on May 7, 2013.

46. Glenn Rifkin, "After South Boston, A Restaurant Was Easy," *The New York Times* (January 4, 2012), http://www.nytimes.com/2012/01/05/business/smallbusiness/after-south-boston-opening-a-restaurant-didnt-seem-so-risky.html. Retrieved on May 7, 2013.

47. "Barbara Lynch," West: Advancing Women in the Business of Science & Technology, http://www.westorg.org/barbara-lynch-bio retrieved on May 7, 2013.

48. Ibid.

49. Rifkin.

50. http://barbaralynch.com/about/ retrieved on May 7, 2013.

51. Ibid.

Concept, Location, and Design

LEARNING OBJECTIVES

After reading and studying this chapter, you should be able to:

- Recognize the benefits of a good restaurant name.

- Explain the relationship between concept and market.

- Explain why a restaurant concept might fail.

- Discuss some qualities of successful restaurant concepts.

- Identify factors to consider when choosing a restaurant's location.

- Identify factors to consider when developing a restaurant concept.

- List restaurant knockout criteria.

Courtesy of Columbia Restaurant

Restaurant Concepts

The objective in planning a restaurant is to assemble, on paper, the ideas for a restaurant that will be profitable and satisfying to the guest and owner/operator. The formulation of these ideas is called the *restaurant concept*, the matrix of ideas that constitutes what will be perceived as the restaurant's image. The concept is devised to interest a certain group of people (or groups of people), called a *target market*. Marketing is the sum of activities intended to attract people to the restaurant. This includes determining what group or groups (target markets) are most likely to react favorably to the concept.

In this section, we discuss *restaurant concepts*. Later sections discuss the relationships among concept, business plan, site selection (restaurant location), and marketing. Concept, location, ambience, and marketing are interdependent. Concept development applies to any foodservice operation, from a hot dog stand to a luxury restaurant, from quick-service to theme restaurants.

The challenge is to create a restaurant concept that fits a definite target market, a concept better suited to its market than that presented by competing restaurants, and to bring it into being. This is known as being *D&B*—different and better. If a restaurant concept is too similar to the competition, there is a good chance of being sued. In 2007, Matador in Seattle was sued by the owner of Peso's, Brian Hutmacher. Hutmacher claimed Matador so closely imitated Peso's in appearance and food that customers confused the two![1] The restaurant business is intensely competitive. There is always a better concept coming on stream—better in atmosphere, menu, location, marketing, image, and management. If a restaurant is not competitive, another restaurant down the street, across town, or next door will take away its customers.

This challenge does not mean that a new restaurant must be built. Plenty of existing restaurants and other buildings can be taken over. The challenge is to develop and install a new concept, acknowledging the possibility that it may be necessary to modify it as competition and other conditions change.

The best concepts are often the result of learning from mistakes. Just when you think you have your concept figured out, guess what? You don't. Also, just when you think it's hopeless, the clouds break, a rainbow appears, and the concept will be reborn. It may be something completely different from what you started with.

Every restaurant represents a concept and projects a total impression or image. The image appeals to a certain market: children, romantics, people celebrating special occasions, fun types, people seeking a formal or a casual venue. The concept should fit the location and reach out to appeal to its target market(s). In planning a restaurant concept, location, menu, and decor should intertwine. When a concept and image lose appeal, they must be modified or even changed completely.

Concept comprises everything that affects how the patron views the restaurant: public relations, advertising, promotion, and the operation itself. Concept frames the public's perception of the total restaurant. It includes the building, its curbside appeal, and its exterior decor. Does the restaurant invite people to venture in, or is it neglected and dirty in appearance? Decor, menu, and style of operation are part of the concept. Concept includes the personality of the owner, the appearance of the dining room staff, the music, and the tone of the place. Particularly important are the menu and the food and its presentation. Symbols, as seen in the sign, logo, colors, upholstery, and lighting, are aspects of concept. The right music reinforces the concept. The concept provides the framework on which to hang the image. The following are 10 tips for developing a restaurant concept:

1. Make your concept different enough from the competition.
2. Don't let your concept be too far ahead of the current times.
3. Don't price your menu out of the market.
4. Pay attention to food costs during menu development.
5. Make your concept profitable.
6. Good concepts are on-trend.
7. Make your concept easily identifiable.
8. Take inspiration from others.
9. Make sure the concept and location fit.
10. Love your concept.[2]

An interesting new concept in New Orleans is from the Commander's Family of Restaurants in the French Quarter, where the family business began in the 1950s, with SoBou. "We're South of Bourbon (ok—it's really southeast), in the land of civilized drinking and worlds away from the oversized beers and bad frozen drinks," SoBou's website states.[3] The modern Creole saloon is inspired by street food and has a beverage focus.

As the SoBou concept developed, cocktails and the warmth of a saloon or tavern environment were very much on their mind, but it focused on dishes people crave. For SoBou, "the food is always center stage, but stage right are the cocktails and stage left is the wine."[4]

When you think of Nashville's food scene, you probably think of barbecue or fried chicken. Chefs Josh Habiger and Erik Anderson want to change that reputation with their 32-seat tasting-menu restaurant.[5] The open kitchen is laid out in a U-shaped curve, and the two chefs prepare an ever-changing seven-course dinner. It's pricey, at $100 a person, but the high price didn't concern Habiger and Anderson. "Yes, guests are more focused on their money, so they want to get more quality for their dollar," Habiger says. "This is more of an experience; it's like a sporting event." The menu is flexible to accommodate both availability of ingredients and the chefs' whims. "We can do whatever we want," Anderson says. "The plating style has a modern look, but what goes on those plates can change at a moment's notice."[6]

CONCEPT: CLEAR-CUT OR AMBIGUOUS?

Many restaurants lack clear-cut concepts. The symbols, furnishings, service, and all of those things that make up the atmosphere of a restaurant are not integrated into an image that is projected for everyone to see. Logos (identifying symbols), signs, uniforms, menus, and decor should fit together into a whole that comes across to the public as a well-defined image.

Concepts can be purposefully ambiguous, but most restaurants are made more visible psychologically if they project a theme, a character, and a purpose. A concept is strengthened if it immediately establishes an identity, one that is vivid, easily remembered, and has a favorable ring. The name *Wendy's* was chosen because of its identification potential and because it was easy to pronounce; it also tied in easily with the theme "old-fashioned hamburgers." And it also happened to be the nick-name of the daughter of R. David Thomas (then president). Taco Bell gained instant recognition because the word *taco* is synonymous with Mexican food.

Y DON'T OPEN A RESTAURANT UNLESS YOU . . .

1. Have experience in the restaurant business, especially in the segment in which you plan to operate.
2. Don't mind giving up your evenings and long weekends—not to mention mornings and afternoons.
3. Are able to accept personal risk. Have money to lose—oops! we mean capital to start a high-risk business.
4. Have a concept in mind and menus developed.
5. Have completed a detailed business plan.
6. Have personal and family goals established for the next several years.
7. Have the patience of a saint and two active thyroid glands!
8. Have identified a quantifiable need in the market for the type of restaurant you are considering opening.
9. Have an exit plan—the restaurant business is easy to enter but potentially costly to exit.
10. Can afford a lawyer and an accountant experienced in the restaurant business.

The name of the restaurant is part of the image. The Spaghetti Factory suggests quick service, low cost, and a fun place for Italian food. El Torito suggests a Mexican theme, and T.G.I. Friday's portrays a fun image—however, people who do not know that T.G.I. Friday's is a restaurant would not know what to expect. Coco's is even less descriptive—a patron would hardly know what to expect.

Courtesy of the San Diego Convention & Visitors Bureau
View of diners from above.

The restaurant name can tell the customer what to anticipate—Pizza Palace, New China House, Taco Bell, Hamburger Heaven. No one really expects to meet grandma at Grandma's Kitchen, but the name suggests a homey, friendly place, one without escargots on the menu.

The Seven Grains suggests a health-food restaurant, as does The Thinnery. Well-known British names like Trafalgar Square suggest a British atmosphere and menu. Mama Mia's reflects an Italian menu. La Campagne projects a country French theme; Long John Silver's and Red Lobster suggest seafood restaurants.

Naming a restaurant after the owner has proven successful for centuries, even though the restaurant may use a first name, as in Al's Place. The personal name implies that somebody by the name of Al is going to be around to see that things go well. Stuart Anderson is not likely to be found at any one of the many Stuart Anderson's Cattle Ranch restaurants, but the feeling is that he may be somewhere in the wings watching out for his guests. Naming a restaurant after the proprietor suggests that someone has pride of ownership. The personally named restaurant evokes an image of someone who cares, hovering in the background.

One restaurant on Union Street in San Francisco has a great name, Sushi Chardonnay. You know what to expect. Another good name is Cantina Latina, a casual restaurant with a Latin theme, or how about Eat Here, the name of a new restaurant by award winning chef Sean Murphy. A name that tells people what to expect, one that is easy to remember, and one that people can pronounce is a great asset worth thousands in advertising and promotion dollars—because you don't have to spend them on name recognition.

Courtesy of Sean Murphy
Eat Here—what a great name for a restaurant!

PROTECTING THE RESTAURANT'S NAME

Lawsuits over restaurant names do happen. Even if an owner of a new restaurant were named Howard Johnson, he would be wise not to call his restaurant Howard Johnson's because of trademark regulations. Once selected, a name may be difficult to change without serious financial loss. Ray Kroc, who built McDonald's restaurants, had to pay several million dollars to the original McDonald's owners to continue using that name and format. The proprietary right to a restaurant name not already in use begins with usage and signs, promotional campaigns, and advertising material.

If another party uses your restaurant name, you should take action against that person by proving that you, the challenging party, used the name first. Loss of the right to use a name means changing signs, menus, and promotional material. It can also mean court costs and, perhaps, the loss of power that has been built into the name by a superior operation.

THE MCDONALD'S CONCEPT AND IMAGE

To illustrate concept, look at McDonald's—the greatest restaurant success story of all time. The concept is the all-American family restaurant—clean, wholesome, inexpensive, and fun. Ray Kroc would not allow a jukebox, cigarette machine, or telephone in McDonald's because it encouraged people to "overstay their welcome." In the company's advertising, McDonald's food servers are wholesome, bursting with health and goodwill. Ronald McDonald, the jolly clown, is better known in the minds of children than any other fictional character except Mickey Mouse and Santa Claus. Ronald is fun; therefore, McDonald's is fun. McDonald's TV advertising has reached into the American psyche and implanted the idea that eating at McDonald's is unalloyed joy. Image presentation is consistent and easy to understand; simplicity is portrayed in uncluttered, quick, efficient service.

The simple, straightforward menu is one key to the effectiveness of McDonald's advertising.

While the term *concept restaurant* is relatively new, concept restaurants have been around for some time. The person who took the retired railroad dining car in the 1920s and made it into a diner had the makings of a concept restaurant. In the 1930s, Victor Bergeron converted a garage into a schmaltzy Polynesian restaurant and called it Trader Vic's—a concept restaurant. The Rib Rooms, popular in the 1950s and 1960s, were an adaptation of Simpson's on the Strand in London, a famous rolling-beef-cart restaurant going back many years.

Theme restaurants, which follow a particular ethnic menu and decor or are built around a particular idea, are concept restaurants. The concept can be ambiguous, as is the case with Bennigan's, Chili's, Houlihan's, and Applebee's, where it is difficult to ascertain any particular theme other than bric-a-brac or American bistro.

Decor and menu at these restaurants are fun and stimulating. In the men's room, straps from an old trolley car may be hanging over the urinals. The customer may find himself facing a mirror enclosed by a horse collar. Decorative surprises are the norm. The exterior may be painted an odd color, such as blue-green, or sport a brightly colored red-and-white awning. The concept features are humor, self-deprecation, full service, high-quality food, good value, and a place where people can relax.

Courtesy of Columbia Restaurant

Flamenco dancers entertain diners at the Columbia Restaurant in Tampa, Florida.

GODZILLA

A restaurant in San Francisco, named Godzilla after the original movie, was recently forced to change its name. This happened when the more recent version of the movie opened across the street. TV cameras noticed the restaurant name and crowds; a reporter interviewed the owner, and when a movie executive saw the 30-second TV clip, he contacted the copyright owners. A few days later, a letter arrived from the lawyers of the movie's copyright owners advising the restaurant owner that he was capitalizing on the movie's name and that he must change the name or face a lawsuit.

Some concept restaurants make a virtue of the rustic and the antique by using exposed wood and unpainted old barn siding. An array of antique artifacts can produce a novel effect and, if selected and placed well, can be an inexpensive way to decorate. The owner can count on minimum maintenance.

Defining the Concept and Market

In selecting a concept for a restaurant, define it precisely in the context of which markets will find it appealing. A typical coffee shop with counter and booth service, for example, may appeal to the working family or the traveler on an interstate highway. Ask yourself:

- Will a quick-service place with drive-through, walk-up, and table service appeal to the young family, teenagers, and children?
- Will an upscale restaurant with a view, opening at 5 P.M. to serve dinners, appeal to upper-middle-class patrons?
- Is a Mexican restaurant with hybrid Mexican decor and inexpensive food appealing to the middle class for an evening out?
- Is a pizza house with beer and wine appealing to the young family as a fun place?
- Is a coffeehouse menu in a dinner-house setting, including a few European menu touches, the right concept? Or should it be a stepped-up coffee shop with a few dinner items?
- Does the restaurant offer authentic French, Chinese, or Japanese food? If so, does it have an authentic French, Chinese, or Japanese family operating it? La Campagne, for example, depends on a chef who is highly skilled in classical French cuisine. Authentic Mexican restaurants usually have Mexican (or Mexican American) chefs. Japanese chefs are expected to be behind the grills at Benihana restaurants.

A quick-service ethnic restaurant does not need the authenticity required of a full-service ethnic restaurant. This fact is amply demonstrated in such chains as Taco Bell and Del Taco, which are staffed by teenagers without regard to ethnic background. A quick-service Mexican or Italian restaurant can be operated easily once the format is learned.

Whatever the concept, there must be a market to support it, a clientele who walk or drive to the restaurant and who want the kind of service, food, price, and atmosphere offered. A restaurant cannot exist without a market. One must fit the other. The market may constitute only a small percentage of the total population in an area—for instance, travelers on a nearby freeway, occupants of office buildings in the area, passersby in a shopping mall, or people willing to drive half an hour or more to experience the sort of excitement offered by the restaurant. There must also be a market gap, a need for the concept offered.

Figure 3.1 suggests the relationship between the market and the restaurant. The concept and market are central to the restaurant, supported by the menu, prices, service, quality, location, atmosphere, food, and management.

All aspects of the concept help determine whether a location is right for a particular market. Chuck E. Cheese's pizza parlors cater to children and specialize in children's parties. A shopping mall site offers the parking, security, and convenience that define a good location for this restaurant; the market consists of the families who patronize the mall. Coffee-shop patrons are often freeway travelers but also can be families within the community. All factors—the food, the seating, the type of service, the entire format—select out a particular market, perhaps an age group and an income level. Promotion and advertising can change the image to attract new markets, to a certain extent. Usually, however, promotion and advertising concentrate on an established market—teenagers, families, drivers, office personnel, mall shoppers, and so on.

Census tract surveys are helpful in assessing the number of people in the proposed restaurant catchment area and their demographics (age, occupation, income, sex, ethnic background, religion, family formation, and composition). This information assists in determining whether the concept has the market to support it. The US Census Bureau revealed in 2009 that American consumers racked up $337.7 billion in charges for retail and restaurant services, down 10.1 percent from the previous year.[7] As unemployment remains high and the economy is slow to recover, restaurants continue to struggle.[8]

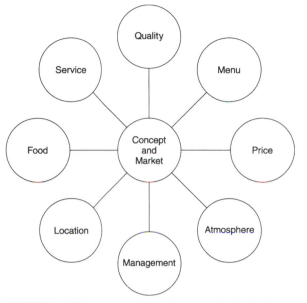

FIGURE 3.1 The concept and market comprise the hub around which the restaurant develops.

Successful Restaurant Concepts

T.G.I. Friday's, Outback, Red Lobster, and many others, both chain and independent, have remained successful over the years because they have stayed close to the guest and concentrated on quality and service. Most cities have an array of exciting restaurants. Some are owned and operated by celebrity chefs, such as Wolfgang Puck's Spago and Chinois in Las Vegas.

Some celebrities (usually with business partners) enjoy trying their hand at restaurants. Sports celebrities who own restaurants include Walt Frazier, Greg Norman, Ray Bourque, Mike Ditka, Brett Favre, Billy Sims, John Elway, Tony Hawk, Michael Jordan, Albert Pujols, Yao Ming, and Wayne Gretzky.[9,10] Other celebrities have also gotten into the act. Robert DeNiro owns Nobu, with worldwide locations. Jay-Z owns the 40/40 Club. Justin Timberlake owns Southern Hospitality. But even big names do not guarantee success: Jennifer Lopez, Ashton Kuchter, and Britney Spears have all opened—and closed—restaurants.[11]

A concept created by Lettuce Entertain You Enterprises is Papagus, an authentic taverna that offers hearty Greek delights in warm, friendly, rustic surroundings. *Mezedes,* a variety of traditional bite-size offerings, may be enjoyed with Greek wine and ouzo. The display kitchen adds an experiential atmosphere and offers specialties such as spit-roasted chicken, whole broiled red snapper, traditional braised lamb, spanakopita, and baklava.

The Lettuce Entertain You Group has several outstanding theme restaurants in the Chicago area and beyond. They include Scoozi, which recalls an artist's studio and serves Italian country cuisine; Café Ba-Ba-Reeba, a Spanish restaurant featuring tapas, the popular hot and cold "little dishes of Spain"; Shaw's Crab House, a premier seafood house that features the Blue Crab Lounge, an oyster bar offering oysters on the half shell, clams, lobster, and crab dishes. The main dining room serves more than 40 fresh seafood items plus chicken and beef.

Corner Bakery Café literally grew out of baking fresh bread for Maggiano's Little Italy. It offers fresh specialty breads in a bakery atmosphere serving breakfast, lunch, and dinner. Among the newer concepts are Big Bowl, serving fresh Chinese and Thai foods, and De Pescara, an Italian seafood house. Wildfire, an American steak, chop, and seafood restaurant concept, has an aura reminiscent of a 1940s dinner club. At Magic Pan Crêpes Stands (*crêpes* is the French word for "pancakes"), crepes have been folded, rolled, and wrapped around various items for years. Among the fillings are cherries royal, chicken divan, spinach soufflé, chocolate Nutella, and crêpes Suzette. R. J. Grunts, the original Lettuce Entertain You restaurant, has catered since 1971. Music and decor are reminiscent of the 1960s and 1970s, in a casual eclectic setting. The restaurant is known for its award-winning chili, oversized cheddar burgers, and daily vegetarian specials. Room service will deliver some of your favorite Lettuce restaurant dishes right to your door.

THE HARD ROCK CAFE

The Hard Rock Cafe is one of the most successful restaurant chain concepts of all time. Peter Morton, then a young American college graduate in England, realized that London did not have a true American-style hamburger joint. In the late 1960s he borrowed about $60,000 from family and friends and opened two restaurants named The Great American Disaster.

Morton quickly realized that London needed a restaurant that not only served American food but also embodied the energy and excitement of music past and present. With this objective in mind, he opened the first Hard Rock Cafe (HRC) in London in 1971. The restaurant offered a hearty American meal at a reasonable price in an atmosphere charged with energy, fun, and the excitement of rock and roll.

HRC was an immediate success. Each HRC restaurant is decorated with memorabilia of rock-and-roll stars, including David Bowie's two-tone black-and-white Vox guitar from the movie *Absolute Beginners*, Jimi Hendrix's beaded and fringed suede jacket, Elvis Presley's gold-studded white stage cape, one of John Lennon's guitars, Madonna's bustier, and one of Elton John's outfits.

In 1982, with backing from film director Steven Spielberg, actor Tom Cruise, and others, the first Hard Rock Cafe in the United States opened in Los Angeles. There are now Hard Rock Cafes in San Francisco, Chicago, Houston, Honolulu, New Orleans, San Diego, Sydney, Maui, Las Vegas, and Aspen, to name a few.

Courtesy of Hard Rock Cafe

The Hard Rock Cafe's theme is a rock-and-roll hall of fame.

DANNY MEYER: A RESTAURANT SUCCESS STORY

Danny Meyer, president of Union Square Hospitality Group, is recognized by his peers as one of the nicest people you will ever meet. He has genuine warmth and a passion for what he does. His values and commitment to excellence have catapulted him to the pinnacle of the New York restaurant scene, where he manages his restaurants and jazz club.

Meyer was born and raised in St. Louis, Missouri. He grew up loving to cook, remembering practically every meal he had ever eaten, adoring festive family get-togethers, and longing to try new restaurants and return to old favorites. During his childhood, Meyer's family often hosted French children of the Relais & Châteaux patrons with whom his father did business. As a result, many meals at his St. Louis home had a Gallic touch and always included a bottle of *vin rouge*.

Courtesy of Danny Meyer

Danny Meyer, president of the Union Square Hospitality Group.

During college, Meyer worked for his father as a tour guide in Rome and then returned to the Eternal City to study international politics. He minored in the study of trattorias, spending at least as much time at the table as he did in the classroom. After graduating he was successful in a couple of jobs—one of which was as a six-figure salesperson for a maker of anti-shoplifting tags. But he gave up his job as the leading salesperson in the company when he decided to pursue his true passion for food and wine.

Meyer gained his first restaurant experience as an assistant manager at Pesca, an Italian seafood restaurant in the newly named Flatiron District of New York City. He then returned to Europe to study cooking as a culinary *stagiaire* in both Italy and France. He would stroll for hours in Rome and scrutinize the menus outside the restaurants before deciding on which one to dine in that evening. In 1985, at the age of 27, Danny created and launched a new breed of American eatery pairing imaginative food and wine with caring hospitality, comfortable surroundings, and outstanding value. Danny Meyer opened a kind of take-off of an Italian trattoria for just $75,000—half of that coming from skeptical relatives. Union Square Hospitality's sales are estimated at over $70 million a year.[12]

A critical success from the outset, Union Square Cafe has twice garnered the coveted three-star rating from *The New York Times*. The restaurant is widely noted as having sparked the dramatic resurgence of the Union Square neighborhood over the past decade. In July 1994, Meyer opened Gramercy Tavern with chef-partner Tom Colicchio. Gramercy Tavern is a renewal of the classic American tavern, offering refined American cuisine and warm hospitality in a historic landmark building.

Union Square Cafe earned the *Zagat Survey*'s number-one ranking as New York's Most Popular Restaurant for an unprecedented six consecutive years from 1997 through 2002. Gramercy Tavern was ranked number-two Most Popular in *Zagat* from 1999 to 2002. In 2003, Gramercy Tavern overtook its sibling restaurant Union Square Cafe (now ranked number two) to become New York's most popular restaurant.

In late 1998, Meyer began welcoming guests to two more restaurants—Eleven Madison Park and Tabla—each situated in a stunning art deco building that overlooks 150-year-old Madison Square Park in the heart of "Silicon Alley." Eleven Madison Park is a breathtaking, grand restaurant featuring Chef Daniel Humm's bold New York cuisine with a French soul.

In spring 2002, Meyer and his Union Square Hospitality Group partners opened Blue Smoke and Jazz Standard at 116 East 27th Street, offering New York

Courtesy of Danny Meyer

Gramercy Tavern is New York's favorite contemporary American cuisine restaurant.

mouthwatering real barbecue and soulful live jazz. Blue Smoke and Jazz Standard have been packed to the rafters since they opened, and were named "Best Barbecue" and "Best Jazz," respectively, by the editors of Citysearch.com. Blue Smoke has led the list of *New York* magazine's "Where to Eat."

In the summer of 2004, Shake Shack, a "roadside" food stand, opened in Madison Square Park, serving burgers, hot dogs, frozen custard, beer, wine, and more. Danny has also opened restaurants at the Museum of Modern Art—The Modern, Terrace, and Café 2; they bring his unique flair to harmonizing food and art.

Meyer describes his philosophy as *enlightened hospitality*—if your staff is happy, then your guests will be, too. Meyer gives each of his 400 employees a voucher to dine in one of the restaurants every month. They have to write a report on the experience; Meyer enjoys reading them. Ever the coach and teacher, he says that it is better to have your staff tell you what's wrong than for you to have to tell them.

Meyer is an active leader in the fight against hunger. He serves on the boards of Share Our Strength and City Harvest. He is equally active in civic affairs, serving on the executive committee of NYC & Co., where he also chairs the Restaurant Committee. He is an executive committee member of the Union Square Local Development Corporation and is chair of the Madison Square Park Conservancy. Meyer has been featured on numerous television shows and has spoken at national conventions.

Danny Meyer and his restaurants and chefs have won an unprecedented 10 James Beard Awards, including Outstanding Restaurant of the Year; Outstanding Wine Service; Humanitarian of the Year; Who's Who of Food and Beverage; Outstanding Service; and Best Restaurant Graphic Design. He has coauthored *The Union Square Cafe Cookbook* and *Second Helpings from Union Square Cafe*, both of which have been reprinted many times.

Meyer manages his 12 restaurants, a catering operation, and jazz club with an extraordinary team of partners called the Union Square Hospitality Group. He lives in New York with his wife, Audrey, and their four children.

A more recent exciting concept from California is Stacked: Food Well Built, a full-service restaurant where guests get exactly what they want. Guests are able to choose from a list of ingredients and create their own meal or select a signature item from the American food line up of burgers, pizza, salads, and mac 'n' cheese. The ingredients are flavorful and fresh and the proteins are grilled to order. And speaking of ordering—that is done via an IPad. Visit stacked.com to see for yourself.[13]

Restaurant Life Cycles

Nearly all restaurants have an almost human life cycle: birth, growth, maturity, senescence, and death. There is nothing mystical about the life cycle of restaurants, nor is there an absolute inevitability about a restaurant's success. Restaurants can be revived on occasion, and a few seem to improve with age. Delmonico's in New York City had a life span of over 75 years but finally expired as successive generations of the Delmonico family lacked the interest and enthusiasm of earlier generations. In the years that followed, others bought the building and used the name to open "Delmonico's" and today, the restaurant proudly boasts the label *America's First Restaurant: Since 1837.*[14] However, several other restaurants would dispute this. Chain operations rise and fall in a similar manner. The largest restaurant chain in the United States during the 1930s was Child's Restaurants, also in New York City. The chain was finally purchased by a hotelier because of its tax-loss value to him.

Horn & Hardart had a successful concept that represented the art deco generation and the new industrial strength that emerged after the Great Depression. The concept was the automat. Customers placed coins in a slot over one of a row of boxes and removed a food item from the box. There was a full selection of good-quality food, ranging from hot entrées to petit fours. Behind the boxes were people working in the kitchen to prepare and put up the food. The concept worked well for a number of years, but, over time, automats became history.

A major reason for a restaurant's decline could be the changing demographics of the area in which it is located. Areas rise and fall economically and socially. The restaurants within them are likely to follow suit. Fashions change. The all-white decor of some of the hamburger chains that flourished in the 1950s became less attractive when other chains moved to color. Top management ages, and the aging is reflected in the operations. The restaurant concept that excited the public when first introduced becomes tired after several years, and its power to excite fades as newer concepts are introduced in the same community. Menus that were entirely satisfactory at one time are no longer appealing.

Restaurant designs and buildings that were novel and attractive when new lose their luster when compared with newer, larger, more expensive designs. In the 1960s, a restaurant investment of a few hundred thousand dollars was enough to produce an imposing building—which by the mid-1970s looked uninteresting compared with restaurants with investments of $1 million to $3 million. As restaurant chains were purchased by conglomerates such as W. R. Grace and General Mills, huge sums of money became available for glamour restaurant investments that introduced a new dimension of scale and luxury into the restaurant business.

Current popular restaurant concepts are high-tech, casual contemporary, ethnic, designer, and celebrity restaurants. In the past few years, Mexican, Chinese, Japanese, and Thai restaurants have become popular. Northern Italian restaurants were hot trends, but have cooled somewhat as a result of the popularity of low-carb diets. Pizza and pasta offered at below $10 provide around two hours of affordable, upscale dining. In saturated markets, a restaurant's being new no longer guarantees customers.

Courtesy of Lettuce Entertain You

Scoozi is an outstanding theme restaurant that gives the impression of an artist's studio.

Go Roma is a 8-year-old "real easy Italian" chain that has been raking in the accolades for its cuisine. It was founded by some executives from Lettuce Entertain You, creator of numerous successful restaurant concepts including Maggiano's Little Italy. To get into a Go Roma, based in Northbrook, Illinois, you need $750,000 in net worth and $250,000 in liquid assets per restaurant. The company prefers experienced multiunit restaurant operators.[15]

Concept Adaptation

Most concepts that have not been tested need some adaptation to the particular market. One highly successful restaurant opened featuring seafood. The menu, however, was not popular, so it was altered. Several months passed before the place was profitable, but the owner wisely had adapted to the market demands. One of the super hotels in downtown Los Angeles featured dessert soufflés in its restaurant for several months. The soufflés were so popular that four extra personnel had to be employed to keep up with the demand. Restaurant volume of sales increased to the point that the sweet soufflés were no longer needed to entice patrons to the restaurant, and the soufflés were dropped from the menu. They had been used to build volume, but because they were high in labor cost and tended to slow down seat turnover, they were deleted from the menu with no appreciable drop in patronage.

Concept development has always been important in the restaurant industry, but it is becoming more so now that dining districts are developing in almost every community. The restaurant cluster may include family restaurants, fine dining, casual, fast casual, and a variety of quick-service restaurants. An area of just a few blocks may include chain representatives from Bob Evans, Flemings, Applebee's, Red Lobster, Taco Bell, Burger King, Arby's, and Pizza Hut, plus several ethnic restaurants. Each has its own identity. Are they all competing with each other? To an extent, yes; these restaurants may cannibalize each other's guests. Generally, however, different menus and prices attract different markets.

As soon as a restaurant format goes stale for a market, a new concept must be developed. Nearly every major chain is undergoing renovation, adding color, changing its seating arrangements, perhaps trying garden windows, hanging plants, private booths, menu variety, different uniforms, or new menu items.

CHANGING OR MODIFYING A CONCEPT

Many highly successful concepts that have worked well for years gradually turn sour. The customer base and the demographics change. Morale and personal service may decline. Anthony's Fish Grotto, a well-established seafood restaurant, experienced sales decline over five consecutive years. Extreme changes were needed; the owners decided to hired consultants.

Changes in management policy and operations turned Anthony's around. First, the owner wrote a *mission statement* that included a vision of what Anthony's would look like in the future. The books were opened to employees—a major innovation. The top-down style of management was replaced by teams that worked on employee scheduling and ideas for a new image. A serving team came up with waitstaff schedules that satisfied all 40 services at one unit. A savings team reduced costs of linen and china.

The concept team worked with designers to create a dining area in the La Mesa, California, store that creates the impression of being in an underwater cave, brightly lit and colorful. The design includes waterfalls and sea animals jutting out from the walls. The new design has helped to attract baby boomers, along with their children.

COPY AND IMPROVE

In coming up with a concept for a new restaurant, be a copycat. Look around for winners. Examine their strong points; look for their weak points; find a proven format. Learn the system to avoid mistakes—then improve on it. Initiate and adapt. Great composers build magnificent symphonies on borrowed melodic themes. Similarly, great restaurants take over elements of established restaurants.

There is no such thing as a completely new restaurant concept—every concept is built on ideas from other concepts, through modifications and changes, new combinations, and changes in design, layout, menu, and service. It is pure braggadocio to claim to have a completely new concept. If that were true, there would be no customers because the restaurant would be so strange that people would avoid it. Accepting the fact that every restaurant builds on hundreds of predecessors makes good sense and can help you avoid big mistakes. So be a copycat—but a critical, creative copycat.

Besides copying the format, learn the system by actually working with it before trying to establish your own restaurant. Merely observing an operation is not enough. Dozens of details must be learned, any one of which, if not known, may spell unnecessary trouble. Buying from the wrong vendor, using the wrong temperature for cooking an item, omitting a particular spice in a dressing, or using the wrong formula for a bun can result in high costs and stress for the operator.

A number of Mexican restaurants have been put together by non-Mexicans and are successful partly because several of the key kitchen personnel and wait personnel are Mexican Americans, who lend authenticity to the restaurant. It is probably not wise to try a full-service ethnic restaurant unless the owner/operator is from that ethnic background or has been immersed in it. Another alternative: Go with a business associate who is of the appropriate ethnic background.

You need not be a social analyst to define carefully the potential market if you copy an already successful restaurant. Creative copycats may borrow ideas from a number of operations, reconfiguring them as needed. The style of service may be drawn from a coffee shop, the method of food preparation from a dinner house; the menu can be drawn from a combination of several successful operations in the area, plus one or two modifications in preparation, presentation, or service. The pricing policy could be a combination of policies already well received by the public. Do not try to establish new taste patterns or vary far from the norm.

WHEN A CONCEPT FAILS

Provided the operator is competent, a failing restaurant need not be sold. The concept can be changed to fit the market. Conversion from one concept to another can take place while the restaurant is doing business. The name, decor, and menu can be changed, and customers who have left may return if the new concept appeals to them. The old concept may have gotten tired. Customers simply may be bored. Customers who enjoyed the old concept may have moved away and been replaced by a new market. Or a new concept, complete with decor, price, and service, may better appeal to the same market and siphon customers away from the competition.

In the worst case, a recession hits and customer count at all restaurants drops. Customers may trade down. For example, those who formerly patronized an upscale dinner house now go to a neighborhood coffee shop. The coffee-shop patron turns to quick service. Those who cannot afford to eat out at all drop out of the market completely. The smart restaurateurs downscale their menu prices to retain market share and even build volume. Luxury restaurants seldom lower à la carte prices; instead, they offer a fixed-price meal at a lower price than if the same food were ordered à la carte.

Restaurant Symbology

Restaurant symbology—the logo, the line drawings, even the linen napkins and the service uniforms—helps to create atmosphere. In the 1890s, César Ritz dressed his waiters in tails, which helped entice the elite from their mansions to his hotel restaurant, the Carlton in London. Chart House restaurants create a different image by dressing their servers in attractive Hawaiian shirts and blouses, as does Tommy Bahama's. The restaurants have a contemporary, nautical decor and are designed with a natural look that harmonizes with the setting. Extensive use of wood and glass gives them a warm feeling. Their biggest draw is their locations, which are nearly all at water's edge.

Symbols include pirates, clowns, and kings. Ronald McDonald is part of McDonald's restaurants' decor and a personalizing element. So, too, are the miniature playgrounds offered by some of McDonald's restaurants. Burger King, which gives children cardboard crowns, competes for customers' attention with Ronald McDonald and Mickey Mouse.

Large companies spend tens of thousands on the graphics that represent them. Restaurant chain logos, often replications of their outdoor signs, are carefully crafted to fit the image the company wishes to project. The independent operator can take cues from the larger companies to come up with symbols and signs that reflect the restaurant's concept.

Multiple-Concept Chains

Single-concept chains, such as McDonald's and Subway, have had the greatest success of any restaurants in history. Having a single concept permits concentrated effort on one system. Nevertheless, the single-concept restaurant chain is changing to a multiple-concept chain, which offers several advantages. Conceivably, a multiple-concept restaurant chain could have five or more restaurants in the same block, each competing with the others, each acquiring a part of the restaurant market.

In fact, this has been done for a long time in order to minimize costs, and will probably be seen more often in the future because of its success in attracting different markets. As early as the 1950s, Lawry's had two separate concept restaurants, across the street from each other, in Los Angeles. The general public had no idea that they were owned by the same company. One aspect of the concepts was directly competitive: Both restaurants featured beef. The company felt that if it did not add another competing restaurant, someone else would, and the area would support two, but only two, beef restaurants.

Generally, where restaurants are clustered, each concept is somewhat different from the others, and as many as 12 or 15 different concepts can be enclosed in the same mall shopping area—as at Marina Del Rey, a comparatively small area near the Los Angeles airport, which has more than 36 restaurant concepts clustered together.

Ruben's and Coco's also share some locations and reduce labor costs by having one general manager for both restaurants with an assistant manager for each.

Within a large market area, such as Los Angeles, Chicago, or New York, the same company may have several concepts, all close to one another but with slightly different decor and menus. Customers do not like to feel they are eating in the same restaurant all over the area, so the restaurants are varied somewhat and carry different names.

The largest of all restaurant companies, Yum Brands Inc., has four concepts: KFC, Taco Bell, Long John Silver, and Pizza Hut. They stand alone, double, or even more concepts.

Sequence of Restaurant Development: From Concept to Opening

Two or more years can pass from the time a concept is put together until a location is obtained, architectural drawings are made, financing is arranged, the land is leased or purchased, approvals for building are secured, construction bids are let, a contractor is selected, and—finally—the building is put in place. The sequence of events (Figure 3.2) may include 15 steps:

1. Choosing a location
2. Business marketing initiated
3. Layout and equipment planned
4. Menu determined
5. First architectural sketches made
6. Licensing and approvals sought

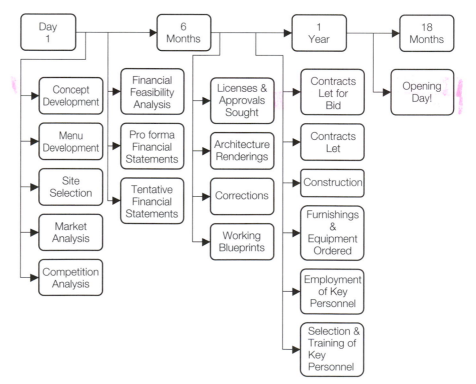

FIGURE 3.2 Timeline shows the sequence of restaurant development.

7. Financing arranged
8. Working blueprints developed
9. Contracts let for bidding
10. Contractor selected
11. Construction or remodeling begun
12. Furnishings and equipment ordered
13. Key personnel hired
14. Hourly employees selected and trained
15. Restaurant opened

In some cases, the time may be reduced, especially when taking over an existing restaurant or altering an existing building. Restaurant chains with preplanned restaurant concepts generally reduce the timeline by 6 to 12 months.

Planning Services

The person building a restaurant should employ an architect experienced in restaurant design. The architect, in turn, may hire a restaurant consultant to lay out the kitchen and recommend equipment purchases.

The builder may employ one of the relatively few restaurant consultants or can turn to restaurant dealers who double as planners or employ planners. The consultant works for a fee or a percentage of cost. The dealer may also charge a fee, but is likely to reduce or eliminate it if the equipment is purchased from him or her.

The best guide in selecting a planner/consultant is that person's experience and reputation. Remember that any kitchen can be laid out in a variety of ways and still function well. The consultant/planner will require a signed design agreement, including agreed-on fees. The agreement spells out what services will be completed by the designer and usually includes:

- Basic floor plan
- Equipment schedules
- Foodservice equipment electrical requirements
- Foodservice plumbing requirements
- Foodservice equipment
- Foodservice equipment elevations
- Refrigeration requirements
- Exhaust air extraction and intake requirements
- Seating layout

Courtesy of City Zen
Restaurant interior at City Zen Restaurant.

Common Denominators of Restaurants

In formulating a restaurant concept, the planner considers the factors common to all kinds of restaurants. An analysis of these common denominators may suggest a concept that is a hybrid of two or more classifications. Fast-food restaurants take on the character of coffee shops, vending operations may offer limited service, cafeterias may take on the appointments of luxury restaurants, and so on.

Common denominators of restaurants can be compared: the human needs met by the restaurant, menu prices, degree of service offered, space provided for each customer, rate of seat turnover, advertising and promotion expenditures, productivity per employee, labor cost, and food cost. The planner picks and chooses from among the common denominators to come up with a concept believed to be most appealing to a particular market.

UTILITY VERSUS PLEASURE

What is the purpose of a particular restaurant? Is it there to provide food for nutritional purposes or for pleasure? Up to 75 percent of the meals eaten away from home are for utilitarian purposes, while the other 25 percent are for pleasure. The distinctions are not clear-cut. Depending on the individual, the quick-service experience may be thrilling or boring. For the child, McDonald's may be full of excitement and fun. For a sophisticate, McDonald's can be a drag. The family that visits a Burger King or a Wendy's may find the experience as exhilarating as depicted in the TV commercials. For them, the utilitarian restaurant is a fun place, perhaps more pleasurable than an ultra-expensive French restaurant. McDonald's (and some other fast-food restaurants) has further blurred the line by adding play areas and party rooms. This is a far cry from Ray Kroc's original plan to keep McDonald's entertainment-free to encourage quick turnover.

As a general rule, however, pleasure dining increases as service, atmosphere, and quality of food increase. Presumably, pleasure also increases as menu price increases. Many factors intrude on such straight-line correlation.

DEGREE OF SERVICE OFFERED

As seen in Figure 3.3, restaurant service varies from none at all to a maximum in a high-style luxury restaurant. As menu price increases, so, usually, does service: the higher the price, the more service provided. At one end of the spectrum, the vending machine is completely impersonal—no service at all. At the other end, the luxury restaurant, a captain and two buspersons may attend each table. Service is maximal. The customer pays for the food but also for the ambience and the attention of service personnel.

It is interesting to compare the productivity and profitability of a luxury restaurant with those of a casual or popular-concept restaurant. The casual restaurant can quickly train personnel replacements and pay relatively low wages. The French restaurant relies on years of experience and polished skills. It is also relatively inefficient. The chain restaurant relies on system and replication, the French on individuals.

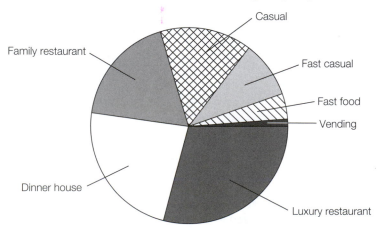

FIGURE 3.3 Different kinds of restaurants require different levels of service.

The chain markets its restaurants; the French restaurant attracts limited patronage with ambience, personality, word of mouth, and public relations.

Restaurant service breaks down into seven categories: vending, quick service, fast casual, casual, family restaurant, dinner house, and luxury restaurant. Figure 3.4 shows that different kinds of restaurants have different seat turnover levels.

The degree of service offered probably correlates with menu price and pleasure—at least, that is the expectation of the diner. Here again, there are many exceptions, and as the expectations are purely psychological, a number of factors can intrude on the correlation.

TIME OF EATING AND SEAT TURNOVER

Utilitarian eating is often accomplished in double-quick time, while the customer of a luxury restaurant who spends $75 to $100 per person for an evening out may savor every minute of the total experience, plus the pleasure of anticipating the dining experience and the pleasure of remembering it. Telling one's friends about the truffled turkey can be worth the price of the meal, a conversation piece adding luster to the dinner. At the other end of the spectrum, the stand-up diner in New York City can hardly be expected to be enthralled by the experience.

The seat turnover and speed of eating correlate with the restaurant classification, but not perfectly (see Figure 3.4). In some restaurants, the family style can offer speedy service and fast turnover and still provide an enjoyable atmosphere for its customers. Turnover is also highly correlated with the efficiency of the operation; turnover in two restaurants of exactly the same type can vary widely because of layout and management.

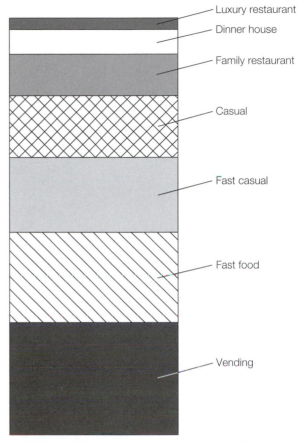

FIGURE 3.4 Different kinds of restaurants have different seat turnover levels.

SQUARE-FOOT REQUIREMENTS

Figure 3.5 suggests the amount of space per customer needed by each type of restaurant. The restaurant customer, in effect, rents space for dining. The drive-through restaurant provides no dining space at all; the customer's automobile is the dining room. Coming up the scale a bit, the customer may walk to a counter and receive some service. The coffee shop provides counter and booth seating and a nominal kitchen, while the luxury restaurant needs upholstered chairs and 15 to 20 square feet of space per patron, plus the kitchen equipment to handle the more extensive menu.

The square-foot requirements and the turnover in patrons per seat per hour are listed in Figure 3.6.

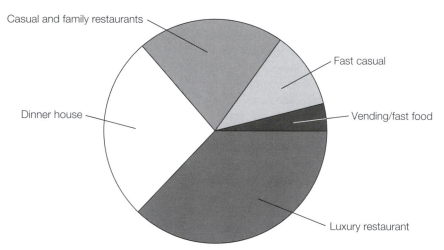

FIGURE 3.5 Different kinds of restaurants have different space-per-guest requirements.

	Dining Room (square feet per seat)	Turnovers in Patrons (per seat per hour)
Fast casual	10–12	1.75–3.0
Dinner house	15–17	1.25–1.75
Deluxe restaurants	13–18	0.5–1.25
Casual restaurants	11–15	1–2.5

Source: Jay R. Schrock

FIGURE 3.6 Different kinds of restaurants have different square-foot requirements and turnover rates.

MENU PRICE AND COST PER SEAT

Menu pricing correlates highly with the degree of service offered, the time of eating, the labor cost, the amount of space offered the customer, and the cost of the restaurant itself.

It might be expected that the cost per seat of a restaurant varies directly with the other factors mentioned. This is true to an extent, but there are wide variations. Some of the chain dinner houses cost $18,000 per seat or more, whereas a small neighborhood restaurant might cost from $6,000 up. Some of the quick-service restaurants are very costly per seat, much more so than the family restaurant. Cost per seat thus does not correlate well with the restaurant classifications presented.

CORRECT NUMBER OF SEATS

Theoretically, a given location will support a given number of seats with a particular concept. A 120-seat restaurant may be right for location X, while a 240-seat restaurant would be wrong. Restaurant chains go through a period of evolution to arrive at the right size to suit their concept. Companies such as McDonald's, Denny's, and Pizza Hut have developed as many as three sizes of restaurants to fit different locations.

Surveys show that 40 to 50 percent of all table-service restaurant customers arrive in pairs; 30 percent come alone or in parties of three, 20 percent in groups of four or more. To accommodate these parties, consultants recommend tables for two that can be pushed together. Booths for four, while considered inefficient for some restaurants, are ideal for family places. Larger groups can be accommodated at several small tables placed together, in booths for six, or at large round tables. The floor space required per seat will vary according to the restaurant's service or atmosphere. Luxury and table-service restaurants require 15 to 20 square feet per seat, coffee shops and luncheonettes should allot about 12 to 17 square feet for each seat, while cafeterias need just 10 to 12 square feet per seat or per stool.

Courtesy of Hard Rock Cafe
The Hard Rock Cafe's theme has been popular for years.

For the beginning restaurateur, it is probably better to build too small than too large. If the restaurant is excessively large for the location, it will be only partially filled. A crush of customers creates ambience and excitement.

Some restaurants are too large for their markets. Better to shut down some rooms, if possible, so that customers can be seated with other customers. Few people like to sit in a large room with only a handful of other people present.

ADVERTISING AND PROMOTION EXPENDITURES

In advertising and promotion, expenditures may vary according to the type of restaurant. Figure 3.7 shows the percentage of sales spent on advertising and promotion among types of restaurants. The vending machine operator spends little or nothing in advertising. Quick-service restaurants are likely to spend 4 to 5 percent of their income on advertising, more than is spent by the casual, fast casual, or family restaurant or the dinner house. At the far end of the spectrum, the restaurant featuring fine food may spend heavily on public relations. Promotion may take the form of entertaining food columnists; the proprietor's being seen at the right places at the right times and with the right people, and the cost of paying a public relations firm for keeping the restaurant in the news.

LABOR COSTS AS A PERCENTAGE OF SALES

Productivity per employee correlates highly with the various elements, moving from a high point at the quick-service end of the classification scale to a low point in a luxury restaurant or at a country club. Here, too, there are exceptions, depending on management skill, the layout of the restaurant, and the menu.

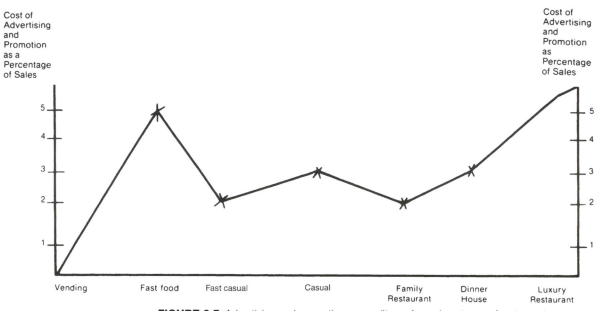

FIGURE 3.7 Advertising and promotion expenditures for various types of restaurants.

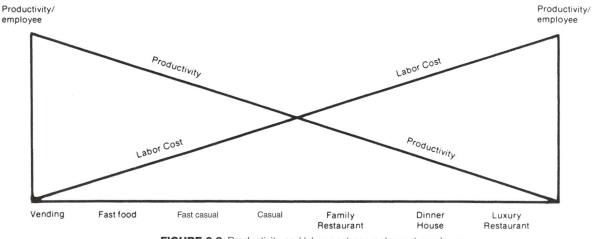

FIGURE 3.8 Productivity and labor cost per restaurant employee.

As might be expected, labor costs vary inversely with productivity, as shown in Figure 3.8. Quick-service restaurants operate at comparatively low labor costs. Labor costs are covered in more detail in Chapter 8.

PLANNING DECISIONS THAT RELATE TO CONCEPT DEVELOPMENT

Who Are the Target Markets, the Customers? Children, teenagers, young married couples, families, businesspeople, retirees, low-income people, high-income people, the adventurous, the sophisticated—anyone who is hungry could be your target market.

Buy, Build, Lease, or Franchise? Building is usually the most time-consuming of these options and can require two or more years from concept to completion. Arranging for financing, employing an architect, buying the land, getting the necessary approvals, and formulating contingency plans all eat up time and money. In franchising, the problem is to pick the right operation and to recognize that most major decisions have already been made and will continue to be made by others.

Food Preparation from Scratch or from Convenience Items? How much of the food will be prepared on the premises? How much will be purchased ready for heating? How many of the menu items will be prepared from mixes, soup bases, and other convenience food items? Some restaurants prepare everything possible from fresh ingredients. Others prepare everything possible from convenience items and have a definite policy of cutting preparation time to the minimum. Most restaurants make some items and buy others. Chain operations often produce some foods in a commissary, then have them delivered for final preparation at the various unit restaurants. Even upscale restaurants usually purchase most of their desserts and pastries.

A Limited or an Extensive Menu? Will the location and the concept support a limited menu, or does the concept call for an extensive menu requiring a large population base to support it?

How Much Service, Limited or Full? The operator can pick from a wide range of service degrees, from vending to walk-up, carry-out, cafeteria, drive-through, and on up to luxury full service. Which best fits the concept and market?

Young Part-time Employees or Older Career Employees? Much of today's foodservice industry is staffed by teenagers, people in their early twenties, and people who receive minimum or slightly above minimum wage. Some restaurants employ a range of age groups and depend on career employees rather than part-timers. Most restaurants offer at least some part-time positions.

Paid Advertising or Word-of-Mouth Advertising? How will the target markets be reached—paid advertising, public relations, promotions, or largely by word of mouth? A number of successful restaurants have a definite policy of no paid advertising. Others rely heavily on paid advertising, still others on promotion or a combination of advertising and promotion, particularly the use of coupons.

Grand or Quiet Opening? Will you open with a bang and fanfare, or open quietly on Monday morning and allow the crew to ease into volume operation?

Electricity or Gas? This decision is not an either/or proposition—some pieces of equipment can be gas fired, others wired for electricity—but the decision is an important one because installation is only part of the total cost. What is the cost of operating gas versus electric equipment, and what are the advantages of each type? Regional utility rates are a factor. In some locations, electricity is cheap; in others, it is expensive.

PROFITABILITY

Now for the famous last-but-not-least factor: *profitability*. Without a doubt, the most profitable restaurants are in the quick-service category. The larger quick-service purveyors have produced dozens of millionaires and more than a few multimillionaires. A number of franchisees have acquired chains within the chain, multiple units clustered within an area. With predominantly minimum-wage personnel, high sales volume, the use of systems, and excellent marketing, the quick-service business is the all-out winner.

Oddly enough, few restaurant-management students opt for quick-service management, believing it lacks the variety, glamour, and opportunity for self-expression found in restaurants offering more service and style. The professional restaurateur sees the restaurant as an ego extension. The investor usually cares most about profitability and what it takes to maximize profits.

Mission Statement

A mission statement drawn up by the restaurant owner can encapsulate his or her objectives for the business. The statement may be brief, such as the one for Max's Restaurant:

> To be the most admired restaurant of choice where people celebrate and cherish great food and excellent service every day, all the time.[16]

Or it could be more encompassing, as in Restaurants Unlimited's Clinkerdagger restaurant in Spokane, Washington:

> Clinkerdagger is the premier place to spend an unforgettable dining experience. Greeted with the glow of the fireplace and the warmth of our staff, our goal is to delight you with our exquisite menu selection and our gracious approach to hospitality.[17]

A mission statement can be explicit about the market(s) served, the kinds of food offered, and the atmosphere in which the food will be served. The ethical standards to be followed can be stated as part of the mission statement or written as a separate code of conduct. The goals to be followed in relating to patrons, employees, vendors, and the community can be included. Darden Restaurants (which includes Red Lobster, Longhorn Steakhouse, Olive Garden, Bahama Breeze, Capital Grille, and Seasons 52), states something of the moral character of the company:

> At Darden, we have a passion to make a meaningful difference in the lives of others, which is captured in our core purpose: to nourish and delight everyone we serve. We work to achieve that goal by delivering great guest and employee experiences and by enhancing the quality of life in the communities where we do business through volunteer involvement and philanthropic support![18]

Several advantages accrue to the restaurant owner/management that takes the time to spell out a mission statement. The exercise forces owners to think through and put in writing an explicit statement about what the restaurant is all about, a statement that is sharp and to the point and can focus the energies of management and employees and set forth the responsibilities of the enterprise in its relations with patrons, employees, vendors, and the public.

Mission statements can include input from employees. Discussions with employees can mobilize their thinking about the restaurant's purpose and reason for existence. There should be no hesitation about stating the profit motivation and such goals as cleanliness, customer service, and customer delight.

A code of ethics or conduct may strike some people as naive. It is "meant to encapsulate an organization's beliefs and values, which must be internalized and used as a guide in all training sessions, given to all new employees, and explained in detail."[19] It places a burden on restaurant owners, managers, and employees to live up to the code, reminding them that ethical behavior begins at the top and assuming a commitment to following the highest standards in personal cleanliness, food protection, service, and employee relations. One clause can address striving to price food to provide fair value and fair profit to investors. It does no harm to state that the restaurant expects employees and vendors to be scrupulously honest and pledges to do the same.

A mission statement is a useful part of the work plan needed to support a loan application from the Small Business Administration, bank, or other loan source. A mission statement should contain these three elements:

1. The purpose of the business and the nature of what it offers
2. The business goals, objectives, and strategies
3. Philosophies and values the business and employees follow

Concept and Location

What makes a good location for a restaurant? The answer depends on the kind of restaurant it is and the clientele to which it appeals. Is the location convenient and accessible for the potential clientele, the target market of the restaurant? The restaurant appealing to the professional for lunch usually must be relatively close to where professionals work. For some groups, the only food service in which they are interested is one within the building. For others, it is anywhere but within the immediate area, providing they can be back in their offices within an allotted lunch period.

Roadside restaurants, especially those on superhighways, are favored by the automobile traveler. Locations within a community (rather than on the edge of town) and on a major highway are plus factors. Brand-name restaurants such as McDonald's, Olive Garden, and Outback Steakhouse appeal to the stranger in the community looking for a known standard of quality and price. The traveler knows the menu prices and is fairly certain of the food quality and sanitation standards in a McDonald's, whether it is located in Massachusetts or New Jersey.

Will the size of the potential market support a particular type of restaurant? A quick-service hamburger restaurant may need only a population of 5,000 to support it, while a Polynesian restaurant might require 200,000. A casual restaurant may do well with only a few thousand potential customers, while a gourmet restaurant may need 100,000 people in its potential market. The marketing manager for one upscale dinner-house chain feels that a population of 250,000 within a 5-mile radius of one of their restaurants is needed for support. If the unit is located on a freeway, the radius might be extended to 10 miles.

The price structure of a restaurant is a major determinant in establishing its market. The $45-average-check seafood restaurant may appeal to 5 to 10 percent of the population, while a $12-average-check Mexican restaurant may appeal to 60 percent. Neither restaurant needs a major highway location to be successful. The public is more apt to search them out because of the specialized menu and service and because, normally, there are fewer of them from which to choose.

Criteria for Locating a Restaurant

The semimonthly magazine *Restaurant Business* publishes an annual Restaurant Growth Index, the purpose of which is to list the best and worst places to open a restaurant in the United States. Quite correctly, the editors say that selecting a restaurant site or a restaurant city is both a science and an art. Certain areas have too many restaurants. A few are good places to buy or build a restaurant, depending on the area's share of employed persons, working women, income level, population age, and food consumed away from home. Certain towns are losing population, others gaining. According to the Bureau of Labor Statistics, Bismarck, North Dakota has an unemployment rate of 2.9 percent. On the other end of the spectrum, Yuma, Arizona, had an unemployment rate of 28.4 percent. A diverse economy, often including energy or health fields, provides some protection against a recession.[20]

While this information is valuable, more important is the amount and intensity of competition already existing, information that can be learned only by on-site study or experience. Help can be had from a local or regional expert on the local situation. It is well known that restaurant competition is intense in major cities.

LOCATION CRITERIA

Restaurant personality, style of service, menu price, and management call for particular criteria in site selection. What is good for one restaurant might not be good for another. The focus is on the potential market. How convenient will it be to the customers' place of residence or work? Will they feel that they are getting value for their money whether the menu price is low or high? Chain-restaurant executives ordinarily define site or location criteria carefully based on experience. Some of the more obvious location criteria follow:

- Demographics of the area: age, occupation, religion, nationality, race, family size, educational level, average income of individuals and families. This information is available at the US Census Bureau (www.census.gov) and Demographics Now (www.demographicsnow.com).
- Visibility from a major highway
- Accessibility from a major highway

- Number of potential customers passing by the restaurant (travelers going through a community, drivers, local workers)
- Distance from the potential market
- Desirability of surroundings

These factors are then weighed against costs: leasehold cost, cost of remodeling an existing building, cost of buying an existing restaurant.

Some location factors are critical, and if a site does not meet them, it must be ruled out as the restaurant location. Establishing the critical factors in determining location is your first job.

The atmosphere of a restaurant must fit the location. Even though it may be part of a chain, your restaurant can be different from the other units. The ethnic background of a community, its income level, and number of children per family are important. McDonald's, Burger King, and Wendy's are moving away from having a standard design for all locations. If the neighborhood is affluent and the demographics indicate an older population, the restaurant is likely to be broken up with more partitions, suggesting gracious dining rather than the fast-food look favored by younger populations.

SOME RESTAURANTS CREATE THEIR OWN LOCATION

Dinner or family-style restaurants need not place the same high priority on convenience of location necessary for casual and quick-service establishments. In effect, the restaurant creates the location if the food service and atmosphere are desirable. The point is proved by the many undesirable locations that have failed as restaurants for as many as 10 different owners but are taken over by an eleventh and within a few weeks are packed with customers.

Because this is true, developers and community officials are often eager to entice a successful restaurant operator into a new shopping center or an area that has fallen on bad times. Decaying communities offer particularly attractive terms to operators with a proven track record. A successful restaurant can attract hundreds of people and rejuvenate a shopping center, mall, or other area.

A colorful personality restaurant may be successful in a location relatively poor with respect to surroundings, distance from market, accessibility, and convenience. Such a restaurant would be that much more successful in a prime location. One owner of a successful chain of Mexican restaurants in California considers the usual location factors relatively unimportant. He feels, and experience has proved, that people will search out his restaurants. Consequently, he buys failing restaurants located in less desirable locations, remodels them, and attracts a large clientele. Other restaurateurs say that even with the best location, it is difficult to succeed in the restaurant business—so you should only choose the best. Prime locations, however, require a good deal more money for lease costs.

SOURCES OF LOCATION INFORMATION

Location decisions are based on asking the right questions and securing the right information. Real estate agents are prime sources. A few specialize in restaurant brokerage. The real estate agents involved (there is usually at least one) are primarily interested in making a sale and gaining a commission. Real estate commissions are ordinarily based on 6 percent of the building's selling price and 10 percent of the selling price of raw land. A $200,000 land deal brings the agent up to $20,000 in commission. (Keep in mind that commissions often can be negotiated.) With this kind of incentive, it is little wonder that the agent may push a sale to the disadvantage of the buyer or the seller. To protect their interests, owners need multiple sources of location information. The agent usually can provide valuable information about the site and probably knows the community, its income level, growth patterns, traffic flows, restaurant competition, and the restaurant scene in the area.

Other sources of information are the chamber of commerce, the banks, the town or city planner, and, believe it or not, other restaurant operators. Town and city planning officials can provide traffic and zoning information. Current zoning information is critical, but no more so than what zoning officials are planning for the future. Is an area scheduled to be rezoned? Can a lot be split? Zoning reflects politics, and even if one group of officials plans one way, the next group may change the plan. The builder hopes for a lot to be rezoned up. Sometimes it is rezoned down. A change in zoning classification can mean a change in value of hundreds of thousands of dollars.

A number of communities have placed moratoriums on building for reasons such as protecting the environment or maintaining the status quo. Rapidly growing communities sometimes stop all building because utility or sewage systems are incapable of keeping up with the growth. In areas not served by a public sewage system, the construction of a restaurant may not be feasible because of the need for a sewage system with a large drainage field. An existing restaurant in such an area may be in a favorable competitive position for several years.

Building a restaurant is always nerve-racking, but it can be disastrous for an investor who encounters unexpected delays in getting permits, materials, and labor. A Howard Johnson's franchisee who was building a restaurant was unable to get the orange-colored roof for a number of months, which almost sent him into bankruptcy. Some communities refuse to allow a particular design of restaurant, and more and more building codes are specifying low-key architecture with minimal signage.

A look at the highways on the outskirts of some cities tells why the planning commissions are placing more restrictions on restaurant buildings and signs. Restaurants and motels crowd each other, each with a large neon sign, giving the strip an unsavory appearance.

Basic demographic information about the people in the area can be obtained from the US Census Bureau (www.census.gov/population/metro/data/metrodef. html). The number of renters or homeowners, income levels, and so on for the particular site in question can be abstracted from delineation files in a few minutes. A plethora of information about people in a given area is available from government sources. Specialized demographic research companies such as NPD Group/Crest or Scarborough will provide the information within a day or two for a moderate price. The larger chains use such companies routinely, but the individual should probably also use them to save time. Information such as population growth, decline, density, income levels, number of children, ethnicity, and other consumer facts are readily available for any given area in the United States. These companies do not research information themselves; they merely collect it from other sources and put it into usable form. All such information is valid only if it is relevant. Location experts working for chains have made big mistakes in selecting sites that were not right for a particular restaurant. The novice site analyst may have more problems.

A mom-and-pop operation may produce a living for its owners in a small town, while a restaurant with a heavy capital investment would be a loser economically. What might be an excellent location for a posh restaurant in one year could be a loser the next, as competition moves in and the fickle elite restaurant diners move on to the new "in" place.

Locations wax and wane in desirability, depending on a number of conditions, including the general economy, the nature of the residents of the area, the presence or absence of new or declining buildings, changing traffic flows, and security. This means that the restaurant operator must be continually alert to general conditions in an area and be ready to change the menu or change the concept, if necessary, or even move out.

Census tracts used to be the standard measure. Now ZIP plus Four (extended ZIP codes), which can contain as few as 15 households or only one business park, is more widely used to gather information.

With the proliferation of chains and changing lifestyles, people are less inclined to travel far to a restaurant. As a result, decision makers have to be even more precise in determining where new restaurants should go.

TRAFFIC GENERATORS

Look for built-in traffic generators, such as hotels, business parks, ball parks, indoor arenas, theaters, retail centers, and residential neighborhoods. Olive Garden, the chain of Italian dinner houses operated by Darden Restaurants, pursues a two-pronged growth strategy in which it moves into new markets as well as fills out markets it already operates in. To reduce development costs, the chain purchases restaurant sites and converts them to its own units.

KNOCKOUT CRITERIA

Failure to meet any one of the following criteria should knock out a site as a restaurant location. There would be no point in exploring that site further.

- *Proper zoning:* If a site is not zoned for a restaurant and it is not likely that it can be rezoned, there is no point in pursuing that site.
- *Drainage, sewage, utilities:* If a site is impossible to use because of the unavailability of certain utilities, or if there is a possibility of being washed out by a flood, or if it has major drainage problems, it must be rejected.
- *Minimal size:* The plot must be of at least the minimal size for a particular restaurant. A freestanding coffee shop ordinarily calls for something like 40,000 square feet. The plot must be big enough, in most cases, to permit adequate parking spaces. A 200-seat restaurant, for example, in some cities calls for a least 75 parking spaces. Other building codes specify at least half as many parking spaces as seats in the restaurant.

■ *Short lease:* If a lease is available for less than five years, the site may be undesirable for most restaurant styles.

■ *Excessive traffic speed:* Traffic traveling at an excessive speed (more than 35 mph) past a location distracts from a site. Thruway and interstate highways are exceptions when off- and on-ramps are convenient to the site.

■ *Access from a highway or street:* This is very important. An easy left turn into the lot may be an important criterion. In one instance, a new traffic light preventing a left turn reduced the volume of sales of a restaurant by half. The site may be all right for a style of restaurant different from one that depends on high traffic flow.

■ *Visibility from both sides of the street:* The fact that a site is cut off from view may rule it out as the location for some styles of restaurants.

OTHER LOCATION CRITERIA

■ *Market population:* Each style of restaurant depends on a certain density of foot or car traffic past the location and/or a minimum residential population within a given radius of the location. Many restaurants call for a resident population of 15,000 to 20,000 within a two-mile radius. Some sites call for 50,000 cars to pass the location each day.

■ *Family income:* A high-average-check restaurant normally calls for families of high income within a two- to five-mile radius. A lower-average-check restaurant could well succeed in a lower-income area.

■ *Growth or decline of the area:* Is the area getting better or worse economically? Is the population rising or declining? If the trend is worse, the restaurant's life span may be brief.

■ *Competition from comparable restaurants:* Is the area already saturated with hamburger restaurants, coffee shops, family restaurants, or dinner houses?

■ *The restaurant row or cluster concept:* The idea is older than the medieval fair. It can be found in the row of snack bars, preserved in Vesuvian ash, in Herculaneum in Italy dating back to the first century A.D. Putting a number of restaurants together may add to the total market because people will come a greater distance to a restaurant row than to separately located restaurants. However, in a restaurant row, only one or two hamburger restaurants may be viable. The usual cluster concept may site 35 or 40 restaurants in a small area, but ordinarily each offers a somewhat different theme, menu, and atmosphere. If the restaurant row is located in a particularly charming area, such as Marina del Rey in southern California or the Wharf area in San Francisco, each restaurant adds to the total ambience. The whole is greater than the sum of its parts. A restaurant row must be part of or near a large population base.

SUBURBAN, NOOK-AND-CRANNY, AND SHOPPING MALL LOCATIONS

Depending on menu and style of operation, restaurants do well in a variety of locations: suburbs, cities, near schools, in shopping centers, industrial parks, stadiums, and in high-rise buildings. McDonald's, for example, after a heavy emphasis on suburban expansion, turned to the nooks and crannies, those locations that are completely walk-up, without parking. Being a part of a shopping mall has many advantages, but the high cost of rent may preclude the success of some restaurants. Also, some styles of restaurants do much better in shopping malls than others, although almost every type of restaurant does well in one shopping area or another. Finding the correct area is the real trick.

Should the restaurant be placed within the covered mall itself or be freestanding on mall grounds? The management of Fuddruckers restaurants chooses the latter. Their clientele, mostly children accompanied by parents, gains the security of the mall and its parking facilities without being lost among the dozens of other mall stores.

The character of the operation should fit the character of the shopping mall. The Magic Pan, with its high-priced crepes and omelets, high-style appointments, and rotary crepe-pan cooking center, should be located where value is appreciated in terms of decor rather than quantity of food—that is, a mall serving an affluent community. A McDonald's restaurant was put in a posh Lexington Avenue area of New York City—and failed. A McDonald's as part of a military base shopping center is usually a winner.

MINIMUM POPULATION NEEDED TO SUPPORT A CONCEPT

How much population is needed to support a particular style of restaurant— 5,000 people, 10,000, 25,000, or 50,000? When a nationally advertised chain such as McDonald's or Burger King comes into a smaller community, that restaurant is likely to have a higher frequency of repeat patronage than it would in a large city. The fewer resources for entertainment a town or city has, the larger portion of business the restaurant will receive. Big cities have shops, restaurants, and thousands of options for the consumer. Put a McDonald's in a quiet little town like Kona on the big island of Hawaii and see what happens. People who do not know how to spend their free time because there are few choices are more apt to frequent a center of activity like a quick-service restaurant. It is new, it is fairly inexpensive, the food is in the American menu stream, and that is where the people assemble.

DOWNTOWN VERSUS SUBURBAN

Many restaurants have faded or failed because of the exodus of the middle class from the downtown area, leaving the restaurant perhaps a luncheon crowd but no one for dinner. The situation has changed back in a number of cities. Townhouses are being built, and the two-person income has enabled many families to rent high-priced downtown apartments. The high density of people living on any one block of New York City helps account for the large number of New York restaurants.

A restaurant's business may be tied to entertainment. When a popular movie is showing, crowds come; when a poor movie is showing, the restaurant has empty seats. Downtown restaurants appear in unusual places: in basements, in lobbies of old apartment buildings, in storefronts, on riverfronts, in department store complexes. Old churches become restaurants, as do converted firehouses, railroad stations, and libraries. Rents can be cheaper, depending on the neighborhood, or they can be considerably higher than in the suburbs, as much as double per square foot.

That an area, whether downtown or suburban, already has more than enough restaurants does not necessarily mean that a new one will not succeed. Is there a market gap to step into? Most towns and cities have more than enough restaurants. The proposer of a new one thinks that his or her place will better satisfy a particular market, provide more interest, be more exciting, have a more charming decor, provide more theater, serve higher-quality food, and so on. New restaurants continually displace old ones.

AVERAGE TRAVEL TIME TO REACH RESTAURANTS

Most diners-out select restaurants that are close by, near home, work, or shopping. Generally, restaurant patrons will travel an average of 15 to 18 minutes to reach a hotel, steak, full-menu, or fish restaurant. People often spend about 10 minutes when going to cafeteria and department-store restaurants. In other words, consumers are willing to spend more time traveling to eat in a full-service specialty restaurant and for meals that are family occasions. People will travel an hour or more to reach a restaurant with a high reputation, especially if the meal celebrates an occasion. The same people want fast food or take-out food to be only a few minutes away.

MATCHING LOCATION WITH CONCEPT

A particular site may be right for a coffee shop but wrong for a dinner house or a fast-food place. It may be right for an In-N-Out Burger restaurant but wrong for a sit-down hamburger restaurant. The size of the lot, visibility, availability of parking, access from roads, and so on, all have an impact on the style of restaurant that will fit a location.

Restaurant sites have been known to fail six or more times running and then become highly successful with a new concept that fits the area and the competition. Sometimes, when a restaurant begins to fade, the owner feels that nothing much can be done except to do a better job, spend more on advertising, perhaps replace the current employees. This may be true, but often the only thing that will save the restaurant is a change of concept.

RESTAURANT CHAIN LOCATION SPECIFICATIONS

Restaurant chains usually have location specification details spelled out for use by real estate agents and potential franchisees. For example, this list shows critical criteria that might be selected by a restaurant:

- Metropolitan area with 50,000 population
- 20,000 cars per 24 hours on all streets of exposure; 24-hour traffic, at least four-lane highways

- Residential backup, plus motels, shopping centers, or office parks
- Minimum 200-foot frontage; approximately 45,000 square feet of land (If the restaurant is in a shopping center, a freestanding pad for a 5,000-square-foot building and adequate parking are necessary.)
- Area demonstrating growth and stability
- Easy access and visibility
- Availability of all utilities to the property, including sewer

The same company illustrates how its restaurant would be placed on a parcel of land. Minimum width of the parcel would be about 170 feet, length about 200 feet. Motorists must be able to enter the property by making left turns from the street. Typical layouts for this company are shown in Figure 3.9.

Here are the site criteria for a Carl's Jr.,[21] a quick-service hamburger restaurant that now includes Hardee's and La Salsa.

- Freestanding location in a shopping center
- Freestanding corner location (with a signal light at intersection)
- Inside lot with 125-foot minimum frontage
- Enclosed shopping mall location
- Population of 12,000 or more in 1-mile radius (growth areas preferred)
- Easy access of traffic to location
- Heavy vehicular/pedestrian traffic
- An area where home values and family income levels are average or above
- Close to offices and other activity generators
- A parcel size of 30,000 to 50,000 square feet
- No less than 2 or 3 miles from other existing company locations

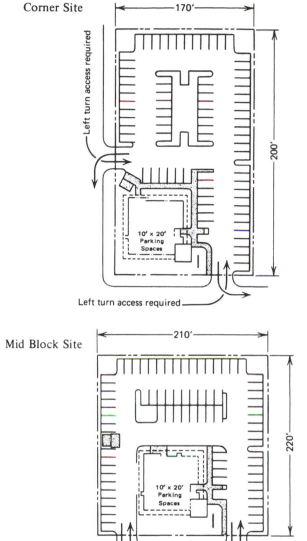

FIGURE 3.9 Typical freestanding family/casual restaurant layout

Owners of nearly all new quick-service restaurants consider installing drive-through windows, which in some locations are used by more than half the patrons.

TAKEOVER LOCATIONS

Being short of capital or wishing to minimize risk, the beginning restaurateur often starts by leasing or buying out an existing restaurant. The restaurant may be failing; the operator may wish to retire. If a restaurant is a failure, the new entrepreneur

Courtesy of Cohn Restaurant Group

Blue Point Coastal Cuisine is a popular seafood restaurant in San Diego's Gaslamp Quarter.

feels that he or she can do it better, or has a better concept for the location. Takeover situations can always be found.

Terms for the restaurateur can be favorable—little cash required and the building and equipment available for lease. The new restaurateur thinks: How can I lose? But he or she can and often does lose because the location is not right for the restaurant concept or format.

Often, the entrepreneur changes the concept from a coffee shop to a dinner house or family restaurant with hammer and nails. The exterior may be covered or repainted, and the interior decor changed by adding or removing booths, moving walls, lowering or raising ceilings, or adding artifacts or color. If the restaurant is successful, a takeover in another location is undertaken. Once the concept has proven itself, the company begins to select its sites more carefully, according to strict criteria, and builds its own restaurants or finds interested investors to build according to specification.

RESTAURANT TOPOGRAPHICAL SURVEYS

Ray Kroc, founder of McDonald's, liked to pick locations for his restaurants from a helicopter. Flying over a community, he could see the churches, schools, and traffic patterns.

An alternative to this approach can be achieved using a town or city map and plotting the location of existing restaurants on the map. This bird's-eye view provides a valuable perspective.

Nearly every restaurant in a community is listed in the Yellow Pages of a phone book, and it is not difficult to classify restaurants in a way that will identify potential competition. If the planned restaurant is a coffee shop, all the coffee shops in the area should be marked on the map; they constitute direct competition. Seeing all of the restaurants in an area on a map or on Google Earth gives some idea of the degree of restaurant saturation.

Of the hundreds of restaurants located in Pomona Valley, east of Los Angeles, quick-service restaurants predominate and compete vigorously with each other. The hundreds of restaurants might all do well in a more heavily populated urban area, which means that the number of restaurants is excessive, a not-unusual situation. Only two or three high-style, high-check-average restaurants can be supported. Several Mexican restaurants can be sustained. A few other ethnic restaurants do fairly well, as long as the owner is the operator and is helped by family. The would-be restaurant operator in this Pomona Valley area would determine if the selected concept is needed. Is there a market gap, a group of people not being served the kind of food or offered the kind of service and atmosphere that the proposed concept would provide?

COST OF THE LOCATION

Finally, and critically, can the concept and the potential market support the location selected? A restaurant has two potential values, its real estate value and its value as a profit generator. The two values should be considered separately. On the one hand, a restaurant building may actually detract from the real estate value, especially if the building has failed as a restaurant one or more times or is unattractive. On the other hand, the real estate value may be greater than the operational value.

A restaurant buyer is concerned with the real estate value, a potential lessee less so. A person wanting to lease a restaurant, however, must consider the real estate value (or its potential value) because, if the value increases, the owner will increase the rent—unless the lease agreement is written to prevent such an increase.

Potential changes in property zoning by local or state zoning boards can affect market value. Will highway changes be made in the near future that will affect the value of the property? Is the area going downhill or being revitalized? Is the area getting better or worse for a particular kind of restaurant? As an area changes, the kind of restaurant that will be supported also changes. A declining-income area may need a lower-average-check restaurant, a quick-service restaurant, or a coffee shop. As affluence grows, more dinner houses can be introduced.

🍷 CANTINA LATINA

One example of a takeover location is Cantina Latina, which is the dream turned into reality of Amanda Garcia and her son, Christian, and daughter, Alexandra. One of Amanda's fondest memories was playing accordion with her church group as a young girl in Colombia. During concerts, the aroma of fresh bread baking and hot chocolate steeping was the impetus for taking long breaks. When she was a teenager, life transported her to the island of Puerto Rico, where she discovered the exotic flavors of roast pork, sweet ripe plantains, and rice with pigeon peas, and her Costa Rican husband, Albert.

Next stop was Los Angeles, where she was introduced to the exquisite Mexican food and the joys of motherhood. Later the family moved to Tampa, where they built one of the first major tortilla factories in the Southeast. After a few years they sold that business and traveled extensively throughout Costa Rica, the Caribbean, and Mexico, wishing that someday they would open their own Latin American restaurant.

A family partnership was formed, and the name Cantina Latina, brainstormed over a few margaritas, was registered. They searched for several weeks to find a suitable location. Finally, one was found in a plaza in Sarasota, close to a high-volume supermarket across from a major shopping mall. The location was good—with plenty of visibility, easy access, and parking. There had been a restaurant at the location, but it was run down. In fact, the stoves and other kitchen equipment did not work. After lengthy negotiations with the previous owners' lawyers, a price was agreed on for the furniture and fixtures. Then a five-year renewable lease was signed with the building's owner. The cost per square foot was excellent value for the Garcias, and the common area maintenance (CAM) fee was reasonable.

(continued)

Cantina Latina opened on December 27, 2002, and there's a good reason for that—by opening in the 2002 tax year, they were able to take some deductions for that year. Before opening, the Garcias had to obtain all the necessary permits and get the licenses required for operating a restaurant. All licenses take a lot of paperwork but are necessary. In Florida, the Bureau of Alcohol Tobacco and Firearms (ATF) issues the liquor license. This involved a visit to the local police station for fingerprinting, and the ATF did an extensive background check. Eight weeks later, the Garcias had their liquor license. For the Health Department permit, it was necessary to register with the state, county, and city. They took the Safe Serve certificate and called the health department shortly before opening, and after an inspection were issued a permit.

Cantina Latina's concept initially called for a kind of TJ Fat's style of service—where guests ordered at the counter, seated themselves, and were served their food. After a while, the Garcias asked their guests if they would prefer table service, and they said yes. So, the service style was changed to please the guests. The Garcias are now on their way to success, by virtue of having selected a great concept, with delicious food in a convenient location at a value price. A copy of the menu and beverage list is shown in Chapter 4.

Courtesy of Cantina Latina

Cantina Latina is the creation of Amanda Christian and Alexander Garcia.

The cost depends on location. The cost of construction may be $200 to $250 per square foot, exclusive of land. A lease may run as high as $20 per square foot or more per month. If restaurateurs pay only $1.50 per square foot per month for a lease, they cannot expect to get the same traffic compared with a location that costs $14 per square foot. Many restaurants that opt for the high-rent district are operating with a smaller footprint—less square feet—in an effort to balance the higher lease costs. They are also doing more take-out meals. Like everything else, you get what you pay for.

VISIBILITY, ACCESSIBILITY, AND DESIGN CRITERIA

Visibility and accessibility are important criteria for any restaurant. Visibility is the extent to which the restaurant can be seen for a reasonable amount of time, whether the potential guest is walking or driving. Good visibility is vital to a quick-service restaurant and may be slightly less important to a full-service restaurant. There is a higher correlation between the quick-service restaurant and good visibility.

Accessibility relates to the ease with which potential guests may arrive at the restaurant. Parking, for example, may be a problem, as may access from the freeway or other traffic artery.

The restaurant has been likened to a theater. Restaurant design has two main components. The first is the stage setting and various props that the audience or guests experience; this is called the front of the house. The second is backstage, or the kitchen, storage, and service areas. The space allocation for backstage is usually 30 percent of the total square footage, depending on the type of restaurant.

The design of both the back and the front of the house needs to correlate with the theme of the restaurant. Design and the volume of business are reflected in each area: the exterior, the entrance and holding area, the bar or beverage area, the dining area (including the table arrangements), the kitchen, and receiving (including access for deliveries), and storage and trash areas. Space is a major issue in restaurant design because it costs money yet is vital to maintaining a balance between the overcrowded restaurant and the more spacious restaurant with too high an average check.

One of the most important elements in a restaurant is its lighting. With the wrong lighting, the restaurant's entire design will suffer; with the right lighting, the entire restaurant design could flourish.

Color should be selected in tandem with lighting because the two need to be in harmony. Color and light interact with one another to create a mood. Darker colors tend to "come out" and make a room look smaller, although they may also give a feeling of greater intimacy. Lighter colors tend to recede and make a room appear larger. Pastel colors help guests relax more than do primary colors. Quick-service restaurants use bold colors (and hard seats) combined with bright lights to ensure that guests move on after about 20 minutes.

Many restaurants use color as a mark of recognition, whether it is on the actual building or on awnings. These may have the psychological effect of attracting people to the restaurant.

The layout of the dining area, especially the tables and seats, the traffic lanes, and service areas, requires careful consideration and usually several mock-up scale drawings. Designers can do this on computers. Will the tables have cloths? If so, what color? Or will there be a wooden, tile, or other hard surface? Will there be cloth or paper napkins? Will the seats be wooden, upholstered in fabric, or vinylized? Will there be a hardwood floor, tile, or carpet? These and many other questions need answers that will conform to the overall theme of the restaurant.

Courtesy of Tihany Design, Photo by Peter Paige

Remi, in New York, is an Adam Tihany-designed restaurant that is both elegant and festive.

Courtesy of the author

Generic layout of a restaurant dining table.

Location Information Checklist

To avoid overlooking location factors, the major chains develop checklists of information for evaluating a site, a recapitulation of the factors that experience has shown to be important for their style of operation. All of the information called for in the checklist might not be needed to judge a particular site, but the list can call attention to factors that might otherwise be overlooked. The checklist is most relevant when evaluating a potential building site.

1. Dimensions and total square footage of site
2. Linear footage of site frontages
3. Distance and direction from nearest major streets
4. Average 24-hour traffic on each frontage street
5. Number of moving traffic lanes past location, widths, medians
6. Traffic controls affecting the location
7. Posted speed limits of adjacent streets (Some chains specify that traffic past a location not exceed 35 mph.)
8. On-street parking
9. Parking requirements: stall size, aisle width, number of stalls required
10. Landscaping and setback requirements for parking lot
11. Topography regarding necessary grading, slope characteristics, streams, brooks, ditches, flood conditions
12. Type of soil (natural and undisturbed, loose fill, compacted-fill soils); visible boulders, rock outcroppings, lakes, ponds, marshes
13. Drainage (public gravity-fed storm system; retention system on-site required)
14. Existing structures
15. Type of energy available (natural gas, LP gas, electric power)
16. Sanitary sewer availability
17. Underground utilities
18. Present zoning classification; any restrictions on hours of operation
19. Use and zoning of adjacent property
20. Building limitations
21. Character of surrounding area within 1 mile (office and industrial, tourist attractions, retail areas and shopping centers, motels and hotels, theaters, bowling alleys, schools, colleges, hospitals)
22. Population and income characteristics (number of people within one to several miles, typical occupations, median annual family income, ethnic makeup, housing value ranges, trade area population)
23. Agencies requiring plan approval:
    - Federal Housing Authority (FHA)
    - Water resources
    - State conservation authority
    - Local planning commission
    - Local health department
    - Environmental Protection Agency (EPA)
    - Other
24. Status of annexation for sites not in municipal limits

25. Signage (pole-maximum area, height allowed, setback; building-area allowed; remote entrance signs, area allowed, height allowed)
26. Construction codes:
    ■ Building
    ■ Mechanical
    ■ Plumbing
    ■ Fire
    ■ Building regulations covering design for people who are handicapped
    ■ Other approvals required to obtain building permit
27. Restaurant competition within one mile of site (fast-food, cafeteria style, family restaurants, coffee shops, dinner houses)
28. Offering price of property

In addition, real estate brokers submitting the information are asked to supply location maps, assessors' maps, plant maps, legal descriptions, zoning maps, chamber of commerce data, aerial photographs, and other available data.

Summary

The concept should reflect the requirements of the market and location menu; service and decor should complement the concept.

Successful concepts exist for both independent and chain restaurants. Some concepts that were successful are now no longer in use. This suggests that fads come and go. Many so-called gimmick restaurants have stood the test of time. The restaurant life cycle varies from a few weeks to several years. The more focused the concept is on a target market, the greater the chance of success. Concepts often must change to keep in step with changing markets and economic conditions.

The sequence of restaurant development has many steps between concept and operation. A mission statement will help keep the restaurant operation on a straight course of action toward a common goal.

Key Terms and Concepts

Degree of service

Different and better

Mission statement

Profitability

Protecting the restaurant name

Restaurant concepts

Sequence of restaurant development from concept to opening

Topographical survey

Utility versus pleasure

Review Questions

1. In concept development, you select a given style of service: counter tray, cart, arm, or French. Which will fit your concept best, and why?
2. Which kind of restaurant is likely to have the greatest productivity per hour? Which will require the most advertising and promotion and the most dining

room space per customer? Which has the greatest likelihood of the highest return on investment?

3. Roughly what percentage of meals eaten out are purely for pleasure?
4. Most college and university students majoring in hotel and restaurant management are not interested in fast-food restaurants. Why not? What distinct advantages do such restaurants have? What disadvantages?
5. What is the relationship between your logo and your restaurant concept?
6. Suppose your name is Joe Smith. Would you have any legal problem naming your restaurant Smith's?
7. Comment on the statement "Behind every restaurant there is a concept."
8. List five factors that together help formulate a restaurant concept.
9. How are restaurant image and concept related?
10. In what way do several existing restaurants close to a site affect the desirability of that site for another restaurant?
11. Can a particular site be wrong for one restaurant, right for another? Explain.
12. The desirability of a given restaurant location changes with time. Give three reasons why this is true.
13. Why may a community give favorable terms to a reputable restaurant operator to start a restaurant in a section of town that is deteriorating?
14. What location criteria would you suggest for a restaurant featuring diet foods?
15. What colors would you suggest for a high-style Italian restaurant?
16. A luxury, white-tablecloth restaurant has a rheostatic lighting control. How would you use it and for what purposes?
17. Why would you (or why would you not) use upholstered soft seating in a quick-service restaurant?
18. What kind of restaurant location can exist without parking?
19. In building a restaurant, what amount of money should you expect to invest per seat?
20. Suppose you have $80,000 with which to start a restaurant and no possibility of borrowing additional capital. What kind of restaurant should you consider, and how would you go about getting started?

CASE STUDY: Wurstkuche

History and Concept

Wurstkuche is the purveyor of exotic grilled sausages in downtown Los Angeles and Venice Beach, California. The company was started in November of 2008 by Joseph Pitruzzelli and Tyler Wilson, two cousins with big ambitions and no previous restaurant operational experience. Before the formation of Wurstkuche, Pitruzzelli worked at an industrial design firm in San Francisco that specialized in designing bars, restaurants and night clubs. Meanwhile, Wilson was an undergraduate student at the University of Southern California studying business management. Although they had never worked in restaurants before, they felt that they had the right combination of knowledge and experience to be successful in the restaurant business.

Staff and Customers

At Wurstkuche, the philosophy for success is to strive for employee satisfaction, guest satisfaction, and an overall sense of community. Pitruzzelli and Wilson wanted to create an excellent dining experience, as well as a great place to work. They believe that managing customer's expectations largely contributes to guest satisfaction. Heavy emphasis is placed on equality of service, which means that all customers are treated equal regardless of who they are. Wurstkuche invites a wide range of clientele that includes construction & railroad workers, business professionals, lawyers, young professionals, college students, international communities, etc. One of the goals set out for this restaurant venture was to encourage people of all walks of life to get to know one another, while enjoying a unique dining experience.

Pitruzzelli and Wilson believe that employee satisfaction is equally as important as guest satisfaction in Wurstkuche's overall success. They strive to achieve a high level of employee satisfaction by maintaining fair and equitable business practices, while striving to create a work environment that is community driven, much like their clientele base. Because they believe that all of their employees are essential to the restaurant's success, they want to ensure that their employees know that they are important, and then reward them for their hard work. Therefore, all tips from customers are pooled together and every employee gets a certain percentage, from the dishwasher to the bartender.

Challenges

There have been a variety of challenges over the first few years, working to sculpt Wurstkuche into the restaurant that it is today. Wurstkuche relies heavily on their staff to produce customer satisfaction. One of the biggest ongoing challenges is to instill a passion for being at work and to ensure that the staff continually delivers excellent customer service and enjoyable experiences time in and time out. Although turnover is high in the Los Angeles restaurant industry, Pitruzzelli and Wilson are strong believers of internal promotion. Most of their employees started from the bottom as food runners and worked their way up through the line of service. They are continuously faced with educating leaders and managers for the company by determining what drives people and then innovating different techniques to encourage their employees to take ownership of the company.

Strategy for Expansion

Wurstkuche's demand saw rapid growth in the first two years, steady growth in the third year, and now business is starting to level off. Currently, Pitruzzelli and Wilson are considering developing a third location in Denver, and possibly more in the future. The strategy for expansion revolves around targeting Metropolitan areas with emerging culture that have urban energy to them. They have a five year goal of expanding to 10–15 new locations. The new challenge is building more of the same concept and reproducing the philosophy, principles, energy, culture and experience in each location. Pitruzzelli and Wilson want to create a timeless experience that continues to evolve with changes in the market and the economy over time.

QUESTIONS

1. Is Wurstkuche's concept clear-cut or ambiguous?
2. Do you believe there is a market to support the concept throughout cities in California? What other locations would work for this concept?
3. Would the restaurant be more successful if the concept was changed or modified in some way? How and why?
4. Does the fact that one of the owners worked at an industrial design firm that specialized in restaurant design benefit the restaurant? How and why?
5. How do you expand the business, but also maintain the brand identity without diluting it down to the idea of just building a lot of properties?

Endnotes

1. Laura Onstot, "Pesos to Matador: You Stole My Concept!" *Seattle Weekly News* (September 9, 2008). Available at http://www.seattleweekly.com/2008-09-10/news/peso-s-to-matador-you-stole-my-concept. Retrieved June 2009.
2. Adapted from: Lorri Mealey, "Top 10 Tips for Developing Your Concept." Available at http://restaurants.about.com/od/decidingontheconcept/tp/Concepttips.htm. June, 2009.
3. SoBou, "SoBou: A Spirited Restaurant South of Bourbon." Available at www.sobounola.com. Retrieved on Sept. 20, 2012.
4. Ibid.
5. Nevin Martell, "20 Hottest New Restaurants," FSR (March 2012). Available at http://www.fsrmagazine.com/new-concepts/20-hottest-new-restaurants.
6. Ibid.
7. "Census Bureau says retail and restaurant sales down 10.1 percent in April." *Portland Business Journal* (May 13, 2009). Available at portland.bizjournals.com/portland/stories/2009/05/11/daily33.html. June 23, 2009.
8. Sam Ro, "Rosenberg: Restaurant Sales Haven't Looked Like This Since the Start of the Last Recession," *Business Insider* (March 14, 2013). Available at http://www.businessinsider.com/rosenberg-warns-of-restaurant-indicator-2013-3.
9. Arthur Bovino, "The 20 Best Athlete-Owned Restaurants," *USA Today* (March 25, 2013). Available at http://www.usatoday.com/story/travel/destinations/2013/03/23/the-20-best-athlete-owned-restaurants/2011221/
10. Leah Goldman, "The Ultimate List of Restaurants Owned by Professional Athletes," *Business Insider* (Nov. 24, 2010). Available at http://www.businessinsider.com/15-awesome-restaurants-started-by-pro-athletes-2010-10?op=1.
11. Rachel Shapiro, Samuel Prime, Chris Godley, "22 Celebrity-Owned Restaurants: The Hits and Misses, The Hollywood Reporter (Feb. 6, 2012). Available at http://www.hollywoodreporter.com/gallery/celebrity-owned-restaurants-pics-279280#1.
12. Katie Kramer, "Shake Shack Founder Expands His Empire," CNBC, (October 14, 2010), http://www.cnbc.com/id/39679233. Retrieved on May 4, 2013.
13. Stacked.com retrieved on May 5, 2013.
14. Delmonico's website. "About: Delmonico's History." Available at http://www.delmonicosrestaurantgroup.com/restaurant/about-history.html4.
15. Carol Tice, 5 Little Restaurant Chains You Can Buy Into Now, Forbes. Retrieved from http://www.forbes.com/sites/caroltice/2012/06/01/5-hot-little-restaurant-chains-you-can-buy-into-now/ on September 20, 2012.4.
16. From Max's Restaurant Vigan City, Philippines.
17. Clinkerdagger website. www.clinkerdagger.com. And personal conversation with Tera on May 5 2013.
18. Darden Restaurants website. http://www.darden.com/commitment/community.asp. Retrieved April 23, 2013.
19. Hrayr Berberoglu, "Ethics in Business," FoodReference.com. Available at www.foodreference.com/html/artethics.html. Retrieved June 2012.
20. Jacquelyn Smith, "The Cities with the Best and Worst Unemployment Rates," Forbes (January 23, 2013). Available at http://www.forbes.com/sites/jacquelynsmith/2013/01/23/the-cities-with-the-best-and-worst-unemployment-rates/.
21. Personal conversation with Karl Karcher, March 14, 2000.

Menus, Kitchens, and Purchasing

Daniel Boulud

Chef Daniel Boulud, owner of some of the country's finest restaurants, author of numerous cookbooks, and creator of gourmet products, has culinary roots that can be traced back to his family's farm near Lyon, France—a place profoundly tied to the rhythms of the seasons, produce fresh from the fields, and delicious home cooking. Yet it is in his sophisticated New York restaurants that this chef has truly mastered the dining scene. In fact, Daniel Boulud is today considered one of America's leading culinary authorities, with a cooking style marked for his unique use of time-honored French technique applied to the finest seasonal American ingredients.

After his nomination as best cooking apprentice in France, Daniel went on to train under the renowned chefs who would become his mentors: Roger Vergé, Georges Blanc, and Michel Guérard. Now Boulud himself serves as a mentor to the talented young cooks he has been working with here in the United States for almost 25 years.

Courtesy of Daniel Boulud

Before making his way to the U.S., Daniel spent two years as sous chef in the Les Etoiles restaurant of Copenhagen's Plaza Hotel. Eager to come to America, Boulud landed in Washington, D.C., as the private chef to the European Commission. Soon after, he moved to New York City, which he has called home ever since. During his first years in New York, Daniel opened the Polo Lounge at The Westbury Hotel and later Le Régence at the Hotel Plaza Athenee.

From 1986 to 1992, Daniel was executive chef at Le Cirque. During his tenure there, the restaurant was regularly voted one of the most highly rated in the country. In 1992, Daniel earned the James Beard award for "Best Chef of New York City."

The year 1993 was an important turning point for Boulud, the year in which he set out on his own to open his much-heralded restaurant Daniel. Not long after opening, Daniel was rated "one of the 10 best restaurants in the world" by the *International Herald Tribune* and would soon become a member of the prestigious Relais & Châteaux organization. Daniel himself was declared "Outstanding Chef of the Year" in 1994 by the James Beard Foundation, with the latter having already named him "Best Chef: New York City" in 1992. After five successful years, the chef-restaurateur relocated Daniel to its grand Park Avenue home. Since the restaurant's 1998 relocation, Daniel Boulud has also been named "Chef of the Year" by *Bon Appétit* magazine, and the restaurant has received *Gourmet* magazine's "Top Table" award, a coveted four-star rating from *The New York Times* as well as *Wine Spectator*'s "Grand Award" and New York City's top ratings for cuisine, service, and decor in the Zagat Survey.

In 1998, Daniel Boulud opened Café Boulud. The contemporary Café Boulud is an elegant French-American restaurant with an international accent and a three-star rating from *The New York Times.* It has established itself as a destination for Manhattan's café society, a spot with the cosmopolitan chic of a Parisian rendezvous. The chef created his first restaurant outside of New York City when he launched another Café Boulud in 2003 at the legendary Brazilian Court Hotel in Palm Beach, Florida. DB Bistro Moderne, which Daniel opened in 2001, serves as his interpretation of updated bistro cooking rooted in French tradition. It is a relaxed and fast-paced Manhattan restaurant located in the City Club Hotel on West 44th Street, just steps from Times Square and the theater district.

Boulud created Daniel Boulud Brasserie in 2005. "The restaurant is reminiscent of beautiful places you've seen, but is like no place you've ever been," explains Chef Daniel Boulud of his restaurant at the Wynn Las Vegas Resort. A splendid waterfront setting sets the tone, at once Alpine lakeside *auberge* and Mediterranean seaside resort. The menu abounds with the kind of straightforward cooking that Boulud calls "French comfort food" adapted to this modern rendition of a bustling French brasserie on the Las Vegas Strip.

CHAPTER
4

The Menu

LEARNING OBJECTIVES

After reading and studying this chapter, you should be able to:

- Identify factors to consider when planning a menu.

- List and describe some common menu types.

- Discuss methods for determining menu item pricing.

- Identify factors to consider when determining a menu's design and layout.

Courtesy of Sysco

The menu is the heart of any restaurant; it showcases everything you have to offer for food and beverages. Menus are as diverse as the number of different types of restaurants. Planning a menu is an interesting challenge; here are a few dos and don'ts when it comes to menus:[1,2]

■ Check out the competitions' menus and websites. Study their menu to see the number and type of items, the prices and range of offerings. Look for similarities and differences between your prospective menu and theirs.

■ Ask yourself, how will my restaurant and menu be different from and better than the others?

■ The theme of the menu, its design and colors, should reflect the theme and decor of the restaurant.

■ Use a clear, easy-to-read font like Times New Roman 14 point so guests can read it, and have a pair of reading/magnifying glasses handy in case a guest has difficulty in reading the menu.

■ Have a couple of focus groups read your menu and give you feedback.

■ Incorporate local names into the descriptions of dishes, such as Washington Lobster Roll, to make them sound more appealing.

■ Specialty menu items can have a star or other insignia to draw attention to them, as well as appropriate placement on the menu (this is described later in this chapter).

■ Use a symbol for potential ingredients that may trigger allergies in guests, such as peanuts or eggs.

■ For the layout, use one or two columns, not more, as the menu will look too crowded.

■ Don't use the clipart that comes as part of your computer software; your menu will look as if it was done at home. There are websites (e.g., shutterstock.com, corbisimages.com) that provide beautiful illustrations and will give your menu a professional appearance. Pay for the rights to use the art; trying to use it for free could lead to legal problems (besides the fact that it is unethical).

■ Don't use too much technical jargon. *Sauté* is fine, but keep it simple and don't use words or terms that guests are unlikely to know.

■ Avoid saying exactly how many pieces of food come in a dish, such as itemizing a menu by saying "six jumbo shrimp" when describing a shrimp cocktail. Simply saying "jumbo shrimp" will suffice. This way, you can adjust the number based on market price to keep your food costs in line.

■ Don't laminate your menu. Instead invest in menu jackets, which allow you to easily change the menu.

Kitchen space is often a limiting factor for many restaurants. Preparation; the cold kitchen; pastry, dessert, and bread production; and service frequently require more space than most restaurants have available. Short of knocking out walls, something has to give. If the restaurant is open for lunch and dinner, the schedule may not leave sufficient time for desserts to be prepared. (If it is open only for dinner, pastries and desserts might be prepared in the morning.) Perhaps they can be purchased. It is not uncommon for restaurants to purchase special desserts rather than make them.

Considerations in Planning a Menu

New restaurateurs who have found a great location often focus more on that than on the food. Many restaurateurs begin to plan the design and decor and even the marketing and promotional activities before they have completely decided on the menu. However, the menu and menu planning should be front and center in the restaurant business. Guests come to restaurants for a pleasurable dining experience, and the menu is the most important ingredient in this experience.

One of the most important factors for patrons when deciding on a restaurant is the quality of food. This challenges operators to provide tastier presentations, offer healthier cuisine, and create new extraordinary flavors to please guests. These and other factors are critical to the menu's and the restaurant's success. The many *considerations in menu planning* attest to the complexities of the restaurant business.

Considerations in menu planning include:

- Capability of cooks and consistency of preparation
- Equipment capacity and layout
- Seasonal availability of menu ingredients
- Price and pricing strategy
- Nutritional value
- Accuracy in menus
- Menu items
- Menu types
- Menu engineering
- Menu design and layout
- Standardized recipes
- Menu trends

The menu is the most important part of the restaurant concept. Selection of menu items requires careful analysis. An analysis of competing restaurants will help in terms of positioning the restaurant with respect to the competition and for product differentiation. In some restaurants, the guests and servers are also asked for input, which makes for consensus building and a feeling of ownership of certain dishes. The menu must reflect the concept, and vice versa. The restaurant concept is based on what the guests in the target market expect, and the menu must satisfy or exceed their expectations. Responsibility for developing the menu may begin with the chef, individually or in collaboration with the owner/manager and, perhaps, cooks and servers. Even New York superstar chef Bobby Flay, who has three high-profile restaurants, television cooking shows, and cookbooks, admits that sometimes "your feelings will betray you." He remembers that several years ago, when he opened Bolo, his Spanish-inspired restaurant, "I had this great idea for a lobster and duck paella using arborio rice. I was so adamant about how good it would be and how well it would do. It bombed."[3]

A café menu for an 85-seat restaurant featuring pastas may consist of about seven appetizers, including pastas, two salads, soup of the day, and 12 to 14 entrées

Concepts are best developed from the menu. When you really know your menu, you can develop a concept.

Using the analogy of restaurants to theaters, the menu is the playbill or program. The cooks and servers are the actors, and the decor is the stage set.

(pastas, chicken, meat, seafood, vegetarian—perhaps a steak, grilled chicken, and a couple of fresh fish dishes). The meat can be grilled, sautéed, or poached and the vegetables steamed. The makeup of this menu is based on the considerations just listed, and now discussed in greater detail.

Capability/Consistency

The *capability* of the chefs or cooks to produce the quality and quantity of food necessary is a basic consideration. The use of standardized recipes and cooking procedures will help ensure *consistency*. A standardized recipe is one that, over time, has been well tested. It lists the quantities of ingredients and features a simple, step-by-step method to produce a quality product. The menu complexity, the number of meals served, and the number of people to supervise are also elements that have an effect on the capability and consistency of the restaurant kitchen. Today, chefs and cooks are more innovative and creative in their approach to the culinary arts. The Culinary Olympics, local chefs' associations, and the many fine foodservice and culinary programs at colleges and universities have done much to improve the creativity of chefs and cooks.

Equipment Capacity and Layout

In order to produce the desired menu items, the proper *equipment* must be installed in an efficient layout. A systematic flow of items from the receiving clerk to the guests is critical to operational efficiency. Chain restaurants and experienced independent operators carefully plan the equipment for the menu so as to achieve maximum production efficiency. Menu items are selected to avoid overuse of one piece of equipment. For example, too many menu items that are broiled may slow service because the broiler cannot handle them. Most menus begin with a selection of appetizers that do not use the stovetops and grills to avoid conflict with the entrée preparation. Some appetizers are prepared and placed in the refrigerator, ready to be served cold. Others may be prepared and then fried.

Availability of Ingredients

Are the menu ingredients readily available? *Availability* requires that a constant, reliable source of supply at a reasonable price be established and maintained. High-quality ingredients make a high-quality product, and fresh must be just that—fresh! Almost all food items are available everywhere—at a price. The operator takes advantage of the seasons when items are at their lowest price and best quality. The ups and downs in food prices can be partially overcome by seasonal menus or even daily menus, as is the case with the California Cafe, where general manager Volker Schmitz has the menu on his computer. This enables him to quickly remove an item from the menu in the event that a hurricane in the Gulf of Mexico or frost in California or Florida dramatically increases the price of fresh fish, fruit, or vegetables. A decision is made either to adjust the price or take the item off the menu.

Price and Pricing Strategy

Price is a major factor in menu selection. The guest perception of the price–value relationship and its comparison with competing restaurants is important. Another important factor is a value-creation strategy. There are two basic components of value creation: what you provide and what you charge for it. To build perceived value, you need to (a) increase the perception of value of what you provide, (b) lower the price you charge for it, or (c) both. Factors that go into building perceived price-value include:

- Amount of product (portion size)
- Quality of the product (dining pleasure)
- Reliability or consistency of the product
- Uniqueness of the product
- Product options or choices (including new products)
- Service convenience (such as speed of service)
- Comfort level (such as courtesy, friendliness, and familiarity with the business)
- Reliability or consistency of service
- Tie-in offers or freebies included with the purchase

Are you selling a Cadillac or a Chevrolet? If you sell a costly Cadillac, you need to charge a Cadillac price; if it's a Chevy, a Chevy price. The most common pricing mistake of independent operators is trying to sell a Cadillac at a Chevy price.

The concept and the target market will determine the parameters of menu prices. For example, an Italian neighborhood restaurant may offer appetizers and salads in the $3.95 to $6.95 range and entrées in the $8.95 to $14.95 range. A quick-service Mexican restaurant might have a limited menu offering food in the $1.99 cents to $4.89 range. The selling price of each item must be acceptable to the market and profitable to the restaurateur. Questions to ask when making this decision include:

- What is the competition charging for a similar item?
- What is the item's food cost?
- What is the cost of labor that goes into the item?
- What other costs must be covered?
- What profit does the operator expect?
- What is the contribution margin of the item?

Consider each factor. In the dynamic marketplace of the foodservice industry, competition continually changes. Individual and chain restaurants rise and fall. New

Courtesy of Bern's Steak House

Guests enjoying an evening at Bern's Steak House in Tampa, Florida.

restaurants are opened, old ones are closed. New management plans, new building designs, new advertising, and, more slowly, newer modified foods are forever appearing. Competition, however, usually determines menu price more than any other factor.

We know that food cost and portion size and control are the best indicators of the price to charge for dishes on a menu. For example, if we are aiming for a 33 percent food cost we can add up the cost of all the ingredients of a menu item—say chicken Cordon Bleu, which costs $3.50 to produce, including vegetables and bread and butter. It would need to sell for at least $10.30. Now, if the restaurant across the street has a similar dish on the menu for $12.95 then you could price yours at $10.50 and look like a hero.

FACTORS IN PRICING

Menu items are selected to complement the restaurant image and appeal to its target market. For example, hamburgers come in a variety of prices, depending on whether they are self-served or table served, their size, their garnish, the atmosphere, and convenience in reaching the restaurant. No one expects to get a hamburger served on a white tablecloth at the same price as one served from a counter. At 21 in New York, a hamburger costs more than $30 and is served with green beans, preserved tomatoes, caramelized onions, and choice of potato.[4] By contrast; a quick-service restaurant burger costs about $2.99.

A walk-up select-your-own steak may cost a third less than one served at a table in a quiet, attractive dining room, such as Bern's Steak House in Tampa, Florida. Bern's is a large establishment with multiple rooms and expensive decor, including murals of French vineyards, antiques, columns, and Tiffany lamps. Bern's reputation has been built over the past 40 years by creating an aura around its beef. The restaurant buys only U.S. prime beef, which is then aged for an additional 4 to 10 weeks in specially built lockers controlled for humidity and temperature. The menu lists six basic cuts, from Delmonico to porterhouse. They are available in any thickness and broiled to eight levels of doneness.[5]

MENU PRICING STRATEGIES

There are two main *menu pricing strategies*. A comparative approach analyzes the competition's prices and determines the selection of appetizers, entrées, and desserts. Individual items in each category may then be selected and priced. The cost of ingredients must equal the predetermined *food-cost percentage*.

The second method is to price the individual menu item and multiply it by the ratio amount necessary to achieve the required food-cost percentage. This method results in the same expected food-cost percentage for each menu item. It is not the best strategy. An expensive fresh fish item may be priced too high when compared to the customer's perception of value or to the prices charged by the competition. A glass of iced tea might have a beverage cost of 15 cents and sell for 75 cents, when it could be priced at $1.50.

This may lead to a weighted average approach, whereby the factors of food-cost percentage, contribution margin, and sales volume are weighted. This strategy allows for the stars to save the dogs. The stars are the high-selling items with the greatest contribution margin (gross profit). These items are strategically placed on the menu at focal points that will attract the greatest attention. A problem with this approach is that averages are relied on to separate the high-selling items from the low-selling items. Guest choices can tilt the food-cost percentage.

CALCULATING FOOD-COST PERCENTAGE

Food cost is reflected in pricing. The cost of food varies with sales (a variable cost). When stated as a percentage of sales, food cost provides a simple target for the chef and management to aim for, becoming a barometer of the profitability of the restaurant.

Traditionally, menus were priced by using a fixed markup, or multiple, based on food cost. The system worked fairly well in that other costs tended to be fairly predictable in a well-managed restaurant with a steady market. If, for example, 33 percent of the sales figure was used as a food-cost percentage target and other costs were steady, the main food items were multiplied by 3 to arrive at a sales price. A number of items, such as coffee, tea, cola, desserts, and soups, were sold at a much lower food-cost percentage. They balanced the higher-cost menu items and waste, which made it possible to achieve the target cost of 33 percent.

Steakhouses came along, and their operators saw that the traditional factor markup did not apply. Steaks could be purchased precut and sold at a price that would permit a 40 percent food cost, or higher, and still the operation was successful. The reason was that the labor cost in preparing and serving steak ran 15 to 20 percent, or even less, as a percentage of sales. The lower labor cost permitted a higher food cost. Operators use food and labor costs as a combination known as prime cost, which should be close to 55 to 60 percent of sales. This allows for a 15 to 20 percent operating profit. The food-cost percentage is the most frequently quoted percentage in the restaurant business. It is generally calculated weekly or monthly. The method of calculating a simple food-cost percentage is:

Opening inventory + Purchases − Closing inventory

= Cost of food consumed

Food cost/Sales of food = Food − Cost percentage

Opening inventory	$10,000
+ Purchases	$66,666 purchases + Storeroom requisitions
Total food consumed	$76,666
− Closing inventory	$10,000
= Cost of food consumed	$66,666

If total sales were $200,000 for the month, the food cost of $66,666 divided into the $200,000 would produce a food cost of 33 percent. This is a basic calculation, which becomes more complex when transfers, returns, breakages, mistakes, guest returns, spillage, employee meals, promotional meals, and so on are factored into the equation. The method of calculating a more complex food-cost percentage is:

Opening inventory + Purchases = Total available for sale

- − Returns to supplier
- + Cooking liquor
- − Lounge and bar food (promotional and giveaway)
- − Promotional food
- = Cost of food

Taking a food inventory is time-consuming and complicated. The storeroom and kitchen must be orderly to make the work of the auditor or inventory-taker easier. One method requires that prices be marked on the food items or recorded in the inventory computer file or a book.

CONTRIBUTION MARGIN

When you know the contribution margin, you can make better decisions about whether to add or subtract a product line and how to price your product or service. The *contribution margin* is the difference between the sales price and the cost of the item. The amount left over when the cost of the item is deducted from the selling price (the gross profit) is the contribution that is made toward covering the fixed and variable costs. It works like this: If restaurant A offers a steak on the menu that costs $5 and sells for $14.95, the contribution margin is $9.95 for every steak sold. The margin of $9.95 goes to pay the fixed and variable costs, including 15 percent for surrounding plate costs, such as vegetables and sauces, and leaves some over for profit. Profit is the amount left over after all expenses have been paid.

Nutritional Value

Restaurant guests, some more than others, are becoming increasingly concerned about the *nutritional value* of food. This is creating a higher demand for healthier items, such as chicken and fish. In fact, two-thirds of all seafood is eaten in restaurants. Fish and shellfish have far less fat than other protein foods. Seafood is lower in cholesterol and sodium, and has high amounts of the highly polyunsaturated omega-3 fatty acids, which are thought to help in heart attack prevention. Greater public awareness of healthy food and individual wellness has prompted operators to change some cooking methods—for example, they are broiling, poaching, steaming, casseroling, or preparing rotisserie chicken instead of frying. Kentucky Fried Chicken, to divert attention from the word *fried* in the title, changed its name to KFC. The company also changed its cooking oil, which included some animal fats, to 100 percent vegetable oil. Some restaurants place a heart sign next to menu items that are recommended for guests with special low-fat dietary needs. A few restaurants put the number of calories beside each item on the menu. Most chain restaurants have taken steps to provide lighter and healthier food. Since 2010, fast-food restaurants with more than 20 branches have had to post this information where customers can see it.[6] Most (if not all) put the information on their websites as well. As an example, McDonald's publishes the complete nutritional breakdown of its menu items, has detailed nutrition information on its website, and has changed its cooking oil for potatoes from animal fat, high in cholesterol, to 100 percent vegetable oil, which is cholesterol free.

Consumers are generally more concerned about a food's fat content than about cholesterol and sodium. A number of restaurants offer menus with leaner meats and more seafood and poultry. Bob Wattel, executive vice president of Lettuce Entertain You Enterprises in Chicago, notes that, on the whole, heart-healthy menu items have sold well. Some of the best sellers in Lettuce's program include tuna *asada* with papaya relish, charred tuna pizza, and angel hair pasta with shrimp and artichokes. The trend toward healthier foods appears to be here to stay, giving seafood a leading role in menu planning. Wholesome and Hearty Foods, located in Portland, Oregon, encourages people to "eat positive." It specializes in a variety of Gardenburgers. The "Original" Gardenburger is made with mushrooms, onions, rolled oats, brown rice, cheese, and spices.

There is no doubt that much of the public believes that healthy eating contributes to prolonging our active lives. Already established restaurants are offering more choices for health-conscious customers with greater guest interest in lower-fat menus. Quick-service restaurants are under pressure due to fast food ties to obesity. McDonald's discontinued its "supersize menus" due to low sales. The movie *Supersize Me* was also reported to play a hand in the dropping of the supersize menu.

Increasing numbers of restaurants are serving *vegetarian*, *vegan*, and the latest craze, *raw fare*. Vegetarian restaurants, such as Radha located in Manhattan and New World Vegetarian in Oakland, California, do not serve meat: no beef, poultry, fish, or their byproducts. Vegan restaurants such as Good Karma in San Francisco and Strictly Roots in Manhattan are stricter than vegetarian restaurants. They exclude everything a vegetarian restaurant excludes, plus all dairy products. Vegans also refrain from wearing clothing that involves the death or suffering of animals (such as leather, silk, and fur). Some vegans refrain from consuming honey. Raw bars or restaurants such as Raw Energy Organic Juice & Café in Berkeley, California, do not serve food heated above 116°F. Some restaurants simply offer a vegetarian dish or two; others, like Grassroot Organic Restaurant in Tampa, Florida, target, expand, and combine their menu to appeal to vegetarians, vegans, and those seeking a raw diet.

Offering more nutritional and natural food is a challenge. Chipotle, whose mission is to change the way people think about fast food by offering foods with integrity, such as naturally raised proteins like beef, pork, and chicken, has two main challenges. First is availability, trying to get enough naturally raised protein and making it available to all its stores. The second is price; guests are prepared to pay a little more: say, $6, but not $15 for a burrito. The solution for Chipotle is to keep supply in balance with its economic model.[7]

Several cities have now banned *trans fatty acids*—commonly termed trans fats—which are a type of unsaturated fat and may be monounsaturated or polyunsaturated. Most trans fats consumed today are industrially created as a side effect of partial hydrogenation of plant oils. The process changes a fat's molecular structure, raising its melting point and reducing rancidity (thus, increasing its shelf life), but this process also results in a fat becoming trans fat. Eating trans fat increases the risk of coronary heart disease—it not only increases the LDL cholesterol (the bad cholesterol) but also decreases the HDL cholesterol (the good cholesterol). Several restaurants and companies have, of their own volition, removed trans fat from their menus and product lines.

In 2012, California banned foie gras—a fattened duck or goose liver dish that animal-welfare advocates say is inhumane because it requires the force-feeding of animals. Massachusetts passed a law limiting students' access to junk food during the school day.[8] In New York, Mayor Michael Bloomberg banned sugary drinks exceeding 16 ounces; however, in March 2013 a state Supreme Court judge struck down the ban before it could be implemented, calling it "arbitrary and capricious." Bloomberg vowed to appeal, saying, "I've got to defend my children, and yours, and do what's right to save lives."[9]

Those looking for restricted foods may not be totally out of luck, however. Most laws and food codes are at the state, or even county, level. They're also difficult to enforce, say food experts. "Any time there's an attempt to ban a food, it just makes the food sexier, like Prohibition," says Douglas Powell, a professor of diagnostic medicine and pathobiology at Kansas State University, where he runs the food safety blog Barfblog. That leads to grassroots groups that fight the legislation, and efforts among eaters to find ways to still buy restricted foods.[10]

GLUTEN-FREE COOKING AND MENU ITEMS

It is important for restaurants to stay current with food allergies and intolerances. The gluten-free diet stems from a certain percentage of the population that is unable to process a particular protein. This autoimmune problem is called celiac disease. People with celiac disease cannot metabolize the gluten protein. Their body will recognize this normally digested protein as a pathogen and will start to attack its own cells, specifically the intestinal track. This damaged intestinal track will then negatively affect the body's nutrient absorption. Although some individuals may have a minor digestive issue, extreme cases can lead to hospitalization and even death. Some common symptoms are: ". . . abdominal pain, bloating, diarrhea, weight loss, lactose intolerance, and malnutrition."[11]

Scientifically speaking, gluten is very important in cooking because this protein will add structure and elasticity to baked goods. For example, different types of wheat flour will result in many different textures in bread, cakes, and pastries. The texture will be different depending on the percentage of gluten in the flour being used. *Cake flour* (with a low gluten percentage) will give the baker a softer texture, whereas *bread flour* (with a high gluten percentage) will give a baker the ability to produce strong artisan type breads. Gluten can be found in many grains including wheat, barley, rye, and oats. The absence of this protein in breads that depend on them will most definitely affect the overall quality.

A knowledgeable chef should not only know about alternate recipes and substitutes but will also be able to recognize when certain food products contain gluten. It may not be just as simple as being able to identifying the "bread" ingredient. Gluten can also be found in many other *processed* foods that at first may seem safe for the celiac-challenged restaurant guest. Following is a list of some common gluten containing-products that might be overlooked:[12]

- Some types of beer
- Soy sauce
- Nondairy creamer
- Glucose syrup
- Miso paste
- Various seasonings
- Certain brands of baking powder
- Certain vitamin capsules

Some common substitutes for wheat flour are rice flour, garbanzo flour, and tapioca flour. Although mimicking gluten can be a bit challenging for the chef, there are many modified recipes that will come close to the original. Pasta, for example, is classically made with wheat flour. However, rice flour pastas can be made from scratch or purchased easily in most grocery stores and will give a gluten-free result. Texture is probably the most recognized difference in gluten-free pastas and breads. The gluten-free breads will typically come out of the oven with a very dense texture. This is because the gluten substitutes are heavier and lack the elasticity factor. A common trick is to add more yeast and sugar or to also just cook the bread in smaller portions. Gluten-free breads tend to overcook on the outside and while leaving the inside undercooked. Lowering the oven temperature at certain points may solve this problem. Xanthan gum may also be used to give the dough a bit of elasticity. As you may gather from this discussion, finding a proven recipe is the key. Creating your own gluten-free breads and pastas will require much trial and error with alternative ingredients.

Most gluten-free guests will request dishes made with the following basic ingredients:[13]

- Fruits and vegetables
- Meat
- Milk-based items
- Potatoes, rice, corn, and beans
- Cereals made without wheat or barley malt
- A wide variety of specialty foods made with alternative grains

Many chefs have also noticed recently that some guests will request a gluten-free meal even though they do not have any celiac symptoms. Many of these guests simply want a healthy vegetable based meal that is free of many of the high calorie starches found in most restaurant fare. They have concluded that one way to possibly guarantee a low calorie meal is by requesting it to be prepared gluten-free.

According to the National Institutes of Health, about 1 in 133 people have celiac disease, and many more go undiagnosed.[14] Due to the seriousness of this disease, restaurant employees should have answers to all gluten ingredient questions as they relate to their existing menus. On the one hand, failing to execute a gluten-free request can result in a very sick guest and might lead to legal ramifications. On the other hand, being able to give your guests an incredible gluten-free experience may result in adding more value to your overall brand.

FOOD ALLERGY SAFETY PRECAUTIONS AND STAFF PROPERLY TRAINED TO HANDLE ATTACKS

Up to 50 million Americans, including millions of kids, have *an allergy* which causes various reactions, *affecting* a *person's* eyes, nose, throat, lungs, skin, or *gastrointestinal tract.*[15] The reaction usually triggers the body to defend itself against what it believes to be a harmful intruder. Typically, what happens is that the body will release many chemicals into the bloodstream, which will usually include histamine. Some symptoms will include minor breathing or skin discomforts. The most serious symptom involves what is known as anaphylaxis. Since the best defense against an allergic reaction is avoiding the specific ingredient, a common tool used in many restaurants is the *chef card*. This card will be given to the guest and they will be asked to write on the card all of the ingredients that the chef should avoid. The Food Allergy & Anaphylaxis Network has a helpful list of ingredients that a chef should avoid specific to certain diets: primarily soy, milk, peanuts, wheat, and eggs.

It is estimated that about 12 million Americans suffer from some type of food allergy.[16] These individuals will suffer from many different symptoms upon digestion of their particular allergic food. More serious cases will even result in long-term hospitalization and even death. There are approximately 150 to 200 deaths per year as a result of food allergic reactions. Although many of the allergic reaction cases will happen at home, many will also occur at restaurants.

In a large party, known food allergies of a few individuals will have an effect on the entire menu. Restaurateurs should take this into consideration when dealing with food allergy menu challenges. Many food allergic guests will have a list of their favorite restaurants. They will trust these locations and may frequent them often. Of course, if they bring their friends, this only benefits the restaurateur. Some restaurateurs cater specifically to these types of guests. Vegan restaurants have seemed to be the most tolerant and creative with food allergic diners. However, many restaurants are finding out that special attention given to the food allergic diner can be a great way to build a long-term relationship with their guests.

Whatever type of cuisine is being served, the restaurant employees will need to be extremely knowledgeable of all ingredients being used on the menu. Today, the waitstaff must be as well versed on the menu as the cooks and chefs. This may be challenging because sometimes not all of the ingredients may be listed on the menu or even the recipe. For example, let's say that the sauté cook normally sears off proteins in an olive oil blend. However, this cook, on one occasion, runs out of this oil and finds the closest neutral oil available: soybean oil. Sautéing in soybean oil is a very popular method. However, this would not be a good substitution if the guest has a soy allergy. Chefs and servers should also be aware of garnishes that could taint a perfectly cooked special meal for an allergic guest.

There is a lot of responsibility for the restaurant when serving food allergic guests. First, the staff should be tested on all ingredients and which ones could pose allergy problems for their guests. Second, and most important, communication between the guest, server, and chef must be present. The allergy may be serious enough to warrant changing linens and avoiding steam from nearby tables or other plates of food en route. If a guest mentions that he or she is allergic to a certain ingredient, it is the server's job to ask follow-up questions. For example, a guest may have a nut allergy. If this is mentioned, then the server should ask specifically, "What nuts exactly"? Some individuals are allergic to peanuts and choose to avoid all nuts when dining out. However, a guest with a peanut allergy might actually enjoy eating pistachios and walnuts. Digging deep and asking the right question should be part of the FOH training.

If an unfortunate allergic reaction happens to a guest, the restaurant should immediately call 911. There should be no hesitation in calling for medical assistance *even* if the guests states that their symptoms will pass.

VEGANISM AND VEGETARIANISM, AND RAW FOODS DIET

Many people and cultures in the world practice veganism and vegetarianism. Although discussions on eating a diet free of animal products can be traced back thousands of years, the term *vegetarian* was coined around the early 1900s. The term *vegan* came shortly after. The vegetarian or vegan will have dietary concerns, but might also take into consideration ethical and/or environmental topics.

It is important to distinguish the difference between being a "vegan" and a "vegetarian." Living a vegan life involves much stricter rules and puts more limits on what the person can consume. Whereas the vegan will eat only plants and vegetables, the vegetarian will choose to add butter, milk, eggs, and cheese to their diets. Ethical vegans will take it a step further and not even use certain animal byproducts such as honey, wool, silk, or fur. There are also subcategories of vegetarianism: pesco-vegetarian, lacto-vegetarian, ovo-vegetarian, and lacto-ovo-vegetarian. These four address including fish, dairy, or eggs into their vegetarian diet.

The number of vegetarian and vegan restaurants has been growing over the years. In Great Britain, for example, the number of vegetarian restaurants increased 50 percent from 2007 to 2010.[17] A 2011 poll conducted by Harris Interactive indicated that about 5 percent of Americans identify as vegetarians (half of those as vegans) and that 33 percent of Americans (vegetarian or not) are eating vegetarian foods ". . . a significant amount of time."[18] The interesting findings from this poll suggest that even people that do not consider themselves true die-hard vegetarians will occasionally eat a vegetarian meal at a restaurant.

There are many helpful websites to help the diner choose which restaurants cater to vegetarians or vegans. The Happy Cow Healthy Eating Guide sorts all vegetarian restaurants by US city, and encourages people to start rating these locations.[19] Restaurants are finding out that most vegetarian guests will not be satisfied with just a bowl full of steamed vegetables. The contemporary chef will need to become knowledgeable of vegetarian and vegan options even if their location is not solely dedicated to the non-meat-eating guest. This includes healthy and nutritionally dense ingredients as well as effective cooking methods that will magnify the flavor of vegetable dishes. For example, reduction, roasting, marinating, dehydrating, and infusing are examples of methods that can increase the intensity of even plain tasting vegetables. Searching for unique flavor profiles have given many restaurants and edge over the competition.

Another recent diet trend has been the raw food practice. This method includes consuming all foods from the raw state, including even meats. Some of the raw and unprocessed foods might include: a juiced carrot, nonpasteurized milk, sashimi, and Carpaccio. Many proponents of the diet believe that foods cooked over a certain temperature will lose certain nutritional value. Raw food dieters would not warm or heat up their food items in a recipe. All items would be cut, sliced, chopped, puréed, or juiced fresh on site. Many vegans share this raw food method for the same nutritional reasoning. The raw food practice is less of a diet and more of a chosen preparation philosophy. Certain Paleo-diets, which include eating meat, may also follow a similar raw food method.

It should be noted that many nutritionists believe that putting so many restrictions on your diet will tend to negatively affect your nutrient intake. Although vegan, vegetarian, and raw food diets have become popular over the years, people must be aware of the many challenges faced by this group of people:[20]

1. Heart health challenges
2. Vitamin B_{12} deficiencies
3. Iron and calcium deficiencies

DIVERSITY IN DIET PLANS AND CROSS-CULTURAL PREFERENCES

Diet plans have been around for thousands of years. If you took the time to catalog all of the known diet fads, you would come to the realization that often times, they do not include sound nutrition. Successful strategies in healthy eating take into consideration the long-term span of an individual's life. Certain diets may be labeled "fads" if their main goal is to only cause a person to lose weight quickly and not have any long-term nutritional benefit. An individual might eventually find this diet to be unrealistic in the grand scheme of their lifestyle.

The Atkin's diet, which concentrates on eating very few carbohydrates and high amounts of animal protein, was actually known as *banting* back in the late 1870s. William Banting was an English casket maker who invented a low-carb diet that he claims helped him lose 50 pounds.[21] There was also the story of the obese William the Conqueror, who decided to drink only alcohol in the year 1087 until he lost enough weight to comfortably ride his horse. Ironically, months later and still obese, he fell from his horse, ruptured his organs, and died.[22]

Although there have been many different kinds of "fad" diets and diet plans of the past centuries, they often originate from the traditions, culture, or learned behavior of a particular geographic region. For example, many Romans would conduct a detox diet that consisted on just grapes and water for several weeks in order to cleanse the intestines. Today's nutritional experts have used the term *pyramid* to describe what each human being should consume over a period of time. Rather than just a "diet plan," these food pyramids are used to describe lifelong requirements in a particular culture. Over the years, food pyramids have been changed and modified by nutritionists after better understanding what truly is in specific ingredients. There are also specific pyramids for different ethnic groups. This would make sense because not every country or ethnic group would have the exact same fruits, vegetables, starches, and meats. Certain grains and spices, for example, may define one ethnic group from another. Certain cooking methods that are used in one group of people may not be used in another. Different flavor profiles may also dictate the exact structure of an ethnic groups pyramid.

It would make sense that different cultural preferences would create different foundations for healthy eating. Many food pyramids now exist for different cultures:[23]

- Mediterranean Diet and Pyramid
- Latino Diet and Pyramid
- African Diet and Pyramid
- Asian Diet and Pyramid

All of these ethnic diets contain regional specific variations from almost all of the following categories: grains, tubers, vegetables, fats, fresh fruits, herbs, spices, dairy, fish, shellfish, meats, water, and alcohol. One common recommendation among all of these pyramids is individual portion control. Each ethnic cuisine will have its own signature flavor and style. For example, Mexican food will be heavily flavored with tomato, chili, garlic, and cilantro, while Indian cuisine will use a wide variety of vegetables and may include chicken or lamb. However, even though these two cuisines are on opposite sides of the globe, they also currently use similar fruits and vegetables such as onion, mangos, lemons, and rice. The combinations of flavor and cooking methods are probably a better way to describe different cuisines besides just a list of ingredients.

Flavor

Flavor is the sensory impression (taste) of a food or beverage. Other factors that come into play when determining the taste of a dish are aroma, texture, sight, and sound. In other words, taste involves all the senses. Many foods are altered with flavorings to change the taste.

With the new millennium, it is clear that the American foodservice industry is on the expressway to a broader range of ethnic and international foods with expanded flavor profiles. Consumers are embracing ethnic cuisines like never before, as restaurateurs begin to use flavor as the main tool to differentiate themselves from each other.

There is no doubt that the American palate is craving an increase in the breadth and complexity of flavor in foods. There are big flavors, spicy flavors, fresh flavors—flavors from a world of diverse cultures that are rapidly changing American restaurant food.[24]

Courtesy of Ophelia's
Flavor abounds in this ostrich dish.

Some chefs feel that fusion cuisine has run its course and that Americans want their food to taste familiar, with just a hint of a foreign influence—perhaps a predominant flavor, ingredient, or cooking method. Terms like *marinated* and *smoked* are being featured on more menus, once again indicating a trend to more flavorful foods.

According to John Li, vice president of Bloomin Brands, other forecasted menu trends include a focus on healthy flavors, portion control, humble foods, authentic ethnic, and exotic endings. Figure 4.1 shows a menu from Union Square Cafe—*yum*—very flavorful.[25]

Accuracy in Menus

Given the trend toward more flavorful food, it makes sense to promote flavor with menu descriptions such as aromatic, spicy, tangy, crisp, smoked, charbroiled, marinated, fresh, crunchy, wood-fired, sizzling, and the like.

Most states have statutes stipulating that businesses (including restaurants) may not misrepresent what they are selling. Restaurants must be accurate and truthful when describing dishes on the menu. *Accuracy in menus* means that if the trout on the menu comes from an Idaho trout farm, it cannot be described as coming from a more exotic-sounding location. Similarly, if the beef is described as prime, then it must be prime, judged according to US Department of Agriculture standards; butter must be butter, not margarine; and fresh cream must be fresh. Some restaurants have been heavily fined for violations of accuracy in menu. At least two class-action lawsuits challenging the accuracy of dietary data on restaurant menus have operators wondering if trendy menu-labeling mandates will open the floodgates for similar litigation.[26]

New York became the first municipality to enact a menu-labeling calorie count requirement. Since then, in response to pressure from guests, many restaurants have made the nutritional values of their menu items available.

Appetizers

Bibb and Red Oak Leaf Lettuce Salad with Grated Gruyère and Dijon Vinaigrette	11.50
USC's Green Salad with Garlic Croutons and Oregano Vinaigrette	8.50
Black Bean Soup with Lemon and a Shot of Australian Sherry	8.50
Heirloom Tomato Salad with Crumbled Coach Farm Goat Cheese, Sweet Onions & Basil	13.00
Risotto with Rock Shrimp, Cucumber, Jalapeño and Cilantro	13.50
Tagliarini with Sweet Corn, Roasted Tomatoes, Pancetta and Gorgonzola Cream	12.00
Penne alla Norma – Sicilian-Style Pasta with Roasted Eggplant, Tomato and Ricotta Salata	11.00
Fettuccine Papalina al Tartufo – with Prosciutto, Parmigiano Reggiano and Black Truffle Butter	12.50
Strozzapreti alla Campidanese – Pasta Twists with Saffron, Tomatoes, and Sweet Fennel Sausage	11.50
Insalata Siciliana- with Crispy Sardines, Roasted Peppers, Green Olives and Caciocavallo	13.00
Sheep's Milk Ricotta Gnocchi with Wilted Arugula and Lemon Cream	12.50
Terrine of Spiced Duck Foie Gras with Peach-Fig Chutney	15.00
Union Square Cafe's Fried Calamari with Spicy Anchovy Mayonnaise	11.25

Main Courses

Herb-Roasted Organic Chicken with Summer Vegetable Panzanella	26.00
Indian Spiced Vegetables – Glazed Eggplant, Potato Bread, Mushroom Basmati, Chick Peas & Spinach	23.00
Sautéed Wild Striped Bass with Roasted Roma Tomato Vinaigrette, Greenmarket Summer Squash, Baby Zucchini and Cipollini Onions	27.00
USC's Grilled Marinated Filet Mignon of Tuna with Gingered Vegetables and Wasabi-Mashed Potatoes	30.00
Seared Wild Alaskan Salmon with Balsamic Butter, Sautéed Spinach, Sweet Corn and Shiitake Mushrooms	28.00
Crispy Lemon-Pepper Duck with Peach-Fig Chutney, Farro and Swiss Chard	26.00
Grilled Lamb Chops *Scotta Dita* with Potato-Gruyère Gratin and Sautéed *Insalata Tricolore*	29.00
Grilled Smoked Black Angus Shell Steak with Mashed Potatoes and Frizzled Leeks	29.00

Michael Romano, Executive Chef-Partner

Courtesy of Danny Meyer

FIGURE 4.1 The menu from the popular award-winning Union Square Cafe features a cuisine of America with rustic Italian flavor.

Specials for Thursday Dinner

Iced Oysters	Salutation Cove (PEI) Steamboat (WA) Totten Inlet (WA)	1.95ea
Cocktail	USC's Campari Citrus Cooler – *Campari, Aranciata and Lime*	9.00
Chef's Soup	Hearty Split Pea with Bacon and Herbed Croutons	8.50
Appetizer	*Tonnarelli all' Aragosta* – Housemade Square-Cut Spaghetti with Roasted Lobster-Heirloom Tomato & Basil Sauce	14.00
Entrée	Pan Seared Scallops with Sautéed Chanterelles, Roasted Brussels Sprouts, Crispy Cardoons and Golden Tomato-Pancetta Butter	28.50
Cheeses	Taleggio (Lombardy) – *Soft-ripened raw cow's milk with salty & nutty nuances*	9.50
	Saint-Maure (Loire, AOC) – *Ash coated, pleasantly salty fresh goat's milk*	
	Bingham Hill Sweet Clover (Fort Collins, CO) – *Rich, nutty, semi-firm raw sheep's milk*	
Dessert	Greenmarket Apple Pie with Caramel Ice Cream	8.50

Featured Wines by the Glass

Lieb Cellars Pinot Blanc (North Fork) 2001	GLASS	9.00
	BOTTLE	35.00
Bedell Cellars, Merlot (North Fork) 2000	GLASS	9.25
	BOTTLE	35.00

Weekly Specials

Monday	USC's Lobster "Shepherd's Pie"— with Mushrooms, Mashed Potatoes, Spinach, Carrots and Lobster Sauce	29.00
Tuesday	Roast Dry-Aged Prime Rib *au Jus* with Twice-Baked Gruyere Potatoes and Sautéed Green Beans	32.00
Wednesday	*Porchetta Arrosta* — Roast Suckling Pig with Rosemary, Garlic, Sautéed Greens and Herb-Roasted Potatoes	28.00
Thursday	*Bollito di Vitello* — Fork-Tender Veal Steamed in White Wine with Braised Vegetables, Aromatic Herbs and Tangy Salsa Verde	28.50
Friday	Roman Style Roasted Baby Lamb with Sautéed Wild Mushrooms, Eggplant and *Fagioli all'Ucceletto*	29.50
Saturday	Grilled Rib Steak for Two with Béarnaise Sauce, Grilled Red Onions and Potato-Gruyère Gratin	30.00 Per Person
Sunday	*Osso Buco* – White Wine-Braised Veal Shank with Sautéed Dandelion and Crispy Polenta	28.00

Vegetables and Condiments

Sautéed Broccoli Rabe "Mama Romano Style"	5.00	Creamy Polenta with Mascarpone, Toasted Walnuts and Crumbled Gorgonzola	6.00
Union Square Cafe's Mashed Potatoes with Frizzled Leeks	5.00	Sautéed Spinach with Lemon and Extra-Virgin Olive Oil	6.50
Fagioli alla Toscana – Simmered White Beans with Savory Herbs and Pecorino	5.00	Grilled Slices of Sweet Red Onion	4.50
		Hot Garlic Potato Chips	5.00

The Union Square Cafe Cookbook
&
Second Helpings from Union Square Cafe
Autographed Copies, $35.00 each

FIGURE 4.1 (*continued*)

Menu Items

In the interests of sustainability and their bottom line, restaurateurs are increasingly seeking out menu items that use local ingredients. This not only ensures a fresher product but also saves transporting it across several states. Additional sustainable measures include selecting cooking methods that require the use of less gas or electricity.

Independent restaurant menus tend to be more creative and adventurous than those of chain restaurants. The chefs tend to have a more extensive culinary background and a flair for innovation. Chain restaurants appeal to a broader section of the market and therefore have menu offerings that reflect items popular with the mass market.

The *menu items* selected will depend on the type of restaurant. The number and range of items on the menu is critical to the overall success of the restaurant. If the menu offerings are too extensive, there will be problems in getting the food to the guests in a timely manner. A family restaurant, for example, is mainstream for all ethnic groups and needs to offer a range of popular menu items. A balance is achieved by offering a selection of hot and cold appetizers, soups, and salads. Entrées might include several types of meat, poultry, fish, pasta, and dessert. Soups might include a popular favorite like vegetable beef, plus a daily special. Salads, which could also be served as a main dish, would likely include house salad, chef's salad, or Oriental chicken, fajita, or Caesar salad. Entrée dishes reflect the basic American family-type meal, including charbroiled chicken, baked halibut or codfish, fried shrimp, steaks, burgers, and a variety of sandwiches. Desserts may include a selection of ice creams and cakes or pastries. A choice of salad dressings is usually offered.

Adding new items to the menu can be risky. The large chain restaurants with decisions made at headquarters must reduce their risk, because the failure of menu items at several restaurants can be very costly. Most chains use a rational decision-making process in one form or another. The steps that chains use in this process vary; not all of them are appropriate for every type of restaurant. The following steps are useful in determining whether to add an item to the menu:

1. Create an objective and a timetable.
2. Develop a list of possible menu ideas.
3. Narrow that list down.
4. Test those ideas with consumers.
5. Build prototypes.
6. Internally narrow the prototypes down.
7. Test and renew the prototypes in selected restaurants.
8. Put the prototypes on the menu.

Independent restaurants can simply put on a new item as a special and, if it's popular, add it to the main menu.

Today, not only high-profile and fine-dining restaurants are shaping the industry; even chain restaurants are taking a role.

Obviously, the public is much more acquainted with star chefs like Emeril Lagasse, Wolfgang Puck, Charlie Trotter's, Jean-Georges Vongerichten, and Danny Meyer, but you do not have to be a star chef to help shape the industry. For example, Einstein/Noah Bagel Corporation, Famous Dave's, and Panera Bread all have received Menu Masters Awards.

APPETIZERS AND SOUPS

Six to eight appetizers are adequate for the majority of restaurants. Most of these can be cold or cooked ahead and zapped in the microwave for speed of service and to avoid use of equipment being used for the entrées.

To accommodate a variety of guest tastes, offer a balance in the appetizer list by selecting an item from each generally accepted group of offerings. For example:

- Chilled fresh tiger prawns cooked in saffron lemon tea with couscous semolina, almonds, bell pepper, angel hair, and avocado
- House-smoked duck breast served with baby corn and wild rice
- Ravioli of Pacific prawns served with fresh thyme cream sauce and diced bell pepper
- California potpourri salad served with almond raspberry vinaigrette and tender lettuce and oak leaves, dressed with warm goat cheese and rosemary

The selection of appetizers should be interesting enough for the guest to want to try one but not so filling as to detract from the entrée. It is a good idea to ensure that at least some of the appetizers utilize kitchen equipment that is separate from the equipment used for the entrée. An examination of some family restaurant menus indicates heavy use of the fryer for such items as chicken strips, onion rings, fried zucchini, and fried mozzarella. One of the nonfried or partially fried items could be nachos supreme (crispy tortilla chips with spicy ground beef, Mexican-style beans, cheddar cheese, green onions, chopped tomatoes, black olives, guacamole, and sour cream, with salsa on the side).

Independent dinner restaurants tend to be more adventurous than chain restaurants. Typical appetizers might include shiitake mushrooms in a sherry herb garlic sauce with Indonesian spice; smoked salmon served with capers, lemon, grapes, fresh fruit, and cheddar cheese; baked Brie coated with almonds and served with fresh fruit; shrimp cocktail; Dungeness crab with sherry cream dressing; fresh oysters; and marinated artichokes.

Presentation of the appetizer is important because it is generally the first item guests see and taste. Consider whether appetizers on the dinner menu will be the same as the ones on the luncheon menu.

The kind and number of soups to offer depend on the restaurant concept and the guests. Soups may be categorized as thick, thin, clear, cream, cold, or chowder. Some menus might include a popular favorite such as chicken noodle and a daily special, or more exotic Louisiana clam chowder with Tabasco butter.

SALADS

With the increase in the variety of salad items and their year-round availability, salads have become the preferred starter in a growing number of restaurants. Typically, salads are served before the meal, as a light appetizer. Today more Americans are ordering them as main courses. Restaurants are adding new ingredients to give guests more variety.

The variety of ingredients that combine to make salads is almost endless. Salads range from a classic garden salad, to salads with Mandarin oranges and almonds, or crispy noodles and chicken topped with a light Oriental dressing. Salads made with chicken, beef, seafood, fruits, and vegetables topped with exotic dressings are increasing in popularity, as guests are looking for ways to add fruits and vegetables to their diet. Traditional Caesar and Cobb salads are top main-dish salad choices.

Even traditional hamburger restaurants such as McDonald's and Wendy's have added healthier, lighter fare to their menu. Today, McDonald's offers a variety of choices of premium Caesar and Southwest salads with assorted toppings.

ENTRÉES

Generally, in a table-service restaurant, there should be at least eight entrées. This allows for a minimum selection cooked in a variety of ways (baked, broiled, sautéed, fried, grilled, poached, and simmered). To maintain a balance, there should be an item or two from each of the major meat, pasta, poultry, seafood, and fish categories. One item, such as chicken, can be cooked in different ways: lemon herb chicken (broiled), grilled chicken breast marinated in ginger vinaigrette, chicken fajitas (sautéed), or chicken in the style of Burgundy (simmered).

DESSERTS

Desserts may include a selection of fruits, pies, cakes, ices, and pastries. When properly merchandised, they can boost the average check and profit of the operation.

Most restaurants cannot afford the luxury of a pastry chef. However, there are alternative ways of offering high-quality desserts to restaurant guests. They may be purchased from a local pastry shop or bakery. Another way is to purchase a tart base and add fruit and yogurt to it. Some restaurants have a sundae bar where guests serve themselves ice cream and frozen yogurt and add a variety of toppings.

MATCHING/PAIRING WITH WINE[27]

In the past, food and wine pairings used to be classics, such as oysters with Chablis or a beef roast with Claret (a Bordeaux red or a red Beaune wine, both from France).

Today's menus take their inspirations not only from Europe but also from Asia, Latin America, and once-ignored corners of the United States, and the wines come from every continent except Antarctica.

The new classics couple a type of wine with a general class of food, with the recipe serving as an example. For instance, baked goat cheese frequently shows up on menus in salads, on a designer pizza, or incorporated into a baked mélange. The accompanying wine is a Sauvignon Blanc. That works well when goat cheese is part of a fruit course, where a crisp, dry wine such as Sauvignon Blanc fits better than it might with the cheese course at the end of the meal.

Another example is seared ahi tuna. Its naturally purple-red meat turns gray when cooked, but it is juicy and jewel-like when raw. Taking a cue from sushi bars, which serve tuna raw, modern cooks not only serve uncooked tuna with Japanese seasonings as an appetizer but also have devised ways to impart a little more flair by seasoning and quickly flash-cooking the surface of a block of tuna. The black and gray of the cooked surface frame the translucent red center. A wine to complement this contemporary classic would be a Chardonnay, whose spicy flavors from barrel fermentation and buttery undertone cozy up to the heady flavors and textures of the lightly cooked tuna.

With grilled salmon, the wine of choice today seems to be a Pinot Noir. The trend toward red wine with salmon appears to have started in the Pacific Northwest, where wine drinkers discovered that Oregon Pinot Noir goes well with fish.

Smoked tomatoes have appeared on menus recently, adding a distinctively sweet-and-smoky flavor to any dish that calls for fresh tomatoes. Pasta primavera is not the same anymore. To match this new classic, try a modern-style Chianti with a tinge of smokiness from aging in small oak barrels. Combine it with the pasta and smoked tomatoes, and the flavors practically reverberate.

Menu Types

Restaurants in the French tradition offer menus that feature about the same number of items in each category and follow the classical sequence of dining: first the hors d'oeuvres, followed by soup, then seafood, entrées, *grillades* (grilled meat items), legumes (vegetables), salads, and, finally, desserts.

The really fancy restaurants are likely to offer several specialties of the house or chef. Dinner-house menus separate similar entrées: beef in one section, seafood in another. House specialties may be offered as a group. Many menus have breakfast items, dessert items, and beverages grouped in separate sections.

Coffee shops usually offer a separate page of breakfast items even though they may be available around the clock. The typical table-service restaurant uses three or even four menus—for breakfast, luncheon, and supper. Separate children's menus with smaller portions and lower prices may also be provided.

À la carte menus offer individually priced items. Most restaurants use this type of menu.

A table d'hôte menu offers a selection of several dishes from which patrons choose to make a complete meal at a fixed price. There might be a choice of items for appetizers, soups and salads, entrées, and desserts. For the guest, the advantage of this type of menu is value. With the price fixed, the guest is assured of a meal at a guaranteed price. The advantage for the restaurateur is that the number of menu items is limited.

Some restaurants add a list of daily specials to an à la carte menu. These items take much of the pressure off the kitchen staff, especially on a busy night, because approximately 70 percent of guests may order from this "select" menu insert.

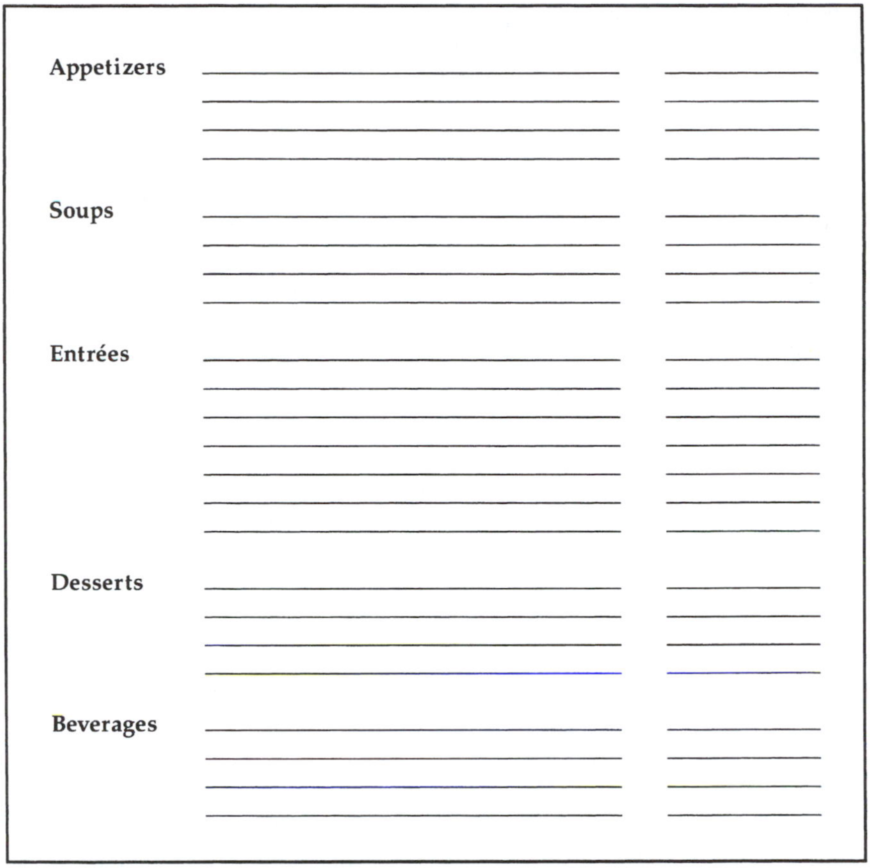

Appetizers

Soups

Entrées

Desserts

Beverages

FIGURE 4.2 Sample of a menu format showing the sequencing of items.

Other *menu types* include the du jour menu, which is a list of food items served only on a particular day. Du jour literally means "of the day," as in "soup du jour." Cyclical menus, which repeat in cycle every few days (normally 7, 10, 14, or 28 days), are generally used in institutions.

The California menu is so named because, in many California restaurants, guests may order any item from the menu at any time of the day. Many restaurants have a separate menu for each meal—breakfast, lunch, dinner, and perhaps brunch. Figure 4.2 shows the format for a simple one-page menu.

The tourist menu is occasionally used to attract tourists' attention to a particular restaurant. Generally, this kind of menu underlines value and acceptability to a guest who may be traveling in a foreign country where the food may be decidedly different.

LUNCH AND DINNER MENUS

From the viewpoint of both guests and restaurant operators, the lunch menu is different from the dinner menu. Today, most lunch guests have about 45 minutes in which to order and enjoy a meal. This means that the menu needs to be easy to read and the kitchen must be capable of producing the food quickly. In most cities, a psychological price barrier keeps lunch menu prices under $10. At dinner, when guests have more time to enjoy a leisurely meal, both the portions and the prices tend to be a little larger.

DEGUSTATION (CHEF'S TASTING) MENUS

A number of exclusive restaurants are offering their guests a *dégustation menu*— meaning "to taste with relish" or "a careful, appreciative tasting of various foods" and focusing on the gustatory system, the senses, high culinary art, and good company. The French term *dégustation* is still commonly used in English-language contexts, even though standard Anglicized spelling and pronunciation exist.

A degustation menu is a sample of the chef's best dishes. They are served in several courses, showcasing the chef's flair for combining flavors and textures. Without a doubt, degustation menus take a lot longer to serve than normal dining menus.

Modern degustation probably comes from the French kitchens of the early twentieth century and is different from earlier meals with many courses because these meals were served as full-sized meals at each course. Degustation is more likely to involve sampling small portions of all of a chef's signature dishes in one sitting. Usually consisting of eight or more courses, it may be accompanied by a matching wine degustation, which complements each dish.

SUSTAINABLE MENUS

Seasonal, sustainable ingredients drive the menu at many contemporary restaurants. One example is Founding Farmers, a 250-seat upscale casual operation in Washington, DC. The restaurant is bankrolled by the 42,000-member North Dakota Farmers Union. Given that the livelihoods of these farmers depend on small-scale agriculture, their attachment to this concept is highly personal. The Founding Farmers restaurant further leverages the sustainability angle by having the restaurant meet both leadership in energy-efficient design standards and Green Certified Restaurant operational standards.[28] The food is billed as "homemade and "scratch-made" traditional American classics inspired by the heartland with sustainably farmed produce, including locally sourced items and in-season vegetables and fruits whenever possible."

Another example comes from Ubuntu, a Napa Valley restaurant that has its own garden, where executive chef Jeremy Fox says that the cooks treat those vegetables with care and respect not just to meet his standards, but to meet their own.[29]

KIDS' MENUS

Restaurants that cater to families usually have a separate kids' menu—one using bold colors and catchy make-believe characters. Children like fun and humor. Children like small prizes to take home, and they like to be involved and treated as more grown-up than they really are. Burger King introduced Big Kid meals to capture the preteen crowd. Others followed suit.

Many restaurants—McDonald's, for example—set aside play areas for children. Almost any restaurant can set aside a kids' corner (if only in self-defense). Some upscale restaurants would just as soon have parents leave the kids at home.

Most restaurants can provide fun placemats, crayons, and small, take-home prizes for kids. Someone on the staff who likes children and enjoys serving them should be the one to wait on them. Someone who is "cool," uses kid-friendly vocabulary, and is lively and laughs easily, is best for the job.

Restaurants serving pancakes can make a funny face on the top pancake with a few berries or colored forms. Take a hint from McDonald's and come up with your own mascot—an animal, silly character, or monster man. The character can be male or female. Kids also enjoy innocuous creatures such as make-believe spiders, big bugs, and other crazy creatures.

RESTAURANTS IN LAS VEGAS REPRESENT THE BEST COUNTRYWIDE

The best 25 restaurants in Las Vegas are as good as the best 25 restaurants in any city in the world. Today, Las Vegas is probably the de facto capital of American cooking, the place where the nation's greatest chefs come together at the table.

Several years ago, Benihana may have been the best restaurant in town. A few years ago, a California Pizza Kitchen opened, and people were delighted because they were able to get something other than buffet-line prime rib and 75-cent shrimp cocktails.

When New York New York opened, it offered restaurants familiar to Manhattan-savvy diners: Chin Chin, Il Fornaio, and Gallagher's Steakhouse. Then Rio brought in Jean-Louis Palladin, dean of French chefs in America. Not to be outdone, The Mirage had James Beard Award–winning chef Alessandro Stratta at Renoir, where the paintings there are real Renoirs, but he moved to Wynn Las Vegas in 2011. Bellagio has Le Cirque and Todd English's Olives restaurants.

For steakhouses, you can choose among The Palm, Gallagher's, Morton's of Chicago, Emeril Lagasse's new Delmonico, and Smith & Wollensky. French chefs include Jean-Louis Palladin, Charles Palmer, Jean-Georges Vongerichten, Joachim Splichal, Jean Joho, and Eberhard Muller. There are several different Wolfgang Puck restaurants in Las Vegas: Spago, Trattoria del Lupo, Postrio, and the Wolfgang Puck Bar & Grill.

Menu Engineering

Over the years, several approaches to menu engineering have been recommended. No matter which is adopted, the important point to remember is that there should be a balance between a menu too high in food cost, which results in giving food away, and too low in food cost, which rips off the customer. Expect some items on the menu to yield a higher margin than others.

Professor Jack Miller developed one of the earlier approaches to menu engineering. The winners were menu items that not only sold more but also were at a lower food-cost percentage. In 1982, professors Michael Kasavana and Donald Smith proposed *menu engineering*. In this approach, the best menu items—the stars—are those that have the highest contribution margin per unit and the highest sales. In 1985, Professor David Pavesic proposed a combination of three variables:

food-cost percentage, contribution margin, and sales volume. Under this method, the best items are called *primes*—those with a low food-cost percentage and a high contribution margin weighted by sales volume.[30]

Professors Mohamed E. Bayou and Lee B. Bennett proposed an approach to menu analyses and engineering whereby each item at each meal is analyzed. Breakfast, lunch, and dinner items are analyzed to compute their measure of profitability. They recommend analysis by:

- Individual menu items
- Categories of menu offering (e.g., appetizers, entrées)
- Meal periods or business categories (e.g., the breakfast meal period, the banquet business)[31]

Menu management software applications can help answer such questions as:[32]

- What is the most profitable price to assign a menu item?
- At what price level and mix of sale does a foodservice operation maximize its profits?
- Which current menu items require reprising, retention, replacement, or repositioning on the menu?
- How should daily specials and new items be priced?
- How can the success of a menu change be evaluated?

Menu engineering is a management application that takes a deterministic approach in evaluating decisions regarding current and future menu pricing, design, and contents. This application requires that management focus on the number of dollars a menu contributes to profit, not simply monitor cost percentages.[33] For a more detailed review of menu engineering, consult one of the Wiley cost-control texts, such as *Food and Beverage Cost Control* by Lea R. Dopson and David K. Hayes.[34]

Dr. Pavesic recommends that restaurant operators first think of the psychological factors that influence guests' price perception. He suggests some guidelines in menu pricing:

1. Use odd-cents increments for digits to the right of the decimal point.
2. Do not write price increases over old prices.
3. Resist increases that raise the dollar amount of the item.
4. Give items that have been drastically increased in price a less noticeable spot on the menu.
5. Try reducing large portions before raising prices. Some restaurant operators suggest taking the items off the menu or changing the dish because regular guests might notice the smaller portions and feel that they were being cheated.
6. Never increase the price on all menu items.
7. Put "market-priced" on items that fluctuate wildly in price.
8. Do not list menu items according to cost, and make sure that menu prices appear after an item's description rather than in a straight column."[35]

Odd-cent menu pricing is widely used in fast-food restaurants. Pricing an item using the 98-cent approach may not be appropriate for unit-scale restaurants, and it certainly should not be used for fine-dining establishments. Many of these price items end in 95 cents. For example, lobster at $19.95 seems appropriate, while $19.98 does not.

Menu Design and Layout

Menu design and layout have been called the silent salespersons of the restaurant. The overall menu design should reflect the ambience of the restaurant. With the aid of graphic artists and designers or the personal computer, menus can be designed to complement decor and ambience.

The menu size may range from a single page up to several pages and be of a variety of shapes; however, menus are generally 9 by 12 inches or 11 by 17 inches. The printing may be elaborate or simple. Both the printing and the artwork should harmonize with the overall theme of the restaurant. The names of the dishes should be easy to read and understand. The menu cover is a symbol of the restaurant's identity.

For menus of more than one page, the outside cover may have the name of the restaurant and a picture appropriate to its style. The layout, typeface, illustrations, graphic design, paper color, and menu copy are a matter of personal choice. Several menu design–related websites feature menu borders and other graphics. Today's personal computers can easily create menus du jour using special software packages. The advantages of making your own menus are flexibility and the ability to recollect daily specials (that way, servers won't forget them!). Money is saved on expensive designers and print shops, records are easily kept, and great graphics are just a mouse click away.

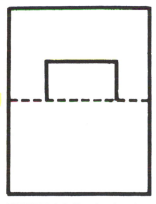

FIGURE 4.3 Focal point of a single-page menu.

We tend to better remember the first and last things that we see or hear. When reading menus, people are also attracted to images, graphics, and icons that will increase sales of particular items—those with the best contribution margins, one hopes.

The layout and sequence of the menu may be a single page encased in plastic laminate. If the menu is more extensive, there is more space on the back for the desserts and beverages.

The focal point of a single-page menu is just above the center, an ideal place to list a special item that may be highlighted to increase sales. This item should also yield a good profit margin because it is a high-selling item. Figure 4.3 shows the focal point of a single-page menu and Figure 4.4 shows the focal point of a two- or four-page menu.

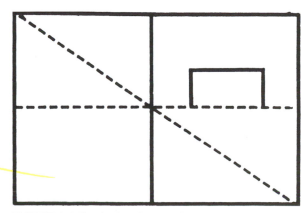

FIGURE 4.4 Focal point of two- or four-page menu.

Menus with two or more pages may be laid out in an appealing way with a signature item or special dishes highlighted or boxed in the focal points. Beverages may appear on the back page or even as a suggestion to accompany a certain dish.

More elaborate menus include additional folds and more pages. Some menus have three panels, while others have inserts for featured specials. Color photographs and graphic designs assist chain guests in making a selection. The Olive Garden has won awards for its picture menu. It and many other fine restaurants use photographs to depict menu dishes. Considering that many restaurant guests eat with their eyes, the picture menu is an effective merchandising tool.

Figure 4.5 shows the menu for Chez Panisse, Alice Waters's renowned Berkeley restaurant. Figure 4.6 shows the menu for Cantina Latina, a new Latin-themed restaurant in Sarasota, Florida.

The paper on which the menu is printed should reflect the atmosphere of the restaurant. In fine dining, use a low-key, expensive paper, and have an inexpensive reduced-size menu available for customers to take with them. A quick-service restaurant may rely completely on a lighted display menu located above the service center. Coffee-shop menus often use a heavy stock paper, enclosed in plastic, with color photos of menu items. The restaurant that changes menu items frequently, perhaps daily, may use a blackboard or a desktop computer to produce the menu.

When starting a new restaurant, it is more cost effective to print two or three menus in the first few weeks and months of operation, as guests' choices determine which menu items are popular and which are not. If a restaurant operator prints an elaborate and expensive menu, it will cost even more when changes are required and new menus are printed.

In an effort to encourage guests to spend more some restaurants are placing the menu prices close to the menu description and not on the far right because they feel that many guests' eyes are scanning the prices and not the food descriptions. This design will make it difficult for guests to compare prices and settle for the cheap dish. Importantly, the design will help force guests to read the food description.[36]

Standardized Recipes

Standardized recipes are used to maintain consistent food quality. A carefully developed recipe helps cooks because the portion size, ingredients, weights, and production steps, including cooking methods and time, are clearly indicated. Restaurant guests will be offered consistently high-quality food. The standard recipe also acts as a control device in that the same ingredients in the same amounts are used over time.

Menu Trends

Trends in the restaurant industry, specifically when relative to menus, are always linked to the behaviors of an entire population. Of course, we can also focus on certain areas of the country as well as consider multiple demographic variables such as age, income, and ethnic group. Defining a specific dining behavior or demand in

Downstairs Dinner Menus

MONDAY, OCTOBER 13 $50
Cipollini onion tart with DeeAnn's garden lettuces
Epaule d'agneau farcie: shoulder of Niman Ranch lamb stuffed with chard and olives, with
    wide noodles and herbs
Baked Bartlett pear with raspberry ice cream

TUESDAY, OCTOBER 14 $65
Elizabeth David's heirloom tomato salad with crème fraîche and herbs
Bay scallops sautéed *à la provençale*
Spit-roasted Sonoma County Liberty duck with quince sauce, Chino Ranch carrots, flat black
    cabbage, and crispy potatoes
Warm chocolate fondant with hazelnut ice cream

WEDNESDAY, OCTOBER 15 $65
Roasted pepper salad with fresh anchovies
Giuliano Bugialli's lasagne verde
Spit-roasted Niman Ranch pork loin with fig and cipollini onion compote, haricots verts, and
    straw potato cake
Three fall sherbets with *pizzelle*

THURSDAY, OCTOBER 16 $65
Warm wild mushroom toasts with DeeAnn's garden lettuces
Potato gnocchi with wilted escarole and garlic
Spit-roasted Hoffman Farm chicken with fried onion rings and green beans with red peppers
Raspberry-almond meringue

FRIDAY, OCTOBER 17 $75
An aperitif
Two color tomato soup with fried polenta sticks and basil oil
Garlic and cheese soufflé with herbs and garden salad
Grilled last of the season local king salmon with bacon, chardonnay sauce, and fennel mirepoix
Pear and frangipane tart

SATURDAY, OCTOBER 18 $75
An aperitif
Fall tomato and hook-and-line caught Atlantic cod salad with basil
Tuscan farro and shell bean soup
Grilled Paine Farm squab with garlic sauce, fried eggplant, and braised fall greens
Tiramisù

Service charge: 15 percent   Corkage: $20 per bottle, limit two (750 ml.) per table.   Sales tax: 8¼ percent
Most of our produce and meat comes from local farms and ranches that practice ecologically sound agriculture.
Other fish varieties may have to be substituted.   www.chezpanisse.com
1517 Shattuck Avenue, Berkeley, California 94709   Reservations: (510) 548-5525
Courtesy of Alice Waters

FIGURE 4.5 At Chez Panisse, in Berkeley, California, only the finest fresh and organic
ingredients are used.

Courtesy of Cantina Latina

FIGURE 4.6 The menu page for Cantina Latina features moderately priced items from Latin America. The restaurant is featured in Chapter 3.

cuisine among a certain population would then qualify as a food trend. Many food trends have shown their endurance and have lasted many years. For example, the Mediterranean food craze became popular in the 1990s and is still holding strong. Restaurant menus in the United States capitalized on this trend and were very successful. The Mediterranean trend eventually spawned other related trends: Spanish, Greek, and Southern Italian. Organizations and media outlets will often try to predict the year's upcoming food trends. Some of these predictions become only short-lived fads, whereas others may become long-lasting trends.

If we look over the past few years, we will find that several trends dominate the landscape. These trends seem to always be in the soothsayer's conversation on new menu trends:[37]

- Using locally grown and sourced ingredients (produce, meats, wine, and beer, etc.)
- The development of healthy menu items for children (healthy sides, portion control, nutritional density, exciting flavors)
- Sustainable food practices

Of course, there are many other food/menu trends that may gain a foothold in the restaurant industry as predicted by experts. However, these top three have seemed to grab attention over the past few years. US diners are becoming much more educated and informed than ever before due to the dominant presence of social media tools. Also, the knowledge that our population has been suffering from an obesity epidemic over the past couple of decades may be another reason.

Some other food/menu trends worth mentioning that have made the top 20 lists of many experts would include:

- Mobile food business (food trucks)
- Culinary cocktails
- Smartphone apps

Restaurant and Institutions magazine suggests the following menu trends in the next few years:[38]

1. Pot roast and brisket and stew: These comfort foods appeal to value-minded diners.
2. Asian plus Latin is a dynamic duo: The Twitter-driven hype over Los Angeles's Kogi truck and its Korean tacos gets at least some credit for this latest fusion craze.
3. Midday dining: During the recession, diners cuts back most on dinner, so many restaurants turned to speed-and value-oriented lunch specials for a greater share of the lunch dollars.
4. Beer, there, and everywhere: Restaurant beer sales are rising in part because guests perceive a specialty beer as an affordable luxury. Seasonal labels, promotion of menu pairings, and themed dinners along with beer-centric eateries all help add to the sales.

5. Premium hamburgers: "Premium burgers represent the ultimate marriage of value and indulgence, so it's no wonder that chains are following the lead of high-end chefs and nudging up America's favorite sandwich a few notches."[39]

6. Downscale dining from big-name chefs: Famous chefs are opening taco bars and sandwich shops.

7. Meatless meals: American's aren't quite embracing vegetarianism en masse, but eschewing meat more often in the interest of health and environmental sustainability is most defiantly in vogue.

8. Fast, casual fine dining: Special menus cut the cost of multicourse meals and/or reduce dining time.

9. Low-carbon-footprint dining: Reducing carbon footprints—the total amount of greenhouse gases produced by a particular activity—offers a holistic approach to going green.

10. Smoking: "From the subtle notes of fruitwoods to the more assertive marks of mesquite and hickory, smoking lets chefs imbue layers of flavor into products without adding fat, sugar, or sodium."[40]

Other identifiable trends are more nutritious kids' meals, farm-branded ingredients, gluten-free/food-allergy-conscious meals, and sustainable seafood. Calorie information is also a hot topic.[41]

According to a National Restaurant Association survey, the top 10 menu trends for 2013 are as follows:[42]

1. Locally sourced meats and seafood
2. Locally grown produce
3. Healthful kids' meals
4. Hyper-local items
5. Sustainability as a culinary theme
6. Children's nutrition as a culinary theme
7. Gluten-free/food allergy-conscious items
8. Locally produced wine and beer
9. Sustainable seafood
10. Whole grain items in kids' meals

Looking at food trends in a city like Boston we find in their restaurants several interesting flavor trends:[43]

■ "Tuna tartare gives way to house-made charcuterie, Italian flavors to Southern, then Asian, ones. Yesterday's risotto is replaced by today's grits— at least until grains like freekeh (roasted wheat) and quinoa begin to encroach."[44]

■ Vietnamese sandwiches called Banh mi feature French bread filled with meat, fish, or tofu, pickled vegetables, cucumbers, cilantro, chilies, and mayonnaise.

■ Homemade ramen noodles and soup is "cult-y comfort food" in Japan. It had appeared largely on late-night menus and in pop-up restaurants but is starting to have a presence on regular menus.

- Meatballs turn up everywhere, made with pork, beef, veal, or shrimp. They are sometimes served in red sauce or sweet-and-sour sauce, with Asian herbs.
- Flatbread is a pizza-like crust topped with things one might put on a pizza. Flatbread just sounds trendier.
- Chinese cha siu bao, steamed buns filled with pork, are a dim sum staple. The New York restaurant Momofuku made them a hot item; as chefs increasingly incorporate Asian flavors, we will see more.[45]

Summary

Menus and menu planning are the most crucial elements of the restaurant. The many considerations in menu planning help us realize the scope and depth of general planning necessary for successful operation. The two main approaches to menu pricing strategies are comparative and individual dish costing. Contribution margins vary from item to item, with the higher food-cost percentage items yielding the greater contribution margin. The various types of menus and menu items are discussed, together with menu design and layout.

Key Terms and Concepts

Accuracy in menus	Menu engineering
Availability	Menu items
Capability	Menu pricing strategies
Chef card	Menu types
Considerations in menu planning	Nutritional value
Consistency	Price
Contribution margin	Raw fare
Equipment	Vegan
Food-cost percentage	Vegetarian
Menu design and layout	

CASE STUDY: Salt "Gastropub"

Introduction

"Salt" is New Jersey's first gastropub, which was opened by Bradley and Laurie Boyle in April of 2008. In case you're not already familiar with the concept, a *gastropub* is simply a pub that serves better-than-average fare, which originated in England in the early 1990s. "Salt Gastropub" features upscale food served in a casual setting without the pretense of a fine-dining establishment. Its menu items are complemented by its vast assortment of quality beers, wines, and specialty cocktails, all of which are reasonably priced to encourage frequent patronage. The name "Salt" was chosen after much deliberation and debate, but the idea was simple; what better way to sum up a concept that is focused on great food than to name it after the key ingredient used in all food preparations—salt.

Background

In 2001, Bradley and Laurie opened their first restaurant, "Bula," in Newton, New Jersey. They owned and operated Bula for eight years before they decided it was time for a larger restaurant operation with a different concept in mind. While driving through the Township of Byram, New Jersey, one day, they discovered a "roadhouse-style" building that was for sale in a rustic setting with highway frontage. Bradley and Laurie seriously considered purchasing the building for its ideal location, architectural potential, and with hopes that they could get if for a good deal, which they did. Bradley and Laurie spent six months trying to get the approval for an SBA loan. The timing was a key factor in getting their loan approval, as the economy began to struggle shortly after.

Customers and Employees

Before it was Salt, the previous business was a local dive bar known as 76ers Waterloo Inn that attracted a rough and often rowdy crowd. Bradley and Laurie wanted to cater to a completely different market from the previous concept, and they knew it would be a challenge to change the location's reputation and give people a reason to come to the establishment. Furthermore, they wanted to be a pillar of the community, as the building is located in a family-oriented community. There is a huge emphasis placed on "the Salt family," which encompasses the staff, customers, and the community. The employees have bought into this philosophy and embrace the culture.

The Menu

When creating the menu, they wanted it to be approachable, with familiar items and ingredients prepared in a unique way; all they while keeping the theme of traditional English pub fare in the background. For this reason, some of their most popular items include

Fish 'n' Chips using beer-battered tilapia; Bangers and Mash using pork sausage in sweet apple gravy with creamy smashed potatoes; and garlic and rosemary marinated Hangar Steak. The key to the entire restaurant is the extensive beer selection, which consists of over 70 beers to choose from, most of which are either craft or imported. At Salt, they make an effort not to serve mainstream beer brands; however, there are a select few available for the everyday guy who yearns for the staple American brand.

Success and Challenges

Since opening in April of 2008, Salt's business has grown every quarter. Overall, it has seen approximately 35 percent increase in business in the past four years. Bradley and Laurie attribute their success to "the perfect storm" of factors that worked out in their favor. They had the right concept for a struggling economy, combining a reasonable price point, good food, and a casual setting and live entertainment, all of which resulted in a desirable experience. Most important, they embedded themselves in the community, and the community embraced them in return by supporting their business. Finally, they maintained an active presence through advertising, social media, and participating in various events to give the restaurant recognition. In 2010, Bradley was featured as a contestant on Food Network's hit television show *Chopped*, which gave the restaurant instant notoriety and significantly increased demand.

Bradley and Laurie have faced various challenges over the past four years at Salt. One of the biggest challenges has been handling the various customer concerns that arise. There is currently a notion in the hospitality industry that "the customer is always right." This can be difficult because customers can be extremely demanding, and the fact is that they are not always right. The Boyles have stated, "We have had suggestions on colors we should paint the bathrooms, the type of music we should have, the beers we should serve, the uniforms we should use, the hours we should be open, to just about anything you can imagine. We love the suggestions, and get a kick out of a lot of them . . . but Salt was a well-thought-out concept that had been developed over years, and we are what we are and always stick to our guns."[46]

QUESTIONS

1. What elements of the menu do you think have contributed to the restaurant's overall success?
2. Should the owners focus on offering items with good nutritional value? Why or why not?
3. How can the owners further improve the menu?
4. In their previous restaurant, Bula, Bradley and Laurie offered bread service with their meals. They used a local bakery and served artisan breads. When they opened Salt, they took this into consideration to determine whether they should offer bread service.
   a. Do you think it is a good idea to serve bread at Salt? Why or why not?
   b. What are some alternatives to bread service?

Review Questions

1. How would you prioritize the considerations in menu planning for your restaurant?
2. There is a trade-off between a fully qualified chef and lower costs. How can a balance be achieved to leave a reasonable return for the owners?
3. To achieve maximum efficiency in your restaurant's kitchen, who should be involved?
4. Discuss how the equipment and menu must harmonize to create a smooth operation.
5. Ask several restaurant owners/managers how they arrived at their menu prices, and compare their answers with the methods suggested in the text.
6. Use sample menus to analyze:
   How many items are in each course?
   What equipment will be required for each?
   Select a few items and determine what you would expect their food-cost percentage to be.
7. How seriously should restaurant operators become involved with the nutritional content of foods the chefs serve?
8. Describe the sources of the menu items that will be featured on your menu.
9. Describe how your menu will look when presented to guests.
10. What will your restaurant food-cost percentage be? How will you achieve it?

Endnotes

1. Lorri Mealey, "Restaurant Menu Design; How to Design a Restaurant Menu," About.com. Restauranting, http://restaurants.about.com/od/menu/a/Menu_Design.htm. Retrieved April 27, 2013.
2. Lorri Mealey, "What to Skip When Writing Your Restaurant Menu," About.com, Restauranting, http://restaurants.about.com/od/menu/a/Skip_Menu.htm. Retrieved April 27, 2013.
3. Michael Sanson, "Will It Fly?" *Restaurant Hospitality* (March 1, 1998), http://business.highbeam.com/1021/article-1G1-20932058/fly. Retrieved on May 8, 2013.
4. Personal conversation with Club 21, June 27, 2013.
5. Bern's Steakhouse website. www.bernssteakhouse.com/BottomMenu/Menu/DinnerMenu/tabid/78/Default.aspx. July, 2012.

6. Wendy Rotelli, "Are Restaurants Required to Provide Calorie or Nutrition Info?" Restaurants.com (March 2, 2013), http://www.restaurants.com/blog/are-restaurants-required-to-provide-calorie-or-nutrition-info/#.UXxEAIK6V8V.

7. Personal conversation with Michael Hartsaw, Business Development Manager, Sysco Foodservice. March 24, 2013.

8. Kelli B. Grant, "Farewell Foie Gras (and 5 Other Banned Foods)," http://blogs.smartmoney.com/advice/2012/07/02/farewell-foie-gras-and-5-other-banned-foods/. Retrieved September 20, 2012.

9. Michael M. Grynbaum, "Judge Blocks New York City's Limits on Big Sugary Drinks," *New York Times* (March 11, 2013). http://www.nytimes.com/2013/03/12/nyregion/judge-invalidates-bloombergs-soda-ban.html?pagewanted=all&_r=0, p. 1.

10. Ibid., p. 1.

11. Scott Adams. "Unsafe gluten-free food list." Celiac.com. http://www.celiac.com/articles/182/1/Unsafe-Gluten-Free-Food-List-Unsafe-Ingredients/Page1.html. 2007.

12. Karen Eich Drummond and Lisa M. Brefere, *Nutrition for Foodservice and Culinary Professionals*, 6th ed. (Hoboken, NJ: John Wiley & Sons, 2007), p. 399.

13. The Food Allergy & Anaphylaxis Network, *Welcoming Guests with Food Allergies* (FAAN, 2008), http://www.foodallergy.org/document.doc?id=143.

14. "Celiac Disease Statistics," Celiac.com (June 26, 2007), http://www.celiac.com/articles/1164/1/Celiac-Disease-Statistics/Page1.html

15. "Allergy Facts and Figures," Asthma and Allergy Foundation, http://www.aafa.org/display.cfm?id=9&sub=30 retrieved on May 8, 2013,

16. Ibid.

17. Denis Campbell,"Vegetarians gain more options for fine dining with 50% rise in foodie eateries." *Guardian* (April 30, 2010). http://www.guardian.co.uk/lifeandstyle/2010/apr/30/vegetarian-restaurants-uk-boom. April 30, 2010

18. "New Harris Interactive poll shows vegan eating doubles since 2009." *Examiner.* http://www.examiner.com/article/new-harris-interactive-poll-shows-vegan-eating-doubles-since-2009. December, 2011.

19. "Happy Cow: The Healthy Eating Guide." Happy Cow. http://www.happycow.net/. 2012.

20. Lila Roe, "Negative side effects of a raw foods diet." Livestrong (May 30, 2011). http://www.livestrong.com/article/411904-negative-side-effects-of-a-raw-foods-diet/.

21. Dan Fletcher, "Fad diets." *Time* (December 15, 2009), http://www.time.com/time/magazine/article/0,9171,1950931,00.html.

22. Ibid.

23. "Heritage Pyramids and Total Diet." Oldways. http://oldwayspt.org/resources/heritage-pyramids. 2012.

24. Annie Corapi, "The Ten Healthiest Ethnic Cuisines," CNN (August 25, 2010). Available at http://www.cnn.com/2010/HEALTH/08/25/healthiest.ethnic.cuisines/index.html

25. John Li, Senior Vice President, Research and Development Bloomin Brands, presentation to USF Hospitality Management class May 3, 2013.

26. Lisa Jennings, "Industry Braces for Menu-Labeling Liability Litigation," *Nation's Restaurant News*, New York: Vol. 42, Iss. 25 (June 23, 2008), pp. 1–3.

27. This section draws on Harvey Steiman, "Made for Each Other," *Wine Spectator* 24, no. 11 (October 31, 1999), pp. 45–71.

28. Bob Krummert, "Green from the Ground Up," *Restaurant Hospitality,* Cleveland: Vol. 92, Iss. 11 (November 2008), pp. 11–14.

29. Ibid.

30. David Pavesic, "Taking the Anxiety Out of Menu Pricing," *Restaurant Management* 2, no. 2 (February 1988), pp. 56–57.

31. Mohamed E. Bayou and Lee B. Bennett, "Profitability Analysis for Table Service Restaurants," *Cornell H.R.A. Quarterly* 33, no. 2 (April 1992), pp. 49–55.

32. Mahmood A. Kahn, Michael D. Olsen, and Turgurt Var, Eds., *VNR's Encyclopedia of Hospitality and Tourism,* Michael M. Kasavana, "Computers in the Foodservice Industry," New York: Van Nostrand Reinhold, 1993, pp. 270–271.

33. Ibid.

34. Lea R. Dopson and David K. Hayes, *Food and Beverage Cost Control* (Hoboken, NJ: John Wiley & Sons, 2010).
35. Pavesic, pp. 56–57.
36. B. Venkatesch, "Designing a Restaurant Menu Differently," *Businessline,* Chennai: (January 4, 2009).
37. Michael Hartsaw, Restaurant Development Manager, Sysco Foodservice. Presentation to a USF class, April 24, 2013.
38. Janet Helm, "Top Dining and Restaurant Trends in 2010, Nutrition Unplugged (November 30, 2009), http://nutritionunplugged.com/tag/gourmet-food-trends/.
39. Ibid.
40. Ibid.
41. National Restaurant Association website. Restaurant.org (December 1, 2009).
42. "What's Hot: 2013 Chef Survey," National Restaurant Association. Available at http://www.restaurant .org/Downloads/PDFs/News-Research/WhatsHotFood2013.pdf. Retrieved on September 21, 2012.
43. Devra First, "Changing Trends on Boston Restaurant Menus," *Boston Globe* (July 31, 2012), http:// www.boston.com/ae/restaurants/2012/08/01/changing-trends-restaurant-menus-what-out-and-upcoming-boston-menus/zV10rgpvMGR8cGnWE00dMN/story.html. Retrieved on September 20, 2012.
44. Ibid.
45. Ibid.
46. Personal conversation with Bradley and Laurie Boyle January 14, 2013.

CHAPTER
5

Planning and Equipping the Kitchen

LEARNING OBJECTIVES

After reading and studying this chapter, you should be able to:

- Identify factors to consider when planning a kitchen's layout.

- Discuss the benefits and drawbacks of an open kitchen.

- Explain selection factors for purchasing kitchen equipment.

- Identify various cooking techniques.

Courtesy of Sysco

This chapter states principles of kitchen planning and the selection of kitchen equipment. Kitchen planning involves the allocation of space within the kitchen based on equipment needs, spatial relationships within the kitchen, and the need to keep traffic flows within the kitchen to a minimum. In the kitchen, food is received and processed (prepared) before cooking, and cooked food is moved to a serving station.

The second part of the chapter presents examples of the most commonly used kitchen equipment, their use, and their performance characteristics.

When an existing restaurant is bought, the buyers are often too concerned with survival to think much about changing the layout or the equipment. If they have the capital, they may ask a restaurant equipment dealer to evaluate the current equipment and suggest kitchen layout changes. Some restaurant equipment dealers are quite knowledgeable about layout planning. Others are not.

Restaurant companies and institutions usually turn to experienced, professional planners to draw up plans for building a new or modifying existing kitchen configurations of large, complicated kitchens.

An overall objective of layout planning is to minimize the number of steps waitstaff and kitchen personnel must take. In quick-service restaurants, equipment is placed so that servers take only a few steps. The same principle applies in fine-dining restaurants, even though a particular dish may pass through five hands before being picked up by waitstaff.

Full-service restaurants are usually laid out so that the kitchen flow is from the receiving area to the cold and dry storage spaces to the pre-prep area, where bulk ingredients are measured and cans opened, to the prep area, where vegetables are washed and peeled and fish, meat, and poultry is cut. The flow continues to the cooking area, where soups and stocks are prepared and other cooking takes place. The last station is where final prep takes place (food is finished, plated, and readied for pickup by staff).

Baking and pantry areas (desserts and sandwiches) may be set off by themselves. If feasible, dishwashing and pots and pans are best kept off to one side, out of the traffic flow. The restaurant configuration and limitations often require special layout and design. Ventilation and necessary airflow and building codes may pose special problems.

Figure 5.1 illustrates the flow of a kitchen where food is received, stored, prepped, cooked, and plated.

Arriving at the best layout for complicated kitchens is a highly sophisticated skill and art. John C. Cini, president and CEO of Cini Little, an international foodservice and hospitality business and also a design consulting firm headquartered in Rockville, Maryland, said, "Great thought is put into every one of our designs,

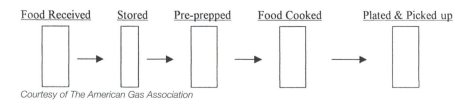

Food Received   Stored   Pre-prepped   Food Cooked   Plated & Picked up

Courtesy of The American Gas Association

FIGURE 5.1 Kitchen flow.

taking into consideration the activities that actually occur during the food preparation, cooking, and serving processes."[1]

A designer with experience in operations has the advantage of being able to relate to and anticipate the behaviors of the personnel who will utilize the facility. For example, one cannot assume that staff members will understand or obey the design intent of a facility. The designer must realize that servers typically take the shortest and most convenient route from any one place to another. Chefs want their work organized in a manner that minimizes excess activity and unnecessary steps. If these concepts are not incorporated into a design, the workers may implement their own makeshift accommodations to satisfy their needs. This diminishes the value of the design and decreases the efficiency of the operation. The efficiency and comfort of the staff is important to the operation. Recent trends, such as ergonomics (the applied science of equipment design intended to reduce staff fatigue and discomfort), influence foodservice facility design. This may include lowering counter heights to make the task of slicing deli meats easier or providing a floor covering that does not tire the body as quickly.

Outside pressures in the form of legislation and public policy also affect foodservice design. For example, compliance with the provisions of government plays a major role in maintaining standards to accommodate the needs of workers and customers who are disabled. These influences are responsible for widening aisles and making equipment more readily accessible. Sanitation is another large factor in foodservice equipment. Designers must understand National Sanitation Foundation standards and apply them to the actions of the workers. By providing a safe work environment, the restaurant benefits by limiting injuries, maintaining morale, and reducing employee turnover. Customers benefit from a decrease in foodborne illness, better service, and an overall higher-quality dining experience.

Cini lists trends in kitchen equipment and their use:

- New equipment combines refrigerated bases with kitchen ranges and grill tops. This enables chefs to have raw foods at hand, so that they need not turn around to open a refrigerator.
- Self-cleaning hoods and ventilators that trap odors and fumes can be automatically controlled by pumps that spray hot water and detergent on the hoods during off hours, thereby limiting grease buildup.
- Combination oven/steamers allow cooks to use either moist or dry heat, or a combination of both. Vegetables can be steamed, cookies can be baked, and meat can be braised with one piece of equipment.
- Induction heating, which has been used in the past for exhibition cooking and in cafeterias, allows chefs to prepare food in full view of customers while eliminating wild heat, excess grease, and noisy ventilators.
- Kitchen equipment now includes computers that automatically control ovens. A bakeshop worker can program the oven to bake different breads at different temperatures and levels of humidity for specific times. Desired oven temperatures can be saved in the computer's memory.[2]

The American Gas Association has published examples of kitchen plans to show the workflow within a typical kitchen layout (see Figure 5.2).

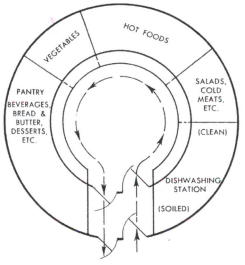

CIRCULAR
Ideal but impractical

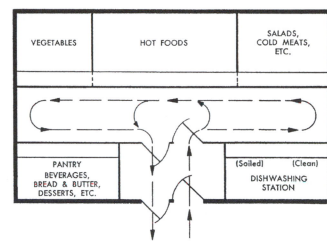

RECTANGULAR
Kitchen Entrance on Long Side

This is usually the preferred layout of the serving area of a restaurant kitchen. The shortened paths indicate the travel if all stations need not be contacted.

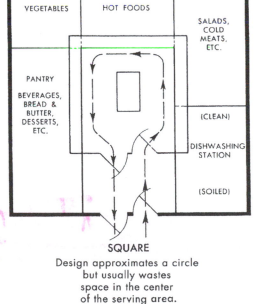

SQUARE
Design approximates a circle but usually wastes space in the center of the serving area.

Courtesy of The American Gas Association

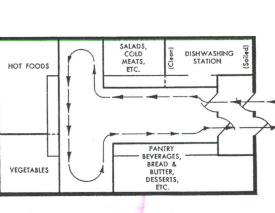
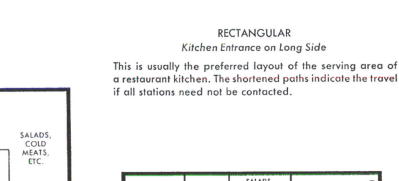

RECTANGULAR
Kitchen Entrance on Short Side

Hot foods must be carried considerable distances and waiters at the various stations may be obstructing traffic to and from the dining area.

FIGURE 5.2 Serving area: Some workflows are better than others.

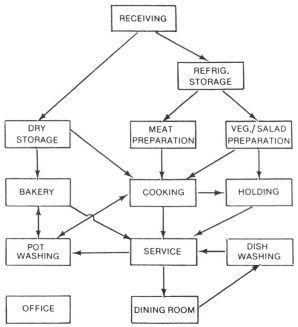

Courtesy of Dr. Arthur C. Avery, Professor Emeritus, Purdue University

FIGURE 5.3 Arrangement of work centers.

The plans show the movement of food from delivery through the various workstations and on to the guest. As the diagram shows, circular workflow patterns are not efficient. Square designs also waste space in the center of the service area. The preferred kitchen plan is rectangular in shape, providing the shortest paths when not all stations within the kitchen are contacted.

Dr. Arthur C. Avery, professor emeritus at Purdue University, studied kitchen efficiency and created arrangements of *work centers* in a typical service restaurant that has a fairly limited menu. A flowchart (see Figure 5.3) traces the movement of food from storage and preparation areas to the center of the kitchen, where the food is cooked. From the cooking area, the food goes to the service area, and from there into the dining room. System elements are interdependent; cooking is dependent on meat preparation, meat prep on refrigeration, refrigeration on receiving.

Avery suggests these methods of increasing kitchen efficiency:

- Use purveyors that have a wide base of supply (so that fewer deliveries are needed).
- Use conveyors to take food to service areas.
- Place service stations in the dining room with silver, beverages, soups, and other items to reduce back-and-forth traffic to the kitchen.
- Use automatic conveyors to take racks from the dining room through the dishwasher and then back to the dining room.[3]

Back-of-the-House Green

Given the high and increasing cost of electricity, gas, and water, it is smart to cut utility costs without sacrificing service, quality, style, or comfort. Induction cooking, which is generally more energy efficient than gas or conventional electrical heat, is one way of greening the back of the house; another is by using the innovative high-speed ovens. This new variety of hybrid equipment has been developed to meet the Leadership in Energy and Environmental Design (LEED) Green Building Rating System, a voluntary building certification program.[4]

According to Energy Star, a branch of the U.S. Environmental Protection Agency, as much as 80 percent of the $10 billion annual energy bill for the commercial foodservice industry does no useful work. These lost energy dollars are often wasted in the form of excess heat, ventilation, and refrigeration, or generated by inefficient appliances.[5]

Restaurants that purchase their equipment wisely can cut their energy costs 10 to 30 percent. Energy Star estimates that by outfitting a kitchen with equipment they currently qualify, the typical restaurant owner would save approximately $2,500 annually in gas and electric bills.[6] One often-overlooked high-energy user is the hood because it sucks up all the air you just spent lots of dollars to cool down. Thankfully, there is now a new generation of super-efficient exhaust hoods. These new exhaust ventilators use high-efficiency filters to take advantage of the flow of thermal air currents to keep the amount of air wasted to a minimum. Some have the addition of a real energy saving switch or computer program to vary the speed and amount of air extraction. Exhaust ventilators do not need to be on at full speed all the time.[7]

Exhaust systems of today can save 40 to 50 percent of treated make up air by lowering the cfm draw, which relieves the HVAC system. For example, if a system draws 5,000 cfm and a Halton M.A.R.V.A.L. system draws 3,500 cfm, that is a substantial difference and relieves the HVAC system and would represent significant savings.[8]

Open Kitchen

Open kitchens (also called exhibition kitchens) have their own equipment and are growing in popularity. By taking down the walls that separate chefs from diners, restaurants are creating more interactive and upbeat atmospheres. According to Roland Passot, chef/owner of the highly regarded La Folie in San Francisco and owner and chief culinary officer of the Bay Area's Left Bank restaurants, "The benefits of having an open kitchen are that it brings energy to the dining room, creates a show for the customer, like watching a performance, and it gives the customer a sense of being on the 'inside,' similar to a reality TV show."[9]

Sometimes an open design focuses on highlighting the kitchen; other times it could highlight a piece of equipment. A steakhouse focuses on the cooking of meat, an Italian restaurant on pizza. These focal points are highlighted by lighting the dining room slightly less than the kitchen. Standard kitchen equipment, such as refrigerators, is placed in other parts of the kitchen that are not visible. Standard food preparation is not usually featured.

The open kitchen is reserved for what is glamorous: bright, shiny ladles, stainless steel and copper utensils—perhaps a stainless-steel counter where food is picked up by staff. A hole in the counter can be used for dropping garbage into a container. A few exhibition kitchens cook by induction coils. Some open kitchens use under-the-counter refrigeration units to conserve space and expedite work. The area set aside for open kitchens costs about 25 percent more than in a standard kitchen. Figure 5.4 shows the floor plan of an open kitchen.

There are also some drawbacks to having an open kitchen. The noise level of a completely open kitchen must be reduced with washable acoustic tile in the ceiling. The dining room and banquet rooms must feature carpet, upholstered chairs, and washable window drapes, plus acoustic ceilings. A few visually open kitchens are enclosed in glass, which eliminates the noise problem. The fact that chefs and cooks are completely exposed to guests means that every word and every gesture is visible. Cooks and chefs must be able to control themselves under pressure. Guests

The California Café Bar & Grill in Schaumburg, Illinois, by Engstrom Design Group, serves California cuisine. The open kitchen, visible from all 200 seats in the restaurant, directs views away from the adjacent Woodfield Mall and its huge parking area. The kitchen is divided with a granite-topped pass shelf that is clad in wood veneer on the restaurant side. Work counters are maple butcher block or stainless steel. The back wall of the open kitchen is covered in ceramic tile and stainless steel, and acid-etched copper panes hide the exhaust hood. The floors are quarry tile. Actual cooking ingredients are set on metal shelves on the wall behind the pantry. Noise is mitigated in the dining room with a combination of drop-in acoustical ceiling tiles, carpeting, fully upholstered booths, and heavy draperies dividing open, private, and semiprivate dining areas.

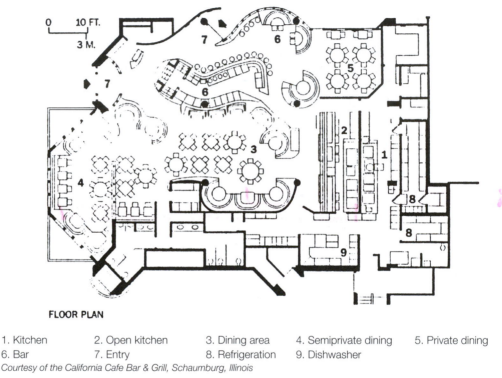

FLOOR PLAN

1. Kitchen	2. Open kitchen	3. Dining area	4. Semiprivate dining	5. Private dining
6. Bar	7. Entry	8. Refrigeration	9. Dishwasher	

Courtesy of the California Cafe Bar & Grill, Schaumburg, Illinois

FIGURE 5.4 Open kitchen floor plan.

might also feel that since they can see the chefs and/or cooks, it is all right to talk to them. Complaints or praise could pose problems on a busy shift.

Costas Katsigris, Ed Norman and Chris Thomas in their book *Design and Equipment for Restaurants and Foodservice: A Management View, Third Edition*, assembled a number of tables that show the range in space needed for various restaurant activities (see Figures 5.5 to 5.9.).[10] The tables can be used as reference when buying, building, or modifying a restaurant. In general—there are many exceptions, depending on the restaurant service—kitchens are about half the size of the dining room, and the space needed for seating varies, so check with your local fire code:

Deluxe—15 to 20 square feet per seat

Medium—12 to 18 square feet per seat

Banquet—10 to 15 square feet per seat

Type of Service	Kitchen Square Footage per Dining Room Seat	Total Square Footage in the Back of the House per Seat
Cafeteria/commercial	6–8	10–12
Coffee shop	4–6	8–10
Table service restaurant	5–7	10–12

Source: Jay R. Schrock

FIGURE 5.5 Dimensions for commercial foodservice kitchens.

Meals Served per Day	Receiving Area Square Footage
200–300	50–60
300–500	60–90
500–1,000	90–130

Source: Carl Scriven and James Stevens, Food Equipment Facts (New York: John Wiley & Sons, 1999)

FIGURE 5.6 Space dimensions for receiving areas.

Meals Served per Day	Dry Storage Square Footage
100–200	120–200
200–350	200–250
350–500	250–400

Source: Carl Scriven and James Stevens, Food Equipment Facts (New York: John Wiley & Sons, 1999)

FIGURE 5.7 Space dimensions for dry storage.

Number of Doors	Height (inches)	Width (inches)	Depth (inches)	Cubic (feet)
1	78	28	32	22
2	78	56	32	50
3	78	84	32	70–80

Source: Carl Scriven and James Stevens, Food Equipment Facts (New York: John Wiley & Sons, 1999)

FIGURE 5.8 Full-door reach-ins.

Size of Unit	Square Footage	Cubic Feet
5′9″ × 7′8″	35.7	259.9
6′8″ × 8′7″	47.4	331.8
7′8″ × 7′8″	49.0	340.2
8′7″ × 11′6″	86.4	604.8

Source: Carl Scriven and James Stevens, Food Equipment Facts (New York: John Wiley & Sons, 1999)

FIGURE 5.9 Walk-ins (all 7-feet, 6-inches height).

The space needed in the back of the house varies as well:

Deluxe—7 to 10 square feet per seat
Medium—5 to 9 square feet per seat
Banquet—3 to 5 square feet per seat[11]

Kitchen Floor Coverings

Kitchen floors are usually covered with quarry tile, marble, terrazzo, asphalt tile, or sealed concrete—materials that are nonabsorbent, easy to clean, and resistant to the abrasive action of cleaning chemicals. In areas where water is likely to accumulate (e.g., near the dishwasher), neoprene matting provides traction, making walking and standing less stressful than they are on hard surfaces. In all kitchen areas, the surfaces should be covered with nonskid material. The number-one cause of restaurant accidents is slipping and falling. Older employees who fall may break bones or suffer a concussion. The same rule applies in dining rooms with even more urgency. Plaintiffs who have fallen and broken bones have won large lawsuits against restaurants.

Building codes do not permit carpeting in kitchens. Coving—the curved, sealed edge on kitchen perimeters that eliminates sharp corners and gaps—is essential. Perhaps the most effective way to prevent slips and falls in kitchens and elsewhere in a restaurant is to enforce a rigid rule that anything spilled, including water, be wiped up at once.

Kitchen Equipment

Selection of *kitchen equipment* may seem simple or complex, depending on your level of experience. Independent restaurants may be copies of existing restaurants, more or less duplicating kitchen layout and equipment. Operators taking over an existing restaurant are likely to continue using the equipment already there. Equipment dealers are ready to make recommendations. Figure 5.10 shows one suggested layout. Restaurant shows, where dozens of equipment manufacturers display their wares, are staged each year; the largest is one managed by the National Restaurant Association in Chicago. Each year a similar one is held in New York City and another in California. Tens of thousands of foodservice operators attend these shows to see new developments in food and equipment. Another major trade show is the North American Foodservice Manufactures (NAFEM) show, which is held every two years.

Today, there are advancing trends in sustainable kitchen equipment. The Energy Star program is a joint program of the U.S. Environmental Protection Agency and the U.S. Department of Energy. They help homes and businesses save money and protect the environment through energy-efficient products and practices.[12] Ideas for conservation of energy and water include the installation of Energy Star kitchen appliances, Energy Star compact fluorescent lamps, low flow prerinse spray nozzles at the dish machine, and flow restrictors on faucets.

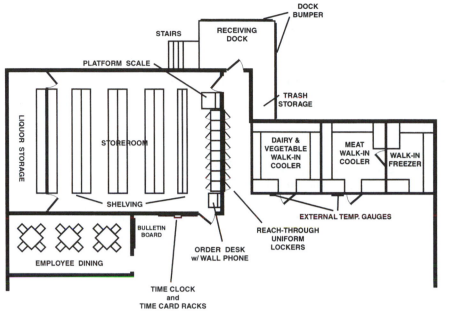

FIGURE 5.10 The back of the house.

The National Restaurant Association recommends the following for reducing water waste:

- Thaw frozen foods in the refrigerator.
- Purchase a water-efficient dishwasher and wash only full loads.
- Soak pots and pans before hand washing.
- Cook vegetables with a minimum amount of water and use cooking water for soup stock.
- Train your staff to turn off the water promptly.[13]

In addition, the National Restaurant Association recommends the following for reducing electricity waste:

- Use fluorescent lighting for indoor and outdoor fixtures.
- Install timers or occupancy sensors.
- Focus light on areas where it's most needed.
- Reduce the burden on your electrical system, don't turn on all electrical equipment at the same time.
- Make sure the size of an appliance suits your needs (and reduce size where possible).
- Reduce the number of times a day you adjust your thermostat
- Change dirty air filters on air conditioners.[14]

As previously discussed, professional restaurant planners are available for a fee to plan, lay out, and recommend restaurant equipment. They can also help in developing, changing, or modifying concepts.

CATEGORIES OF KITCHEN EQUIPMENT

The standard equipment needed in restaurant kitchens can be divided according to purpose or *categories of kitchen equipment*:

- Receiving and storing food
- Fabricating and preparing food
- Preparing and processing food
- Assembling, holding, and serving food
- Cleaning up and sanitizing the kitchen and kitchenware

SELECTING THE RIGHT EQUIPMENT

Anyone selecting kitchen equipment, beginner or veteran, faces some common questions:

- Of the equipment available, which will be the most efficient for the menu, item by item, and for menu items contemplated in the future?
- What is the equipment's purchase cost and operating cost?
- Should the equipment be gas fired or electric?
- Will the equipment produce the food fast enough to meet demand?
- Is it better to buy a large unit or two or more smaller units?
- Are replacement parts and service readily available?
- Is reliable used equipment available?
- Is more energy-efficient equipment available?

For additional help, please consult fee-based food facilities designers via the FCSI.org website. Generally, the saving made by using their services about pays for their fees, and a better design is made.

MATCHING EQUIPMENT WITH MENU AND PRODUCTION SCHEDULE

The menu determines the equipment (see Figure 5.11). Look at the menu, item by item. What equipment is needed to prepare each item? Other variables include:

- *The projected volume of sales for each menu item:* What size of equipment or how many pieces of equipment will be needed? Do not overequip. Market conditions may force menu changes.
- *Fixed or changing menu:* A fixed menu needs fewer kinds of equipment.
- *Menu size:* Large menus may call for a greater variety of equipment.

STORAGE

Cold storage reach-in units	Cold storage walk-in units

FABRICATION AND PREPREPARATION

Breading machines	Cutters and slicers	Mixers
Can openers	Knife sharpeners	Peelers

PREPARATION AND PROCESSING

Broilers	Hot dog cooking equipment	Revolving tray ovens
Cheese melters	Hot plates	Steamers
Convection ovens	Microwave ovens	Steam-jacketed kettles
Display cooking equipment	Mobile mini-kitchens	Steam boilers
Egg cookers	Ovens	Tilting fry pans
Frying equipment	Proof cabinets	Ventilators
Griddles and grills	Ranges	Waffle bakers

ASSEMBLY, HOLDING, AND SERVING

Beverage equipment	Dispensing equipment	Mobile buffet and banquet equipment
Coffee brewers	Food reconstitutors	Shake and soft-serve equipment
Coffee ranges	Hot serving equipment	Toasters
Cold serving equipment	Infrared warmers	Dish-dispensing equipment

CLEANUP AND SANITATION

Cleaning and sanitizing	Dishwashing equipment	Glass washers
Compactors	Disposers	Water-heating equipment

FIGURE 5.11 Electric equipment found in restaurants.

- *Speed of service desired:* Fast service may call for equipment of larger capacity. Reduced cooking time translates into higher seat turnover in the dining room.
- *Nutritional awareness and equipment selected:* Interest in nutrition brings an increased interest in the method of food preparation used. Frying is avoided to cut down on consumption of fats. Baking, broiling, and steaming are more healthful ways to prepare meat, fish, and fowl.

Multiple uses for equipment means less kitchen space must be allocated to equipment. *Slow cooking* with ovens can be done during the night, freeing up oven space for daytime use. Small-quantity, staggered cooking for vegetables can be done with a relatively small piece of steam-pressure equipment.

TOTAL COST VERSUS ORIGINAL COST

The initial cost of equipment is but one factor in the cost equation. What about life expectancy and parts replacement? How often must the magnetrons in a microwave be replaced? How long do the infrared lamps last? The thermostatic controls in the fryer? Even more important is the cost of energy each piece of equipment consumes. In most locations, gas is much less expensive than electricity, sometimes dramatically so. Electric equipment requires warm-up time. Gas heat is immediate. Cost of warm-up time is considerable on equipment that is used intermittently. Over the period of a year, the operational cost differential becomes an important factor in the choice of equipment. The initial cost of upgrading to energy-efficient equipment may be high in the beginning, but over time you earn that money back in lower utility bills.[15]

SELECTING THE MOST EFFICIENT EQUIPMENT FOR THE PEOPLE AND SKILLS AVAILABLE

Too often a kitchen is loaded with equipment that is seldom or never used. Select only those pieces of equipment that are most efficient and necessary for the menu. Many European kitchens and small restaurant kitchens in the United States prepare outstanding food using only a stovetop burner, pots and pans, a few knives, and other small equipment. A few seafood restaurants produce a high volume of food using only deep fryers. McDonald's restaurants are built around a griddle and deep fryers. Several other large hamburger chains revolve around a conveyor-type broiler.

DESKILLING THE JOB WITH EQUIPMENT

Much of the new kitchen equipment is designed to reduce or eliminate cooking skills. One of the best examples of this type of equipment is the conveyor broiler used by several fast-food hamburger chains. The employee needs only to place frozen patties of hamburger on the conveyor belt, which carries the patties through flames directed from above and below. The movement of the conveyor belt is timed so that when the patties drop out at the other end of the broiler, they are done. There is no need for the employee to know when to turn the patties, how to control the griddle temperature, or how to clean the griddle. The same is true of the new conveyor pizza ovens.

Automatic crepe-making machines are controlled so that a perfect crepe is produced automatically, without timing or turning.

The grooved griddle de-skills broiling. The griddle maintains a constant temperature, and meat is merely placed on it. There is no need to raise or lower a rack to control temperature, as must be done with traditional broilers.

The quartz-fired griddle produces heat from above as well as from below and eliminates the need for turning the food.

Cook-chill and *sous vide* are two techniques that have gained in popularity. The cook-chill process enables chefs to safely (and efficiently) prepare large amounts of food for long-term storage in a refrigerated environment. Food is prepared and rapidly chilled to prevent bacterial growth and is available in portions of various sizes. Consistent quality and substantial reduction in labor cost and stress levels are the result in the kitchen. Food is prepared to restock inventory rather than to order. One of the best applications of cook-chill is when cooking batches of food in a centralized kitchen for later use in a satellite facility. This method not only extends shelf life, it also lowers production costs. For example, the cook-chill system processes about 70 percent of the food made at Morongo

Casino, Resort & Spa thus allowing the kitchen to operate with approximately 30 percent fewer employees.[16]

Sous vide is popular in Europe, especially in France, where it was developed. With this technique, food is prepared in the restaurant kitchen, often during slack times. It is then individually vacuum packed and refrigerated for future use. Perhaps the best application of sous vide is for à la carte menu restaurants and for a group of restaurants that share a centralized production kitchen. Cooking sous vide is easier than the fancy name suggests. Ingredients are simply sealed in a plastic bag and, later, placed in a water bath and finished off—by searing or other method—once the item is at the correct temperature.[17]

Equipment Stars

The principal pieces of cooking equipment—the stars—are selected to best prepare the principal menu items. The other equipment is arranged around the stars and constitutes the supporting cast. In older kitchens, saving money and reducing waste means replacing outdated equipment. Again, the cost is high in the beginning, but over time you earn that money back in lower utility bills.[18]

The stars of a hamburger restaurant are the griddle (or broiler) and the deep-fat fryers. The same is true for coffee shops and pancake restaurants. In a full-service restaurant, stovetops, ovens, and broilers dominate the scene. In a Chinese restaurant, the star is the wok, a large basinlike pan around which the supporting equipment is arranged.

In planning a kitchen and selecting equipment, think of the dominant menu items, those expected to have the highest volume of sales. Place the cooking equipment for these items to support the cooking stations. Preparation of these foods can take place elsewhere, but preferably close by.

STOVE/OVEN

Probably the most prominent piece of equipment in the full-service kitchen is the traditional range, the combination stove and oven, fired by gas or electricity. These are often also the biggest energy users in the restaurant. For a shortcut to the biggest energy and cash savings, attention should be focused on what are likely to be the kitchen's biggest energy users: broilers, hot top ranges, boiler-based steamers, pasta cookers, conveyor ovens, and combination ovens.[19] Take broilers, for example. Cutting out only one hour each day of broiler "on" time can translate to a savings of around $450 annually. If your restaurant operates with a profit margin of around 5 percent, you'll need about $9,000 worth of sales to earn $450.[20]

The kitchen is often planned around the stove/oven. With the availability of *convection ovens*, steam-jacketed kettles, and *tilting skillets*, some kitchen planners deliberately eliminate the range, regarding it as cumbersome and inefficient. Newer equipment that transfers heat more efficiently than the old space-consuming range is preferred. Important pieces of cooking equipment are the

Courtesy of the Vulcan Hart Company

Stoves with burners and griddles sell for about $1,750 to $2,500.

oven, tilting skillet, *combination convection and microwave oven*, *convection steam cooker*, the microwave oven, and the deep fryer. The range-top stove, however, is still probably the workhorse of a full-service restaurant kitchen.

The sectionalized griddle, whose surface has sections separately controlled for temperature, can cook different foods at different temperatures at the same time: 300°F for eggs, 350°F for sausages, and 400°F for small steaks. The sectionalized griddle provides flexibility. If only hamburgers are to be cooked, all sections can be set at the same temperature, or one section can be set at a lower temperature for slower cooling in case customer demand is unpredictable.

Griddle tops are usually made of steel boilerplate, ½ to 1 inch thick. The thicker ones are less likely to warp. Some tops are made of sheet aluminum, and one brand is made of steel with a chromium surface. The griddle surface itself can be on a stand, mounted on a table, or set as part of a range top. To achieve even temperature across the griddle surface, a heat pipe has been introduced.

To determine the size of griddle needed, planners project the volume of food to be cooked during peak periods and the time required for each item to cook. If a hamburger requires four minutes to cook and 100 are needed during the peak hour, 25 hamburgers must be cooked at one time. One griddle is needed. Suppose that eggs, pancakes, and other foods will also be ordered during the peak period. Two griddles are called for. Two griddles, placed side by side, enable two cooks to work simultaneously. Two griddles also permit a trainee cook to watch, work, and learn alongside an experienced cook. Most coffee shops install two griddles side by side, even though both may be needed at the same time only an hour or two each day. Alternatively, a sectionalized griddle with separate controls for each griddle may do the job.

To maximize the griddle during peak periods, some foods may be precooked in a steamer, and then finished quickly on the griddle during mealtime. Steamer technology has come a long way in recent years. Today, they can rank among the more energy-efficient kitchen appliances.[21]

Griddles require adjacent worktables for holding and getting food ready. In purchasing a griddle, Professor Avery recommends buying only those that preheat to 350°F or 400°F in 7 to 12 minutes. To conserve energy, he recommends covering a griddle not in use with a metal or, preferably, a pressed-foam cover.

Griddles serve multiple purposes. They can substitute for a solid-top range; perhaps one part is used as a griddle, the other as a stovetop. Griddles are used for browning and cooking meat, cooking pancakes and eggs, and toasting buns and sandwiches.

More recently, the grooved griddle has been widely used for cooking steaks. In many fast-food restaurants, it has replaced the broiler. The ridges in the griddle produce marks on a steak similar to a broiler's, and the grooves allow fat and juices to drain off, avoiding most of the smoke created by the conventional broiler. Another consideration: The grooved griddle uses less fuel than a broiler. The grooved griddle is popular with chain operators because much less skill is required to cook meat. Hamburgers cooked by a grooved griddle are less likely to be burned. With a hot broiler, if the cook looks away for a minute or two, the hamburger becomes a charburger.

DEEP-FRYING EQUIPMENT

Manufacturers produce fryers designed for water boiling with thermostats that go up to 212°F (as opposed to 390°F for deep-fat fryers). Operators use these *deep fryers* to boil seafood, vegetables, and pasta products.

Pressure fryers are fryers whose lids, when closed, act to create pressure within the fry kettle. Increased pressure reduces the cooking time by as much as one-half, mainly because less evaporative cooling occurs. Some pressure fryers include moisture injection systems. The water injected turns to steam.

Deep-fat fryers can act as cooking pots; when filled with water, they can be used for quick-cooking vegetables, cooking hams or frankfurters, reheating foods, hard-boiling eggs, cooking macaroni or spaghetti, or holding canned or containerized foods. (Electric fryers cannot be so used; water will affect the heating element.)

A number of restaurants that serve fresh vegetables blanch them in a deep fryer, remove them, and immediately cover them with ice to stop the cooking process. Blanched vegetables can be held in a refrigerator for later service. Final preparation is done by sautéing the vegetables and serving them immediately.

Courtesy of the Vulcan Hart Company

Deep-frying equipment. Electric or gas-fired kettle for holding fat or oil in which baskets can be immersed for frying food. Temperature usually can be controlled in a range of 325° to 400°F.

LOW-TEMPERATURE OVENS

Low-temperature ovens that permit low-temperature roasting and baking are widely used in the restaurant business to reduce shrinkage of meat and to hold meat so that it can be served to order from the oven. One such oven, the electric-fired Alto Sham, is popular for roasting beef. A large coffee shop chain buys 2- to 3-pound tips (meat cut in chunks near the sirloin). The tips are cooked for four hours at 250°F and held at 140° to 150°F. All of the meat is cooked to the rare stage or a little above. If medium beef is called for, the ends are used. When well done is ordered, a hot au jus is poured over the meat to bring it to the well-done stage.

FORCED-AIR CONVECTION AND TURBO OVENS

A *forced-air convection oven* is similar to a conventional oven except that a fan or rotor, usually located in the back, makes for rapid circulation of the air and quicker heating of the food. Preheating and cooking times are considerably less than with the conventional oven. Directions for baking with a convection oven must be followed exactly; otherwise some foods, such as sheet cakes, will dry out excessively

Courtesy of the Vulcan Hart Company

A conventional oven. Standard or range ovens heat food by heating the air in a chamber. This air surrounds food and cooks it.

on top. A pan of water is placed in the oven when baking some foods to humidify the oven air and reduce moisture loss in the food.

Turbo Chef Ovens work about 15 times quicker than conventional ovens so Pizza Inn can offer high-quality pizzas with diverse ingredients in about three minutes. Pie Five Pizza Co. uses a Turbo Chef oven in its fast casual model that allows guests to choose their own toppings while walking through a Chipotle-like line queue. Turbo Chef Ovens have a belt width of 21 inches and they don't require hood ventilation.[22]

MICROWAVE OVENS

The cooking chamber of the microwave oven is usually small and of lesser capacity than that of larger conventional or other types of ovens. Magnetrons in the top of the oven emit microwaves. These electromagnetic waves of 915 or 2,450 megacycles penetrate foods in the chamber and are absorbed by food materials containing water, agitating the water and fat molecules to produce heat, which is conducted to other kinds of molecules surrounding them. Cooking by microwave relies completely on radiated energy to penetrate food and set up intermolecular friction, which heats the food.

There is no preheating time, because once the microwaves are produced, they travel at the speed of light and enter the food almost instantaneously. Compared with standard ovens, relatively small quantities of food can be prepared at one time in microwave ovens. However, they are excellent for reheating small quantities of food.

Strangely, some materials are transparent to the waves and are not heated by them. Glass, china, and paper containers do not absorb the waves. Metal reflects the waves, so metal containers are not used in microwave ovens.

Because microwaves are absorbed preferentially by water, cooking is not uniform. Instead of heat being applied to the surface of the food, then being conducted slowly into the interior, microwave energy heats the food under the surface as well. The surface is left uncooked and relatively cool, unless the oven contains a special browning unit with infrared heating elements.

Advantages and Disadvantages of Microwave Cooking Microwave cooking has several advantages over conventional methods of cooking. The energy can be directed; there is no heat loss to the kitchen from the oven; and the speed of cooking is amazingly fast for small quantities of food.

Without a browning unit and used correctly, there is no spillage or sputtering, which makes for easy cleaning. There is little fire hazard.

The principal disadvantage of the microwave oven for commercial kitchen use is its relatively low capacity. It is usually the fastest-cooking device available for heating, defrosting, or cooking one or a few small items, such as a single casserole, hot dog sandwich, lobster tail, or trout. All of these are high-moisture items. As additional items are placed in the oven, heating or cooking time may increase by 75 percent or more per item. A microwave oven can bake a single Idaho potato in five to seven minutes, compared with an hour for a conventional oven. Two potatoes almost double the baking time in the microwave oven. The conventional oven bakes 2 or perhaps 50 potatoes in the same one-hour period.

The second major disadvantage of the microwave oven is a result of its very advantage: its speed. A few seconds short or long, and the food is under- or over-done. Different food materials heat at different rates. For example, bread in a frozen sandwich heats faster and is overheated before the filling is thawed; fat and water heat faster than muscle. Also, microwaves do not evenly distribute in a food, which results in uneven heating and cooking. Other variables are involved, making microwave ovens the most complex to use of all cooking equipment in the present-day kitchen. In restaurants, microwave ovens are mostly used to heat finished food items. When a quantity of over 8 pounds of food is to be cooked, the microwave oven cooks no faster than a conventional oven. Some practical uses for microwave ovens are:

Courtesy of the Vulcan Hart Company

A grill is now a popular piece of restaurant equipment, predominantly used for meats and fish.

- Reheating previously cooked foods
- Quickly heating desserts
- Defrosting
- Special-request orders
- Precooking

The principal use for the microwave oven is probably for reheating frozen foods that have already been cooked. It has little value for producing baked-dough items or any food that involves a leavening action.

INFRARED COOKING EQUIPMENT

Like microwave energy, infrared waves, transmitted at the speed of light, can penetrate the vapor blanket that surrounds moist food when heated. Infrared wavelengths used for cooking are only microns in length. Wavelengths of about 1.4 to 5 microns are said to be the most effective for cooking foods. Several specialized infrared ovens are marketed for the purpose of reheating frozen foods. Infrared broilers and ovens, which reduce cooking time, are also being produced.

Relatively new equipment on the market uses infrared emitters above and below a conveyor belt or in compartments resembling a standard oven. Electrically fired, the emitters can be temperature controlled separately, depending on the product being cooked. An 8-ounce filet mignon, for example, can be cooked in 10 minutes using 700°F temperature on both the top and bottom deck. A 9-inch deep-dish pizza takes 14 minutes using 575°F on the lower deck and 650°F on the upper deck. A 12-ounce soufflé is done in 12 minutes using 530°F for both decks. Cookies are done in 7 minutes using 500°F.

HOT-FOOD HOLDING TABLES

Food being held almost always loses quality, but in many restaurants there is little choice but to hold some of it prior to service. Hot tables constitute the serving containers in cafeteria service; here, warming tables patterned after the old bain-marie (water bath) are used. The bain-marie is simply a tank holding heated water in which hot foods in pots or crocks are placed to keep food warm and to avoid cooking. The modern steam table is heated by gas, electric, or steam elements controlled by a thermostat.

The more sophisticated warming tables are sectionalized to permit specific temperatures for particular foods: soup at 180°F, meats at 145° to 150°F, and vegetables at 140°F. Those tables containing heated water keep the foods moist and delay their drying out. The typical hot-food table holds a number of steam table pans 12 by 12 inches in size.

It should be remembered that although hot tables are not cooking appliances, foods held above 140°F are still cooking. Foods to be held any length of time should, therefore, be slightly undercooked.

REFRIGERATORS AND FREEZERS

A *refrigerator* or *freezer* can be thought of as two boxes, one inside the other, separated by insulation. Heat is withdrawn from the inside box by a cooling system. The insulating material is usually polyurethane foam. The cooling system consists of a compressed gas that is allowed to expand within the cooled interior. An expansion valve permits the gas to expand into an evaporator. As it expands, the gas absorbs heat and is returned to the compressor where, under pressure, it becomes a liquid.

Refrigerators require a minimum of 2 inches of polyurethane insulation; freezers require 3 inches.

Large restaurants need considerable refrigerator and freezer space, usually large enough for a person to walk into; such coolers are called walk-in boxes. Refrigerator drawers and undercounter refrigerators permit storage at point of use. Reach-in refrigerators conserve energy. Multiple-rack units on wheels permit maximum storage and save energy in moving food in and out of refrigerators. See-through glass or Plexiglas doors reduce the need for opening. Kitchen planners recommend this amount of refrigerator space on a per-meal basis for a luxury restaurant:

Meat/poultry	0.030 cubic feet
Dairy products	0.015 cubic feet
Produce	0.040 cubic feet

Walk-in boxes are often placed adjacent to food-receiving areas. Doors can be installed on two sides, one on the receiving side and one on the exit side toward the preparation area. Food can then be received at one side of the box and taken out on the other when needed.

Compressors should be located away from the kitchen or in the basement so that heat generated by their use is not dumped into the kitchen itself, and so that the noise of the compressors is unobtrusive.

For efficient functioning, coils within the refrigerator must be kept defrosted and free of ice. If the coils are icy, the cooling system cannot pick up heat within the box and transport it away.

Blast chillers and freezer technology allows operators to move product through the danger zone more quickly. Unique *Dynamic Fresh System* guarantees intensive, but delicate extraction of heat, preserving food's quality, freshness, and nutritional properties while naturally increasing its shelf life.[23]

ICE MACHINES

Restaurants need at least one ice machine for producing ice for ice water and for such beverages as soft drinks, iced tea, and—if liquor is served—a variety of alcoholic drinks. Machines are available for producing small-size cubes ideal for tall drinks, which make a tall drink look even taller. A survey conducted by equipment manufacturer Enodis found the most frequent purchase of restaurant operators was an energy-saving ice machine.[24] This shows that energy savings is on the restaurant owners' minds. A broader survey, conducted by the National Restaurant Association, found that slightly more than half of all operators had purchased energy-saving equipment in the past two years.[25]

Ice cubes are good for beverages served at banquets. The larger size melts more slowly and lasts longer. Crushed ice lowers the temperature of a beverage quickly and is also used as part of a salad bar, oyster bar, or juice display.

The hotter the climate, the more ice capacity is needed. A bar often has its own ice machine. A 100-seat restaurant with a bar probably needs an ice machine capable of producing 400 pounds of ice during the hours of operation and having a storage capacity of 540 pounds (see Figure 5.12).

Some experts advise against buying one central machine, which, if broken, leaves the restaurant without ice. Rather, purchasing two or more smaller machines and locating them near their points of use is recommended.

PASTA-MAKING MACHINES

Many restaurants that feature pasta have purchased their own pasta-making machines, and each week they produce various types of pasta: macaroni, vermicelli, fettuccine, and the like. With the low cost of flour, and if volume of sales warrants,

Restaurant Type	Realistic Average	Production/Storage Recommendations
Informal (with soft drinks)	0.5–1 lb. person	400–540 lb. for 125–200 seats
Formal (no liquor)	0.5 lb. person	300–540 lb. for 100–125 seats
Formal (with liquor)	1.5 lb. person	800–750 lb. for 200 seats
Drive-ins	0.5 lb. person	—
Fast food	0.25 lb. person	800–750 lb. per $1 million of sales
Cafeterias (iced salad bar)	0.5 lb. person	—
	10 sq. ft. display	200–400 lb. crushed ice
Cocktail lounges (with restaurant)	1 lb. person	400–540 lb. for 125 seats
Bar (no food)	0.5 lb. person	200–170 lb. avg. or 300/235 lb
Taverns (mostly beer with limited food)	Small 100 lb./day	100 lb./65 lb. (for possible under-bar application)
	Medium 200 lb./day	200/170 lb.
	Large 300 lb./day	300/235 lb.

FIGURE 5.12 Ice-sizing guide suggested for temperate climate.

the purchase of such a machine pays for itself in a short time. Operation of the machine is fairly simple. Different pasta products are produced simply by changing an extruder head through which the dough is forced.

SPECIALTY COOKING EQUIPMENT

As might be expected, special foodservice equipment has been developed for special menus. Hot food items on a Mexican menu, for example, are best served at higher-than-average temperatures. Some Mexican restaurant operators use convection ovens. Characteristically, a chili sauce or a cheese sauce covers entrées, which are placed under a cheese melter for a short time just prior to service. A Salamander is an overhead, broiler-type piece of equipment, usually several feet long and just wide enough to hold a plate. It is used for toasting, browning, and finishing. It is recommended for preparation of lobster, garlic bread, and au gratin potatoes.

Restaurants that feature salads may have a spin dryer in which centrifugal force whips off excess moisture from salad greens. Places that use frozen entrées may use a special quartz-fired oven for quick reheating.

Special spaghetti cookers, dough mixers, pasta-making machines, pizza ovens, and an array of other special cooking equipment are available. Old equipment is constantly being adapted to new uses.

New forms of energy are also being developed. Stovetops that use magnetic induction coils for energy are a novelty at this time but could be commonplace in the future.

Several chains have developed special equipment for producing featured items in front of the patron. Crepe-making machines are a good example; the machines are located near the restaurant entrance or other focal point, where patrons can watch the crepes being made.

None of the heavy-duty electrical equipment operates on the standard 110/120 volts installed for residential use. A revolving-brush glass washer may operate on 110-volt wiring, but equipment calling for large amperage needs the heavy-duty wiring carrying 208, 240, or 480 volts. Heavy-duty motors may call for 208/240-60, one-phase current; others call for 440/480-60, three-phase current. Booster heaters call for as much as 550 volts. Rewiring a kitchen to fit a particular piece of equipment can be costly.

Natural gas requires a different size jet and different settings from that for LP (low-pressure) gas. The heating qualities of the two are quite different.

EVAPORATIVE COOLERS

Evaporative coolers installed in kitchens reduce the cost of cooling considerably where humidity in the outside air is low, as in desert areas. The coolers take in outside dry air and pass it through loosely woven pads. Water from the regular water supply is either dripped or pumped over the pads. As the fresh air is drawn by a blower through the pads, it is cooled and filtered. Water in the wetted pads evaporates and, as it does so, absorbs the heat as it changes from water to vapor. This is evaporative cooling, known as the heat of fusion energy involved when matter changes from one form to another.

Evaporative cooling, although inexpensive, is not usually satisfactory for the dining room because the air brought in from the outside absorbs moisture. On muggy days or in climates with high humidity, moisture accumulates in the dining room. The kitchen, however, is a different matter. There air movement to the outside is usually rapid, air being pulled up the exhaust ducts to rid the kitchen of noxious fumes, odors, and accumulated heat from the cooking equipment. Evaporative coolers are used even in St. Louis, known for its high humidity.

Because evaporative coolers have no need of compressors, they operate at approximately 25 percent of the cost of operating a refrigerated air-conditioning unit of similar cooling capacity.

Evaporative coolers can be used in combination with refrigerated air-conditioning, relying on evaporative cooling except on the hottest, most humid days. Evaporative cooling is a relatively inexpensive way of making the kitchen a much more pleasant and efficient place to work, provided outside humidity is low.

OTHER EQUIPMENT

Numerous other small kitchen items are available that may be useful for a particular menu. Such items include ice cream holding units, display cases, cream dispensers, meat patty–making machines, garbage disposals, infrared heating lamps, drink dispensers, dough dividers, and bakers' stoves.

Because so many restaurants go out of business, used equipment is almost always available from equipment dealers. Few items fall more drastically in value after purchase. Once bought, restaurant equipment may drop as much as 80 percent in value. Restaurant equipment auctions may offer excellent used equipment. Used items without moving parts are about as good used as new. Examples are sinks, wire shelving, worktables, steam tables, cutting boards, kitchen utensils, and cooling racks. Refrigeration units may need only compressor replacement. Old mechanical equipment, however, may not be a bargain, because of the difficulty of locating replacement parts. Purchasing used equipment can be a mixed experience. There are some bargains but there are a lot of dogs out there— just be a smart shopper.

Maintaining Kitchen Equipment

Maintenance of equipment is a little like preventive medicine. By following certain practices, major problems can be avoided. Moving parts, when properly oiled, last longer. Removing grease and dirt from compressors helps ensure that they are not overworked. Clean griddles operate better than those with grease deposits on their surfaces. Gas burners adjusted for gas-air mixtures provide more heat. Checking electric wires for loose connections or frayed insulation can avert fires and equipment breakdown.

Restaurant equipment is generally thought to have a life expectancy of about 10 years. When properly cared for, however, equipment can last much longer. For best maintenance information, consult the instructions provided by the manufacturer. The old quip, "When everything else fails, read the instructions" is just too true. Restaurant operators are likely to be more people-oriented, sales-oriented, and food-oriented than mechanically inclined. A schedule of maintenance helps and is one of those details that make a good restaurant both a work of art and a nuts-and-bolts business.

Often restaurant operators give little thought to regular maintenance of kitchen equipment. They are too involved in other problems and in keeping up with the demands of the day-to-day operation—purchasing and receiving food, replacing personnel, handling complaints, and seeing to it that the operation moves smoothly. Knowing this, chain operators often employ a full-time mechanic who moves from restaurant to restaurant, performing maintenance checks or who can be called to handle breakdowns of equipment. Because every piece of equipment eventually breaks down or deteriorates, especially if it has moving parts, it pays to establish and follow a system of maintenance that forestalls breakdowns or emergency situations.

The place where most equipment headaches occur is in the dish machine. It is not uncommon for the hot-water booster heater, used to raise the temperature to the 180°F needed for dish sanitation, to break down. As a result, thousands of dishes are washed without the benefit of sanitization. As water is heated in the booster, minerals in the water tend to precipitate out and be deposited on the walls and in the pipes of the heater. These deposits can be removed by periodic flushing; open the drain valve and drain 2 to 5 gallons of water from the tank, then run the water until it flows clear. If the local water contains a high percentage of lime or other minerals, the heater may need to be drained monthly.

Repair of dish machines is usually beyond the capacity of the manager or kitchen personnel. This means that a mechanic must be brought in. In the time that it takes to repair the machine, the dish machine room can become bedlam. Inevitably, dishware breakage is high.

If the dish machine water is heated by steam, there is usually a steam trap through which the condensate flows. The condensate, which is in the form of water, then flows back into the boiler, where it is reheated and converted to steam again. The steam trap is intended to permit the condensate—but not the steam—to pass out of the heater. The trap blocks the steam and frees it to condense into water before it leaves the heater. The trap can jam shut or open. If it jams open, the steam blows through the trap, wasting energy and causing problems in other parts of the system. If it jams shut, neither steam nor condensate can pass through, and no water will be heated. Many installations include a test valve that can be operated to see if the trap is working. Follow the instruction sheet provided by the manufacturer.

Because the steam trap prevents steam from passing out into the heater, one way to determine if it is operating is to put on canvas-type work gloves and simultaneously grasp the pipe leading into the trap and the one leading out. If the trap is working, there will be a marked temperature difference. The trap should allow only condensation and the steam that has condensed to flow back to the heater. If steam is blowing through the trap, both the entering pipe and the exit pipe will be at the same temperature. The trap is probably stuck open, wasting steam.

When the dish machine breaks down or there is no hot water, dishes can be washed in cold water and sanitized by using diluted Clorox or other compounds used for cold-water sanitization. (Bar glassware is usually sanitized in cold water.) The spray nozzles inside the dish machine are there to provide a forceful spray onto the ware being washed. Lime deposits build up in the nozzles, which must be cleaned periodically by inserting a wire in the openings.

Low-temperature dishwashers may be leased. In this case, the leasing company assumes responsibility for maintenance and operation. The lessor may also offer to train new dish machine operators. In the traditional dishwashing machines, wash water is raised to 140°F and rinse water to 180°F—a considerable expense. The low-temperature machines operate with water temperatures as low as 100°F. Germicidal chemicals, rather than heat, are used to kill the germs. Some restaurant chains that have shifted to low-temperature dishwashing have cut ware-washing costs in half.

Meeting with the Health Inspector

Before a restaurant can officially operate, it must pass a rigorous examination by a public health official. Public health officials and planning boards, quite rightly, want to assure the public that eating in restaurants under their jurisdiction is safe. To this end, local health officers draw up extensive requirements for floor covering, number of toilets, foodservice equipment, lighting, fire exits, and other factors that bear on the hazards associated with restaurant operation. Requirements vary from place to place. One community may insist on toilet stalls for the handicapped and imperme-able floor covering in toilet stalls and in kitchens; another jurisdiction may not. Floor drainage systems, exhaust ductwork, distances between dining room tables, number of seats permitted, number of parking spaces required, number of entrances and exits to the parking area and to the restaurant—all must meet safety requirements.

It is a good idea to submit a plan review during the planning stage, including the construction drawings and equipment list and get an initial sign-off then; when final inspection come it should be easy to get a sign-off. Also you can call the health department and say I am going to buy XYZ restaurant do you have any suggestions regarding that particular restaurant?

Even if a building has been used as a restaurant for years, a new owner must pass the health and building inspector's close scrutiny. A new owner or lessee may find that a number of changes are required. All proposed building modifications must be approved. Often the eager operator is astonished and frustrated to learn that the linoleum floor installed in the restrooms must be taken up and replaced. The delays can be extremely costly because a number of people may already be on the payroll, interest expenses continue, and the cash flow expected is delayed. There is no way the restaurant can open until it passes the health inspection and the building inspection. Approval for building equipment and modifications must be secured beforehand. It can be hazardous for the operator to assume that approvals will be forthcoming.

Summary

Kitchen planning precedes equipment purchasing. Some restaurant equipment deal-ers also assist in laying out a kitchen and selecting equipment. The kitchen plan helps ensure an easy flow of food in and out of the kitchen. The idea is to place the equipment in such a way that the distance between it and the staff members who use it is minimized. Professional planners, assisted by drafters, are available for a fee. Planners may also recommend equipment that fits the menu and the restaurant's clientele and make sure that the chef and kitchen crew have the knowledge and skills to operate the kitchen. The purposes, uses, limitations, and prices of restaurant equipment are discussed. Decreasing energy use is another result of good kitchen planning and equipment selection.

Key Terms and Concepts

Broilers	Freezer
Categories of kitchen equipment	Kitchen equipment
Combination convection oven and microwave	Low-temperature dishwasher
	Low-temperature ovens
Convection oven	Refrigerator
Convection steam cooking	Slow cooking
Cook-chill	Sous vide
Deep fryer	Tilting skillets
Forced-air convection oven	Work centers

Review Questions

1. Before equipment selection takes place, what factors must you evaluate? Use at least three examples of equipment in your discussion.
2. What are the advantages of microwave ovens? Why are they not used more widely in restaurant kitchens?
3. Why are low-temperature dishwashing machines growing in popularity?
4. What conditions favor purchasing a tilting skillet for your kitchen? A vertical cutter/mixer? A convection oven?
5. In starting a restaurant, what used equipment would you consider buying? What equipment would you want to buy new?
6. Will you install gas or electric kitchen equipment, or both? What factors will affect your decision?
7. Kitchens are generally becoming smaller in relation to dining areas. Why?
8. You forecast your restaurant to gross $1 million per year in sales. Will you include a bakery section in your kitchen? Explain.
9. What are these pieces of kitchen equipment used for?
   a. Bain-marie
   b. Ridged griddle
   c. Infrared broiler
   d. Charbroiler
   e. Convection oven
10. What are two advantages of reach-in refrigerators and under-shelf refrigerators over the bigger walk-in boxes?
11. Explain the statement, "The menu determines the kitchen equipment."

CASE STUDY: Steuben's Food Service

Company Background

Steuben's Food Service was founded in 2006 by Josh Wolkon, a successful restaurateur in Denver, Colorado. Steuben's Food Service includes an independent restaurant in uptown Denver specializing in unique comfort cuisine, as well as a food truck service, which regularly circuits through the city providing both residents and travelers alike with quality food and exceptional service. At Steuben's, heavy emphasis is placed on providing a unique dining experience that cultivates a sense of comfort and familiarity. The menu consists of a variety of regional American classics, which serve to inspire memories of favorite dishes from their customer's pasts. This is where Steuben's differentiates itself from other restaurants in Denver, bringing national appeal to a local spectrum.

Inspiring Success

When Steuben's opened in 2006, it was busy from day one. In the first year of operation, Steuben's raked in approximately $70,000 per week ($364,000 annual revenue). From that point on, Steuben's made a name for itself, which resulted in annual business growth due to a successfully run operation and positive word of mouth. From 2010 to 2011, Steuben's experienced 17% sales increase, and then in 2011, Steuben's was featured on Food Network's *Diners, Drive-Ins and Dives*. Subsequently, demand continued to grow and sales increased an additional 12 percent from 2011 to 2012, amounting to approximately $6 million in annual revenue.

A Worthy Proposal

In 2011, Wolkon was approached by a third-party business, who presented an investment proposal for a licensing agreement to use Steuben's brand and concept to open a location in Denver International Airport. At the time, airports in large cities were looking to better represent their city by adding more independent and less commercial restaurants. By partnering with this business, Wolkon believed he would be doing a great service to the local Denver traveler, as well as worldwide visitors, by providing the experience, service, and food quality of the Steuben's brand in the airport's Terminal C. The licensing agreement would not require Wolkon to put up any money on his end, and he would receive a piece of the location's profit in the form of a licensing fee.

QUESTIONS

1. Do you think Steuben's should license its brand to a third-party and expand its business or remain as an independent operator in one location? How does planning play into this decision?
2. Are there other opportunities to expand the brand without possibly compromising Steuben's current brand and philosophy?
3. How would Wolkon benefit from the licensing agreement for the Terminal C proposal in terms of the expenses of purchasing kitchen equipment?
4. What are the advantages and disadvantages of offering a food truck service, in terms of equipment?

Endnotes

1. Courtesy of John C. Cini, president and CEO of Cini Little, July 3, 1999.
2. Ibid.
3. Arthur C. Avery, "Up the Productivity," *Commercial Kitchens,* Baltimore, Maryland, American Gas Association, 1989, pp. 205–214.
4. Dan Bendall, "Back of the House Green," *Restaurant Hospitality,* 92 (1) (January, 2008), pp. 60–62.
5. Dan Bendall. "Green Friendly Equipment," *Food Management,* 43 (4) (April 2008), pp. 76–78.
6. Ibid.

7. Ibid.
8. Personal conversation with Ed Norman, president MVP Services Group Food Facilities Design and Hospitality Consultants, Chicago, IL.
9. Bob Ecker. "The Kitchen Is Now Open." *Wave Magazine* Online. www.thewavemag.com/pagegen .php?articleid=25360&pagename=article. August 2009.
10. Costas Katsigris, Ed Norman and Chris Thomas, *Design and Equipment for Restaurants and Food-service: A Management View*, 3rd ed. (Hoboken, NJ: John Wiley & Sons, 2008). This is by far the best book available on the subject. Costas Katsigris is director of the Food and Hospitality Service Program at El Centro College in Dallas, Texas. Chris Thomas is a professional writer specializing in food and wine topics.
11. Ibid.
12. Energy Star, www.energystar.gov/index.cfm?c=about.ab_index. August 2009.
13. "How to Make Your Operation More Environmentally Friendly." National Restaurant Association. http://cf.restaurant.org/profitability/openrestaurant/howto/enviro/. Retrieved on May 9, 2013.
14. Ibid.
15. Jeff Breeden, "Lower Your Energy Bills Now." *Restaurant Hospitality* (August 1, 2009), www .restaurant-hospitality.com/operational_tips/lower_energy_bills_0809/index.html.
16. Christophe Douheret, "F&B Production Costs Lowered by Cook-Chill Process," Indiangaming .com (June 2007), Food & Beverage column. www.indiangaming.com/istore/Jun07_Douheret.pdf. August, 2009.
17. Nathan, "Why Cook Sous Vide?" Modernist Cuisine (January 15, 2013), http://modernistcuisine. com/2013/01/why-cook-sous-vide/. Retrieved on May 9, 2013.
18. Breeden.
19. "Boosting Restaurant Profits with Energy Efficiency. A Guide for Restaurant Owners and Managers." www.fypower.org/pdf/BPG_RestaurantEnergyEfficiency.pdf. August, 2009.
20. Ibid.
21. Ibid.
22. "Media Center, " June 1, 2012, http://www.turbochef.com/commercial/site.php?PAGE_TYPE= CONTACT_US&nav_id=47&press_id=125&archive=0&page_id=0&sub_page_id=0onOctober3, 2012.
23. "Dynamic Fresh System Lets You Do Your Best Work," Irinox, http://www.irinox.com/en/company/ refrigerated-cabinets/dynamic-fresh-system.html. Retrieved on May 10, 2013.
24. "Going for the Green," *Restaurant Hospitality*, www.restaurant-hospitality.com/features/rh_ imp_17256/index.html. Retrieved August 2009.
25. Ibid.

Food Purchasing

LEARNING OBJECTIVES

After reading and studying this chapter, you should be able to:

- Explain the importance of product specifications.

- List and describe the steps for creating a purchasing system.

- Identify factors to consider when establishing par stocks and reordering points.

- Explain selection factors for purchasing meat, produce, canned goods, coffee, and other items.

Courtesy of Sysco

This chapter covers the basic elements of food purchasing. When setting up a *food-purchasing system*, think in terms of:

- Establishing standards for each food item used (product specification)
- Establishing a system that minimizes effort and losses and maximizes control of theft
- Establishing the amount of each item that should be on hand (par stocks and reorder points)
- Identifying who will do the buying and who will keep the food-purchasing system in motion
- Identifying who will do the receiving, storage, and issuing of items

The dynamics of *purchasing* have changed in several key ways: Restaurants are creating partnerships with a select few purveyors—the rationale being that you get more loyalty and spend less time ordering and receiving multiple times, with some deliveries coming at awkward times. Purveyors say that the freight costs are the same for 1 or 100 boxes.

Sustainable Purchasing

Restaurants are also moving toward buying more locally, cutting down freight costs. Buying locally strengthens regional economies, supports family farms, preserves the local landscape, and fosters a sense of community.[1] However, buying local does not necessarily mean that it is a sustainable product. Sustainability includes buying food as locally as possible, but also involves food production methods that are healthy, do not harm the environment, respect workers, are humane to animals, provide fair wages to farmers, and support farming communities.[2]

A growing number of restaurateurs are increasingly adopting sustainable purchasing practices by purchasing animals that have not been raised in confinement, given antibiotics or hormones, or fed animal byproducts. An example being, avoiding the purchase of chickens and eggs from large factory farms where the chickens are raised in small cages or large overcrowded barns.[3] There are also concerns with the purchasing of fish, by buying only fish that are not endangered limits the variety used in foodservice but helps fish stocks to rebuild their numbers.

Natural food purchasing is gaining momentum. Although more expensive, some operators find their guests are requesting more organic items on the menu. Additionally, there is an increasing demand for health enhancing foods that are rich in antioxidants and phytonurtrients.[4]

Restaurateurs are letting the menu drive business, and many change menus and prices four times a year. Maintaining a close relationship with suppliers helps with advance warnings of pending price increases and lack of availability. For example, a year ago the price of live cattle was 65 cents a pound. Now it is $1.05 a pound, not slaughtered, trimmed out, or transported. One week the price of tenderloin is up 95 cents a pound over the previous week; the next week, turkey is available at a big discount. If they have fancy menus printed, these changes make it difficult for restaurants to control costs.

Good suppliers are now more like consultants who are interested in your long-term success. They help you purchase the best product for the menu application. For instance, chicken comes in many forms: whole, breast only, four pieces, a quarter, eight pieces plus wings and legs, or thighs separated. The breast comes in various sizes—4 to 10 ounces, randomly; generally two breasts together are less expensive than when separate. The larger the bird, the older and tougher it is.

Freezing techniques have advanced to the point where, for example, fishing boats are out for longer periods—it's too expensive to return to port every night, so they stay out for days or, in some cases, months. With a process called *flash freezing*, fish are immersed in a liquid chemical that gets them to −265°F so fast that water molecules do not crystallize.

Moreover, prepared products have improved. Guests expect better-quality foods, and innovative food processors have responded. For example, frozen chicken rotisserie is a good, consistent quality product that can go on the grill. It is more expensive, but it will reduce labor costs and better control waste.

Vegetables can now be harvested and, within two hours, be blanched, frozen, and ready for the cook to prepare for service. They are often more consistent than market price. With salads, items like romaine lettuce can fluctuate in price from $19 to $45 per case. With processed lettuce, you have virtually no labor costs and *know* that you will get 25 salads to a bag and four bags to a box, versus separating and breaking into bite-size pieces and washing the lettuce. Plus, if there is a lot of moisture on the product, the shelf life will be short.

It's all a question of knowing what's available, when it's available, and at what price. So, planning a menu should begin by consulting with a supplier.

The National Restaurant Association's Foodservice Purchasing Managers Executive Study Group offers useful purchasing recommendations: a reduction in the number of suppliers and a move to partnering with them. This increases information on markets and aids in forecasting future supply availability and price movements. This is one strategy to beat the market; however, it is still crucial to define market prices accurately. One of the best ways to accomplish this is to negotiate a long-term contract (annual, at a fixed cost, with downside protection if feasible). Suppliers for some perishable items may be invited to bid on a range of items for a week

Courtesy of Sysco

A supplier, chef, and manager discuss new menu suggestions.

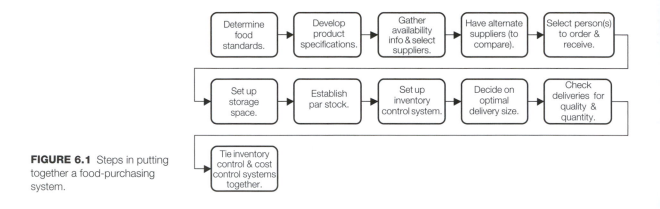

FIGURE 6.1 Steps in putting together a food-purchasing system.

or a month. This process allows the restaurateur to control the process. Primarily composed of chain personnel, The National Restaurant Association's Foodservice Purchasing Managers Executive Study Group is also open to NRA members who specialize in purchasing at independent foodservice operations and who carry a purchasing title.[5]

Food standards (specifications) are set, preferably in writing, before a restaurant opens. The amounts to purchase are based on a forecast of sales, which, without a sales history, is admittedly a guesstimate. Here, previous experience with a similar kind of restaurant is most valuable.

The same procedures are followed for buying other supplies—paper goods, cleaning materials, glassware, and so on. Purveyors are contacted, credit is established, and the food is received and stored.

When in operation, *par stocks* (the reasonable amount to have on hand) and *reorder points* (the stock points that indicate more should be ordered) are established. Figure 6.1 illustrates the steps in putting together a food-purchasing system. Figure 6.2 shows the detail that Red Lobster goes into for the product specification of one type of shrimp.

Food-Purchasing System

Purchasing can be thought of as a subsystem within the total restaurant system, which, once installed, can be set in motion, repeating itself. There are 11 steps in putting together a purchasing system:

1. Based on the menu, determine the food standard(s) required to serve the market. Will vegetables be canned, fresh, or frozen? What cut and grade of meat is appropriate for each meat item on the menu? Will fish be fresh or frozen, or some of both?

2. Develop product specifications—detailed descriptions of what is wanted based on consultation and best information available—and place responsibility for product consistency and quality on the supplier.

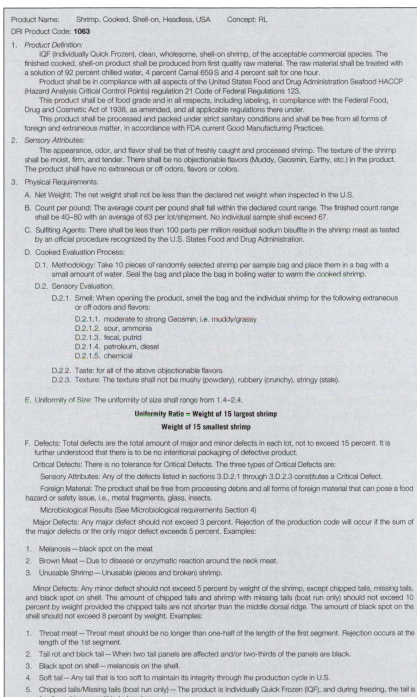

Product Name: Shrimp, Cooked, Shell-on, Headless, USA   Concept: RL

DRI Product Code: **1063**

1. *Product Definition:*

    IQF (Individually Quick Frozen), clean, wholesome, shell-on shrimp, of the acceptable commercial species. The finished cooked, shell-on product shall be produced from first quality raw material. The raw material shall be treated with a solution of 92 percent chilled water, 4 percent Carnal 659 S and 4 percent salt for one hour.

    Product shall be in compliance with all aspects of the United States Food and Drug Administration Seafood HACCP (Hazard Analysis Critical Control Points) regulation 21 Code of Federal Regulations 123.

    This product shall be of food grade and in all respects, including labeling, in compliance with the Federal Food, Drug and Cosmetic Act of 1938, as amended, and all applicable regulations there under.

    This product shall be processed and packed under strict sanitary conditions and shall be free from all forms of foreign and extraneous matter, in accordance with FDA current Good Manufacturing Practices.

2. *Sensory Attributes:*

    The appearance, odor, and flavor shall be that of freshly caught and processed shrimp. The texture of the shrimp shall be moist, firm, and tender. There shall be no objectionable flavors (Muddy, Geosmin, Earthy, etc.) in the product. The product shall have no extraneous or off odors, flavors or colors.

3. Physical Requirements:

    A. Net Weight: The net weight shall not be less than the declared net weight when inspected in the U.S.

    B. Count per pound: The average count per pound shall fall within the declared count range. The finished count range shall be 40–80 with an average of 63 per lot/shipment. No individual sample shall exceed 67.

    C. Sulfiting Agents: There shall be less than 100 parts per million residual sodium bisulfite in the shrimp meat as tested by an official procedure recognized by the U.S. States Food and Drug Administration.

    D. Cooked Evaluation Process:

    D.1. Methodology: Take 10 pieces of randomly selected shrimp per sample bag and place them in a bag with a small amount of water. Seal the bag and place the bag in boiling water to warm the cooked shrimp.

    D.2. Sensory Evaluation:

    D.2.1. Smell: When opening the product, smell the bag and the individual shrimp for the following extraneous or off odors and flavors:

    D.2.1.1. moderate to strong Geosmin, i.e. muddy/grassy
    D.2.1.2. sour, ammonia
    D.2.1.3. fecal, putrid
    D.2.1.4. petroleum, diesel
    D.2.1.5. chemical

    D.2.2. Taste: for all of the above objectionable flavors
    D.2.3. Texture: The texture shall not be mushy (powdery), rubbery (crunchy), stringy (stale).

    E. Uniformity of Size: The uniformity of size shall range from 1.4–2.4.

    Uniformity Ratio = Weight of 15 largest shrimp

    Weight of 15 smallest shrimp

    F. Defects: Total defects are the total amount of major and minor defects in each lot, not to exceed 15 percent. It is further understood that there is to be no intentional packaging of defective product.

    Critical Defects: There is no tolerance for Critical Defects. The three types of Critical Defects are:

    Sensory Attributes: Any of the defects listed in sections 3.D.2.1 through 3.D.2.3 constitutes a Critical Defect.

    Foreign Material: The product shall be free from processing debris and all forms of foreign material that can pose a food hazard or safety issue, i.e., metal fragments, glass, insects.

    Microbiological Results (See Microbiological requirements Section 4)

    Major Defects: Any major defect should not exceed 3 percent. Rejection of the production code will occur if the sum of the major defects or the only major defect exceeds 5 percent. Examples:

    1. Melanosis — black spot on the meat

    2. Brown Meat — Due to disease or enzymatic reaction around the neck meat.

    3. Unusable Shrimp — Unusable (pieces and broken) shrimp.

    Minor Defects: Any minor defect should not exceed 5 percent by weight of the shrimp, except chipped tails, missing tails, and black spot on shell. The amount of chipped tails and shrimp with missing tails (boat run only) should not exceed 10 percent by weight provided the chipped tails are not shorter than the middle dorsal ridge. The amount of black spot on the shell should not exceed 8 percent by weight. Examples:

    1. Throat meat — Throat meat should be no longer than one-half of the length of the first segment. Rejection occurs at the length of the 1st segment.

    2. Tail rot and black tail — When two tail panels are affected and/or two-thirds of the panels are black.

    3. Black spot on shell — melanosis on the shell.

    4. Soft tail — Any tail that is too soft to maintain its integrity through the production cycle in U.S.

    5. Chipped tails/Missing tails (boat run only) — The product is Individually Quick Frozen (IQF), and during freezing, the tail is fragile and is susceptible to breakage.

    A. Dehydration: There shall be no dehydration in the product.

    B. Decomposition: There shall be no decomposition in the product.

Courtesy of Red Lobster

FIGURE 6.2 Example of a food product specification.

3. Gather product availability information and select supplier(s) based on reliability of service, price, and honesty. Obtain samples of the food and test them in order to select the best.
4. Have alternate suppliers in mind for comparison.
5. Select person(s) to order and receive supplies, and give him/her (them) authority to reject delivery of individual items. Make sure that the person ordering is different from the person receiving and that management authorizes or places each order, even for meat and other perishables.
6. Set up storage spaces for maximum utilization.
7. Establish the amount needed to be stocked (par stock) for each item.
8. Set up an inventory control system.
9. Decide on optimal delivery size to reduce cost of delivery and handling.
10. Check all deliveries for quality and quantity or weight.
11. Tie inventory control and cost control systems together.

PURCHASING CYCLE

A purchasing cycle can be set up that rolls along efficiently, a system that repeats itself day after day with minimal demands on the operator (see Figure 6.3). Even though under constant review, each part of the cycle is changed slowly, only as customers and menu change and as new products and purveyors are considered. Product specifications need only be reviewed, not reset, each time food is ordered. Par stock and reorder points are relatively fixed and change only as sales volume changes appreciably or as the menu changes. (Product specifications and par stock are explained in detail later.) Major suppliers are changed infrequently. Receiving, issuing, and recording are carried out systematically, and the information becomes the basic data for the cost control system.

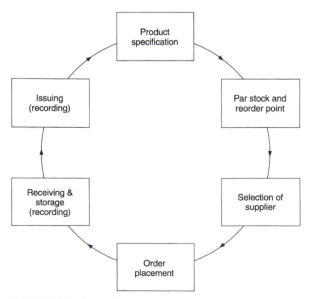

FIGURE 6.3 Purchasing cycle.

WHO SETS UP THE SYSTEM? WHO OPERATES IT?

In the usual restaurant, the manager, in consultation with the chef, decides on product specification, selects purveyors, and has a figure in mind for par stock and reorder point. It is recommended that one person, and one person only, who has a clear understanding of food cost control and of the restaurant market, should set up and operate the food-purchasing system. That person is usually the manager. Too often it is a nonowner chef with purveyor friends who get the orders and charge high prices. Experienced restaurant operators do not let a purveyor "par up" the restaurant. Purveyors are in the business of selling food, beverages, and related items to restaurants.

FOOD QUALITY STANDARDS

Standards for food quality are set to serve a particular market. The standards required for a particular restaurant or chain is determined by the owner and chef/cook in a small restaurant or a group of interested stakeholders in a chain. Quality relates to value in that a higher-quality product will provide the guest with increased satisfaction over a lower-quality product.

Some operators serve fresh fish only, never frozen. If fresh fish is unavailable, no fish is served at all. Some restaurants use only fresh vegetables. Others use all frozen. Others use canned vegetables. A chain of highly successful dinner houses specifies that all items be breaded to order and deep-fried at once. No frozen breaded items are used. This chain believes that the quality of frozen items is lower than items breaded by hand and cooked immediately.

BUYING BY SPECIFICATION

Although many restaurants do not spell out in detail a specification for each food item purchased, the specification is usually well outlined in the operator's mind. Each operation needs a quality of food that fits its market. The quality needed varies with the market and also with the food item being produced. Canned vegetables used in a made-up dish need not be of fancy grade. Meat for grinding into hamburger may well come from US good or even lower-graded meat and still be satisfactory. Canned beef may be satisfactory for deli (thinly) sliced sandwiches. Apples for use in apple pie need not be of the same quality as those to be eaten out of hand, where appearance is important.

It might be expected that buying by grade alone would be sufficient to assure the quality desired. Not so. Canned vegetables, for example, vary considerably within a grade because of different growing conditions experienced in one part of the country as compared with another. Most large foodservice operations conduct can-cutting tests annually, after the fruit and vegetable crops have been harvested and canned. Beyond knowing unit cost, the operator wants to compare the color, texture, taste, and uniformity of products.

HOW MUCH INVENTORY?

Every food item has a shelf life—the length of time it can be stored without appreciable loss in quality or weight. Nearly every food that contains a large amount of water shrinks with storage. Even under ideal refrigeration of −20°F, ice cream shrinks. Consider also the dollars tied up in *inventory*, which represents money that draws no interest and does no work for the enterprise. There should be no more inventory than what is actually needed to cover the operation from one delivery date to another.

This target cannot be realized if the operation has delivery problems or is some distance from a source of food materials.

The temptation is to buy a large quantity when a price reduction is available—which may be fine for liquor, where little is affected by storage—but this requires extra handling space and time for most items. Some storerooms have been seen to hold as much as a year's supply of canned fruit merely because a salesperson convinced the food buyer that the fruit was a good buy or that the buyer would receive a prize or gift certificate for the purchase.

Par Stock and Reorder Point A food-purchasing system calls for a par stock and a reorder point for each food item. These are based on quantities used, storage space available, and availability of the product. A steakhouse may have a policy of ordering meat once a week and base the order size on forecasted sales for the upcoming week. Milk may be delivered twice a week, based on a standing order. Fresh produce may be delivered every other day.

When it comes to the par stock for canned foods, the amount that is considered a safe inventory may be ordered only when the supply is down to a specified amount, such as one case—the reorder point. Management may wish never to have more than one case of a certain wine on hand and will order only when down to the last two bottles. A fast-moving item may require 10 cases as par stock.

Par Stock Based on Preprepared Foods The operator with a fixed menu has an advantage in buying. Preprepared of entrées can be done in terms of prepared items—so many trays stored under refrigeration. At the Pump Room in Chicago, which has been an institution since 1938, the entrance is lined with hundreds of photos of celebrities who have dined there over the years. The restaurant serves fine American cuisine and is noted for its prime rib and roasted duck. Its par stock calculations are based on the previous quarter's numbers. One beef rib is preprepared for each 60 expected guests and 10 ducks for each 100 guests. The figure fluctuates on holidays and in winter.

In a restaurant where several items are preprepared and stored, purchasing can be based on the par stock of preprepared and stored items, not on raw food in the refrigerator or freezer, where inventory control is tighter. The savvy restaurant operator will call vendors frequently, even daily, because prices vary considerably. Fresh vegetables, meat, and fish are good examples of items on which to get frequent price quotations, especially in a high-volume restaurant.

MECHANICS OF ORDERING

Opinions vary as to the best way to place orders for food and supplies. Some experts recommend calling for competitive prices before ordering anything. This is time-consuming. It may also pit the supplier against the operator, and the supplier eventually passes on the excessive costs of making small deliveries to the operator. Other operators deal only with one or two trusted suppliers. Still others get much of their food at local supermarkets.

In many instances, a restaurant operator pays as much or more than the casual shopper does for a product. The supplier has the cost of delivery to the door and, usually, the cost of providing credit and other service, which must be recouped if the supplier is to stay in business.

The standing order is a predetermined order that is filled regularly—so much milk per day, so much bread, and so on. The standing order can vary with the day of the week. On Monday, so much milk is delivered; on Tuesday, so much additional milk; and so on.

Large restaurants have a more formal purchasing system that includes a purchase order. This is a form with three or four copies; one or two copies go to the supplier, one of which accompanies the delivery. The buyer keeps a copy for company files. A fourth copy may be kept by the person doing the receiving in the restaurant. Storage is discussed in Chapter 9.

Types of Purchasing

BUYING FROM FULL-LINE PURVEYORS

Most of the populated areas of the United States have food distributors such as Sysco. These distributors carry a large line of the supplies and foods needed by a restaurateur, which makes for one-stop shopping. The full-line distributor can offer more than product in the usual sense, providing merchandise and promotional material and training in the use of certain products and preparation of some foods. Buying from a full-line distributor saves the operator time in placing and receiving orders. Most of the larger distributors use computers for receiving online orders and simplified billing procedures. The large full-line distributors specify certain amounts for orders, which a specialized distributor may not require. One-stop buying eliminates the need for daily shopping but does not completely eliminate the need for price comparison. Companies like Sysco do a weekly exotic fruit and vegetable list called *The Market Report*. For example, 22 types of tomatoes are available at various times of year.

CO-OP BUYING

Another type of distribution that can be found in many areas is co-op buying. The co-op management agrees to supply products at cost plus enough of a markup to cover the cooperative's cost. A co-op is a nonprofit institution that is able to provide restaurant food and supplies at a lower cost than the profit-oriented purveyors.

BEWARE

Avoid aligning yourself with a supplier, who, in turn, has suppliers who are not certified by quality inspectors. Specialty foods are often produced by newcomers to food processing who are not aware of the dangers of food contamination and the real possibility of transmitting serious diseases via food. All food processors in this country are subject to health regulations, including periodic health inspections. However, the quality and frequency of such inspections vary widely from one state to another, and a small meat packer or processor of specialty foods such as tofu may be in violation for months or even years before discrepancies are found and corrected. For example, raw peanuts are subject to a fungus growth called aflatoxin that can permanently damage the liver. Without proper inspection of equipment, peanuts and peanut butter can reach the market contaminated in one form or another without anyone knowing it.

Courtesy of Sysco
Portion cut pork loin chops.

One small food-processing plant that we visited—a tofu plant—used old diapers in place of fresh cheesecloth, and mouse droppings were casually brushed off a strainer that was then used without further sanitizing. A visit to any small food processor soliciting your trade may pay for itself.

Buying Meat

Because meat is the most costly food item in most restaurants, it deserves the most thought in drawing up food specifications. Fortunately, the federal government, through the *United States Department of Agriculture (USDA)*, provides a great deal of information about all commonly purchased meat. Other useful information is available from the National Livestock and Meat Board, headquartered in Chicago.

Principal factors in meat buying are the cut of the meat (what part of the animal), the USDA grade of the meat (its fat content, tenderness, and cost), and the style (its form: carcass, wholesale cut, or ready-to-serve portion). Restaurant patrons (the market), through the menu and price, mostly determine the best kind of beef to buy. A high style of beef house may need loins from which to cut and age prime steaks. A hamburger house may need grass-fed beef. Both operators must satisfy their patrons. Meat may also be purchased locally, a more sustainable approach. The restaurant Bethany's Table in Portland, Oregon, is now purchasing whole steers that are raised by small lot farmers and butchered in small USDA approved local shops. At $1 per pound on the hoof, $2 per pound hanging weight, $2.50 per pound cut and wrapped, it's worth a try.[6]

PURCHASING MEAT[7]

Given that meat is one of the more expensive menu items, we need to make our purchasing decisions carefully. Beef, veal, pork, and lamb are frequently used on restaurant menus. They are prepared using a variety of cooking methods according to guest preferences. Operators can save money and reduce by using a lower meat grade from an older, tougher, but more flavorful animal when a moist heat cooking method is used.

Beef can be purchased as a *side of beef*, which, as the name suggests, is half a cow that can then be butchered into the desired cuts. This may work for some larger and some high-end restaurants, where butchering meat is making a comeback. The advantage is that cutting the meat fresh costs less than prebutchered meats. The disadvantage is that once the desired cuts have been removed, the remaining carcass needs to be dealt with. Many other restaurants use *selected cuts* of meat, either fresh or frozen; that way they don't have to pay a butcher or devote space for butchering; they simply find it more efficient to order exactly what they want fresh or frozen.

The *as purchased* (AP) has a price spread for a *portion cut* that needs nothing more than cooking. The AP price for the *wholesale cut* such as a whole loin, which can be butchered into sirloin steaks obviously coats less than a portion cut and more than a side of beef. The federal government has set standards of identity for meat products. Meat buyers should use the *Institutional Meat Purchase Specifications (IMPS)* numbering system for meat items. These numbers take the part of a meat specification. For example, if a restaurant orders a 1112 ribeye steak, it will get a particular style and trim. All the specifications and numbers are listed in the *Meat Buyer's Guide (MBG)*, published by the North American Meat Processors Association (NAMP). This is very helpful for restaurants as they can simply order by the number.

GOVERNMENT INSPECTION AND GRADES OF MEAT

The inspection of meat for wholesomeness has been mandatory since 1907. Federal inspection falls under the jurisdiction of the United States Department of Agriculture's (USDA) Food Safety and Inspection Service (FSIS). The main inspection system the FSIS uses is the Hazard Analysis of Critical Control Point (HACCP) described in Chapter 9. Meat that passes the rigorous United States Department of Agriculture inspection is marked with a federal inspection stamp. A quality grading system exists for beef, lamb, pork, and veal; the grades are:

1. *Prime:* The best product available, tender and very juicy.
2. *Choice:* Contains at least 5 percent fat. Three levels: high, medium, and low. Choice is similar to prime, although the animal has been grain fed for 90 to 180 days, for medium 120 days, and low 90 days.
3. *Select:* A very lean product that contains 4 percent fat. This grade is popular in supermarkets. It is a low-cost item and is more healthful than higher-quality grades. But it lacks flavor.

The grading is determined by the marbling content of the rib eye between the twelfth and thirteenth bone.[8]

Lamb quality grades are based primarily on the color, texture, and firmness of the flesh; the proportion of meat to bone; and the amount and quality of the "feathering," which is the fat streaking in the ribs and the fat streaking in the inside flank muscles. The grades for lamb are: prime, choice, good, and utility.

Pork quality grades are almost exclusively based on yield. The most important consideration is the amount of finish, especially as it relates to color, firmness, and texture. Feathering is also an important consideration. Grain-fed pork makes better-quality products, which are far superior to those animals that are given other types of feeds. The quality grades for pork are: No. 1, No. 2, No. 3, No. 4, and Utility. If fresh pork is used on the menu it is far better to use No. 1 or No. 2 quality grades only.

Veal quality grades are based on the color, texture, and firmness of the flesh; proportion of meat to bone; quality and firmness of the finish; and amount and quality of feathering. High-quality veal will have a pink color and smooth flesh. The quality grades for veal are: Prime, Choice, Good, Standard, Utility, and Cull. Prime and choice are intended for restaurant use.

BUYING AND RECEIVING MEAT

The *first step* in buying meat is to get a copy of the Meat Buyer's Guide (MBG).

Then, *step two* is to determine exactly what meat the restaurant needs. Fresh meats are selected on the basis of US grades and IMPS numbers, while processed convenience items are typically selected on the basis of packers' brands. It is always wise to prepare specifications for each item. Representatives for major suppliers like Sysco or US Foods can help prepare specifications.

Step three is to request bids for the purchase specifications. This is done by asking for quotes from purveyors. Bids are normally for three to six months in the future. Buyers also consider the reputation of the purveyor based on dependability and service.

The receiving and storage of meat are an important part of the restaurant food system. If, as with most restaurants, there is no scale at the receiving dock, then there should be one inside the kitchen to weigh and check the meat. Some operators actually check the meat inside the cooler to keep it in good condition. The question of who should check it in is up to the owner but a manager is better than the chef or jointly to reduce the possibility of pilferage and collusion. In any event, the meat should be checked for freshness, an example being a cherry red color for beef and a pleasant smell. If the color is a darker red and there is an unpleasant odor, then the meat is old. Pork is difficult to check for odor because it deteriorates from the inside out, not the outside in.

The receiver should check the temperature of the meat, which should be 40°F, minimally, for fresh and 0°F, minimally, for frozen meat. Then look for weight, count, and sizes. Remember to weigh only the actual piece of meat, not the container or packing materials.

Fresh meat should be stored at a temperature of 35° to 40°F and in a meat refrigerator separated from cooked meats. Frozen meats should be stored at −10°F. Meats should be dated and rotated when being used.

Buying Fresh Fruits and Vegetables

According to the National Restaurant Association's "What's Hot" 2012 survey, the number-one trend among chefs was buying local produce. According to the survey, buying local keeps money in their state and gives customers the sense that they know where their food is coming from. Trends number three and four are closely tied to the buy-local trend as well: sustainability and locally produced beers, wines, and spirits.[9]

Many operators, especially those with higher-priced menus, feature fresh fruits and vegetables. If these are really fresh and cooked minimally, they taste better than frozen or canned fruit. The cost of purchase and preparation is also higher.

Courtesy of Ophelia's
Fresh fruits add to a delicious dessert.

Ever since Lorenzo Delmonico, name restaurateurs have made a point of ferreting out the finest produce possible, often visiting the wholesale market early in the day or buying from a small farmer who specializes in certain fruits or vegetables. The proprietor of one French restaurant features tiny zucchini fresh daily when in season. Many operators, including a few chain operators, feature fresh strawberries year-round, even though they must be imported from Mexico, New Zealand, and Chile.

Restaurants with lower-priced menus are likely to feature fruit that is in season. The most popular fruits—apples, bananas, and oranges—are available year-round. Figure 6.4, prepared by the USDA, shows what to look for in fresh vegetables. Local vegetables may be

ASPARAGUS

Purchase Units:

Cartons	15-16 pounds
Pyramid Crates	30-32 pounds

Select firm, crisp, smooth, and clean spears with compact tips and good green color extending down near the base. Spears that are ridged, crooked, or have spread tips or excessive amounts of white at base are likely to be tough.

Watch For: Wilted, flabby spears or mushy condition of tips, which indicate age and have objectionable flavor.

AVOCADOS

Purchase Units:

Cartons and Flats	12-15 pounds

Select avocados having a fresh, bright appearance, heavy, medium-size, fairly firm, or just beginning to soften. Irregular light brown markings on the skin have no effect on the flesh.

Watch For: Dark, sunken spots may merge and form irregular patches. If the surface is deeply cracked or broken, this is an indication of decay.

BEANS, GREEN OR WAX

Purchase Units:

Baskets	bushel	28-30 pounds
	½ bushel	14-15 pounds
Crates	bushel	28-30 pounds
Cartons		28-30 pounds

Select young, tender, well-formed beans that are free from blemishes and are fresh and crisp. Look for bright color in either green or yellow podded varieties. Beans should snap or break in two pieces before bending double.

Watch For: Wilted and dry beans, which are signs of aging after picking, resulting in poor flavor. Older beans with enlarged seeds, which are likely to be tough and fibrous.

BROCCOLI

Purchase Units:

Crates	4/5 bushel	15-20 pounds
Crates, Wirebound		20 pounds
Baskets	8 quarts	6 pounds
Cartons	14 bunches	20-23 pounds

Select bunches having a deep green color, compact firm surface with small individual buds, and fresh appearance.

Watch For: Soft, slippery, watersoaked spots or irregular brown spots, which are signs of decay. Heads that are spreading, wilted, turning yellow or have many enlarged flower buds are old and probably will have an off-flavor.

BRUSSELS SPROUTS

Purchase Units:

Wooden Drums		25 pounds
Flats	12 10-ounce cups	7½ to 8 ounces per cup
Cartons		25 pounds

Select sprouts having fresh, bright green color, tight fitting and firm outer leaves.

Watch For: Sprouts with yellow or otherwise discolored leaves or sprouts which are soft, open or wilted. Small holes or ragged leaves may indicate worm damage.

CABBAGE
Purchase Units:

Crates	1 3/5 bushels	50-55 pounds
Cartons		45-50 pounds
Mesh Sacks		50-60 pounds

Select well-trimmed heads having green, fresh outer leaves and heads, which are firm and heavy for their size, free from signs of insects and bad blemishes. Stock out of storage is usually lacking in green color, but may be otherwise satisfactory.

FIGURE 6.4 What to look for in fresh vegetables.

bought at local farmers' markets, some grocery stores, and the local farms themselves. The group *Community Supported Agriculture* has become a popular way to buy local, seasonal food directly from a farmer. A farmer offers a certain number of "shares" to the public. Typically, the share consists of a box of vegetables, but other products from the farm may be included. Interested consumers purchase a share and in return receive the seasonal produce each week throughout the farming season. Not only do you get fresh vegetables, but you get to develop a relationship with the farmer who grows your food and learn more about how food is grown.[10]

When selecting fruits and vegetables personally, these guidelines apply:

- Select freshly picked, mature items and use them as quickly as possible. This especially applies to such items as sweet corn, which begins losing sugars (they change to other carbohydrates) once it is picked. Vitamin loss also begins with picking. Some fruits, such as avocados and bananas, are picked early and ripened later. Other fruits, such as pineapples, do not ripen after they are picked.
- Handle fruits and vegetables as little as possible to avoid bruising.
- Distinguish between blemishes that affect only appearance and those that affect eating quality.
- Check on maturity of items.
- Avoid vegetables and fruits that are overripe or show decay.
- Be conscious of size and count. Use off sizes when possible; they may be better buys.
- Know sizes of containers and check on their contents. Watch for loose or short packs, or packs with one quality on top and another on the bottom.

Most operators are unable to visit wholesale markets personally and rely on distributors for delivery. Grade standards can be used. The USDA maintains inspection services at principal shipping points and terminal markets and has developed these standards. They are helpful, but because of rapid perishability of produce, it is difficult to rely on grades alone. The buyer specifies grade, size, count, container size, and degree of ripeness. Local food is fresher and tastes better than food shipped long distances from other states or countries. Local farmers can offer produce varieties bred for taste and freshness rather than for shipping and long shelf life.[11]

According to the Environmental Defense Fund and Restaurant Associates' (a New York City–based foodservice) Green Dining Best Practices, when sourcing produce you should follow these practices:

- Go organic. Organic produce meets USDA standards if it is grown without synthetic pesticides or fertilizers.
- Go seasonal. Where and when a food is grown has a significant impact on its environmental footprint.
- Buy imported produce with credentials. When what you are looking for is not available locally, buy those certified by a credible third party that can vouch for environmentally friendly growing practices.
- Reduce transport greenhouse gases. Buying from local farms reduces transport distances. Look to buy from those that choose the most efficient modes of transportation.[12]

USDA WHOLESALE PRODUCE GRADES

Grade standards are necessarily broad. Fruits and vegetables differ widely in quality, according to type and growing conditions. Federal standards must have broad tolerances to encompass all the variations. A set of fruit and vegetable *grade standards* is available from the Fruit and Vegetable Division, US Department of Agriculture, Washington, DC 20250. The grades and standards follow:

- *US Fancy:* This grade applies to highly specialized produce, a very small percentage of the total crop. This grade is rarely used on most commodities because it is too costly to pack.
- *US No. 1:* This grade is the most widely used grade in trading produce from farm to market and indicates good average quality.
- *US Commercial:* This grade applies to produce inferior to US No. 1 but superior to U.S. No. 2.
- *US Combination:* This grade applies to produce that combines percentages of U.S. No. 1 and U.S. No. 2.
- *US No. 2:* This grade applies to what is usually considered the lowest quality practical to ship. Produce of this grade usually has much poorer appearance and more waste than US No. 1.
- *US No. 3:* This grade applies to produce used for highly specialized products.

Small supermarket chains may offer produce at prices below vendor prices because their buyers pick and choose relatively small lots of produce in which the large chains are not interested. Restaurants also can feature produce sold as loss leaders in supermarkets. The quality of fruit that is to be used in soup or chopped up in a fresh fruit cup need not be the same as that offered raw or on a fresh fruit plate. Premium-size produce need not be purchased when it is to be cut up. Celery for soup and watermelon for fresh fruit cups are examples.

CANNED FRUITS AND VEGETABLES

A great deal of information is available about canned fruits and vegetables, much of it developed by the USDA and by the Food and Drug Administration (FDA). Quality standards and the standard of fill of container are concerns of the FDA. The FDA also requires labeling on most food items containing several ingredients. The common or usual names of all ingredients, listed in descending order of their presence by weight, must be on the container. Some products turn out to be mostly filler. All foods shipped interstate come under the jurisdiction of the FDA. State and city laws regulate items produced and sold within the states, but most of these laws resemble the federal laws.

Operators who frequently use canned fruits or vegetables perform can-cutting tests, usually in the late fall, after the picking season. In these tests, labels on cans from various vendors are covered, and the contents are graded for taste, texture, color, uniformity, price, and size. They can also be compared as to how well the contents hold up on a steam table. An important comparative measure is drained weight. The results of these tests are often surprising: The less expensive products may turn out to be superior.

Some soup bases contain more salt than anything else; salt is cheaper by the pound.

Salt (sodium chloride), the most widely used flavor additive to food in the world, has many values—when used in moderation. Americans, however, generally use too much. Less than ½ teaspoon a day satisfies the daily current salt requirement. Yet Americans typically consume 3½ teaspoons each day.

If a little is needed, why use a lot? Overuse can damage the kidneys, interfere with nutrient absorption, and contribute to high blood pressure. Excessive salt intake sets up people with heart disease for congestive heart failure.

Most canned and bottled products contain too much salt. For example, a 10-ounce can of chicken broth contains almost 1,000 milligrams of salt.

Summary

Successful foodservice operators establish standards of food quality that please the clientele served. They also establish a purchasing system that helps ensure that the food is purchased, stored, and accounted for so that theft, waste, and overproduction are minimized. The National Restaurant Association research has shown that sustainable practices are significant factors to today's consumers when choosing a restaurant. Forty-four percent say they are likely to make a restaurant choice based on a restaurant's efforts to conserve energy and water. Six out of 10 say they are more likely to visit a restaurant that offers food that was grown in an organic or environmentally friendly way.[13]

Basic to such a system is the establishment of food standards appropriate to the kinds of customers served and the prices that can be charged to achieve a profit. The percentage of fat in the hamburger, the size of the fried egg, the ingredients in the milkshake, and the grade of meat in the steak are examples of the information needed to establish food standards. The standards are expressed in terms of food specifications used in ordering and monitoring food purchases.

In independent restaurants, the responsibility for food purchasing usually rests with the manager. Standards and specifications are set at headquarters for chain operations. Purchasing controls are necessarily tight because theft is a strong possibility. Collusion among vendors, managers, and employees happens. It is wise to keep storeroom keys tightly controlled by issuing them to only one or a few people.

Receiving and storage practices are spelled out. Canned and dried goods can be stored so that the most frequently used items are easiest to get.

Items that must be refrigerated or frozen are kept in separate locations.

Government standards for such items as meat, fish, and poultry can be used in establishing the standards used by the restaurant. For restaurants that use a lot of canned goods, annual can-cutting tests that compare brands of canned goods for quality and price are useful. Several examples of food specifications are given. Inventory control—the amount of food to be ordered and stocked—can be built into the purchasing system by reference to past records. Excessive inventories tie up capital and space and lead to food waste. Establishing reorder points (when to reorder specific items) and par stocks (amounts normally stocked) are part of a purchasing system.

The number of vendors used in a policy matter is based on the reliability, prices, and trustworthiness of the vendor(s). In larger towns and cities, reliance on full-line purveyors may save time and money. Some vendors offer training for restaurant personnel in dish machine use and coffee brewing, for example.

A *food-purchasing system* includes periodic review of current buying practices and customer preferences and a readiness to change any part of the system as necessary.

Key Terms and Concepts

Food-purchasing system	Par stock
Food standards/specification	Portion cut
grade standards	Reorder point
Institutional Meat Purchase Specifications (IMPS)	Selected cuts
	Side of beef
Inventory	Wholesale cut
Meat Buyer's Guide	

Review Questions

1. Define *par stock* and *reorder point*.
2. How will you select the coffee to be served in your restaurant?
3. What is a can-cutting test?
4. Hamburger used in most fast-food restaurants probably is of what USDA grade?
5. What are two disadvantages in using USDA prime beef?
6. Who should be in charge of food purchasing?
7. How is the food-purchasing system related to the food and beverage cost-control system?

CASE STUDY: Farm Burger

Introduction

Farm Burger is a "farm and table" burger joint that was opened by George Frangos and Jason Mann in April 2010. Farm Burger seeks to create a superlative burger experience that directly connects the consumer to the producer. Farm Burger partners with local farmers, ranchers and butchers in order to maintain an organic, sustainable and humane system of beef production from pasture to processing and then directly to the restaurant. The burgers are made from 100 percent grass-fed beef. This means that the cattle roam freely through the pasture, grazing at their leisure, and they are never fed antibiotics, hormones, or grain. Farm Burger's dedication to their craft and practice sustains a high quality product for their customers.

There are currently two Farm Burger locations in the Atlanta area. The first location was opened in Decatur, Georgia, which is dominated by residential urban communities. The second location was opened in Buckhead, Georgia, just 18 months after the Decatur property proved to be viable. The Buckhead location is positioned in a very active business district that drifts into the city of Atlanta. Although its sales are approximately 30 percent lower than the Decatur property, Buckhead sees a heavy lunch crowd Monday through Friday that predominantly consists of business professionals working in the area.

Success

Farm Burger's philosophy for success lies in several universal values, which the owners believe are mandatory at every Farm Burger location. Heavy emphasis is placed on a strong sense of integrity with their food product, namely their beef, which is always held to a high standard of quality. There is a strong culinary base behind their menu items, which combine flavor, uniqueness and authenticity. The owners strive to educate and train their staff to be friendly, outgoing, and knowledgeable with a goal of continuously exceeding customer's expectations. With all the success they have achieved in such a short amount of time, there are still many challenges faced both short-term and long-term.

Challenges

One of the biggest challenges they face is controlling the price of their beef product. Because they are committed to serving 100 percent grass-fed beef that is high in quality, George and Jason must pay a higher price to their farmers than what many others pay for regular beef that comes from a feedlot. Generally, farmers will keep their cattle on grass for one year, and then sell the cattle to a large feed lot, which will pay an average price of $0.60 per pound. At the same time, Farm Burger offers to pay a premium of $0.80 per pound for the farmers to keep their cattle on grass. The biggest challenge comes when the demand for beef rises, because the price rises along with it. When this happens, farmers know they can get more for the cow. If the purchase price for the cow rises 30 to 40 percent, the farmer can expect to get approximately $0.90 per pound at a feedlot. This would require Farm Burger to raise the premium they pay to $1.10 per pound to get the bid for the cow. This in an ongoing challenge that requires constant negotiation, as the price of beef fluctuates throughout the year.

The owners feel that the increase in social media outlets can present another challenge at times. With an array of social media platforms to choose from, people can get their opinion out much quicker, easier, and more widespread. As a result, word of mouth becomes much harder to control. In the past, if someone had an issue or concern while at a restaurant, he or she would talk to the manager. This presents an opportunity for restaurants to fix the problem on the spot and hopefully prevent customers from leaving unhappy or spreading negative word of mouth. Now, people can simply post a negative comment on a social media platform without giving a restaurant the opportunity to address the problem.

Goals

Although there are continuous challenges at their current properties, the owners feel that as long as their ventures are successful, they will continue to expand the concept. Currently, they are in the process of finalizing plans to expand to a third location in Dunwoody,

Georgia. This location combines a strong residential community with a business district, which is basically a hybrid location with features of each of the other two properties. Their philosophy for expansion revolves around allowing opportunities to present themselves.

QUESTIONS

1. Do the owners of Farm Burger practice sustainable purchasing? Briefly describe.
2. If the demand for beef rises and the price in the feedlot market increases 30 to 40 percent, Farm Burger will be required to pay a premium of approximately $1.10 per pound, which is $0.30 per pound more than average for the beef that produces their main menu items. What can the owners do to make up for the additional cost and balance their expenses in order to maintain a healthy profit?
3. Why is it important for the owners to maintain accuracy when planning for purchasing of food products, especially their meat products?
4. What can the owners of Farm Burger do to increase annual sales 30 percent in the Buckhead location to match sales at the Decatur property?

Endnotes

1. "How to Buy Local," *Food Routes,* www.foodroutes.org/howtobuylocal.jsp. Retrieved August 2009.
2. "Eat Local, Buy Local, Be Local. What Is Local?" *Sustainable Table.* www.sustainabletable.org/issues/eatlocal/. Retrieved August, 2009.
3. Carolyn Walkup, "College Foodservice Learning to Live Green," *Nations Restaurant News,* 42 (26) (June 30, 2008), p. 49.
4. "Chains Opt for Healthy Dining," *Lodging Hospitality* 63, (13) (September 1, 2007), p. 10.
5. "Certification Adds Professionalism to Purchasing," *Nation's Restaurant News.* findarticles.com/p/articles/mi_m3190/is_n12_v26/ai_12083793/. Retrieved August, 2009.
6. "Be in the world, what you want to see in the world." Bethany's Table website. www.bethanystable.com/community-pages/buy-local/. Retrieved August 2009.
7. This section draws heavily on Andrew Hale Feinstein and John M. Stefanelli, *Purchasing: Selection and Procurement for the Hospitality Industry,* 5th ed. (Hoboken, NJ: John Wiley & Sons, 2002), pp. 451–485.
8. Personal conversation with Mike Hartsaw, Manager Sysco, Florida, November 28, 2012.
9. Lorri Mealey, "Top Trends for Restaurant Menus: The NRA What's Hot in 2012 Menu Trends," About.com, http://restaurants.about.com/od/menu/tp/Top-Trends-For-Restaurant-Menus.htm.
10. "Community Supported Agriculture," Local Harvest, www.localharvest.org/csa/. Retrieved August 2009.
11. Buy Fresh, Buy Local. http://guide.buylocalca.org/whyLocal.html. Retrieved August 2009.
12. "Sustainable Food Purchasing: Produce." Environmental Defense Fund, http://innovation.edf.org/page.cfm?tagID=35058. Retrieved August 2009.
13. "National Restaurant Association Trade Show Serves Up Green." Sustainable Life Media. www.sustainablelifemedia.com/content/story/strategy/national_restaurant_association_trade_show_serves_up_green. Retrieved August, 2009.

Restaurant Operations

Concept of Aria Restaurant

The contemporary American concept of Aria was developed due to two factors: space allocation and the passion of Gerry Klaskala, the chef-owner. Aria was located in a small area, so the owners decided to go the small, upscale route. The second factor in deciding on the concept was Gerry Klaskala's passion for contemporary American cooking.

LOCATION

Aria Restaurant is located in Atlanta, Georgia, in a building previously occupied by another restaurant. Klaskala came across the location after checking the area; at the time, the restaurant was up for sale. Klaskala made an offer to buy, and today this establishment is known as Aria.

MENU

Chef-owner Gerry Klaskala prepared the menu at Aria. It is based on his own soul-searching and what current cuisine was out there when the restaurant was opening. The menu constantly evolves. It focuses on items that are categorized as "slow food" prepared with patience.

Courtesy of Aria Restaurant

Braised, roasted, stewed, and simmered savory meats are offered. There are also daily specials with fresh seasonal selections.

AWARDS

Since opening, Aria has received a number of awards:

- One of the country's best restaurants in 2000, *Esquire* magazine
- One of the top five restaurants in Atlanta, *Gayot Dining Guide*
- Gerry Klaskala received the 2001 Robert Mondavi Culinary Award of Excellence
- The Top 22/The Definitive List of the Best New Restaurants in America, *Esquire* magazine
- John Kessler's Top 50 Restaurants, *The Atlanta Journal-Constitution*
- Best New Atlanta Formal Restaurant, *Bon Appétit*
- Two of Atlanta's 10 Best Chocolate Desserts, *Atlanta Homes & Lifestyles*
- Culinary Award of Excellence, Robert Mondavi Winery
- Tops local lists for best restaurant, best chocolate desserts, best food and wine pairings, and most romantic

PERMITS AND LICENSES

Klaskala went to various governmental agencies (the police department, health department, and so on) to fill out and submit several applications. Since the building had been a restaurant, he did not have to deal with zoning issues, because everything was already established. He just had to register a new corporation.

MARKETING

The owners of Aria did not do marketing per se. They relied on editorial write-ups through public relations before opening.

CHALLENGES

The major challenge of opening Aria was getting sales up past the breakeven point. They did this very quickly.

FINANCIAL INFORMATION

Aria Restaurant's annual sales are $2.5 million. It has about 800 guest covers a week. Guest checks average $75 to $100 per person.

A breakdown of sales percentages follows.

- Percentage of sales that goes to rent: 2 percent
- Percentage of food sales: 55 percent
- Percentage of beverage sales: 45 percent
- Percentage of profit: 15-plus percent

WHAT TURNED OUT DIFFERENT FROM EXPECTED?

The opening of Aria went pretty much as planned. The one thing that was not planned was the occurrence of 9/11. After September 11, 2001, "sales dropped like they were going off a cliff." Aria is very dependent on travelers and conventions. Eventually sales went back up, but it took about a year.

ADVICE TO PROSPECTIVE ENTREPRENEURS

Follow your passion and the money will come.

Learn more about Aria Restaurant at www.aria-atl.com.

Bar and Beverages

LEARNING OBJECTIVES

After reading and studying this chapter, you should be able to:

- Explain how to obtain an alcoholic beverage license.

- Identify factors to consider when developing the design and layout of a bar.

- List guidelines for suggesting wines to accompany menu items.

- Identify a restaurant's legal liability regarding the sale of alcoholic beverages.

- List ways in which bartenders and others can defraud the restaurant bar and beverage operation.

Courtesy of David Laxer

Given today's social concerns about alcoholic beverage consumption and the high costs of litigation, creating and operating a restaurant bar and beverage operation presents challenges. By creating a convivial place for *responsible alcoholic beverage service*—one with a pleasant atmosphere that reflects the furnishings, decor, lighting, music, and service—restaurateurs can offer a place for relaxation, socialization, and entertainment. In some restaurants, bars are used as a focal point or a centerpiece; T.G.I. Friday's is an example. Others, like the Olive Garden, use the bar more as a *holding area*.

Beverage sales in restaurants can account for a significant portion of total sales. Today, a reasonable split is about 25 to 30 percent beverage sales and 70 to 75 percent food sales.[1] A ratio any higher than this in favor of beverage sales will attract undue attention from the *Department of Alcoholic Beverage Control (ABC)* or Alcoholic Beverage and Tobacco (ABT) department as well as prosecuting attorneys in court during a "driving under the influence" (DUI) case.

Beverage sales yield more profit than food sales—a bottle of wine simply needs storage for a few days, then opening. A bottle of wine may be purchased for $9 and sold for $27 to $36. A measure of Scotch may cost 70 cents and sell for $3.50. The cost of production is much less in the bar than in the kitchen; consequently, the margins are greater.

Alcoholic Beverage Licenses

Each state has a Department of Alcoholic Beverage Control. In California, for example, the department was created by constitutional amendment as an executive branch of the state government. The director of Alcoholic Beverage Control heads the department and is appointed by the governor. The department has the exclusive power, in accordance with laws enacted, to license and regulate the manufacture, importation, and sale of all alcoholic beverages in the state.

TYPES OF ALCOHOLIC BEVERAGE LICENSES

A license issued under the ABC act is a permit to do that which would otherwise be unlawful. Such a license is not a matter of right but is a privilege that can be suspended or revoked by the administration because of violation of the act or department rule. There are several types of retail licenses. The most common include:

- *On-sale general:* Authorizes the sale of all types of alcoholic beverages—namely, beer, wine, and distilled spirits—for consumption on the premises.
- *Off-sale general:* Authorizes the sale of all types of alcoholic beverages for consumption off the premises in original, sealed containers.
- *On-sale beer and wine:* Authorizes the sale on the premises of all types of beer, wine, and malt liquor.

- *Off-sale beer and wine:* Authorizes the sale of all types of beer, wine, and malt beverages for consumption off the premises in original containers.
- *On-sale beer:* Authorizes the sale on the licensed premises of beer and other malt beverages with an alcoholic content of 4 percent or less by weight.[2]

HOW TO APPLY FOR A LICENSE

For restaurants, there are two main kinds of *alcoholic beverage licenses:* a general liquor license and a beer and wine license. Both licenses must be applied for from the state liquor authority. The application process can be lengthy—up to several weeks—and may not always be a smooth ride. States have jurisdiction over the sale of alcohol, and some are more stringent

Courtesy of Roy's New York City. Photo by Paul Warhol

The bar at Roy's New York City welcomes guests to a restaurant with a multiaward-winning wine list to match the Hawaiian-inspired Euro-Asian cuisine

than others in granting licenses. For new licenses, a state like New York, which is liberal when it comes to granting licenses, is quite different from neighboring New Jersey, which is stricter. In New Jersey, the number of new licenses is limited by increase in population. In addition, new licenses must be approved not only by the state but also by city officials. In order to be granted a license, a restaurant must meet certain regulations. In California, to obtain a general license, a person must find and purchase a licensed restaurant or an ABC license for sale. When the restaurant is purchased, the license becomes part of the escrow. Subject to regularity approval, the ownership of the license will change with the ownership of the restaurant. In the counties of some states, new licenses are being issued only when, for whatever reason, an old one is no longer being used. Because so few new licenses are being issued, the price is going up and restaurateurs are having to pay a lot extra to obtain a liquor license.

When purchasing a restaurant, make sure that you have a clause in the contract that says that with the approval of state and local authorities, the liquor license will transfer to you. The current price of a license in many states is about $20,000 to $25,000. Licenses can be moved within but not outside the county. Once an application is filed, an investigation is conducted to ensure that the applicant is not a felon nor on probation. In California, a 30-day posting period of the application is required. Most investigations take approximately 45 to 50 days. The license can average about 75 days for a person-to-person transfer, and 90 days for an original.[3] In Florida, a beer-only license costs $280; a beer and wine license, $392; and a beer, wine, and spirits license, $1,820 (though this may vary according to the county).[4]

Notices stating that a license has been applied for must be placed in the newspaper and posted in the window of the restaurant. This notice must be posted for a minimum of 30 days. After 45 days, providing there are no protests by residents, the police department, the sheriff's department, or others, and assuming the zoning allows it, a conditional-use permit is issued.

Once a license is obtained, liquor may be purchased only from a wholesaler or manufacturer. Each state and county has its own regulations, and prospective restaurateurs should consult with their respective ABC departments for relevant local information.

Bar Layout and Design

Deciding on the bar layout and design can be intimidating for most people. Novices have made costly mistakes by overlooking important aspects. If you can afford to hire a specialist in restaurant design, then do so—but make sure the person has experience in planning bars. Alternatively, have a bartender look over the plans to double-check the practicality of the proposed bar.

A number of factors affect bar location and the design of restaurant bars:

■ Type of restaurant
■ Overall design and layout of the restaurant
■ Intended prominence of the bar
■ Number of bartenders required to operate the bar and beverage service
■ Volume of business expected
■ Degree of self-sufficiency of the bar
■ Electric and water supply
■ Construction costs of providing electric and water supply
■ Distance to the storeroom and the dispensing system
■ Location of the beer kegs and cooling equipment

Courtesy of the 21 Club

A private dining room at the 21 Club where guests may enjoy selection from the extensive wine list.

Restaurant operators have a constant dilemma of balancing the ideal bar setup with their particular situation. Should the bar be along a wall or in the center of the room? In most restaurants, it is less costly to set up the bar along a wall. Center bars may be suitable for some high-volume restaurants, but, unless they are well planned and built with expensive cabinetry, they can look unsightly to guests.

FRONT BAR, BACK BAR, UNDER BAR

The bar setup is divided into three areas: the *front bar*, the *back bar*, and the *under bar*. The front bar is both the place where guests may belly up to the counter and where the bartender prepares drinks. The workstation has storage space for equipment, beverages, speed racks, ice, and glasses.

The back bar—usually the back wall of the bar—is for aesthetics and functions as a storage and display area. The lower part houses refrigerated storage cabinets, and the upper part often has a mirror or other decor and a display of *premium-brand liquors*. The sales volume will determine the amount of refrigerated storage space required. One refrigerator may be needed for wine and a separate one for beer. Most restaurants use the back bar to add atmosphere by displaying premium spirits and liqueurs. This display is a form of subliminal advertising.

The under bar is the part where the bartender prepares the drinks; it includes the part under the front counter. The main equipment in the under bar is the speed rack, which contains the *well (or pouring) brand liquors*. It should be located in a convenient position to allow the bartender to work quickly and efficiently. The speed rack is generally centrally located at waist level. The speed rack holds several of the most common pouring brands, called house brand: Scotch whisky (two bottles), bourbon, vodka (two bottles), gin (two bottles), rum, tequila, vermouth (two bottles), and cordials.

Only restaurants with very high volume have an ice machine at the bar; most have one in or near the kitchen. However, a sanitary ice bin is critical for a bar operation. The ice bin requires drainage; smaller restaurants manage with a bus pan lined with a plastic bag. Above the ice bin is an area where the bartender places glasses during the preparation of drinks. Kegs of draft beer may be located either under the bar or in a nearby storeroom. The name and logo of the beer is usually displayed on a *pull handle* supplied by the distributor and located in view of the guests on the bar counter or, occasionally, on the back bar counter. For draft beer to be at its best, the plastic lines from the keg need to be cleaned each week with a cleansing agent to remove any buildup of impurities.

PLACEMENT OF A BAR WITHIN A RESTAURANT

As so many things do, the location of a bar within the restaurant depends on the target market. Is it made up of the working class or some other demographic group? Is the bar to be featured by bright lighting, or is it to be a service bar located out of public view? Is the bar seating made up of stools, and is the bar stock of bottles to be prominently displayed? Will wine be displayed separately in a temperature-controlled glassed-in section? How many chairs will the bar have?

The floor plan of Roy's New York restaurant (see Figure 7.1) shows the bar as item 6, located so that it has easy access from the entrance (item 1). If the restaurant operator wants to highlight the bar, it is usually prominently lighted and placed near the restaurant entrance. Some bars provide comfortable seating in which customers can relax. Most bars seat customers on small bar stools that almost require the customer to lean on the bar. The seats are placed close enough to encourage

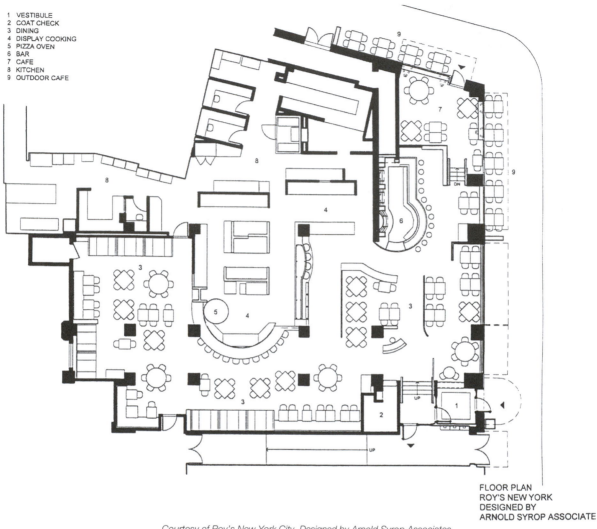

1 VESTIBULE
2 COAT CHECK
3 DINING
4 DISPLAY COOKING
5 PIZZA OVEN
6 BAR
7 CAFE
8 KITCHEN
9 OUTDOOR CAFE

FLOOR PLAN
ROY'S NEW YORK
DESIGNED BY
ARNOLD SYROP ASSOCIATE

Courtesy of Roy's New York City. Designed by Arnold Syrop Associates
FIGURE 7.1 Roy's New York floor plan.

conversation. At Roy's New York, the layout is such that display cooking (item 4 in the drawing), which adds interest for diners as they can see items being cooked, backs up the kitchen (item 8).

Beverages

Given that restaurants make a higher profit margin on beverages as compared to food, it makes sense to have an appropriate beverage program and menu. During these challenging economic times, restaurant operators are putting a new twist on the old adage.

Operators are stirring up their beverage menus and drink promotions and creating more premium offerings that allow them to charge premium prices.[5] Currently, restaurants are selling such nonalcoholic drinks as a piña colada with strawberries and pineapple juice, a strawberry and cranberry juice with ginger ale and fresh lime, and specialty drinks such as "berry good lemonade," which is a combination of strawberry mix and lemonade.[6] A beverage program and menu begins with cocktails.

COCKTAILS

A *cocktail* is a style of mixed drink. According to Jerry Thomas, who wrote the first drink book ever published in the United States, a cocktail was a mixture of distilled spirits (gin, cognac, vodka, rum, or tequila), sugar, water, and bitters.[7] The word has come to mean almost any mixed drink containing alcohol.[8] A cocktail today usually contains one or more types of liquor and one or more mixes, such as bitters, fruit juice, soda, ice, sugar, honey, milk, cream, or herbs.[9] The earliest known printed use of the word *cocktail* was in *The Farmers' Cabinet,* April 28, 1803. And for good measure, the first cocktail party, that most essential of American institutions, was thrown by Mrs. Julius S. Walsh of St. Louis in May 1917. The *St. Paul Pioneer Press* reported that "Positively the newest stunt in society is the giving of cocktail parties."[10]

During Prohibition (1920–1933) when the sale of alcoholic beverages was illegal, cocktails were still consumed illegally in establishments known as speakeasies. The quality of alcoholic beverages was lower than previously used.[11] Cocktails became popular again in the 1960s and have remained so with names like the martini, tequila sunrise, grinch, sex on the beach, angel's kiss, orgasm, piña colada, Shirley Temple (nonalcoholic), Manhattan, kamikaze, and many others.

Cocktails are divided into two categories according to volume: short drinks, up to 3.5 ounces, and tall drinks, up to 8.5 ounces. The secret of a good cocktail lies in the following factors:[12]

- The balance of the ingredients
- The quality of the ingredients
- The skill of the bartender

Cocktails can stimulate an appetite or provide a conclusion to a fine meal. These days, cocktails may even be healthy. Spencer Warren, proprietor of the

Courtesy of the Columbia Restaurant

Richard Gonzmart in his temperature-controlled wine cellar at the Columbia Restaurant in Tampa, Florida, winner of the *Wine Spectator* Best Award of Excellence and the Award of Excellence from Distinguished Restaurants of North America.

Firehouse Lounge in Pittsburgh's downtown, uses antioxidant-rich pomegranate and acai berry juices—they contain 10 times the antioxidants of red grapes as well as assorted other vitamins and minerals.[13]

The rebirth of cocktails seems to be taking place led by the plethora of Vodka and Rums entering the market place. Many of the vodkas are flavored, from far-away places advertising their origins or have uniquely designed bottles. Martinis' have also been popular with many variations on the old standard. This trend has been going on for some time and one may find Blue Martinis, Chocolate Martinis and an assortment of local signature martinis and hotels and restaurants attempt to market their latest creations.

The trend started with the Old New Orleans rum distillery in 1995, and now there are 12 such distilleries in the United States. The trend has not been limited to the USA the Naked Turtle is a small brewer of white rum distillery in St. Croix. There are some great rums from some unlikely places like the Drum Circle Distillery on Siesta Key in Sarasota Florida. Other well-known names in the beer-brewing business have moved on to rums as the craft beer market has become saturated. Dogfish Head Craft Brewers in Delaware and Roque Ales Brewing on Oregon are both distilling rum. The rums range from dry to sweet and from white to dark chocolate brown. This craze is leading to new pleasures and delights in new and more exciting cocktails. The majority of these distillers have signed pledges to help promote responsible alcohol consumption. Always remember: As a member of the hospitality industry, it is in our best interest to promote safe alcohol consumption so our guests enjoy themselves and return safely.

SPIRITS

Whisky is one of the popular spirits that has been distilled in Scotland and Ireland for centuries. In fact, the word *whisky* comes from the Celtic word *visgebaugh,* meaning "water of life." Whisky is "a spirit or liquor made from a liquid that has been fermented and distilled from grain. Sometimes the grain has been malted, sometimes not. It is aged, often for long periods of time, in wooden barrels (usually oak). This barrel-aging smoothes the rough palate of the raw spirit and adds aromatic and flavoring nuances along with the base amber hue."[14] Consequently, a spirit has a high percentage of alcohol, gauged by its proof content. Proof is equal to twice the percentage of alcohol in the beverage; therefore, a spirit that is 80 proof is 40 percent alcohol.[15] Spirits are traditionally enjoyed before or after a meal, rather than with a meal. Most spirits may be enjoyed straight or "neat" (without ice or other ingredients), or they may be consumed with water, soda, juices, or cocktail mixes.[16]

Whisky from Scotland is called scotch, and most aficionados drink it neat or with a little water (when using the term *Scotch whisky,* there is no e). Some extol the virtues of single malt scotch of which there are several brand names each with their own distinguishing characteristics. Most whiskey is blended, a craft practiced by the blender who uses judgment based on years of experience to produce the Johnnie Walker or Chivas Regal.

Bourbon has a special place in American history. In Colonial New England, rum was popular, but after the separation with England, whiskey became the favorite alcoholic drink. That is, until George Washington levied a tax on this whiskey. So, the farmers moved south in order to carry on production, but when the rye crop failed, they mixed corn and found the result very enjoyable. Since the experiment happened in Bourbon county Kentucky, the name bourbon stuck. Bourbon is now produced mainly from corn and is aged up to six years in charred barrels that give bourbon its distinctive mellow taste. Jack Daniel's, George Dickel, and Maker's Mark are among the better-known brands.

WHITE SPIRITS

Gin, vodka, rum, and tequila are the most common so-called white spirits.

Gin, originally known as Geneva, was first produced in Holland, but it was the British who shortened the name to gin. They used almost anything to make it. Often gin was made in the bathtub in the morning and sold all over London at night at hole-in-the-wall dram shops. Naturally, the quality left a lot to be desired; however, the poor drank it up to the point of national disaster.[17] Gin became popular as the foundation of many drinks such as the martini, gin and tonic, gin and juice, and Tom Collins.

Vodka is made from several different ingredients, predominantly barley, corn, wheat, rye, sugar beet molasses, and potatoes. Because vodka lacks color, flavor, and odor, it is often combined with juices or other mixes whose flavors predominate.[18] Vodka has increased in popularity in part because it "leaves you breathless." There are several popular brands of vodka, some with special flavorings.

Rum comes dark or light in color. Dark rum is distilled from molasses and light rum is distilled from the fermented juice of sugar cane. Rum is mostly produced in the Caribbean islands of Barbados (Mount Gay), Puerto Rico (Bacardi), and Jamaica (Myers). Rums are used in mixed drinks like rum punches, daiquiris, piña coladas, and rum and cokes.

Tequila is distilled from the agave tequilana, a type of cactus, called *mezcal* in Mexico. Tequila can be white, silver, or golden. White is not aged, silver is aged up to three years, and golden is aged in oak barrels for up to four years. Tequila is used in margaritas and tequila sunrise cocktails as well as shooters.

Cognac is distilled from wine and regarded by connoisseurs as the best brandy. By French law, cognac can only come from the Cognac region of France. Cognacs are aged in oak barrels from two to four years or more. Because cognacs are blends of brandies of various ages, no age appears on the label; instead, letters signify the relative age and quality. For example, VSOP must be aged at least four years.[19]

Brandy is also distilled from wine and comes from California and South Africa. It is used in the "well" for mixed drinks, while premium brandy, aged for at least two years in white oak, may be used for after-dinner drinks.

NONALCOHOLIC BEVERAGES

Nonalcoholic beverages are those that do not have any alcohol. They include sodas, juices, nonalcoholic beers, dealcoholized wines, and nonalcoholic cocktails or

Go to several restaurant bars and watch the bartenders, noting how many steps they require and how easy or difficult it is for them to make the drinks. This should help you set up your restaurant's bar.

mocktails, such as the Shirley Temple, Virgin Mary, and virgin piña colada. Bottled waters, power drinks, and coffee and tea round out the nonalcoholic beverages most restaurants offer.

Considering the excellent margins on nonalcoholic beverages it's a wonder not more restaurants tout their beverage menus. The typical margin on a fountain drink is about 85 percent. Margins can be pushed further by offering specialty drinks; for example, a 20-ounce fountain drink sells for $1.59; but a line of a mix of various soft drinks and fruit juices can up the margin considerably. The cost of a soda fountain drink is 31 cents and a specialty mix costs 40 cents but sells for $2.49.[20] At Berryhill Baja Grill in Houston, the signature drink has become the mint lemonade, a blend of freshly squeezed juices and mint. The lemonade is displayed in a large glass container on the counter next to the cash register so guests cannot miss it when they place their orders. The mint lemonade sells for $2.50, versus $1.89 for a fountain drink.[21] That may not seem like much, but when you sell thousands of them it adds up, especially if you have a chain of restaurants.

Bartenders

The recruitment and selection of a great bartender is, obviously, critical to the success of the beverage operation of a restaurant. Here are the top 10 tasks bartenders are responsible for:

1. Collect money for served drinks.
2. Check ID for legal age.
3. Balance cash receipts.
4. Avoid liability for intoxicated guests.
5. Ensure clean glasses, utensils, and bar equipment.
6. Execute beverage orders from *staff or guests.*
7. Serve wine, spirits, cocktails and bottled or draft beer.
8. Clean bars, work areas, and tables.
9. Mix ingredients to prepare cocktails and other drinks.
10. Serve snacks or food items to guests seated at the bar.[22]

During the morning shift, bartenders cut fruit, make mixes for drinks like piña coladas and margaritas, set up the bar, and prepare for service. They count the cash and place it in the till. The swing shift comes on duty at 4:00 P.M. and stays through the happy hour and evening rush. The closing shift comes on duty at 6:00 P.M. and continues the service of guests until closing. They also stock the bar and make out requisitions. Many restaurants require a bartender to first spend time on the floor of the restaurant as a food server in order to become familiar with the restaurant and its operational procedures.

Prerequisites for successful bartenders are a positive attitude, the ability to talk to people, honesty, patience, maturity, integrity, and the ability to make guests come back.

Basic Bar Inventory

The selection of a basic bar inventory depends on the type of restaurant. For example, a trendy upscale restaurant will carry several premium brands that a neighborhood Italian restaurant will not.

A new concept in planning for a more sustainable bar includes the addition of organic, *biodynamic,* and/or local alcohol. Along with meeting other criteria, once alcohol has been certified organic for three years, it can be considered biodynamic.[23] If organic or biodynamic alcohol is not available in the area, the next best option is local. Look for alcohol produced in your region, because that means that it wasn't transported across the country or the world, and that it has a smaller carbon footprint.[24]

The basic inventory shown here is for a contemporary casual/upscale restaurant of 120 seats in the historic area of a major convention city.

Wine by the glass	House: A good no-name red/white
	A Cabernet Sauvignon
	A Chardonnay
	A Merlot
	A Sauvignon Blanc
Champagne	Korbel
	Moët & Chandon
Sherry	Fino
Cognac	Rémy Martin
Gin	Tanqueray, Gordon's
Vermouth	Martini & Rossi Red/White
Vodka	Absolut
	Grey Goose
	Smirnoff
Rum	Bacardi
	Captain Morgan
	Mount Gay
Tequila	Cuervo Gold and 1800
	Sauza Hornitos
Scotch Whisky	Chivas Regal
	House
	Johnnie Walker Red/Black/Gold and Green
	Glenlivet
Rye Whiskey	Wild Turkey
	Canadian Club
	Templeton Rye
	Jim Beam

Cordials and Liqueurs	Baileys
	Chambord
	Cointreau
	Drambuie
	Grand Marnier
	Kahlúa
	Tia Maria
Draft Beer	Budweiser
	Bud Light
	Michelob Ultra
	Michelob Light
	AmberBock
	Rolling Rock
	Killian's
	Samuel Adams
Bottled Beer	Budweiser
	Bud Light
	Corona
	Heineken
	Samuel Adams
Soda	Coca-Cola
	Diet Coke
	Dr. Pepper
	Sprite
Bottled Water	Evian, Dasani, Fuji, Zepherhills
Juice	Apple
	Cranberry
	Orange
	Pineapple
	Tomato

One tip in creating your wine list is to use unfamiliar wines so that people do not know the cost. When customers see that you are charging $30 for a wine widely advertised and sold in supermarkets for $8, they feel ripped off. Use a wine that is good but one the guests will not compare to liquor store prices.

Wines

Wine, the fermented juice of freshly gathered grapes, is produced in many temperate parts of the world. In Europe, for example, France, Spain, Italy, Germany, and other countries produce excellent wine from several different grapes. In North America, California, Oregon, Washington, and New York states, along with British Columbia and Ontario, are the better-known wine-producing areas. In South America, Chile, Argentina, and Uruguay are the main wine producers. Australia's states of New South Wales, Victoria, and South Australia produce excellent wines. New Zealand also has a good selection, as does South Africa.

Soil, climate, and cultivation all have a significant impact on the wine's character. Too much or too little of one essential element will mean a poor-tasting wine. Too much sun will dry out the grapes and the yield will be small. Too much rain and the grapes will not get enough sun to ripen properly.

Wines are first categorized by color: red, white, or rosé. Then they are further classified as light beverage wines, still, sparkling, fortified, and aromatic. Most wines are still, meaning they don't contain any bubbles.

In the United States, wines are named by the variety of grape. Several well-known white wines are Chardonnay, Sauvignon Blanc, Pinot Blanc, White Zinfandel, Pinot Grigio, and Riesling. Among the better-known red varietal wines are Cabernet Sauvignon, Merlot, Pinot Noir, Zinfandel, and Petite Syrah.

A wine connoisseur would describe the most noted white and red wines in the following way:[25]

Chardonnay is the most popular wine grape in North America. It is the classic white of Burgundy in France but is grown in many locations around the world. It is one of the three grape varieties most commonly used in the making of Champagne,

Did you ever wonder why there are so many descriptions about an individual wine? The answer is that you could say *I like it* or *I don't like it,* but that would be a very short conversation and would not distinguish great wines from good wines or acceptable wines from poor wines. The fact is that wines depend on many factors—the variety of grape, the climate, the soil type, the elevation, the temperature, rainfall amount and time of year, the sugar content of the grapes at time of harvest, the winemaker's skill and taste, the fermentation process, the aging time, and the type of container used for aging. These are just a few of the things that affect the glass of wine you may be serving tonight.

If you look at a list of great wines, you will see that some years the wine is considered better than others. The winemaker may use the same the process but the grapes most likely will have been subjected to different weather conditions. If there were more rain than normal just before harvest it would lower the brix sugar concentration. One degree brix is one gram of sucrose sugar for each one hundred grams of a solution. So you see that wine is very complex and has very delicate flavors.

Most flavors are distinguished through your nose by way of the olfactory nerves. Don't believe your nose has a big impact on your taste? Try this: Take a jellybean any color but do not look at it; it is a surprise. With one hand, hold your nose tight closed and with the other hand pop the jellybean, which you have not looked at, into your mouth. Chew it up then quickly let go of your nose.

Wow, see what happened. As you start chewing, you will not be able to distinguish the flavor the jellybean, but the moment you release your nose, the aroma of the jellybean is immediately identifiable. The reason for not looking is that your brain will have some memory of what an orange or any other flavor should taste like. You have had this sensation before when you were sick and your nose was stuffed up and you didn't want to eat because the food was not so appealing. Most of what you tasted was from your memory of what the food should taste like. Your tongue has only four taste sensations (well, some say five: salt, sour, bitter, sweet, and savory). All the others sensations we call *taste* actually come from your olfactory nerves in your nose, and that is where wine descriptions of flavor and aromas get their start in the nose.

or sparkling wine, as it is called outside of the Champagne region of France. Chardonnay is aged in oak barrels or stainless steel vats. Some people will use the term *unoaked,* which means no oak was used. Instead nonporous containers were used to age the wine—albeit the aging time may differ greatly. Wine that is aged in stainless steel vats is a product of New World wines, non-European. Chardonnay is the most popular white grape of North America. Its flavors include lemon, pear, honey, vanilla, and some buttery flavor. With grapes from warmer climates such as Southern California, flavors include white peach, pineapple, melon, mango, banana, nutty, and buttery. When aged in oak barrels, more of a richness and depth of flavor is imparted to the wine from the wood, but this is a matter of individual taste. Chardonnay pairs well with cheeses such as brie, cheddar, and gruyere and with foods such as chicken, turkey, and many Chinese, Indian, and Japanese dishes, as well as spicy foods.

Sauvignon Blanc is a very distinctive, aromatic, grassy white wine, but in some climates can develop a bit of sweetness. It is classic in white Bordeaux, where it is often blended with Semillon grapes to mellow the tartness. Some of the best Sauvignon Blanc wines come from the Loire Valley of France. Although much is made of the Sauvignon Blanc from France, many of the best now come from Australia, Chile, and North America. Flavors include floral, honeydew, white, peach, banana, lemon, apricot, gooseberry, green apple, and sometimes slightly smoky/oaky (when fermented in oak barrels).

Cabernet Sauvignon, the king of red grapes, is one of the most distinctive and important red wine grapes, and one of the most widely planted varieties in wine regions all over the world. Wines from the Cabernet Sauvignon grape need time to mature, but can develop great complexity with age. It is the primary grape of top vineyards in Bordeaux's Medoc and Graves districts and is the signature grape in most of California's top red wines. Cabernet Sauvignon and oak go together like a hand and glove. The oak lessens the large amount of tannins common in the wine and imparts great flavors to the wine. Tannins give wine its astringent quality. Flavors include blackcurrant, blackberry, cherry, chocolate, prune, and oak (from the barrels). Cabernet Sauvignon is a full-bodied wine with firm tannins. The wines are rich in color, aroma, and depth, and they have long-lasting flavor. The wine pairs well with red meats, especially grilled meats, chocolate, cream sauces, and things with black pepper. It does not go well with spicy foods.

Pinot Noir is the queen of red wines and is a grape of aroma and finesse. This is the grape of the great red Burgundies and one of the main grapes used in the making of Champagne. The name *Pinot Noir* is from the French for pine and black. Pinot Noir also grows very well in the milder climates of northern California and also in Oregon, Northern Italy, Chile, and New Zealand. Flavors/aromas include strawberry, raspberry, cherry, plum, when young; when the wine matures, flavors include figs, prunes, chocolate, and violet. Pinot Noir is low in tannin, and the wines can be "silky" in texture and fantastically fragrant.

Riesling is considered by many as the premier white wine grape after Chardonnay. Riesling was initially the grape of the Rhine region of Germany but now the grapes are grown worldwide. Rieslings are typically light-bodied, pale yellow, and lower in alcohol than many other white wines. They are most often drunk young but will become sweeter with age. Yet this wine has a floral bouquet.

Pinot Grigio, or Pinot Gris, as they are call the world over, is a white wine grape that could be a distant relative of Pinot Noir, but the two are very different. This grape has a bluish-gray skin. The name *Gris* is French for gray. The color of the wine is a light lemon to straw yellow, depending on the winemaker and location. The flavor is acidy and crisp like apple.

Pinot Blanc wines may be made from any or all of the Pinot grapes: Pinot Blanc, Pinot Gris, Pinot Noir, and or Auxerrois Blanc. As was said earlier, Pinot Noir is a deep purple red grape, so in making white wine or Champagne the grape juice should not stay in contact with the grape skins. It is difficult to find Pinot Blanc wine made from just one variety, but the best examples are aged in oak barrels and are high in acid with an aroma of apple and citrus.

Zinfandel is a very nice red grape that can be made into a red or white Zinfandel wine. The red Zinfandel juice remains in contact with the skin and the white Zinfandel, which may also be a rose or blush wines depending on the length of contact with the grape skins after the grapes are crushed. The Zinfandel grape has a very high sugar content, which results in a high alcohol content when fermented. It is also has a large amount of tannins and slightly spicy flavor. The white or rose is much less complex and has much less tannins. In some cases the alcohol content can reach or exceed 14%. In the United States, the white Zinfandel is more popular than the red. The red Zinfandel has flavors of blackberry, black raspberry, and peppercorn but can vary greatly, depending on harvest. The white Zinfandel is lighter in body and much less complex. It is sweeter and has softer fruit aromas.

If you are a server or bartender, it is advisable to learn which foods go with which menu items. It will be a relief to your guests and increased tips for you. Many people want to order wine with meals but are a bit timid for fear of making a mistake. Ease their anxiety and make wine suggestions at a couple of different price points.

There are very good wines on the market that are not expensive, so shop around, and as you try wines, make some notes so you can find them again. I have seen two Pinot Noirs rated at 88 points where one is $23 and the other is $5.99. So it does pay to shop and take notes.

WINEMAKING

Wine is made in six steps: crushing, fermenting, racking, maturing, filtering, and bottling. Grapes are harvested in the fall, after they have been tested for maturity, acidity, and sugar content. The grapes are picked and quickly sent to the pressing house to remove the stems and crush the grapes. The juice that is extracted is called *must*.

The second step in the winemaking process is *fermentation* of the must, a process that occurs naturally due to yeasts on the skins of the grapes. Additional yeasts are also added. The yeasts convert the sugar in the grapes to ethyl alcohol, until little or no sugar is left in the wine. The degree of sweetness or dryness in the wine is controlled by adding alcohol, removing yeasts by filtration, or adding sulfur dioxide.

Red wine gains its color during the fermentation process from the coloring pigments of the red grape skins, which are returned to the must.

Once the fermentation is complete, the wine is transferred to racking containers. There it settles before being poured into stainless-steel vats or oak barrels (for better wines). Barrel-aged wines gain additional flavor and character during aging. Throughout the aging process, red wine extracts tannin from the wood, which gives longevity to the wine. Some white and most red wine is barrel aged between 2 and 24 months. After maturing, the wine is filtered to help stabilize it and remove any solid particles in a process called *fining*. The wine is then *clarified* by adding either egg white or bentonite, which removes impurities as it sinks to the bottom of the vat. The wine is then bottled.

Fine *vintage* wines are kept for a few years to further mature in the bottle and are drunk at their peak, several years later. White wines mature more quickly than red wines and are often consumed within a few months of bottling. However, the better white wines are also aged a few years. The better red wines are aged several years to reach their peak of perfection.

In Europe due to the variable climate, wines from some years are much better than others; these better years are declared vintage years, and wines from those years command a higher price. Experts judge the relative merits of a wine based on a 1-to-10 point scale. The *Wine Spectator*'s 100-point scale is also a good guide for selecting wine.

Following is *Wine Spectator*'s 100-point scale and what it indicates:[26]

95–100—Classic; a great wine

90–94—Outstanding; superior character and style

80–89—Good to very good; wine with special qualities

70–79—Average; drinkable wine that may have minor flaws

60–69—Below average; drinkable but not recommended

50–59—Poor; undrinkable, not recommended

Champagne, like wine, should be stored lying flat in a rack so the cork is kept moist. The best storage temperature is between 50° and 55°F and served in an ice bucket at a temperature of 43° to 47°F. Here are the six steps for presenting, opening, and serving Champagne:

1. In a formal restaurant, the bottle is presented to the guest partially wrapped in a cloth napkin, with the label up. This is to double-check that it is the correct bottle, as ordered.

2. Then the bottle is placed in or returned to an ice bucket to await opening.

3. Great care must be taken when opening a bottle of Champagne or sparkling wine: Do not shake it; first remove the wire and foil around the top of the bottle, then point the bottle away from guests. While gently holding the top of the cork with the napkin, twist the cork in one direction only—not back and forth—until it gently pops out of the bottle.

4. When the cork pops out, continue holding the bottle at a 45-degree angle to let the gases out for about five seconds. If the bottle is held upright, Champagne as well as gas will come out.

5. Serve Champagne in two pouring motions: First fill the glass and wait for the bubbles to subside, then top it off to three-quarters full.

6. As with all wines, first offer the host a taste, then pour the guests a glass before returning to the host to top off his or her glass.

SPARKLING WINES

Champagne, sparkling white wine, and sparkling rosé wine are known as *sparkling wines*. The "sparkling" part comes from the addition of carbon dioxide, which can be either naturally produced or infused into the wine. The best-known sparkling wine is champagne, which is mostly used for celebrations. Champagne owes its unique sparkling quality to a second fermentation in the bottle, a process called *méthode champenoise*. French and international law stipulates that champagne can come only from the champagne region of France; all other sparkling wines can only use *méthode champenoise*.

FORTIFIED WINES

Sherries, ports, Madeiras, and marsalas are *fortified wines*, meaning that brandy or wine alcohol has been added to them. The brandy or wine alcohol gives a unique taste and increases the alcohol content of the wine to about 20 percent. Fortified wines are sweeter than regular wine. Each has several subgroups with a range of aromas and tastes. Fortified wines range from dry to sweet and light to dark in color. They can be enjoyed anytime and are also used in cooking.

Sherry (which comes from Spain) is normally drunk before a meal. Port (which comes from Portugal) is enjoyed after a meal and goes really well with cheese.

AROMATIC WINES

Aromatized wines are fortified and flavored with herbs, roots, flowers, and barks. These wines can be sweet or dry. Aromatic wines are better known as aperitifs, which are normally enjoyed before a meal to stimulate the digestive juices.

Among the better-known aromatic wines are Dubonnet (red is sweet, white is dry); vermouth (red is sweet, white is dry); Byrrh (sweet); Lillet (sweet); Punt e Mes (dry); and St. Raphael (red is sweet, white is dry). These aromatic wines are enjoyed by themselves or mixed with other drinks in a cocktail.

 WINE TASTING

Wine tastings can enhance a restaurant's appeal and help guests enjoy and learn more about wines. Wine appeals to three senses: vision through its color, smell through its aroma, and taste. Connoisseurs enjoy a three-step ritual when tasting wine; each step is designed to maximize the enjoyment and complement the wine's appeal to each sense.

1. Hold the wineglass up to the light to see its color. Is it clear and bright? The deeper the color, the fuller the wine flavor will be.

2. Swirl the wine around the glass to release more of the aroma, then sniff the wine. The wine will reveal its characteristics and flavor (cabernet sauvignon, for example, should smell of cherry and plum, and be slightly peppery) and give an indication of the taste to follow.

3. Taste the wine by rolling it around your mouth so that it touches the taste buds while at the same

(continued)

time sucking in a little air between your lips. This helps release the complexities of the wine.

The *Wine Lovers' Manual* provides this list of wine-tasting terminology:[27]

1. **Aroma:** Wine aromas are generally positive, describing the wine before it is tasted. Many of the aromas will be the same as the flavors after tasting the wine. In wine speak folks will refer to primary and secondary aromas (e.g., fruity, oak, vanilla, spicy, toast, butter, cream etc.).

2. **Astringent:** Gives a pucker, drying sensation in the mouth. This sensation is caused by the tannins, acids that are types of phenols. They coat the tongue and cause the drying sensation. There is generally more tannin acid in young red wines such as Cabernets, Zinfandel, Merlot, and many other reds.

3. **Balanced:** This describes harmonious balance of a wine's components (sweetness, acidity, tannin, alcohol, oak, etc.).

4. **Body:** The density or viscosity of a wine. It is the fullness feeling in your mouth and usually ranges from light- to full-bodied. A light-bodied wine has more of a feel of water in your mouth, where a full-bodied wine has more the thickness or consistency of milk.

5. **Bouquet:** No to be confused with the aroma of a wine, this refers to the scent that a wine develops over time by chemical reactions after fermentation.

6. **Complex:** A wine that is multidimensional and well balanced in terms of flavor and aroma.

7. **Crisp:** A lively sensation on the palate, similar to tartness.

It is typical of wines high in acidity.

8. **Floral:** The aroma of flowers can be found in white wines such as Riesling and Gewurztraminer (carnation, jasmine, orange blossom, rose petals, grapefruits, etc.) and red wines such as Pinot Noir (roses, violets, etc.).

9. **Fruity:** Characteristic of a sweetness. The richness and body comes from ripe grapes. Specific fruits are often used in the description.

10. **Nose:** Total of all the aromas and odors that the nose can smell.

11. **Oaky:** Oak barrels used during the aging process create a specific aroma.

12. **Spicy:** Common aromas in wine include cinnamon, cloves, anise, and black pepper found to a great degree in most red wines.

WINE BOTTLES AND GLASSES

It is helpful to know the wine bottles and glasses by their shape, as they are identified by their shape. The *Wine Lovers' Manual* provides this useful guide:[28]

Wine bottles:

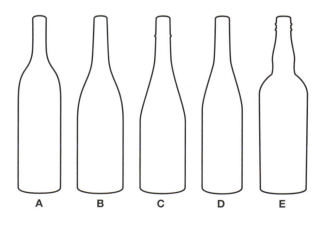

A   B   C   D   E

A-Bordeaux bottle; this slope-shouldered bottle is pale green and this bottle shape is widely used, used in Burgundy, Loire, and the Rhone. It is also used for Shiraz and widely used by new world winemakers.

B-Burgundy bottle; is green widely used throughout the New World for Chardonnay and Pinot Noir,

C-Champagne bottle; is thick green glass, with gentle sloping shoulders and a deep indentation on the bottom. The thick glass and indent are necessary because the pressure inside the bottle can approach 90 pounds per square inch. That is the pressure of a bicycle tire. This bottle is also used for most sparkling wines.

D-Mosel and Alsace; is a slender green glass bottle, it is smaller in diameter and taller that the other bottles. It is also used for Rhine wines which are traditionally brown colored glass.

E-Fortified wines; this bottle is most commonly used for Port, Madeira and Sherry. These bottles are quite strong and sometimes vintage port bottles have a bulge in the neck which supposedly to help catch any sediment as the port is poured.

According to the *Wine Lovers' Manual,* "Wine glasses are not only drinking tools—with proper glasses, you can enjoy its color, bouquet and taste while discovering the wine's complexity, balance and harmony of individual character."[29]

HOW TO SELECT A WINE LIST

Creating a wine list can be fun, and to do so you can involve future guests—that's the tasting part. Before the tasting experience, however, let's be practical and see how much budget and space you have. Remember, the wine has to be purchased, so the larger the list, the more money will be sitting in the wine storeroom. Plus, white wine will need to be stored in a wine refrigerator prior to service. Some wines can be securely displayed near the entrance—to imply that wine should be enjoyed with the meal. This also adds to the ambience of the restaurant.

The wine selection offered should be appropriate for the restaurant. Naturally, an Italian restaurant will feature wines from Italy, along with some from California and perhaps other countries. A casual American regional restaurant can offer wines from America: California, Washington, and Oregon, for example.

Next, consider the varietal type of grape and, most important, what's on the menu. Pairing food with wine is critical to the enjoyment of the meal, as wines can either complement or detract from a dish.

Another thing to consider is the layout and format of the menu and wine list. Today, a number of restaurants put the two together so guests can more easily make their selection. A wine can be suggested alongside each dish on the menu.

The more popular varietal white wines are champagne and sparkling wine. Unless you have a large restaurant, you should select one of each. To save writing out each varietal name on the wine list, just use the term *selected white wines.* Select one or more from various regions and countries. Advice can always be obtained from wine suppliers—but remember, they will want to dominate your list with their products. Be sure to have a test of a selection of each type.

Courtesy of Carmel Café

The bar at Carmel Café is inviting and profitable.

Select wines that will be good to accompany the menu and be priced for your guests. The typical restaurant's percentage cost for wines is 30 percent. Thus, if a bottle costs $10, it would sell for $30 or a rounded number close to that. Wines are best listed with the most expensive first or mixed up, but not from the least expensive to the most expensive. Wine by the glass is usually offered, with a couple of house and a couple of better varietal wines available.

Red wines should be stored at room temperature and white wines in a cool place and chilled before service. You can purchase special wine refrigerators, but the cost must be balanced against the type of restaurant and the wine consumption. If the white wine is kept in a cool place, it can be refrigerated before service—this means careful preparation and turnover of bottles in readiness for each meal service to ensure always having chilled bottles ready. See Figure 7.2 for a sample wine list from an upscale contemporary restaurant. The number of bottles offered in each category is perfect for this restaurant.

Wine lists apps are now available for iPads and other mobile devices and can carry descriptions of hundreds of wines. Restaurants using them report a significant increase in wine sales. According to the website for Restaurant Wine List Pro (billed as the number 1 wine list app for restaurants and wine bars), "With Restaurant Wine List Pro you can update your wine inventory on the fly, and each iPad linked to your list will automatically update to display your current wine selections!"[30] The app allows customers to find out about the style, flavors, pairings, and regions of the wines on your list. It also makes it easy to highlight the wines you wish, and remove them at any time.[31]

Another app, designed for Android devices, is Vinipad. According to its website, "Vinipad combines design and functionality making this application both suitable for professional users and an extension of your business brand."[32]

WINES WITH FOOD

The combination of great food and wine is one of life's greatest pleasures. Today, anything goes, meaning that if a guest wants a red wine with a white meat, that's okay. Patrons should feel comfortable with any choice of wine with a meal. A restaurateur may want to be able to give advice as to what wine best complements a certain dish. Over the years, experience has shown that:

■ White wine is best served with white meat—pork, turkey, chicken, veal, fish, and shellfish.
■ Red wine is best served with red meat—beef, lamb, duck, and game.

RED WINES

FRANCE

BORDEAUX

403 Château Batailley Pauillac 2006....95
404 Château Moulin de Bernat 2009....44
406 Château Magne Figeac St. Emilion 2009....48
407 Château Rauzan Segla Margaux 2006....75
408 Château Moulin de Cabanieu Medoc 2009....38
410 Château La Rose de Palenne "Organic" 2009....39
803 Château Mouton Rothschild, Pauillac 1996....995
808 Château Mouton Rothschild, Pauillac 2001....395

RHONE

454 Andre Brunel Chateauneuf de Pape 2009....59
455 Aline Bonfils Gigandas Cuvee Tradtional 2009....55
456 Domaine Fondreche Nadal 2009....44
457 Michel Gassier Nostre Pais Red 2010....39
458 Domaine Belle Hermitage 2007....69
459 Domaine Grapillon D'Or Gigondas 2010....59

BURGUNDY

460 Dom Joblot Givry Clos de la Servoisine 2006...69
461 Dom Collotte Les Champ Salomon Marsannay 10...59
462 Monnot Volnay Ier Cru Clos des Chênes 2008....75
463 Dom Lécheneaut Nuit-St-George 2007....89
464 Jayer Gilles Hautes Côtes de Nuits 2007....55
465 Domaine Yvon Clerget Volnay 2009....72
468 Joblot Givry Clos du Cellier Aux Moines 2008....65
469 Monnot Beaune Ier Cru Les Toussaint 2008....50

BEAUJOLAIS

472 Pierre-Marie Cuvee Traditionale 2010....36
473 Thibault Liger-Belair Moulin-a-vent 2010....49

ITALY

501 Lafo'a Colterenzio Cabernet 2001.....55
502 Fenocchio Barolo Villero 2003....68
504 Rendola Brunello di Montalcon 2004....75
505 Marina Cvetic Merlot, 2008....56
306 Casale Del Giglio Madreselva 2008/09....58
507 L'Oca Ciuca Brunello di Montalcino 2004....69
508 Contemassi Brunello di Montalcino 2004....65
509 Tenuta Vitanza Quadrimino Rosso 2005....59
510 Castellani Amarone Cinque Stella 2007....115
511 Carpazo Rosso di Montalcino 2010....45
513 Villa Erbice Amarone 2006....89
514 Carpazo Brunello di Montalcino 2007....79
515 Borgo Scorpeto Chianti Classico 2009....69
518 Ronchi di Giancarlo Rocca Barbaresco 2006....63
519 Anna Maria Abbona Dolcetto di Dogliano 2008....75
520 Aurelio Settimo Rocche Barolo 2007....85
522 Montefalco Rosso 2007....26
523 La Selvaccia Brunello di Montalcino 2004....69

SPAIN

582 Layer Cake Granacha, 2010....36
583 Resalte Crianza Ribera del Duero 2009....45
584 Honoro Vera Monastrell "Organic" 2011....24

HALF BOTTLES OF RED

550 King's Estate Pinot Noir, Oregon 2010....29
551 Nozzole Chianti Reserva 2008....24
552 Freestone Pinot Noir, Sonoma 2008....40
554 Bodega Amalaya Malbec, Argentina 2010....18

NORTH AMERICA

MERITAGE & PROPRIETARY BLENDS

705 Stolpman "La Cuadrilla", Central Coast 2011....40
706 Col Solare, Columbia Valley 2007....85
707 Chalk Hill Red, Sonoma County 2009....115
708 Sean Minor Red, Napa Valley 2009....42
709 Jax Vineyards Y3 Taureau, Napa Valley 2010...38
710 Gundlach Bundschu Mountain Cuvee, Sonoma 2010....42
713 Opus One, Napa Valley 2009...275
902 Dominus, Napa Valley 2000......190
910 Dominus, Napa Valley 2002, 03, 04, 05......180

CABERNET SAUVIGNON

602 Falcone Family Vineyards, Paso Robles 2009....55
604 Silver Oak, Alexander Valley 2008....130
605 Keenan, Napa Valley 2008, 2009....79
606 Caymus, Napa Valley 2010....120
607 Fisher Estate Vineyards, Sonoma 2006, 07, 08....110
608 Richard Perry, Napa Valley 2008....89
609 Turnbull, Napa Valley 2009....69
610 Layer Cake, California 2010....39
612 Mica by Bucella, Napa Valley 2009....98
613 Fisher Unity, Napa Valley 2010....69
614 Ty Caton, Sonoma County 2009....59
615 Gundlach Bundschu, Sonoma County 2008....69
616 Raymond "Reserve Selection", Napa Valley 2009....69
617 Lancaster Estate, Sonoma County 2008....125
618 BV George de la Tour Reserve, Napa Valley 2008....195
619 Caymus Special Select, Napa Valley 2010....175
620 Grgich Hills, Napa Valley 2009....79
621 Hewitt, Napa Valley 2009....135
622 Jax Vineyards, Napa Valley 2008....75
623 Joseph Phelps, Napa Valley 2010....105
624 Jordon, Alexander Valley 2009....85

PINOT NOIR

651 Hook and Ladder, Russian River Valley 2011....42
652 St. Innocent, Willamette Valley 2011....45
653 Miura, Monteray 2008....49
654 Chandon, Carneros 2010....40
655 Sean Minor, Carneros 2010....42
656 Robert Goyette, Sonoma County 2010....44
657 MacPhail, AndersonValley 2009....69
658 Lemelson "Thea's Selection", Willamette Valley 2008....52
659 Walt "La Brisa Vineyards", Sonoma 2010....65
660 Rusack, Santa Barbara 2009....69
662 Belle Glos Los Altarus, Santa Rita Hills 2011....59

MERLOT

671 Duckhorn, Napa Valley 2010....79
672 Stags' Leap Winery, Napa Valley 2009....55
673 Ty Caton, Sonoma County 2009....55
674 Provenance, Napa Valley 2009....45
675 Keenan, Napa Valley 2007, 2009....49
676 Decoy by Duckhorn, Napa Valley 2010...52
678 Gainey, Central Coast 2008....44
868 Chalk Hill Merlot, Sonoma County 1998, 1999...145

OTHER REDS

782 Laurel Glen Za Zin Old Vines Zifandel, Lodi 2010...39
783 Amavi Syrah, Walla Walla 2010....52
784 Seghesio Sangiovese, Alexander Valley 2009....44
785 Martinelli Syrah "Terra Felice", Sonoma County 2008....52
786 Marietta Cellars Petite Sirah, Alexander Valley 2009....39

NEW WORLD REDS

752 Jules Taylor Pinot Noir, NZ 2011....36
753 Boekenootskloot "The Chocolate Block" S. Africa 2010...59
756 Zorzal Gran Terrior Malbec, Argentina 2010...48
757 Archaval Ferrer Malbec, Argentina 2011....48
758 Archaval Ferrer "Quimera" Red, Argentina 2010.....69

Courtesy of Ophelia's

FIGURE 7.2 A wine list from Ophelia's on the Bay Siester Key, Florida.

Courtesy of Charlie Trotter

Charlie Trotter's offered an incredible selection of wine, including some 30 by the glass, to complement the dining experience.

- Champagne can be served throughout the meal.
- Port and red wine go well with cheese.
- Dessert wines, which tend to be sweeter than others, best complement desserts and fresh fruits that are not highly acidic.
- When a dish is cooked in wine, it is best served with wines of that variety.
- Regional food is best served with wine of the same region.
- Wines are best not served with salads with vinegar dressings, chocolate, or strong curries, all of which are too strong or acidic for it.

Food and wine are described by flavor and texture. Textures are the qualities in food and wine that we feel in the mouth, such as softness, smoothness, roundness, richness, thinness, creaminess, chewiness, oiliness, harshness, and so on. Textures correspond to sensations of touch and temperature, which we can easily identify—for example, hot, cold, rough, smooth, thin, or thick. Regarding the marrying of food and wine, light food with light wine is always a reliable combination. Rich food with a full-bodied wine can be wonderful as long as the match is not too rich. The two most important qualities to consider when choosing the appropriate wine are richness and body.

Flavors are food and wine elements perceived by the olfactory nerves as fruity, minty, herbal, nutty, cheesy, smoky, flowery, earthy, and so on. A person determines flavors by using the nose as well as the tongue. The combination of texture and flavor is what makes food and wine a pleasure to enjoy; a good match between the food and wine can make special occasions even more memorable. Some restaurants offer wine tastings as special promotional events.

To delve a little deeper into food and wine paring let's look at roast or grilled beef. According to FoodandWinePairing.org, "It would be best to pair a wine that is big enough to keep up with the beef's full flavor and has enough tannin to balance the fats in the beef. (In case you are not familiar with tannins, they are similar to what you taste when you drink tea from a cup of tea which has had a tea bag sitting in it for too long.) That mouth-puckering flavor comes both from the grapes and the wood barrels the wine is aged in—when provided in balance—provides a great flavor that helps cleanse your palate."[33] For a chicken dish with a cream sauce, select a full-flavored wine like a Chardonnay or a white Burgundy. For a fish dish, select a Sauvignon Blanc for a light-flavored fish and possible sauce or a Chardonnay for a fuller-flavored fish dish.[34]

Responsible Alcoholic Beverage Service

Managing alcohol risks by practicing responsible alcoholic beverage service is vital to ensuring guest safety and the security of the restaurant, as well as protecting the bottom line. Creating a responsible alcoholic beverage service program is, in itself, a powerful lawsuit defense. These guidelines from the American Hotel and Motel Association's *Lodging* magazine focus on safety and lawsuit preparedness:

1. Write a responsible alcohol-serving mission statement outlining your position on drinking and safety. Once the mission is written down, the operator has a basis from which to complete the policy and plan.
2. Review local and state liquor laws.
3. Assess the operation's clientele.
4. Make a plan for developing and maintaining relationships with law enforcement officials and transportation organizations.
5. Establish a comprehensive program of ongoing staff training.
6. Create a schedule of management audits of policy and practice.
7. Create a system of actions that demonstrate support for responsible and enjoyable drinking.[35]

Responsible alcoholic beverage service programs should also include responsible actions—for instance, having a trained person at the door to check IDs for proof of age, to discourage patrons from leaving with alcohol, and to prevent intoxicated patrons from driving. Restaurant and bar operators should encourage a designated-driver program, offering free or reduced-cost nonalcoholic drinks to a driver. Also, provide taxi numbers to servers for use with intoxicated guests. Another good practice is to encourage food consumption. Finally, all incidents of concern should be recorded. The time of day, date, situation, response, patron identity, alternative transportation offered, and names and addresses of witnesses are all things that should be noted if possible.

A responsible alcohol service program, such as ServSafe Alcohol or Learn2Serv, are highly recommended as a further methods of training employees on the law and responsibilities of alcoholic beverage service, how alcohol affects the body, and techniques for responsible alcohol service and service in difficult situations.[36]

Dramshop laws enacted by state legislators bring alcohol awareness training to the forefront because, without it, the restaurant risks losing its liquor license. In most states, the servers of alcoholic beverages can be held accountable for drunken-driving accidents under state statutes or under common-law liability. Serving liquor to an intoxicated person is a criminal act in some states. Judgments against places serving alcohol can be so large as to wipe them out of business. With an oversupply of lawyers looking for lawsuits, cocktail lounges and bars are ready targets. Publicity about the number of deaths caused by drunken driving has focused attention on the problem and made alcohol awareness training a must where liquor is served to the public.

Many people serving liquors—bartenders, servers, and managers—are first concerned with sales volume. Concern about drunkenness comes only after a customer causes a problem. Happy hours and two-for-ones do increase liquor consumption and move the drinker toward drunkenness.

Bartender training stresses the absolute necessity of requesting proof of age from suspected minors.

Many restaurants cut off any person who appears to have had a little too much liquor, especially those who become belligerent. Judging the level of alcohol intoxication, however, is difficult. In carefully controlled tests conducted at the Rutgers Center of Alcohol Studies, social drinkers, bartenders, and police officers were able to judge levels of intoxication of subjects accurately only 25 percent of the time. The three groups were able to tell when subjects were sober but underestimated the intoxication level of the subjects who had been drinking.

Third-Party Liability

Owners, managers, bartenders, and servers may be liable under the law if they serve alcohol to minors or to persons who are intoxicated. This is known as *third-party liability*. The penalty can be severe. The legislation that governs the sale of alcoholic beverages is called dramshop legislation. Dramshop laws, or civil damage acts, were enacted in the 1850s and dictated that owners of establishments that serve alcohol are to be held liable for injuries caused by intoxicated customers.

To combat underage drinking in restaurants and bars, a major brewery distributed to licensed establishments a booklet showing the authentic design and layout of each state's driver's license. Trade associations, such as the National Restaurant Association, have, together with other major corporations, produced a number of preventive measures and programs aimed at responsible alcohol beverage service. As mentioned earlier in the chapter, the major thrust of these initiatives is awareness programs and mandatory training programs such as ServSafe Alcohol and Learn2Serve. These programs promote responsible alcohol service. They also teach participants about alcohol and its effects on people, the common signs of intoxication, and how to help customers avoid drinking too much.[37]

Responsible alcohol service programs offer bonuses to those who implement them, such as reductions in insurance premiums and legal fees.

Controls

If the liquor inventory is not properly controlled, losses from spillage, theft, and honest mistakes can seriously affect the restaurant's bottom line, so think of a liquor bottle as a $100 bill and guard it accordingly. The loss or smuggling of liquor occurs in virtually all restaurants. It is safer to assume that, given a chance, people will steal it one way or another.

To avoid or solve liquor *control problems*, institute a weekly or biweekly audit. This may be done by an outside auditor, which is recommended for larger and higher-volume restaurants, or internally, with the correct equipment. For large or high-volume restaurants, the audit begins with a physical count of all open and full bottles of liquor and wine, and beer kegs are weighed. Any other inventory, such as bottled beers and cordials, are counted. The sales and purchase figures are factored in, and the auditor is able to calculate the pouring-cost percentage. The source and volume of lost liquor may then be identified and a plan developed to investigate the losses and prevent recurrence.

Restaurants that use an external audit service receive a printout each week giving management/owners the information they need to target problem areas. Generally, the outcome is a reduction in smuggling and an increase in net savings. The cost of audits range from $175 to $300, depending on the site of the inventory and frequency of audits.

For operators who want to conduct their own audit and calculate liquor-pouring cost, suppliers offer systems that use a computer, a portable scale, and a bar-code scanner.

CONTROLLING LOSSES

Several other commonsense measures can be incorporated into the control of the bar and beverage operation:

- Limit bar access to bartenders and make them accountable for the pouring-cost results.
- Give incentive bonuses for good results.
- Require that drink orders be rung into the register before the drinks are made.
- Use a remote system in which servers must ring up the order before it goes to the bartender.
- Install a surveillance camera.
- Install an alarm on the bar door.
- Do not allow bags to be brought into the bar.
- Provide lockers in another area.
- If bartenders make mistakes, have them written off and signed for by management.
- Cushion bar floors to reduce breakage.
- Set up a system that allows employees to report incidents anonymously.
- Be careful in hiring employees for the beverage operation; check references and do background checks.

WAYS TO STEAL IN A RESTAURANT OR BAR

In the food and beverage industry, it is estimated that 25 percent of employees steal regardless of the controls in place; 25 percent will not steal regardless of the controls in place; and 50 percent will steal if given the opportunity. The controls in place in a restaurant determine whether 25 percent are stealing or 75 percent are. The *Practitioners Publishing Company's Guide to Restaurants and Bars* suggests 99 ways to steal in a restaurant or bar. Some of the more likely ones to happen to a restaurant are listed below. The imagination shown in stealing from bar operations is exceeded only by some lawyers when billing clients.

Among the many ways that bartenders can steal are:

■ *Short ringing*—Bartenders enter a lower amount on the terminal and charge the guest the full amount, then pocket the difference. The way restaurant owners can prevent this is to hire a spotter to watch the bartender or use a surveillance camera or both.

■ *Bringing in his or her own bottle*—Bartender brings a bottle from outside and pockets the amount of sales from that bottle. This can be prevented by marking all bottles and checking them.

■ *Giving drinks away*—Bartender give guests a free drink in the expectation of a larger tip. This can be avoided by employing a spotter or using a surveillance camera, or both.

■ *Not entering the sale*—Bartender does not ring up the sale. Using a spotter or surveillance camera can help avoid this.

■ *Short changing*—Bartender only gives partial change, as in ten dollars for twenty. A spotter or a surveillance camera will be able to detect this.

■ *Short pouring*—Bartender pours less than a full measure. This can be avoided by employing a spotter or a surveillance camera.

■ *Altering credit card entries*—Bartender alters the amount of the credit card sale. This can be avoided by vigilant management.

Restaurateurs that pay attention to details like expensive beverages and treat them as if they were 100-dollar bills instead of bottles will get the attention of bartenders and others who might otherwise steal from the restaurant. In order to incentivize bartenders some operators reward them for meeting the anticipated pouring cost.

Some coffee vendors offer to train restaurant employees in coffee brewing and may clean the coffee brewing machine periodically at no charge. Aficionados of coffee are legion, and many agree that the brew should be held at a temperature of 185°F for no longer than 30 minutes.

Coffee and Tea

Like everything else on the menu, the coffee must fit the clientele. The operator's choice may not be that of the market being served. Preferences vary around the country, and people tend to like the coffee with which they grew up. Widely traveled people often move toward a stronger coffee with a heavier roast.

Coffee served in restaurants is a blend, with mountain-grown coffees predominating. Probably the best way to select coffee is to serve it to a taste panel of typical patrons and use the one they choose.

Generally speaking, coffees are divided between the robust, heavy-flavored coffees and the lighter, milder, mountain-grown coffees. Two separate coffees from a small country may differ widely. The degree of roast and the manner in which the coffee is brewed have a marked effect on the final flavor. It is not enough merely to buy the most expensive coffee.

Coffee vendors often supply the restaurant operator with a coffee-making machine on a no-cost lease basis provided the operator agrees to buy all of his or her coffee from the vendor. Sometimes the vendor charges a few cents more per pound of coffee—which, over time, pays for the machine. For a beginning restaurateur who is short of capital, such offers are welcomed. (Ice cream cabinets are often provided on a similar basis.)

According to the Environmental Defense Fund and Restaurant Associates coffee totals $70 billion in restaurant sales each year. Some growers are using mass production methods using an excess of chemicals and pesticides. These chemicals end up polluting waterways and harm wildlife habitats. More sustainable means of growing coffee beans does exists. The Environmental Defense Fund and Restaurant Associates' Green Dining Best Practices suggests restaurants buy their coffee from credible suppliers that are Rainforest Alliance Certified (this certification ensures sustainable farm management, conservation of natural habitat, and responsible pest control). You can further ensure sustainability by buying coffee labeled organic.[38]

Tea and in particular, iced tea, which some people call the Champaign of the South, can make $900 profit on a 32-count case of loose-leaf iced tea. So it is no wonder it is one of the "suggested" beverage offerings of many restaurants.[39]

Summary

Restaurant bar and beverage operations present operators with challenges and opportunities. The challenges begin with training or transferring a liquor license and operating with strict controls. Establishing and maintaining a program is not only critical to the restaurant's success but is also socially responsible. Opportunities exist for creating exciting cocktails and for the combination of wine with food.

Key Terms and Concepts

Alcoholic beverage license

Aromatized wines

Back bar

Biodynamic alcohol

Bourbon

Brandy

Cabernet Sauvignon

Chardonnay

Cognac

Control problem

Department of Alcoholic Beverage Control

Fortified wines

Front bar

Gin

Holding area

Merlot

Petite Syrah

Pinot Blanc

Pinot Grigio

Pinot Noir

Premium-brand liquors

Pull handle

Responsible alcoholic beverage service

Riesling

Sauvignon Blanc

Tequila

Third-party liability

Under bar

Vodka

Well brands

Whisky

White Zinfandel

Wine

Zinfandel

Review Questions

1. Outline the steps involved in obtaining a liquor license.
2. Draw a rough sketch of a bar layout.
3. Write a mission and prepare a responsible alcoholic beverage service program.
4. Suggest six entrées and wines to accompany them.
5. List the ways that your restaurant bartender might try to steal from you and explain what preventive measures you will install to ensure 100 percent control of your beverages.

CASE STUDY: Classic Restaurant Concepts[40]

Background

Classic Restaurant Concepts is a private company based out of Framingham, Massachusetts, which formed in 1997 by a group of investors who wanted to open up independent Irish-pubs throughout the Massachusetts area. The group was headed by Skip Sack, a restaurateur, most notably known for his ownership of the Red Coach Grill and expansion of the Applebee's Neighborhood Grill and Bar franchise. The idea for Classic Restaurant Concepts came when Skip Sack heard about the Irish Pub Company, a restaurant design company in Dublin, Ireland, which develops concepts for Irish pubs from the ground up. Sack believed that there was an opportunity to open up an Irish pub around the Boston area and partnering with Irish Pub Company would ensure the development of a successful concept.

to open a second restaurant only a year later in the Government Center building, in downtown, Boston, Massachusetts. Seeing the potential this location could offer to the right restaurant venture, Classic Restaurant Concepts developed a similar but ultimately different Irish pub concept called The Kinsale, named after the epicurean capital of Ireland.

In October of 2001, the company sought out a third restaurant venture in Cambridge, Massachusetts, called The Asgard, which donned a Nordish-Irish theme. The restaurant was developed in a similar manner as the previous two, but unfortunately, opened just two weeks after the tragedy of September 11th. The restaurant struggled tremendously during the first year of operation, but survived, and gradually picked up business over the years. Currently, the restaurant serves as one of the premier dining establishments around the Cambridge area.

Three Leaves

The first restaurant opened by the company was called "Desmond O'Malley's," which was located in Framingham, Massachusetts. Partnering with the Irish Pub company gave the restaurant a truly "authentic" feel, from the furnishings and décor to the colors painted on the walls. The development was very detailed and fully imported, which made it a more expensive process, but completely unique from other Irish pub concepts in the area. The success of the first restaurant prompted the company

Challenges

In the early 2000s, Desmond O'Malley's lost its liquor license for three weeks, during which time it was unable to serve alcohol beverages of any type. However, the restaurant remained open and served food, offering gift certificates to all customers who came in to dine at the establishment. Sales during the "dry" period dropped from $60,000 per week to $10,000–$12,000. Unfortunately, when it finally got its liquor license back, the business did not return with it, and Desmond O'Malley's was forced to close its doors for good. After closing Desmond O'Malley's, Classic Restaurant Concepts converted the building space into a steakhouse concept, straying away from the Irish pub" concept in attempt to make the location work, as they still had a lease to pay on the building.

The steakhouse entailed a fancy atmosphere with a moderately priced menu, averaging $50 per check. Business was strong for a year and a half until the recession hit, decreasing business by approximately 25 percent. Once again, the restaurant shut its doors, and Classic Restaurant Concepts went to work on another concept for the location. Next, the company negotiated a deal with David Ortiz of the Boston Red Sox for a restaurant called "Big Papi's" Grille, which garnered a lot of potential for success. In the beginning, business was booming; however, after about a year of steady business, the appeal tapered off and demand decreased, possibly due to the fact that the restaurant was in Framingham, which is located 16 miles from downtown, Boston. After several years of marginal business, the company closed the doors for a third time when the lease on the building expired, opting not to renew its contract on leasing the building.

Moving Forward

Currently, Classic Restaurant Concepts is in the process of signing a lease with Harvard University for a third location in Harvard Square, a location in high demand for restaurateurs. The building is owned by Harvard University, which is very selective about whom it leases its properties to, and concurrently, Harvard charges a high price for the property. Additionally, Classic Restaurant Concepts must convert the building from an office space to a restaurant, which requires heavy renovation of the physical structure of the building, which includes the addition of a roof deck. The company is putting a lot of resources into this venture, with the intention of opening either a bistro or a gastropub in the new location. Financially, Classic Restaurant Concepts seeks to evenly balance its food and alcohol sales. Classic Restaurant Concepts decided that it wanted a food-oriented business that offers great pub atmosphere as well. It optimistically seeks to open the new restaurant within 18 months.

QUESTIONS

1. What additional things could Classic Restaurant Concepts have done to attract and retain business during the time that it lost its liquor license?
2. Make a list of the basic bar inventory you would include for the new location in Harvard square. Explain why you have chosen these selections.
3. How would the basic bar inventory differ between an Irish-pub concept and a gastropub concept?
4. What are the pros and cons of seeking an even balance of food and alcohol sales?

Endnotes

1. Jennifer Hudson-Taylor and Douglas Robert Brown, *The Food Service Professional Guide to Building Restaurant Profits: How to Ensure Maximum Results* (Ocala, FL: Atlantic Publishing Group, 2003), p. 17.
2. California Department of Alcoholic Beverage Control. www.abc.ca.gov/permits/licensetypes .html. September 2009.
3. Ibid.
4. My Florida website, December 28, 2012, www.myfloridalicense.com/dbpr/abt/documents/fee_ chart.pdf. Retrieved April 29, 2013.
5. Dina Berta, "Restaurants Belly Up to the Bar," *Nation's Restaurant News, 42* (28) (July 21, 2008), pp. 35–39.

6. Ibid.
7. Jerry Thomas, *How to Mix Drinks* (New York: Dick & Fitzgerald Publishers, 1862).
8. Grey Regan, *The Joy of Mixology* (New York: Potter Publishing, 2003), p. 24.
9. Dale DeGroff, *The Craft of the Cocktail* (New York: Potter Publishing, 2002), p. 15.
10. Eric Felten, "St. Louis—Party Central," *Wall Street Journal* (October 6, 2007), P.W 4.
11. Eric Felten, "Celebrating Cinco de Drinko," *Wall Street Journal* (November 28, 2008), P. B 2.
12. John R. Walker, *Introduction to Hospitality Management,* 4th ed. (Upper Saddle River, NJ: Pearson, 2013), pp. 324–325.
13. Stephen Beaumont, "Antioxidant-rich fruits like acai, pomegranate give cocktails a healthful trendy kick," *Nation's Restaurant News 42*, (10) (March 10, 2008), p. 34.
14. "All About Scotch Whisky," www.tastings.com/spirits/scotch.html. Retrieved April 29, 2013.
15. John R. Walker, *Introduction to Hospitality,* 6th ed. (Upper Saddle River, NJ: Pearson, 2012), p. 320.
16. Ibid.
17. C. Katsigiris and M. Porter, *The Bar and Beverage Book,* 3rd ed. (Hoboken, NJ: John Wiley & Sons, 2002), p. 139.
18. Walker, *Introduction to Hospitality*, p. 323.
19. Ibid., p. 324.
20. Berta, pp. 35–39.
21. Ibid.
22. "Occupational Details: Bartenders." Nevada Workforce Research & Analysis Bureau. www.nevadaworkforce.com/cgi/databrowsing/occExplorerQSDetails.asp?menuchoice=&soccode=353011&geogArea=3201000000. Retrieved September 2009.
23. "Your Sustainable Bar: Make It Organic, Biodynamic, or Local," *Sustainable Life.* www.thesustainablecoach.com/2009/07/your-sustainable-bar-make-it-organic.html. Retrieved on September 14, 2012.
24. Ibid.
25. *Wine Lover's Manual 11 Uncorked: Comparing and Pairing*. Retrieved December 2012. http://classicwinesofcalifornia.com/images/Wine_Lovers_Manual_II.pdf. And Dr. Jay R. Schrock, Professor Emeritus, University of South Florida.
26. "Wine Basics," www.wine.com/v6/aboutwine/wineratings.aspx?ArticleTypeId=2. Retrieved December 8, 2012.
27. Classic Wines of California," Wine Lovers' Manual (Mango Press, 2013), http://www.gourmetnotes.com/uploads/basic_20wine_20guide_20112007.pdf.27.
28. Ibid. And Dr. Jay R. Schrock, Professor Emeritus, University of South Florida.
29. Ibid.
30. http://www.winelistpro.com/download.html. Retrieved on December 20, 2012.
31. Ibid.
32. https://play.google.com/store/apps/details?id=air.com.vinipad.android&hl=en. Retrieved on April 29, 2013.
33. http://www.foodandwinepairing.org/wine_pairing_board.html. Retrieved November 14, 2012.
34. Ibid.
35. *Lodging.* www.lodgingmagazine.com/ME2/Default.asp. September, 2009.
36. National Restaurant Association. www.nationalrestaurantassociation.com/pressroom/pressrelease.cfm?ID=381. Retrieved September 14, 2012.
37. ServeSafe website. www.servsafe.com/. Retrieved on September 14, 2012.
38. "Sustainable Food Purchasing: Coffee and Tea," EDF+Business, http://business.edf.org/food-water/restaurants-and-dining/sustainable-food-purchasing-coffee-and-tea. Retrieved April 30, 2013.
39. Personal conversation with Michael Hartsaw, manager, Sysco Florida, November 28, 2012.
40. The author gratefully acknowledges the courtesy of Skip Sack, owner.

Operations, Budgeting, and Control

LEARNING OBJECTIVES

After reading and studying this chapter, you should be able to:

- Describe front-of-the-house operations.

- Describe back-of-the-house operations.

- Identify ways to control food, beverage, and labor costs.

- Discuss methods of guest check control.

Courtesy of Roy's New York City. Photo by Paul Warhol

Restaurant Operations

Restaurant operations are split between the back and front of the house. In the *back of the house* are the areas that include purchasing, receiving, storage, issuing, food preparation and service, dishwashing area, sanitation, accounting, budgeting, and control. *Front of the house* refers to the operations and people who interface with customers in the dining areas.

Front of the House

Front of the house refers to the hosts, bartenders, servers, and busers. There is an opening manager and a closing manager. If necessary, each area of the restaurant will have an opener, a swing-shift person, and closers, so as to spread the staff to cover the shift in the most-effective manner. However, guests often call for reservations or directions and receive a first impression of the restaurant by the way they are treated. Guests also receive a first impression known as *curbside appeal*—or, would you even stop or get out of the car? The visual appeal of the building and parking area are important to potential guests. Is the pathway to the entrance door clean, or are cigarette butts littering the sidewalk? Are the doors clean, or do they have fingerprints all over them? Is the host's greeting welcoming? Each of these adds up to that important first impression of a restaurant.

The first thing restaurant managers do is to forecast how many guests are expected and share that information with the kitchen. A *guest count* is arrived at by taking the same day last year and factoring in things like today's weather, day of the week, and so on. Figure 8.1 shows a *daily flash report* for a large-volume restaurant. Notice the daily sales for the month of October and the sales for the same day last year. Keeping accurate records is vital in the restaurant business. Having last year's sales is helpful in planning for this year. This report also has the number of guests and the average check, together with month-to-date sales and variances. The forecast is also used for staffing levels to ensure an appropriate level of service. Different restaurants have different table configurations. In the high-rent district, tables are often 24 inches square and about the same distance from each other—waiter, there's an elbow in my soup! The best tables are those that can go from a deuce to a foursome with flaps or become a six-top when spread open. Servers can then arrange for parties of various numbers without too much trouble. The restaurant is set, the tables laid, the bar is stocked and ready. Then the front-of-the-house staff have a quick-service meeting to go over the specials of the day and perhaps a training detail. This is followed by a family-style meal for all front-of-house staff. Then it's action stations!

Many upscale restaurants use Open Table, a reservation service available on the web or via the restaurants website. It allows guests to reserve tables at times selected by the restaurant. Now here is a good hint. If a guest calls your restaurant for a table of four at 7 P.M. offer them one at 6:30 or 7:30 P.M. so that you get an extra turn on those tables, which equals more profit.

Hosts greet guests and seat them by rotation in sections, so as not to overwhelm any one server. Hosts generally give guests menus and inform them of the name

As Of 09/30	Sales To Date 3,852,448.64 — Daily Sales	GST/$ CH	Retail	Sales To Date 2013 4,105,336.69 — Daily Sales	GST/$ CH	Retail	MTD 2014	MTD 2011	Daily Flash MTD Variance 2013-2014	YTD	YTD	YTD Variance
01-Oct	5,048.39	357/14.39	88.99	5,923.31	341/18.81	490.58	5,048.39	5,923.31	874.92	3,857,497.03	4,111,260.00	253,762.97
02-Oct	7,416.94	505/14.96	142.70	8,412.06	597/14.87	465.63	12,465.33	14,335.37	1,870.04	3,864,913.97	4,119,672.06	254,758.09
03-Oct	10,436.67	648/16.52	268.89	18,958.86	1089/17.75	374.78	22,902.00	33,294.23	10,392.23	3,875,350.64	4,138,630.92	263,280.28
04-Oct	16,149.93	1048/15.94	558.73	20,744.17	we/1344/15.81	513.93	39,051.93	54,038.40	14,986.47	3,891,500.57	4,159,375.09	267,874.52
05-Oct	19,897.08	we/1348/15.26	673.68	13,074.03	we/898/14.96	333.77	58,949.01	67,112.43	8,163.42	3,911,397.65	4,172,449.12	261,051.47
06-Oct	13,655.00	we/900/15.65	431.06	8,807.25	598/15.19	281.35	72,604.01	75,919.68	3,315.67	3,925,052.65	4,181,256.37	256,203.72
07-Oct	9,439.82	595/16.77	542.42	10,037.79	669/15.73	488.29	82,043.83	85,957.47	3,913.64	3,934,492.47	4,191,294.16	256,801.69
08-Oct	8,714.72	648/13.96	335.88	9,979.03	641/16.13	364.62	90,758.65	95,936.50	5,177.95	3,943,207.19	4,201,273.19	258,066.00
09-Oct	10,105.22	696/14.74	157.95				100,863.77					
10-Oct	9,042.58	637/14.89	442.49				109,906.35					
11-Oct	16,940.07	1126/15.74	785.41	we			126,846.42					
12-Oct	19,019.89	we/1254/15.69	667.20	we			145,866.31					
13-Oct	15,433.36	we/1026/15.57	545.95				161,299.67					
14-Oct	8,469.89	h/r/550/16.11	386.68				169,769.56					
15-Oct	5,073.38	r/355/15.85	554.68				174,842.94					
16-Oct	9,241.20	603/16.07	452.89				184,084.14					
17-Oct	11,505.97	723/16.66	540.74				195,590.11					
18-Oct	17,775.63	1198/15.34	609.30	we			213,365.74					
19-Oct	18,692.93	we/111317.21	453.42	we			232,058.67					
20-Oct	12,137.37	we/850/14.63	301.73				244,196.04					
21-Oct	9,338.07	635/15.18	320.65				253,534.11					
22-Oct	9,752.52	679/14.94	397.92				263,286.63					
23-Oct	9,011.51	599/16.03	590.73				272,298.14					
24-Oct	12,925.34	708/19.12	615.76	we			285,223.48					
25-Oct	17,504.63	964/18.97	783.48	we			302,728.11					
26-Oct	18,790.51	we/1315/14.72	570.62	we			321,518.62					
27-Oct	13,365.76	we/960/14.29	354.40	we			334,884.38					
28-Oct	12,104.74	781/15.74	349.72				346,989.12					
29-Oct	8,119.43	556/15.17	316.84				355,108.55					
30-Oct	7,016.80	466/15.37	149.89				362,125.35					
31-Oct	6,425.25	425/15.78	281.74				368,550.60					
Total	388,550.60		13,672.54	95,936.50		3,312.95						

	2012	2013	2014	Average
JAN	265,910.27	277,170.15	267,633.02	270,237.81
FEB	465,575.02	393,856.56	406,657.17	422,029.58
MAR	517,305.12	619,728.81	656,074.68	597,702.87
APR	563,230.27	564,188.03	639,666.97	589,028.42
MAY	471,499.80	482,067.26	556,313.22	503,293.43
JUN	428,233.94	429,103.38	414,830.33	424,055.88
SUBTL	2,711,754.42	2,766,114.19	2,941,175.39	

	2012	2013	2014	Average
JUL	427,282.31	447,676.15	487,680.15	454,212.87
AUG	371,443.39	372,076.64	388,821.95	377,447.33
SEP	225,733.12	266,581.66	287,659.20	259,991.33
OCT	307,391.00	368,550.60	0.00	225,313.87a
NOV	328,428.24	321,977.07	0.00	216,801.77a
DEC	294,560.80	270,770.83	0.00	188,443.88a
PTD TOTAL	4,666,593.28	4,813,747.14		4,105,336.69

FIGURE 8.1 A daily flash report for a large restaurant shows daily sales for the month of October, the number of guests and average check, month-to-date and year-to-date sales, and variances and sales for the same date last year.

of the server. Occasionally, guests will be asked to wait—only a few minutes, it is hoped. This wait is also done to help space out the orders, which helps avoid the kitchen getting too slammed.

The server introduces him- or herself, explains the beverage specials, and takes and brings the beverage order while the guests are deciding what to have from the menu. Specials of the day are explained and any questions are answered. Servers need to be knowledgeable about the menu so as to describe and "suggestively sell" dishes.

Once the order is taken, it is given or sent to the kitchen, the appropriate cutlery is checked for each guest, with soup spoons added or removed as needed. The buser or server may bring bread or similar items to the table, followed by the server bringing the beverage order and serving it.

Appetizers are brought to the table and served—each to the correct person, without having to ask who's having what. As this table is enjoying the meal, the server keeps an eye on the guests but also takes care of three or four other tables.

Entrées are served and cleared, the table is cleaned, the dessert cutlery is brought down to the side of the guest (if it's on the table), and dessert menus are given to the guests. Coffee and after-dinner liquors are also suggested. Eventually, the check is requested and presented.

The manager makes sure everything goes smoothly, by helping guests and staff in any way that will make for a more enjoyable dining experience. Managers need to spend time with guests, ensuring that they return soon with their friends. This is a universal concept among restaurants. Sam Harrison is the owner of two restaurants in London, Sam's Brasserie in Chiswick, and Harrison's in Balham. In an interview for *Caterer & Hotelkeeper* magazine, he discussed the importance of having good relationships with customers:

> In these difficult economic times, we have to give people a reason to return to our restaurants. Of course people will return for good food and a value for money, but a big part of the decision is down to how they feel they have been treated and looked after. Being made to feel special as a customer is not something you forget in a hurry, and by making our customers feel valued we are hopefully building long-term relationships.[1]

Danny Meyer, president of Union Square Hospitality Group, describes his restaurants as machines. The cleaning takes place overnight. At 6:00 A.M. the lunch cooks arrive. Deliveries are received, the cooks cook, and the bakers bake. Managers arrive at 8:30 and servers at 10:15. In between, the chef and sous chef may be shopping for fresh produce. Once the setup is complete at 11:00 A.M., all servers and cooks have a family lunch. During this time they go over the service notes and lunch specials. At 11:30, the final touches are completed—uniforms checked, the seating chart finalized. After lunch, there is a managers' meeting to review the lunch and prepare for dinner. The dinner cooks arrive at 2:30 P.M. and the dinner servers at 4:30. They all have a family meal at 5:00 P.M. The specials and any particular service details are discussed, and the evening dinner service begins. Managers also have a debriefing after the service and record all important points in the logbook.

Managers and chefs watch the clock to be sure that as the restaurant gets quieter, staff are thanked for their shifts and get off the clock. Sounds simple, doesn't it? When you think of the number of guests served at a restaurant like Union Square Cafe, your respect for Danny Meyer and his partners greatly increases.

Operationally, the owner/manager goes through the elements of management to constantly deal with the many challenges of running a restaurant and meeting or exceeding the goals set. The elements of management are planning, organizing, communicating, decision making, motivation, and control. Goals are set for each *key result area (KSA)*. For example, sales goals include the number of guests per meal every day and the average

Courtesy of Sysco
Chefs conducting a taste test.

check. Planning also includes working with the chef/cook to determine the amount of each menu item to prepare and the specials to add to the menu.

Several restaurants use the *Red Book* to assist in managing the restaurant; it aids from planning to control. *Red Book Solutions* has developed an entire line of products and solutions to help full-service restaurant managers and owners address their biggest concerns: food safety/compliance, increasing sales, employee retention, and customer service as well as task compliance management, team communication management, crisis management, key metric variance and corrective action, and training reinforcement.[2] In the *Red Book*, which is now available in an electronic format, the manager records important information, such as sales, specials, any short orders from suppliers, who's quit, who's fired, who's hired, and any occurrences from the shift.

Another aspect of planning is that the chef gets a dollar amount for a combination of hourly labor, food, and kitchen supplies purchases, an example being 38.5 percent. This and other aspects of planning link to all the other elements of management.

Schedules and checklists help organize the restaurant. A *lead sheet* lists staff on both shifts so you can easily see who's on duty. There is also a list of staff and phone numbers plus part-timers on call. There is a preshift meeting to go over any service details and specials. For motivation, restaurants might have sales contests to see who can sell the most of a particular item, usually wine or cocktails. Prizes vary from DVDs to televisions. It's amazing to see how pumped some staff members get over such competitions. An example of control is to keep the cost of goods sold below 52 percent and give managers a bonus on the results. The good thing about pegging this bonus on the total cost of goods sold is that it ties the back and front of the house together. So managers are watching for waste, portion control, and so on.

Some restaurants use the services of a *shopper* who makes a reservation at the restaurant, arrives, and has a meal like any other guest—albeit anonymously. The shopper completes a report on the restaurant. Figure 8.2 shows a sample shopper's

LOCATION ID	Location Name	
FILL ID	Date	9/17/07
EVALUATOR ID	Day	Wednesday
Location Address	Arrival Time	6:10pm
City, State	Departure Time	7:30pm
Phone	Total amount Spent	**$61.18**
	Guest Demographic	#Adults 2 #Males 1
		#Kids 0 #Females 1

PHONE CALL	YES	NO	**Comments**
Was the phone answered within 3 rings?	☒	☐	Terri answered after two rings.
Was the greeting appropriate?	☒	☐	Cheerful voicel
Was the person friendly?	☒	☐	
Was your question answered without hesitation?	☒	☐	All questions were answered.

ENVIRONMENT–Initial Impression		
Was the parking lot free of debris?	☒	☐
Was the exterior of the building in good repair?	☒	☐
Was the landscape well maintained?	☒	☐
Was the entrance dean and free of debris?	☒	☐
Was the waiting area clean?	☒	☐
Were the windows and doors clean?	☒	☐
Were all of the light bulbs functional?	☒	☐
Were the light fixtures, fans and rafters dust free?	☒	☐
Were the floors clean?	☒	☐

ENVIRONMENT–Table Preparation			
Was the seating area neatly arranged?	☒	☐	
Was the Tabletop clean?	☒	☐	
Were the chairs clean?	☒	☐	
Were the menus clean and grease free?	☒	☐	
Were the utensils clean?	☒	☐	
Were the condiment containers full and clean?	☒	☐	There were no condiments at the bar
Were the ashtrays clean and empty?	☒	☐	☒ N/A

ENVIRONMENT–Atmosphere

Was the atmosphere appropriate?	☒	☐		
How was the music sound level?	☒ Perfect	☐ Too Loud	☐ Too Soft	
How was the lighting level?	☒ Perfect	☐ Too Bright	☐ Too Dark	
How was the restaurant temperature?	☒ Perfect	☐ Too Hot	☐ Too Cold	

ENVIRONMENT–Restroom

Which restroom did you visit?	☒ Mens	☒ Ladies	
Was it odor free?	☒	☐	
Was the area clean?	☒	☐	
Was toilet paper available?	☒	☐	
Were paper towels available?	☒	☐	One paper towel holder was empty but the other one had paper.

Courtesy of John Horn, The Anna Maria Oyster Bar, Sarasota, Florida

FIGURE 8.2 Restaurant shopper's report.

SERVICE

Hostess/Host-Appearance   Name   Carry
   Description (required) Gender: F Hair Color: Blonde Hair Length: Shoulder Height: 5'1" Weight: 100

	YES	NO	Comments
Was her/his overall appearance neat?	☒	☐	Black Top and Tan Slacks
Was she/he friendly?	☒	☐	

Hostess/Host-Service

	YES	NO	Comments
Were you immediately greeted?	☒	☐	She was seating a customer and we asked if we could sit at the bar and she said "Yes! certainly."
Was the greeting warm and friendly?	☒	☐	
Were you given an estimated waiting time?	☐	☐	☒ N/A
If YES, what time period was given?		Minutes	
If YES, were you seated within the time period given?	☐	☐	☒ N/A
Were you offered a choice of seating?	☐	☐	N/A
Were you escorted to your table?	☐	☐	N/A
Were you given menus when seated?	☐	☐	N/A
Were children given a menu and crayons?	☐	☐	☒ N/A
Were you told who your server would be?	☐	☐	N/A

Server-Appearance   Name   **Jim**
   Description (required) Gender: **M** Hair Color: **Salt/Pepper** Hair Length: **Short** Height: **5'7"** Weight: **145**

	YES	NO	Comments
Was her/his overall appearance next?	☒	☐	Tropical Shirt and Tan Shorts
Was she/he friendly?	☒	☐	

Server–Service

	YES	NO	Comments
Were you greeted within a reasonable time?	☒	☐	
Was the greeting warm and friendly?	☒	☐	
Were your utensils delivered before your food?	☒	☐	
Were your beverages served in a timely manner?	☒	☐	If NO, how long?
Was your appetizer served in a timely manner?	☒	☐	If NO, how long?
Were your entrées served in a timely manner?	☒	☐	If NO, how long?
Were your dessert served in a timely manner?	☐	☐	If NO, how long? NA
Was your order correct?	☒	☐	
Was your satisfaction verified within 2 minutes of receiving your order?	☒	☐	
Was your satisfaction verified once more during your meal?	☒	☐	
Were your non-alcoholic drinks refilled without question?	☒	☐	
Was your table cleared as needed?	☒	☐	
Were you offered a to-go container?	☐	☐	Not Needed
Were your items placed in the to-go container for you?	☐	☐	N/A
Was your check presented in a timely manner?	☒	☐	
Was your check correct?	☒	☐	
Was your check processed in a timely manner?	☒	☐	
Was your receipt returned and change counted back?	☒	☐	

FIGURE 8.2 (continued)

	YES	NO	Comments
Server–Suggestive Selling			
Were you offered specific drinks?	☐	☒	
If you ordered beer, was a pitcher suggested?	☐	☐	☒ N/A
Did the server suggest specific appetizers?	☒	☐	Jim told us to check out the Specials on the Shrimp Menu.
Did the server suggest specific entrées?	☒	☐	Jim did a great job of making suggestions and
Did the server suggest coffee?	☒	☐	of answering questions about the different
Did the server suggest dessert?	☒	☐	menu items.
The Team–Teamwork			
Did the team members ID younger patrons?	☒	☐	
Did the team work together to get food served?	☒	☐	
Did the team work together to keep tables cleared?	☒	☐	
Did the team interact and contribute to the atmosphere?	☒	☐	
Were all of the team members friendly?	☒	☐	
Were you thanked for your visit?	☒	☐	
Were you invited to return?	☐	☒	No one present at the door when we left.

The Manager　　　　Name　　**Not Observed**

Description (required) Gender:　　Hair Color:　　Hair Length:　　Height:　　Weight:

Was the Manager visible in the dining area?	☐	☒	
Did the Manager greet you at any time?	☐	☒	
Was the Manager interacting with customers?	☐	☒	We did not see anyone acting in a management position.

PLEASE LIST ADDITIONAL TEAM MEMBERS THAT INTERACTED WITH YOU DURING YOUR VISIT.

Position　　　　　　　　　　　　　　Name
Description (required)　　Gender:　　Hair Color:　　Hair Length:　　Height:　　Weight
Comments
Position　　　　　　　　　　　　　　Name
Description (required)　　Gender:　　Hair Color:　　Hair Length:　　Height:　　Weight
Comments
Position　　　　　　　　　　　　　　Name
Description (required)　　Gender:　　Hair Color:　　Hair Length:　　Height:　　Weight
Comments

PLEASE LIST AND RATE ITEM ORDERED, EVEN IF THEY ARE NOT REIMBURSABLE
MENU

	Ratings	1–Poor Presentation	2–Good Taste	3–Great Temperature	List Receipt Price	Would you order again?
Beverages						
2–Vodka Tonic		☐1 ☐2 ☒3	☐1 ☐2 ☒3	☐1 ☐2 ☒3	8.50	☒Yes ☐No
2–Coffee		☐1 ☐2 ☒3	☐1 ☐2 ☒3	☐1 ☐2 ☒3	3.38	☒Yes ☐No
		☐1 ☐2 ☒3	☐1 ☐2 ☒3	☐1 ☐2 ☐3		☐Yes ☐No
Appetizers						
2–Coconut Shrimp		☐1 ☐2 ☒3	☐1 ☒2 ☐3	☐1 ☐2 ☒3	11.98	☒Yes ☐No
		☐1 ☐2 ☒3	☐1 ☒2 ☐3	☐1 ☐2 ☒3		☐Yes ☐No
		☐1 ☐2 ☐3	☐1 ☐2 ☐3	☐1 ☐2 ☐3		☐Yes ☐No

FIGURE 8.2 (continued)

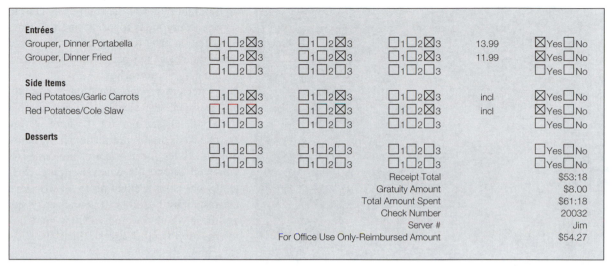

Entrées					
Grouper, Dinner Portabella	☐1 ☐2 ☒3	☐1 ☐2 ☒3	☐1 ☐2 ☒3	13.99	☒Yes ☐No
Grouper, Dinner Fried	☐1 ☐2 ☒3	☐1 ☐2 ☒3	☐1 ☐2 ☒3	11.99	☒Yes ☐No
	☐1 ☐2 ☐3	☐1 ☐2 ☐3	☐1 ☐2 ☐3		☐Yes ☐No
Side Items					
Red Potatoes/Garlic Carrots	☐1 ☐2 ☒3	☐1 ☐2 ☒3	☐1 ☐2 ☒3	incl	☒Yes ☐No
Red Potatoes/Cole Slaw	☐1 ☐2 ☒3	☐1 ☐2 ☒3	☐1 ☐2 ☒3	incl	☒Yes ☐No
	☐1 ☐2 ☐3	☐1 ☐2 ☐3	☐1 ☐2 ☐3		☐Yes ☐No
Desserts					
	☐1 ☐2 ☐3	☐1 ☐2 ☐3	☐1 ☐2 ☐3		☐Yes ☐No
	☐1 ☐2 ☐3	☐1 ☐2 ☐3	☐1 ☐2 ☐3		☐Yes ☐No

Receipt Total	$53:18
Gratuity Amount	$8.00
Total Amount Spent	$61:18
Check Number	20032
Server #	Jim
For Office Use Only-Reimbursed Amount	$54.27

FIGURE 8.2 (*continued*)

report. Notice how it covers all areas of the restaurant and service. Other forms offer a scale of 1 to 5, for example, for the shopper to score the restaurant and express an overall percentage result.

Back of the House

The back of the house is sometimes called the "heart" of the operation. A successful restaurant operation depends on the back of the house functioning smoothly. The kitchen is the center of production and must be run properly, producing an excellent food quality and presentation and meeting costing goals.

The chef, having set the menu for the day—this might be either a permanent menu with specials or a daily menu—will have checked inventory at the close the previous night to ensure sufficient food quantities for the anticipated orders of the next meal period, and completed a purchase order that was given to an office assistant or owner/manager to place with vendors. The chef made out a *production sheet* for each station, detailing all the tasks necessary to bring the food quantities up to par stock of prepared items and to complete the preparation on time. As the prep cooks arrive, they are given their assignments and begin to prepare the various menu items for the anticipated number of guests according to the standardized recipes. Most of the prep work is done during the early morning and afternoon.

The chef makes sure that all menu items are prepared in accordance with the standardized recipes and that the line is ready for service. During service, either the chef or a manager may act as a caller—in an attempt to control the ordering and expediting of plates at the pass. All handwritten orders must be easily read or must come through on the kitchen printer so that the kitchen cooks can put

Courtesy of State Street Eating House, Sarasota

Thanking a crew member for a great shift.

up the right plates at the right time. During service, everyone is focusing on timing and presentation. The food must be at the right temperature yet not be overcooked; flavorful but not overpowering.

After the service, the food is properly put away and the cleanup is done, the par stocks for all stations for the next service are checked, orders are made, and production schedules for all stations are done. As you well know, it's a never-ending challenge that is so fascinating to all who love the restaurant business. It sounds easy, but ask those who know and you may get a different story. Don't forget to thank the crew for a great shift!

Some tips for restaurant managers are given by the Foodservice Where House. They cover a variety of management topics. Good managers do not appear overnight, and sometimes restaurant managers need instruction and practice in order to effectively run the business, supervise employees and satisfy customers. The following top-ten list suggests ways restaurant managers can improve their businesses:[3]

1. *Manage costs effectively:* To be successful, operators must efficiently and effectively manager food, beverage, labor and other costs.
2. *Increase sales:* Increasing sales is key to the success of an operation.
3. *Be consistent:* Be consistent in all aspects of food, beverage, and guest service.
4. *Deliver superior service:* Service, service, service, it's all about delighting the guest.
5. *Manage time wisely:* Timing is critical in the restaurant business so it is important to manage time by having a "game plan."
6. *Create a positive work environment:* Create a wonderful work environment and you will become the employer of choice.
7. *Motivate the team:* Find out what motivates your team—back and front of the house—and use incentives, bonuses, and competitions that team members think are rewarding. Praise employees whenever possible.
8. *Be a good example:* Be a role model for your associates to admire and respect.
9. *Discipline consistently:* Ensure that all employees know the policies and procedures. Be fair and consistent in dealing with inappropriate actions.
10. *Reward as often as possible:* Ensure that all employees are aware of the standards expected of them and reward as often as possible when an employee meets or exceeds standards.

Control

In the restaurant business, you first have to know how to steal the chicken before you can stop someone else from stealing the chicken. There is so much food and beverage in a restaurant that, unless management and owners exert tight control, losses will occur. If portion control is not used, you might as well put a few dollars on each plate as it goes out of the kitchen. "Control is like saying, how do you eat an elephant—you take a lot of little bites," says Stephen Ananicz, chief operating officer of the Childs restaurant group. Ananicz offers this advice: "Don't 'manage' to cut costs—manage to build revenue."[4] Buy the best product and use standardized recipes, and weigh and measure frequently. When checking in produce and dry goods, the worst thing you can do is to allow someone to sign for it or even to just look at the boxes. There might be rotten stuff packed at the bottom. Really check the expensive items to see that they are what you ordered—quantity, quality, and weight. So pull things out and check that you get what you're paying for. Don't over- or under-order—order a realistic expectation for the number of guests and the choices of menu items they are likely to make. Do a daily inventory of high-priced items like meats.

Restaurants can use programs like ChefTec, which shows the actual food cost compared with the ideal food cost. This is known as *food optimization*. It works like this: Take every item on the menu and cost it out by ingredients. At the end of the day, run a *product mix*, which tells how many items were sold; multiply each menu item by the number sold, and that will give you what food should have cost for the day. ChefTec will also cost, scale, and store recipes; write recipe procedures using cut and paste, customizable fonts, colors, and a culinary spellchecker; instantly analyze recipe/menu cost by portion and yield; attach photos, diagrams, videos, or company logos to recipes; print kitchen-readable recipes; calculate costs based on highest or most recent prices paid for ingredients; save recipes in HTML; and share data via the Internet.

For inventory control, ChefTec can preload an inventory list of 1,900 ingredients; import purchases from vendors' online ordering systems; track vendor pricing from purchasing bids; compare vendor pricing from purchases or bids; instantly see the impact of a price increase on recipes; automate ordering with user-set par levels; and generate customized reports detailing purchases, bids, and credits. Nutritional analysis is also a part of the program. ChefTec serve a vast cross-section of the foodservice industry including restaurants, hotels, caterers, motels, educators, and others. Today, ChefTec is the leader in recipe and menu costing, inventory control, purchasing, ordering, and nutritional analysis software.[5]

CALCULATING THE FOOD-COST PERCENTAGE

The *food-cost percentage* should be calculated at least monthly. The formula is

$$\text{Food-cost percentage} = (\text{Cost} \div \text{Sales}) \times 100$$

So, if an item cost $1 and sold for $4, the food-cost percentage would be $(1 \div 4) \times 100$, or $.25 \times 100 = 25$ percent.

But to calculate the food-cost percentage, first we need the cost of food sold. Let's use a hypothetical example.

Opening inventory	$500
+ Purchases	200
	700
− Complementary & staff meals & spoilage	50
− Closing inventory	400
= Cost of food sold	250

In our example, let's assume that sales are known to be $1,000. So here, ($250 ÷ $1,000) × 100 = .25 × 100 = a food-cost percentage of 25 percent.

All you have to do is remember is

$$\text{Cost} = \text{Opening inventory} + \text{Purchases} - \text{Spoilage} - \text{Employee meals} - \text{Closing inventory}$$

and

$$\text{Food-cost percentage} = (\text{Cost} \div \text{Sales}) \times 100$$

Taking the actual inventory can be a pain, but if the storeroom and coolers or refrigerators are clean and tidy and you have a list of all the items typed out or, better yet, entered into the computer or handheld device, it will be much easier and quicker to compute. In fact, if you keep inventory and expense information in an Excel spreadsheet (or restaurant software such as ChefTec), your computer can make these calculations for you. Make sure that the items are listed as they appear on the shelves. Experienced operators take spot inventories of expensive items and do a quick check on the number of sales of those particular items to see that there is no pilferage.

DETERMINING THE FOOD COST OF A PARTICULAR ITEM ON A MENU

Say a hamburger plate sells for $10.50 in your pub. The edible plate cost (EDC) for this item is $3.25. The plate cost includes everything that is served on the plate: bun, burger, tomato slice, lettuce, onion slice, and fries. What is your food-cost percentage?

The food-cost percentage is a simple division problem. Taking the plate cost (EDC) of $3.25 and dividing the menu price (MP) of $10.50 will give you a food-cost percentage (FC%) of 31 percent. Note that the following food-cost formulas are all the same formula:

$$FC\% = EDC \div MP$$

$$EDC = FC\% \times MP$$

$$MP = EDC \div FC\%$$

One of the challenges in obtaining a food-cost percentage is that you don't know the cost of particular food items months out. Clever chefs cost their dishes using the highest forecasted annual price—for example, on salmon, which fluctuates a lot in price—to compute all food costs for the year. That way they can achieve the goal of, say, a 28 percent food cost. This method allows for some price fluctuation and gives a slight buffer on plate costs when the price is below the highest.

Some restaurant operators give a bonus to all back-of-the-house employees if the food and labor costs and profit percentages are met. One operator does this quarterly, and line-level employees receive an extra $100 or more in their paychecks.

RECYCLING TO REDUCE COSTS

One form of control many restaurants overlook is recycling. At the end of the night at most restaurants, leftover food, paper, bottles, and cardboard typically are put in a dumpster in the back alley destined for a landfill. Separating garbage is dirty; it requires people and time to do it. But the fewer times the dumpster needs to be emptied, the less you will have to pay for trash pickup.[6] When the savings are considered, it is worth the effort—and besides, it does something good for the planet.

Recycling has become business as usual for 65 percent of restaurant operators. Approximately 74 percent of operators said they use a back-of-house recycling program, while 43 percent said they use a program in the front of the house.[7]

Some local governments offer monetary assistance for recycling. In addition, trash handlers may have service plans that include recycling and can cost $20 to $50 less per ton than conventional garbage pickup.[8]

Making small changes to a daily routine can help any restaurant. For example, a color-coded system for staff to get in the habit of recycling can result in thousands of dollars in savings a year.

Liquor Control

Liquor control is critical to the success of the restaurant. There is too much opportunity for abuse and theft. The cycle begins with management deciding which brands to have for the well or house, then setting a par stock of beverages to have on hand. Management also decides on the selling price and markup for beer, wine, and liquor. This will set the standard for the *beverage-cost percentage*. Once the standard is set, there is something to measure actual performance against. The normal pouring cost for beer is 24 to 25 percent. Thus, if a beer costs $1.10, it should sell for about $4.50. Now, the pricing level and markup is your choice. It could be that you want to sell domestic beer at $4.75 or $5.00. If it still costs $1.10, then the pouring cost percentage will go up and you will make more money. You will best know the price points for your guests.

Wine should have a pouring cost of 26 to 30 percent. So, for a 30 percent cost, if a bottle of wine cost $10, the selling price is $33.30. If you wanted a 33 percent pouring cost on wine, then the selling price would be $30 or, better yet, $29.99.

Liquor pouring costs should be 16 to 20 percent of sales. Thus, for a 20 percent pouring cost if a shot of premium Johnnie Walker Gold cost 83.33 cents, it would need to sell for $4.16, or a rounded figure. The size of the bottle and the measure poured will also influence the pouring cost percentage. For example, if the scotch comes in a quart bottle and you are using a 1.5-ounce measure, then you would expect to get 21 measures out of the bottle. Some bottles are liters and will need to be computed into US measures. Mixed drinks complicate things because they use a base liquor plus a small amount of two or three other liquors. Fortunately, the popular cocktails can be recorded in the point-of-sale (POS) system and costed out accordingly. The number of mixed drinks is recorded and the correct amount of liquor allocated to the cost of each drink is

Courtesy of Christian Hershman

Chef/Proprietor Christian Hershman managing the numbers.

charged, so that when the cost of beverages is calculated, it will include the correct amount.

Combined, the beverage pouring cost should be 23 to 25 percent of beverage sales. In order to obtain this pour-cost percentage, restaurant operators get to make their own rules on pouring. We will insist that all drinks are poured using the pour spout or a jigger—no free pouring—and nothing is served unless there is a check. Management needs to observe the bar, using a surveillance camera and spotters if necessary.

There are several software solutions available to aid in liquor control. Using a reliable bar inventory control software program will lower pour costs and raise bottom line profits. Bar Cop's liquor, wine, and beer inventory control software tracks bar inventory fast and accurately, which helps to keep profits where they belong.[9]

The beverage inventory must be secure at all times. The storage area must be kept locked, with only one key available to the manager. New bottles should be issued only when an old bottle is returned. All bottles should have an indelible stamp of the restaurant on them, and the liquor bottles must have the state tax stamp when sold by the wholesaler or distributor—it is a different color from the stamp on bottles sold in retail stores.

If one server steals one drink per shift, the revenue lost can exceed $3,000 per year.[10] The iBarControl solutions is the first Windows Mobile solution for hospitality inventory control. It allows two methods of counting partial items. It is the first product in hospitality to offer a Bluetooth wireless scale interface as well as a wireless scanner.[11] By quick and easy weighing of partial items, iBar assures accuracy for true inventory control. Real counts by real clients reveal that a 63-bottle back bar can be counted in as little as 8 minutes with the iBarControl system.[12]

Beverage inventory is usually done by "eyeball," measuring bottles of liquor in tenths. The amount is recorded either on a sheet or directly into a program on a computer or handheld. The total value of liquor is added and recorded. Wine and beer bottles are counted and priced. Then a total beverage inventory value is arrived at. This value is expressed as a percentage of beverage sales—not total sales. A formula similar to the food-cost percentage is used:

Opening inventory	$1,000	
− Plus purchases	500	
		1,500
− Less complementary & spillage	50	
− Less closing inventory	750	
		800
Cost of goods sold		700

If we assume beverage sales were $2,800, then the beverage-cost percentage would be 25 percent.

As with the food purchasing, have the bartender make out an order and turn in the empty liquor bottles when requesting new ones. A copy of the order should go to the person receiving the beverage delivery. (You should not rely on the delivery person's sheet but on your own order.) A manager must carefully check everything into the secure storeroom, and issues must be made only when a proper requisition is given in exchange for the bottles.

Figure 8.3 shows the projected food and beverage sales and costs, the actual sales and costs, and the variance for a volume restaurant. Notice how it is more

Optimum Costs				
	04/30/2014	05/31/2014	06/30/2014	07/31/2014
Restaurant 1				
Food				
Sales	253,943.77	254,048.06	197,163.00	240,348.79
Cost	70,624.89	70,848.51	56,608.45	68,858.42
%	27.81%	27.89%	28.71%	28.65%
Actual Sales	372,505.78	298,191.75	236,082.62	269,029.44
Actual Costs	113,267.63	97,768.77	76,762.95	87,325.46
Actual %	30.41%	32.79%	32.52%	32.46%
Variance	2.60%	4.90%	3.80%	3.81%
Liquor				
Sales	81,736.01	70,985.71	47,267.47	58,580.56
Cost	13,081.09	11,537.95	7,667.29	9,670.63
%	16.00%	16.25%	16.22%	16.51%
Actual Sales	83,531.47	69,673.86	49,798.18	61,300.67
Actual Costs	13,683.82	13,059.45	8,669.18	11,438.24
Actual %	16.38%	18.74%	17.41%	18.66%
Variance	0.38%	2.49%	1.19%	2.15%
Beer				
Sales	32,687.61	26,292.40	18,474.87	24,519.25
Cost	8,222.21	6,454.98	4,482.31	6,115.70
%	25.15%	24.55%	24.26%	24.94%
Actual Sales	33,373.99	26,963.20	20,221.85	24,975.13
Actual Costs	8,371.40	7,612.03	5,701.85	6,005.33
Actual %	25.08%	28.23%	28.20%	24.05%
Variance	−0.07%	3.68%	3.93%	−0.90%
Wine				
Sales	28,264.48	23,012.59	14,514.90	16,206.65
Cost	7,299.89	6,294.22	3,761.61	4,237.88
%	25.83%	27.35%	25.92%	26.15%
Actual Sales	28,982.50	23,279.45	16,569.78	16,741.21
Actual Costs	8,027.93	5,474.96	3,759.38	4,856.56
Actual %	27.70%	23.52%	22.69%	29.01%
Variance	1.87%	−3.83%	−3.23%	2.86%

FIGURE 8.3 Projected and actual food and beverage sales cost.

difficult to achieve the percentages when the sales drop as they did in August. Management skill is required to get the percentages in times of lower sales.

Controllable Expenses

The term *controllable expenses* is used to describe those expenses that can be changed in the short term. Variable costs are normally controllable. Other controllable costs include salaries and wages (payroll) and related benefits; direct operating expenses, such as music and entertainment; marketing (including sales, advertising, public relations, and promotions); heat, light, and power; administration; and general repairs and maintenance. The total of all controllable expenses is deducted from the gross profit. Rent and other occupation costs are then deducted to arrive at the income before interest, depreciation, and taxes. Once these are deducted, the net profit remains. Figure 8.4 is a sample income statement showing controllable expenses.

Given the thin profit margins, higher energy costs, and the desire to become more sustainable, restaurateurs are looking for ways to reduce their energy bills. "Most restaurants are energy-intensive facilities where significant energy-saving opportunities exist through wise operation and equipment selection."[13]

Among the energy audit options for saving power are:

- Reduce air conditioning and heating use during unoccupied hours by adjusting the thermostat.
- Use window shades to reduce air-conditioning needs.
- Turn off unneeded lights.
- Use more efficient lower-wattage or compact florescent bulbs.
- Regularly service and adjust the heating, air conditioning, cooking, ice making, and refrigeration equipment as needed.
- Turn off equipment that is not in use.
- Make sure automatic controls work correctly and are set appropriately.
- Lower water temperature settings.
- Use higher-efficiency outdoor lighting, with reflectors where possible.[14]

A number of states also offer incentives to improve energy efficiency. Visit the US Department of Energy (apps1.eere.energy.gov/states) for further details.

A restaurant's profit is typically only 3 to 9 percent of total revenue. EN-ERGY STAR claims that if you follow their cost-effective recommendations, your investment in energy efficiency can give you up to a 30 percent return.[15] For more information, visit the ENERGY STAR website (www.energystar.gov).

However, energy-monitoring systems probably aren't the best way for restaurants to demonstrate a long-term commitment to becoming more sustainable. More long-term options include biodegradable takeout packaging and the installation of solar panels. Energy-monitoring systems do offer immediate, measurable, and consistent energy savings and the opportunity to realize a return on investment within a year.[16]

	Statement Period				
	Projected Amount (Thousands)	Percentages	Actual Amount	Percentages	Variance
Sales					
Food (Schedule D-1)	750.0	75.0			
Beverage (Schedule D-2)	250.0	25.0			
Total sales	1,000.0	100.0			
Cost of Sales					
Food	232.5	31.0			
Beverage	55.0	22.0			
Total cost of sales	287.5	28.8			
Gross profit	712.5	71.2			
Other income (Schedule D-3)	4.5	0.5			
Total income	717.0	71.7			
Controllable Expenses					
Salaries and wages (Schedule D-4)	240.0	24.0			
Employee benefits (Schedule D-5)	140.0	4.0			
Direct operating expense (Schedule D-6)	60.0	6.0			
Music and entertainment (Schedule D-7)	10.0	1.0			
Marketing (Schedule D-8)	40.0	4.0			
Energy and utility (Schedule D-9)	30.0	3.0			
Administrative and general (Schedule D-10)	40.0	4.0			
Repairs and maintenance (Schedule D-11)	20.0	2.0			
Total controllable expenses	480.0	48.0			
Rent and other occupation costs (Schedule D-12)	50.0	5.0			
Income before interest, depreciation, and taxes	187.0	18.7			
Interest	15.0	1.5			
Depreciation	23.0	2.3			
Total	38.0	3.8			
Net income before taxes	149.0	14.9			
Income taxes	50.0	5.0			
Net Income	99.0	10.7			

*Telephone, insurance, accounting/legal office supplies; paper, china, glass, silvers, menus, landscaping, detergent/cleaning suppliers, and so on.
Source: Adapted from Raymond S. Schmidgall, *Hospitality Industry Managerial Accounting*, 2nd ed. (East Lansing, Mich.: Educational Institute of the American Hotel and Motel Association, 1990), 94.

FIGURE 8.4 Income statement showing projected and actual controllable expenses.

Labor Costs

In most full-service restaurants, the largest variable is *labor cost*. Depending on the type of restaurant and the degree of service provided, labor costs may range from approximately 16 percent of sales in a quick-service restaurant to 24 percent in a casual operation and up to about 30 percent in an upscale restaurant.

Projecting payroll costs requires the preparation of staffing schedules and establishing wage rates. Staffing patterns may vary during different periods of the year, with changes occurring seasonally or when there are other sales variations. These changes are identified and categorized on a schedule form used to project any single week's payroll activities and to compare them with guest count/sales projections.

Restaurant operators should make a budget at the beginning of the month, and break it down to a daily dollar amount, then to hours in the kitchen. Hosts and servers are likely to be at minimum wage, so it's the kitchen where it is important to keep control with an hourly wage of $9 to $14. Do a labor pro-forma—write out a schedule without names:

> 3 prep cooks
>
> 2 cooks
>
> 1 pantry
>
> 1 dishwasher
>
> Cost of labor = 7 hours × Average wage × Cost per shift

Software programs can give a cost of labor, but you can also work it out. A rule of thumb is 9.2 percent for front-of-the-house labor costs as a percentage of sales and 13 percent for back-of-the-house costs. Front-of-the-house staff planning goes like this: If you have 25 tables and want 4 table sections, then 4 × 6 = 24, so you need 6 servers to cover the tables every night.

If you are open seven days a week and each server works a four-day workweek, you can calculate how many total shifts/week, or how many servers, are needed to cover every shift. The math looks like this:

$$7 \text{ days/week} \times 6 \text{ servers/day} = 42 \text{ servers/week, or } 42 \text{ shifts}$$

$$42 \text{ shifts} \div 4 \text{ shifts/week} = 10.5 \text{ shifts/week}$$

You can't hire half a person, but you can hire one person part time, so 0.5 shifts/week is acceptable. But this is based on 25 tables, and they had better be filled! Otherwise, the servers will be standing around. If you know that you will not be using all 25 tables, then downsize the staffing level accordingly. Don't forget the busers: You need three or four per busy shift; fewer on quieter ones.

In the bar, depending on the volume of business, if you are open for lunch and are busy, you need one bartender and one or two at night. It's a good idea to cross-train a couple of servers to assist in the bar if necessary and to cover days off. The host desk also needs to be covered for each shift. Calculating for lunch and dinner seven days a week and including days off, that can mean three or four people. In all areas, certified trainers will help new servers and other workers get up to speed. These trainers receive additional compensation for their efforts. Training definitely helps reduce labor turnover. A form like Figure 8.5 can be used both for projecting expected payroll amounts for any future period and for comparing these projections at a later time for cost-control purposes.

| JOB TITLE | RATE | HOURS PLANNED | | | | | | | WEEKLY TOTAL | | SUMMARY | |
		SAT.	SUN.	MON.	TUES.	WED.	THURS.	FRI.	HOURS	AMOUNT		
											PROJECTED SALES	
											ESTIMATED PAYROLL	
											PAYROLL RELATED	
											TOTAL PAYROLL	
											% TO SALES	
											DATE PREPARED	
											PREPARED BY	
TOTAL HOURS												
PROJ. CUST. COUNT											APPROVAL	
PROJ. CHECK AVER.												
ESTIMATED SALES		$	$	$	$	$	$	$	$			

UNIT NAME   UNIT NUMBER

FIGURE 8.5 Form for projecting expected payroll amounts.

In some cases, it may be desirable to complete this effort for each of the 52 weeks in the coming year. More often, some standardizing can accommodate expected variations, and three or four standard weeks can be established and used as a basis for shorter calculations. (Many weeks develop a pattern and can be duplicated.) The more accurate the breakdown, the more precise the result. Figure 8.6 illustrates a summary of expected staffing and resulting payroll costs, utilizing a breakdown into four categories of restaurant staffing: management and administration, production, service and cashiers, and sanitation. The breakdown allows for planning by activity as well as for control of both employee hours and payroll dollars.

Payroll and related costs fall into two categories: variable (percentage ratio to payroll) and fixed (dollar amount per employee on the payroll). Variable items include those mandated by law: Social Security (FICA), unemployment insurance (state and federal), workers' compensation insurance, and state disability insurance. The fixed items usually refer to employee benefits and include health insurance (an amount per employee per month), union welfare insurance (also an amount per employee per month), life insurance, and other employee benefits.

Employee meals can be treated as payroll costs or as part of food cost and wages. It is more common to find employee meals treated as food cost for a restaurant operation. Operators need to establish a value for employee meals; the IRS treats them as a nontaxable benefit.

 Wendy's, in one cost-cutting mode, trimmed unit payrolls by 30 hours per week. This was achieved by finding a different way to pan meat and by weighing cash on scales so no one has to count it. Another labor-saving method is using a Jacuzzi-like power washer to scrub pots, pans, and condiment pumps.

The average check for lunch is $9 and dinner $16

I. Management and Administration

1	General Manager	$50,000 + Bonus
2	Assistant Managers (open & close)	48,000
1	Office Clerical	20,000
		118,000

II. Production

1	Kitchen Manager		35,000 + Bonus
7	Line Cooks	@ Avg. 9.50 per hour	138,320
3	Dishwashers	@ 6.00 per hour	37,440
4	Prep Cooks	@ 7.00 per hour	58,240
			$269,000

III. Service

3	Hosts @ 6.00 per hour	37,440
20	Servers and Busers @ 6.00 per hour	249,600
3	Bartenders @ 6.00 per hour	37,440
3	Cashiers @ 6.00 per hour	37,440
		$360,920

IV. 1	Sanitation @ 6.25	$13,000

Recapitulation

I	Management and Administration	118,000
II	Production	269,000
III	Service	360,920
IV	Sanitation	13,000
	TOTAL	$760,920

FIGURE 8.6 Projected payroll costs for a hypothetical casual restaurant with sales volume of $2.7 million.

When determining the number of staff to schedule for a restaurant, take the number of seats and decide how many tables/seats to give each server. Take expected sales into account—on a Monday lunch, sales may be $3,000, but on a Friday, $6,800. So, obviously, more staff are needed for Friday. In the kitchen, the various stations need to be covered: pantry; boxes (stoves, convection ovens, and steamers, so named because they look like boxes); grill/sauté; fryer/breader; wheel person; expediter; and dishwasher. In the volume restaurant described here, everyone must pull together—if one section gets behind, everyone is in trouble. The wheel person has to really have it together. Although this person might never cook a thing, he or she must coordinate the food coming from all the stations and double check that plates are correct by the order. It is easier when the order goes from the servers' POS directly to each station—this saves someone having to bark out the orders at the *pass* (a term for the hot plate area where plated items are passed to the food servers). Figure 8.7 shows an actual versus projected payroll for a week. Notice the projected and actual sales and projected and actual costs for back and front of the house as well as the total per day and week to date.

One successful restaurant has begun a manager's bonus for each of its four restaurants. The managing partner and four managers are each eligible for a monthly $1,000 bonus, based on meeting or exceeding performance goals. Figure 8.8 shows the cost-of-goods-sold (COGS) bonus scale expressed for three different sales volume levels. In the month of August, the total cost of goods sold came to 56.60 percent and sales were $36,612, so no bonuses were given.

If we look at the right-hand column, we can see at the bottom of that column + 56.5% = $0. If the COGS had been, say, 56.5 percent, then each manager

Payroll: Actual vs Projected
Week of May 26–June 01, 2014

	23 MON	24 TUE	25 WED	26 THUR	27 FRI	28 SAT	29 SUN
Projected Sales	$3,000	$4,500	$4,600	$4,600	$6,800	$5,400	$5,200
WTD Projected Sales		$7,500	$12,100	$16,700	$23,500	$28,900	$34,100
Actual Sales	$3,673	$4,307	$3,773	$5,148	$6,851	$5,103	$4,527
WTD Actual Sales		$7,980	$11,753	$16,901	$23,752	$28,855	$33,382
Daily + or − %	22.44%	−4.29%	−17.98%	11.91%	0.75%	−5.49%	−12.94%
Actual vs Projected Sales	$673	($193)	($827)	$548	$51	($297)	($673)
WTD + or −		$480	($347)	$201	$252	($45)	($718)
Weekly + or − %	22.44%	6.40%	−2.87%	1.20%	1.07%	−0.16%	−2.11%
BOH							
Projected BOH Labor	$398	$440	$470	$467	$640	$561	$515
WTD Projected BOH		$838	$1,308	$1,775	$2,415	$2,976	$3,491
Actual BOH Labor	$438	$492	$446	$460	$616	$503	$474
Daily BOH Labor %age	11.93%	11.42%	11.82%	8.94%	8.99%	9.85%	10.46%
WTD Actual BOH		$930	$1,376	$1,837	$2,453	$2,956	$3,429
Daily + or − %	10.14%	11.80%	−5.11%	−1.44%	−3.73%	−10.35%	−8.05%
Actual vs Projected BOH	$40	$52	($24)	($7)	($24)	($58)	($41)
WTD + or −		$92	$68	$62	$38	($20)	($62)
WTD BOH Labor Percentage		11.66%	11.71%	10.87%	10.33%	10.24%	10.27%
FOH							
Projected FOH Labor	$246	$248	$284	$275	$458	$310	$307
WTD Projected FOH		$494	$778	$1,053	$1,511	$1,821	$2,128
Actual FOH Labor	$291	$312	$283	$275	$380	$309	$316
Daily FOH Labor Percentage	7.92%	7.25%	7.50%	5.35%	5.55%	6.05%	6.99%
WTD Actual FOH		$603	$886	$1,161	$1,542	$1,850	$2,167
Daily + or − Percentage	18.18%	25.85%	−0.34%	0.18%	−16.96%	−0.42%	3.08%
Actual vs Projected FOH	$45	$64	($1)	$0	($78)	($1)	$9
WTD + or −		$109	$108	$108	$31	$29	$39
WTD FOH Labor Percentage		7.55%	7.54%	6.87%	6.49%	6.41%	6.49%
Total Labor							
Total Projected Labor	$644	$688	$754	$742	$1,098	$871	$822
WTD Projected Labor		$1,332	$2,086	$2,828	$3,926	$4,797	$5,619
Actual Total Labor	$729	$804	$729	$736	$996	$812	$790
WTD Actual Labor		$1,533	$2,262	$2,998	$3,994	$4,806	$5,596
Actual vs Projected Total	$85	$116	($25)	($6)	($102)	($59)	($32)
WTD + or −		$201	$176	$170	$68	$9	($23)
Projected %	21.47%	15.29%	16.39%	16.13%	16.15%	16.13%	15.81%
WTD Projected %		17.76%	17.24%	16.93%	16.71%	16.60%	16.48%
Actual %	19.85%	18.67%	19.32%	14.29%	14.55%	15.90%	17.45%
WTD Actual %		19.21%	19.25%	17.74%	16.82%	16.66%	16.76%

FIGURE 8.7 Payroll: actual versus projected.

MANAGERS' BONUS AUGUST 2008				JULY 28–AUG 24, 2011

COGS Bonus Scale

Volume +55,000 per week		Volume 40–55,000 per week		Volume <40,000 per week	
<50.0%	$1,000	<51.0%	$1,000	<52.5%	$1,000
<51.0%	$750	<52.0%	$750	<53.5%	$750
<52.0%	$500	<53.0%	$500	<54.5%	$500
<53.0%	$250	<54.0%	$250	<55.5%	$250
<54.0%	$100	<55.0%	$100	<56.5%	$100
+54%	$0	+55%	$0	+56.5%	$0

2009 Total Volume	$146,448.00	Wkly Avg	$36,612.00
2009 Food Volume	$127,409.76	87.00%	
2009 Bev Volume	$18,306.00	12.50%	
2009 Retail Volume	$732.24	0.50%	
Food Purchases	$52,714.00	41.37%	36.00%
Supplies	$0.00	0.00%	0.00%

Total Food Purchases	$52,714.00	41.37%	36.00%

Bar Purchases	$5,190.00	28.35%	3.54%

Total Purchases	$57,904.00	39.54%	39.54%

Labor	$24,987.00		17.06%

Total Cost of Goods S	$82,891.00		56.60%

Total Bonus: $0.00

Bonuses Paid

John	$0.00	DJ	$0.00
Fred	$0.00	Jenn	$0.00
Gary	$0.00	Shawn	$0.00
		Sean	$0.00

Total	$0.00

Date Paid

Authorized

FIGURE 8.8 Managers' bonus. Unfortunately, no one received a bonus this month.

would have received $100. In this restaurant's case, discussion is taking place about whether to include training in the labor costs. This seasonal restaurant has a more transient labor market than others, so staff turnover is an issue. Of course, it can be argued that management/leadership should minimize labor turnover. What do you think?

Guest Check Control

If not controlled, guest checks are like blank checks that the operator has already signed. Without check control, a server can give food and beverages away or sell them and keep the income.

Without guest check audits, the checks can be padded in favor of the server or the guest. Numbered guest checks are issued to servers. Each check must be accounted for and at least a spot check of the additions and correct prices made.

If guest checks are not strictly accounted for, servers face a great temptation. The server may bring in his or her own checks, present them to the guest, and pocket the payment. Guest checks can be altered and substitutions made if the checks are not numbered. To avoid such temptations, most restaurants require that the server sign for checks as received and return those not used at the end of the shift.

Checks can be issued by the book, 150 to a book. For tight control, every guest check is audited, addition is checked, and every check is accounted for by number. Guest check auditing may be done in a central office in the case of a restaurant chain, or in someone's home for an independent restaurant. Most restaurants use the duplicate-check system to maintain tight control. The second copy of the check is handed to the cook in return for the food. No check, no food. Every food item is recorded on a guest check, even a cup of coffee.

Some operators control restaurant income by having servers act as their own cashiers. Servers are, in effect, set up in business for themselves. They bring their own banks of $50 in change; they do not operate from a cash register but out of their own pockets; they deposit their income in a night box at the bank.

No food can be taken from the kitchen or liquor from the bar without being "paid for" by a duplicate check. If, indeed, no food is issued from the kitchen to anyone without the duplicate check, the checks provide an adequate record of sales. Much more responsibility is placed on the server. This system does not require a cashier, but the servers must be able to add and subtract and perform the same functions as the cashier.

A bookkeeper totals all of the checks of each server, and this amount is compared with the amount deposited to the restaurant account by the server at the end of the shift. It is often said that being a server is like being in business for oneself. This plan carries the analogy one step further.

One restaurant that we stumbled on in London may have the answer: The servers have to pay the cooks *cash* for each dish they take out of the kitchen. Now that's an interesting twist!

Few restaurants employ a full-time bookkeeper, especially one on the premises. Restaurant Adventures, a small chain of restaurants in California, has a different idea.[17] Each of these restaurants grosses more than $1 million in sales annually and each has an owner do the books to save money in the afternoon to save money. The day's business is completely recorded and analyzed by dinner time, including labor, food, and other percentage ratios. The smaller restaurant is likely to employ a part-time person in his or her home who does the restaurant bookkeeping on a day-by-day basis. An accounting firm is employed to prepare monthly statements and help with income taxes. Chain operations ordinarily do most of the bookkeeping and operating analysis at the home office. Recordkeeping at the unit level is minimal.

Streamlining was attained by reducing the average time for drive-through service from 160 to 100 seconds. That jump in efficiency enabled operators to crank another 30 to 40 cars through the line at peak periods. Window sales increased from 56 to 63 percent of sales.

Productivity Analysis and Cost Control

Various measures of productivity have been developed: meals produced per employee per day, meals produced per employee per hour, guests served per waitperson per shift, labor costs per meal based on sales. Probably the simplest employee productivity measure is sales generated per employee per year (divide the number of full-time equivalent employees into the gross sales for the year). An easy and meaningful measure is to divide the number of employees into income per hour. Some restaurants achieve a $70 per hour productivity rate. When labor costs get out of line, the manager can analyze costs per shift or even productivity per hour to pinpoint the problem.

Without knowing what each expense item should be as a ratio of gross sales, the manager is at a distinct disadvantage. He or she should know, for example, that utilities ordinarily do not run more than 4 percent of sales in most restaurants, that the cost of beverages for a dinner house ordinarily should not exceed 25 percent of sales and could be much less, and that occupancy cost should not exceed 8 percent of gross sales in most cases. Operating ratios must be in terms of what is appropriate for a particular style of restaurant: coffee shop, fast-food place, or dinner house (see Figure 8.9).

Sales	100%
Cost of sales	33.0%– 43.0%
Gross profit	57.0%– 67.0%
Operating expenses	
Controllable Expenses	
Payroll (including manager)	23.0%– 33.0%
Employee Benefits	13.0%– 5.0%1
Direct operating expenses	13.5%– 9.0%1
Music and entertainment	10.1%– 1.3%1
Advertising and promotion	10.8%– 3.0%1
Utilities	13.0%– 5.0%1
Administrative and general	13.0%– 6.0%1
Repairs and maintenance	11.0%– 2.0%1
Occupation Expenses	
Rent, property tax, and insurance	16.0%– 11.0%
Interest	10.3%– 1.0%1
Franchise royalties (if any)	13.0%– 7.0%1
Income before depreciation	12.0%– 19.0%
Depreciation	10.7%– 5.0%1
Net profit before income tax	15.0%– 15.0%

Source: Figures were developed by the Small Business Reporter *in California*

FIGURE 8.9 Operating ratios

Moreover, the ratios must be appropriate for the region. Restaurant labor costs, for example, are usually low in the South as compared to the North.

Summary

Restaurant operations are divided into front and back of the house. The chef, to make a production schedule for the day based on the par levels required, the volume of business expected, and the estimated guest menu selection, uses standardized recipes. The chef monitors production and checks dishes as they leave the kitchen. Either the chef or a manager is at the pass to ensure a smooth expedition of all plates.

In the front of the house are an opening and a closing manager. The opening manager checks on the expected level of business—based on the prior year's business, the day's weather, and any other relevant factors. Stations are assigned to servers and a service meeting is held to inform everyone of the specials and any training detail to focus on. Then they have a meal followed by action stations. The manager and servers ensure that the service goes well and that guests are delighted.

Control of food and beverage items is critical to the overall success of the restaurant. Inventory taking and the calculation of food- and beverage-cost percentages are described. Controllable expenses are discussed and examples are given for controlling using income statements. Labor is the largest controllable cost, and examples are given to plan and monitor labor costs. Productivity analysis, operating ratios, and seat turnover are also discussed.

Key Terms and Concepts

Back of the house	Key result area
Beverage-cost percentage	Labor cost
Controllable expenses	Liquor control
Food-cost percentage	Operating ratios
Front of the house	Pass
Guest count	Production sheet

Review Questions

1. Detail how back- and front-of-the-house restaurant operations will be in your restaurant.
2. Describe your food control system.
3. Outline your beverage control system.
4. How do you control restaurant labor costs?
5. What are the ratios for your restaurant?

CASE STUDY: Big Shanty Smokehouse

The Family Business

Big Shanty Smokehouse is a family-owned and -operated barbecue restaurant in Kennesaw, Georgia. The restaurant was opened in February of 2008 by Chic Dillard, his wife, Sissy, and their daughter, Shannon. After working in the restaurant industry for so many years, Chic decided that he wanted to start his own restaurant in 2007. At the time, all members of the Dillard family were working in different restaurants, and the family wanted to do something together. One day, on the way home from playing golf with his son in Kennesaw, Chic passed a "For Sale" sign in the window of a small shack, and felt that the building called to him. The Dillards felt that the building looked like a little barbecue smokehouse and the location called for a barbecue concept. The name "Big Shanty Smokehouse" was coined as a way for the Dillards to make the restaurant a part of the history of Kennesaw, as the city was known as "Big Shanty" before the Civil War.

Why Barbecue?

The Dillards did not have any previous experience with barbecue restaurants before opening Big Shanty Smokehouse; however, they felt that barbecue is like any type of cuisine in that if you stick to the basics and let the food stand on its own, you are more likely to succeed in making a great product. When the restaurant opened, the menu was simple and featured only three smoked meat options: chicken, pork, and ribs, along with three side options: potato salad, baked beans, and cole slaw. They use smoke to flavor the meat, and they only lightly sauce and spice the meats before serving, because they feel the meat has enough flavor to stand on its own.

Over time, the menu has been further developed, and additional items have been added. The integration of a catering service has allowed the restaurant to bring in different items to run as specials that you might not expect to see at a typical barbecue restaurant, such as prime rib and barbecue tacos.

Food, People, and Community

The Dillard's philosophy for success combines attention to detail, the level of service provided, and a commitment to quality. The Dillards believe that it is important to develop a good rapport with their customers and to provide them with exceptional service at all times. Their customers are very diverse, ranging from residents of country club communities to the trailer park down the street. They serve many families, elderly customers, business lunch-goers, and entire Little League teams during baseball season. When customers come into the restaurant with a question, they're going to get someone who has all the answers to their questions.

Big Shanty Smokehouse relies on the lunch and dinner rush to propel annual revenue. It offers "family-style" group meal packages catered to family's on-the-go who want a quick fix that is much tastier and healthier than the typical fast-food meal. Part of the reason service is so efficient is because the current employees have been there for such an extended period of time; they know what they are doing and they take pride in their job. With that in mind, one of the biggest challenges that the Dillards face is bringing in new people and training them to interact with customers and to service them at a level that is up to speed with the more veteran employees and the Dillards themselves.

The Biggest Challenges

There are also challenges that are out of the Dillards' control, such as when the price of pork or beef raises several cents per pound. This presents a challenge because the Dillards want to keep their prices down in order to maintain customer satisfaction and demand, but they don't want to sell themselves short, either. One way the Dillards offset this dilemma is to minimize wasted product by using all available product in some way. For instance, they make their own sausage with the trimmings from ribs and brisket, and they sell chicken wings separately from the whole smoked chicken that is used as pulled meat on the menu.

Big Shanty Smokehouse opened for business in February of 2008, just two months before the economy crashed. In the first year of operation, the restaurant struggled to manage enough cash flow to keep the business up and running. However, eventually it began experiencing enough demand necessary to exist comfortably. In the four years that Big Shanty Smokehouse has been open, there has been a 30 percent increase in sales each year. In October 2011, the restaurant cut back from being open 6 days a week to only 5 days, but the restaurant continues to increase revenue. The future goal for the Dillards is to maximize all that they can out of the current location through expansion of the property to create additional seating, along with maximizing the potential of their catering services.

QUESTIONS

1. How can the Dillards control their rising food costs?
2. How much does the economy play into the success or failure of a starting restaurant business?
3. Is Big Shanty's "barbecue" concept more or less risky that other possible concepts considering their geographics, demographics, product offered, and customer behavior?
4. What makes a restaurant successful?
   a. What control factors play into the overall success of a restaurant venture?
   b. Why do you think this particular restaurant succeeded?
5. What are some additional things the restaurant could offer to increase its efficiency and generate additional revenue?

Endnotes

1. Sam Harrison, "Great Service Moves Forward," *Caterer & Hotelkeeper,* 199, (4582), (June 19–June 25, 2009), p. 19. ABI/Inform Trade and Industry. Retrieved October, 2009.
2. Red Book Solutions. http://www.bettermanagers.com/Retrieved on May 13, 2013.
3. Monica Parpal, "Top 10 Restaurant Management Tips," Restaurant Equipment and Supplies, http://www.foodservicewarehouse.com/restaurant-equipment-supply-marketing-articles/restaurant-management-and-operations/top-10-restaurant-management-tips/c28052.aspx. Retrieved on November 14, 2012.
4. Personal conversation with Stephen Ananicz, chief operating officer of the Childs restaurant group January, 12, 1013.
5. Culinary Software Services. ChefTec. www.culinarysoftware.com/css-home.htm. Retrieved on November 16, 2012.
6. Monica Parpal, "Benefits of Recycling in the Commercial Kitchen," Restaurant Equipment and Supplies, http://www.foodservicewarehouse.com/restaurant-equipment-supply-marketing-articles/going-green/benefits-of-recycling-in-the-commercial-kitchen/c28135.aspx retrieved on May 13, 2013.
7. "Recycling and Waste Reduction," National Restaurant Association, http://www.restaurant.org/Industry-Impact/Conservation/Recycling. Retrieved on May 13, 2013.
8. Parpal, "Benefits of Recycling."
9. Bar Cop Inc., www.barcop.com. Retrieved on November 17, 2012.
10. http://www.barkeepapp.com/index.html. Retrieved on May 13, 1013.
11. Ibid
12. Ibid.
13. "Energy Efficient Fact Sheet." Energy Ideas Clearing House. www.energyideas.org/documents/factsheets/03_022_Rest_Tips_fct.pdf. October 2009.
14. RH Staff, "Ten Tips to Tame Your Energy Tab." Restaurant Hospitality, October 1, 2006), http://restaurant-hospitality.com/observer/rh_imp_14817/. Retrieved October 2009.
15. Energy Star, "ENERGY STAR for Restaurants." www.energystar.gov/index.cfm?c=small_business.sb_restaurants. Retrieved October 2009.
16. Christine LaFave, "Control Freaks," *Restaurants & Institutions,* 119 (6), (June 1, 2009), p. 49. ABI/Inform Trade and Industry. Retrieved October 2009.
17. Personal conversation with Samantha Williams Restaurant Adventures. May 13, 2013.

Food Production
and Sanitation

LEARNING OBJECTIVES

After reading and studying this chapter, you should be able to:

- Discuss America's culinary heritage.

- Explain the main elements in receiving and storing perishable and nonperishable items.

- Describe the key points in food production.

- Discuss the various types of food poisoning and how to avoid them.

- Develop and maintain a food protection system.

Courtesy of Sysco

Our Culinary Heritage

Before we delve into food production, let's first get a taste of our *culinary heritage* because it brought us to where we are today and brings hope of a bright tomorrow.

For many, the background information of the kind given in this chapter provides depth and feeling. American cooking is formed on a matrix of national cuisines, the confluence of foods and food preparation methods from numerous national and racial groups. The early American colonists brought from England the love of beef and lamb. Once they arrived in the New World, the colonials quickly adapted to Indian corn; in fact, it became a staple food for a number of years. Later successive streams of immigrants—Irish, Scots, Germans, and Scandinavians—added their own foods and methods of preparation. Potatoes, originally from the Inca Empire in South America, became a staple brought to this country via Europe.

As wheat and other grains became plentiful, bread formed a part of every meal. Many Americans grew up on meat and potatoes, bread, and milk. Meat and bread as sandwiches, milk in milkshakes, and potatoes in french fries dominate today's fast-food restaurant menu.

Roast beef and steak are the basics of the beef and steakhouse restaurants. The Midwest and South have their favorite barbecued beef and pork emporia. The meat, potatoes, and bread syndrome is the despair of fancy food writers, yet these foods are highly nutritious and obviously satisfying to the American public.

Later came the Italians with their cheeses and pasta dishes. Italian restaurants have spread across the country, and pizzerias can be found in almost every community.

When Chinese laborers were brought in to help build the railroads and work in the West, they brought their own cookery techniques and food combinations.

Coffee shops have their sources in Vienna and in the seventeenth-century coffeehouses of England and France.

The family restaurant might trace its beginnings to the "ordinary," the boardinghouse style of food service found in the taverns of Britain and early America.

For the more complicated, subtle dining experience, we look to the French.

Mexicans, and before them the Spanish, provided the backdrop for today's Mexican restaurant. More recently, specialized foods from the Orient—India, Thailand, Korea, and Japan—have appeared in specialty restaurants.

Whenever there are Jewish communities, there are the Jewish ethnic foods and deli restaurants.

The menus are the common denominator of restaurants; they offer foods that originated from around the world prepared by methods that are an amalgam of various cookery styles, sharpened by food science, other restaurants, and the food section of the daily newspaper. All cuisines are worthy of study, but this book is about restaurants so we will focus on only a few, less understood yet influential cuisines.

Native American Influence

Native Americans have had a lasting, yet sometimes overlooked, influence on American cuisine today. Foods like cornbread, turkey, cranberry, blueberry, hominy, grits, and mush were adopted into the cuisine of the United States from Native American groups.[1]

Early American Indians residing in the Eastern Woodlands (now the eastern United States and Canada) planted crops of corn, beans, and squash. These crops are today commonly referred to as the "three sisters." Native Americans residing in the South formed the foundation of today's Southern cuisine. They made use of corn crops by grinding it into meals or by liming it with an alkaline salt to make hominy (i.e., masa). Potatoes were often used in similar ways to corn.

Native Americans diets included several fruits and vegetables. Pumpkin, various types of beans, squash, peppers, blackberries, raspberries, and tomatoes were all introduced to settlers through Native Americans. Diets were also supplemented through hunting game. Meat staples included venison, rabbit, squirrels, and raccoons.

African American Influence

Soul food is a term used for an ethnic cuisine, food traditionally prepared and eaten by African Americans of the Southern United States.[2] Although the term *soul food* only dates back to the 1960s, the selection of food can be trace back to Africa. In the early 1600s, the first Africans were brought to America to work as slaves. Many Africans brought fruits and vegetables with them to eat on their journey. The seeds of these fruits and vegetables would have a lasting influence on American cuisine. They include seeds from foods such as watermelon, okra, black-eyed peas, and eggplant.

At this point in time there were no refrigerators. Meat was smoked in a smokehouse to prevent spoilage. When it was time to prepare the meat for eating it was barbecued, roasted, boiled, or combined with other ingredients to make stews. To prepare birds they would use methods such as frying, baking, roasting, or simmering (to make broths, stews, and/or gravy). Vegetables were generally boiled or fried. Meals were cooked in open fires using black kettles or were barbecued in open pits.[3] Notable influential African American dishes include cornbread, greens, gumbo with okra, red beans and rice, southern-style black-eyed peas, sweet potato pie, and fruit cobbler.[4]

Italian Influence

Say "Italian food" and we think of spaghetti and pizza, but Italy has a rich culinary tradition and offers a variety of foods. Historically, Italians cultivated fine cuisine long before the French. In the ancient period, wealthy Romans spent lavish amounts of time and money on food and drink.

The Italian and French influences have much in common, for it was from Italy that much of the French fascination with food came originally. In the sixteenth century, when Florence led the Renaissance, a little girl of 14, Catherine de' Medici, went to France in 1533 to become the bride of Henri, Duke of Orleans, the second son of King Francis I of France. With her came a couple of her cooks, chefs who were particularly well informed about the preparation of sweets; Catherine was particularly fond of gelato, a water ice.

The Medici fortune had been built in part on the spice trade, largely salt, pepper, saffron, ginger, nutmeg, and cloves. Catherine brought some of the Italian art of cookery with her, along with an interest in olive oil, oranges, sugar, artichokes, broccoli, beans, and the tiny new peas, which the French later called *petits pois*. Rice had been brought in from the Orient, and Catherine ate it regularly as a child in the form of risotto.

Crusaders had brought spinach to France. Even today, the word *Florentine* in a dish means that it probably contains spinach in some form. Truffles came along from Italy, as did a taste for songbirds, a liking for sweetbreads, and the wine custard known as *zabaglione* in Italian, which in France became *sabayon*. Keynotes of Florentine cooking were sauces and simplicity. The aromatic herb basil was an Italian import.

In the eighteenth century, an Italian by the name of Procopio opened an ice cream parlor in Paris serving liqueurs, pastries, cakes, and delicate water ices.[5]

French Influence

The lexicon of cookery reflects the contribution of the French to the culinary scene: dishes developed by the French and terms referring to styles of food preparation, presentation, and service. We blanch, fricassee, and poach, all terms of French origin. Foods are prepared with almonds (*almandine*) and on a skewer (*en brochette*), terms that are commonly used. When it comes to classic culinary terms, the vast majority are straight from the kitchens of France.

Most foodservice experts rank French cookery near or at the top of various national cuisines. Menus of luxury restaurants in US hotels and restaurants reflect the French concern for subtlety of flavor through sauces, the use of butter and cream, the emphasis on quality of food, and appetizing combinations of food. Perhaps more than other national groups, the French have long been concerned with the nuances and complexities of food. Much of the ingenuity of the French chef appears in various classical dishes that have been adopted by the Western culinary world.

Common French sauces found in luxury restaurants include hollandaise (emulsified egg yolks and butter with lemon juice or white wine and pepper), béarnaise (similar to hollandaise plus tarragon, shallots, and chervil), and meunière (hot butter and lemon juice). Veal Cordon Bleu (veal, ham, and cheese) is a common veal dish. Tournedos Rossini (filet of beef plus a slice of pâté de foie gras) and bouillabaisse (a stewlike soup containing several fish and shellfish) are typically French.

The French have heavily influenced the style of foods and even their shape in dinner restaurants: potatoes duchesse (mashed and mixed with egg yolk, salt, and pepper); potatoes Anna (cylindrically sliced and cooked in layers of clarified butter); potatoes Parisienne (cut into small balls); and potatoes château (barrel-shaped and roasted). Quiche has been popularized in some chain restaurants. Quiche Lorraine, a thin-crusted pastry flan stuffed with bacon, chopped ham, egg yolk, milk, or cream is widely served.

FRENCH CHEFS DOMINATE CULINARY HISTORY

Of all of the hundreds of thousands of cooks in history, only a few are recorded. Nearly all of them are French. In 1671 Vatel, maitre d'hotel to the Prince de Conde, gained dubious distinction by committing suicide when the fish failed to arrive for an important banquet. The prince had invited King Louis XIV and an entourage of several hundred for a spring hunting weekend at Chantilly Castle. When the fish failed to arrive, Vatel stabbed himself three times.

François Pierre de La Varenne became well-known because of his cookbook, *Le Cuisinier François* (1651). La Varenne disapproved of heavy masking sauces for meat, preferring au jus mixed with lemon or vinegar and thickened when necessary with a roux or egg yolks. It was he who invented sauce duxelles, the popular mince of mushrooms, shallots, and onions seasoned and simmered in butter and oil until almost black. Unfortunately for La Varenne, the mixture was named after his master, the Marquis de'Uxelles.

The name Carême signifies classic cuisine. Antoine Carême, not one to hide his light under a chef's hat, stated that his goal was to "present sumptuously the culinary marvels with which I enriched the tables of kings."[6] He did, in fact, work for royalty, including for a short time the Prince Regent of England, where for one banquet in 1817, Carême prepared 116 dishes. Carême was much impressed with set pieces, the centers of attention of the classical style of dining. These pieces sometimes took on architectural quality in the form of fish aspics, poultry galantines, and baskets of fruit, creations in spun sugar. A Carême dessert we all remember is Charlotte Russe, a concoction of lady fingers, Bavarian pudding, and whipped cream. Carême died in 1833 at just 48 years old.

Felix Urbain-DuBois, chef of the King of Prussia, is chiefly remembered for his book *La Cuisine Classique*.

In modern times, the chef whose name every gastronome knows is Georges Auguste Escoffier, whose happy association with César Ritz and the fact that he was a capable organizer and author have emblazoned his name in gastronomic history. Of great social importance for Escoffier was his friend and sponsor, Edward Albert, Prince of Wales and later King Edward VII.

Perhaps the most inventive of chefs, Escoffier enjoyed beautiful women and the invention of dishes to which he attached their names. A few of these are still popular: Riz à l'Imperatrice (named for the Empress Eugénie); Peaches Alexandra (for the wife of the Prince of Wales); Peaches Melba (for his friend Dame Melba, the famous Australian opera star).

Part of the reason we eat frog's legs today may be traced to Escoffier and the Prince of Wales. Asked by the prince to prepare an intimate theater supper, Escoffier put together a dish that he called Les Cuisses de Nymphes à la Aurore (the thighs of nymphs at dawn). The next morning, Marlborough House, the royal residence, called to ask for the recipe, only to learn that the party had eaten frog's legs in a paprika-shaded wine sauce to resemble the dawn. The sprigs of tarragon suggested seaweed.

The English, never known for culinary adventurousness, had never eaten frog, but since the prince liked them, the snobs of London were soon calling for them. (It took longer for America to come around to frog's legs. As late as World War I, the American doughboys in France called the French the derisive term *Frogs*.)

Escoffier's book, *Le Guide Culinaire*, or as it appeared in this country, *The Escoffier Cookbook*, written in 1903, became the bible for thousands of cooks for many years. It is still referred to with some reverence.

During the 1960s and 1970s, the most popular food commentator in the United States was "The French Chef," Julia Child (neither a chef nor French), who detailed the art of French cooking over dozens of television stations and in her cookbooks. The French are still very much with us.

French chefs have been in demand in the homes of the rich and in expensive restaurants, especially since the French Revolution of 1789, when many of their employers were killed. Some chefs went into business for themselves in Paris, a few emigrated to the United States; many served in the stately homes and clubs of England. Name restaurants in the West world often employ French chefs and others apprenticed on the Continent, since most have been intensively trained, often starting at the age of 14.

The word *restaurant* itself is of French origin, derived from the soup recommended by physicians of the time as a *restorant* (restorative). Paris is credited with having the first restaurant opened by a Monsieur Boulanger in 1765. Supposedly this inscription in Latin appeared over the door: *"Venite ad me omnes qui stomachs laboralis et ego restaurabo vos"* ("Come to me all those whose stomachs cry out in anguish and I shall restore you").

The French and Chinese are known for their attention to gastronomy and the willingness to devote time and talent to its elaboration. The various sections of the French kitchen suggest the high degree of specialization that can be found in a large French restaurant. Such a specialized kitchen with its own hors d'oeuvres maker, ice cream maker, fish cook, meat cook, vegetable cook, and cheese specialist is, of course, rare.

FRENCH SAUCES AND SEASONINGS

The French influence in seasonings is widespread, especially the use of bay leaf, parsley, thyme, and chervil. In the past we tended to think of French cookery in terms of butter, cream, pâté de foie gras (fat goose liver paste), delicate fish dishes in pastry cases, wines, and an array of cakes and pastries.

Sauces, particularly those thickened with roux (equal quantities of fat and flour), were the hallmarks of the French cook. The professional chef knew at least 100 sauces, usually learned over a period of years as an apprentice.

To better understand the contribution of the French to the culinary scene, look at the attention to detail that has gone into the subject of sauce cookery. French cuisine includes literally hundreds of sauces, but basically there are five "mother," or leading, sauces, each with a number of variations. These basic sauces are shown in Figure 9.1.

Sauces can be remembered by color: white, blond, brown, red, and yellow. In the white sauces, the liquid is milk or cream. Fish, chicken, or veal stock is used in the blond sauces. Reduced meat stock is the vehicle for the brown sauces. Egg yolks provide

Name	Ingredients
Béchamel	Milk (simmered with a clove and studded onion) + White roux
Velouté (chicken, fish, or veal)	White stock + White roux
Brown or Espagnole	Brown stock + Brown roux
Tomato	Tomato + Stock + Roux (optional)
Hollandaise	Butter + Egg yolks

FIGURE 9.1 Leading, or "mother," sauces.

most of the liquid for the yellow sauces. The thickening agent is likely to be roux (pronounced roo, a mixture of flour and fat) for the white, blond, and brown sauces.

Most widely used of all the warm sauces is white sauce. In the original French version, béchamel, it was made with veal stock. Variations of the white sauce include Mornay (the most widely used) and Sauce Newburg, which has paprika, shallot, sherry wine, and butter added. Another of the mother sauces, the velouté sauces (meaning velvety smooth sauces), are made from thickened veal, chicken, or fish stock.

Of course, the French are not the only inventors of sauces. We have many of our own, an example being the à la king sauce, which is a white sauce to which chicken or other meat, sliced pimientos, and green peppers (and sometimes mushrooms) are added. American home cooking features gravy, the drippings from meat thickened with flour or cornstarch.

The French are much more sophisticated when it comes to brown sauces, as seen in Figure 9.2. The French brown sauce starts with stock prepared from beef bones, chopped vegetables, and a bag of herbs. Preparing espagnole sauce from scratch is time-consuming, and with labor costs rising can become quite expensive.

The American cook often starts with a sauce or soup base. Hollandaise, another French offering, is widely used, and béarnaise sauce, a derivation of hollandaise, is often seen on sophisticated menus.

Ketchup, probably the most widely used sauce of all, is not usually thought of as sauce. But sauce it is, albeit served at room temperature, and it is very similar to the basic tomato sauce.

Demi-Glace		Espagnole + Brown stock (reduced)
Fond Lie/		
Jus Lié		Brown stock + Cornstarch and seasoning
	Bordelaise	Reduction of red wine, shallots, herbs, seasoning, and garnished with bone marrow
	Chasseur (French for Hunter)	Mushrooms, tomato, and white wine
	Diable (Deviled)	Reduce white wine, chaopped shallots, and crushed pepper. Add demi-glace, simmer. Add cayenne to taste.
	Madeira	Reduce demi-glace and add Madeira wine.
	Marchand De Vine (Wine Merchant)	Reduction of red wine and shallots
	Mushroom	Sauté sliced mushrooms, minced shallots in butter, add demi-glace, simmer, add sherry, and a drop of lemon juice.
	Perigeaux	Garnish Madeira sauce with finely diced truffle.
a	**Robert**	Sautéed onions in butter with a white wine reduction to which demi-glace is added, plus dry mustard and a pinch of sugar dissolved in a little lemon juice.

FIGURE 9.2 Classic small brown sauces—A partial list.

Adapted from Wayne Gisslen, Professional Cooking, *7th ed. (Hoboken, NJ: John Wiley & Sons, Inc., 2011), pp. 188–189.*

Though paying homage to tradition, the French kitchen is also flexible. The traditional warm sauces, heavy with saturated fats and flavor, are still with us, but younger French chefs have invented ways of avoiding calories while retaining flavor. Fresh foods, lower fat, and the avoidance of roux-thickened sauces are being featured. Voilà: *nouvelle cuisine* (new cuisine) and *cuisine minceur* (pronounced man sir, the "cuisine of thinness").

Instead of roux-thickened sauces, pureed fruits and vegetables are used and liquids are reduced by cooking to appropriate thickness. As in the diet restaurants of the United States, nouvelle cuisine emphasizes veal, fish, fruit, and salads. It reduces the use of table sugar and places more emphasis on sugars found naturally in fruits and vegetables. An example of a tomato sauce without a thickening agent: puree a fresh tomato in a blender and use the result, nothing else, as a sauce.

Courtesy of Carmel Café
Shrimp Ceviche at Carmel Café and Wine Bar.

Traditional French cookery, especially that of haute cuisine (the complex, expensive cookery), was concerned with working over foods: long cooking times, the making of forcemeats, shaping and turning vegetables, and combining foods in familiar ways. Nouvelle cuisine espouses unusual marriages of fruits and vegetables, shorter cooking times, and often an emphasis on *au natural* foods, cooked not at all. Hors d'oeuvres for a reception might feature crudités: raw carrots, cauliflower, celery, and the like.

About the same time that nouvelle cuisine was being introduced—the early 1980s—Alice Waters opened Chez Panisse, in Berkeley, California. One of the things that made Chez Panisse special was that it offered fresh local ingredients. It did not offer an à la carte menu but simply a table d'hôte menu featuring whatever was fresh that day.

The 1990s and early 2000s saw the popularization of *fusion cuisine*—a blending of the techniques and ingredients of two different cuisines, such as Japanese and French, Mediterranean and Chinese, or Thai and Italian.

Today because of fusion cuisine and other influences, a new American cuisine has evolved using methods and ingredients from other cultures. Regional American cuisine has also become more prominent. Another recent trend is the Spanish small-plate concept that evolved from tapas, where people can eat four or five appetizers, which gives them the chance to enjoy more variety. A number of renowned chefs offer guests inspired cuisine that is local and international, fresh and organic.

Receiving

Smart restaurateurs arrange with suppliers for all deliveries to be delivered at times convenient to the restaurant—usually between 8 and 11 A.M. and 2 and 4 P.M. For those restaurants only open for dinner, receiving hours of 8 A.M. to 3 P.M. allows for items delivered to be prepared for that evening's dinner.

It is critically important that a copy of the order be available for the receiver (to ensure that no item was forgotten) and to check that the quality and quantity was accurate per the order. Even more important is to have a member of management check and sign for all deliveries. All items should be checked for quantity—size, weight, and number—and quality. Some restaurants also verify price before signing.

Few restaurateurs have the time to check all items, so they check the higher-cost items, knowing that their system will show if there is a shortage of an item. One successful restaurateur's system showed that there was a 400-pound shortage of potatoes in one month. When the general manager started to weigh every bag of potatoes, the scale showed short deliveries. The supplier agreed and found that the grower was not weighing the potatoes. The restaurant received a credit for the short deliveries. This situation underlines the necessity of occasionally spot checking every item on the delivery sheet.

Restaurants that have purchase order specifications (often made up with the help of the supplier) find it easier to check the condition and quality of orders. Some useful industry tips for receiving are:

- Keep the receiving area clean and tidy.
- Check for product freshness: Use your eyes, nose, and, yes, mouth if necessary.
- Maintain an accurate weighing scale for easy checking of the weight of items. Remember to take the packaging off and weigh the raw product.
- Check all the items you want to; don't be hurried by the delivery person.
- Check the temperature of items to be sure that frozen items are still frozen and items that should be chilled are chilled. If the temperature is 50°F and it should be 43°F, have the item replaced.
- Once the delivery is received, it must be dated, labeled, and stored in the proper place.

Storage

Courtesy of Ophelia's
A delicious appetizer.

Part of the food production system is to store food and other supplies so that they fit into the overall system. This means storage arranged for easy receiving, easy issuing, and easy inventory control. In the dry-goods storeroom, canned, packed, and bulk dry foods are stored according to usage. The most-used foods are stored closest to the door, the least-used foods in the less accessible corners and shelves.

Once a system of storage has been arranged and the items are stored according to usage, a form can be made up listing the items in the sequence in which they are stored. The spreadsheet is then used in taking a physical inventory.

As foods are received, they are stored at the backs of shelves, the older items moved forward to be used first. This rotational system helps ensure that items are not allowed to become too old.

The rotation of goods has no relation to any system of costing foods or other merchandise. In costing an inventory, the *last-in, first-out (LIFO)* system costs the item at the price paid for the merchandise purchased last. The *first-in, first-out (FIFO)* system uses the price actually paid for the item. During a period of inflation, the two costs could be quite different. Whichever method is selected, it must be used consistently. Changing methods requires the approval of the IRS.

Convenience foods usually come in a form that makes it possible for them to be stored in a minimal amount of space. Other items are received in a form that should be processed immediately to reduce the amount of storage needed. Lettuce is a good example. Crated lettuce can be uncrated, trimmed, cored, and placed core side up under ice in less space.

Many operators buy only salad greens that have already been washed and cut. Both time and space are saved, but the quality may be lower than if the greens were prepared on the premises. To ensure freshness, a frequent turnover is essential.

In order to maximize the shelf life of a product, it is important to store all items at the correct temperature. A guide to storage temperatures follows:

Dry storage	50°–75°F
Produce	37°–40°F
Meat & poultry	33°–38°F
Dairy	33°–38°F
Seafood	33°–38°F
Frozen foods	0°–15°F

Managers should be present at delivery times and see that everything is properly stored.

Depending on the size and operation of the restaurant, the storage area and walk-ins may be open to the prep cooks; in most restaurants they are of necessity. In order to safeguard against theft, most smart restaurateurs treat their kitchen staff right by paying them a good salary, feeding them, and providing a good working environment. They also take inventory twice a month and calculate their food-cost percentage.

To help facilitate ordering and inventory taking, a perpetual inventory method can be used. In this system, a record of the inventory level of an item and a column for withdrawals and total remaining is kept on a clipboard.

Food Production

Similar to creating an employee schedule, the production sheet depends on *business levels.* Future business levels are affected by many variables: past history, holidays falling on different days of the week compared to last year, social activities, new construction in the area, weather and recent food trends and so on. The key to success, as Chef Joe Askren explains, is to concentrate on the six to eight high-cost protein items and not lose sleep over the other 400 items in the entire inventory.[7]

"Let's get in the mind of a chef." What is he or she is thinking when preparing a production sheet and or production strategy? The actual production sheet is formatted around the menu while taking the different BOH stations into consideration.

For example, if the sauté station was responsible for five menu items, then the production sheet would be formatted accordingly. A protine might be listed at the top of the sauté section followed by every single ingredient needed to prepare all components for that specific menu item. This method would hopefully flush out any crossover such as asparagus being used on multiple items. Chef Askren says the three universal questions in doing a production plan are: Where are we? Where do we want to be? How do we get there?[8]

Planning, organizing, and producing food of a consistently high quality is no easy task. The *kitchen manager*, *chef*, or cook begins the production process by determining the expected number of guests for the next few days. The same period for the previous year can give a good indication of the expected volume and breakdown of the number of sales of each menu item. The product mix (a list of what was sold yesterday) will give an indication of what needs to be prepped (prepared) in order to bring the item back up to its par level—and par levels for Monday, Tuesday, and Wednesday will be different from later in the week.

The *kitchen manager/chef* then gives the food order to the general manager. In some cases a kitchen manager/chef is authorized to order directly him- or herself.

Every morning the chef or kitchen manager determines the amount of each menu item to prepare. The *par levels* of those menu items in the refrigerators are checked, and a *production sheet* is completed for each station in the kitchen. (See Figure 9.3.) Most of the *prep* (preparation) is done in the early morning and afternoon. The prep sheets (production sheets) give the quantity of each menu item to be prepared. Use of prep sheets increases efficiency and productivity by eliminating guesswork. Taking advantage of slower times in which to prepare food allows the line cooks to do the final preparation just prior to and during the meal service. Kitchen managers make up their own production sheet based on the menu. The production sheet can be split into sections by station or equipment: mixer, stove, oven, pantry, and so on.

The *cooking line* is the most important part of the kitchen layout. It might consist of a broiler station, window station, fry station, salad station, sauté station, and dessert station, to name just a few of the intricate parts that go into the setup of the back of the house.

The kitchen is set up according to what the guests order more frequently. For example, if guests order more broiled or sautéed items, the size of the broiler and sauté station set up must be larger to cope with the demand.

Teamwork, a prerequisite for success in all areas of the hospitality and tourism industry, is especially important in the kitchen. Due to the hectic pace, pressure builds, and unless each member of the team excels, the result will be food that is delayed or not up to standard, or both.

Organization and performance standards are necessary, but helping each other with preparing and cooking is what makes for teamwork. Teamwork in the back of the house is like a band playing in tune, each player adding to the harmony. Another example

Courtesy of Sysco
A delicious dessert.

FRI-SAT   PREP/WEIGHT WATCHERS

DAY PREP   DATE:

PG	DAY PREP	SHIFTS	PAR	INV	PREP
82	TOMATO WEDGES 1X=1/6TH. PAN	2	1X		
82	SLICED TOMS 1X=LAYER 1/3 RD.PAN	2	1X		
82	DICED TOMS 1X=1/6TH. PAN	2	8X		
21	PICO 1X=1/6TH. PAN	3	11X		
15	GUAC 1X=1/6TH. PAN	2	3X		
81	CUCUMBER 1X=1/6TH. PAN	2	2X		
138	TRI-COLORED STRIPS MIXES/WELL	2	2X		
137	WHITE CORN CHIPS/LIGHTLY SALTED	2	5X		
120	BACON BITS COOKED 1X=5#	2	5#		
80	DICED EGGS 2 OZ	2	20		
32	SALAD 3.5 OZ. PORTION	3	50		
32	SALAD 7 OZ. PORTION	3	50		
35	ROMAINE 4 OZ. PORTION	4	30		
35	ROMAINE 8 OZ. PORTION	4	40		
31	ORIENTAL 4 OZ. PORTION	4	30		
31	ORIENTAL 8 OZ. PORTION	4	30		
31	ORIENTAL 2 OZ. PORTION	4	25		
13	COLE SLAW 1X=1-1/6TH. PAN	4	6X		
80	WING CELERY 1X=1/2 LEX	4	2X		
	WW. SALAD MIX 7 OZ. PORTIONS	3	20		
	WW. ROMAINE LEAVES WHOLE	4	20		
99	WW. SHRIMP SALAD SETS	4	8		
101	WW. VEGGIE QUESA MIX 1X=14/5 OZ	4	5X		
90	WW. BLK/CORN SALSA 1X=12#20 DISH	3	8X		
33	SPINACH SALAD (PORT=2.5OZ EA)	4	15		
33	SPINACH SALAD (PORT=5OZ EA)	4	15		
71	RED PEPPER/RED ONION (2OZ/1OZ)	4	30		
107	COBB SALAD SET (1/4 CUP EACH) (6OZ)	4	10		

PG	HOT PREP	SHIFTS	PAR	INV	PREP
128	HERB GARLIC MASH POTATOES (1X=3P)	2	1X		
127	FETTUCCINI 10#=24/10 OZ	2	1X		
133	MEXI RICE 1X=18/6 OZ	4	4X		
132	ALMOND RICE 1X=19/6 OZ	4	8X		
103	WW WHITE RICE 1X=43/3 OZ	4	45		
45	COUNTRY GRAVY 1X=11/6 OZ	4	1X		
139	WINGS 10 PORTION=5DRUMS/5 WINGS	4	40		
130	POT PIE LIDS 12/TR/SUGAR WATER	4	20		
131	RIBLETS CASES COOKED	6	3CS		
91	WW GRILLED LEMON HALVES 1X=1EA	4	50		
	COUNTRY POTATOES 1X=1EA	4	5		
18	4 CHEESE PANINI SETS	4	5		
19	PANINI SPREAD (1X=12-30#)	6	5X		
27	CRANBERRY TURKEY SET	4	10		

PG	MISC PREP	SHIFTS	PAR	INV	PREP
5	GARLIC BUTTER BROCCOLI(4 OZ)	4	200		
108	WW BROCCOLI (6 OZ PORT)	4	60		
3	TERIYAKI BOWL VEG 1X=9/8 OZ	4	4X		
1	BROCCOLI FLORETTES 1 EA/3 OZ	4	25		
80	SLICED MUSHROOMS 1X=10# BOX	4	10X		
25	VEGGIE PIZZA 1X=16/5 OZ	6	5X		
136	SAUTEED ONIONS 1 PAN=10#	4	20X		
135	SAUTEED GR. PEPPER 1X=10#	4	10#		
204	TOSTADAS (1/2 AND WHOLE)	2	30/30		
22	QUESA FILLING 1X=26/6 OZ	4	4X		
100	WW LEMON HERB 2 OZ PORTION	4	5		
92	WW CILANTRO DRESSING 1X=2QTS	4	1X		
92	WW CILANTRO DRESSING (PORTION)	4	10		
106	WW TERRI SAUCE 1X=21/1.5 OZ LADLE	4	2X		
105	WW SALSA RANCH 1X=26/1.5 OZ LADLE	4	1X		
98	WW BBQ RANCH 1X=21/1.5 OZ LADLE	4	5X		
12	ROAST GAR. BRUSHETTA (1X=12-1/4CUP)	3	2X		
49	BOURBON STREET MELT SAUCE	6	2X		
51	REMOULADE SAUCE	6	1X		
50	ROASTED ASIAGO SAUCE (1X=44-#20)	6	2X		
73	FAJITA 5.5 OZ MARINADE	6	2X		
53	FAJITA SAUCE (1X=4 CUPS)	6	1X		******

PG	FREEZER PREP	SHIFTS	PAR	INV	PREP
61	ONION PEELS 6 OZ 1X=CASE	90	2CS		
61	SWEET POT FRIES 6 OZ 1X=1CS	90	2CS		
61	BONELESS WINGS 1EA=6 OZ BAG	90	4CS		
61	BUTTERMILK SHRIMP (1X=1CS 10EA)	90	2CS		
61	BATTERED FISH 1X=1CS/4EA PIECES	90	1CS		
61	BROWNIES 1X=1EA	4	15		
61	BLONDIE 12CT 1X=1EA	4	15		
61	APPLE CHIMI 1X=1EA	4	15		
61	APPLE PIE 1X=1EA	4	15		
207	KEY LIME PIE	6	12		

PG	PORTIONING	SHIFTS	PAR	INV	PREP
70	POT PIE 1X=12/10 OZ PORTIONS	8	12		
63	BAKED BEANS 1X=18/4 OZ	6	40		
60	ALFREDO SAUCE	6	25		
205	KEY LIME PIE SAUCE (1X=10/3 OZ)	6	1X		
114	ANGLAISE SAUCE (1X=10/3 OZ)	6	2X		
115	MAPLE SAUCE 1X=12/4 OZ	4	10		
110	APPLE-BUTTER SAUCE 1X=15/2 OZ	4	45		
206	MARGARITA LIME BUTTER (1X=26/#20)	6	1X		
64	BEEF MIX 1X=1BG/8-9 OZ PORTIONS	4	5X		
64	BEEF MIX 1X=1BG/2 OZ PORTIONS	4	24		
46	HABANARA SAUCE 1X=10/4 OZ	10	15		
	ALMONDS 1X=1EA/1 OZ	14	60		
	ALMONDS 1X=1EA/2 OZ	14	60		
	BLACK BEANS 1X=16/1/4 CUP	4	1X		
	HONEY BBQ PORTION 1X=24/3 OZ	6	30		
	ORANGE GLAZE 1X=1EA/3 OZ	6	50		
	TERI SAUCE (3 OZ PORT)	10	30		
	CHIPOTLE CHICKEN 1X=1BG-21/4 OZ	6	2X		
	CHIPOTLE CHICKEN 1X=1BG-28/4 OZ	6	2X		
155	GARLIC BREAD 1X=1 LEX	3	5LEX		
	CHX ROLL UP SETS 4OZ CHK/8OZ CHEESE	6	30		
65	CLUB GRILL SETS 1X=1EA(3 OZHAM/TURKEY)	4	15		
68	FAJITA FLOUR TORTS 1X=4 EA	4	30		
66	BABY BACK RIBS-FULL/BAGGED/DATED	2	20		
66	BABY BACK RIBS-HALF/BAGGED/DATED	6	10		
153	BURGERS PREP- 1X=1CS/5 PER BAG	10	2CS		
	PORTION RIBS 10 OZ/WRAPPED/DATED	6	ALL		
96	WW TERRI SHRIMP SKEWERS 1X=2EA	2	25X		
24	SEASONED SHRIMP 1X=13/7 PCS.	4	5X		
158	PLAIN SKEWERS(1X=2 SKEWERS BAG)	4	20X		
	DICED CELERY (1/4 CUP PORT)	2	20		
	BL. CHEESE CRUMBLES (1/4 CUP PORT)	6	20		
	MANDARIN ORANGES (1/4 CUP PORT)	6	15		
67	CRANBERRY (1 OZ) PECAN (1 OZ)	6	15		

PG	O'CHEESES	SHIFTS	PAR	INV	PREP
	JACK/CHEDDAR 1/4 CUP 1 BAG=88	10	2 BAG		
	PIZZA CHEESE 1/2 CUP 1 BAG=35	10	1 BAG		
	PARM 1/4 CUP 1 BAG=42	10	2 BAG		
	WW. LOW FAT CHEESE 1/4 CUP 1X=42	10	2 BAG		
72	PHILLY CHEESE SAUCE 2 OZ/1X=18	8	20		
11	BLUE CHEESE 1X=12#40 DISHER	3	5		
23	QUESO CHEESE MIX 1X=4-1/6 PANS	6	4X		
20	PARM TOPPING 1X=7/320 DISHER	6	3X		
	PEPPER JACK CHEESE (1/4 CUP)	6	2BG		
	BISTRO PORT (5.5 OZ) 5 SHAKE TABASCO	6	30		
	CRAB CAKE (2EA PORT)	6	1 BG		
	RED ONION SLICE (4 RINGS 1/2 CUT)	4	30		
52	APPLE WALNUT DRESSING (1X=16/2 OZ)	4	2X		
28	GRANNY SMITH APPLES (3X=12 PORT)	2	1X		
	ZESTY RED SAUCE	6	1X		
200	SHREDDED BEEF MIX (1X=32/12 DISHER)	6	2X		
202	SOUTHWEST VEGETABLE (1X=14 1/4 CUP)	4	4X		
4	FAJITA VEG SET	4	4X		
203	HONEY LIME CILANTRO VIN (1X=14/4 OZ)	4	3X		
201	ENCHILADA SET (CERAMIC SKILLET)	4	20		

Courtesy of Anna Maria Oyster Bar

FIGURE 9.3 Production worksheet.

of organization and teamwork is T.G.I. Friday's five rules of control for running a kitchen:

1. Order it well.
2. Receive it well.
3. Store it well.
4. Make it to the recipe.
5. Don't let it die in the window.[9]

A kitchen team in full swing, preparing and serving quality meals on time, is an amazing sight.

Production Procedures

Production in the kitchen is critical to the success of a restaurant since it relates directly to the recipes on the menu and how much product is on hand to produce the menu. One way to increase sustainability is to have menu items that require less cooking times, items that are prepared using less heat, and items that are prepared through cooking methods that require less heat and cooking time. Think about how much energy (and money) is saved by serving menu items such as salads, sushi, fruits, etc.!

In addition, timing is vital if guests are to get their food quickly. Thus, controlling the production process is a challenge.

The first step in creating the production sheets is to count the products on hand for each station. Once the production levels are determined, the amount of production required to reach the level for each recipe is decided. When these calculations are completed, the sheets are handed to the cooks.

It is important to make the calculations before the cooks arrive, taking into consideration the amount of prep time that is needed in order to produce before the rush. For instance, if a restaurant is open for lunch and dinner, enough product should be on hand by 11:00 A.M. to ensure that the cooks are prepared to handle the lunch crowd.

When determining production, par levels should be changed according to sales trends. This will help control and minimize waste levels. Waste is a large contributor to food cost; therefore, the kitchen should determine the product levels necessary to make it through only one day.

Products have a particular shelf life, and if the kitchen overproduces and does not sell the product within its shelf life, it must be thrown away. More important, this practice allows for the freshest product to reach guests on a daily basis.

After the lunch rush, the kitchen checks to see how much product was sold and how much is left for dinner. (Running out of product is unacceptable and should not happen. If proper production procedures are followed, a restaurant will not have to cancel anything on the menu.)

After all production is completed on all stations, the cooks may be checked out. It is essential to check out the cooks and hold them accountable for production levels. If they are not checked out, production will slide, negatively impacting the restaurant and the guests.

The use of production sheets is critical in controlling how the cooks use the products. Every recipe has a particular spec (specification) to follow. When one deviates from the recipe, the quality goes down, consistency is lost, and food cost goes up. That is why it is important to follow the recipe at all times.

Production starts with *mise-en-place* (the assembly of ingredients and equipment for the recipe). The backbone for every service in the restaurant is having all the specific ingredients for the recipes prepped ahead of time. Stocks and sauces are done weekly; garnishes are prepped in the late afternoon, and marinated meats the day before or early in the day of use, and so on. Experience goes a long way in gauging how much product to prep. For example, what if you have 350 guests in two hours?

Mise-en-place also includes presentation hardware such as china, lids, under-liners, and paper doilies. Most recipes and methods of production include *batch cooking*—for example, making a batch of parsnip purée that will yield 12 appetizer orders but only yield 6 entrée orders. Cooks may make last-minute decisions on batch cooking based on business levels. The shelf life of a batch of soup will assist the cook in deciding whether to make two batches or three batches. For instance, a seafood-based soup may only be allowed to be shelved 24 hours verses a cream of mushroom soup that may have a shelf life of three to five days. Cooks may also batch cook separately sauces at the beginning of a shift to ensure consistency in flavor and texture.

Lead line cooks and/or sous chefs should always approve production sheets created by line-level employees. The best case scenario would be to prepare your production sheet a shift or even a day in advance. For example, dinner service cooks, after breaking down their line after service, will create their production sheets on the same night. This production sheet will then be handed to the chef, who will then use it to place a food order for the following day(s). Often times, critical items are not ordered and production is at a standstill due to a haphazardly created production sheets. This, then, causes a backup in the next day's production and may even lead to a menu item being eliminated from the night's menu, leading to unhappy customers. Having tight par levels and reordering points in your system helps the ordering process.[10]

Other common problems:

- Assuming you have it . . . but the ingredient was not properly rotated.
- Incorrect production sheet = overprepping or underprepping.
- Not tasting or critiquing "batch" recipes. When in doubt, throw it out and start over again. Wasting product is bad, but giving improperly cooked/seasoned food to a guest is even worse!

Everything should be set up at the station—the proper number of pans, containers, sauce bins, and so on—and cooks should try to avoid calling for extra ingredients.

During production, it is important that standards are maintained for quality and inventory control: the right size, measurement, portion, temperature, and compliance with food safety. Chefs need to work to a time frame and constantly check production for quality and quantity.

Normally, the menu for lunch is different from that for dinner. An inventory needs to be taken after the lunch service to see what was consumed and what can be used for dinner and what needs to be prepped.

After every meal service, it is important to clean the station and begin the preparations for the next service.

Once again, a production schedule is used to plan and organize stations. Both the quantity of an item and a timeline for the steps of production are listed so that the chef can check on progress.

Dinner normally has a more complicated menu with more selections available, which adds to the workload.

Staffing and Scheduling

Practicing proper staffing is absolutely critical to the successful running of a kitchen. It is important to have enough staff on the schedule for the restaurant to handle the volume on any shift. Often, it is better to overstaff the kitchen rather than understaff it, for two reasons. First, it is much easier to send an employee home than it is to call someone in. Second, having extra staff on hand allows for cross-training and development, which is becoming a widely used method.

Problems can be eliminated if a manpower plan is created, for example, to set levels for staffing needs. These levels should be adjusted according to sales trends and a regular basis.

Foodborne Illness

Posted in the kitchen of a large university is a sign "Cleanliness Is Next to Godliness." Restaurant patrons may not believe in the religious implication of the statement, but they place implicit trust in the integrity of restaurant operators, believing that food served will be clean, free of harmful germs and foreign materials.

The United States Public Health Service identifies more than 40 diseases that can be transferred through food. Many can cause serious illness; some are even deadly. A foodborne illness is a disease that is carried or transmitted to human beings by food.

There are three types of hazards to safe food: biological, chemical, and physical. Of these three, biological hazards cause the highest percentage of foodborne illness outbreaks. Disease-causing microorganisms, otherwise known as pathogens, such as bacteria, molds, and yeast, are considered biological hazards.

Whether it's cookie dough or meat products that are contaminated prior to arrival at a restaurant, it still severely taints the restaurants image. And while restaurants are not always associated directly with these food poisoning outbreaks, the industry nevertheless has felt the repercussions as concerned consumers react to an environment clouded by a growing fear of the food they consume.[11] In 2009, nine people died and more than 700 were sickened after they consumed foods containing salmonella-laced peanut products made by Peanut Corporation of America in

Blakely, Georgia. After the tainted items were traced back to PCA, federal inspectors examined the company's facilities in Blakely and discovered filthy conditions there. In other incidents, 1,300 people became ill when they ate raw serrano peppers containing the rare saintpaul strain of salmonella. The FDA was eventually able to trace the source to peppers raised on a farm in Mexico.[12]

In December 2012, a Casper, Wyoming, Golden Corral had to temporarily shut down to sanitize the restaurant after more than 300 cases of foodborne illnesses were linked to it. Diners came down with norovirus, the most common form of food poisoning. Kelly Weidenbach-Virgil, Wyoming's state epidemiologist, noted that several of Golden Corral's employees had continued to work while sick, and one or more of those ill or previously ill employee working in the food-handling area might have been "an important contributing factor in the propagation of this outbreak."[13]

BIOLOGICAL HAZARDS—BACTERIA

Bacteria, single-celled microorganisms that are capable of reproducing in about 20 minutes, cause the highest number of biological foodborne illness. Under favorable conditions, one bacterium can become a colony of one million bacteria in less than six hours, more than enough to cause serious illness.[14] By understanding bacteria, we can destroy or control them and render them harmless. Like all living organisms, bacteria, need sustenance to function and multiply.

Bacteria can cause illness in two ways. The first is via disease-causing bacteria, known as *pathogens*, which feed on nutrients in hazardous foods and, given favorable conditions, multiply rapidly. Other bacteria, while not harmful themselves, discharge toxins as they multiply. These toxins poison humans who eat food containing them.

Pathogenic bacteria can cause illness in humans in one of the three ways: intoxication, infection, or toxin-mediated infection.[15]

The best-known example of intoxication is botulism, a toxin produced by some bacteria; it cannot be smelled, seen, or tasted. Unlike many other bacteria, high temperatures do not destroy botulism, so special care is required in food handling to avoid illness.

Salmonella is the best-known example of infection caused by bacteria. The bacteria live in the intestines of chickens, ducks, mice, and rats. Under favorable conditions, *salmonella* bacteria may cause illness to humans. Cooking foods to a temperature of 165°F or higher can kill them.

Toxin-mediated infection has characteristics of both intoxication and infection. Examples are *Clostridium perfringens* and *Escherichia coli* 0157:H7 (*E. coli*). After ingestion, these living organisms establish colonies in human or animal intestinal tracts, where they produce toxins. Young children and the elderly are vulnerable to these bacteria.

From time to time, the general public's faith in the safety of restaurant food is badly shaken by an outbreak of foodborne illness in a relatively few restaurants, cases that are widely publicized in the news and that frighten the public. A few such instances have resulted in death and caused serious financial damage not only to the restaurant where the outbreak occurred but to the restaurant industry in general.

Food protection practices are not easy to enforce. It must be assumed that all employees carry potentially dangerous bacteria and are shedding them in their feces and urine and from noses and mouths.

To ensure clean hands and nails, double hand washing, using a fingertip brush, must be done. Proper hand washing includes using water as hot as the hands can comfortably stand, using a brush for the fingernails, and rubbing the hands together using friction for 20 seconds. The fingernail brush is not used during the second wash.

Should paper towels or heat be used to dry hands? Other food protection practices are discussed in the sections that follow.

CAUSES OF FOODBORNE ILLNESS

Any kind of food can be the vehicle for foodborne illness. However, generally, the high-protein foods that we eat regularly are responsible for most foodborne illnesses. The foods are classified as potentially hazardous by the US Public Health Service and include any food that consists in whole or in part of milk or milk products, shell eggs, meats, poultry, fish, shellfish, edible crustaceans (shrimp, lobster, crab, etc.), tofu and other soy-protein foods, plant foods that have been heat treated, raw seed sprouts, or synthetic ingredients.[16]

Thousands of cases of stomach upset in the United States are traceable to restaurant food. The result of neglected food protection is seen more dramatically in some foreign countries. Many North American visitors who travel to developing countries come down with foodborne illness.

The foodservice operator should consider the cultural backgrounds of employees and understand that food sanitation practice and attitudes toward cleanliness vary widely from one culture to another. The Japanese are known for their emphasis on sanitation. In Tokyo, persons with colds wear face masks to curb the spread of the cold to others. Other cultures place less emphasis on cleanliness and sanitation.

In developing countries, the germs most likely to cause intestinal upsets are strains of *E. coli*, whose germs pass from bowel to hand to food. *E. coli* causes a majority of the tourist symptoms commonly experienced in developing nations. Food protection problems increase in hot, humid climates where cockroaches are endemic, flies abound, and rodents are searching for food and shelter.

In the United States, outbreaks of *E. coli* have been traced to producers of spinach, romaine lettuce, clover sprouts, hazelnuts, and frozen pizza, among others.[17]

Although sanitation rules are straightforward and relatively simple, consistent implementation demands constant attention and concern. Habits are like giant flywheels; once learned and set in motion, they are difficult to change. Sanitarians are unanimous in their praise of the wonders of soap and water.

The NRA's *Sanitation Operations Manual* discusses a number of cases of foodborne illness in which the causes were tracked down.[18] Here is what typically happens in restaurants when food is not well prepared:

■ In a large downtown restaurant, many patrons became ill after eating a Thanksgiving Day meal. Salmonella was allowed to grow in the turkey and gravy because the food was held between the noon and evening meal at a low temperature in the danger zone. A cook was identified as carrying a positive salmonella culture.

- At a sandwich shop, 22 cases of salmonella infection were traced to the owner and two employees. Barbecued pork was chopped by hand on a pine cutting board. The pork was not refrigerated for two hours.
- For a catered picnic, 100 pounds of potato salad was put in a tub while still warm, then placed in a walk-in refrigerator overnight. Salmonella was present and grew because the interior of the potato salad never cooled; the temperature was 50°F. Salmonella was found in the stool culture of the person who made the salad.
- Roast beef is sometimes infected with *Clostridium perfringens*. Beef was sliced on a wooden cutting board and contaminated by the liquid from plastic bags enveloping the turkeys previously cut up on the board.
- Staphylococcus poisoning at a drive-in restaurant was caused by a high staph count in chocolate and other cream pies. The pies had been stored in a refrigerator at a temperature between 52° and 60°F.

The three disease-causing microorganisms most commonly associated with foodborne illness in the United States are *Staphylococcus aureus*, salmonella, and *Clostridium perfringens*.

Staph bacteria live in our noses and on our skin and are concentrated in large numbers in boils, pimples, and other skin infections. Staphylococci present a special problem. In a favorable environment, they produce enterotoxins impervious to boiling water temperatures or the other temperatures commonly associated with food production. This means that you cannot destroy the staphylococci poisons. High-protein foods such as meats, poultry, fish, eggs, and dairy products that involve human handling are usually associated with staphylococci food poisoning. The microorganisms thrive and grow rapidly at temperatures above 44°F and survive to about 140°F or higher in certain circumstances.

Salmonella is the name of some 2,000 closely related bacteria that continually cycle through the environment in the intestinal tracts of people and animals. First discovered in swine by Dr. Daniel E. Salmon in 1885, salmonella occurs in hundreds of different species, essentially as infections in animals and animal products such as eggs, meat, and milk. Researchers believe that only 1 percent of the infections caused by salmonella germs are reported.

Clostridium perfringens ranks third as a cause of foodborne illness. The bacteria are present in the soil, the intestines of animals, including humans, and in sewage. It has been called the cafeteria germ because it grows so well in food left standing at temperatures between 70° and 170°F. A problem with *perfringens* is that while the vegetative cells of the germ are destroyed at normal cooking temperatures, the spores are not.

Clostridium perfringens is a natural contaminant of meat and is commonly found in the intestinal tract of healthy humans. It is around most of the time. Meat that has been cooked and then left out at room temperature for some time is almost certain to develop this bacteria.

Streptococcus *food infection*, found in contaminated nasal or oral discharges, is spread by sneezing or poor food handling and can cause scarlet fever and strep throat. Foods contaminated with excreta by unclean hands also cause intestinal strep infections.

Bacillus cereus organisms are found in soil, water, and dust. Keeping hot foods hot, cold foods cold, and preventing cross-contamination controls this bacteria.

Shigella dysenteriae is another serious threat in foodservice. As few as 10 germs of this kind in a salad can make healthy people ill.

Parasites also cause infections. Trichinosis, fish tapeworm, and some kinds of amoebas are the parasites that North Americans are most likely to encounter.

Viral infections—the common cold and hepatitis—are other hazards found in the restaurant. Viruses are transmitted to food by humans. Luckily, viruses do not multiply in food. Unfortunately, heat does not kill them.

Raw or insufficiently cooked pork can support the parasite *Trichinella spiralis*, which burrows into the muscles of the host. Fish tapeworms in some fish taken from infected waters are another hazard and make the practice of serving any raw fish questionable. Tapeworms, also found in raw beef, attach themselves to the intestinal wall of the host and can grow to 30 feet in length.

Some foodborne diseases are parasites that have quite serious consequences.

Amoebic dysentery, for example, is not a self-limiting diarrhea and can last for months. Bacillary dysentery, a self-limiting diarrhea that is widespread in the tropics, may have an onset period of about two days and last about six days.

Cholera is spread by ingesting food and liquids contaminated by sewage that contain the virus *Vibrio comma.*

Infectious hepatitis is dangerous, often lethal. Unlike food poisoning, which usually runs its course in a few days, infectious hepatitis has a long incubation period, 10 to 50 days, before its symptoms of yellow discoloration, severe loss of appetite, weight loss, fever, and extreme tiredness set in. Caused by a virus, infectious hepatitis is found in feces and urine of infected persons and in raw shellfish harvested from infected waters.

The paradox of foodborne illness is that most of it can be avoided by clean hands and by following a few simple precautionary practices. Salmonella presents no problem if suspect foods are heated to 165°F or higher. Make sure the hands do not brush the hair, fingers are not in the nose, and the hands are washed after changing money or working with any potentially contaminated object, such as garbage.

How does one know which of the three principal pathogens is the cause of foodborne illness? One cannot be sure, but the symptoms manifested are a clue to the microorganisms at fault. All three types of bacteria cause vomiting and diarrhea. *Staphylococcus aureus* (staph) symptoms appear two to six hours after eating infected food and last a day or two. Salmonella symptoms normally show up later, 12 to 36 hours after eating, and last longer—two to seven days. *Perfringens* symptoms appear as diarrhea and pains 8 to 24 hours after consumption and often end within a day.

Microorganisms for causing foodborne illness are not visible to the naked eye.

Staph germs are grapelike cells; salmonella are rod-shaped cells that cluster together. *Perfringens* germs are also rod-shaped but not clustered together like salmonella.

The most frequently cited errors in food handling are:

1. Failure to cool food properly
2. Failure to heat or cook food thoroughly

3. Infected employees who practice poor personal hygiene at home and at the workplace
4. Foods prepared a day or more before they are served
5. Raw, contaminated ingredients incorporated into foods that receive no further cooking
6. Foods allowed remaining at bacteria-incubation temperatures
7. Failure to reheat cooked foods to temperatures that kill bacteria
8. Cross-contamination of cooked foods with raw foods, or by employees who mishandle foods, or through improperly cleaned equipment[19]

CONTROLLING OR DESTROYING BACTERIA

Bacteria, like other living things, have a comfort zone. In order to grow, bacteria require food and moisture, the proper pH, and time. The food on which bacteria thrive is called potentially hazardous. Among the potentially hazardous foods are those high in protein, like meat, milk and dairy products, and especially eggs, fish, and shellfish. Items like custard, mayonnaise, hollandaise sauce, and quiche are particularly susceptible to contamination.

Temperature is the most important element for bacteria survival and growth; it is also the easiest for restaurateurs to control. The temperature danger zone—between 40° and 140°F—is the range in which bacteria can thrive and multiply most rapidly. Outside of these temperatures, bacteria become dormant, only to reactivate when more favorable conditions return.

It is critical for operators to heat the internal food temperature to a minimum of 140°F. Other safe practices include:

1. Hold foods at internal temperatures of at least 140°F.
2. Heat foods rapidly to avoid the danger zone.
3. Heat small quantities at a time.
4. Heat foods close to service time.
5. Do not use a steam table to reheat foods; instead, heat them rapidly to an internal temperature of 140°F, then transfer them to the steam table for holding.
6. When hot foods must be cooled, chill them quickly in an ice bath or with running water.
7. Place cooked foods in the refrigerator above uncooked foods; this will help avoid cross-contamination.
8. Do not thaw foods at room temperature.
9. Thaw foods gradually in the refrigerator. Put them in a container to prevent them dripping onto other foods.

The golden rule in restaurant operations is to keep hot foods hot and cold foods cold. By controlling the environment in which bacteria may grow and thrive, restaurant operators can prevent outbreaks of foodborne illness. Additionally, raw foods should not be stored above ready-to-eat products, so as to prevent drippings from contaminating food.[20]

Bacteria thrive on protein foods that contain moisture and are neutral or slightly acidic. Generally, microorganisms do not grow in foods that are highly acidic or highly alkaline.

BACTERIA AND TEMPERATURE

Most bacteria, harmful or not, are destroyed by heat. For example, heat of 180°F is used in the final rinse of dishwashing machines.

Chemical sanitation is most effective at temperatures between 75° and 120°F. Three commonly used chemical sanitizers are chlorine, quaternary compounds, and iodine. If, for some reason, the usual dishwashing methods are not available, chlorine performs well if at least 50 parts per million of water are used for one minute. Dishes and utensils are immersed for one minute in solution at least 75°F in temperature.

Microwave heat, as used in microwave ovens, acts by the agitation of water molecules in the food. Because of unequal water distribution in the food and uneven microwave distribution in the oven, food cooked in a microwave is not heated properly. An important guideline to ensure that the safe internal temperature is achieved in microwave cooking is to add a minimum of 25°F to the recommended internal cooking temperature of food when prepared the conventional way. This means, for example, that chicken cooked in a microwave oven should have an internal temperature of 190°F instead of the usual 165°F recommended. Figure 9.4 shows the minimum safe temperatures for various hot foods.

VIRUSES

Viruses are another type of microorganism of concern to restaurant operators because they can cause foodborne illness such as hepatitis A and Norwalk virus. Viruses do not require a hazardous food in order to survive. They can survive on any food or surface, do not multiply, and are not as affected by heat or cold as are bacteria. They simply use the food or other surface as means of transportation. Once the virus enters a body cell, it takes over, forcing the cell to assist in the production of more viruses.

Outbreaks of foodborne or waterborne diseases are usually caused by unfiltered drinking water, shellfish from polluted waters, and, especially, poor personal hygiene. Foods not cooked after handling are those most likely to cause a viral disease. Examples include salads, baked products, milk, sandwich meats, fish, and shellfish.

Product	Temperature
Pork, ham, sausage, and bacon in a microwave	170°F (76.6°C)
All foods previously served and cooled that are reheated	165°F (73.9°C) within two hours
All poultry and game birds	165°F (73.9°C)
Stuffed meats	165°F (73.9°C)
Stuffing	165°F (73.9°C)
Pork, ham, and bacon in another heating element	150°F (65.6°C)
Potentially hazardous foods	140°F (60°C)
Beef roasts (rare)	130°F (54.4°C) for two hours
Beef steaks (rare)	130°F (54.4°C) (or as customer requests)

FIGURE 9.4 Minimum safe internal temperatures for various hot foods.

A hepatitis outbreak in Los Angeles in 2007 had health officials examining the cost and benefits of mandatory vaccinations for foodservice workers. Health officials issued warnings to 3,500 people who had attended more than a dozen events catered by the company, including a *Sports Illustrated* bash celebrating the magazine's swimsuit issue.[21]

CHEMICAL CONTAMINANTS

The increased use of pesticides has caused concern about the chemical contamination of foods. Besides pesticides, other types of chemical contamination can, and do, occur along the food supply chain:

1. Restaurant chemicals like detergents, sanitizers and similar products are poisonous to humans.
2. Overuse of preservatives like sulfating agents (used for maintaining the freshness and color) and nitrates (used as a curing agent to prevent bacterial growth and as a flavor enhancer).
3. Acidic reaction of foods with metal-lined containers.
4. Contamination of food with toxic metals (may occur when carbonated beverages that pass through copper pipes).

There is a common misconception that cleaning products have to be packed with strong chemicals to be effective. Many excellent sustainable cleaners are now available made from 100 percent nontoxic, biodegradable ingredients. They work just as well as the others, without the detrimental health effects.[22] Natural products, such as baking soda, vinegar, and lemon may also be use as cleaning agents.

Many outbreaks of foodborne illness are caused by humans who do not observe proper personal hygiene. By not washing hands frequently, especially after dealing with potentially hazardous foods, and by not wearing protective gloves when handling foods, employees may contaminate foods. Even healthy people can carry microorganisms like staphylococci in their mouth, throat, and nose. Other microorganisms passed on by humans are shigella, *Clostridium perfringens*, salmonella, and hepatitis A. The way to prevent outbreaks of foodborne illness caused by humans is to practice personal cleanliness.

Because germs are ubiquitous in restaurants, management should set the tone that every staff member is also a sanitarian—a person constantly aware of the importance of personally controlling pathogens. There is a right and a wrong way of carrying utensils and serving food (see Figure 9.5). Parts of food handling courses cover the subject.

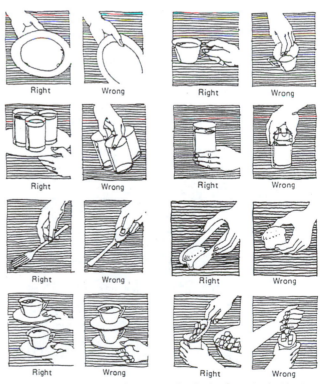

Source: Applied Foodservice Sanitation, A Certification Coursebook, *4th ed. (Educational Foundation of the National Restaurant Association, 1995), p. 141.*

FIGURE 9.5 Sanitary ways to carry utensils and serve food.

Hazard Analysis of Critical Control Points

Because of the necessity of avoiding any kind of illness among astronauts, the National Aeronautics and Space Administration (NASA) developed a program that attempts to ensure that space fliers do not become ill from foodborne diseases. The program, called Hazard Analysis of Critical Control Point (HACCP), presents methods for systematically ridding kitchens of pathogens. The system follows seven basic steps:

1. Identify hazards and assess their severity and risks.
2. Determine critical control points (CCPs) in food preparation.
3. Determine critical control limits (CCLs) for each CCP identified.
4. Monitor CCPs and record data.
5. Take corrective action whenever monitoring indicates a CCL is exceeded.
6. Establish an effective recordkeeping system to document the HACCP system.
7. Establish procedures to verify that the HACCP system is working.[23]

The first step is to decide what hazards exist at each stage of a food's journey through the kitchen and to decide how serious each is in terms of overall safety priorities. On your own checklist, this may include these items:

- Reviewing recipes; paying careful attention to times for thawing, cooking, cooling, reheating, and handling of leftovers
- Giving employees thermometers and teaching them how to use them; correctly calibrating the thermometers
- Inspecting all fresh and frozen products upon delivery
- Requiring hand washing at certain points in the food preparation process and showing employees the correct way to wash for maximum sanitation
- Adding quick-chill capability to cool foods more quickly in amounts over 1 gallon or 4 pounds

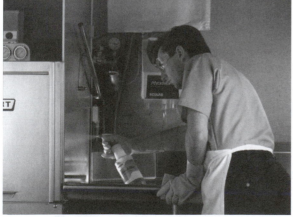

Courtesy of EcoLab, Inc.

Sanitizing the dishwasher is an important step in maintaining a sanitary operation.

There are as many of these possibilities as there are restaurants.

The second step is to identify critical control points. A CCP is any point or procedure in your system where loss of control may result in a health risk.

If workers use the same cutting boards to dice vegetables and debone chickens without washing them between uses, that is a CCP in need of improvement. Vendor delivery vehicles should be inspected for cleanliness; product temperatures must be kept within 5 degrees of optimum; expiration dates on food items must be clearly marked; utensils must be sanitized; and the list goes on and on.

The third step is to determine the standards and limits for what is acceptable and what is not in each of the CCP areas in your kitchen.

The fourth step in the HACCP system is to monitor all the steps you pointed out in step 2 for a specific period of time to be sure each area of concern is taken care of correctly. Some CCPs may remain on the list indefinitely for constant monitoring; others, once you correct the procedure, may be removed from the list after several months. Still others may be added to the monitoring list as needed.

The fifth step kicks in whenever you see that one of your CCLs (see step 3) has been exceeded and corrective action must be taken.

The sixth step requires that you document this whole process. Without documentation, it is difficult, at best, to chart whatever progress your facility might be making. If there is a problem that affects customer health or safety, having written records is also very important.

Finally, the seventh step requires that you establish a procedure to verify whether the HACCP system is working for you. This may mean a committee that meets regularly to discuss health and safety issues and to go over the documentation required in step 6.

Common Food Safety Mistakes

Some of the most common food safety risks in day-to-day food production fall into three key areas: time/temperature abuse, cross-contamination, and poor personal hygiene. Following are useful tips to avoid them.

TIME/TEMPERATURE

Here's the drill: The danger zone in which bacteria thrives lies between 40° and 140°F. Keep all cool foods below 40°F and all hot foods above 140°F.

- Invest in digital thermometers with long probes or thermocouples. (Some new thermometers even record temperatures for recordkeeping.) Make use of oven and refrigerator thermometers.
- Randomly take temperatures of sample food shipments to ensure that proper chilling temperature is maintained through transport. Food shipments that require cold storage must be chilled immediately.
- When cooling hot foods, place them into shallow pans and cool them with an ice bath or a cooling paddle, or use ice as an ingredient before placing them in the cooler. Placing hot foods in the cooler not only raises the cooler temperature, but many foods simply won't cool to 40°F within the four hours prescribed.
- Cook foods to the temperature recommended in the Food and Drug Administration (FDA) Food

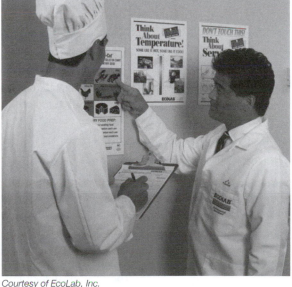

Courtesy of EcoLab, Inc.

Setting up a cleanliness program is critical to food production and the sanitation of restaurants.

Code. Reheat foods, one time only, to 165°F. Once foods are cooked or reheated, temperature must be held above 140°F.

■ Prepare foods in batches; avoid leaving large quantities of food at room temperature during preparation.

CROSS-CONTAMINATION

Most cross-contamination occurs in food preparation. It is easy to engage in unsanitary food practices without realizing the dangers. Picking up a spoon by the bowl is like sticking your fingers in someone's mouth. Picking up ice has the same effect. Handling money definitely transfers germs to the hands. Sneezing in the hand has the same effect.

Have you ever seen a server grab a piece of pie and shovel it in his mouth while picking up an order for the dining room? He has almost certainly contaminated his hands. Dragging on a cigarette and failing to wash the hands afterward also means germs from the mouth go onto the hands.

The following guidelines will reduce cross-contamination:

■ Buy a plentiful supply of color-coded cutting boards and dedicate the colors to specifics foods: chicken only, vegetables only, bread only, for example. Wash the board in hot water and sanitize after every use. When boards go black, that's bacteria growing in the scores. Throw them out!

■ Buy nonabsorbent, washable mats to anchor cutting boards instead of using towels that can absorb contaminated juices. Replace mats between each cutting job.

■ As with cutting boards, dedicate knives to specific foods, and clean and sanitize them between all cutting jobs. Label the drawers where the knives are kept so that they stay dedicated.

■ Wipe down the slicer blade with a clean, hot cloth between jobs and sanitize.

■ Invest in an antiseptic block (a block of solidified sanitizer that you slice on the slicer).

■ Clean and sanitize the counter between each cutting job.

■ When storing foods in the cooler, follow this rule: Cooked foods and foods to be served raw go on top shelves, uncooked raw foods go on bottom shelves. This eliminates the chance of contaminated juices dripping onto ready-to-eat foods.

■ Buffets are prime situations for cross-contamination. Tongs, ladles, and spoons get dropped, switched in the bins, touched by many hands, coughed on—you name it. They need to be cleaned and sanitized, or replaced, every half hour.

Approaches to Food Safety

Overall responsibility for foodservice has been given to the FDA. States and local health authorities draw up ordinances that specify standards and practice for the protection of employees and patrons and provide for regular inspection and enforcement of the ordinances. The FDA provides a model ordinance that is the basis for most local health ordinances.

A public health license to operate a restaurant is required; the license can be revoked if standards are not met or if a dangerous health hazard is found or suspected.

When operating a new restaurant facility or taking over an existing one, a sanitarian or other health officer makes an inspection and may call for changes, such as the installation of sneeze guards over salad bars or changes in plumbing, floor coverings, and number or kind of toilet facilities. Most jurisdictions require a toilet for the people who are physically handicapped.

While the requirements and inspections may appear onerous to the operator, they should be welcomed as a means of safeguarding the public and avoiding problems that could destroy a restaurant. Some restaurant chain operators want more, not less, food protection and monitoring and hire their own bacteriologists to perform regular bacteria counts on foodservice equipment and on such items as glass, china, and flatware.

Regular physical examination of personnel is an excellent practice, one that too few restaurateurs follow because of time and cost. At the very least, newly hired employees should be given physical examinations for no other reason than to protect current employees and to learn of any physical limitations, and to counter claims that a disability was caused on the job. Some health departments provide free or low-cost exams.

That a person is examined and found healthy does not in any way reduce the necessity for following all the rules for food protection. Individuals can harbor infectious agents in their bodies. These people, known as carriers, can transmit the disease to others without themselves exhibiting symptoms. A number of outbreaks of disease have occurred through such carriers.

All states and many local communities monitor restaurants for cleanliness and adherence to food protection ordinances. Most, however, lack the staff to do more than a few inspections. Several states mandate that all foodservice employees complete a food protection course and become certified food handlers.

A number of municipalities have assigned to their public health director the responsibility for ensuring that every restaurant employee completes an elementary course in food protection. Certificates and pins are awarded to those who pass the course. With high employee turnover, however, it is virtually impossible to enforce health codes that mandate such courses. Management interest in food protection and insistence on sanitation is the only practical way to protect employees and the public from diseases that are most certainly present when hundreds of people sit down to eat in a public restaurant.

Many restaurants require kitchen staff to wear gloves when handling food. This lessens the risk of contamination.

Uneven enforcement of regulations causes some confusion in the industry. For example, in some communities, public health officers do not permit tables to be set, prior to serving a meal, with glasses, cups, knives, forks, and spoons unless the glasses and cups are inverted and the knives, forks, and spoons are wrapped or otherwise covered.

Food Protection as a System

Up to a point, the more sanitation practices that can be built into a system, the more likely they will be carried out. The system includes details that can be otherwise overlooked. Personnel trained in the system are carried along by it. One of the reasons for the success of chains like McDonald's is its emphasis on the sanitation

LOCATION: _____ DATE: _____ TIME: _____ DAY: _____

Does this Heritage Restaurant meet the following acceptable cleanliness standards?

	Yes	No		Yes	No		Yes	No
EXTERIOR			RESTROOMS (MEN'S)			DISH AREA (CONT.)		
Parking Lot			Floor			Garbage Cans		
Planters			Urinals			Floor		
Weeded			Stools			Walls		
Watered			Wash Basin			Ceiling		
Dumpster Area			Mirrors			Dish Racks		
Grease Area			Wastebasket			Mops and Buckets		
Front Door			Toilet Paper			Employee Table		
Walks			Seat Covers			WALK-IN		
Lights			Towels			Floors		
Signs			Soap Dispenser			Walls		
Back Door Locked			Other:			Ceilings		
Other:			RESTROOMS (WOMEN'S)			Racks Labeled		
INTERIOR			Floor			Containers		
Floors Swept			Stools			Labels and Dates		
Floors Clean			Wash Basin			FREEZER		
Door/Handles			Mirrors			Floors		
Greeting Sign			Wastebasket			Racks Labeled		
Floor Drains			Seat Covers			Containers		
Windows			Towels			STOREROOM		
Window Sills			Kotex dispenser			Floors		
Walls			Soap dispenser			Racks		
Ceilings			Other:			Shelves		
Vents			KITCHEN			Walls		
Light Fixtures			Floor			Containers		
Light Bulbs			Walls			Labels		
Table Bases			Ceiling			OTHER:		
Chairs			Light Fixtures			OTHER:		
Counter Stools			Ovens			OTHER:		
High Chairs			Shelves			EMPLOYEES		
Counter Top and Front			Sinks			Waitstaff Appearance		
Other:			Work Tables			Uniforms		
EQUIPMENT			Mixer			Name Badge		
Cigarette Machine			Slicer			Hair		
Coffee Makers			Steam Tables			Cooks' Appearance		
Cash Register			Filters			Hat and Scarf		
Cutting Bar			Grills			Clean Aprons		
Waitstaff Stations			Reach-ins			Utility Appearance		
Wait Station Stock			Cold Table			SERVICE STANDARDS		
Wait Station Cleaned			Grease Traps			Greeting		
Fountain Area			Other:			Service Times		
Pie Case Area			Other:			Cooperation		
Reach-ins			Other:			Customer Awareness		
Menus			UTILITY AREA			Cooking Times		
Salt and Peppers			Dish Machine			Service Priorities		
Sugar Dispensers			Sinks			Waitstaff Callbacks		
Creamers			Shelves			Managers' Appearance		

Comments: _____

Supervisor's Signature: _____ Manager's Signature: _____

Source: Courtesy of Heritage Restaurants

FIGURE 9.6 Heritage Restaurant's inspection report.

system. "Why is that toothpick on the floor?" asks a McDonald's inspector. "Why hasn't that table been cleaned?" "Why is the restroom not cleaned?"

To systematize sanitation practices, they should be built into the manager's daily schedule, as shown in Figure 9.6.

The Waffle House, Inc., an Alabama-based chain, provides an inspection schedule that takes managers through the day. When the dayshift manager arrives at 6:30 A.M., he or she arrives and checks the building for appearance. The manager checks around the building for paper, trash, and beer cans. Five minutes later, the manager checks the front door glass, the floor, the booths, the restrooms, and the floor behind the counter. At 10:30 A.M., the floor is swept; at 2:00 P.M., it is mopped. At 4:30 P.M., the whole unit is gone over for cleanliness. At 9:00 P.M., a manager checks the cash register and supplies.

To take care of major cleaning, a weekly cleaning schedule is laid out. Each day something major is cleaned: the back bar on Sunday; grills and light globes on Monday; sidewalks and blinds on Tuesday; ceiling and booths on Wednesday; refrigerators and under the dishwashing machine on Thursday; display case and music machines on Friday; menus, office window, and parking lot on Saturday.

Each operator can design and copy a checklist that fits his or her restaurant. The checklist can be a reminder to check those things that, over time, may be overlooked. Without a checklist, the unacceptable becomes acceptable. The dirty carpet is overlooked; the soiled uniform becomes normal. If used on a regular basis, the checklist systemizes sanitation. Final responsibility for sanitation must remain a management priority.

Summary

Our culinary heritage draws heavily on the cuisines of other countries, notably Italy, France, China, and to a lesser extent several other countries. The cuisines of Native Americans and African Americans also influenced our culinary heritage. French chefs dominated our culinary history.

The French influence in seasonings and sauces is evident in the use of the leading, or mother, sauces: béchamel, velouté, espagnole, hollandaise, and tomato.

Nouvelle cuisine was introduced as people became more health conscious and was followed by fusion cuisine: the blending of techniques and foods from two cuisines. Today, a number of renowned chefs offer guests culinary delights including natural and local foods.

For the purpose of this chapter, food production begins with receiving. Restaurateurs need to specify convenient delivery times; check everything, especially the most expensive items; weigh everything and check for freshness; check temperature; and ensure that what is delivered is what was ordered.

Storage is a part of the food production system where items are stored according to their special needs. Items are labeled and dated then stored in rotation with storage temperatures controlled.

Kitchen managers/chefs plan their food production by determining the expected number of guests for the day and next few days, then making a production schedule to bring the stock of prepped food up to the par stock level. Each station on the line will make its mise-en-place, then prep and cook as orders come in. Plates are prepared, garnished, and checked by the expediter.

Restaurants, like hospitals and schools, are public places where people from many walks of life and backgrounds come together. Every person carries harmful microorganisms or viruses that can be transmitted by food or drink. The restaurant operator is necessarily engaged in preventing that transfer of pathogens, a relentless war in which hot water, heat, refrigeration, and chemicals are used. Vermin and insects are excluded from the kitchen and cleanliness is part of the restaurant's credo. The National Restaurant Association Educational Foundation publishes a number of booklets on the topic of sanitation. The NRAEF website can be viewed at www.nraef.org.

Key Terms and Concepts

Basic, leading, or mother sauces	Food protection system	Par levels
Batch cooking	Fusion cuisine	Pathogen
Clostridium perfringens	Infectious hepatitis	Prep
Cooking line	Kitchen manager/chef	Production sheet
Culinary heritage	LIFO and FIFO	Salmonella
E. coli	Mise-en-place	Shigella
Food infection	Nouvelle cuisine	Soul food
Food poisoning	Outbreak	Staphylococcus

Review Questions

1. Describe the French influence on our culinary heritage.
2. What were Escoffier's contributions to the culinary world?
3. Name the five *mother,* or leading/basic, sauces.
4. Explain the terms *nouvelle cuisine* and *fusion cuisine*.
5. Outline the main elements of food production.
6. What can you, as a restaurant owner, do to avoid food poisoning in your operation?
7. Describe the common germs associated with food poisoning.
8. If you are manager of a restaurant, what are your daily food protection and sanitation responsibilities?

CASE STUDY: PDQ

Who and What Is PDQ[24]

PDQ is a fast casual chicken sandwich and salad chain that was started by Bob Basham, co-founder of Outback Steakhouse and Nick Reader, chief executive of MVP–holdings in Tampa, Florida. The first PDQ restaurant opened on October 30, 2011, and currently, the chain includes four quick-service restaurants in and around the Tampa Bay area. The name PDQ stands for "pretty darn quick" to most people, and the restaurant maintains a dedication to the speedy production of food items; however, PDQ also means "people dedicated to quality," which serves as the foundation of its operation. PDQ was founded on some of the same principles as both casual dining restaurant chain

Outback Steakhouse, as well as fast-food restaurant chain In-N-Out Burger. Both chains are dedicated to similar core beliefs, such as quality products, simplicity of menu, and a slow-growth approach in the beginning of the company's existence.

The idea for PDQ came when Basham was approached by the owner of a small restaurant in Cornelius, North Carolina called Tenders, which offered chicken tenders and other items similar to what is now offered at PDQ. The owner of Tenders believed that his vision and beliefs were similar to those of Outback's, and he wanted to create a franchise of restaurants with the same philosophy in mind. Who better to get invested in this project than Outback's very own Bob Basham, who eventually took over the daily operations of Tenders, reinvented the concept, and built a new string of restaurants in Tampa. PDQ owners pride themselves in the way they differentiate their concept from typical fast-food restaurants. They are conveniently located in the same high-trafficked business districts and neighborhoods as many of their biggest competitors, but they believe that they have created a niche that makes them unique.

Competitive Advantage

PDQ has an advantage in curb appeal, with buildings that are fashioned more like fast-casual restaurants than fast food. The building décor is trendy with vibrant colors and contemporary architecture. Also, there is a commitment to traditional hospitality components that are near and dear to the owners, who have taken them from casual dining and translated them to the QSR business. At PDQ, there is no squawk box at the drive-through, because they believe that a warm greeting at the door can be conceptualized by having a welcoming greeting at drive-through. Additionally, there is a sense of personalization of service by asking customers to provide their name when they order food, and then delivering their orders by name when ready. One of the biggest reasons PDQ has been successful thus far is that the owners continuously look at some of the common things QSRs struggle with and prevent these things from occurring at the onset.

Their philosophy for success is generated from three major components, including a commitment to the quality and freshness of the product offered, speed of service delivery, and the cleanliness of staff and the establishment. According to Basham, "The idea of fast-food has gotten twisted and you are seeing long lines in the restaurant as well as in the drive-throughs during peak business hours, when working people are in a hurry to grab a bite to eat." Unlike other fast-food restaurants to date, PDQ has an openly visible hand-washing sink with a sign above it affirming "cleanliness and quality go hand in hand." This provides customers with physical assurance that the people who work with their food maintain an acceptable level of cleanliness. The kitchen area is also openly visible to allow customers to see their food being cooked and served, which inspires a sense of trust.

While PDQ has been successful since opening in 2011 under the leadership of veteran operators, such as Bob Basham and company, it still faces many challenges with being a new restaurant concept in a very demanding market full of firm competition. Many other establishments in the area have been in operation much longer and have already carved out a loyal customer base. Originally, the first PDQ was opened in South Carolina. The food was similar to what is now being served at the popular PDQ chains in Tampa; however, the building and décor were more like the typical fast food chains such as Dairy Queen, McDonald's and Chick-fil-A. The business never took off at that location, and over time, the restaurant was forced to close its doors. The fact that the first PDQ failed accounted for an increased degree of risk in transferring the idea over to Tampa.

Challenges and Goals

Basham stated that "one of the biggest challenges of opening a new restaurant is making the unit level economics work. You might have a model for your concept, but the question is whether or not that model is feasible." The owners of PDQ aim for a slow-growth approach in southern markets, while maintaining focus on the restaurants it currently has. Basham said, "Many times, owners make the mistake of wanting to expand too quickly, and when they do, they lose focus on the current operation because their focus shifts to the execution of the new operation, and the previous establishment could suffer." One of the biggest goals moving forward is achieving the capacity to establish an environment that is grounded by opportunity for internal growth. Basham believes in rewarding employees for their hard work by guaranteeing them an array of growth opportunities based on their performance. It is essential to put people first, which includes your employees and your customers. Success is measured by sales and profits, and these are the people that make that happen.

QUESTIONS

1. How does PDQ differentiate itself from its competitors?
2. What are the benefits of PDQ's food production process?
3. How does PDQ maintain a reputation of cleanliness and good sanitation?
4. What is slow-growth expansion? Is it important to maintain a slow-growth approach to expansion? Why or why not?

Endnotes

1. Native American Cuisine. www.native-american-online.org/native-american-food.htm. Retrieved on November 18, 2012.
2. African American Registry. www.aaregistry.com/african_american_history/2676/Soul_Food_a_brief_history. Retrieved on November 18, 2012.
3. "Stamp on Black History. Cooking African American Style." http://library.thinkquest.org/10320/Recipes.htm. Retrieved on November 18, 2012.
4. Victoria Breckwich Vasquez, "Healthy African-American Cuisine," University of California at Berkeley. http://berkeley.edu/news/berkeleyan/1997/0129/healthy.html. Retrieved on November 18, 2012.
5. Marjory Bartlett Sanger, *Escoffier, Master Chef* (New York: Farrar, Straus and Giroux, 1976).
6. "A Collection of Culinary Quotations," http://onthetable.us/culinaryquotes.shtml. Retrieved on May 14, 2013.
7. Personal correspondence with Chef Joe Askren, January 6, 2013.
8. Ibid.
9. Personal conversation with James Lorenz May 14, 2013.
10. Ibid.
11. Paul Frumkin, "Lawmakers in Washington must act quickly to stem tide of food borne illnesses," *Nation's Restaurant News, 43* (25) (July 13, 2009), p. 17.
12. Ibid.
13. Dan Flynn, "Wyoming Norovirus Spread Mostly in Golden Corral," *Food Safety News* (February 8, 2013), http://www.foodsafetynews.com/2013/02/wyoming-norovirus-was-spread-inside-the-golden-corral/#.UYEyQ4K6V8U
14. Wayne Gisslen, *Professional Cooking*, 7th ed. (Hoboken, NJ: John Wiley & Sons, Inc., 2011), p. 17.
15. Ibid, p. 17.
16. USDA website, www.fsis.usda.gov/Fact_sheets/Foodborne_Illness_What_Consumers_Need_to_Know/index.asp. Retrieved on November 19, 2012.
17. Centers for Disease Control and Prevention, "Reports of Selected E. coli Outbreak Investigations," http://www.cdc.gov/ecoli/outbreaks.html.
18. The National Restaurant Association, *The Sanitation Operations Manual,* 1200 Seventeenth Street, N.W., Washington, DC 20036-3097.
19. The National Food Safety Certification Program, ed., *Applied Foodservice Sanitation, A Certification Coursebook,* 4th ed. (The Educational Foundation of the National Restaurant Association, 1995), p. 46.
20. Tom Wray, "Serving Up Safety," *National Provisioner, 222* (9) (September 2008), pp. 62–66.
21. "LA Hepatitis Outbreaks Spur Vaccinations." CBNNews (March 9, 2007), www.hepatitisblog.com/2007/03/articles/hepatitis-a-watch/la-hepatitis-outbreaks-spur-vaccinations/. Retrieved September 2009.
22. "Green Home Non-Toxic Cleaning." www.greenhome.com/products/housekeeping/#1. Retrieved September 2009.
23. Costa Katsigris and Chris Thomas, *Design and Equipment for Restaurants and Foodservice*, 3rd ed. (Hoboken, NJ: John Wiley & Sons, Inc., 2008), pp. 209–210.
24. Personal interview with Bob Basham, March 27, 1013.

FOUR

Restaurant Management

Concept of Niche Restaurant

Niche Restaurant was founded by Chef Jeremy Lycan and Sommelier Jody Richardson following the closing of the restaurant 302 West in April of 2006. In 1987, 302 West opened its doors as a "contemporary American restaurant" that focused on an all-American wine list and continental cuisine. Jody Richardson had been with 302 West for six years, Jeremy Lycan, three years. Just before 302 West closed, 12 members of its staff met to discuss the opportunity of working together again. This was the beginning of what today is known as Niche Restaurant. The staff who carried over were comfortable, prepared, and well-trained to continue the concept.

LOCATION

For a location, the owners wanted to find a building with character, personality, and unique architecture. They wanted the site to be controllable and not too large. After looking at various locations, they came across exactly what they wanted. The building, previously occupied by a French restaurant, needed some work, but it had the uniqueness the owners wanted for Niche. In addition, it had great foot traffic, being located directly on the main strip on Third Street in Geneva, Illinois. "The dining room at Niche is the canvas, the background to an excellent dining experience, not intrusive but soothing."

MENU

The owners wanted to carry over the menu concepts from 302 West. The creativity of the entire kitchen staff contributes to the menu at Niche. This results in great attention to details of flavor, texture, and presentation. Menu items change on a daily basis and are developed according to seasonal availability. "It encompasses

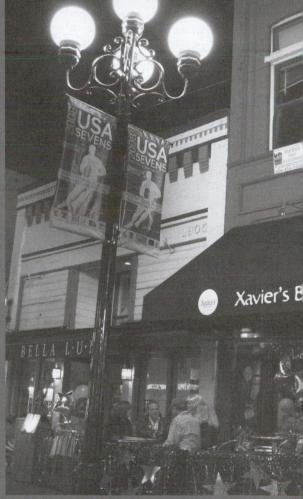

Courtesy of the San Diego Convention & Visitors Bureau

the best the season has to offer and a constantly evolving menu allows for creativity and flexibility." Niche obtains its foodstuffs through local growers and mushroom hunters.

WINE LIST

Niche Restaurant also features an all-American wine list. They buy their wine only from boutique wineries that do not sell wine by the pallet. On the guest-friendly menu, each varietal is described by origin and flavor profile. Niche offers over 140 wines by the bottle and 12 wines by the glass; each wine is American and produced in small quantities. Jody Richardson developed the wine list for 302 West, where it won the Wine Enthusiast Award of Distinction.

PERMITS AND LICENSES

The building Niche was to be located in was previously a restaurant. This made the obtaining of permits and licenses a bit easier than it would have been had the building not been a previous restaurant. Some of the licenses, such as the liquor license, were transferred over. The owners completed applications for other permits and licensees, which were then sent to the mayor for approval. Niche Restaurant is an LLC (limited liability corporation).

MARKETING

The owners and staff were the main facilitators of the restaurant's marketing. Marketing techniques

included the creation of a Web site, press releases, and a quarterly newsletter. Niche restaurant was fortunate to have the mailing list of 302 West carry over to them. They sent postcards and the quarterly newsletter to the people on the mailing list before opening. The restaurant's central location also helped with marketing.

CHALLENGES

The main challenge of opening a restaurant for the owners of Niche was finding capital investors. Then the search began for the right location. They also had to make the decision to keep the concept of 302 West and make every facet of the location congruent with the contemporary American design. They wanted to keep Niche classic yet contemporary. The small details of setting the restaurant up were another challenge, from finding creamers that matched their china to picking the right carpeting.

FINANCIAL INFORMATION

Niche Restaurant's annual sales were expected to reach $1.3 million in their first year. They have about 320 to 350 guest covers a week. Checks average $65 to $70 per person. A breakdown of sales percentages follows.

- Percentage of sales that goes to rent: approximately 6 percent
- Percentage of food sales: 58 percent
- Percentage of beverage sales: 37 percent

- Percentage of other (i.e., gift certificates): 5 percent
- Percentage of profit: 7.2 percent

WHAT TURNED OUT DIFFERENT FROM EXPECTED?

While most of the staff at Niche was brought over from 302 West, two positions had to be filled. The owners thought that since the staff had worked together so closely for so long, it would be hard to bring in new people who could adapt to the tight-knit group and fit in well. To their surprise, it was not as hard as they thought. The two new hires fit right in with the family.

MOST EMBARRASSING MOMENT

When asked about her most embarrassing moment, owner Jody Richardson told a story about an opening party that her investors put on. She was asked to give a brief speech to thank everyone for their help in the development and opening of Niche Restaurant. Jody explained that she is not a public speaker by nature. During her speech, she thanked everyone by name. Afterward she realized that she had forgotten to mention one person.

ADVICE TO AVOID THIS AND OTHER EMBARRASSING MOMENTS

Don't speak before you think and don't be an open book! Learn more about Niche Restaurant at www. nichegeneva.com.

Restaurant Leadership and Management

LEARNING OBJECTIVES

After reading and studying this chapter, you should be able to:

- Describe the characteristics of effective leaders.

- Discuss some important factors that must be considered when leading restaurant employees.

- Know several important management concepts.

- Discuss conflict management.

- Describe the process of conflict resolution.

Courtesy of Sysco

Leading Employees

Restaurant corporations of excellence regard their employee resources as their most valuable asset and competitive advantage. Progressive employers seek to become the *employer of choice*. We need to realize that the *leadership* of employee resources is critical because we don't manage our employees, we lead them. We manage finances, we lead employees. This is a fundamental paradigm shift. The restaurant experience is intangible, meaning that one restaurant is much the same as the other. What makes the difference is the human element of service, service, and service![1]

You may already be, or soon may be, a leader in the restaurant industry. Being a *leader* is exciting; there are challenges, opportunities, and rewards. If you are a leader, your company has invested its trust in you and has expectations of your performance. But how do you feel? Well, you wouldn't be alone if you felt some apprehension because you are responsible not only for your work, but also for the work of others. We hope you get off to a great start with this book and wish you success in your career.

Ever wonder about the impact that leaders have on the success of a restaurant company? Here is an example: On Restaurant Row in one city, one family restaurant has had 12 different busers in two months. In the restaurant next door, the food is superb one week and terrible the next. The bar on the corner cannot find a decent bartender, much less keep one. Across the street, one restaurant had a near-riot in the kitchen resulting from an argument between the cooks and servers. The Italian restaurant two doors down is losing customers steadily because its service is so poor. But the oldest restaurant on the block is packing them in night after night, with staff who have been there for years.[2] In many of the city's restaurants, the employee turnover rate is very high. Every seven days we turn thousands of employees in this industry. We don't have a "labor" crisis. We have a turnover crisis. Service is poor and guests complain, but then that's just part of the game, isn't it? Yet several restaurants in town have few *staffing* problems and happy guests.

Throughout the city a common cry in the restaurant industry is that you just can't get good people these days. People don't work hard the way they used to, they don't do what you expect them to, they come late and leave early or don't show up at all, they are sullen and rude, they don't always speak English—the complaints go on and on. The rotten help you get today must cause all the problems. Is this true? If it is true, what about those establishments where things run smoothly? Can it be that the way in which the workers are led has something to do with the presence or absence of problems? You bet it does! In this section, we explore the leadership aspect of a restaurant.

In the hospitality industry, almost everything depends on the physical labor of many hourly (or nonmanagerial) workers: people who cook, serve tables, mix drinks, wash dishes, mop floors. Few industries are as dependent for success on the performance of hourly workers. These employees make the products and they serve the customers—or drive them away.[3]

How well these employees produce and serve depends largely on how well they are led. If they are not led well, the product or the service suffers and the restaurant is in trouble. It is the people who lead these employees who hold the keys to the success of the operation.

If you were to ask any hospitality leader what his or her greatest challenge is, the likely answer would be finding and keeping great employees motivated. Given the high turnover in the hospitality industry and the resultant cost, we begin to understand some of the leadership challenges that human resources professionals face.

The idea that a manager or supervisor must be a leader comes as a surprise to people who have never thought about it before. In terms of hospitality leadership, the following definition is appropriate: Leading is the process by which a person with vision is able to influence the activities and outcomes of others in a desired way.[4]

Leadership begins with a vision, a mission, and goals. *Vision* is the articulation of the mission of the organization in such an appealing way that it vividly conveys what it can be like in the future. Vision instills a common purpose, self-esteem, and a sense of membership in the organization. The *mission statement* describes the purpose of the organization and outlines the kinds of activities performed for guests.

Mission statements normally have three parts: First, a statement of overall purpose; second, a statement explaining the values employees are expected to maintain in the daily decision-making process; third, a declaration of the major *goals* that leaders believe are essential as well as how to attain the goals. Goals should be relevant to the mission, specific and clear, challenging yet achievable, made in collaboration with employees, and written down with the strategies and tactics of how to meet the goals. The importance of vision, mission, goals, *strategy*, and *tactics* is critical to the success of the company, and supervisors do much of the crucial work.[5]

In a work situation, the company installs the leader. In the hospitality industry the term *leader* often refers to a manager at a lower organizational level who supervises entry-level or other employees who themselves do not have supervisory responsibilities. The employees are expected to do what the boss tells them to do—that's just part of the job, right?

But if employees simply do what they are told, why is labor turnover so high, productivity so low, and absenteeism so prevalent? Why is there conflict between employees and management? The truth of the matter is that the leader is supposed to be leading the employees, but that does not guarantee that the employees will put all of their efforts into the job. This is where leadership comes in.

The hospitality industry is composed of 70 percent part-time, short-term people. They are "only working here *until*"—until they get out of high school, until they get out of college, until they have enough money to buy a car, or until an opening comes up someplace else. It is not uncommon to hear a young hourly employee say, "I'll keep this job until I can get a real job," for what they often mean is that they plan to switch from an hourly to a salaried position.

LEADERS AND ASSOCIATES

Restaurants are dependent on large numbers of people to fill low-wage entry-level jobs that include washing dishes and pots, busing tables, hosting, prepping the same or similar food every day from the same steam table. Employees sometimes take these jobs either because no special skill, ability, or limited experience is required, or because nothing else is available.

Often, they are frequently taken for granted, ignored, or spoken to only when reprimanded. Given the nature of the work and the attitudes of management and sometimes of other workers, it is no wonder that turnover is high.

Another level of hourly worker is the skilled or semiskilled: cashiers, bartenders, cooks, and servers. These jobs are more appealing, the money is better, and there is a chance for advancement. Yet here, too, you often find temporary workers—students, moonlighters, people who cannot find anything in their own fields—people working there *until*.

Many employers assume that their employee will not stay long, and most of them do not. According to Dr. Jay R. Schrock the turnover rate for hourly workers in full-service operations is 100 percent.[6] That means that your typical full-service restaurant will lose every one of its hourly employees during one year and have to fill every position. If we were to ask workers to explain why they left their jobs, the most frequently cited reasons would likely be more money, a better work schedule, and more enjoyable work. Given this alarming statistic of 100 percent turnover we need to examine human resources leadership in hospitality beginning with the characteristics of leaders.

CHARACTERISTICS OF LEADERS

If we were to examine great leaders of the past we would likely come up with a list of characteristics and traits like this from the *U.S. Guidebook for Marines*.

Courage, decisiveness, dependability, endurance, enthusiasm, initiative, integrity, judgment, justice, knowledge, loyalty, tact, and unselfishness. Of these, a Marine would likely say that integrity is the most important. Integrity to a Marine means to do something right even if nobody is aware of it.[7]

Effective leaders have six traits that distinguish them from nonleaders: drive, the desire to influence others, honesty and moral character, self-confidence, intelligence, and relevant knowledge.

A person's *drive* shows that he or she is willing and able to exert exceptional effort to achieve a goal. This high-energy person is likely to take the initiative and be persistent.

Leaders have a *desire to influence others*. This desire is frequently seen as a willingness to accept authority. A leader also builds trusting relationships with those supervised, by being truthful. By showing consistency between their words and actions, leaders display *honesty and moral character*.

Leaders have *self-confidence* to influence others to pursue the goals of the organization. Employees tend to prefer a leader who has strong beliefs and is decisive over one who seems unsure of which decision to make.

Influencing others takes a *level of intelligence*. A leader needs to gather, synthesize, and interpret a lot of information. Leaders create a vision, develop goals, communicate and motivate, problem-solve, and make decisions. A leader needs a high level of *relevant knowledge,* technical, theoretical, and conceptual. Knowledge of the company, its policies and procedures, the department, and the employees are all necessary to make informed decisions.[8] Effective leaders are able to influence others to behave in a particular way. This is called *power*. There are four primary sources of power:[9]

1. *Legitimate power*, which is derived from an individual's position in an organization

2. *Reward power*, which is derived from an individual's control over rewards
3. *Coercive power*, which is derived from an individual's ability to threaten negative outcomes
4. *Expert power*, which is derived from an individual's personal charisma and the respect and/or admiration the individual inspires

Many leaders have a combination of these sources of power to influence others to goal achievement.

The Nature of Leadership[10]

Now, you may wonder, "What is a leader, and how is it any different from being a manager?" These are good questions. As a part of the management staff, one is expected to produce goods and services by working with people and using resources such as equipment and employees. That is what being a manager is all about. A leader can be defined as someone who guides or influences the actions of his or her employees to reach certain goals. A leader is a person whom people follow voluntarily. What you, as a supervisor, must do is to direct the work of your people in a way that causes them to do it voluntarily. You don't have to be a born leader, you don't have to be magnetic or charismatic; you have to get people to work for you willingly and to the best of their ability. That is what *leadership* is all about.

Although it is true that many leadership skills are innate and that not all managers make great leaders, it is also true that most managers will benefit from leadership training. Moreover, natural leaders will flourish in an environment that supports their growth and development.

Figure 10.1 shows the seven steps to establishing a foundation for leadership development.

1. Commit to investing the time, resources, and money needed to create a culture that supports leadership development.

2. Identify and communicate the differences between management skills and leadership abilities within the organization.

3. Develop quantifiable measurements that support leadership skills. These include percentage of retention, percentage of promotables, and percentage of cross-trained team members.

4. Make leadership skills a focus of management training. These include communication skills (written, verbal, nonverbal, and listening), team-building skills (teamwork, coaching, and feedback), proactive planning skills (transitioning from managing shifts to managing businesses), and interpersonal skills (motivation, delegation, decision-making, and problem-solving).

5. Implement ongoing programs that focus on leadership skills, such as managing multiple priorities, creating change, and presentation skills.

6. Know that in the right culture, leaders can be found at entry level.

7. Recognize, reward, and celebrate leaders for their passion, dedication, and results.

FIGURE 10.1 The seven steps to establishing a foundation for leadership development.

In theory, you have authority over your people because you have *formal authority*, or the right to command, given to you by the organization. You are the boss and you have the power, the ability to command. You control the hiring, firing, raises, rewards, discipline, and punishment. In all reality, your authority is anything but absolute. *Real authority* is conferred on your subordinates, and you have to earn the right to lead them. It is possible for you to be the *formal leader* of your work group as well as have someone else who is the *informal leader* actually calling the shots.

The relationship between you and your people is a fluid one, subject to many subtle currents and cross-currents between them and you. If they do not willingly accept your authority, they have many ways of withholding success. They can stay home from work, come in late, drag out the work into overtime, produce inferior products, drive your customers away with rudeness and poor service, break the rules, and refuse to do what you tell them to, create crises, and punish you by walking off the job and leaving you in the lurch. Laying down the law, the typical method of control in hospitality operations, does not necessarily maintain authority; on the contrary, it usually creates a negative, nonproductive environment.

What it all adds up to is that your job as a leader is to lead and coach a group of employees who are often untrained, all of whom are different from each other, and many of whom would rather be working somewhere else. You are dependent on them to do the work for which you are responsible. You will succeed only to the degree that they permit you to succeed. It is your job to get the workers to do their best for the enterprise, for the customers, and for you. How can one do this?

As a distinguished leadership expert noted, "Managers are people who do things right, and leaders are people who do the right things." Think about that for a moment. In other words, managers are involved in being efficient and in mastering routines, whereas leaders are involved in being effective and turning goals into reality. As a human resources leader, your job is to *do the right things right,* to be both efficient and effective. An effective supervisor in the hospitality industry is one whom, first, knows and understands basic principles of management, and second, applies them to managing all the resource operations.

In the hospitality industry we use a technique referred to as *LBWA, leadership by walking around,* spending a significant part of your day talking to your employees, guests, and peers. As you are walking around and talking to these various people, you should be performing three vital roles discussed in this book: listening, coaching, and troubleshooting.

Employee Input, and What's in It for Me?

Any restaurant that wants to optimize its potential will have extensive employee input into not only the vision and mission but also how to achieve or exceed them. Employees who are engaged with these processes will feel "in on things" and be more likely to go the extra mile to delight guests and create the all-important guest loyalty. Employees can have input into the menu, the beverage menu, service methods, tip arrangements, shift selection and allocation, cost reductions, recycling programs, and energy reduction.

It's natural for employees to think or request, "What's in it for me?" because if they are going that extra mile they surely need recognition and rewards for outstanding accomplishments.

Policies and Procedures

Restaurant policies and procedures are necessary even for small restaurants because without them we all know chaos prevails. Policies and procedures are the "ground rules" of how to "play the game"; for example, how should a person who is repeatedly late be treated? Well, if there is a clear policy and procedure for that, it is easier to enforce, and besides, employees will respect an operator who has policies and procedures in place. One large and successful restaurant operator, Cracker Barrel, has an interesting policy on fraternization. Managers and supervisors are not allowed to fraternize with employees. For example, they should not go drinking together after a shift or attend baseball games together; unless it is a company-sponsored event, no fraternization is allowed. Can you guess why? Because they don't want to leave themselves open to getting sued for discrimination or harassment if Maria did not get the shift she wanted because . . . or if someone else did get seemingly preferential treatment.

Courtesy of the San Diego Convention & Visitors Bureau
Good planning makes for a smooth production.

Management Topics

Most management texts outline the elements of management as planning, communicating, organizing, decision making, motivating, performance management, and control.

PLANNING

Planning provides the direction for the organization to go in order to be successful. It is the process of setting goals and determining how best to accomplish them. Planning is the foundation of all the other elements of management. There are two main types of planning—strategic (long range, 3–10 years) and operational (short term, 1–12 months).

Strategic plans are devised to steer the organization toward its vision and mission. Owners and managers look ahead to plan where they want the organization to be in 5 or 10 years. One way organizations do this is by strengths, weaknesses, opportunities, and threats (SWOT) assessment. This *SWOT assessment* is done by comparing the organization to its competitors and the general business

> - ■ Forecasting
> - ■ Determining where the organization is and where it wants to be
> - ■ Setting goals and strategies to achieve the goals
> - ■ Evaluating results

FIGURE 10.2 Steps involved in the planning process.

environment. Each restaurateur or restaurant company can decide what the points of comparison are. These could include taking the guest cycle beginning with location, reservations (if the restaurant takes them), to curbside appeal, parking, greeting, holding area, menus, food quality, timeliness of food, presentation of food, service, atmosphere of restaurant, noise level, decor, and cleanliness of restrooms. Figure 10.2 shows the steps involved in the planning process.

Planning takes time but pays dividends when everyone is on the same page and making progress.

Forecasting *Forecasting* is a part of planning that aims to predict what will happen in the future. In a restaurant situation, we need to forecast the number of guests to expect and prepare for. Obviously, the better job we do in "guesstimating" the numbers, the easier it will be to make or exceed the goals set. If a restaurant is already in existence, we can examine past guest counts, sales, and even menu selections in order to plan for the next few days.

Determining where the organization is and where it wants to be operationally: The owners and employees need to determine where the organization is, meaning that it has a level of guest satisfaction and guest loyalty that is measurable. There are also opinion surveys that can influence guest restaurant selection—good ratings in Zagat can help a restaurant, as some guests are influenced by this and other similar guides. Let's say that a restaurant has a poor service rating; it would be a no-brainer to want to improve this score. This can easily be planned for by setting a goal of 90 percent on guest comments (up from the current 75 percent). In terms of profit, if current profits are, say, 4 percent return on investment, it would be smart to plan how to increase that ROI up to 15 percent.

Goal Setting and Strategies *Goals* and strategies should be set for each of the key result areas of restaurant operations. Among the key result areas are:

- ■ Guest satisfaction
- ■ Guest loyalty
- ■ Sales
- ■ Labor costs
- ■ Food and beverage costs
- ■ Energy costs
- ■ Direct operating expenses and so on

An example of goal setting would be for sales of $20,000 per week for the month of July. Another would be for 100 percent guest satisfaction or 95 percent or whatever number you like. Similarly, goals can be set for food costs (say 27 percent) and beverage costs (say 22 percent) and so on. Strategies are how the goal is met or exceeded. So, for the goal of $20,000 sales per week, a good marketing and sales plan is required to be in place and active. Promotions and sales and service training, including emotional intelligence (making a connection and bonding with guests so they will want to return), will also contribute to this goal being met. A strategy for ensuring that the food cost percentage is met is to check the cost of goods sold on a regular basis. The same applies to the labor costs; not only will effective scheduling work but also constant monitoring of sales and labor costs will ensure no surprises at month's end.

ORGANIZING

The purpose of *organizing* is to get a job done efficiently and effectively by completing these tasks:[11]

- Divide the work to be done into specific jobs and departments.
- Assign tasks and responsibilities associated with individual jobs.
- Coordinate diverse organizational tasks.
- Cluster jobs into units.
- Establish relationships among individuals, groups, and departments.
- Establish formal lines of authority.
- Allocate and deploy organizational resources.

So, how does this relate to restaurant leadership and management? Well, whether you're a part of Darden restaurants' management team or owner of your own restaurant, good organization is a must for success in the restaurant business. What should the organization of a restaurant be like? It depends on the size and complexity of the company. Is it a standalone restaurant or a chain of several restaurants? Large chains may be organized into areas with a vice president or area director for each. The company would likely have a VP for operations, marketing, finance, human resources, and franchising. For small chains, a president or an operations director may run the entire chain.

Each store will have its own organization—for example, a full-service restaurant with front and back of the house and departments clearly defined. For example, the kitchen can have separate fry, sauté, broil, grill, prep, salad, dessert, and appetizer stations. Such work specialization improves efficiency.

DECISION MAKING

Operating a restaurant requires countless decisions every day. Most decisions are made quickly and easily but some require more thought or information or both. The more challenging decisions go through the eight-step *decision-making process*:[12]

- *Identification and definition of problem:* Identifying the problem or challenge is important; otherwise, we may never know if we have fixed the problem or merely patched it only to have it surface again.
- *Identification of decision criteria:* Once the problem has been identified and defined, we need to determine the criteria relevant to the decision. Suppose

the problem was the price and availability of a menu item, then the decision criteria might be the following: Get prices and availability from other suppliers, take the item off the menu, or change the dish by using other ingredients.

■ *Allocation of weights to criteria:* We all know that some elements of a decision are more important than others, so putting a number for its weighting makes sense—of course, we often do this instinctively.

■ *Development of alternatives:* A listing of the various alternatives is presented.

■ *Selection of alternative:* The best alternative is selected.

■ *Implementation of alternative:* The decision is put into action.

■ *Evaluation of decision effectiveness:* The degree of success as a result of the decision is gauged.

There are two major types of decisions, programmed and nonprogrammed. A *programmed decision* relates to decisions that occur on a regular basis, such as what to do when the stock of something goes below par, or when a guest makes a request for a booth. A *nonprogrammed decision* is one that rarely happens so it is handled differently. Some examples would be which software program to use for a restaurant's front- and back-of-the-house operations, or which supplier to use.

COMMUNICATING

In the restaurant business we spend most of our time *communicating* with guests and associates. Fast-paced restaurants require quick and accurate communications. From personal greetings from greeters or hosts, to introductions by service staff, communication is important as it imparts an impression of the restaurant to guests. Communications are equally important between front- and back-of-the-house staff, namely, servers and cooks. Here the communication of what the guest ordered is normally written or punched onto a screen so it quickly transmits to the cooks in the kitchen. We have all probably experienced occasions where the communication broke down and misunderstandings escalated into unfortunate situations.

Courtesy of the San Diego Convention & Visitors Bureau

A manager communicating with guests.

Interpersonal communications include verbal, nonverbal, body language, and verbal intonation. The best way to communicate is verbal face to face, as there is an opportunity for immediate feedback. *Nonverbal* communication is without words. It can be a sound like a bell telling a server that an order is ready for pickup. *Body language* is an expression on a guest's face as she or he complains about something or the cook's gesture to a server as she asks about an order. Reading facial expression is an important part of communication because it can give a good idea of how the person talking is feeling. *Active listening* is really hearing and understanding what is being said. Most of us could probably work on improving our listening skills because we are either thinking of what we are going to say next or not agreeing with what is being said instead of actively listing.

MOTIVATING[13]

When you lead a restaurant team, you will have certain expectations of your employees. You will expect them to do the work they have been hired to do—to produce products and services to the quality standards set. You may wonder if their performance will meet your expectations, and you may have some plans for improving their productivity. But you may not realize what these employees expect from you and how you meet their expectations may have as much to do with their performance as your expectations of them.

Motivation refers to what makes people tick: the needs and desires and fears and aspirations within people that make them behave as they do. Motivation is the energizer that makes people take action; it is the *why* of human behavior. In the restaurant, motivation goes hand in hand with productivity. The big question is how to motivate poor performers to realize their potential and raise their productivity, and how to keep good performers from going stale in their jobs or leaving for a better opportunity.

Actually, you cannot motivate people to do good work. Motivation must come from within. The one thing you as a leader can do is turn it on, to activate people's own motivations. To do this you must get to know your associates and find out what they respond to. It might be the work itself. It might be the way you lead. It might be the work environment. It might be their individual goals: recognition, achievement, challenging opportunities, money, or whatever. Figure 10.3 shows the relationship of key motivators: needs, desires, fears, and aspirations.

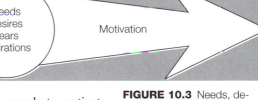

FIGURE 10.3 Needs, desires, fears, and aspirations lead to motivation.

In sum, motivation is a complicated business, and getting people to motivate themselves to do their jobs well has no one simple answer. It takes something of an experiential approach; you try to find out what each person responds to (you can always ask them!), and if one does not work, maybe the next thing will. Remember that recognition, rewards, and positive reinforcement work wonders.

PERFORMANCE MANAGEMENT[14]

Performance management is an important part of overall restaurant management. Performance standards form the heart of the job description and they describe the what's, how-tos, and how-wells of a job. Each performance standard measures three aspects about each unit of the job:

1. What the employee is to do
2. How well it is to be done
3. To what extent it is to be done (how much, how soon)

If you develop a full set of performance standards for each job that you are responsible for, you have the basis for a management system for your associates and the work they do. You can use them to describe the jobs, to define the day's work for each job, to train associates to meet standards, to evaluate associates' performance, and to give them feedback on how they are doing. You can use performance standards as a basis for rewarding achievement and selecting people for promotion.

Intelligent and consistent use of a performance standard system reduces or eliminates those five major reasons for low productivity and high turnover. Associates are told clearly what to do. They are taught how to do it. They know how well they are doing because there is a goal standard of measurement. A manager can help and support associates with additional training or coaching when a standard is not being met. All this makes for much better relationships between associates and management.

CONTROL

Control deals with keeping track of costs, inventory, percentages, and other factors that keep the organization profitable and compliant with regulations. The subject of control is covered in Chapter 8.

Restaurant Management Issues

There are many restaurant management issues, but here are some of the most important and most likely to happen.

SEXUAL HARASSMENT[15]

As a restaurant manager or owner, you need to be able to recognize and confront *sexual harassment*. The Equal Employment Opportunity Commission (EEOC) issued guidelines on sexual harassment in 1980, indicating that it is a form of gender discrimination under Title VII of the 1964 Civil Rights Act. The EEOC states, "Unwelcome sexual advances, requests for sexual favors, and other verbal or physical conduct of a sexual nature constitute sexual harassment when this conduct explicitly or implicitly affects an individual's employment, unreasonably interferes with an individual's work performance, or creates an intimidating, hostile, or offensive work environment."[16] This definition of sexual harassment is known as the *quid pro quo* definition. *Quid pro quo* means that something is given in exchange for something else. In this type of sexual harassment, submission to or rejection of a sexual favor is used as the basis for employment decisions regarding that employee. The employment decision may be an increase in pay, a promotion, or keeping your job. Only management or supervisors can engage in quid pro quo harassment.

There are almost 100,000 EEOC cases a year, of which about 35,000 are based on race, 30,000 based on sex, and 38,000 based on retaliation. Additionally, 7,500 sexual harassment charges and 3,700 pregnancy discrimination charges are made and $365 million in monetary relief was gained by charging parties.[17]

Here is an example from the EEOC regarding a restaurant that allowed a male employee to abuse a female employee.[18]

Dinos Restaurant Allowed Male Co-Worker to Abuse Female Employee, Federal Agency Charged

SOUTH BEND, IND. A Michigan City, Ind., restaurant will pay $20,000 to settle a second sexual harassment lawsuit brought by the U.S. Equal Employment Opportunity Commission (EEOC), the agency announced today.

The EEOC charged in its suit (Case No. 3:11-cv-0306-TLS-CAN in U.S. District Court for the Northern District of Indiana, South Bend Division) that the restaurant owner, Faros, Inc., violated federal law when it failed to respond to complaints that a male server sexually harassed a female coworker for over several months including, sexual innuendo and propositions that escalated to unwanted touching at least twice. The EEOC further charged that Faros, Inc. retaliated against the harassed employee by reducing her wages after she complained.

Such alleged conduct violates Title VII of the Civil Rights Act of 1964. The EEOC filed suit after first attempting to reach a pre-litigation settlement through its conciliation process.

In addition to monetary settlement, the consent decree, which will remain in effect until September 2016, requires Faros, Inc. to comply with prohibitions against further discrimination and retaliation, and continue the policy, training and posting obligations mandated by the Consent Decree which resolved the EEOC's first sexual harassment lawsuit against Faros, Inc. (Case No. 3:10-cv-00407-RL-CAN).

"There is no excuse for permitting employees to touch, proposition or barrage their coworkers with offensive sexual statements at work," said EEOC Regional Attorney Laurie Young. "Employers must make eradicating such conduct from their work places a priority."

Another example of sexual harassment occurred at a Caesars Palace property, where the EEOC asserted that male supervisors would demand and/or force female workers to perform sex with them under threat of being fired. Women, predominantly Spanish speakers, were forced to have sex with their supervisors. To make matters worse, management failed to address and correct the unlawful conduct, even though women complained about it. Further, the EEOC said, when workers complained about the unlawful conduct, they were retaliated against in the form of demotions, loss of wages, further harassment, discipline, or discharge. Caesars paid $850,000 to settle the suit.[19]

In another case, a Subway franchise paid $166,500 for a disability harassment lawsuit. The EEOC charged in the case that the Subway owner and one of his managers subjected Ms. Gitsham to a disability-based hostile work environment, including teasing and name calling, because she is hearing impaired and wears hearing aids. Ms. Gitsham was forced to resign her position after both the owner and human resources/training manager repeatedly mocked her privately and in front of employees, creating a hostile workplace, with taunts such as: "Read my lips," and, "Can you hear me now?" and, "You got your ears on?"[20]

Another type of sexual harassment is *environmental sexual harassment*. In this case, comments or innuendos of a sexual nature or physical contact are considered a violation when they interfere with an employee's work performance or create an "intimidating, hostile, or offensive working environment." In this situation, the harassment must be persistent and so severe that it affects the employee's well being.

A final type of sexual harassment is *third-party sexual harassment*. Third-party sexual harassment involves a customer or client and an employee. The customer or client may harass an employee, or the other way around. For example, a male customer may harass a female bartender.

The following examples of sexual harassment include an example of quid pro quo, environmental, and third-party sexual harassment. See if you can determine which is which.

1. Beth is a new employee who works as a cook's assistant in a crowded kitchen. The men in the kitchen are constantly making crude, sexually oriented comments and jokes, and leave their X-rated magazines in full view of anyone walking by. Beth feels very intimidated and ill at ease. Unfortunately, the situation doesn't improve over the first two months, and Beth feels too stressed to continue working.

2. For the past few nights, after the dining room has closed, Susan's boss has asked her to go to his place for a drink. Although Susan has gone out with him and some friends once before, she is not interested in pursuing a relationship with him. When she tells him she is not interested, he tells her that a dining room supervisor job will be opening soon and that he could make sure she gets it if she takes him up on his invitation.

3. Barbara is a regular customer at a popular after-work bar where Bob works as a bartender. Barbara finds Bob to be a very good-looking fellow, so much so that she can't keep her eyes, or hands, off him. Bob doesn't like the attention Barbara gives him, but he feels he can't do much about it since she is the customer.

Such instances of sexual harassment can cost a company lost productive time, low morale, harm to its reputation, court costs, and punitive damages to harassment victims. In each of the situations just described, there is an element of sexual harassment. While the second situation represents the typical exchange of sexual favors for employment opportunities, the first situation is an example of environmental sexual harassment in which the working environment was intimidating, hostile, or offensive due to physical, verbal, or visual (such as pornographic pictures) sexual harassment. The third situation represents third-party sexual harassment.

As a manager you are responsible for recognizing, confronting, and preventing the sexual harassment of both female and male employees by other employees or by nonemployees such as guests or people making deliveries. "An employer can be liable for customers who harass employees when the employer knew or should have known of the harassment and failed to prevent it."[21] Both you and your employer will be considered guilty of sexual harassment if you knew about, or should have known about, such misconduct and failed to correct it. If you genuinely did not know that sexual harassment took place, liability can be averted if there is an adequate sexual harassment policy and the situation is corrected immediately.

Following are some specific actions that you can take to deal effectively with the issue of sexual harassment:

■ Be familiar with your company's sexual harassment policy. Figure 10.4 is a sample policy. This policy should include disciplinary guidelines for people who are guilty of sexual harassment and guidelines for harassers who

---

I.   Policy

   The policy of XYZ Restaurants is that all of our employees should be able to enjoy a work environment free from all forms of discrimination, including sexual harassment. Sexual harassment is a form of misconduct that undermines the integrity of the employment relationship, debilitates morale, and therefore interferes with the work effectiveness of its victims and their coworkers. Sexual harassment is a violation of the law and will not be tolerated or condoned.

II. Definition of Sexual Harassment

   Sexual harassment consists of unwelcome advances, requests for sexual favors, and other verbal or physical conduct of a sexual nature when:

   1.   submission to such conduct is made either explicitly or implicitly a term of condition of an employee's employment, or
   2.   submission to or rejection of such conduct by an employee is used as the basis for employment decisions, or
   3.   the conduct interferes substantially with an employee's work performance or creates an intimidating, hostile, or offensive work environment.

   Sexual harassment is not limited to actions of restaurant employees. Customers and clients may also be victims, or perpetrators, of sexual harassment. Following are examples of sexual harassment.

   • Unwelcome intentional touching or other unwelcome physical contact (such as pinching or patting).
   • Unwelcome staring or whistling.
   • Unwelcome sexually suggestive or flirtatious notes, gifts, or electronic or voice mail.
   • Offering an employment-related reward in exchange for sexual favors.
   • Verbal abuse of a sexual nature.
   • Unwelcome display of sexually suggestive objects or pictures such as pinups.
   • Conduct or remarks that demean or are hostile to a person's gender.

III. Coverage: XYZ Restaurants

   XYZ Restaurants prohibits sexual harassment during work hours or while on company property by all employees and by all nonemployees, such as customers and suppliers.

IV. Responsibilities

   XYZ Restaurants managers are responsible for preventing sexual harassment and educating employees about this subject. They are also responsible for setting a good example, taking every complaint seriously, investigating complaints fairly, and maintaining confidentiality.

   XYZ Restaurants request that any employee with a complaint regarding sexual harassment make every effort to promptly present the complaint to their immediate supervisor or the human resource director. If the complaint involves the employee's immediate supervisor, or if the employee feels uncomfortable discussing the complaint with the immediate supervisor, the employee may speak to another supervisor.

V.   Investigation Procedures and Disciplinary Action

   Once a supervisor has received a complaint, he or she is to immediately contact the human resource department. After notification of the employee's complaint, a fair and confidential investigation will be initiated. The human resource director will review the results of the investigation for possible disciplinary action.

   If warranted, disciplinary action up to and including termination will be imposed. Retaliation against employees who file complaints or assist in investigating complaints may also result in discipline up to an including termination.

FIGURE 10.4 Sample sexual harassment policy.

retaliate against those who turn them in. This policy may also include a formal complaint procedure for employees to use if they think they have been victims of sexual harassment, with provisions for immediate investigations and prompt disciplinary actions when appropriate.

- Educate your employees on how to recognize sexual harassment, how to report it when it occurs, and the steps that will be taken if an employee is guilty of sexual harassment.
- When an employee informs you of a possible case of sexual harassment, investigate the situation promptly according to your company policy. Your investigation is much the same as that done for any possible case of misconduct as just described. Don't assume that anyone is guilty or innocent.
- When you witness an example of sexual harassment, follow your policy and take appropriate and timely disciplinary action.
- Provide follow-up after instances of sexual harassment. Check with victims and witnesses that harassment has indeed stopped and that no retaliation is taking place.
- Prevent sexual harassment by being visible in your work areas, being a good role model, and taking all reported incidents seriously.

CONFLICT MANAGEMENT

We may wrongly assume that all conflict is bad for individuals and the organization. This is simply not so—some conflict is not only natural, but also productive, experts say; learning how to manage it, however, does not come naturally.[22] Every relationship and every conflict has a past, present, and future, and resolving conflicts effectively requires that we deal with all three.[23]

Conflict management is the application of strategies to settle opposing ideas, goals, and/or objectives in a positive manner. Managers are often put in the middle of conflicts. They must know how to manage themselves, as well as the situation, positively and delicately. Managers must be able to separate their own emotions and feelings from the situation at hand. They need to be able to act, not react!

It is tempting as a manager to ignore conflict, or to just tell your employees to get along. However, Wolf Rinke, a professional speaker and author, says, "If you decide as a manager that all conflict is bad, then employees will make sure no bad information gets to you."[24] If you discourage reports of friction, you might shut off a crucial flow of information that could lead to innovation.

An article for Food Service Warehouse states, "Conflicts may stem from friction with other employees or negativity toward a workplace policy. Employees may take issue with the owner's management style, or become jealous of another co-worker's more favorable job responsibilities. Employees may have a scheduling conflict that turns into a major problem, or they may feel bullied while at work. Any of these can become grounds for conflicts, both minor and serious."[25]

Everyone's needs are important and everyone deserves respect. "In workplace conflicts, differing needs are often at the heart of bitter disputes. Recognizing the legitimacy of conflicting needs and acknowledging them with concern and understanding opens pathways to positive problem solving, team building, and improved relationships."[26]

There are many ways to manage conflict. For the purpose of this chapter, we will use a five-step approach to conflict management, which is illustrated in Figure 10.5.

The first step is to *analyze* what is at the center of the conflict. To do this, supervisors need to ask themselves questions, as well as those involved in the conflict. Here are a few questions to ask:

- Who is involved?
- How did the conflict arise?
- Can a positive spin be put on the situation?
- Are there any secondary issues?
- Have positions been taken?
- Is negotiation plausible?
- Is there a way to serve all interests at hand?
- Are there external constraints/influences?
- Is there a previous history of the conflict?

After the main source is identified and the source of the conflict is understood, it is helpful to brainstorm and write thoughts and ideas of resolution on paper.

The second step to managing conflict is to determine the type of *strategy* that will be used to resolve the conflict. Some examples of commonly used resolution strategies are collaboration, compromise, competition, accommodation, and avoidance.

Collaboration results most often when concerns for others are of high importance. This type of strategy results in a win/win outcome. Both parties cooperate with each other and try to understand the other parties concerns, while also expressing their own. The parties both put forth a mutual effort and come to a solution that is completely satisfactory for both parties.

Compromise results from high concern for one's own interest or one's own group interest accompanied by moderate to high interest for the other parties involved. Both parties try to resolve the conflict by finding a resolution that partially satisfies both of them, but completely satisfies neither. This type of strategy either produces a win/win or lose/lose outcome, depending on if the solution chosen is the most effective. This varies, depending on the situation at hand.

Competition results when there is a high concern for one's own interest or one's own group. The outcome could vary from win/lose to lose/win, depending on who prevails. This strategy is not ideal, as it may cause increasing conflict, the losing party may try to even the score.

Accommodation is the result of low concern for your own interests or the interest of your group, which produces a lose/win outcome. The opposing party is allowed to satisfy its interest, while one's own interests are neglected.

Avoidance is exactly what it sounds like. Both parties avoid conflict and neither party takes action to resolve it. This produces a lose/lose outcome. In the hospitality industry, this strategy is generally useless because employees work in close quarters. This makes it virtually impossible to avoid each other.

The third step to managing conflict is to start *prenegotiations*. This is a key part of the conflict management process. Being effective at negotiating is a fundamental

Step 1: Analyze

Step 2: Strategy

Step 3: Pre-negotiate

Step 4: Negotiate

Step 5: Implement

FIGURE 10.5 Five step conflict management process.

skill for supervisors. During this step, there are several sub-steps. Initially, both of the parties involved in the conflict should be given the opportunity to come forth and offer a negotiation. If neither party is willing to come forth, then an outsider, in this case the leader, must step in.

Next, the situation should be *reassessed*. The key parties involved in the conflict must be willing to cooperate with each other in the resolution process. The issues should be laid out on the table. From here what is negotiable, as well as what is not negotiable, must be determined. The parties involved should agree upon what information is significantly related to the conflict, as well as how communication and decision making will take place. All of this should be completed before moving on to the fourth step.

The fourth step to managing conflict is to begin the *negotiation* phase. All parties must be able to express their concerns and interests; they must also be willing to listen to each other. As a manager you will be considered the neutral third party. This means that you should not judge or favor either of the parties' ideas or suggested options. You are there to facilitate a healthy discussion and keep the parties focused on the cause of conflict and how it is to be resolved (not to assign blame to a particular party).

The parties involved in conflict should make a list of options that may help resolve the conflict, as well as satisfy their interests. After the lists of possible solutions are completed the options should be discussed and evaluated. Which option would best resolve the conflict and satisfy the most interests should be determined together. A commitment ought to be made to carry out the agreements, and both parties must feel assured that the other will carry out their part.

The final step is for the parties to *implement* the negotiations made. As a supervisor you need to support the resolution and continue to communicate. It is also beneficial to continue monitoring the situation, in order to be certain that the agreement is in fact being carried out.

CONFLICT RESOLUTION[27]

Handling conflict in restaurants can be a challenging task. As a manager, you should always first keep the best interest of your company in mind. In Herb Kindler's book *Conflict Management: Resolving Disagreements in the Workplace* and Robert Friedman's article "Knock out On-the-Job Conflicts, Complaints with Six Simple Steps," published in *Nation's Restaurant News,* the authors discuss the following guiding principles for handling conflict.[28]

First of the guiding principles is to *preserve dignity and respect*. This means to preserve the dignity and respect of all parties involved in the conflict, including yourself. The focus should stay on resolving the conflict, not on the individual characteristics of the parties involved. As a manager, you should never talk down to an employee, especially during a conflict; this could result in them feeling like they are being attacked. If you make everyone feel respected, this will lower defenses and help the process of resolution.

Second is to *listen with empathy and be fully present and identify the issues*. As you listen, determine what issues may have created the conflict. In some cases, the real issues may be beneath the surface. The flash point of a festering disagreement may ignite and result in serious consequences. An example is the hoarding of cutlery in a restaurant by some employees. When it is discovered that there is a shortage of spoons, in particular, and another employee finds out where they are being hidden a fight breaks out.

Don't daydream while an employee is trying to voice their opinion. Listen carefully to everyone involved and withhold any judgments until everyone has had a chance to speak. Try to see from each differing perspective, put yourself in each of the individual's shoes. Give everyone a chance to speak with you on an individual, one-on-one basis. Give them your full attention and make direct eye contact. Most importantly, make sure that your employees feel heard. There is nothing worse than being left with the feeling that your opinion (or words) does not matter.

Third is to *and find a common ground without forcing change and agree on the issues*. Recite for the participants what you perceive to be the issues and ask them to agree with you or correct you. Appealing as it may seem, as a manager it is important to not try to force others into changing. People don't change for others, they change for themselves. They change only when they believe that they will benefit from the change. Therefore, throwing weight around as a superior will result in getting nowhere. It is also important for your employees to trust and respect you. If they believe that you are always looking out for their best interest, they are more likely to believe in you, and look up to you as their *mentor*.

Fourth is to *discuss solutions*. The parties involved have some idea of how they want the situation to be solved—ask them for suggestions.

Fifth is to *honor diversity, including your own perspective*. According to *Webster's Dictionary, diversity* is defined as a "difference, variety, or unlikeness." To *diversify* is to give variety to something; to engage in varied operations; to distribute over a wide range of types or classes. During this step it is important to honor diversity, as well as foster diversification.

Sixth is to *agree on the solutions and follow up*. Discuss solutions with each participant until there is agreement on the issues. Keep detailed notes or have a recorder. Then, once agreement has been reached, document it and have the participants sign it. Then follow up to see if the agreement holds or needs further discussion.

Okay, so let's say everyone has differing viewpoints on a certain issue. This can lead to a creative way of searching for the right resolution, or it can result in feelings of isolation. All too often the search for a resolution during a conflict is a hasty one. When we rush, we rush others into an agreement. We don't let them have time to understand what really matters to them, or come to an independent viewpoint from that of the group, a phenomenon known as *groupthink*. Let's say you are the only person in a group that holds a different viewpoint, you will probably end up conforming to the group and not speaking your opinion. What you should do, of course, is to speak out and let your voice be heard.

We all know the cost of a lawsuit is very high, but in the case of employment litigation, many companies find that the cost of defending themselves against the charges of unfair employment practice is extremely high, often exceeding the amount of the employee's claim of damages. Cases for unfair employment practices may drag on for years, with increased legal expenses. So it makes sense to have an in-house dispute resolution process.[29]

ALTERNATIVE DISPUTE RESOLUTION

Alternative dispute resolution (ADR) is a term for problem-solving and grievance resolution approaches to address employee relations and disputes outside the courtroom. The purpose of ADR is to provide employers and employees with a fair and private forum to settle workplace disputes. With ADR a process is in place to offer the following options:[30]

- *Open-door policy*: Employees have the opportunity to meet with managers to discuss issues.
- *Third-party investigations*: A neutral third-party, from inside or outside the organization, confidently investigates complaints and proposes resolutions.
- *Fact finding*: A neutral third-party person or team from outside the organization examines the facts of the complaint and presents them in a report.
- *Peer review*: A panel of employees, or employees and managers, work together to resolve the employee complaints.
- *Mediation*: A voluntary and confidential process in which a neutral third-party facilitator trained in mediation techniques negotiates a mutually acceptable settlement. The steps in the process are gathering information, framing the issues, developing options, negotiating and formalizing agreements. Participants in the mediation process create their own solutions and settlements are not binding.
- *Arbitration*: Disputes are settled by an arbitrator and may be either binding or nonbinding according to the wishes of the participants. An arbitrator or panel of arbitrators hears both sides of an issue and then makes a determination.

As Nancy Lockwood, a human resource content specialist with the Society for Human Resource Management, suggests, the advantages of ADR are that the total cost is less than traditional means of resolving workplace disputes, legal costs are contained, the time spent on investigations is reduced, and workplace productivity is not compromised.[31] Figure 10.6 shows the steps in an alternative dispute resolution process.

Darden Restaurants has a dispute resolution program in place to address employee questions and complaints on a variety of Darden and employee-related issues. A cornerstone of that program is the open-door policy, where employees are encouraged to speak to their direct supervisor or manager about their problem or concern. If the employee is unable or uncomfortable speaking to their direct supervisor, they are encouraged to speak to their senior member of management, the Darden senior vice president of human resources, or the appropriate employee relations department.

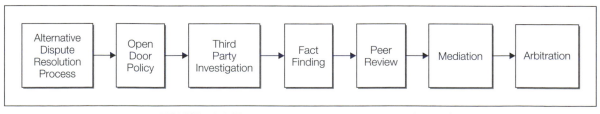

FIGURE 10.6 The steps in an alternative dispute resolution process

To encourage reporting, appropriate confidential, toll-free hotline phone numbers for each restaurant concept and the Restaurant Support Center are communicated through posters located in all restaurants and through other means. The applicable phone numbers and methods of communicating them to employees are listed.[32]

Summary

Restaurant corporations of excellence regard their employee resources as their most valuable asset and competitive advantage.

Leadership begins with a vision, a mission, and goals. *Vision* is the articulation of the mission of the organization in such an appealing way that it vividly conveys what it can be like in the future.

Mission statements normally have three parts: First, a statement of overall purpose; second, a statement explaining the values employees are expected to maintain in the daily decision-making process; third, a declaration of the major *goals* that leaders believe are essential as well as how to attain the goals.

Goals should be relevant to the mission, specific and clear, challenging yet achievable, made in collaboration with employees, and written down with the strategies and tactics of how to meet the goals.

Effective leaders have six traits that distinguish them from nonleaders: drive, the desire to influence others, honesty and moral character, self-confidence, intelligence, and relevant knowledge.

Leaders create a vision, develop goals, communicate and motivate, problem-solve, and make decisions.

Any restaurant that wants to optimize its potential will have extensive employee input into not only the vision and mission but also how to achieve or exceed them.

Planning provides the direction for the organization to go in order to be successful. It is the process of setting goals and determining how best to accomplish them.

Strategic plans are devised to steer the organization towards its vision and mission. Owners and managers look ahead to plan where they want the organization to be in 5 or 10 years.

Forecasting is a part of planning that aims to predict what will happen in the future.

Goals and strategies should be set for each of the key result areas of restaurant operations.

The purpose of organizing is to get a job done efficiently and effectively by completing these tasks.

Operating a restaurant requires countless decisions every day. Most decisions are made quickly and easily but some require more thought or information or both. The more challenging decisions go through the eight-step decision-making process.

A programmed decision relates to decisions that occur on a regular basis, like what to do when the stock of something goes below par or when a guest makes a request for a booth.

A nonprogrammed decision is one that rarely happens so it is handled differently. Some examples would be which software program to use for a restaurant's front- and back-of-the-house operations, or which supplier to use.

In the restaurant business we spend most of our time communicating with guests and associates. Fast-paced restaurants require quick and accurate communications. *Interpersonal communications* include verbal, nonverbal, body language, and verbal intonation. The best way to communicate is verbal face to face as there is an opportunity for immediate feedback.

Motivation refers to what makes people tick: the needs and desires and fears and aspirations within people that make them behave as they do.

Performance standards form the heart of the job description and they describe the what's, how-tos, and how-wells of a job. Each performance standard has three things about each unit of the job.

Conflict management is the application of strategies to settle opposing ideas, goals, and/or objectives in a positive manner. The EEOC provides guidance on dealing with discrimination and harassment issues.

Alternative dispute resolution (ADR) is a term for problem-solving and grievance resolution approaches to address employee relations and disputes outside the courtroom.

Key Terms and Concepts

Accommodation	Leader
Alternative dispute resolution (ADR)	Leadership
Avoidance	Leadership by walking around (LBWA)
Collaboration	
Communicating	Mentor
Competition	Mission statement
Compromise	Motivation
Conflict management	Nonprogrammed decision
Decision-making process	Organizing
Diversify	Performance management
Diversity	Programmed decision
Employer of choice	Sexual harassment
Forecasting	Strategic plans
Goals	SWOT assessment
Groupthink	Vision

Review Questions

1. Define the term *vision*.
2. What is the purpose of a mission statement?
3. Discuss the three parts of a mission statement.
4. What do you think are the most important characteristics of effective leaders, and why?

5. What is meant by the term *real authority?*
6. What is the purpose of forecasting?
7. Discuss why Title VII of the 1964 Civil Rights Act was passed.
8. Briefly describe the steps in the conflict management process.
9. Define the terms accommodation, avoidance, compromise, and competition, as they pertain to conflict management.
10. What are the six guiding principles for handling conflict?

CASE STUDY: Eat Here[33]

To fully appreciate the concept of Eat Here we need to introduce the colorful character of Sean Murphy, owner of the acclaimed Beach Bistro on Anna Maria Island, near Sarasota, Florida—a long way from his hometown of Halifax, Nova Scotia. According to the Beach Bistro website, "Sean graduated from Dalhousie Law School, the 'Harvard of the North.' Avoiding a career in law and Canadian winters, he followed his passion for food to New Orleans and learned the restaurant trade under the tutelage of industry renowned Archie Casbarian at the world-famous Arnaud's."[34] In the early 1980s Sean and wife, Susan, found their way to Sarasota, where Sean worked at the Colony on Longboat Key until he was able to save enough to launch his own restaurant.

The Pursuit of Perfection

The Beach Bistro opened in 1985 shortly after Hurricane Elena had rocked Sarasota. Sean explained why he was doggedly determined to open on schedule: "We had spent all our money and were overdrawn by $800 . . . Opening night, we took in $848."[35]

The Bistro's focus from inception was perfection. One of Sean's favorite advisories is, "If you pursue perfection you will achieve a high degree of excellence a good part of the time." The Bistro endeavors to procure the very best American food product and serve it at its best. The Bistro serves only fresh grouper, Prime American beef, domestic lamb, and the "best smoked salmon in the free world."

The Bistro's "relentless pursuit of excellence in food and service" earned regional acclaim from the *Sarasota Herald,* the *Tampa Tribune,* and the *St. Petersburg Times.* It was awarded its first Florida Trend Magazine's Golden Spoon in the early 1990s as one of the Top 20 Restaurants in Florida. Throughout the 1990s, the restaurant earned national recognition and was consistently awarded the highest Zagat ratings in the region.[36]

In September of 2005, Beach Bistro was invited to perform a James Beard Foundation dinner at the Beard House in New York, "the Temple" of American Culinary Art. In 2006 the Bistro expanded the Bar and introduced a casual bar menu featuring The World's Best Grouper Sandwich and the acclaimed Steak Sandwich. That same year, it also began offering a few outdoor tables for dining (When the weather is right, the Gulf views are spectacular).

In 2010, Sean and Susan introduced another Anna Maria Island restaurant—Eat Here, a Gulf Coast cookery serving an upscale-casual menu and craft beer from select microbrewers. In 2011, the Beach Bistro was once again awarded the top Zagat rating in food and service on the Gulf Coast of Florida. In November of that year, a second Eat Here location was opened in Sarasota, receiving rave reviews from the beginning.

The Beach Bistro is currently an eight-time recipient of Florida Trend Magazine's Golden Spoon Award and has been enthroned in the Golden Spoon "Hall of Fame." Its wine list regularly receives the Wine Spectator Award of Excellence for offering "one of the best wine lists in the world." It is included in Zagat's Top Restaurants in America and is lauded by the guide for "the best food on the Gulf Coast . . . as good as any in New York or Paris." Sean's ambition has been the same since the Beach

Bistro first opened: "to provide you with one of the best dining experiences that you have ever had."[37]

Eat Here

Eat Here (what a great name for a restaurant) personifies the character of its creator. Eat here, Murphy says, offers smaller plates than Beach Bistro and does it in a more relaxed atmosphere. The menus, for example, are printed on regular paper, stapled together, and given to customers on clipboards. The napkins are cotton kitchen towels. Eat Here has 70 seats downstairs, 40 on the patio, and 50 upstairs, which also includes a cool patio.

Eat Here has a food cost percentage of 28 percent, Labor 33 percent, alcohol 8 percent, beer 3 percent, and wine 14 percent. Sean gets all this for a 4 percent of sales lease. (the industry average is 8 percent). The cost of opening was $300,000 downstairs and $200,000 upstairs.

Sean says, "It has a cool and hip feel, but it's still casual and welcoming."

Finally, the Eat Here model depends on a quick and easy opening. The Holmes Beach location was built-out in a month and cost about $250,000—ultra-fast and inexpensive in the restaurant industry. Murphy brought on two passive partners for Eat Here. One, part-time Longboat Key resident Skip Sack, once owned multiple Applebee's and is a past president of the National Restaurant Association. Sack helps Murphy look for new locations.

"I think it's a great concept because it's a niche no one else is doing," Sack says. "It's not like a chain."

The Eat Here idea, Murphy says, goes back five or six years, when he saw guests shift their attitudes about dinner out. "I began to notice dining out was becoming much more about being entertained," he says. He noticed the trend at the Beach Bistro. Although the shift to new dining-out attitudes is a big reason behind Eat Here, the number one lesson he teaches budding restaurant owners is that food comes first. "It's always about the food," Murphy says. "You have to get an 'A' every time." Eat Here's signature dishes are seafood stew, pot roast, lobster taco, and heart attack hot dog.

A third location was eyed at university town center close to Lakewood Ranch, a large upscale master planned community in Manatee County, but Sean got wind of the fact that Chris Sullivan, a founder of the Outback chain, was about to open his latest concept, Carmel.

QUESTIONS

1. What is your opinion of Eat Here as a concept?
2. What do you think about the menu?
3. Do you think Eat Here can become a chain with several stores—if so, how?
4. What would you do next if you were Sean Murphy?
5. Based on what you know, prepare an income statement for Eat Here.

Endnotes

1. John R. Walker, *Introduction to Hospitality* 6th ed. (Upper Saddle River, NJ: Prentice Hall, 2012), p. 535.
2. John R. Walker and Jack E. Miller, *Supervision in the Hospitality Industry: Leading Human Resources,* 7th ed. (Hoboken, NJ: John Wiley & Sons, 2012)), p. 1.
3. Ibid.
4. Walker, p. 469.
5. Walker and Miller, p. 9.
6. Dr. Jay R. Schrock, professor emeritus, University of South Florida.
7. Walker and Miller, p. 9
8. Larry J. Gitman and Carl McDaniel, *The Future of Business,* 5th ed. (Cincinnati, OH: South-Western Publishing, 2005), p. 209.

9. Ibid.
10. This section is from Walker and Miller, pp. 13–14.
11. Walker, p. 521.
12. Ibid., pp. 553–554.
13. This section draws on Walker and Miller, p. 178.
14. Ibid., p. 213.
15. This section draws on Walker and Miller, pp. 364–366.
16. U.S. Equal Employment Opportunity Commission, "Facts About Sexual Harassment," www.eeoc. gov/sexual_harassment.html. Retrieved May 2, 2013.
17. Data compiled from US Equal Employment Opportunity Commission website, "Enforcement and Litigation Statistics," http://www.eeoc.gov/eeoc/statistics/enforcement/. Retrieved May 2, 2013.
18. This profile is from US Equal Employment Opportunity Commission, "Michigan City Restaurant to Pay $20,000 to Settle Second EEOC Sexual Harassment Suit," EEOC (December 20, 2012), http:// www.eeoc.gov/eeoc/newsroom/release/12-20-12c.cfm.
19. U.S. Equal Employment Opportunity Commission. "Caesars Palace to Pay $850,000 for Sexual Harassment and Retaliation," EEOC (August 20, 2007), http://www.eeoc.gov/eeoc/newsroom/ release/8-20-07.cfm. Retrieved November 29, 2012.
20. U.S. Equal Employment Opportunity Commission, "Subway Franchise to Pay $166,500 for Disability Bias, Jury Rules in EEOC Lawsuit," EEOC (July 27, 2007), http://www.eeoc.gov/eeoc/ newsroom/release/7-27-07.cfm. Retrieved November 29, 2012.
21. www.eeoc.gov/laws/practices/harassment.cfm?renderforprint=1 retrieved on May 14, 2-13.
22. Vicky Hess, "Conflict Management Contributes to Communication," Society for Human Resource Management: Workplace Diversity Library-Employment Issues, January 2007.
23. Morton Deutsch, Peter Coleman, and Eric Marcus, *The Handbook of Conflict Resolution: Theory and Practice* (San Francisco: Jossey-Bass, A John Wiley & Sons Imprint, 2006), p. 161.
24. Paul Moomaw, "Managing Employee Conflict: Be a Coach, Not a Cop," *Restaurants USA* (June/July 1996), http://cf.restaurant.org/tools/magazines/rusa/magArchive/year/issue/article/?ArticleID=175.
25. Monica Parpal, "Resolving Employee Conflicts," Food Service Warehouse http://www.foodser-vicewarehouse.com/restaurant-equipment-supply-marketing-articles/restaurant-management-and-operations/resolving-employee-conflicts/c28039.aspx. Retrieved May 2, 2013.
26. "Carola Hicks," "Six Tips for Managing and Resolving Conflict," Restaurant Central (February 2, 2012), http://www.restaurantcentral.ca/managingresolvingconflict.aspx. Retrieved May 2, 2013.
27. This section was adapted from Herb Kindler, *Conflict Management: Resolving Disagreements in the Workplace* (Boston: Thomson,, 2006), pp. 3–4.
28. Robert Friedman, "Knock out On-the-Job Conflicts Complaints with Six Simple Steps," *Nation's Restaurant News,* 40, (37), (September 11, 2006), p. 30.
29. Stephen Barth, "Why In-House Dispute Resolution Makes Sense," *Lodging Hospitality,* 58 (7), (May 15, 2002), p. 19.
30. Nancy R. Lockwood, "Alternative Dispute Resolution," Society for Human Resource Management, SHRM Research, February 2004.
31. Ibid.
32. Darden Restaurants, "RP-3: Code of Business Conduct and Ethics," March 7, 2011, http://www. darden.com/pdf/corporate/Code_of_Business_Conduct_and_Ethics.pdf .
33. Much of this case is based on a personal interview with Sean Murphy on November 15, 2012.
34. "Meet Sean Murphy," Beach Bistro, http://www.beachbistro.com/meet-sean-murphy-2/. Retrieved November 22, 2012.
35. "Our History," Beach Bistro, http://www.beachbistro.com/our-history/. Retrieved November 22, 2012.
36. Ibid.
37. Ibid.

Organization, Recruiting, and Staffing

LEARNING OBJECTIVES

After reading and studying this chapter, you should be able to:

- Describe the processes for creating job and task analyses.

- Describe the components of a job description, and list the guidelines for creating one.

- Identify legal issues surrounding hiring and employment.

- Determine the legality of potential interview questions.

Courtesy of John Horne/Anna Maria Oyster Bar

Presumably, we have our concept, our location, our menu, health and fire department approval, liquor licenses, and other local permits. We have found finances and taken care of legal matters. Now we think of setting up the jobs and *organizing the restaurant* so that it fulfills its function—to serve guests and produce a profit. In an existing restaurant, improvements in job content and organization may be possible. In a new concept restaurant, tasks have to be defined to form job descriptions, and the job descriptions have to be related to each other. This chapter discusses how to analyze jobs and relate them to each other to form an organization chart. We first look at job descriptions.

Job Descriptions

A well-organized restaurant has written job descriptions and specifications. Few independent restaurants bother to perform job analysis but rely on the owner's or manager's knowledge of the job. Chain operators usually have documented job descriptions and specifications for use by both manager and employees (see Figures 11.1 and 11.2). Often the description and specification are combined for convenience. The importance of good job descriptions cannot be overemphasized. They have been used as evidence in a number of lawsuits and *Equal Employment Opportunity Commission (EEOC)* cases. More important, they help in creating a clear and common understanding of the purpose and expected outcomes of each job. Every restaurant should have one for each position.

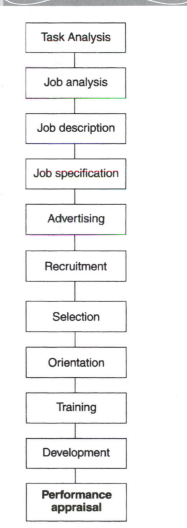

Guidelines for Writing a Job Description
- Describe the job, not the person in the job.
- Do not describe in fine detail, such as would be the result of a time and motion study.
- Use short, simple, and to the point sentences. Use only words and phrases that really contribute to the description.
- Explain technical jargon if used.
- Make the description detailed enough to include all aspects of the job.
- Include the essential functions of the job and the outcomes expected from performing the job.[1]

JOB SPECIFICATION

A job specification lists the education and technical/conceptual skills a person needs to satisfactorily perform the requirements of the job (see Figure 11.3). Once the tasks performed in a job are described, a separate section of the job description form can be developed. Remember, no job requires all the faculties of an individual, which means that many jobs can be performed by people who have disabilities in some areas but are otherwise able to handle the tasks. For example, at the Olive Garden restaurants, workers with disabilities make salads and do the dishwashing.

JOB INSTRUCTION SHEET

Task analysis can be converted into job instructions, which can serve not only as a guide to new employees but also as a quality assurance measure for the maintenance

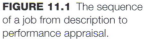

FIGURE 11.1 The sequence of a job from description to performance appraisal.

Position   Assistant Manager

Reports to: Manager

Position overview: Under the general supervision of the manager, subject to the Service Policy and Procedure Manual, assures constantly and consistently the creation of maximal guest satisfaction and dining pleasure.

RESPONSIBILITIES AND DUTIES

A. Planning and organizing

1. Studies past sales experience records, confers with manager, keeps alert to holidays and special events, and so on; forecasts loads and prepares work schedules for service employees in advance to meet requirements.
2. Observes guest reactions and confers frequently with waitstaff to determine guest satisfactions, dissatisfactions, relative popularity of menu items, and so on, and reports such information with recommendations to the manager.
3. Observes daily the condition of all physical facilities and equipment in the dining room, making recommendations to the manager for correction and improvements needed.
4. Anticipates all material needs and supplies, and assures availability of same.
5. Inspects, plans, and assures that all personnel, facilities, and materials are in complete readiness for excellent service before each meal period.
6. Anticipates employment needs, recommending to the manager plans for recruitment and selection to meet needs as they arise.
7. Discusses in advance menu changes with waitstaff to assure full understanding of new items.
8. Conducts meetings of service employees at appropriate times.
9. Defines and explains clearly for waitstaff their responsibilities for relationships with:
   - each other
   - the hostess/host
   - the cashier
   - the guest
   - the manager
   - kitchen personnel

B. Coordinating

1. Assures that waitstaff are fully informed as to all menu items—how they are prepared, what they contain, ounces per portion.
2. Periodically discusses and reviews with employees company objectives and guest and personnel policies.
3. Keeps manager informed at all times as to service activities, progress, and major problems.

C. Supervising

1. Actively participates in employment of new waiters and busers; suggests recruitment sources, studies applications, checks references, and conducts interview.
2. Following an orientation outline, introduces new employees to the restaurant, restaurant policies, fellow employees.
3. Using a training plan, trains new employees and current employees in need of training.
4. Corrects promptly any deviations from established service standards.
5. Counsels with employees on job and personal problems.
6. Follows established policy in making station assignments for the waitstaff.
7. Establishes, with approval of manager, standards of conduct, grooming, personal hygiene, and dress.
8. Prepares, in consultation and with approval of the manager, applied standards of performance for waiters and busers.
9. Recommends deserving employees for promotion and outstanding performers for special recognition and award.
10. Strives at all times through the practice of good human relations and leadership to establish esprit de corps—teamwork, unity of effort, and individual and group pride.
11. Has a responsibility to maintain and keep a keen and constant alertness to the entire dining room situation—a sensitivity to any deviation or problem—and to assist quickly and quietly in its correction, adjusting guest complaints.
12. Greets and seats guests cordially and courteously, to assure a sincere welcome and genuine interest in their dining pleasure.

D. Controlling

1. Controls, according to established policies, standards, and procedures, employees' performance, conduct, dress, hygiene, sanitation, and personal appearance.
2. Studies all evidence of waste—time, materials, and so on—making recommendations for prevention.

E. Other

1. On emergency occasions may serve guests, act as cashier, or perform specifically assigned duties of the manager.
2. Personifies graciousness and hospitality to guests and employees on the basis of "We're glad you're here" and "We're proud to serve you."

FIGURE 11.2 Job description.

Position: Hostess/Host

1. Maturity—capable of relating effectively to elder and younger patrons and employees. Observable personal competence and stability.
2. Education—minimum of a high school education required, some college desired.
3. Experience—prior positions as a waitress/waiter required, experience as a hostess/host desired. Possess ability to perform as cashier and assist in table clearings. Prior supervisory experience desired. Basic understanding of food, service skills, sanitation, and dining room equipment mandatory.
4. Physical requirements—appropriate physical stature, excellent hearing and vision. Observable strength to be able to walk and stand for long periods without noticeable fatigue.
5. Mental requirements—observable average intelligence, ability to retain sense of order and balance of patron seating placements. Ability to relate to several persons concurrently in a pleasing and prompt manner.
6. General character—observable conscientiousness, good grooming, basically pleasant, and exudes an attitude of willing cooperation. Possesses a "taking charge" demeanor of personal authority. Speaks clearly and with acceptable volume and intonation. Possesses personal confidence.

FIGURE 11.3 Sample job specification.

of work standards. Job instructions comprise a list of the work steps performed, arranged in sequential order if there is a natural cycle to the work. It is a short step from job description to job instruction sheet. If the job description is well done, the information can be reorganized, with some information added and some omitted, to form a job instruction sheet. This is used both by trainer and trainee.

Organizing People and Jobs

In one way or another, every restaurant is organized so that these restaurant functions are performed:

- Human resource management and supervision
- Food and beverage purchasing
- Receiving, storing, and issuing
- Food preparation
- Foodservice
- Food cleaning; dish and utensil washing
- Marketing/sales
- Promotion, advertising, and public relations
- Accounting and auditing
- Bar service

All of the functions can be performed by one person, as in a one-person pizza parlor, or by thousands of people, as in a large restaurant chain (see Figure 11.4). An organization chart lays out the lines of communication and relationships between jobs. It also suggests lines of authority, responsibility, and accountability, which means that the jobs themselves must be structured and defined. Who is responsible for what? Who reports to whom? Who has authority for making what decisions? Who is accountable for what? Figure 11.5 shows a simplified organization chart, without job responsibilities.

As the restaurant grows, specialization of function becomes necessary. The owner/manager must delegate most or all of the restaurant functions, except

RESTAURANT MANAGER—Coordinates and directs the entire operation to assure efficient quality, courteous foodservice. Works through supervisory personnel, but in smaller restaurants may directly supervise kitchen and dining room staffs. Must know all of the details involved in every restaurant job.

BOOKKEEPER—Audits guests' checks. May compute daily cash intake and operating ratios, deposit money in bank, and maintain financial records.

ASSISTANT MANAGER—Performs specific supervisory duties under the manager's direction. Generally takes over in the manager's absence. Must be thoroughly familiar with the entire operation and have good management skills.

PURCHASING AGENT AND STORE-ROOM SUPERVISOR—Orders, receives, inspects, and stores all food for distribution to the different food departments. Must be capable of managing an inventory and keeping track of current market prices. This job is sometimes the responsibility of the manager or chef.

FOOD PRODUCTION MANAGER—Responsible for all food preparation and supervision of kitchen staff. Must have thorough knowledge of food preparation and good food standards. Should know how to work with and supervise people.

DINING ROOM MANAGER—Coordinates dining room activities, trains and supervises host/hostess, waiters, waitresses, busboys, and busgirls. Should possess leadership qualities, objectivity, and fairness.

CASHIER—Receives payment for food and beverages sold. May total checks. Must be personable, quick at mental arithmetic, and completely honest.

PANTRY SUPERVISOR—Supervises salad, sandwich, and beverage workers. Should be able to create attractive food arrangements. May be in charge of requisitioning supplies and supervising cleaning crew.

CHEF AND COOK—Prepares and portions all foods served. In large restaurant operations, job can be highly specialized with individual cooks or chefs responsible for a single category, such as vegetables, cold meats, soups, sauces, and short orders.

HOST/HOSTESS—Takes reservations. Keeps informed on current and upcoming table reservations. May present menu and introduce waitperson. Should be attractive, friendly, able to maintain composure when restaurant is busy.

BEVERAGE WORKER—Prepares hot beverages such as coffee, tea, or hot chocolate. May assist in the pantry and help others in the kitchen during rush hours. It is a good beginning position.

KITCHEN HELPER—Assists the cooks, chefs, and bakers by performing supervised tasks. It's a good entry job for the individual who wants to learn food preparation because the kitchen helper is busy measuring, mixing, washing, and chopping vegetables and salad ingredients.

WAITER-CAPTAIN—Supervises and coordinates activities of dining room employees, performing in a formal atmosphere. May be responsible for scheduling hours and shifts, keeping employees' time records, and assigning work stations.

SANDWICH MAKER—Does basically what the name implies, but also is involved in preparing fillings and dressings. This position is an opportunity for a quick, careful worker who may find the job has a touch of creativity. Skills acquired here will help the individual to move to a better-paying position.

SANITATION/MAINTENANCE WORKER—Maintains clean cooking utensils, equipment, walls, and floors. In most modern restaurants, dishwashers and other machines simplify part of the job. This behind-the-scenes position allows the individual to study the various kitchen duties before choosing a particular job or direction for the future. This category includes porters, dishwashers, and potwashers.

WAITPERSON—Takes food orders and serves the foods to customers. These key employees must like people, be poised and have good self-control, be able to coordinate and respond to many requests made at almost the same time. The individual must move quickly and accurately. Many people make this a career position.

PASTRY CHEF AND BAKER—Bakes cakes, cookies, pies, and other desserts. Bakes bread, rolls, quick breads. In some restaurants, must also be skilled in cake decorating.

BUSPERSON—Clears the table, re-sets it with fresh linen and eating utensils, fills water glasses, and helps in other housekeeping chores in the dining area. A fine way to start learning the business.

FIGURE 11.4 Organization chart provides job functions in a large restaurant.

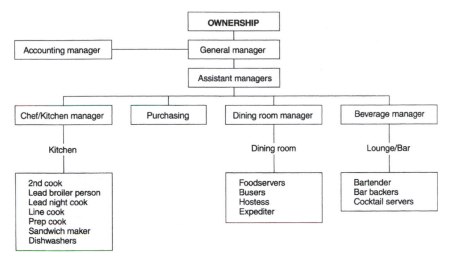

FIGURE 11.5 A hypothetical dinner house/restaurant organization chart.

management, retaining responsibility for planning, overseeing, motivating, and making major decisions—especially financial decisions. People are added and specialists take on responsibilities for purchasing, for food preparation, and for service. Figure 11.6 shows the Red Lobster recruitment process.

Some organization charts are flat—meaning they have fewer levels. This type of organization works well for small and large restaurant businesses, both independents and chains that are informal or less autocratic. A variation of the flat organization chart is the pyramid—especially, the inverted one with guests at the top and managers/owners at the bottom. Figure 11.7 shows an inverted pyramid organization chart.

FIGURE 11.6 Managers/owners are supporting servers who are taking care of the guests.

Staffing the Restaurant

"In the hospitality business, the happiness and satisfaction of your employees translates directly into the satisfaction of your customers, and eventually the bottom line."[2]

The restaurant continues to grow and finally reaches the maximum capacity of sales that can be generated in the location. The owner adds another restaurant by taking over a failed place or perhaps constructing a new restaurant.

Recruitment, preemployment testing, interviewing, selection, and employment are key words in finding the right people and preparing them to work successfully in the restaurant. Figure 11.8 shows the steps involved in staffing the restaurant.

The most important hiring decision is recruiting and selecting the chef. According to Brian Wilber, district manager of Bon Appétit Management Company, a chef is responsible for 60 to 80 percent of an operation's finances and 95 percent of its food costs.[3] Joseph Keller, chef-owner of Como's and Bistro Zinc, never hires a chef until they have worked together in the kitchen. He "auditioned" five for the opening of one of his restaurants by working together in the kitchen for one or two weeks for four to five hours a day.[4] Given the financial as well as interpersonal importance of the job it is essential to have a list of carefully prepared questions about financial and people management skills.

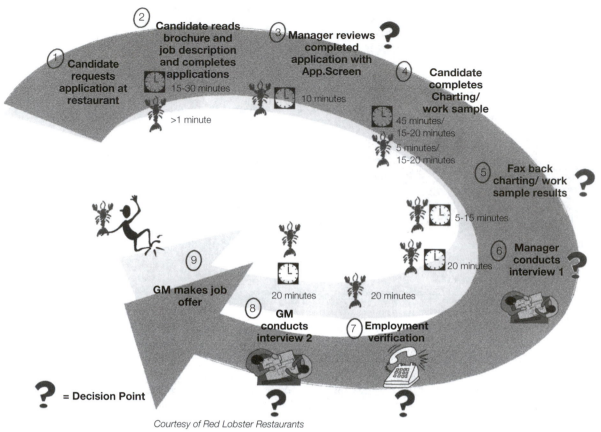

Courtesy of Red Lobster Restaurants

FIGURE 11.7 Red Lobster recruitment process.

Other good questions include asking yourself why someone would want to work with your operation. In today's labor market, chefs can often select with whom they want to work. It's all about getting the right people excited about working with you. When talking with potential candidates, ask them about past employee-management problems/challenges they have had. People who complain or bad-mouth previous restaurants are a sure sign of trouble.

RECRUITMENT

Recruitment is the process by which prospective employees are attracted to the restaurant in order that a suitable applicant may be selected for employment. Recruitment must be carried out in accordance with existing federal and state employment laws and regulations and with civil rights regulations. Restaurants recruit employees from a number of different sources:

- Via the restaurant website and social media
- Recommendations from existing employees
- Internal recruiting, promoting from within

- Local career fairs websites like Eater.com and Shiftgig.
- The Shiftgig and Eater websites can be helpful along with Craigslist.
- Monster.com, which might sound useful but will likely produce a flood of unqualified applicants
- As a result of being a guest lecturer at a college
- Serving as a mentor and having interns work at the restaurant
- Placing an advertisement in a local or community newspaper
- Head-hunting—tactfully talking about your restaurant opportunities when meeting employees who are working at other businesses, including restaurants

Whichever the method of recruiting, the message needs to be consistent. You must tell potential applicants what they want to know:

1. What the job is all about
2. Where you are
3. What the hours are
4. What qualifications are needed
5. How to apply
6. Features of the job—such as wages and benefits

Let applicants know when and how to apply. For example, by email or fax; or in person between 2:00 P.M. and 4:00 P.M., Tuesday. Figure 11.9 illustrates an example of management selection flow from Red Lobster Restaurants.

PREEMPLOYMENT TESTING

Federal and state laws and regulations restrict the use of *preemployment testing* if it is not valid or reliable. The validity of an employment test relates to whether it measures what it is supposed to measure and whether test scores predict successful job performance. A test is said to be reliable if essentially the same results are seen on repeated testing. A test cannot be valid unless it is also reliable.

There is a range of tests for employers to select from: intelligence tests, aptitude tests, and achievement tests. These might or might not be considered necessary for a restaurant, depending on the position available and the desire of the owner or management to utilize a test as a step in the selection of staff.

Some restaurant companies check for substance abuse and honesty, and some use psychological tests in order to select the best possible employees. For example, a cashier position may require a police background check. First, however, a prospective employee would have to sign a waiver. Cooks may also be tested on their culinary skills before they are hired.

INTERVIEWING

Making a hiring decision based on a job interview is not easy, because interviewees are on their best behavior. We are looking for a caring, skilled, outgoing, conscientious, loyal person with good work ethics. How do we determine if a person has all these qualities in the short time an interview allows?

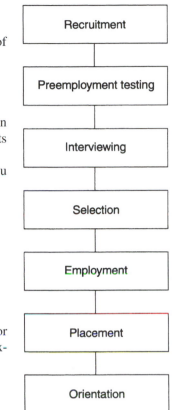

FIGURE 11.8 Steps in staffing the restaurant.

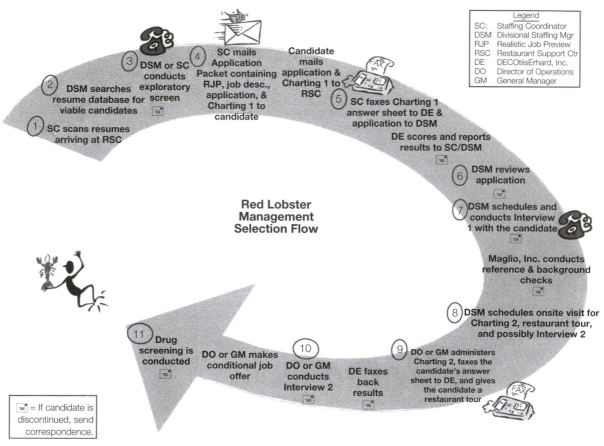

Courtesy of Red Lobster Restaurants

FIGURE 11.9 Red Lobster management selection flow.

Interviews seek to identify certain behavioral characteristics that may determine successful employment practices. They have specific purposes:

■ Gain sufficient information from the candidate to enable the interviewer or a member of management to determine that the applicant is capable of doing the job for which he or she is applying.

■ Give information about the company and the job to help the applicant determine if both are right for him or her.

■ Ask appropriate legal but leading questions that will weed out undesirable workers.

First impressions are important both ways—in other words, the restaurant also needs to make a good first impression. An interview takes careful planning. The setting should put the applicant at ease; it should be comfortable yet businesslike and without interruptions.

Once the applicant has been made to feel welcome, the completed application form is a good starting point for discussion. If the applicant has had nine jobs in 10 years, it would appear that he or she is not a stable employee who, if hired, would stay a long time. If there are gaps in the employment record, be sure to check them thoroughly.

The majority of applicants want to be placed in positions that will allow them to be challenged, to grow and develop. Other applicants may be happy to do the same job year in, year out. A win/win situation is achieved when the goals of the employee and employer overlap—the more overlap, the better. The overlapping circles in Figure 11.10 depict this. If either the employee or the employer has too strong a personal agenda, problems will occur.

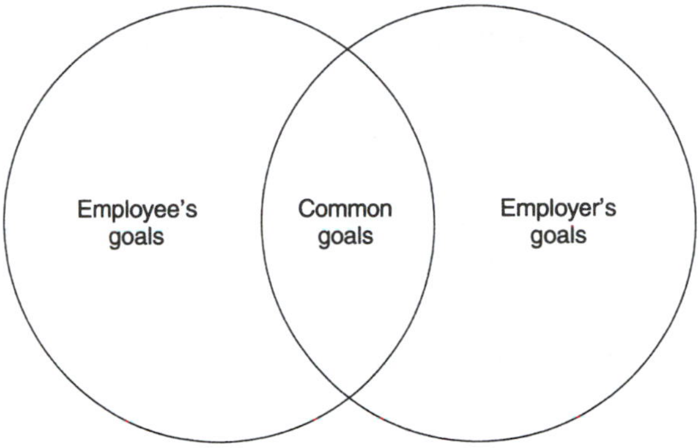

FIGURE 11.10 Venn diagram shows the overlap of an employer's and employee's goals overlap.

Ideal Employee Profiles Because employees constitute such a large part of restaurant ambience, spirit, and efficiency, management decides what type of personnel will fit best with the restaurant's style. Outgoing personalities fit well in the front of house, where staff must be clean-cut, optimistic, healthy, and outgoing. The kitchen can use those who are not so extroverted.

Apparent health and goodwill are obvious assets to all foodservice personnel, adding to the atmosphere, helping to create the eating-out experience.

Obviously, the ideal cook would need training to make an ideal server, and the ideal bartender could be the ideal assistant manager.

Restaurants need to allow for employee development. An employee may start out as a server and become a bartender, followed by time in the kitchen, before moving into an assistant manager's position. Some restaurants have a formal management training program; others will move or promote employees when opportunities arise. In either case, it's important to plan for and give employees the chance to succeed in the restaurant business. Just think of the effect that Norman Brinker has had on the restaurant business. Back in the prime—no pun intended—of Steak and Ale's development, he nurtured several then-assistant managers or managers who are now presidents of large, successful restaurant chains of their own. Chris Sullivan of Outback Steakhouse is an example.

The temptation is to think of a kitchen with a highly trained chef at its head. However, only about one-third of all restaurants employ anyone with the title of *chef*. Sometimes the term *kitchen manager* or *head cook* is used. Large hotels generally have chefs. Full-service restaurants are more likely to have chefs than other restaurants are, and about half of all foodservice operations have someone with the title of chef. Quick-service restaurants may call someone chef, but the title is more name than reality, as few of the skills required of a chef are needed. The highly profitable restaurants are those with relatively fixed menus that require few skills in the kitchen; here, the ideal employees may be teenagers rather than experienced cooks. The dining room may be staffed almost completely by students.

A problem in hiring is determining whether the candidate is underqualified or overqualified, and whether he or she will be satisfied with the job. Another big problem in selecting restaurant personnel is determining the candidate's degree of honesty and responsibility. Cost controls diminish the need for absolute honesty, and productivity standards help ensure responsibility.

CALIFORNIA CAFE BAR & GRILL
APPLICANT INTERVIEW AND RATING FORM
(FILL OUT AFTER INTERVIEW AND ATTACH TO APPLICATION)
(DO NOT WRITE ON APPLICATION)

Date Of First Interview___/___/___/   Manager:_____

Call For Second Interview: 1st try: __/__/__/   2nd try: __/__/__/   3rd try: __/__/__/

Date Of Second Interview:___/___/___/ Time:_____   Manager:_____

Approved For Hire GM's Initial:_____

Department:_____   Salary Requirements:_____

RATE EACH CATEGORY 1 THROUGH 5 :

APPEARANCE & ATTITUDE:_____

KNOWLEDGE:_____

EXPERIENCE:_____

SOCIAL SKILLS:_____   (PERSONAL TRAITS)

STABILITY:_____

             TOTAL:_____
COMMENTS:
_____
_____
_____
_____

REFERENCES CHECKED BY:_____PERSON(S) CONTACTED:_____

DATE:__/__/__/COMMENTS:_____
_____
_____
_____

Date Of Hire:__/__/__/   Rate Of Pay:_____

Checked For Citizenship:_____   Managers Initial:_____
(Or Work Permits)

Foodhandler Card:_____   Review Date:__/__/__/
(If Applicable)

Employee Folder Completed:__/__/__/   MGR/BKPR Initial:_____

Employee folder must contain: Send To Datamasters:
Photocopies of: Drivers Licence & Social Security Card   Copy of W4
                 Other Documentation For Proof Of Work Eligibility   Datamaster New Hire Sheet
                 Signed Parking Policy Sheet etc.
                 I 9 Immigration Form
                 W 4 Tax Form
                 Application & Ratings Sheet
                 Signed Manual Receipt Pages
                 Datamaster New Hire Sheet

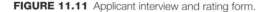

FIGURE 11.11 Applicant interview and rating form.

Interview and Rating Form California Cafe uses an applicant interview and rating form (see Figure 11.11) that managers fill out immediately after the interview and attach to the application form. Managers are not permitted to write on the application form.

For restaurant service jobs, attitude is more important than ability. Prestige restaurants may select only 1 out of 20 applicants. Because of the low wages offered in most restaurants, the operator does not have such a wide choice and must rely on continuous training to meet high service standards. Using a rating form can help interviewers keep track of attitude and other traits not revealed on an application form.

SELECTION

Selection is the process of determining the eligibility and suitability of a prospective employee—not only how well a person can cook or serve but also how he or she will fit in with the team. Personal appearance, grooming, and hygiene are also important. The purpose of the selection process is to hire an employee who will be a team player, a person who will exceed the performance expectations of guests and management.

EMPLOYMENT OF MINORS

The National Restaurant Association and many state restaurant associations have taken a positive approach to improving the industry's reputation as a youth employer.

A concerted effort has also been mounted by a cooperative task force made up of officials from the US Department of Labor (DOL), the US Congress, and the National Restaurant Association to go beyond what is merely required by law to provide a high-quality work experience.

Several leading restaurant chains have found that teenagers, beginning at age 16, are excellent candidates for almost every restaurant job, from busing and dishwashing to cooking and order taking. Some restaurants have teenage shift managers, lead people, and assistants. All of the quick-service chains in this country and a number of table-service restaurants have built outstanding operations around teenagers. The biggest success story of them all, McDonald's, employs a high percentage of teenagers—if possible, part-time only, so that they can perform at peak efficiency during the hours worked. A tired, dispirited employee destroys the character of a restaurant almost as fast as poor food.

Restrictions on Employing Minors A number of federal regulations control the kind of work permissible for minors (under age 16). State laws also apply and may be different from the regulations laid down by the federal government. Where state laws are more restrictive, they take precedence over the federal regulations. The regulations change from time to time, as do their interpretations. The National Restaurant Association spells out the work that may not be done by minors under 16 years of age:

- Work in connection with maintenance or repair of machines or equipment
- Outside window washing that involves working from windowsills, and all work requiring the use of ladders, scaffolds, or their substitutes
- Cooking (except at soda fountains, lunch counters, snack bars, or cafeteria serving counters) and baking
- Work in freezers and meat coolers and all work in preparation of meats for sale (except wrapping, sealing, labeling, weighing, pricing, and stacking)
- Loading and unloading goods to and from trucks, railroad cars, and conveyors
- Work around cars and trucks involving the use of pits, racks, or lifting apparatus or involving inflation of tires mounted on a rim equipped with a movable retaining ring
- Work as a motor vehicle driver or outside helper
- Work in warehouses, except office and clerical work, and at any occupations found and declared to be hazardous by the Department of Labor (DOL).[5]

Minors between 16 and 18 years of age cannot:

- Operate elevators or power-driven hoists
- Operate power-driven shaving machines or bakery machinery
- Operate circular saws, power-driven slices, band saws, and guillotine shears

There are exceptions for students engaged as apprentices or in student-learner programs. Of course, federal and state laws set the absolute standard and may specify additional requirements for employing minors. At age 18, teenagers may legally work at any job. If in doubt, call your local DOL office for an interpretation of the law or regulations. Children under 16 may be employed by their parents in occupations other than those declared hazardous for minors under 18.

Maximum Work Hours and Night Restrictions
- *Ages 14 and 15:* On school days, minors may work a maximum of three hours per day, 18 hours per week; on nonschool days, eight hours per day, 40 hours per week.
- *Age 16 and over:* There are no restrictions on working hours even during school hours. However, if a state law is stricter, it must be followed.

- *Ages 14 and 15:* Minors may not work before 7 A.M. or after 7 P.M. on school days; from June 1 through Labor Day, they may work until 9 P.M.[6]

Because of the restrictions, some employers refuse even to consider minors under age 16.

Federal laws are enforced by the DOL, Employment Standards Administration, Wage and Hour Division, Washington, DC 20210. The US Child Labor Requirements provide for a criminal fine for willful violators.

EMPLOYMENT OF UNDOCUMENTED ALIENS

The *Immigration Reform and Control Act of 1986* makes it illegal for employers to employ undocumented aliens. It is the employer's responsibility to verify the prospective employees' legal immigration status and right to work in the United States. Fortunately, employers are not currently required to verify the authenticity of documents presented, although this might be changing. Many restaurants now use E-Verify, an Internet-based system that allows businesses to determine whether current or potential employees are eligible to work in the United States. According to US Citizenship and Immigration Services, "E-Verify is fast, free, and easy to use—and it's the best way employers can ensure a legal workforce."[7] However, human resource directors are required to do their best to ensure the authenticity of all documents and, in case of doubt, may refer to the Immigration and Naturalization Service (INS). Keep copies of all documents presented in case of a government audit. The I-9 form is proof of having inspected the employees' documentation. Failure to keep appropriate records may result in fines and, potentially, the loss of employees just before opening for Friday night business.

List A documents show both identity and employment authorization:

- US passport
- Certificate of US citizenship
- Alien registration receipt card and/or permanent resident card
- Foreign passport with temporary 1-551 stamp authorizing the individual to work
- Employment authorization document with photograph
- Foreign passport with Form 1-94
- Passport from the Federated States of Micronesia, the Republic of the Marshall Islands, or the Commonwealth of Northern Mariana Islands, with restrictions

List B documents are specific photo IDs. Employees who choose to present a list B document must also present a document from list C, which includes birth certificates, Social Security cards, Native American tribal documents, or US citizen ID cards, for example.[8]

The consequences of hiring undocumented aliens are substantial fines, which is a high price to pay for sloppy recordkeeping and document checking. In late 2011, the owner of French Gourmet in San Diego was fined $396,575 and the manager was fined $2,500 for knowingly hiring undocumented workers at the bakery and catering business. Both also received probation (five and three years, respectively).[9]

EMPLOYEE SOURCES

The most useful source of employees is referrals by reliable current employees. Other sources depend on the area and the employment situation at the time. Possible sources include:

- Current employees via promotion (the first place to look)
- Restaurant website
- Facebook and Twitter
- The Internet
- State employment service
- Schools—high school co-ops, culinary technical schools, colleges, regional occupation programs
- Vendors
- Customers
- Youth groups (e.g., Boy Scouts, Girl Scouts)
- Fraternities, sororities
- Walk-ins
- Minority sources
- Church groups
- Veterans' organizations
- Retiree organizations (a valuable resource that often goes untapped)
- TV (ad time is often available on local cable stations at reasonable rates)
- Community bulletin boards
- Job fairs
- Local partnerships

There are several important legal issues to be aware of when staffing a restaurant. What follows is an overview of the employment laws affecting restaurants.

> They don't necessarily look for experience. When I applied at the Olive Garden, I was applying to be a hostess, but they wanted me to work as a server, and it didn't matter that I had no prior experience because they had a good training program.

Civil Rights Laws

Civil rights laws state that employers may not discriminate in employment on the basis of an individual's race, religion, color, sex, national origin, marital status, age, veteran status, family relationship, disabilities, or juvenile record that has been expunged. Neither may employers retaliate in any way or discharge employees who report, complain about, or oppose discriminatory practices or file or participate in the complaint process.

Federal and state laws on discrimination are similar. The state may be charged with the enforcement of federal civil rights legislation. Different state agencies are charged with enforcing various aspects of the law. For example, in Oregon, the Bureau of Labor processes federal complaints for the EEOC, while the DOL, Wage and Hour Division, deals with sex and age discrimination. Other aspects of the law are enforced directly by the DOL, the Office of Federal Contract Compliance, and the US Department of Health and Welfare. As you might guess, when more than one agency is involved, they do not necessarily agree on the interpretation of the law.

EQUAL EMPLOYMENT OPPORTUNITY

Equal employment opportunity (EEO) is recruitment, selection, and promotion practices that are open, competitive, and based on merit. Merit assessed by clearly defined, job-related criteria ensures that the best applicant is selected for the job.[10]

Providing equal employment opportunity is required by law and applies to discrimination based on race, sex, religion, color, national origin, veteran status, age, and non–job-related mental or physical disabilities. The intention of this legislation is to prohibit discrimination against job applicants or employees for promotion for one or more of the above reasons.

The EEOC is the organization to which employees or job applicants may appeal if they feel they have been discriminated against. If the EEOC agrees, this agency files charges against an individual and/or the organization.

The Immigration Reform and Control Act of 1986 outlaws discrimination against legal immigrants to the United States. It covers all employees, and someone with permanent work authorization cannot be favored over someone with temporary status.

The Age Discrimination Act was passed in 1967 to protect people over the age of 40 from discrimination.

AMERICANS WITH DISABILITIES ACT

The *Americans with Disabilities Act (ADA)* prohibits discrimination against employees who are disabled and requires making "readily achievable" modifications in work practices and working conditions that enable them to work. ADA provides comprehensive civil rights protection for people with disabilities in these areas:

- Employment (Title I)
- All aspects of state and local government operations (Title II)
- Public accommodation, private business serving the public (Title III)
- Transportation (included under both Titles II and III)
- Telecommunication (Title IV)

The law specifically requires that restaurants welcome customers with disabilities by removing barriers that interfere with access to the facilities and services provided.

Today, there are 43 million people with disabilities in the United States and, as the population ages, the number will increase steadily over the next several decades.

Who Is a Person with a Disability? "One out of five Americans is considered disabled, according to the Census Bureau, and the ADA protects any employee who has a mental or physical disability that substantially limits a major life activity, such as working."[10] The ADA defines a

Courtesy of Cafe L'Europe
An employment interview allows the prospective employee and the employer to get to know one another.

person with a disability to be an individual who falls within one of these three categories:

1. An individual with a physical or mental impairment that substantially limits one or more major life activities, such as walking, seeing, or hearing
2. Someone with a history of such an impairment—for example, a history of heart disease or cancer
3. Someone who is perceived as having a disability, such as an individual who is severely scarred or someone who is believed to have tested HIV positive

How Does the ADA Affect Your Restaurant? All areas in a restaurant used by the public are places of public accommodation under the ADA and thus are subject to the requirements of Title III, which regulates access to both a restaurant's physical facilities and to the services it offers. In terms of access to physical facilities, new construction designed for first occupancy after January 26, 1993, is required to meet the ADA Accessibility Guidelines (ADAAG). ADAAG provides technical design requirements to assure that newly constructed facilities are accessible to individuals with disabilities. Alterations undertaken later must also meet the guidelines. However, barrier removal that is readily achievable, defined as easily accomplishable without significant difficulty or expense, is required in all existing buildings.[11]

HIRING PEOPLE WHO ARE PHYSICALLY OR MENTALLY CHALLENGED

Employees usually overlooked are those who are seriously disadvantaged emotionally, mentally, or physically. Hundreds of restaurant operators state categorically that they hire such workers because they are more loyal, try harder, and are more appreciative of having a job than the average employee. Numerous studies support this view.

Ask yourself which restaurant position is the most demanding, least satisfying, most confining, and, usually, at the bottom of the pay scale. The answer is the dishwasher, pot and pan person, or cleanup person. These are the jobs with the greatest turnover. In many restaurants, the dishwashing section is humid and noisy, and sometimes the only people doing the dog work of the kitchen are emotionally disturbed or addicted people. In many restaurants, the dish room has automatic dishwashers, good ventilation, lighting, and protective gloves, which make the job more acceptable.

AIDS[12]

Acquired Immune Deficiency Syndrome (AIDS) cannot be transmitted through the air, water, or food. The only medically documented ways in which AIDS can be contracted are by exchange of bodily fluids, by shared needles (usually associated with drug addiction), by infusion of contaminated blood, and through the placenta from mother to fetus. AIDS is not passed through the daily routines that occur in restaurants. You cannot catch the disease by working with someone who has AIDS or by eating food prepared by someone who has AIDS. The Centers for Disease Control states:

All epidemiological and laboratory evidence indicates that bloodborne and sexually transmitted infections are not transmitted during the preparation or serving of food or beverages, and no instances of HBV or HTLV-III/LAV [the viruses that cause AIDS] transmission have been documented in this setting.

The statement of the Surgeon General is less technical but equally emphatic:

Nor has AIDS been contracted from . . . eating in restaurants (even if a restaurant worker has AIDS or carries the AIDS virus).

Two other laws—the Americans with Disabilities Act (ADA) and the Family and Medical Leave Act (FMLA)—plus any applicable state laws, must be taken into account in your dealings with employees who have AIDS or who are HIV-positive. The ADA law clearly states that people who acquire AIDS (or HIV infection) are covered by the ADA. You cannot discriminate in hiring, in promoting, or in offering benefits to an employee with HIV/AIDS. In addition, if such an employee needs a "reasonable accommodation" to help him or her perform the essential functions of a job, you are required to provide it unless doing so creates an "undue hardship."

Questions to Avoid on the Application Form and During the Interview

The civil rights laws do not prohibit specific questions, but they do forbid discriminatory use of information in selecting employees. The burden is on the employer to show the need for the information requested and how it is used in the hiring decision. If it is necessary to identify applicants by race and sex, the employer should include a statement informing the applicant that the questions are being asked for affirmative action purposes and that the information will not be used in a discriminatory way. Figure 11.12 shows questions to avoid.

- *Name and address:*
  - What is your full name?
  - What is your address?
  - What is your telephone number?
- *Age and citizenship:*
  - Do you meet the minimum age requirement for work in this state?
  - If hired, can you show proof of age?
  - Are you over 18 years of age?
- *Work schedule:* What is acceptable here is a statement by the employer of regular days, hours of shifts to be worked, and the expectations of regular attendance.
- *Physical condition handicap:* It is acceptable to ask if the potential employee is able to perform the essential functions of this job with or without reasonable accommodations.

Questions are appropriate only if asked of all candidates—for example, "Do you know any reason why you might not be able to come to work on time every day?" You may ask if a person has ever been convicted of committing a felony. If the

Protected Class	Inappropriate Inquiries	Comments
Marital status	Are you married? Divorced? Separated?	Since it is illegal to discriminate on the basis of marital status, all these inquiries are inappropriate. One's marital status has nothing to do with one's ability to perform the job, nor is this an effective means of discerning one's "character."
Age	Birth date? How old are you?	If it is necessary to know that someone is over a certain age for legal reasons, this question could better be stated, "Are you 21 or over?"
National origin	Are you native-born or naturalized? Have you proof of your citizenship? What was your birthplace? Where were your parents born?	If it is necessary to know if someone is a US citizen for a job, this question could be asked directly without asking further, which might reveal national origin. If it is necessary to require proof of citizenship immigrant status, employment can be offered on the condition that proof be supplied.
Family relationship	Do you have any relatives currently employed here?	A job cannot be legally refused to someone who has a relative already working for the employer unless either relative would have supervisory or grievance adjustment authority over the other family member.
Mental or physical handicap	Do you have, or have you ever had, cancer? epilepsy? addiction to drugs, alcohol? an on-the-job injury? Have you ever been treated for a mental condition?	A job cannot be refused because of a mental or physical disability that would not prevent the person from performing the functions of the job. If there is a question about someone's physical or mental ability, the job can be offered on the condition that a physician's opinion be furnished indicating that the person is able to do the job with the probability that the person would not harm self or pose danger for others.
Race, sex	What is your race, sex? Furnish a photograph. What is your hair and eye color?	If it is necessary to ask for this information for affirmative action purposes, these inquiries should be accompanied by a statement indicating that the information is needed for affirmative action reporting purposes and will not be used to discriminate. A photograph should not be required; how someone looks has nothing to do with how he or she performs the job.
Sex	Are you pregnant?	Some state laws clearly state that discrimination on the basis of pregnancy is sex discrimination. In order to legally refuse employment because of pregnancy, an employer would have to show there was strong reason to believe the woman couldn't do the job (such as a physician's opinion to that effect) or that the nature of the position would not allow the employer to grant maternity leave without undue hardship. Pregnancy must be treated like other physical conditions under the law.
Injured worker	Have you ever applied for workers' compensation?	It is illegal to refuse to hire because a person has applied for workers' compensation. If it is necessary to know about someone's physical condition to perform a job, it is better to ask for this information directly.
Religion	What is your religious affiliation? What clubs/associations are you a member of? Can you work Saturdays? Sundays?	The first two questions are inappropriate. Religious affiliation is no indication of work ability. Asking for membership information may reveal religious affiliation; club membership is not an indicator of work ability. It may be necessary for an employer to know if an applicant cannot work Saturdays or Sundays because of religious beliefs. However, an employer has an obligation to accommodate those beliefs unless it would cause undue hardship to the business.
Race	Have you been arrested? Have you been convicted of crimes other than minor traffic violations?	Since minority group members are arrested and convicted of crimes at a significantly higher rate than nonminority people, these inquiries could be used to exclude minorities from job opportunities disproportionately more than nonminorities. Asking for arrest records is highly questionable, since being arrested is not a true indicator of guilt. Courts have held that conviction records can be used to deny employment if the crime for which the person was convicted is related to the type of job. For example, an employer could refuse to hire someone convicted of theft and receipt of stolen goods for a job as a bellhop who would handle personal belongings of customers.
	Do you own your own home?	This question may also tend to exclude people from minority groups because they do not own homes in the same proportion as nonminority people. Home ownership is not an indicator of someone's ability to do the job.

FIGURE 11.12 Questions to avoid.

Do not write comments on the application form, because they may be used against you in legal proceedings.

answer is yes, then it's legal to ask what for. You would then need to make a determination about the suitability of placement in the available position. You wouldn't want a person convicted of stealing as a bartender or in charge of the payroll.

You should always ask potential employees about their sanitary attitude, habits, and knowledge. Find out what sanitation training they have had, in order to establish what needs to be learned. It is extremely important to hire employees with excellent personal habits and good attitudes toward safe service.

QUESTIONS YOU CAN ASK

General Opener
- Tell me a little about your work experience.
- What is the most important factor in the success of a restaurant?

Experience
- What is your favorite restaurant and why?
- What is your (foodservice, cooking) experience?
- What are your present duties and responsibilities?
- How well do you think you succeed in meeting those?
- Describe your ideal job.
- How do you see this restaurant helping with your future?

Transportation
- Can you get to and from work reliably for the shifts?

Availability
- What are your available working hours?
- Is there any time you cannot work?
- Are you available to work overtime when necessary?
- Do you have limitations on what shifts you can work?

Hobbies/Interests
- What are your hobbies and interests? (This is a general question that may encourage an applicant to open up.)

Goals/Ambitions
- What are your goals and ambitions? (The restaurant owner may be able to provide assistance, counseling, and overall encouragement to a person who has identified goals.)

- What goals have you established for yourself that are not work-related for the next few years, and why?
- Where do you see yourself three years from now?

Sports
- Which sports do you play or follow?

Languages
- Do you speak more than one language?

Work Experience
- How would your previous employer describe your work?
- What did you like most and least about your former job?
- How did you handle problems such as a drunken or obstreperous customer?

Skills and Specific Job-Related Questions
- Describe how you would prepare an item on the menu (for a cook's position) or the way to serve a particular food item (for a food server).
- What skills do you possess that make you think you should be employed here? What do you think this job and our organization can do for you?
- How long do you think you will be able to work for us?

Other Interview Questions
- How do you plan to achieve your career goals?
- What do you consider to be your greatest strengths and weaknesses?
- How do you think your last employer will describe you when we call to check references?

- How do your coworkers describe you? your subordinates?
- What motivates you to put forth your greatest effort?
- Why should I hire you?
- What qualifications do you have that make you think you will be successful in the restaurant business?
- What qualities should a successful manager possess?
- Describe the relationship that should exist between a supervisor and those reporting to him or her.
- What two or three accomplishments have given you the most satisfaction? Why?
- What led you to choose the restaurant industry?
- Do you have plans for additional education? What have you done to implement those plans?

- Do you think your grades in school are a successful indicator of your abilities?
- In what type of work environment are you most comfortable?
- How do you work under pressure? Give me an example.
- Why did you decide to seek a job with us?
- What do you know about our restaurant?
- What criteria are you using to evaluate the company for which you hope to work?
- What major problem have you encountered, and how did you deal with it?
- Tell me about an unusual request or demand from a guest and how you handled it.
- Give me an example of a situation in which you solved a problem of an angry guest.
- What two or three things are important to you in your job?

MULTIPLE INTERVIEW APPROACH

When plenty of applicants are available, the multiple interview is probably more effective than a single interview by a single person. A first interview may be given and the candidate rated from 1 to 5 on whatever factors are considered relevant to successful job performance. Only those candidates receiving a rating of 5 are given an additional appointment with a second interviewer.

TELEPHONE REFERENCES

Following up references by phone is much more effective than sending a written request, if the caller is adroit in asking questions. The phone call should be directed toward finding out the applicant's strengths and weaknesses. Reference checks are also useful in verifying what the applicant has said about previous wage or salary, job title, and length of employment.

The caller should state his or her name, title, and restaurant, and request to speak to a past supervisor. Then he or she should explain that the applicant has applied for employment and has given the person being called as a reference. After asking "Would you mind answering a few questions?" the caller can review what the applicant said he or she earned and did.

Few people voluntarily make adverse comments about applicants. The tone of voice and what is not said may be more important than the words. With "right to know" legislation and our litigious society, it is wise to ask questions that only relate to the applicant's attendance, such as "How long has *x* been with you?" and the dates work began and ended, and work capability and rate of pay. An important question might be, "Is the person eligible for reemployment?" (Conversely, restaurateurs should not volunteer opinions about former

Bill Nordhem, an experienced Chicago restaurateur, says that, over the years, he has developed a sixth sense about which servers will succeed and which will not. He looks for applicants with a positive mental attitude and willingness to participate in a team effort. "I don't believe in hiring the wrong person. I know in five minutes or less if someone is going to work out. I've learned to trust my gut. Every time I haven't, I've paid the price."[13]

employees, no matter how factual they may be. A former employee could have a friend call and record the conversation. The former employee could then sue for slander.)

Research-minded operators can rate applicants on a scale of 1 to 5 and use the rating as a prediction of success or failure on the job. A follow-up of worker performance can be correlated with the original ratings. Over time, an operator can see how effective his or her judgment has been in predicting employee performance and can change the interviewing process to sharpen the predictions.

Careful Selection of Staff

Taking time and care in selecting personnel is one of the best investments possible. Aside from the several positive reasons already mentioned, there is the need to take a defensive posture in trying to make sure that disruptive, dishonest people are not hired. Lawsuits brought by employees can be disastrous in cost and mental anguish. Some trials go on for years, with lawyers the only winners. Wrongful discharge alleged to involve race, color, creed, marital status, age, handicap, political affiliation, and so on are juicy complaints for lawyers. Lawsuits can be brought for such things as defamation of character, intentional infliction of emotional stress, and sexual harassment. Cases going to a jury trial often result in huge settlements unrelated to much of anything except the skills of the plaintiff's lawyer, who pockets much of the award as legal fees.

Three Main Hiring Objectives
1. Hire people who project an image and attitude appropriate for your restaurant.
2. Hire people who will work with you rather than spend all their time fighting your rules, procedures, and systems.
3. Hire people whose personal and financial requirements are a good fit with the hours and positions you are hiring for.[14]

Attitude and appearance are critical, say many human resource directors. Employers can teach the job skills, not the human and interpersonal skills.

The ADA poses a number of questions. If there are two equally qualified candidates, one of whom is disabled, must the disabled applicant be given hiring preference, even though some modification investment will be required? The most qualified person would get the job. If questioned or challenged, an operator would have to prove how the person who got the position was the most qualified person. Make a bad choice and it will cost you; some experts estimate a poor hiring decision could cost thousands.

Thousands of people with disabilities work in the restaurant industry as dishwashers, kitchen helpers, food servers, cooks, and pot and pan washers.

Many were first trained by a job coach funded by state or federal grants. Totally blind persons can be proficient dishwashers. A number of other jobs require only travel vision—enough sight to move about and generally see what is going on. Defective hearing does not disqualify applicants for many jobs.

FIVE TIPS FOR BETTER INTERVIEWING

Effective interviewing techniques and procedures are a key in recruiting and training the best-qualified managers. Here's a checklist of important tips that can help make you a better interviewer.

1. *Use a job profile based on the job description, a list of duties, responsibilities, and the personal characteristics the ideal candidate has.* This will also help evaluate each candidate's potential once the interview is over.

   If your organization's human resource department has job descriptions for each position on file, review them periodically to make sure that they are up to date and truly reflect each position's responsibilities and necessary qualifications of potential candidates.

2. *Describe the job in reasonable detail at the start of the interview.*

Let the candidate know what his or her day-to-day responsibilities will be, what opportunities there are for growth, how the rest of the management team is structured, and what is expected of the candidate in the larger organizational structure.

3. *Ask the right questions.* Knowing the right questions to ask is a critical part of effective interviewing, so prepare a list of questions in advance and think about how you will ask each. Avoid questions that require a yes/no answer, which discourage candidates from elaborating. Instead, ask open-ended, focused questions like "Think back to a difficult situation you had with an employee under your supervision and tell me how you handled it." Identifying how a candidate handled past conflicts or situations

is a good way to assess how he or she will handle that problem if faced with it again.

4. *Get specific.* A good question to ask a job candidate is, "What specific things did you do in your last job to improve your effectiveness or to improve productivity in your department?" The answer gives you a sense of a candidate's motivation and willingness to surpass the basic job requirements. Candidates who went that extra mile in a former job will probably do the same in your operation.

5. *Take notes.* Hiring decisions are too important to rely on your memory about every candidate you interview, so take good notes during each interview so you can review them later.

SCREENING OUT THE SUBSTANCE ABUSER

Alcohol abuse is a big problem for restaurant managers; it is magnified by the sale of liquor and the high-pressure atmosphere in many restaurants. More recently, cocaine, marijuana, prescription painkillers, and other drugs used by employees have added to management concerns.

Substance abuse impairs performance. More important, addicts frequently steal to support their habit.

Screening out drug abusers in the employment process is step one. Applicants who are habitual users show signs of health deterioration. Reference checks usually do not elicit explicit statements about drug abuse. The employment record can provide indicators: absenteeism, compensation claims, high number of sick days, accidents, late arrivals, and early departures. If the applicant has a history of arguments or fights with other employees or supervisors, substance abuse may have been involved. Tremors, excessive perspiration, slurred speech, and unsteady gait are physical indicators of substance abuse.

PREEMPLOYMENT PHYSICAL AND DRUG EXAMINATIONS

Many restaurants are considering or using preemployment drug and physical exams as a means of avoiding future personnel problems. Physical exams, as long as they pertain to the job, are permissible (e.g., lifting a tray or a stack of dishes). However, restaurants must conform with ADA regulations. Drug testing may be required in order to provide a safe and secure working environment for both guests and staff.

Summary

Staffing the restaurant is extremely important, because effective screening not only selects the best employees but also screens out undesirable ones. Effective recruitment selects people with the most positive service spirit and professionalism. Compliance with existing employment legislation is a must.

The human resource cycle begins with defining jobs and organizing the restaurant. A task is a related sequence of work and a job is a series of related tasks. Task and job analyses examine the details of the work performed and form the basis of the job description. The job specification identifies the qualifications and skills necessary to perform the job. The two main approaches to task and job analysis are bottom up, which is used when the organization already exists, and top down, which is used when opening new restaurants.

Key Terms and Concepts

Age discrimination

AIDS

Americans with
Disabilities Act
(ADA)

Civil rights laws

Equal Employment
Opportunity
Commission
(EEOC)

Immigration Reform
and Control Act

Interviewing

Job description

Job, position, task

Job specification

Organizing the
restaurant

Placement

Preemployment testing

Recruitment

Selection

Task and job analysis

Training

Review Questions

1. How long before opening would you employ your chef? your servers? your hostess?
2. Describe the ideal server, the ideal hostess, the ideal cook. How do they deliver on the experience you intend to provide to your guests?
3. Will you employ undocumented aliens in your restaurant? Give your reasons for your decision.
4. List five employee sources other than newspaper classified ads.

5. In some locations, job vacancy notices bring in literally hundreds of job applicants. If this happens to you, what methods will you use to select the best of them?

6. In checking employee references, how can you improve your chances of getting valid information on the applicant's past performance?

7. Will you use psychological tests in selecting employees?

8. Many people have a drug or alcohol problem. Would you hire such people? How would you avoid hiring such people?

9. Suppose you want to employ only women for your dining room and bar service. Will you be violating the Equal Employment Opportunity laws?

10. How will you prepare for interviewing a chef? What questions will you ask?

11. What is the difference between a job and a position? between a task and a job?

12. Give at least three reasons for performing job analysis.

13. In your restaurant, will your host be a "greeter and seater" or a dining room manager? What factors bear on your decision?

14. Will you bother to draw an organization chart for your restaurant? Justify your decision.

15. In your restaurant, will the sanitation/maintenance employees report to the chef or to you, the owner/operator? What factors bear on this choice? Is there an advantage in having these employees report to someone other than you or the chef?

16. What elements will you include in the job description for a food server? a line cook?

17. What elements will you include in the job specifications for a food server? a line cook?

18. Is a restaurant that performs task and job analysis and writes job descriptions and specifications likely to be more successful than one that does not? Why?

19. What is the value of training a person for working more than one job?

CASE STUDY: Short Street Cakes[15]

Background

Short Street Cakes is an all-natural "southern-style" bakery that specializes in wedding cakes and cupcake production. Short Street Cakes was opened in Asheville, North Carolina, in February 2009 by Jodi Rhoden, a small business entrepreneur and self-taught baker. As a hobby, Jodi began making wedding cakes from home for her friends around the area. As it turned out, Jodi's cake-making skills were heavily in demand throughout the Asheville community. Word spread quickly of the quality and decadence of her cakes.

Next, Jodi got her home kitchen certified, created a menu of her cake offerings, took a business class, and then started a booming home-based cake business. This lasted for three years and provided a great foundation to eventually expand the business outside of her home. Jodi then found an investor to partner in opening a full-fledged bakery, which she called Short Street Cakes.

Repertoire

Jodi has maintained a singular and idealistic approach to her business: "Do one thing and do it well." While Short Street Cakes specializes in creating cakes for weddings and other events, it is not a café. Short Street Cakes has made wedding cakes the backbone of its business, which gives it the capacity to produce a much larger quantity of cakes and styles. Its cake products are fashioned by "Southern-style" recipes as opposed to "European-style," which gives it an advantage over other cake makers in the area who do not use this technique. This is where Short Street Cakes has carved out a niche within its realm of business.

Short Street Cakes produces a repertoire of over 30 different cake styles. Some of its biggest sellers year-round include the Strawberry Short Street, which is a pound cake with fresh strawberries in the batter and a vanilla cream cheese icing, along with even more strawberries to decorate the top. Another favorite is the Triple Chocolate Ganache. This is a deep dark chocolate cake, which also happens to be a vegan-friendly recipe. The cake is complimented by a "super chocolaty" (non-vegan) buttercream ganache, which drizzles down the side and provides the perfect presentation to ensure that first-bite "wow" moment.

Success and Challenges

Short Street Cakes' overall success has been the result of proactively seeking out new customers, while keeping a small and simple operation that maintains focus at all times. Jodi recently purchased advertising for in-room guest compendiums in various hotels throughout Asheville. Because destination weddings represent such a large part of the bakery's business, the advertising gets the name out first to people who visit Asheville to make wedding plans. Above all else, Jodi strongly emphasizes creating a high-quality product using as many local ingredients as possible, all of which are always served "fresh same day." The bakery also offers vegan and gluten-free options, which cater to a certain demographic with a substantial presence in the Asheville area.

There are continuous challenges that arise in the bakery business, and one of the biggest is constantly getting quality ingredients. The current state of the economy has caused the quality of certain products to decline in the market, resulting in a higher price paid for the same quality Jodi

used to get at a lower price. This can present a big problem because Jodi's livelihood is based on particular recipes and ingredients. The smallest difference in an ingredient can significantly alter the end product. Another challenge is showing up for the business 100 percent of the time and maintaining the necessary passion and energy to run it successfully. It is difficult to balance the demands of a restaurant business with a healthy family life. However, Jodi continues to strive to create a valuable experience that is sustainable in the long term for her as an individual, for her staff, and for the business as a whole.

Opportunity Ahead

Recently, a retail space became available in the building next door to Short Street Cakes. The building is conveniently owned by the same landlord, who offered Jodi a very reasonable deal to lease the space if she would like. Owning and operating a café has never been an interest of Jodi's in the past, and there are both positive and negative aspects of significantly expanding the retail business. Additionally, there are opportunities to rent store space in downtown Asheville, which is much more heavily trafficked than the bakery's current location; however, the rent is also twice as much, which would require selling twice as many cupcakes daily in order to break even. Ultimately, Jodi would like to expand her wedding repertoire and increase what she is able to do in terms of design and distance.

QUESTIONS

1. What are some benefits to the ways Jodi's business is structured?
2. What are some of the advantages and disadvantages to expanding the retail business? Would Jodi need to staff differently?
3. If Jodi does expand the retail business, would the building next door be the right location, or would a location in the downtown area be more ideal to creating a successful retail expansion?

Endnotes

1. Philip M. Perry, "Recruiting Employees to Play on Your Team," *Restaurants USA* 19 (November 1999), p. 32.

2. Ed Levine, "How to Keep Restaurant Staff Motivated and Satisfied," Open Forum (October 29, 2010), https://www.openforum.com/articles/how-to-keep-restaurant-staff-motivated-and-satisfied-1/.

3. Virginia Gerst, "The Ten Minute Manager's Guide to Hiring Chefs," *Restaurants & Institutions,* 116 (5), (March 1, 2006), pp. 20–22.

4. Ibid.

5. National Restaurant Association, "Changes in Some Federal Teen-Labor Regulations Take Effect Feb. 14, 2005," Federal Teen-Labor Regulations, http://www.marylandrestaurants.com/laws/documents/TeenLaborLawChanges2005.pdf. Retrieved on May 16, 2013.

6. US Department of Labor, "Fair Labor Standards Act Advisor," http://www.dol.gov/elaws/faq/esa/flsa/028.htm.

7. US Citizenship and Immigration Services, "E-Verify," http://www.uscis.gov/portal/site/uscis/menuitem.eb1d4c2a3e5b9ac89243c6a7543f6d1a/?vgnextoid=75bce2e261405110VgnVCM1000004718190aRCRD&vgnextchannel=75bce2e261405110VgnVCM1000004718190aRCRD. Retrieved May 24, 2013.

8. US Citizenship and Immigration Services, "Documents that Establish Employment Authorization," http://www.uscis.gov/portal/site/uscis/menuitem.eb1d4c2a3e5b9ac89243c6a7543f6d1a/?vgnextoid=27c41921c6898210VgnVCM100000082ca60aRCRD&vgnextchannel=27c41921c6898210VgnVCM100000082ca60aRCRD. Retrieved May 15, 2013.

9. US Merit Systems Protection Board, "Merit System Principles (5 USC, http://www.mspb.gov/meritsystemsprinciples.htm retrieved on May 16, 2013.

10. Phillip M. Perry. "Gray Matters: The Do's and Don'ts of Dealing with Disabilities." National Restaurant Association Online (November 1998), http://cf.restaurant.org/tools/magazines/rusa/magArchive/year/issue/article/?ArticleID=318. Retrieved. June 29, 2006.

11. Tony Perry, "Restaurant's Owner and Manger Fined for Hiring Illegal Workers," *Los Angeles Times* (December 23, 2011), http://articles.latimes.com/2011/dec/23/local/la-me-1223-bakery-owner-20111223. Retrieved May 15, 2013.

12. This section draws from the National Restaurant Association. *Basic Facts About AIDS for Food-service Employees*, and "When an Employee Says." http://cf.restaurant.org/tools/magazines/rusa/magArchive/year/issue/article/?ArticleID=103. June 29, 2006.

13. Nancy Backas, "Training and Personality," *Cheers* 9, (2) (March 1998), p. 58.

14. Stephen Michaellides and Carolyn Watkins. "The Big Talent Search." www.food-management.com/article/12414. June 29, 2006.

15. Courtesy of Jodi Rhoden.

Training and Service

LEARNING OBJECTIVES

After reading and studying this chapter, you should be able to:

- List the goals of an orientation program.

- Compare and contrast behavior modeling and learner instruction.

- List guidelines for effective trainers.

- Describe characteristics of effective servers and greeters.

- Identify the seven commandments of customer service.

- List guidelines for handling customer complaints.

Courtesy of Red Lobster Restaurants

Experience has shown that the most practical and immediately beneficial way of training restaurant employees is the time-tested hands-on method (showing and telling the trainee, then having the trainee do the task). This method prompts immediate rewards and shows where further instruction is needed. The assumption, however, is that the trainer knows the skill being taught and at least some of the principles of learning. It also assumes that the trainer has laid out the steps needed in order to attain competence. From fast food to fine dining, restaurant training programs involve interactive processes to teach employees how to do tasks. But for training to be successful, managers and trainers must get inside the heads of their employees to understand what motivates them to learn.[1] This chapter gives an overview of employee training and the related subjects of employee orientation and development.

In training our trainers, an analogy I like to use is that there are three types of people who attend training programs: prisoners, vacationers, and explorers.[2]

You know who the prisoners are—the 10-year employees who are wondering, "Why am I here?" They are just told to show up and they are unhappy about being there.

You've got vacationers. These are people who are glad to be anywhere but at work. They're easy to recognize, too.

Then you have the explorers. These are the people who are excited to be in the class and about taking the knowledge they will gain and applying it to be more successful on the job.

We need to step back and think about what we are doing in the restaurant business. The next two examples give a clear answer. Chester Kroeger, owner of Fudpucker's restaurants in Destin and Ft. Walton, Florida, says, "Together with wanting to be entertained, guests today go out because they want to be treated special. They want to be served. They want to be taken care of. They want to feel like they matter. If you fail at any point in the course of the guest service experience, you will likely have lost a guest, and potentially many more."[3]

An interesting piece from *Lessons in Service: From Charlie Trotter* by Edmund Lawler sets the tone for this chapter: "Orchestrating the interplay of food and wine is a team of dark-suited servers who move gracefully through the dining room, all but anticipating the guest's every need. Gracious to a fault, the impeccably groomed servers never say no to a guest request. Their mission is to guide the guest through the dining experience of a lifetime—to 'blow their minds.'"[4]

LA phenom chef David Myers says, "We do Navy Seal training, the model training program the Seals created to weed out for their BUDS (Basic Underwater Demolition Seals). In the winter, we have a full day. It starts at 4 A.M., swimming in the ice-cold ocean. Each person has a swim buddy and we're out there going through the Navy Seal hell week exercises. You get low-grade hypothermia while you are doing it. We have doctors there because it's a brutal experience. But, at the end of it, we're a team, ready to go to bat for each other. They learn about winning, leading, success. We do this with everyone, the front of the house included."[5]

Orientation

A well-planned *orientation* program helps new employees become acquainted with the restaurant and feel a part of it. Because much of labor turnover occurs in the first few weeks of employment, it is important to establish a bond between the new

Courtesy of State Street Eating House

Orientation allows new employees to get acquainted with the restaurant and to learn the procedures to be followed.

employee and the restaurant. As with any other program, it is necessary to establish the goals to be accomplished.

There are eight goals for an orientation program:

1. To explain the company history, philosophy, mission, goals, and objectives
2. To make employees feel welcome
3. To let employees know why they have been selected
4. To ensure that employees know what to do and who to ask when unsure
5. To explain and show what is expected of employees
6. To have employees explain and then demonstrate each task so that supervisors can be sure they understand their full job
7. To explain the various programs and social activities available
8. To show where everything is kept (tour of restaurant storerooms, refrigerators, etc.)

Help employees become familiar with the restaurant and the food. For example, at the Olive Garden, everyday training of new employees involves sampling the food. This makes servers better equipped to answer customers' questions and helps build employee confidence.

Part-Time Employees

Part-time employees are both a benefit and a drawback. One of the benefits to the operator is in not having to pay benefits (which may be up to 28 percent of payroll). One of the drawbacks is the possible lack of continuity, which increases the need for training.

The Bureau of Labor Statistics reports that well over half of all persons employed in foodservice occupations work part time. In the quick-service segment, the proportion of part-timers is higher. Part-time employees are good for the industry because they can be scheduled to fit the peaks and valleys in sales. Moreover, the overwhelming majority, reports the Bureau, wants to or can only work part time. Using part-timers means giving more training; most part-timers do not think of foodservice as a permanent career. The result: more people to train, and more people who are not particularly motivated to learn their job.

Training and Development

The objective in *training and development* employees is to produce desired behavior—attitudes and skills appropriate for producing food and service that pleases the restaurant's clientele. Much learning can be programmed; employees are trained to follow a sequence of behavior. Behavior can be taught by role-playing—smile, pour coffee, present the menu, ask about wine. The routine is critiqued by other employees and by managers.

Employee *development*, usually thought of as training for management, is partly programmed, but it is also based on knowledge that provides background for flexible responses to problem situations. What do I do when all the restaurant seats are filled, when I spill spaghetti, when a customer is angry, when the refrigeration or the ice machine cuts out?

Employee development promotes problem-solving ability and provides analytical skills, new perceptions, and methodologies. Development deals with principles, training, with procedure and process. Both types of learning are needed in any business. Learning for management and supervision emphasizes development; on-the-job training is closer to programming. One is more conceptual than the other.

Training can produce robotlike behavior: smile, say, "Thank you," and say, "Good-bye, come again." Training produces skills quickly by breaking them down into segments and piecing them together into sequences:

- Turn the hamburger when the juices rise to the top.
- Cut the steak ¾-inch thick and weigh each piece on a portions scale.
- Make fresh coffee every hour.

In management development, we learn rules or follow models:

- When criticizing an employee, use the plus-minus-plus model: Start with praise, bring in the criticism, end with praise.
- Never criticize in public.
- Every day, everyone needs praise.

Though these rules of supervision are in the nature of principles and are on a conceptual level, they can be programmed and memorized for use as appropriate.

Training suggests doing something to others, teaching people skills they do not have today. "We will train new hires to serve food to and from the left, beverages to and from the right." But what about the exceptions to the program—for example, guests sitting against the wall, where service from the left is awkward or impossible?

Employee development programs deal with perspectives, with attitudes, and with feelings about the restaurant, the job, the customers, and the boss. Can attitudes be programmed? Every coach tries to program the team to have a winning attitude. The restaurant owner also wants spirit and optimism. The old McDonald's slogan, "food, folks, and fun," sums it up neatly.

Here, *leadership* and training merge. *management* works to help employees understand that their needs—for praise, for achievement, for dignity and approval— are congruent with the success of the restaurant. If managers believe it and live it, employees are likely to absorb some of the same spirit. The coach shows the players how to win; in a restaurant, that translates to how to keep dishes and stations clean, how to broil a steak to medium-done, filet a fish, stuff a pork chop, make a Mornay sauce, or set a table.

To a certain extent, problem solving can be programmed. What should be done when something happens that is not taken care of by the system, when the

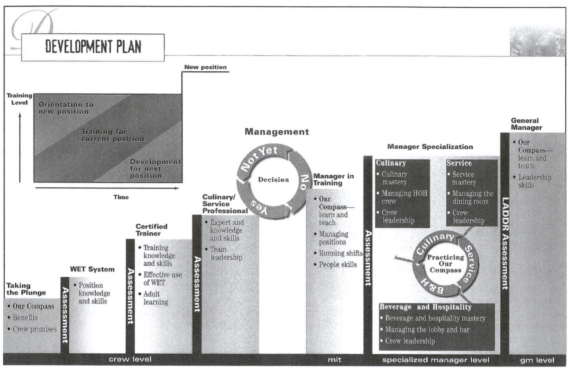

Courtesy of Red Lobster Restaurants

FIGURE 12.1 Red Lobster's development plan.

unexpected happens or a crisis occurs? Just about every crisis that will happen in a restaurant can be considered beforehand and behavior suggested:

■ A robbery

■ A dishwasher breakdown

■ A customer fainting

■ An electricity outage

■ A fistfight in the dining room

■ A drunk spilling his food

■ Coffee spilled on the customer

■ Toilets backing up

■ An argument over the check

■ A customer without funds

Planning for contingencies is part of development. What should be done when there is a mistake in scheduling employees? What should be done when employees fail to show up for work? What about theft of tips? Definite solutions that cover all cases are probably not possible, but the steps to be taken in problem situations can be learned: Keep cool. Think. What are the alternatives? Figure 12.1 illustrates Red Lobster's development plan.

The broad solutions can be programmed; the exact solutions often cannot.

TRAINING PROGRAMS

Most training programs involve comprehensible step-by-step job learning that utilizes job checklists and differing styles of management control. Training programs also tend to emphasize varying types of sales incentives.

To train, the trainer needs to know what should be learned—the tasks that make up a job. Much restaurant training is accomplished by absorption—watching someone and somehow learning the job: "Follow George!" or "Watch Mary." Training by observation has its place. However, it is much better and more efficient to approach training systematically by analyzing a job, breaking it down into the tasks performed, and teaching the tasks in the sequence in which they are normally performed.

Management decides how extensive written job instructions should be. Brevity is an asset, and if the job tasks can be printed on a pocketsize card, the employee has a handy reference. Guidelines for a job can be put together and given to the new employee to augment more comprehensive, detailed job instructions. Both can become part of a training manual. Here is a suggested Training schedule for new employees:

Day 1

Orientation

Lunch

Station tour and observation

Study alcohol awareness

Employee handbook review

Study first third of recipe references

Read training manual

Day 2

On-the-job training shift

Alcohol awareness test (open book)

Employee handbook review due

Recipe review; study second third of recipe references

Study for introduction to kitchen and sanitation tests

Day 3

On-the-job training shift

Introduction to kitchen and sanitation tests

Recipe review; study final third of recipe references

Day 4

On-the-job training shift

Recipe review; study all recipe references

Day 5

On-the-job training shift

Recipe review; study all recipe references

Day 6

On-the-job training shift

Review with the manager

Final test

Training for restaurant jobs and careers is offered in high schools, community colleges, and specialized culinary courses. The Culinary Institute of America is an example. It has campuses in Hyde Park, New York, and in the Napa Valley in California. Courses offered range from basic culinary skills to a four-year bachelor's degree program.

The Lettuce Entertainment training program lasts five days, for eight hours daily. Each new hire studies the company's training guides in the morning on-site and trails a server in the afternoon.

Performance is evaluated on each shift. If necessary, additional training shifts can be scheduled to meet requirements successfully.

Personnel training is the key to keeping satisfied, capable, confident, and competent employees. Training can give employees a feeling of confidence. At one restaurant in Deburne, Texas, the owner wanted to increase sales at his restaurants by 25 cents per guest. That goal was reached one week after the servers participated in a sales training program. An increase of $1.10 was obtained at dinner and 91 cents at lunch. These increases were credited to a script that was developed for the servers to use. Sales prior to the training as well as after were monitored, and employees were able to share a percentage of the profit above their individual sales goals.

Without enthusiasm in training, learning suffers. How many well-informed professors offer dull classes attended by only a handful of students? The best speakers are also entertainers who appeal to the emotions as well as the brain. Professional speakers use gimmicks to gain attention. Humor is carefully put into the presentation. Concepts are condensed into models and slogans. A catchy training slogan that appears on the blackboards in some kitchens reads: "We forgive all mistakes except what you serve to our customers."

Courtesy of The Prado, San Diego, California
Training is a critical link to consistent service.

TRAINING AIDS

The Educational Foundation of the National Restaurant Association (NRA) has developed informative DVDs and CD-ROMs. Five topic areas are currently available: Waitstaff, Back-of-the-House Training, Wine Training, Profits from Produce, and How to Implement Video Training. In addition, individual tapes focus on current foodservice concerns, such as tip reporting, the immigration law, the AIDS issue, and alcohol awareness training.[6]

Several practical guides have been written to meet a variety of operational needs as well. Contact the NRA Educational Foundation, 175 West Jackson Boulevard, Suite 1500, Chicago, IL 60604, (800) 775–2122.

The National Restaurant Association Educational Foundation has developed a Foodservice Management Professional Credential (FMP). This credential has minimum requirements and a certification examination with five sections that must be passed before the certification is awarded. The examination covers the five major areas of competence for foodservice managers: accounting and finance, administration, human resources, marketing, and operations.

With restaurant budgets suffering from recession-related cutbacks, trainers and human resource managers are looking for inexpensive ways to keep employees trained and able to serve customers.[7] Trainers say they are developing their own material, running smaller departments, devising formulas to determine the return on investment for training dollars, and developing low- to no-cost leadership programs.[8] The Council of Hotel and Restaurant Trainers (CHART), in partnership with Maritz Research, announced the release of the State of Training and Development in the Hospitality Industry Report. This is the first report of its kind. It contains answers to budget related questions collected from 140 CHART hotel and restaurant trainer members. The CHART survey showed participants' companies spending, on average, a total of $2 million annually on training, including salaries, benefits, travel, and in-house development of training materials. The results mirror the economic state of the industry, with 53 percent of respondents reporting a decrease in their training budgets over the past 18 months.[9]

COMBINE TRAINING WITH DEVELOPMENT

Probably every job calls for some training and some development. Programming (training) servers provides the base. What should be said when approaching a guest? When do you hand the menu to the person? When is water served? Each job also calls for adaptability—some jobs more than others. Cutting meat calls for little adaptability; supervision calls for a lot.

Should a server be encouraged to make small talk? Small talk is difficult to program. Guidelines would suggest avoiding subjects like politics and religion. Never argue with a guest. Never upstage a guest. What should a server do when propositioned? Be tactful. But where tact is difficult to program, principles can be suggested: Keep your cool. Quickly divert attention to another subject.

Should servers joke with customers? House policy may encourage it or prohibit it, depending on the character of the restaurant. If encouraged, some guidelines may help: Stay impersonal. Stay away from touchy subjects. Keep conversations brief and friendly.

SLOGANS HELP

Most of us like "thought packages," as put together in slogans:

> Plan Your Work, Work Your Plan.
> Use Your Head to Save Your Feet.
> Be Firm, Fair, and Follow Through.
> KISS—Keep It Simple, Stupid!
> Protect Your Employees with Controls.

STEP-BY-STEP TRAINING

It is essential to explain not only how to do something but why it is important. Server training can be broken down and taught step by step. It can also be summarized on a card small enough to be carried around in a pocket for easy reference. T.G.I. Friday's new employees must be validated (checked off) by a back- or front-of-house trainer. There may be up to 30 trainers in a T.G.I. Friday's restaurant. The trainer who is certified gives small-group and individual training in the mornings. New employees must pass a written test and demonstrate competence in both the health card care and alcohol awareness test. In addition, they must pass an individual department test.

For hosts, T.G.I. Friday's has developed a checklist that represents a typical day and is used as a guideline for training.

A typical day for a host working at T.G.I. Friday's is similar to hosting your own party. Think of guests as friends of yours, and treat them in the same manner you would treat honored guests visiting your home.

You are the host of a party on each shift. Greet guests on their arrival, ensure that their dining experience is better than expected, and bid them farewell as they leave. Here is a typical restaurants checklist for a host/ess position:

1. Be in proper uniform.
2. Clock in at scheduled time.
3. Review the cleanliness and organization of the station. Check for restocking of necessary supplies. Bring all areas up to standard. Discuss problems with your manager.
4. Ensure that all menus are clean.
5. Check restrooms to ensure cleanliness standards (continue to check every 15 minutes).
6. Shift responsibilities:
   a. Open the door for each guest.
   b. Greet guests upon entering.
   c. Maintain a cheerful, courteous disposition (*smile*).
   d. Maintain a neat, clean, professional image.
   e. "Read" guests and seat them as soon as possible at an appropriate table. Be alert for:
      ■ Elderly guests
      ■ Guests with children
      ■ Handicapped guests
   f. Present only *clean* menus to guests. Open each menu to the appetizer page and offer assistance if necessary.
   g. Inform guest of your name.
   h. Notify a manager if you perceive that *any* guest is the least bit unhappy.
   i. Properly assist guests when on a waiting list.
   j. Work with busers to ensure that tables are bused and reseated within one minute.
   k. Bid farewell to each departing guest. Ensure that everything was satisfactory and invite them to return.
   l. Answer the telephone within two rings.
   m. Assist in properly setting and aligning tables.
   n. Perform shift change and/or closing duties.
7. Meet with the manager on duty to check out your station and sign your time card.

TRAINING THEORY

Dozens of books have been written on theories of learning and their application to training. Here are proven guidelines for a trainer:

Courtesy of the Cohn Restaurant Group
The first impression a restaurant makes is with the greeting from the host.

- All of us react to discipline and punishment. Examples of discipline: absence of approval, reprimands, lack of apparent progress. Reward might include praise, smile, and recognition.
- Reward (reinforce) desired learning; allow undesired behavior to extinguish itself by not rewarding it.
- Reward or punish immediately after the observed behavior.
- Spaced training is more effective than a long period of training. Spacing allows the learning to be absorbed and avoids fatigue.
- Expect learning to proceed irregularly. There may be periods when no apparent learning is seen but changes are taking place.
- Expect wide differences in the ability to learn. Many restaurant employees are not rapid learners, but once they have learned, they do excellent work. Slower learners are often not bored as quickly as rapid learners.

Much of the theory of learning is incorporated in the following trainer test. Try it out and see how your answers compare with the discussion that follows.

Test Yourself as a Trainer

Answer true or false.

General

1. The restaurant has an obligation to provide employees with the skills necessary to perform the job.
2. Employee turnover is often related to training or the lack of it.
3. Learning by on-the-job training is not the only way to provide necessary learning for new employees.
4. Training low-skilled employees may be just as important as training highly skilled workers.
5. Prior to training, explain the rules and regulations of the company to the new employee.
6. Prior to training, answer the unspoken question in every trainee's mind: "What's in it for me?"
7. Popular persons are certain to make good trainers.
8. Before actual training begins, explain the position as it relates to the total restaurant.
9. A person who performs well on the job is qualified to teach others the skills needed for the job.

10. The ability to train can be developed, to a large extent.
11. A trainer should always be available for social activities with trainees.
12. A trainer should spend as much or more time in preparation to train as in actual instruction.
13. The trainer should have written task instructions before beginning to teach and should list the key points around which instructions are built.
14. The trainer should learn what the employee already knows about the job before starting to train.
15. The trainer should have a timetable with a schedule of instruction for each day and the amount of learning that is expected daily.

Points to Remember while Training

16. In setting instructional goals, give trainees more work than they can accomplish so that they will work toward high standards.
17. When a trainee performs correctly, reward the person with praise—something like, "That's good," or, "You're doing fine."
18. A trainer must never admit past or present errors or not knowing an answer to a question.
19. The best way to handle a cocky trainee is to embarrass the person in front of others.
20. In training new employees, concentrate on speed rather than form.
21. A trainer must continuously be aware of the attitudes and feelings of the trainees.
22. Surprise quizzes and examinations are good ways to ensure performance at a high level.
23. Expect that there will be periods during the training when no observable progress is made.
24. Expect some employees to learn two or three times as fast as others.
25. Both tell and show the trainee how to do the skill involved.
26. When an employee performs incorrectly, say, "No, not that way!"
27. After a task is learned, ask trainees for suggestions on how to improve the task.

In this quiz, the first six statements, according to the experts, are true. To create learner interest, explain the benefits to the person and explain the rules and regulations of the company. Answer such obvious questions as location of the employee dining area and the locker room, if there is one. All of the benefits and the requirements should be explained and gotten out of the way before skill training is started.

Number 7 is false. Popularity does not necessarily correlate highly with being a good trainer. The desire to train is needed, and the ability to train can be developed, to a large extent. Number 8 is true; it is important to see the particular job as a part of the whole. Number 9 is false and Number 10 is true.

Numbers 12, 13, 14, and 15 have to do with getting ready for instruction before actually doing it. All of these statements are true.

Number 16 is false. Training is an occasion when success at every step is important. Standards should be achievable so that employees avoid the experience of failure. Number 17 is true. Number 18 is false; no one expects a perfect trainer.

Number 19 is false. Even when a trainee is out of line, it does no good to embarrass the person. Rather, talk to the person privately.

Number 20 is false. Form comes first; speed comes later.

Number 21 is true; 22 is false. Surprises are not considered good in training.

Number 23 is true. There are times when consolidation of skills takes place and no observable progress is made.

Number 24 refers to a vast range of individual differences found in the general population. It and number 25 are true.

Number 26 represents a negative way of teaching; it is far better to emphasize the positive.

The last item is true. Every task can be improved by new techniques, new methods, new equipment, new skills—or it may be completely eliminated as unnecessary.

Methods for Training Employees

There are as many ways to train employees as there are learning styles. This chapter looks at three methods of training: behavior modeling, learner-controlled instruction, and manager as coach.

BEHAVIOR MODELING

Closely related to role-playing, which has been around a long time, *behavior modeling* is a technique that depicts the right way to handle personnel problems, shows how to interview and evaluate applicants, and demonstrates decision making. Emphasis on interpersonal skills—*people handling*—has always been of great importance in the restaurant or in any management position, but the move to deemphasize theory and emphasize "how to do" is new.

Everyone has had behavior models: parents, schoolteachers, athletic coaches, friends, and others. Which model should one follow?

Behavior modeling uses the innate inclination for people to observe others to discover how to do something new. It is more often used in combination with some other techniques.[10] Systematic exposure to models favored by an organization constitutes the training. Audiovisual materials in which an actor or company executive demonstrates the correct or approved techniques for dealing with problems are used by several foodservice companies. Feedback from peers and videotapes of trainee performance give trainees the advantage of seeing how they look to others and how well they are progressing.

Host International holds training sessions at one-week intervals and asks trainees to take each new skill back to the work situation, where it can be practiced. At the end of each session, the trainee is asked to explain how the skill is put to use.

LEARNER-CONTROLLED INSTRUCTION

A concept called learner-controlled instruction (LCI) has been used by some hospitality organizations for management training with considerable success.[11] *Learner-controlled instruction (LCI)* is a program in which employees are given job standards to achieve and asked to reach the standards at their own pace. Many believe the LCI method is less costly than classroom instruction and reflects employees' different levels of motivation, energy, and ability. The learner is self-motivated and can proceed from unit to unit at a speed with which he or she is comfortable.

To be effective, LCI presumes the availability of learning resources. These can be in the form of books, written practices and policies, and the availability of knowledgeable people willing to pass along their skills and information. A manager's resources manual, assembled by C&C Services of Cucamonga, California, sets up performance criteria for management trainees that lead them through nine modules of learning: bartender, cook, prep, meat cutting, cocktail, cashier, waiter, hostess, and assistant manager. Each learning module is completed when the trainee passes a module test at an 85 percent score and completes the work experience prescribed for the module. If the module is done satisfactorily, the supervisor signs off on it and the trainee can think about passing on to the next module.

The resources suggested for a section on attitude awareness include a book (with discussions of it with a trainer). In learning the bar operation, the trainee is scheduled to work the bar one day per week until competence in bartending is achieved. The bartender written test includes items on glasses used with each drink on the bar list, garnishes to use with various drinks, bar abbreviations used, and the ingredients for all of the drinks served. (Do you know what is in a sex on the beach or a Long Island iced tea?) The management trainees are urged to follow the 2½ times rule—2½ contacts with each patron or party in the restaurant during the course of a meal:

> A hello when the customer comes in equals ½ contact.
>
> A contact during the meal to obtain feedback equals 1 contact.
>
> A contact when the meal is over equals 1 contact.

The trainee checks a certain number of tables every 20 to 30 minutes. It takes only 5 minutes, says the manual, to check four to five tables. If this is done every 15 to 20 minutes, most tables can be covered in an hour.

The proficiency test for the cook module is detailed enough to cover such points as:

> How do you tell when chicken is done?
>
> How do you put out a butter fire?
>
> How do you tell whether the ovens are at the correct temperatures?
>
> How often should you turn a steak?
>
> How many carrots go onto a plate?
>
> How do you cook swordfish?
>
> What should you do if you:
> > a. Drop an order of crab on the floor?
> > b. Drop half a pan of potatoes?
>
> How can you tell when zucchini is done?
>
> What is a sign of old mushrooms?
>
> How long do potatoes keep in a warmer?
>
> How many lemons do you serve on a side dish?

Standards are set up for nearly everything that is done by a manager, who is expected to know about and be able to perform every task in the restaurant. Putting together such a comprehensive LCI program is a large task that can take months. The material is best assembled in loose-leaf form to allow easy insertion and deletion.

Much of the success of an LCI program depends on the cooperation of all concerned. Trainees are scheduled into the various jobs and must learn from incumbent employees as well as from supervisors, who are the main resource to whom trainees turn for information and instruction.

MANAGER AS COACH

A professional training and development program creates a situation in which all concerned win; the customer and the employee enjoy better product, better service, and greater professional satisfaction. "Winning," said Vince Lombardi, the famous football coach, "isn't everything; it's the only thing." In the training experience, there should be no losers, only winners. The training effort is geared so that winning begins with day one. Everyone needs a series of successes; learning favors the success experience.

Just like a football team, a restaurant staff has a coach, a manager, and personnel to train and motivate (*manager as coach*). The operation calls for timing, coordination, signals, and a will to win. Deadlines must be met, morning, noon, and night. Hundreds of expectations must be met on time. Hundreds of variables are involved in the personalities, the food products, the equipment, and skills of the players. Any one or many of the variables can go wrong. When there is a full house, action is at a fever pitch. Tension is high. The manager must be on the premises, calling the signals. The coach coaches. He or she shows people how to perform. Criticism is given if needed. More important, the right way is stressed. Everyone, including the pot-and-pan person, needs positive feedback, reinforcement of the right way, and information on how the game is going.

The goal is to please the customer at a profit. The coach is constantly motivating, triggering the will to win. The coach controls the game in a restaurant more so than in most businesses. Training regimens and systems of play pull the team together into an operating whole.

Like football teams, restaurants rise and fall. The talent changes as players come and go. There is always another restaurant down the street ready to move up in popularity. Coach X may be more knowledgeable than Coach Y, but may not be able to instill the winning spirit into his team. Teamwork is critical to the success of any restaurant.

Coach Y may have been a winning coach, but he has lost his enthusiasm and drive, or he has lost some of his key players and can't seem to get it together without them. He may have lost interest in the team and prefers concentrating on his evenings off. Or he may have made the big time too soon and cannot handle the prestige and the money that go with success. Coach Y, who formerly was out on the floor for every meal, now sits in the office and reads the *Wall Street Journal* during the heavy meal periods. Coach X is on the floor greeting the guests, speaking to the employees, instructing, checking details, and lending a life force to the restaurant.

The word *manage* implies purpose and the mobilization of resources for given goals. A restaurant manager has resources with which to accomplish the purpose of a restaurant: to satisfy patrons at a profit. The resources at the manager's disposal are the restaurant itself, its personnel, its supplies, and its operating capital. Managers have a variety of skills, such as knowing how to motivate, train, delegate, forecast business, plan the menu, and market what is produced. Systems or programs are set up and, once in place, administered by the manager.

You may have heard the expression "If the only tool you have is a hammer, everything starts to look like a nail." If you keep pounding the same way, everyone will become numb to the blows. Well, training with only one tool can quickly become old so here are some pointers to avoid that.[12] The solution is to make sure you have more than one tool at your disposal. Using different items as props can often help, depending on the nature of the group. Recently I observed a class in which one trainer used different animal Beanie Babies to help a group associate different temperature ranges and cooking requirements with different types of proteins.

Graphic association is a very effective way to emphasize an idea. You might use a photo or drawing of raw chicken being stored on a top shelf with some dripping occurring, and overlay that with a large red "X" through the image. You could follow that with a photo of properly stored product with a large green check mark through the image.

Another technique is to use a "spot the error" exercise. For example, if you were doing some preshift training, you might take staff into a cooler where you have intentionally misplaced some items to violate standards and then have the trainee find and correct the errors. Does everyone know that it is bad practice to store a mop standing in a bucket rather than hanging it up? If not, it is an opportunity to explain that some common insects like to hide in wet mops.

Service

It is generally accepted that servers contribute as much to the dining experience as, or perhaps more than, the decor, appointments, background music, lighting, and even the food served.

Guest service, including guest recognition, is important for all restaurants, but particularly so for dinner houses and fine-dining restaurants because they offer more service.

When dining at a white-tablecloth restaurant or a casual burger joint, customers value good table service over any other aspect of the dining experience, according to a recent *Nation's Restaurant News* study.[13] Similarly, service quality is often the most frequent complaint made by restaurant patrons.

Guest relations is an aspect of marketing and sales. Some restaurants are able to become profitable within a few months by not spending a great deal of money on media advertising but by developing a signature complimentary appetizer that is delivered to the table as soon as guests are seated.

The psychology of foodservice as practiced by the server varies tremendously with the type of establishment, from the hot dog emporium to the deluxe dinner house. The teenager in Arby's is probably happy with working as a part of a team of other teenagers in an air-conditioned, well-lighted, well-appointed, and fast-paced establishment. The skills required are minimal: assembly of food orders, a few simple cooking skills, making change. Most important, though, is the customer contact and the pleasure in working with one's peers. Supervision is minimal; most of the motivation comes from the necessity of keeping up with customer demand.

Consider the more complex relationships and skills required in a dinner house. The dining area is usually broken into tables and booths. Each booth forms a separate environment and protects the territorial imperative, the walls visually blocking some stimuli and providing *social distance* from other patrons, facilitating social interaction among those seated within the booth. The booth can be thought of as providing social and psychological security while accentuating the need for group interaction. Group participants are physically forced to look at each other and focus attention on those sitting within the confines of the booth. Its very design establishes intimacy and makes for a more relaxed atmosphere.

The server standing at the head of the booth commands the attention of those seated and tends to interact with them as a group more than as individuals. Everyone hears what everyone else is saying, including what each orders. The server need not repeat answers to questions and can establish a rapport with the individuals as a group, answering questions, explaining the menu, and making suggestions.

Individuals entering a restaurant alone feel like outsiders, compared with the couples and parties. If seated at an exposed table, they may feel even more isolated and uncomfortable. However, the hostess or maitre d' is reluctant to tie up a booth with a single. If the individual is noticeably shy or ill at ease, the decision should be for the booth. One study found that solos appreciated and were made comfortable by fast, friendly service. They did not like sharing a table, nor did they want to be seated in a special section for singles. Men seemed to prefer more attention from servers, while added service disturbed some women. Wine by the glass was appreciated. More women than men said they liked eating alone.

Servers can expect more problems from people seated in open spaces—more complaints about noisy people at neighboring tables, uneasiness, concern over speed of service, and defensive behavior.

Banquet rooms can be expected to produce the same sort of customer behavior. Very often customers are seated next to someone they know only casually, or not at all. It usually takes an aggressive, self-assured person to break the ice of separateness.

Low lighting is favorable for the dinner house, encouraging people to relax and breaking down social distance. Low lighting is also more sustainable, and reduces the costs associated with bright standard incandescent lighting. In a darkened room, people are encouraged to speak and eat more intimately and to focus on those in the party rather than on the distractions of people entering, leaving, or moving around. In the fast-food establishment and in the coffee shop, the lighting tends to be brighter, in keeping with the mood of the customer who wants to eat quickly and move on. Even these establishments are switching over to low lighting. Some Energy Star–qualified light fixtures meeting EPA guidelines for energy efficiency generate approximately 75 percent less heat than standard incandescent lighting.[14]

Here are some service points from Charlie Trotter's award-winning restaurant, which unfortunately closed after a 25-year run in 2012 as one of the, finest restaurant in the world.[15]

- Have your employees walk in the guest's shoes by patronizing similar businesses.
- Ask yourself: "How would I like to be treated if I were a customer?"

- Respect demanding guests; they can bring out the best in you.
- Seek inspiration by visiting the leading company in the field.
- Be mindful of how damaging poorly rendered service can be to your business.
- Invest in your employees as you would your equipment; develop appropriate compensation.
- Tend to the little things. Employees will learn that attention to small and large mattes is equally important.

SERVICE ENCOUNTER

Many servers are skilled performers in the *service encounter*. The heart of a service is the encounter between the server and the customer. It is here where emotions meet economics in real time and where most people judge the quality of service.[16] The dinner house, and especially the lounge, is the stage. Two shows daily—lunch and dinner— deliver the same great performance every time. The server and the guest are both actors in the play. Both knowingly engage in the drama. The payoff for the guest is a feeling of warmth, friendship, and ego enhancement. The reward for the server is the big tip and the excitement of the drama. Matters of service and what constitutes good service are subjective to be sure. In the end, though, the customer's perception is what counts.[17]

For some servers, the play's the thing. They know they are acting and love it. They may also "love" their customers. The guests feed back similar feelings to generate a staged love affair. All smiles and attention, the server hangs on guests' every word and gesture, radiating goodwill and the desire to please.

Once the meal is finished, the play is over, the guest leaves, and the server moves on to the next stage. Should the guest and server meet in the supermarket the next morning, they may scarcely acknowledge each other.

If the dinner house adds liquor to the environment, guests may experience loosening inhibitions, clouded perceptions, and a reduction in anxiety and hostility. Voices rise, suppressed needs surface, conversations become animated, ego guards are lowered, jokes are funnier. This increases the need for restaurant owners, managers, and servers to become aware of and practice responsible alcoholic beverage service.

The traveling person eating alone is uneasy, especially in a dinner house where couples and groups are out having fun. Alienated and self-conscious, he or she wonders about the price of the meal and may order something more expensive than usual to let anyone who might be interested know that he or she can afford it. The traveler may want more rapid service, eating quickly and leaving as soon as possible.

The same person in a group, exhilarated by the presence of friends, can take on a completely different personality. Instead of being impersonal with the server, he or she is now friendly.

If the group is large and made up of relative strangers, as in a banquet setting, servers may become nonpersons. Guests may refer to them in the third person even though they are nearby and can overhear the comments. No one likes to be treated this way. Servers sometimes set themselves up for such treatment by displaying a lack of self-confidence, excessive deference, or over eagerness. Something in human nature, at least in some people, causes them to treat such people as inferiors and even to humiliate them.

Visitors to this country are surprised by the service, especially that given by college students. Many times, the financial and educational level of the server is higher than that of the guests.

Here are a few sage words from renowned restaurateur Danny Meyer of Union Square Hospitality Group. "My appreciation of the power of hospitality and my desire to harness it have been the greatest contributors to whatever success my restaurants have had. I've learned how crucially important it is to put hospitality to work, first for the people who work for me and subsequently for all the other people and stakeholders who are in any way affected by our business-in descending order, our guests, community, suppliers, and investors. I call this way of setting priorities 'enlightened hospitality.' It stands some more traditional business approaches on their head, but it's the foundation of every business decision and every success we've ever had."[18]

WHAT MAKES A GOOD SERVER?

There is a lot of agreement as to what makes a good server. Here are five attributes that restaurateurs look for:

1. *Personality*. It's fine to know the technical aspects of service, but the guest puts more emphasis on the attitude and personality of the server.

2. *Team orientation*. Servers must be willing to participate in a team effort. They have to be willing to contribute to the guests' satisfaction, whether they are in the server's section or not.

3. *Technical knowledge of product*. Servers must have thorough knowledge of both the food and the wine. They need to have tableside confidence.

4. *Ability to read guests and anticipate their needs*. Some guests want lots of attention; others do not want to have their conversation interrupted by a server.

5. *Knowledge of the finer points of service*.

SERVICE PERSONNEL AS A FAMILY

Many managers do whatever possible to create a family feeling among foodservice personnel. They encourage employees to eat and drink on the premises by reducing their price for meals and drinks by a third or even half. Employee parties are sponsored; liquor and sometimes food is provided. (Other operators do not permit their employees to come back even if off duty.)

The serving group, in many ways, is the elite within the restaurant, having the fun of working with guests. In many restaurants, servers are selected, in large part, on the basis of appearance—the best-looking women and the handsomest men.

GREETERS

The host is the first and last person the guest meets at a restaurant, so naturally the impression he or she makes is important. A smiling, well-groomed, friendly person is an asset to the restaurant, but the position calls for more. Hosts who know the restaurant add luster and are able to answer a variety of specific and general questions. The main part of the host's job is to represent the restaurant by offering a friendly

Alex von Bidder, coowner of Four Seasons Restaurant, sometimes makes personal phone calls to his closest guests when their patronage drops. His intention is to show that he cares and to inquire about the guests' welfare. Those phone calls give guests an opportunity to discuss any service failure they may have experienced. By making the calls, von Bidder personalizes his service and gathers relevant information.[19]

greeting and facilitating the seating of guests, even if it means politely asking them to wait a while in the lounge or holding area. Being a great host is an art and takes practice. Another key aspect of the job is knowing how to seat guests so as not to overload a server or the kitchen. That is where experience comes in.

Hosts keep a sheet for reservations, whether they are called in or walk-ins. The sheet has several columns, each representing a table size or *top*, as it is called in the restaurant business—one column for two-tops or *deuces*, one for four-tops, one for six-tops, and one for larger parties. Names of parties are entered under the respective table size. Over time, restaurants gauge their turn time. For example, the deuce waiting time will be faster than that of the four- or six-tops. Full-service restaurants normally allow about 1½ hours for a deuce, 2 hours for a four-top, and 2½ hours for a six-top.

In order to avoid calling out names—and thus annoying other guests—some restaurants give guests a beeper device that lets them know when their table is ready. Hosts know when the table is ready by receiving a signal from the server. If waiting guests have opened a bar tab, it is preferable to transfer that over to the food server to avoid the inconvenience of the guests having to pay the closeout bar tab when being seated. Any beverages from the lounge/holding area should be carried on a tray to the dining area by the hostess. Here, the service calls for a way to remember who was drinking what so as to place the correct beverage in front of each guest.

On arrival at the table, the host might pull out the best seat, perhaps a window view. This seat is normally offered to and occupied by the senior woman of the party. The hostess then assists others in being seated and offers their menus.

A number of restaurants have service standards that they expect to meet or beat. Here are 11 steps of service that set a standard for all to meet:

From the moment guests call to make a phone reservation to the moment they are walking out the door, they judge a restaurant not just on food but also on customer service. Great customer service is what brings them back.

1. Greet guests within one minute.
2. Suggestively sell beverages/take order.
3. Bring beverages by four minutes.
4. Offer to explain the specials and other menu items.
5. Bring appetizers/soups/salads by six minutes.
6. Bring entrées by 15 minutes.
7. Check that everything is perfect within two minutes.
8. Take dessert order.
9. Bring dessert by four minutes.
10. Check everything is perfect.
11. Upon guest request, present the check within two minutes.

Standards like these give servers something to aim for and achieve because otherwise service will be below guest expectations.

SERVER AS INDEPENDENT BUSINESSPERSON

Because so much of their compensation is based on tips, it is too easy to set servers up as private businesspersons, each doing his or her own thing—in effect, operating an independent business on premises leased for nothing. One human resource director—who had better remain anonymous—calls servers "soldiers of fortune."

Such a situation can foster competition rather than cooperation. If any situation calls for teamwork, it is a fast-paced dining room, which requires working in harmony, goodwill, and trust. It is much easier and faster for two service people to serve a party of six than it is for one, and more fun. Normally, a server cannot carry more than four plates, and if it is necessary to make two trips to the kitchen to serve six people, two of the plates will get cold. A party of six or eight usually starts each course together. If they have to wait for all to receive the salad, then all to receive the entrée and, finally, the dessert, the delays become troublesome.

FOODSERVICE TEAMS

Various kinds of dining room service organization exist, the server/buser combination being the most common. Some restaurants operate with servers working two to a team so that at least one team member is on the floor most of the time dealing with the patrons rather than off the floor.

The *team* system differs from the usual server–buser relationship in that buspersons ordinarily confine their work to cleaning and setting up tables. In other situations, the entire serving crew works as a team. Anyone entering the kitchen picks up any order and delivers it, and if a table needs more than one server to flame a dish or to perform other duties, the servers in the general area will pitch in, even though it removes them from their assigned stations. A slogan—"Full Hands In, Full Hands Out"—helps everyone work to help each other.

The team system has one major advantage: Hot food is served hot. Whoever is nearest the setup counter picks up the food and serves it. The check accompanies the order; the number of the table is written on the check. Seats at each table are numbered clockwise, starting at the seat closest to an agreed-on anchor point.

Stations where two servers rotate tables encourage teamwork because each is paying attention to the customers to see when the next table will be leaving, trying to get them out the door.

> Experienced servers learn to read guests and react accordingly. Some guests are in a hurry, some want advice on what to order. Good service means subtle, unobtrusive service. For example, there is no need for the server to arrive at the table with a handful of plates asking who's having what.

Courtesy of Le Bec-Fin

Foodservice at Le Bec-Fin, in Philadelphia, makes for a memorable experience. Here, servers lift the cover off dishes presented to guests.

HARD SELL VERSUS SOFT SELL

Restaurant literature and educational programs uniformly urge service personnel to promote and sell as part of the service job. The rationale is that sales and tips will increase—and, if the sales job is done correctly, guests will have a better dining experience. Discussions with servers bear out the thesis, but there are some qualifications. Undoubtedly, some patrons have a fixed idea of how much they will spend on a particular meal, and such people may resent a hard sell: "Would you like a cocktail?" "Will you have dessert?" "Will you have an after-dinner liqueur?" People may feel pressured and sometimes say so, especially if the server's approach is the hard sell. Those who receive a higher check than expected may avoid the restaurant in the future.

COME-BACK KIDS

There's a story of a group of diners at a restaurant. Everyone's ordering a number of items to pass around, but one customer wants to mix and match an appetizer with an entrée. "Oh, we can't do special orders," apologizes the server. "Why not?" asks the customer. "The chefs really get mad at me," the server responds. "They won't do it even one time because if you should ever come back, you might want it again."[20]

The kind of clientele may determine the best approach, *hard or soft sell.* Low-key, complete service may be what is expected. Other patrons, wanting to live it up, may welcome the hard sell and purposely run up the tab as a kind of self-indulgence. "Nothing is too good for our anniversary"—or business client, or prospective buyer. The expense account (using the company's money) is justification to order the finest!

Servers characteristically compete with each other in the amount of tips received in the course of a work shift. Some servers make 50 or even 100 percent more than others. The service rendered has been perceived by the diner as superior, or the server has manipulated the diner into increasing the check or the tip percentage, or both. Tip and tab go together. Management mostly pushes the thought, "When in doubt, promote."

Aside from selling, service includes a number of other factors and practices, including showmanship, ritualization of wine service, paying attention to what is said by the diner, attention to detail, refilling water glasses, cleaning ashtrays, replacing soiled silver, and so on. The server is attempting to control the behavior of the diner. Call it manipulation, influencing attitude, making friends, maintaining rapport, or what have you, it is still selling. A server who displays skill and confidence is desirable. In most situations, a harassed or timid server may elicit sympathy but can also arouse apprehension or uneasiness in the guest. No doubt, a number of guests want to be courted and wooed, buttered up, and even fawned on. Others may resent this kind of behavior.

Seven Commandments of Customer Service

1. *Tell the truth:* When it comes to customer service, honesty is the best policy.
2. *Bend the rules:* Learn why a rule is a rule in the first place. Once you know the reason for the rule and its boundaries, go ahead and bend it, if that's what it takes to make the system better serve your customer.
3. *Listen actively, almost aggressively:* Customers are ready, willing, and able to tell you everything you need to know. All you need to do is listen.
4. *Put pen to paper:* A letter or e-mail after a conversation can be a terrific way to confirm facts and details or just to say thanks.
5. *Master the moments of truth:* If you pay attention to details—the promises made in your advertising, how long your phone rings before being answered, the look of your parking lot—customers will know and notice.
6. *Be a fantastic fixer:* An effective customer-service recovery process includes these components: apologize, listen and empathize, fix the problem quickly and fairly, offer atonement, keep your promise, follow up.
7. *Never underestimate the value of a sincere thank-you:* It's easy to take regular and walk-in customers for granted. Don't. Customers have options every time they need a service or product. Thank them for choosing to do business with you.

FORMALITY OR INFORMALITY

How formal should the relations between host and guest be? Should the server be seen and not heard? Does the customer want *formality or informality?*

The answers vary with the kind of experience you are trying to deliver. Some restaurants thrive on informality. The servers may appear in tennis shoes and blue jeans, saying, "Hi, I'm Bob, I'll be your server tonight. Please call on me for anything that I can do to make your meal pleasant."

In another, more formal atmosphere, the server may wear a black jacket and speak only when spoken to, with conversation limited to, "Good evening, madam. Good evening, sir," "I hope you enjoy your meal, madam," and so on.

Some general principles apply to all restaurants.

- Restaurants, by their nature, are service oriented, and all personnel should accept this as a continuing challenge to give excellent service. Complaints should be accepted at face value, at least until proven to be without substance.
- The guest's viewpoint is different from that of the employees or the manager. Most complaints are left unspoken. When a complaint *is* voiced, a public relations opportunity emerges. Food should be replaced at once with another of the same or of the customer's choice. A complimentary bottle of wine or an after-dinner liqueur adds a gracious note.
- Never try to explain why things go wrong. A guest is not interested in excuses.
- The general atmosphere at a restaurant should be friendly. A warm smile is almost never out of place.
- Teamwork is always appropriate.
- The little extras, like offering free dessert for the birthday guest or taking a picture of the diners with one of their cell phones, are almost always appreciated.

The famous maitre d' at the Waldorf Hotel in New York, Oscar, considered himself a stage manager and would often approach a table, examine the food, and, even if nothing was wrong, add some little touch or have it whisked away and replaced. He was widely known as Oscar of the Waldorf and produced a large cookbook, despite not being a chef. Today, he is known as the creator of veal Oscar, eggs Benedict, Waldorf salad, and for helping to popularize Thousand Island dressing. Waiters were trained to focus on him. Hand signals let the waiters know what to do. His mien expressed sincere concern for guests' well-being. He was very polite, very formal, tuned in to each guest. The outcome of great customer service is customer loyalty.

SETTING THE TABLE

The table setting should be pleasing and inviting to the guest. Guests notice clean cutlery and flatware that is free from watermarks, fingerprints, and food particles. Avoid watermarks by cloth-drying the flatware immediately as it comes out of the dishwasher. Remember: To avoid fingerprints, train staff and servers to hold the cutlery flatware by the handle.

Experienced maitre d's bend their knees to level themselves with the glassware and can spot a dirty one at a distance. Like cutlery, all glassware should be free of water spots and fingerprints. Dirty rinse water causes spots; chemicals in the rinse water can streak glassware. An improper mix of washing and sanitizing chemicals might lack the action that makes the water sheet off the glass without streaks or watermarks.

When the table setting is complete, it should look pleasing to the eye. This is accomplished by arranging everything symmetrically. Everything should be clean and free from fingerprints.

LESS CHOICE

Pare down the menu. People forget that service often relates to the time it takes for them to decide on what to order. Too many choices are too time-consuming to wade through.[21]

Courtesy of Charlie Trotter
The table setting at Charlie Trotter's was a delight to the eye.
(Charlie Trotter's is now closed)

TAKING THE ORDER

If they have not already done so, servers introduce themselves and take the opportunity to suggest beverages. This is done by describing two or three drink items (depending on the guest). For business convention guests, this might be a special martini—if the bartender is known for that—or a choice of wines. The main thing is to get people to make a selection from a variety of choices rather than a simple yes-no decision. At the initial guest contact moment, the server may also describe food specials, then depart to obtain the beverages while the guests decide on their food order.

The food order should be taken by asking the senior female for her order first, followed by the other women. (The server has to politely take control of the situation to prevent everyone from shouting his or her order.) Then the senior male's order is taken, and so on. The server's team takes the order by seat number from a vantage point (say, the entrance). This allows each plate to be placed correctly in front of the person who ordered the dish. Some restaurants use the clockwise system.

Restaurants generally have a rule as to which side food is served to and cleared from. Beverages are both served and cleared from the right-hand side from and to a tray. Some restaurants clear plates as soon as a person is done eating; others wait until everyone has finished. The method chosen is a matter of preference. It also depends on how busy the shift is and how soon you need the table.

GREETER OR TRAFFIC COP

The greeter in the restaurant is supposed to be just that—a host welcoming the arriving guest, saying a few kind words, and really being pleased to have the person pay the restaurant a visit. As the first representative of the restaurant to interact with the visitor, the host sets the tone for the entire dining experience. His or her welcome, or lack of it, creates a feeling, positive or negative, that colors the entire meal experience.

It has been observed that the rookie who, for the first few weeks of being a host in a busy restaurant, is an outgoing, warm, friendly human being, can easily turn into a traffic cop who orders visitors, "Leave your name and we'll call you," or, "Sit over there until a table opens up." It is quite understandable that, with fatigue, the big hello can become a little hello, or less. It is difficult to smile and act friendly when the individual feels anything but friendly or ready to cope with new problems.

It does not take new hosts long to realize that their pay may be a fraction of that of the servers, yet they may be working just as hard and may be contributing as much or more to the dining experience. With a few exceptions, hosts receive close to minimum wage, while servers may earn three times that amount. Little wonder that hosts lose some zest for doing an outstanding job. However, since the host is the person responsible for making the first impression, it is in the restaurant's best interest to find a way to provide a positive environment. One solution is to give hosts the option of becoming servers as the next vacancy occurs.[22]

MAGIC PHRASES

A coffee shop server leaves an indelible impression on the guest when she says, as the patron leaves, "I hope to see you tomorrow." Phrases recommended at Suso restaurant for use by servers include:

Welcome back.	May I take your plate?
We're happy you're here.	How was your evening?
It's good to see you again.	Sorry to have kept you waiting.
I hope you like it.	I'm sorry; I'll put that right.
I hope you enjoy it.	Have a nice trip home.

Other than the magic phrases, the next 10 server suggestions should be followed thoroughly (if appropriate, depending on the character and style of the restaurant concept):

1. Smile and introduce yourself within one minute.
2. Get down to eye level. Make *eye contact*.
3. Welcome the guests and explain something about the restaurant and any special beverages.
4. Help guests by explaining any entrée they inquire about.
5. Suggest/offer assistance with wine selection.
6. Follow the restaurant's style of service. When serving entrées, use an "anchor" person as the number one, and then serve all plates starting with the eldest female guest. Or use the auction method of asking who's having what (the what is the plate in your hand). Some casual restaurants like this method; formal restaurants use the anchorperson method.
7. Constantly keep one eye on the table, as you never know when guests may need something.
8. Clear plates as you think guests need them cleared; don't interrupt a conversation and don't reach over/across someone.
9. Suggestively describe desserts and after-dinner beverages.
10. Write "thank you" on the back of the check. Doodle on the check, put a happy face on it, and use a tip tray.

Recommended replies in response to a complaint are:

I apologize.

Thank you for letting us know about this.

I'd feel the same way if I were in your position.

You've certainly been patient. We appreciate your taking time to tell us about this.

Keep responses simple and sincere. Accept ownership for the problem, even though you personally may not be responsible.

Courtesy of the 21 Club
Tableside service enhances the guests' dining experience at the 21 Club in New York City.

When a guest orders "incorrectly," accept the responsibility. Avoid making the guest feel stupid. Tact is in order: "Perhaps next time you'd like to try a medium-done steak and be sure to let us know how it is."

One restaurant general manager puts customer relations in this framework: "Unless you are willing to give each customer a little bit of yourself, you shouldn't be in the hospitality field."

DIFFICULT GUESTS

Once in a while, a server is confronted by a *difficult guest* who is determined to prove his manhood or vent hostility on other guests, on the serving personnel, or on the manager personally. A large coffee-shop chain encountering more than its share of such guests because its units are open around the clock insists on a "hands-in-the-pocket" policy, which means that no matter how obnoxious a patron becomes, a manager never considers being physical in handling the situation.

The majority of *handling complaints* falls into employees' hands. Employees have to be trained to problem solve the right way and right away.

The approach is, "What can I do to help?" which is, in itself, quite disarming. The fact that the manager has a pot of hot coffee in hand may also give the patron pause. It matters not how big the manager or whether male or female; the manager who speaks calmly and acts ready to mediate or settle a problem can usually calm the most disruptive person.

If the calm approach fails, the manager may have a system of hand signals for employees, one of which means, "Call the police." Suggesting that the police are on the way (even though that might not be the case) is also effective in emergency situations. If a problem customer is completely unreasonable, the best thing to do is insist that he or she leave. Any food served is on the house.

Bar operators say that an effective approach to anyone drinking excessively is to say, "If you leave, I'll pay for all of your drinks." If the patron is too inebriated to drive, it is often wise to insist on putting the person in a cab and, if necessary, paying the cab fare. The so-called third-party liability feature of the law can place the restaurant at fault for serving too much alcohol. Should the person become involved in an auto accident, the restaurant operator can be sued and, in some cases, held liable for damages, sometimes involving hundreds of thousands of dollars.

If it is necessary to get rid of a problem guest, call the police if you are unable to resolve the problem any other way—or if violence occurs.

STRATEGIES FOR HANDLING COMPLAINTS

No restaurant likes to hear guest complaints. According to Kay McCleery, director of training for Hobee's Franchising Corporation, a win/win result can be obtained by using these action tips:

- Act immediately on a complaint.
- Let the guest know you care.
- Calm the guest by acknowledging the problem and encouraging feedback.
- Tell the guest in an honest way how the problem will be addressed.
- Invite the guest to express his or her feelings.
- Never invalidate or make the guest wrong.
- Offer appropriate and reasonable amends.
- Nurture the relationship by smiling and thanking the guest again.[23]

Other strategies can also make the situation better. Although there are no specific steps to follow for *handling complaints,* operators and staff members can do the following to make irate patrons feel better. These responses are critical to regaining diners' loyalty and encouraging repeat business.

- *Be diplomatic:* The issue is not whether the guest is justified in his or her complaint—as long as diners feel justified, they are. A helpful initial response from you and your staff can go a long way toward salvaging the situation.
- *Remain calm:* Although you may feel that the patron is personally attacking you, try to remember that the person is mad at the situation and not at you. You must put your personal feelings aside and handle the situation in a professional, calm manner. Arguing with an already annoyed guest is a no-win situation.
- *Listen:* When guests become angry, they have to vent that anger in order to feel better. Listen to everything they have to say without interrupting. Just feeling that they are being heard can help ease their anger.
- *Empathize:* The best response you can make when handling complaints is to show empathy. Empathy is the ability to feel as another person feels. Your objective is to identify with the diner's feelings and to let him or her know that you understand. Whatever you do, don't offer excuses for the problem or complaint.

You can show empathy by rephrasing both the contents of the problem and the guest's feelings about it. For example, you might say, "I realize that you are upset about your steak being undercooked, and I understand that it makes you feel angry." Be sure to tell the diner that you are sorry the incident occurred and that his or her feelings are important to the restaurant. Also tell the person that you will take care of the problem immediately.

- *Control your voice:* The volume, speed, and tone of your voice can help defuse difficult situations. Your volume should never go up—even if the diner's does. Speaking in a calm, slow voice will show the diner that you are really concerned about the problem and are prepared to solve it. Sometimes speaking more and more softly helps, too.
- *Get the facts:* Some incidents, such as a lost coat or a charge-card error, may be difficult to resolve. Collect as much data as you can and write everything down. Writing down the details shows the guest that you take the incident seriously and will also help you remember pertinent information.
- *Take care of the problem immediately:* Whether it is an entrée that is not prepared properly or dirty glassware, remove the offending object from the table

---

Restaurant Service Quality

Guest satisfaction levels with restaurant service quality hinge on several key service encounters:

Booking the table (when applicable)
Ease of access
Parking (possibly valet)
The welcome greeting
The host/hostess encounter
Announcing that the table's ready (not ready)
The host/hostess seating guests and presenting menus
The server's introduction
The beverage order
The server explaining the "specials," followed by taking the order

Serving the appetizers
Clearing the appetizers and checking to replenish the beverages
Serving the entrées
Clearing the entrées
Suggestively selling the desserts
Clearing desserts and offering coffee and after-dinner drinks
Bringing check when requested

Each of these items can be given points and scored to arrive at a level of satisfaction for the service at a restaurant.

FIGURE 12.2 Readers tell how restaurants fare.

immediately. If you are unsure what response the diner wants, ask, for example, "Would you like me to take that and bring you the menu?" (or "another glass?").

■ *If you do take back a diner's entrée, offer to keep the meals of the other diners in the party warm in the kitchen so that the group can eat together:* An irate diner may become more so if he or she has to sit there and watch others enjoy their food while waiting for a replacement entrée.[24]

Tact: Always

How many times have you entered a restaurant to be greeted with the words "How many?" or by some comment such as, "The waiting time is 30 minutes," or, "Please have a seat at the bar."

Use *tact* Don't say, "Just one?" or, "Are you alone?" When tables are plentiful, the question could be "Would you prefer a table or a booth?"

How much better to look the guest full in the face, smile, and say, "May I help you with your coat?" Guests want common courtesy, which means recognition, respect, and a friendly welcome. We all know that a principal reason people dine out is the desire for sociability. Failing to meet this basic need is an unnecessary form of deprivation foisted on guests by an unthinking service person who has mixed up his or her priorities. Figure 12.2 shows the key service areas for a restaurant.

Summary

Restaurants often employ teenagers and young adults, many of them working part time and on their first job. Many or most do not expect to make a career in the restaurant field. Wages are low and employee turnover is high. For these and other reasons, training and management development is important.

Training can be broken down into orientation training and job training. The purpose of training is to teach specific ways of doing things.

Management development deals with principles and policies that managers use in relating to employees and customers. Behavior modeling assumes that employees will copy supervisors' attitudes and job performance. Learner-controlled instruction provides learning material that can be studied and learned by individuals at their own pace.

Guest relations is one of the aspects of restaurant keeping that makes it so interesting—and so frustrating. It is a continuous challenge, a challenge that is not for the timid, the tired, or the malcontent. The perfectionist and the thin-skinned cannot win at the customer relations game—there are too many variables. A sense of humor, good health, and a lively intelligence are decided assets. A desire to please and to serve is even more valuable.

Key Terms and Concepts

Behavior modeling	Hard sell/soft sell	Service encounter
Development	Leadership	Social distance
Difficult guest	Learner-controlled instruction (LCI)	Tact
Eye contact		Team
Formality or informality	Management Manager as coach	Training and development
Handling complaints	Orientation	Training schedule

Review Questions

1. In programming first-day employee training, what kind of information should be given priority?
2. What is the difference between employee development and training?
3. Explain the plus-minus-plus model as it relates to criticizing an employee.
4. How are you, as an owner/manager, involved in behavior modeling?
5. What are some advantages of learner-controlled instruction? What is the big disadvantage?
6. Traditionally, employee training in restaurants has been unstructured—that is, there are no formal classes, formal instructional materials, or particular trainers. How will you set up your training program, if any?
7. What kind of orientation training will you give new employees?
8. Does it follow that your chef, who is highly experienced and skilled, will be effective in passing along knowledge and skills? If he or she is not motivated to do so, what can you do?
9. How will you get across your dos and don'ts—your policies about stealing, courtesy to patrons, parking rules, eating on the job, and so on?
10. Service personnel must be aware of the degree of social distance desired by their customers. Explain.
11. As a restaurant manager, a server calls your attention to a booth of four men who are talking loudly, using profanity, and being belligerent. How would you handle the situation?

12. Your restaurant is located near a high school. Recently, several of the students who are patrons have been throwing ice and wadded paper napkins at each other. What should you do?

13. Eye contact is particularly important in patron relations. Explain.

14. In seating a lone woman in a restaurant, what factors should be considered?

15. The degree of psychological tension that is desirable varies with the situation. How can a restaurant manager work to raise or lower the tension to make it appropriate for the situation?

16. What are three phrases suitable for use by a hostess in greeting patrons? What are three phrases for saying good-bye to them?

17. In taking reservations, what factors help determine how much time to allow between seatings?

18. What are the pros and cons of taking lunch or dinner reservations? If you managed a restaurant, would you take them on Friday and Saturday evenings, your busiest nights?

19. What will be your policy in handling guest complaints about the food (the steak is too tough, my soup is cold)?

CASE STUDY: Ophelia's on the Bay

History of Ophelia's

Ophelia's on the Bay is a fine-dining waterfront restaurant in Sarasota, Florida, founded by Stan Ferro, Jane Ferro, and Charles Kelly in May of 1988. Before purchasing Ophelia's, the Ferros were living in Massachusetts, where they owned a seasonal restaurant. The economy in Massachusetts wasn't great, and the Ferros were looking to move somewhere with more opportunity and the potential to start a new restaurant venture. The building was discovered by Stan Ferro's great aunt, Ophelia, who was living in Sarasota. The restaurant happened to be for sale, and she told the Ferros to come down and take a look at it. Although the restaurant was a bit outdated and needed some structural work, the property and location offered great potential.

Courtesy of Ophelia's on the Bay

More than "Floribbean"

The fare at Ophelia's can be described as American Continental fusion cuisine with emphasis placed on both fresh Florida and exotic ingredients that are meant to broaden the guest's palate. Recently, the food at Ophelia's was coined as "Floribbean" cuisine; however, they offer a broad spectrum of international styles of cuisine, including Asian, French, and Mediterranean, as well as the diversification of their products, which encompasses much more than what the term "Floribbean" entails. While some of the menu's fresh local seafood items include Key West shrimp, local grouper, and local snapper, there are also intercontinental items such as Loch Duart Scottish salmon, eggplant crepes, Hawaiian big eye tuna, and filet mignon of Japanese Kobe beef.

Guests and Competitors

Ophelia's has always appealed to people who appreciate the finer things in life. Ophelia's caters to an older and more sophisticated clientele that can appreciate some of the upscale and exotic foods that are offered. However, even with these acquired delicacies,

Ophelia's has always remained competitively priced. Over the years, Ophelia's has received some criticism for its higher than average prices, but the fact remains that you have to pay more for the quality of products used to prepare the food that they want to serve, of which there is an active demand in Sarasota.

Some of Ophelia's biggest competitors belong to the same group as they do, known as "The Sarasota Originals," which includes the more prominent, upscale, and veteran restaurants throughout Sarasota. This group of restaurants has supported each other over the years, and while some of these restaurants serve as major competitors, the Ferros believe that they have a competitive advantage in being the only fine-dining waterfront restaurant in Sarasota. Ophelia's offers approximately 100-seats of dockside dining, featuring a gorgeous waterfront view of little Sarasota Bay, which faces the bird and mangrove sanctuary. The dockside space allows the restaurant to hold many weddings and private event functions.

Secrets to Success

At Ophelia's, success is achieved by anticipating the guests' needs, and then going above and beyond to provide extraordinary service to fulfill their needs. On many occasions, employees at Ophelia's have recommended local activities and events, printed out directions, contacted cab services, and even made reservations over the phone for guests. Ophelia's bases a lot of its business on the vendor relations with local business, especially lodging establishments. Because word-of-mouth is a big source of its business, it is important to keep potential customers informed. Finally, Ophelia's continues to stay active in the community by participating in fundraising and charity events with various organizations, which keeps its name in the minds of consumers and also allows them to give back to the community that has helped progress their continued success.

Challenges of Transforming

Ophelia's may be one of the more veteran restaurants in Sarasota, but it has faced its fair share of challenges over the years. One of the biggest challenges has been adjusting to the times and maintaining a sense of flexibility. For Ophelia's, adjusting to the times means adapting to more sustainable products, being more environmentally conscience, and opening up the variety of foods they offer, by substituting high-priced items, with similar but more reasonably priced items. It requires going outside the box to find alternatives that work without compromising your quality or your identity.

Into the Future

Stan and Jane's daughter, Kristina Grainger, is currently the general manager of Ophelia's. Kristina has worked to bring a younger clientele base back through the doors, while continuing to cater to the current customer base as well. Kristina believes it is important to continuously give new life to the business, because the past generations are going to move on, and you want to appeal to the next generation as much as the last, in order to remain successful. Additionally, Kristina seeks to recapture some of the notoriety Ophelia's enjoyed in the past, such as Wine Spectator and Zagat awards, as well as AAA diamond ratings, which started to slip away with the struggling economy. Kristina believes that it is important to seek to achieve goals that can help the restaurant elevate what it has to offer, and continuously move toward being the best at what it does.

QUESTIONS

1. Create a detailed training plan for a new employee at Ophelia's.
2. What are some things a restaurant can do to achieve a sense of "wow" in the eyes of its guests?
3. What are some ways Ophelia's has succeeded in terms of guest service, and what are some additional things it can do to provide extraordinary guest service?
4. The executive chef at Ophelia's is self-taught in culinary expertise. He began his career as a line-cook at the age of 19, worked his way up to sous chef, and is now executive chef of Ophelia's. Compare and contrast the conceptual knowledge attained in a school setting vs. practical knowledge learned on-the-job from the perspective of a culinary student vs. a restaurant chef.

Endnotes

1. Dina Berta, Jack Hayes, Brooke Barrier, "Hands-on Instruction Makes for Head-Smart, Heart-Happy Employees," *Nation's Restaurant News,* 38, (40), p. 94. October 2009.

2. John Lawn, "Improving the Effectiveness of ServSafe Training," *Food Management* (December 8, 2007), http://food-management.com/food-safety/improving-effectiveness-servsafe-training. Retrieved on May 16, 2013.

3. Chester Kroeger, "Fudpucker's in Restaurant Owners Uncorked," *Schedulefly,* (2011), p. 168.

4. Edmund Lawler, *Lessons in Service from Charlie Trotter.* Berkeley, CA: Ten Speed Press, 2001, p. 1.

5. Libby Platus, "L.A. Phenom David Myers Borrows Some Unorthodox Methods to Get His Team in Shape," *Restaurant Hospitality* 92 (4) (April 2008), pp. 48–49.

6. http://www.restaurant.org/Search?searchtext=training&searchmode=anyword. Retrieved on May 16, 2013.

7. Dina Berta, "CHART Event Tackles Training Budget Cuts," *Nation's Restaurant News,* 43 (29), (August 10, 2009), p. 4. ABI/Inform Trade and Industry. October 2009.

8. Ibid.

9. Anonymous, "Council of Hotel and Restaurant Trainers; CHART and Maritz Partner and Release Report Benchmarking Employee Training Investments and Practices in the Hospitality Industry," *Leisure & Travel Week* (June 6, 2009), p. 59. ABI/Inform Trade and Industry. October 2009.

10. "Training and Development: Behavior Modeling." www.traininganddevelopment.naukrihub.com/methods-of-training/games-and-simulations/behavior-modeling.html. October 2009.

11. Lewis C. Forrest, Jr. "Learner-Controlled Instruction for Management Training," *Journal of Hospitality and Tourism Research.* http://jht.sagepub.com/cgi/content/abstract/13/3/309. October 2009.

12. F. John Reh, "How to Give Positive Feedback." http://management.about.com/cs/peoplemanagement/ht/positivefb.htm. October 2009.

13. "Enhance consumer experiences by tuning in to table service," *Nation's Restaurant News.* http://findarticles.com/p/articles/mi_m3190/is_19_39/ai_n13729085/. September 2009.

14. KJ Fields, "A New Order: Fast-food Restaurants Offer a Menu of Sustainable Features," *Eco-Structure* (May 27, 2009). www.eco-structure.com/retail-projects/a-new-order.aspx. September 2009.

15. Danny Meyer, *Setting the Table: The Transforming Power of Hospitality in Business* (New York: Harper, 2006), p. 2.

16. Richard B. Chase and Sriram Dasu, "Psychology of the Experience: The Missing Link in Service Science," In Bill Hefley and Wendy Murphy (eds.), Service Science, Management and Engineering: Education for the 21st Century (New York: Springer, 2008), pp. 35–40. http://link.springer.com/content/pdf/10.1007%2F978-0-387-76578-5_6.pdf#page-1 retrieved on May 21 2013.

17. "Serving Aces: How Restaurants Are Improving Customer Service Standards," *Restaurants and Institutions.* http://images.centralrestaurant.com/images/trends/pdfs/ServingAces.pdf retrieved on May 21, 2013.

18. Meyer, p. 2.

19. Beth G. Chung and K. Douglas Hoffman, "Critical Incidents: Service Failures That Matter Most," Cornell University School of Hotel Administration Online. www.hotelschool.cornell.edu. June 27, 2006.

20. Jennifer Waters, "Eye on Service," *Restaurants and Institutions* 108 (28) (December 1, 1988), p. 46.

21. Jennifer Waters, "Hurry, Please," *Restaurants and Institutions* 108 (11), (May 1, 1998), p. 119.

22. David Scott Peters, "Restaurant Service: GUEST," *Restaurant Report.* www.restaurantreport.com/management_tips/tip_guest.html. September 2009.

23. Kathy L. Indermill, "Calming Complainers," *Restaurant Hospitality* 74 (10), (October 1990), p. 70.

24. Bob Losyk, "Placating Patrons: How to Satisfy Dissatisfied Customers," *National Restaurant Association* 16 (May 1996), p. 5.

Technology in the Restaurant Industry

LEARNING OBJECTIVES

After reading and studying this chapter, you should be able to:

- Identify the main types of restaurant industry technologies.

- List and describe the main types of software programs.

- Identify factors to consider when choosing technology for a restaurant.

Courtesy of MICROS

Technology in the Restaurant Industry

Ask any restaurant operator about the alphabet soup known as *ASP*s, WAN, LAN, SAN, VPN, SQL, and *POS*, and you may get a puzzled look or a response that adds to your restaurant technology vocabulary. We have come a long way from the mom-and-pop operators and their proverbial cigar box. Independent operators may not require—or be able to afford—the sophistication of technology that chain operators are using. However, it is hard to overlook the progress in making technology available and affordable for independent restaurants. This chapter examines some of the better-known systems used and identifies their applications in the restaurant industry.

One of the biggest trends is technology that improves the guest experience, including online and tableside ordering and credit-card payment.[1] Restaurateurs are also becoming more sustainable and reducing food costs by getting back to basics—including clamping down on waste, repurposing trim, costing items carefully, and employing some creativity. Operators also are using more sophisticated menu-engineering techniques and making use of the latest inventory technologies.[2] Most restaurants divide their technology into two parts: back and front of the house. Many systems integrate these so that operators can input and draw on the information from both programs.

BACK-OF-THE-HOUSE TECHNOLOGY

Back-of-the-house, or *back-office*, restaurant technology consists of product management systems for purchasing, managing inventories, menu management, controlling labor and other costs, tip reporting, food and beverage cost percentages, human resources, and financial reporting. With the economic trend line showing no signs of reversing direction any time soon, the industry's top chief information officers say they are focusing on technology that will help their companies and franchisees weather the storm.[3]

Data Central by Restaurant Magic is a back-office system that is a web-based centralized reporting and document delivery method enabling operators to increase their effectiveness and efficiency. It helps restaurant management to exert control in critical key result areas such as sales, product mix, purchasing, inventory, workforce, cash and information management, and enterprise reporting. Data Central also helps operators keep up to date with accurate and timely results like profit and loss information, which positively impacts cost management decisions and analysis and the ability to compare performance to budget.[4] Data Central increases the effectiveness and efficiency by helping to control critical key result areas such as sales, product mix, purchasing, inventory, workforce, cash and information management, and enterprise reporting.[5]

Purchasing and Inventory Control *Product management* allows managers to track product through each stage of the inventory cycle and to automatically reorder when an item falls below the par stock level. The ingredients for recipes are costed to calculate cost and selling prices. If the purchase price of an item increases, it is easy to enter this information and get the new selling price. Culinary software services solutions like Data Central Restaurant Magic include options, such as importing purchases from vendors' online ordering systems and comparing vendors' pricing from purchases or bills. Additionally, the software allows restaurants to automate ordering with user-set par levels and generate customized reports detailing purchases, bids, and credits. See Figure 13.1. Data Central by Restaurant Magic is used at a number of leading restaurant companies and hotels for recipe and menu costing, inventory control, and nutritional analysis.[6]

A new service offered by Sysco called ChefEx is a catalog of products that, due to their uniqueness, perishability, or sales volume, would not typically be warehoused by an operating company. ChefEx allows increased customer product offerings from small artisan producers nationally. Orders are placed in the normal way, and items are drop-shipped directly to the restaurant; they do not go to the warehouse.

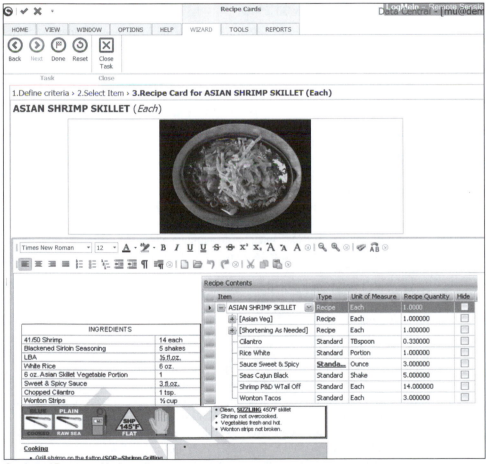

Courtesy of Restaurant Magic

FIGURE 13.1 Data Central from Restaurant Magic Software has recipe and menu costing, inventory control, and nutritional analysis programs.

Inventory Control Back-office systems aid inventory control by quickly recording the inventory and easily allowing new stock to be added. Calculations are done rapidly and monetary tools are given for each item, plus a cumulative total. The software programs prompt when inventory falls below the reorder point. When new menu items are added to the system, they are costed and priced according to the mark-up. With the help of back-office systems, restaurateurs can track "perpetual inventory" if they are interfaced to point-of-sale systems. Perpetual inventory is the inventory that should be on hand. As an example, let's assume that a restaurant has 100 Coca-Cola cans in the beginning of the month and it purchased 100 cans during the month. If the restaurant sold 100 Coca-Cola cans, the perpetual inventory for Coca-Cola cans is 100 units. When perpetual inventory is compared to physical inventory, which is taken usually once a month, the difference can be attributed to waste, theft, or shrinkage.

KITCHEN DISPLAY SYSTEMS

Efficient kitchen coordination is also a necessity in guaranteeing guest satisfaction. *Kitchen display systems (KDS)* provide highly visible, real-time information to manage and control kitchen efficiency. Contrary to some beliefs, these systems are being installed in more upscale restaurants today than in fast-food and casual restaurants.

Fully integrated with point-of-sale (POS) systems, the intuitive, graphical software application is conveniently mounted in the kitchen or food prep area. Visible to the entire kitchen staff, it displays food orders for preparation and monitors the timing of orders for speed of service. When the preparation time for a menu item exceeds the preparation time set by the chef, the color of the order changes indication that this item is taking longer than it should. Obviously, if guests wait more than they should, their satisfaction will decrease. If it takes significantly more time to cook a menu item than it should, not only the color of the item will change in KDS, but also a manager is paged. This provides feedback about the status of each table and captures service times for management reporting.

Features of order preparation include color-coded alerts that indicate exceeded prep times; varied order display options; icon displays for VIP, rush orders, or voids; and display functions, such as "all day," "order done," and "order recall."[7] The displays even can play videos and display the image of courses. Watching a video about how to prepare a menu item in KDS will ensure that the menu items prepared in the kitchen will be consistent. Even new kitchen staff can prepare the items based on the standard operating procedures. Obtainable statistics and reporting include service times for each guest check and table, average prep times for different courses at various prep station, and instantaneous reports on kitchen performance. This will also give the restaurant a chance to improve its staff members' efficiency. For example, if it takes Joe 15 minutes to prepare a cheeseburger instead of 9 minutes, the chef can train Joe to make sure that he prepares the menu item within the time limit. Increased interaction and integration of security and POS systems reduces the impact of employee theft in today's tough economic conditions.

As with table management solutions, certain systems incorporate paging, providing for end-to-end kitchen communication. Whether the restaurant is full, limited, or quick-service, servers will have more time to focus on the guests, and managers can be notified if there are any questions or problems in the kitchen that call for immediate attention. This technology helps to get food out of the kitchen faster, eliminates reheats, reduces labor expenses, and builds better guest rapport.

Mike Snow, information technology director for Silver Diner, says, "With KDS we were able to reduce the amount of recooks because modifiers and special instructions are more clearly displayed. Before KDS we did not have an accurate perception of our ticket times. KDS gives you precise data on ticket times and menu item cook times."[8]

Food Costing When calculating the food (and beverage) cost percentage, a handheld device (personal digital assistant, or *PDA*) can enter the inventory amounts into the system. Bar-code scanning technology is speeding up the inventory-taking process and making it more accurate. When the data are entered into the system, a variance report is generated, and any significant variances are investigated (see Figure 13.2). Technological improvements have made it possible to do a restaurant's food-cost percentage in about one-third of the time it used to take and with more accuracy.

Data Central from Restaurant Magic software solutions integrate programs with recipe and menu costing, inventory control, and nutritional analysis capabilities (see Figure 13.3). The recipe and menu costing program can cost, scale, and store an unlimited number of recipes; instantly analyze recipe and menu costs by portion or yield; update prices; change ingredients in every recipe; cost an entire function or catering job; generate accurate catering bids; add videos for preparation and training; and add pictures of plate turnout, or plate layout, for consistency.

The inventory control features can track rising food costs automatically; compare vendor pricing from purchases or bids; enter invoices; generate customized reports on purchases, price variances, bids, and credits; and lists of ingredients in different languages. Data Central includes a personal digital assistant (PDA) for inventory taking.

Some of the purchasing and ordering features include generating orders: based on par levels; based on lowest price/lowest bid; and for multiple vendors or a single vendor.

The nutritional analysis features a quick and accurate analysis of nutritional values; the ability to add your own specialty items and calculate the nutritional values of these items; and the ability to print "Nutritional Information".[9]

Menu Management There is a definite link between food costing and menu management. *Menu management systems* are food service software programs with an array of functions and features used to more efficiently manage the front-of-house and back-of-house operations in restaurants. San Diego–based Cambridge Investments, operator of 60 Arby's and five Baja Fresh units, is an example. Cambridge Investments use MenuLink to "evaluate managers' produce purchasing, test proposed recipe and pricing changes, and compare actual to expected food usage." The menu management function is used to determine what offers work best, so that coupon building may be directed toward those items. Since MenuLink use began, food and labor costs have both dropped.[10]

Cost of Goods Sold - Detailed (MU)

Date From: 01/16/2013
Date Thru: 01/22/2013

Unit: 144 Mayfair
Period Start: 2013: 01 - 04
Period End: 2013: 01 - 04
Account Reporting Group: All Formats
Account: All Accounts
Show Zero Value Items: Unchecked
Smart Filter: All Records
Problems Only: Unchecked
Display By: Dollars
Unit of Measure Type: N!

Item Description	Beginning Inventory	Bound in Recipe	Total Beginning (+)	Purchases (+)	Trades (+)	Used by Prepared (-)	Special Event (-)	Ending Inventory	Bound in Recipe	Total Ending (-)	Cost of Goods Sold	COGS Account %	Tracking Account %
Account: Meat Costs			**Tracking Account: Food Sales Net**										
Beef Corned	$46.62		$46.62					$25.90		$25.90	$20.72	0.97	0.05
Beef Ground Chuck	$475.68	$13.31	$488.99	$255.00				$228.19	$10.65	$238.84	$505.16	23.69	1.18
Beef Ribeye Shaved	$44.94	$10.26	$55.20	$93.79				$113.33	$3.66	$116.99	$32.00	1.50	0.07
Beef Roast	$57.95		$57.95					$39.90		$39.90	$18.05	0.85	0.04
Corn Dog	$24.75		$24.75					$17.25		$17.25	$7.50	0.35	0.02
Stk Ny Strip LB	$164.18		$164.18					$71.14		$71.14	$93.03	4.36	0.22
Stk Sirloin 4oz	$202.62		$202.62					$144.35		$144.35	$58.27	2.73	0.14
Stk Sirloin 7oz	$819.63		$819.63	$308.06				$307.11		$307.11	$820.57	38.48	1.92
Stk Sirloin 9oz	$567.54		$567.54	$148.43				$138.87		$138.87	$577.09	27.06	1.35
Total: Meat Costs			**$2,427.48**	**$805.28**						**$1,100.35**	**$2,132.39**	**99.99**	**4.99**
Account: Pork Costs			**Tracking Account: Food Sales Net**										
Andoullie Sausage	$40.05		$40.05					$30.22		$30.22	$9.84	1.79	0.02
Bacon Applewood	$147.16		$147.16	$69.91				$115.54		$115.54	$101.53	18.42	0.24
Bacon Bits Diced	$88.66	$7.08	$95.74					$39.85	$3.79	$43.64	$52.10	9.45	0.12

Courtesy of Restaurant Magic

FIGURE 13.2 Details of Cost of Goods Sold.

Previously these transfers were processed manually. With this feature, most of the manual processing will be eliminated.

Labor Management *Labor management systems* interface with both front- and back-of-the-house employee working hours, plus they handle human resource information. Labor management systems include a module to monitor applications (which can now be online and paperless), recruitment, personnel information, I-9 status, tax status, availability, and vacation and benefit information. Labor management systems also do the scheduling based on the forecasted volume of business for each meal period, and managers monitor the schedules to control costs. The actual time worked is recorded, the data on tips are entered and later reported per IRS guidelines, the pay scale and the calculation of paychecks are made, and the check is in the mail.

Windows-based labor schedulers make it easier for restaurant operators to stay on top of controllable expenses. TimePro from Commeg Systems has a time, attendance, and scheduling feature. Once the manager completes the schedule, associates cannot clock in more than 10 minutes early or 5 minutes late without a manager's override. This prevents people from coming in early and taking socializing breaks out back. Obviously, schedules are geared toward expected guest counts and sales. It is better to avoid copying a schedule from week to week; by doing so, either the labor budget or the guests will suffer, since no two sales periods are identical. Forecasts are checked against actual performance, and both figures are checked against the ideal for the time period; then the numbers are tweaked for the next forecast. It does take more up-front work, but once done it not only yields savings but also allows managers to focus on things like pleasing guests.

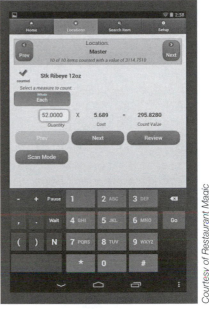

FIGURE 13.3 A mobile inventory from Restaurant Magic.

Courtesy of Restaurant Magic

Savvy restaurateurs guesstimate their sales for the next week and 28 days and compare the numbers with the budget, then update the numbers daily. Managers frequently are on a bonus plan, and meeting labor costs is a big part of the program.

Financial Reporting Back- and front-of-the-house systems may interface by transferring data to and from the central server. Profit (or loss) statements, budgets and variances, daily reports, and balance sheets are prepared with the aid of software programs.

The advantage of this technology is that information is provided in real time, enabling operators to make informed decisions quickly. Quicker decisions allow managers to "keep their fingers on the pulse" of the restaurant.

When the back- and front-of-the-house systems are interfaced, it is easier for management to monitor service times, POS food costs, labor costs, and guest counts. Again, this compilation of information helps managers make more informed decisions.

E-learning Computer-based training, known as *e-learning*, delivered via the Internet or proprietary Internet sites, is expanding knowledge in the workplace. Darden

Restaurant managers and hourly paid workers have used it to learn a new software system. About 85 percent of Fortune 1000 companies have significant e-learning initiatives under way. Darden Restaurants, with more than 130,000 employees and 1,200 restaurants nationwide, uses a PeopleSoft software system so employees can access benefits and other information through Darden's intranet site. Training can now easily take place online with, for example, materials displayed on how each plate should look.

There have been many breakthroughs in training people how to use this type of software. Not too long ago, the training process consisted of people being bogged down with long manuals. Today, the majority of training can be done online, with the click of a button.

Associations such as the National Environmental Health Association (NEHA) offer online training for foodservice professionals. All front-of-the-house employees should take a responsible alcohol service course and all back-of-the-house employees should take (or are required by their state to take) one of three ANSI/ CFP accredited certification exams: Prometric, ServSafe, or The National Registry of Food Safety Professionals.

FRONT-OF-THE-HOUSE TECHNOLOGY

Front-of-the-house technology revolves around the point-of-sale system and wireless handheld devices. New technologies include multimedia lobby displays that promote branding and special offers. Self-service kiosks that allow guests to interact and ease host stand congestion. Servers may greet guests with wireless ordering terminals. Wireless payment-processing units are a convenient, efficient and secure way to interact with customers.[11] Another technological advance designed to improve the guest experience is an in-store dashboard displaying vital restaurant statistics. Systems that monitor spending and hardware and software that aid front-of-the-house operations were among the tools that foodservice CIOs at the 14th annual International Foodservice Technology Exposition said their departments were using to help their companies cut costs and drive customer traffic.[12]

POS Systems *Point-of-sale* (POS) systems are the combination of hardware and software used is any business setting where transactions occur. While the most basic POS systems used in retail businesses function predominately as an electronic cash register, more dynamic and multifunctional versions are commonly used in hospitality businesses. POS systems are used in both the front-of-house and back-of-house operations for an array of purposes, including but not limited to the input of food and beverage orders, electronic cashier transactions, and tracking of sales and payroll. By now, restaurateurs know that having a good point-of-sale system is essential to their business operations. Technological innovation has produced POS systems that are faster, smarter, easier to use, and more reliable.

In today's increasingly competitive restaurant industry, investment in a quality POS system is a standard component of operational costs. The question many owners may have is: "How can I utilize my POS investment to its utmost capability, and what other technology is out there that will help improve operations?" Some of the advantages of POS systems include:

- Elimination of arithmetic errors
- Improved guest check control
- Increased average guest check
- Faster reaction to trends
- Reduced labor costs
- Reduced late charges (if there is a direct interface between a POS and Property Management System in a hotel)

Fortunately, first-rate solutions available today are specifically designed to address these types of objectives. POS systems now work in tandem with applications and tools that enable enhanced management of the total guest experience, table and kitchen operations, back-office systems, business intelligence, and gift and loyalty programs. Furthermore, these individual solutions can be integrated into a complete enterprise solution scalable to fit an independent operation or even a large chain corporation.

The sections that follow highlight some of the latest restaurant technology trends.

The point-of-sale terminal is the workhorse of restaurant operations. It needs to be strong enough to withstand the rigors of daily restaurant use and versatile enough to achieve order-entry and guest-check efficiency.

Restaurant operators are increasingly demanding POS terminals that work within today's conditions while leaving room for expansion or adaptation. Open platform architecture, a leading trend in POS, is giving restaurant operators more flexibility when it comes to choosing operating systems, peripherals, and applications, while improved design is reducing footprint and increasing reliability.

Selecting a POS System Clyde Dishman, hospitality industry vice president of NCR, suggests that because a POS system can cost thousands of dollars, any new restaurant-level system should be pretested in "live" environments. Additionally, because restaurants of all shapes and sizes have varying sets of technology requirements, the system must combine proven hardware with multiple software modules to create flexible and customizable solutions.

NCR's Human Factors Engineering (HFE) team provides the quantitative data for evaluating current store performance levels and user interface designs. HFE concentrates on restaurant performance improvements that allow the restaurant operator to identify areas in which to increase revenues and improve operational efficiency and guest service. HFE has demonstrated the ability to assist the restaurateur in many facets of the business, whether in technology or in purely operational areas, such as workflow design or ergonomic assessments. The two focus areas of HFE are store performance and user-interface design.

The store performance group measures key store-level metrics to assess productivity at the point of sale, as well as ergonomics and technology, and then compares that to other best-in-class restaurant practices. The resulting quantitative data are used to conduct cost/benefit analysis of recommended solutions.

The second focus area relates to the usability of the system. When a restaurant's employees are not productive and customer-service levels are not up to snuff, such problems often can be traced to the design of the POS interface, ranging from complicated screen layouts to inappropriately sized buttons and the poor use of colors for different menu items. HFE quantifies productivity levels of an existing system by surveying the needs of front-line restaurant employees to ensure that any recommended solution is easy to use. For example, HFE developed a series of more than 200 guidelines for touch-screen POS applications, which outline the best practices for designing software that improves productivity, reduces training time, and facilitates usability.[13]

Dishman adds that NCR's Real POS 21 has added a biometric device for fingerprints for restaurant employees. This helps restaurant operators by cutting out the "buddy punching" in timekeeping. It also helps with a manager's override of a void by preventing a manager from giving his or her card to an employee if the manager is busy doing something else. Another good feature of the Real POS 21 is that guests can now also see the display of their order, thus reducing the number of errors and the need to alter the order.

A key element in the installation of any new equipment is how you operationalize it. Subway put in a self-service kiosk near Vanderbilt University; because it took 30 minutes to get the order, the kiosk was removed.[14]

NCR Aloha has a popular POS with a full-range of restaurant products that includes Aloha Table Service (see Figure 13.4), which offers user-friendly ways of entering orders, managing guest checks, running promotions, and processing payments. The management function has a built-in Event Scheduler that lets managers program events that are automatically activated at a specific time. Special messages can be entered to appear on the screen, keeping staff informed. Managers can also access real-time sales results and reporting features such as product mix reports, employee check-in stats, and server sales.

NCR Aloha's virtual order processing communicates between the kitchen and waitstaff. For example, with the menu availability feature, staff members are able to count down selected items or specials as they're ordered so servers never order out-of-stock items. Some of the features of Table Service include intuitive touch-screen interfaces, built-in redundancy, user-customizable screens and screen flow, menu management, integrated customized table floor plan, Microsoft Windows–based performance measurement for servers, open architecture, off-the-shelf nonproprietary hardware, enterprise capabilities, extensive kitchen chit printing options, and simple check- or item-splitting and combining functionality.

Optional packages for NCR Aloha's Table Service also include Aloha credit card, which authorizes, processes, and settles credit card transactions. The NCR Aloha Customer Management includes a database to offer loyalty programs and track vital customer information. The Aloha Kitchen Display System gives the flexibility to route orders to video monitors in the kitchen. Having these monitors increases productivity because it eliminates having someone, such as an expeditor, calling out orders to each station.

NCR Mobile Pay, which is integrated with NCR Aloha, enables consumers to act instead of waiting. "Restaurant patrons can easily review an order, add to it, tip and pay, and take a survey—all directly from their smartphone. NCR Mobile Pay transforms the guest experience while also improving order and accuracy, increasing speed of service and reducing the potential of credit card fraud for restaurant operators."[15]

Courtesy of NCR Corporation

NCR's Real 70 POS System uses the Microsoft Windows platform and Intel Pentium IV integrated touch screen, magnetic stripe reader, and customer display.

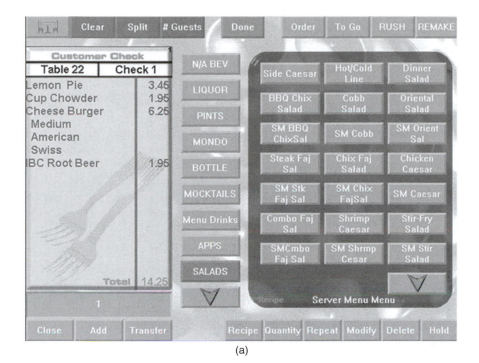

(a)

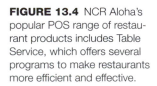

(b)

Art provided courtesy of NCRAloha Technologies

FIGURE 13.4 NCR Aloha's popular POS range of restaurant products includes Table Service, which offers several programs to make restaurants more efficient and effective.

Split Checks

Customer Check		Customer Check		Customer Check		Customer Check	
Table 22	Check 1	Table 22	Check 2	Table 22	Check 3	Table 22	Check 4
Lemon Pie	3.45	BOURBON	3.65	Cheese Burger	6.25	Coco-Strw Appl	2.95
Cup Chowder	1.95	Jack		Medium		Straw Sundae	3.45
IBC Root Beer	1.95	Rocks		American		1/2 Fried Mozz	2.97
Malt	2.95	Bowl Chowder	3.95	Swiss		Hot Fudge Sunc	3.45
Coffee				Steak Faj Sal	9.45		
1/2 Fried Mozz	2.98						
Three For All	7.25						
Quesa	6.50						

| Combine | Add | ✓ OK | ✗ Cancel | Split Items |

FIGURE 13.4 *(continued)*

(c)

Courtesy of Carmel Café

Carmel Café uses tablets for guests to order their food directly from the kitchen.

NCR also offers powerful restaurant reporting and analytics software that can collect data and turn them into actionable information distributed via the cloud. You can use the drilldown viewer options for fast, high-level examination of data, or even to look at the data in minute detail. NCR's web-based and mobile restaurant management software permits data reporting and replication at the site level or across your organization. NCR's Pulse platform "revolutionizes the way restaurant owners, operators and staff communicate and manage the business. The Pulse platform embraces the idea of delivering actionable information and gives you access to store metrics, social media management and much more via your smartphone or tablet device."[16]

Table Management

The guest experience begins from the time patrons are greeted until they exit the restaurant. They are consciously and subconsciously forming an opinion about the restaurant during the seating process, throughout their table service, and while taking care of paying the bill. Efficiency, consistency, and accuracy are the key goals in successfully meeting the expectations of guests and at the same time improving speed of service. When this occurs, faster table turns are achieved, resulting in increased revenue and profit.

Highly developed *table management* software allows for meticulous control of this essential restaurant function. Through easy-to-use automation, the restaurant is able to effortlessly handle time-sensitive guest demands associated with reservations and waiting times. The software makes this possible by streamlining the capture and calculation of the data, resulting in a more accurate quote time and final seating time. Common customer preferences including table location are also built in to the data capture module.

Table management solutions also incorporate alert features via the use of pagers. With the touch of a button, the hostess can alert guests that their table is ready; the pager vibrates, flashes, or even plays a voice mail message.

Manager alerts also aid in crucial situations like servicing VIPs. When a VIP visits the restaurant, managers receive a page or text when the table is set and ready to be seated.

Ed Rothenberg, vice president of restaurant development for MICROS Systems, Inc., a leading supplier of information systems to the hospitality and retail industries, says that "table management, wait lists, and reservations have traditionally been a pen-and-paper function. Using technology allows restaurants to do this more accurately using actual data from the POS." He believes the top benefits of this solution are "more accurate quoting of wait times, less room for error in tracking reservations, expanding a restaurant's reach through accepting Web-based reservations, and the capacity for historical tracking of all customer touch points beginning the moment they walk in your restaurant."[17]

PAY AT THE TABLE

More than ever, consumers are concerned about the security risks that go along with credit card usage. The Federal Trade Commission's *Consumer Fraud and Identity Theft Complaint Data* report stated that credit card fraud was the most common form of reported identity theft, accounting for about a quarter of all identity theft fraud.[18] With this in mind, the restaurant industry is now following the retail industry by offering consumers the ability to make payments without letting their credit card out of their sight. This option, called pay at the table, is on the forefront of new restaurant technology.

When guests are ready to pay for their meal, a server can provide them a hand-held device in which they can verify their bill, swipe their card, include any tip, and print the receipt. Most recently, technology providers have also designed devices that allow the use of debit instead of credit cards, as many consumers prefer to use their secure PIN (personal identification number). The *pay-at-the-table* solution puts guests in control of the payment process and decreases the risk of skimming. This common scam occurs when a server takes the guest's card for payment and runs it through a device to capture the encoded information off the magnetic strip. The server returns the guest's card, with the guest unaware that the card's data has been stolen and he or she is now susceptible to fraudulent charges.

Pay at the table offers two benefits to guests: more peace of mind concerning security issues and the ability to leave the restaurant a little sooner, because they don't have to wait for a server to facilitate payment. Not only does this add to the

Courtesy of Aloha Technologies

FIGURE 13.5 Aloha's popular POS range of restaurant products includes Table Service, which offers several programs to make restaurants more efficient and effective.

overall guest experience, but it also improves the restaurant's table turns and speed of service. Owners particularly consider the ability to perform debit transactions a financial benefit because they incur lower processing fees.

Adam Greenberg, owner of Potomac Pizza in Gaithersburg, Maryland, recently invested in pay-at-the-table technology. He says, "It'll save the customers time; it'll save the servers time."

ASI has the popular Restaurant Manager POS (see Figure 13.5), with easy-to-use training. This, coupled with the seamless integration between Restaurant Manager and the Write-On Handheld POS system, means that servers simply jot down guests' orders and send them to the kitchen with a tap of their stylus. The Write-On Handheld also gives servers easy access to wine lists, daily specials, and recipes.

Handhelds can provide a number of benefits to restaurants, such as faster table turns, because servers no longer need to record each order twice. Another benefit is reduced errors—servers are reminded to ask for details, like cooking temperature or salad dressing. The handheld system prompts servers to enter orders into the system starting with seat number one and then moving around the table. It makes it easy to track specific items to the corresponding guest, which is especially helpful when a food expediter is needed on a busy night. This function also makes it less complicated to provide split checks—even after the order has been totaled. Yet another feature of handhelds is up-sells; because the entire menu is in the palm of their hand, servers can promote or up-sell items more easily. There's no need to visit a fixed POS station and process the order a second time and no need to check with the kitchen to see if an item is sold out.[19] If an item is sold out, it will be displayed on the device so servers will know instantly.

Restaurant Manager comes with a full complement of peripheral devices that include bar-code scanners, cash draws, coin dispensers, caller ID devices, customer displays, Debitek card readers, fingerprint readers, kitchen display units, liquor control devices, magnetic strip readers, order confirmation displays, printers, weighing scales, and video tracking monitors.

PCI DSS

Payment Card Industry Data Security Standard (PCI DSS) can be described as a system of standards established in order to reduce the risk of payment card fraud and prevent the misuse of cardholder information that is stored or being transacted. In 2007, PCI DSS was introduced to enforce compliance by every merchant around the world that accepts credit and debit cards as a form of payment. Failure to comply with the guidelines set forth by PCI DSS can result in fines from payment card issuing brands, banks, and state government agencies, as well as increased payment process fees, lawsuits, the risk of losing credit card payment privileges and negative media attention, which may also result in a loss of business.[20]

The hospitality industry represents the largest percentage of credit card fraud victims. Over 50 percent of all payment card fraud occurs within a hospitality establishment. At the same time, small hotels and independent restaurants encompass the largest amount of noncompliant establishments, who fall in the least demanding category of compliance. It has become increasingly important to satisfy PCI DSS standards for the sake of the merchants and their establishments, as well as the guests, who represent a supposedly protected group of consumers in the hospitality industry. Furthermore, compliance with PCI standards is the morally just thing to do, and a good business practice.[21]

POS Systems

There are several suppliers of POS. IBM offers Linux servers and Sure POS 700 series for restaurants. The Sure POS 700 open platform applications for both Microsoft Windows and IBM 4690 OS allow for customization of applications, peripherals, and displays; they also drive USB technology for plug-and-play setup and automatic configuration. The Sure POS 700 incorporates an onboard 10/100 ethernet local area network (LAN) to handle both Internet and intranet applications.

Sharp has the UP-5900 system, which is also an open platform terminal. Combined with Maitre'D Restaurant Management software, it can drive a variety of software modules and interfaces.

NCR offers the 7454 POS Workstation with open PC-based architecture that is certified for MS DOS and Windows for flexibility. It offers full-screen, full-motion video.

Hardware solutions from NCR and its partners include the fully integrated NCR Real POS 70. It combines the reliability of the Microsoft platform and the industry-leading technology of Intel with the innovation of Authen Tec. The Intel Pentium IV-based terminal sports an integrated touch screen, magnetic stripe reader, and customer display. It also features a newly designed motherboard that is based on Intel's standards-based specification. The motherboard, hard disc, and power supply are placed on user-friendly "sleds," allowing for tool-free access and servicing. That means a terminal that needs servicing can be up and running in seconds. NCR will also certify, support, and offer preloaded operating system images on the NCR Real POS 70 for Microsoft Windows 200, XP Pro, NT, and DOS.[22]

NCR's Compris runs on the NCR 7454 hospitality point-of-sale system. The Compris solution includes a flexible POS application, a back-office component for managing restaurant operations, and corporate tools for remote database maintenance and consolidated reporting. The Windows-based Compris WinPOS is easy to use and has an Advanced Manager's workstation that includes Navigation, which allows inventory, operators to configure their interface with daily tasks and user-defined tabs like cash management or view, print, and balance all POS data at the back office. The system also handles food cost control invoices, receipts, transfers, credits, and waste reports. Reporting includes both theoretical and actual usage and variance tracking. Labor includes controlling labor costs, tracking time and wages, generating time cards, and avoiding employees' clocking in too early or clocking out too late. It provides a full complement of reports: daily, weekly, and period labor costs, employee punches, hours worked, and server totals. The data can be extracted from and imported into a payroll system. Schedule Builder generates simple-to-use schedules for each shift, highlights conflicts, and tracks variances.[23]

Courtesy of MICROS

WS5A MICROS Simphony is a cloud-based POS offering designed for SaaS.

Micros has the Eclipse PC Workstation that combines a small footprint and seams designed to channel liquids off the unit. The Eclipse also supports a number of operating systems, including MSDOS 6.22 and Microsoft Windows, as well as all Micros point-of-sale applications.

POS systems have come down in price and offer the independent restaurateur the convenience of providing information for financials that obviates the need for cash registers and spreadsheets, which are time-consuming and often have to be reformatted and reentered into the accounting journals by bookkeepers or accountants. Today POS systems have credit-card integration and interface with payroll and financial systems. The information is consolidated, and an automated profit-and-loss statement is produced.

Some operators choose a POS for its power beyond the point of sale. These multimedia workstations feature a large hard drive and can run customer promotions or employee training programs when not in use as POS terminals.

For some smaller restaurants, there is the old standby electronic cash register (ECR), which is now offering some of the flexibility of POS. For example, the ECR can be used as a stand-alone unit for a small restaurant.

Wireless POS has been around for a few years, but it is getting better and smaller. How is wireless POS being used in the restaurant business? The general managers at Red Robin use their wireless POS as a tool to notify them of a variety of things, from when team members go on overtime, to violations of underage working rules, to birthdays and anniversaries, and of the need to void or comp a guest check.

Some restaurateurs are concerned about the quality of guest contact during the order-taking process and how that might be negatively impacted by a server doing a POS transaction while standing at the table.

Several restaurant-industry technology trends are becoming more prominent. The main one is increased integration of front- and back-office systems. New technology is constantly being introduced. There is new satellite or cable entertainment; age verification units to confirm a guest's age or ferret out fake IDs; and handheld PDAs that function as pagers, data-entry pads, and inventory control devices.

The cost of installing a POS system will depend on the number of stations required. A 125-seat casual dining restaurant could use two or three stations in the dining area, one in the bar, and printers in the kitchen, plus a managers' station. The total cost would be in the $18,000 to $20,000 range.

If you are opening a restaurant and do not have that kind of money, you can start with a simple cash register and work up to a more sophisticated system as your business grows.

Mobile Phone Technology

In today's technology-based economy, it is essential to own a smartphone device of some type—or it is at least recommended. Mobile phone technology is commonly used throughout the hospitality industry by organizations and their consumers. Hospitality technology companies are constantly developing innovative equipment and software, which serves to encourage a more efficient and effective operation, while establishing a more direct link from the consumer to the end product or service. The various elements of a business's life cycle, including advertising and awareness, brand recognition and purchasing decisions, as well as post-purchase behavior and loyalty, are continuously being influenced by mobile phone technology, which may eventually dictate the entire consumer purchase process. In this section, we will discuss some of the trends taking aim in the use of mobile phone technology by both restaurant organizations and their consumers.

The QR code is used by many Fortune 500 companies in their marketing efforts. The QR code can also be a useful tool for restaurateurs. For example, guests can enter the QR code takeout menu onto their smart phones and even jump the line when a custom-generated QR code is scanned at the point-of-sale.[24] A QR code can also show photos of menu items to help guests decide on what to order. The QR code can add photos to the restaurant's Yelp listing, or to Twitter and Facebook to facilitate social media sharing.[25]

Mobile payment can be described as the transaction between the producer and consumer of a good or service, which allows the consumers to pay for their purchase directly from their phone. This can significantly benefit both the producer and consumer in different ways. Many independent restaurant operations function on a cash-only basis because of the extra cost associated with accepting credit card payment, which limits their capacity and growth potential. The convenience of offering mobile payments provides opportunities to increase a restaurant's customer base and business demand without the added cost of accepting credit cards. Furthermore, accepting mobile payments allows businesses to track the behaviors of their customers. The collection of customer data can be used to predict future trends or forecast levels of business demand.[26] Mobile payments can be a substantial relief for consumers for the purpose of quickness, convenience, and portability. No longer will it be a problem to forget your wallet on a first date. In fact, the burden of carrying extra accessories in your pocket will be reduced, and the fear of losing your wallet in public will be nonexistent. Additionally, you will no longer have to wait around if the credit card machine malfunctions—which, unfortunately for restaurants, happens all too often.

Text messaging is used as an outlet of communication throughout the hospitality industry for a variety of purposes, both personal and public. Text messaging allows for person-to-person communication within an organization, which can be very beneficial in a restaurant setting, when employees want to get in touch with each other without distracting their guests. Furthermore, text messaging is used by organizations to advertise their products directly or indirectly. For example, CMS Text is an independent company used by many hospitality organizations to develop and launch individual mobile marketing campaigns for many different purposes, including the awareness of a new restaurant or concept, the continual recognition of an existing restaurant, or the promotion of a product or service. CMS Text allows businesses to reach a wide range of consumers in a matter of seconds by sending mobile blasts to a database of identified customers.[27]

Many restaurant organizations are using text messaging to positively influence the guest experience; however, there is also multifunctional technology, which offers more capabilities than simply advertising and promotion. Freshtxt is a service offered by Heartland Payment Systems, which integrates restaurant customer management with mobile marketing by combining software and personal text messages. This new software includes a reservation management system featuring a guest wait list and the ability to forecast wait times by table. This service is not only efficient but eco-friendly as well, saving countless pages of paper that were previously used for tracking wait lists and marking table assignments. Freshtxt allows restaurant to use text messaging to alert guests when their table is ready without the hassle of carrying around cumbersome pagers typically used in the past. Furthermore, Freshtxt software has the ability send promotional messages to guests, much like CMS Text.[28]

Web-Based Enterprise Portals

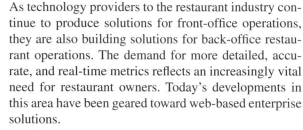

Courtesy of MICROS

mStation image—MICROS's newest workstation combines the need for mobility with the requirement for connectivity.

As technology providers to the restaurant industry continue to produce solutions for front-office operations, they are also building solutions for back-office restaurant operations. The demand for more detailed, accurate, and real-time metrics reflects an increasingly vital need for restaurant owners. Today's developments in this area have been geared toward web-based enterprise solutions.

The primary competency of an Internet portal is its centralization of applications, which offers substantial advantages whether the restaurateur owns an independent restaurant or multiple locations. Content-rich portals provide access to simple management tools for areas such as data warehousing, inventory, menu and pricing analysis, and loss prevention. The ability to set up and manage gift cards and point-based loyalty programs with complete reporting is a key feature of this technology. RTIconnect is an in-store food cost, labor scheduling, cash control and sales reporting system. This technology enables use of an Internet platform to control food costs, schedule employees, view sales reports, and much more—with a customizable easy to use interface. Specific areas include:

- Sales reporting
- Cash management
- In-store profit and loss statements
- Labor management
- Food costs
- Prep
- Ordering
- Task lists
- POS data[29]

Gift Card and Loyalty Programs

Customer relationship management (CRM) is not new to the restaurant industry; however, the capacity for a single vendor to combine the necessary components into one worthwhile CRM solution is a recent development. With so many different innovative approaches to customer database building, prospecting, loyalty campaigning, and general relationship management, integrated CRM solutions deliver a 360-degree view of the guest's activities. All of the activities are tracked and controlled from a central database, allowing restaurant operators to recognize their guests with the most frequent spending patterns and determine the best technique to attract and measure the expansion of new trial, or less frequent, guests into the core customer base. This type of analysis is instrumental in establishing stored-value gift cards and point-based loyalty programs.

Gift cards are helping to increase restaurant revenue. In fact, they may even represent a larger portion of total sales. Most major chains now sell gift cards; they have become a significant revenue producer in the restaurant industry.

The latest CRM solutions give operators the ability to issue and activate cards with fixed or present values; reload, cash-out, and transfer balances from one card to another; look up gift card accounts by name, ZIP code, and phone number; and centrally manage and control the issuance and redemption of cards systemwide.

With point-based loyalty programs, guests can be rewarded by issuing coupons that can be used for subsequent visits; awarding amounts to guest accounts that achieve a certain point level; applying on-the-spot discounts to guest checks; and elevating a guest's status from one program level to another.

Integration is the bottom line. Restaurant operators now have alternatives for merging multiple technology solutions into their overall operations. The most notable benefit to this solution is the ability to work with a single vendor versus several third-party vendors, each with its own technology, service costs, and administrative overhead. Partnering with one vendor contributes to a reduction in staffing requirements, fewer errors, and better intelligence.

Even the finest POS systems require supplementary components to make them more robust, which in turn expands a business's possibilities for growth. By integrating solutions like table management, kitchen display systems, pay at the table, and web-based enterprise portals, restaurants are more likely to improve customer satisfaction, staff productivity, and operational efficiency. The final result: a positive return on investment.

Guest Services and Websites

Restaurant technology has evolved to the point where a restaurant can store and recall guests' preferences for tables, menu items, wines, and servers. Tables may be booked over the Internet at any time by leaving a credit card as a form of deposit to secure the table, especially in large cities at convention times. Hosts can use programs to allocate tables, allowing a certain time—say one and a half hours—before that table is booked again. Guest checks can be split for payment by several people, if need be. Guest bills even come with suggested tip amounts calculated.

More and more restaurants are offering another form of guest services: high-speed Internet access. Starbucks or Panera just might be the next place for your meeting. If you need to access data from an online report, your laptop can retrieve it instantly. And if the meeting gets boring, you can check your e-mail. Other restaurants are using wireless paging to help reduce wait time for guests and loss of pagers for restaurants. When guests give their names to the hostess, they are asked for their cell phone number. This is entered into the "Trinity" system. When the table is ready, a prerecorded message notifies guests. Wireless surveys allow guests to give feedback before they leave the restaurant, and tabletop pagers let guests page their server when they need something.

Restaurant websites need an appealing, user-friendly design and functionality, including accessibility and interactivity. When Joe Public is trying to access your site, can it be done without fault? Other features that are helpful are menus, photos of the restaurant, how to get there, parking information, frequently asked questions (FAQs), and secure transaction capability. Among the higher-scoring restaurant websites are Red Robin, T.G.I. Friday's, Outback Steakhouse, and Hard Rock Cafe.

Cafe Ba Ba Reeba, Chicago's first tapas restaurant, selected Nextology as its software program because it could take care of a dream list of items. The restaurant has a number of special "reservation required" events, such as cooking classes, wine tastings, and shows, so keeping those up to date was very important. It also needed the ability to list specials, menu changes, and other information of interest of its clientele. It now has a site that enables it to take reservations and receive payment for events online. It can also edit, change, and update information on the fly. Michael Cunningham, the general manager, says that Cafe Ba Ba Reeba could not go with a generic website design due to the restaurant's reputation and image. Now his staff is on the phone less and bookings are up.

Restaurant Management Systems

Restaurant operators are increasingly relying on systems to improve the guest experience and enhance the restaurant's performance.

1. *MICROS Alert Manager.* Alert Manager monitors conditions in an operation and compares them to established standards. Exceptions are immediately identified, and a message is sent to the pager, PDA, cell phone, or e-mail of those who need to know. "The MICROS Alert Manager provides exciting new integration with the RES products and the on-premise paging and communications solutions made available by JTECH, a MICROS subsidiary."[30]

2. *Push-for-service.* Push-for-service is a system that a hotel or restaurant with remote areas can use to be notified by guests when they need to order food or beverage items. A great example for a push-for-service system could be in a beach area where guests may not want to leave for security (i.e., they do not want to leave their children by themselves or for convenience reasons). They can simply press a button under their beach umbrella. This will page the

servers for that area. The pager will show the push-for-service number (i.e., Umbrella 12). A server can push a button on notifying the other servers that this request has been taken care of. This push-for-service system can increase guest satisfaction and operational profitability.

3. *Table locator systems.* The introduction of the fast-casual restaurant (the guest orders the food at the counter and the food is brought to the table) has made for quicker order and food service than conventional restaurants. Table locator systems can increase speed of service and guest satisfaction. When the guest orders the food at the counter, the cashier would give the guest an electronic card. When the guest picks a table, she/he inserts this card into a slot. This will indicate the table that the guest chose. It will also activate the timing of the order. When the food is ready, the server can see which table the guest is sitting at. When the food is served, the server can insert her/his card into the slot indicating that the food has been delivered. The total time to cook and serve the food is also kept in the system, allowing the restaurant manager to measure the efficiency of the kitchen and service staff.

Summary

This chapter reviews the technology and its applications for front- and back-of-the-house restaurant operations. POS systems and various software programs are discussed.

Most restaurants divide their technology into two parts: back and front of the house. Many systems integrate these so that operators can input and draw on the information from both programs.

Back-of-the-house, or *back-office*, restaurant technology consists of product management systems for purchasing, managing inventories, menu management, controlling labor and other costs, tip reporting, food and beverage cost percentages, human resources, and financial reporting. Back-office systems aid inventory control by quickly recording the inventory and easily allowing new stock to be added. Calculations are done rapidly and monetary tools are given for each item, plus a cumulative total.

Front-of-the-house technology revolves around the point-of-sale system and wireless handheld devices. *Point-of-sale* (POS) systems are the combination of hardware and software used is any business setting where transactions occur. While the most basic POS systems used in retail businesses function predominately as an electronic cash register, more dynamic and multifunctional versions are commonly used in hospitality businesses.

Key Terms and Concepts

Back-of-the-house technology
Customer relationship management (CRM)
E-learning

Kitchen display systems (KDS)
Labor management
Menu management
Mobile payment

Pay-at-the-table

Payment Card Industry Data Security
Standard (PCI DSS)

PDA

POS

Product management

Table management

Review Questions

1. How would you decide which is the best POS system and restaurant system for your restaurant?
2. Are handheld devices worth the investment for independent table-service restaurants?
3. What is PCI DSS? How is it related to the restaurant industry?
4. How has mobile phone technology affected the restaurant industry?
5. What are some ways that restaurateurs can strengthen customer relationship management within their establishment?
6. What is the difference between front-of-house and back-of-house restaurant technology products? Give examples of each.

CASE STUDY: Carmel Café & *Wine Bar*

Something New

Carmel Café & Wine Bar is a relatively new restaurant chain based out of Tampa, Florida that was started in November of 2010, by Chris Sullivan, co-founder of Outback Steakhouse, along with Terry Ryan, Nancy Shneid and Alex Sullivan. The concept combines a sophisticated lounge environment with contemporary Mediterranean cuisine to compliment the immense wine list, full of exquisite grape varietals from various regions around the world. The concept was developed around the idea of encompassing different culinary influences, allowing the restaurant to offer a greater depth of menu options, as well as appealing to a wider range of clientele. The name "Carmel" was coined after the town of Carmel-by-the-Sea, a quaint and beautiful golf community full of Mediterranean-style restaurants, and located in Monterey, California. There are currently three Carmel locations in and around the Tampa Bay area, as well as one location in Sarasota, Florida, just 60 miles south of Tampa.

At the forefront, Carmel was created with the female diner in mind. Its wine list offers different portion options, including a 3, 6, or 9 ounce glass, as well as a full bottle of wine. The restaurant offers both small and large portions of food items, which caters to the traditional dinner customer, as well as the diner who wants a "tapas-style" or "social-eating" experience. During the construction of new Carmel properties, Chris Sullivan and company partner with a visionary architect from Ybor City, Albert Alfonso, who designs the layout of the restaurants using lighter woods, various types of seating areas, larger tables for community dining, and an overall environment that invites lounging and relaxation. The décor is modern, but uses feminine colors and lower lighting, which creates a sense of ambiance. According to Chris Sullivan, "these are all things that women appreciate".

Technology Trends

At Carmel, each guest is presented with a regular paper menu, as well as a personal electronic "MenuPad," which features a full food menu with pictures and descriptions of menu items, as well as a full wine list, which offers information about the wine's grape varietal, region and recommended pairings with menu items. When customers have selected food or beverage items, they can place their order directly on the MenuPads at their leisure. The idea behind implementing the MenuPads was to ensure that the restaurant remained relevant in the minds of customers, and to give them more control and information regarding what and when they want to order. The purpose of the MenuPads is not to replace the servers but to assist them in creating an excellent dining experience from menu knowledge to speed of service. According to Chris Sullivan, "With the ever-increasing speed of technology comes an increase in the customers' expectations for faster service."

The Toughest Competitor

Carmel's target market is customers with sophisticated palates and an interest in wine exploration, typically between the ages of 25 and 45. The restaurant seeks to develop new locations in higher-income neighborhoods in order to capture its target demographic. Today, one of the biggest challenges of starting a new restaurant concept is the competition that already exists and the new competition that comes into the market. According to Chris Sullivan, "Approximately 60 percent of new restaurant ventures and 33 percent of total restaurant ventures fail annually." With the amount of culinary talent and advanced ideas that enter into the market each year, it becomes increasingly difficult to be one of the few that succeed over the long term, especially in this tough economic time. If a restaurant is serving good food and has a good wine list and consistently executes its service, then it is viewed as Carmel's competition. Currently, Carmel is in negotiations for several sites in Orlando for future development of Carmel properties; however, the uncertainty of the economy has made expansion of a new restaurant chain riskier now more than ever. With these uncertainties at large, the best option moving forward is to take it one step at a time.

QUESTIONS

1. What type of clientele do you believe this concept should target?
2. What are the pros and cons of Carmel's Menu-Pad and overall concept?
3. How can the MenuPad ensure consistency in the kitchen regarding the preparation and appearance of menu items?
4. What are some other forms of restaurant technology trends? What forms of technology do you think are most beneficial to restaurants?

Endnotes

1. Restaurant Technology/Restaurant Trends 2013 Annual Restaurant Technology Study by Hospitality Technology retrieved from.
2. Bret Thorn, "Price Controls Pay Dividends," *Nation's Restaurant News*, 43 (17), (May 11, 2009), p. 43. ABI/Inform Trade and Industry. Retrieved September 2009.
3. Paul Frumkin, "FS/TEC 2009: CIOs Say Software Key to Cold, Hard Cash," *Nation's Restaurant News*, 43 (7), (February 23, 2009), p. 4. ABI/Inform Trade and Industry. Retrieved September 2009.
4. www.restaurantmagic.com. Retrieved on January 15, 2013.
5. Ibid.
6. Personal correspondence with Greg Kingen, VP Sales & Marketing Restaurant Magic Software. Sememeber 3, 2013.
7. "Kitchen Display Systems," http://www.micros.com/Solutions/ProductsAM/KitchenDisplaySystems/. Retrieved on May 21, 2013.
8. Hope B. Byers, "Restaurant Technology Trends: Looking Beyond POS to Improve Restaurant Operations," *Maryland Hospitality* (Winter 2006), p. 10, http://kaytitaylor.files.wordpress.com/2011/03/ramq_0406_sales.pdf. Retrieved on May 21, 2013. Also see "Silver Diner," Micros

Case Study, January 2012, http://www.micros.com/NR/rdonlyres/5849CA60-7690-4578-B16C-c13c1347EC8C/0/SilverDinerCaseStudy.pdf. Retrieved on May 21, 2013.

9. Personal correspondence with Greg Kingen, VP Sales & Marketing, Restaurant Magic Software, September 3, 2013.

10. Lisa Terry. "Building a Better Menu." *Hospitality Technology* (June 2002). www.cbord.com/press/72.pdf. Retrieved September 2009.

11. Karen Sammon, "Guest-focused Restaurant Technologies Should Always Have a Spot at the Table," *Nation's Restaurant News*, 41 (49) (December 10, 2007), p. 22. ABI/Inform Trade and Industry. Retrieved September 2009.

12. Ibid.

13. Personal correspondence with Clyde Dishman. NCR Corporation and www.ncr.com. Retrieved September 2012.

14. Ibid.

15. "Restaurant Reporting and Analytics," NCR, www.ncr.com/products/restaurant/management-software/reporting-analytics.

16. Ibid.

17. Personal correspondence with Ed Rothenberg, November 14, 2012.

18. Federal Trade Commission, *Consumer Fraud and Identity Theft Complaint Data, January–December 2007* (US Federal Trade Commission, February 2008), p. 14, www.ftc.gov/opa/2008/02/fraud.pdf. Retrieved May 31, 2013.

19. Restaurant Manager, an ASI Technology. www.rmpos.com. Retrieved September 2009.

20. Mark G. Haley and Daniel J. Connolly, *The Payment Card Industry Compliance Process for Lodging Establishments* (The American Hotel & Lodging Association, 2008). http://www.ahla.com/uploadedFiles/AHLA/Members_Only/Property_and_Corporate/Property_-_Publications/PCI%20Compliance%20Technology%20Primer.pdf, p. 13.

21. Ibid, pp. 8–9.

22. The author gratefully acknowledges the cooperation and professional courtesy extended by NCR: Clyde Dishman; and Micros Systems: Louise Casamento, Paul Armstrong, and Hope Byers.

23. NCR Corporation brochures.

24. Hamilton Chan, "4 Ways Restaurants Should Use QR Codes," *Mashable* (March 8, 2012), http://mashable.com/2012/03/08/qr-codes-restaurants/. Retrieved on May 22, 2013.

25. Ibid.

26. Jennifer Gregory, "5 Major Benefits of Mobile Payments," *Open Forum* (August 16, 2012). http://www.openforum.com/articles/5-major-benefits-of-mobile-payments/.

27. Cmstext.com, "How It Works" (2012). http://cmstext.com/why-mobile/how-it-works/.

28. Freshtxt.com, "How it Works" (2012). http://www.freshtxt.com/how-it-works/.

29. RTIConnect. www.internetrti.com/software/rticonnect/. Retrieved September 2009.

30. "Manage by Exception to Proactively Control Business Operations," Micros http://www.micros.com/NR/rdonlyres/74E66DF8-78B2-49A6-86C7-64587DAF847A/0/AlertManager2012.pdf. Retrieved May 8, 2013.

PART FIVE

Business Plans, Financing, and Legal Matters

Concept of Panificio Café and Restaurant

Panificio Café and Restaurant is a European bistro. Its owner, Chris Spagnuolo, developed the concept when he was young, based on his grandfather's bakery. Chris attended Syracuse University and traveled to Paris and Rome often. He grew to love the bakeries he visited in Europe.

LOCATION

Panificio Café and Restaurant is located on Charles Street on Beacon Hill, in Boston, Massachusetts. Chris saw a vacancy sign in the window; he decided that the location would be great since it was an underdeveloped area of Charles Street yet it had heavy foot traffic. It was also a commercial and residential area located next to the Charles Street T stop (subway).

Courtesy of Panificio

MENU

Panificio's menu was developed in a number of ways. Some of the items were adapted through the owners (at the time Chris, his brother, and two friends) visiting other restaurants and noting dishes they thought would suit their concept. Some dishes were recipes passed down, like Chris's mother's soups and salads. The menu also adapts to seasonal changes. Chris, who today operates the restaurant on his own, likes to keep the menu fresh with a little French and a little Italian.

PERMITS AND LICENSES

Chris Spagnuolo and his partners obtained their licenses with the help of a lawyer friend of Chris's father. They had to visit the Inspection Service Department in Boston, which comprises five regulatory divisions that administer and enforce building, housing, health, sanitation, and safety regulations mandated by city and state governments. They also obtained licenses at other governmental agencies, including the licensing board and city hall.

MARKETING

Most of the marketing was conducted through word of mouth. When Panificio first opened, the owners handed out business cards, had write-ups in local newspapers, and held various events (parties, catering, etc.).

CHALLENGES

Due to Panificio's location, the major challenge was getting the licenses and permits. In order to operate in this historical district, you have to go through a civic association. The association makes sure that the historical district is preserved, by ensuring that businesses will appeal to the locals and will abide by certain restrictions (no neon signs, specific hours of operation, and so on).

FINANCIAL INFORMATION

Panificio Café and Restaurant is an S-corporation. Annual sales are $1 million. The number of guest covers a week varies due to the nature of the cafe. Some people come in for a muffin and coffee in the morning while others come in for a whole meal during dinner hours. Guest checks average range anywhere from $3 to $23 per person. A breakdown of sales percentages follows.

- Percentage of sales that goes to rent: no more than 7 percent
- Percentage of food sales: 75 percent
- Percentage of beverage sales: 25 percent
- Percentage of profit: 3 to 4 percent

WHAT TURNED OUT DIFFERENT FROM EXPECTED?

It's not all fun and games like you would think. What turned out the most different from what the owner expected was the hours and amount of work he has put into his restaurant. Some weeks he works 60 to 80 hours!

MOST EMBARRASSING MOMENT

Chris says that his most embarrassing moments are when something gets messed up.

ADVICE TO PROSPECTIVE ENTREPRENEURS

The best thing you should do is get a good lawyer and accountant. The lawyer should know about corporations and licenses. You should also do your homework before getting into the business and double-check EVERYTHING!

Learn more about Panificio Café and Restaurant at www.panificioboston.com.

Restaurant Business and Marketing Plans

LEARNING OBJECTIVES

After reading and studying this chapter, you should be able to:

- Describe the various forms of business ownership.

- Discuss the advantages and disadvantages of each form of business.

- Identify the major elements of a business plan.

- Develop a restaurant business plan.

- Conduct a market assessment.

- Discuss the importance of the four *P*s of the marketing mix.

- Describe some promotional ideas for a restaurant.

Courtesy of Panificio

Before embarking on the complex task of setting up any business, especially a restaurant, it is essential to do a *business plan*. This will help increase the probability of the restaurant's success. As with any plan, the more work that goes into it, the better informed the owner/operator and the financial backers are regarding the feasibility and viability of the proposed restaurant. Some operators find that after preparing a detailed business plan, the numbers do not add up—in other words, it is unlikely that the restaurant would be successful. That's okay! All they have lost is the time and effort put into the plan; they have not lost their shirt.

Restaurants, like many other businesses, are experiencing extreme challenges in these difficult times. Yet, for the fearless there are opportunities. It is possible to get into an existing restaurant location with very little money down by negotiating with the landlord and creditors/suppliers for more favorable terms.[1]

Deciding on the concept, location, menu, and decor of a restaurant is a lot more fun than doing the paperwork.

A new restaurant operation has a choice of legal entities under which to operate. These are *sole proprietorships* (individual ownerships) or *partnerships* (with one or several co-owners, but with only a general partner or partners making decisions and legally responsible if things go wrong). There is also the corporation, a legal entity unto itself. An S corporation is a type of corporation that has advantages of both a corporation and sole proprietorship.[2]

A lawyer and an accountant should aid in setting up a business to prevent future problems. Laws—state, federal, and local—must be considered. If you need a liquor license, get it before opening your restaurant. Health and fire department approval and permits must be obtained. Your lawyer or accountant can advise you concerning tax matters. What follows is general information; details and possible changes in laws should be checked with an experienced accountant and lawyer.

The decisions made regarding legal and tax matters are crucial to the restaurant and its owners. It is advisable to hire the best lawyer and accountant you can afford—ones with experience in dealing with restaurants and ones who come well recommended by several sources.

What Business Entity Is Best?

How should a restaurant be operated—directly by the owner, as a partnership with other owners, or as a corporation?

Under the law, all businesses are operated as proprietorships, partnerships, or corporations. Business ventures have a choice of these entities, each with different tax consequences, advantages, and disadvantages. At one point, one business entity provides more advantages; at another time, a different form may be better.

Always consider that one of four things will happen to the restaurant: It will be sold, it will be merged with another company, it will fail, or it will pass to heirs. Also consider that members of a family-operated restaurant will almost certainly disagree at times and that spouses may divorce. Almost inevitably, one person must make final decisions, and some of these will be wrong. Divided responsibility and authority can be dangerous, although input by others can result in a better decision.

The choice of entity affects:

■ Federal income taxes
■ Liability to creditors and other persons

- The legal and/or personal relationships among the owners (if more than one exists)
- The legal life and/or transferal of the business entity

In addition to the choice of a form of business entity, certain other tax choices and elections are made prior to filing the new entity's first federal income tax return. We will examine these in this chapter.

SOLE PROPRIETORSHIP

A sole proprietorship is both the simplest and the most prevalent form of business organization.[3] In the case of the sole proprietor, an attorney or accountant is not needed, though it is better to consult with both. In most states, the new proprietor is required to register the business name (if different from his or her own). From an income tax standpoint, only a Schedule C as part of Form 1040 need be filed as part of the federal income tax returns.

As sole proprietor, the restaurant operator does not draw a salary for federal income tax purposes. He or she reports as income the profit for the year or deducts as an expense any loss for the year. For tax purposes, the proprietor is not an employee; however, his or her income is subject to self-employment tax. The rate is slightly higher than the rate for Social Security taxes, with the same limitation on earnings subject to tax as is the case for an employee. This tax is paid along with the federal income tax. If both husband and wife work in a sole proprietorship, each pays the self-employment tax, up to the total income or the tax limitations, whichever is less.

An individual taxpayer normally reports on a calendar-year basis for federal income tax purposes. Consequently, each year, all of the earnings of the restaurant are taxed in addition to investment income and income earned by a spouse.

Advantages of the Sole Proprietorship   Advantages to being a sole proprietor, as opposed to doing business in corporate form, include these:

- It is simple. You are required, for tax purposes, to keep a formal set of books. (This is highly recommended for financial purposes even when it is not required for tax purposes.) The tax laws and regulations require you to keep those records that will enable you to accurately report your income.
- Because all the earnings are yours, there is no problem about setting a reasonable salary that could be questioned when doing business in the corporate form.
- Funds can be withdrawn from the business, subject to their availability, without tax consequences.
- The business can be discontinued or sold with minimal tax consequences, compared with those arising in connection with the corporate form.

Courtesy of Ingrid Croce

Ingrid Croce, who began as a sole proprietor, outside one of her restaurants. Croce was a pioneer in the development of San Diego's Gaslamp district.

Courtesy of Cohn Restaurant Group

David and Leslie Cohn at one of their restaurants in San Diego's Gaslamp district.

Disadvantages of the Sole Proprietorship Tax disadvantages in doing business as a sole proprietor include these:

- You cannot be a participant in your company's qualified pension or profit-sharing plans. A sole proprietor can set up a Keogh retirement plan for self and employees; however, law limits the amount.
- The owner's liability for all of the restaurant's debts and any tort liability to third parties is unlimited. Theoretically, owners limit their liability by incorporating; however, in many cases—in fact, most—the owners are called upon to endorse or guarantee the corporation's liabilities.
- The sole proprietorship has no legal existence apart from the owner. The death or incapacity of the owner has severe legal implications and results in the termination of the business, unless it has been willed to another person or persons. Often, the willed property must pass through probate, which can be time-consuming and costly in terms of legal fees.

PARTNERSHIP

A partnership is legally defined under the Uniform Partnership Act as any venture where two or more persons endeavor to make a profit.[4] There are two kinds of partnerships: general and limited. General partnerships have complete liability but full management rights. *Limited partnerships*, however, share limited liability with no services performed.

When two or more individuals plan to enter the restaurant business together, they may wish to employ the partnership form of doing business. The tax consequences of doing business as a partnership are basically the same as those for a sole proprietorship. The partnership, however, does file an annual tax return on Form 1065. This is an information return only, as the partnership pays no federal income tax. The partnership return requires a beginning and ending balance sheet, together with a reconciliation of each partner's capital account for the year. Consequently, formal bookkeeping must be done. Also, each partner receives a Schedule K-1 of the partnership tax return form and reports his or her respective income or loss from the Schedule K-1 on the individual tax return.

Partners do not draw deductible salaries from partnerships for tax purposes. Therefore, if a partner receives a salary from the partnership, no payroll taxes are deducted. At the end of the year, each partner reports his or her salary and share of the profits (or losses) on personal tax return Form 1040. The partnership entity is quite flexible for tax purposes and lends itself to situations whereby one partner supplies the capital and another supplies only services or services plus a lesser amount of capital. It is possible to structure almost any type of business arrangement within a partnership as long as the tax consequences are consistent with the business realities.

The partnership, as an entity, has the same problems of legal liability as the sole proprietorship. In addition, each partner can create debts for the partnership. All partners must understand the dangers of this arrangement. Each partnership interest is an asset that can, under certain circumstances, be subject to the legal claims of an individual partner's creditors or other claimants.

Partnerships can be expected to dissolve someday. Death, disagreement, ill health, and other contingencies can make the perfect partnership into a perfect nightmare. Spouses setting up in the restaurant business as partners can see the business fall apart as they quarrel or divorce. In states with community property laws, each divorced spouse is entitled to half the assets, which might mean a forced sale of the restaurant. Partnerships usually work well when things go well. With losses, partners quickly see each other at fault.

Partnerships can be set up in a number of ways. The terms of the partnership may limit partners' liability for debts. Limited partners have no voice in the restaurant operation; managing partners are given this responsibility. There may be dozens of limited partners, with only one or two managing partners.

RESTAURANT AS A CORPORATION

A corporation is a legal entity similar to a person in that it can borrow, buy, and conduct business, and must pay state and federal taxes on profits. Corporations provide limited liability for the owner. Corporation owners cannot be sued for the debts of the corporation unless they personally guarantee them. Working through a corporation offers advantages and disadvantages.

Deciding whether to incorporate often depends on the amount of insurance coverage available. If insurance coverage is available, a restaurant may decide not to incorporate because the insurance will cover and limit the sole proprietor's liability, which might otherwise cause financial ruin in the event of a mishap or lawsuit. In certain circumstances, however, insurance protection may not be available or affordable. In these cases incorporation might be worthwhile because it will provide limited liability.

When incorporating, the first step always should be to consult an attorney. It might cost a bit more than doing it yourself, but in the long run securing legal advice should ensure that all necessary requirements have been met.

The second step should be to select a state in which to incorporate. The state is important because regulations, incorporation costs, and other fees, taxes, and ownership rights will vary.

The big disadvantage of corporate ownership of a restaurant is that it opens the way for double taxation. Profits of the corporation are taxed and then passed on to the owners, where the profits are again subject to taxation as individual income. To avoid double taxation, an S corporation (explained below) can be used.

In setting up a corporation, the entrepreneur must keep in mind that to maintain control, he or she must own 51 percent of the stock. Anything less could mean absolute lack of control and even expulsion from management. Stock in a corporation can be sold to the general public or to individuals.

A corporation is a separate entity and is incorporated under the laws of the state in which it has its principal place of business. The rules for incorporation vary from state to state. The owners of a corporation are called shareholders or stockholders. They elect a board of directors, which has the final responsibility of operating the restaurant. Theoretically, the directors elect corporate officers. The directors can, under certain circumstances, have legal liability to third parties for their actions. The corporation has a legal existence apart from its owners, the shareholders. The latter are not responsible for the corporation's debts, provided they have fully paid for their investment in the company's capital stock and have not guaranteed its debts.

Before deciding to incorporate, the investors must make certain business and tax decisions that will have a vital effect on the future of the business. How much of the investment will be paid into the corporation? A portion may be paid in as capital stock and the balance may be loaned, to be repaid when the company has sufficient funds. From a tax standpoint, placing funds in the corporation as a loan is more advantageous than is stock. The repayment of a loan is tax free, whereas the repayment of stock is taxed as a dividend to the extent of the company's after-tax profits. Interest paid on a loan is tax deductible to the corporation, whereas dividends paid are treated as distribution of profits and are not deductible.

Enough must be paid in as stock to satisfy creditors. If the stock amount is too small in relationship to the amount of shareholder loans, the Internal Revenue Service (IRS) may claim that all of the money paid in is capital and that all repayments are taxable dividends to the extent of corporate after-tax profits. A "thin corporation" has the minimum allowable as capital, the maximum as debt.

Because the corporation is a separate legal entity, the restaurant operator is an employee of the corporation. His or her salary is subject to all payroll taxes, just as that of any other employee is. The operator may also be covered for group insurance. Other corporate *fringe benefits* can be arranged, such as medical expense reimbursement, sick pay, and pension and profit-sharing plans. What is a reasonable salary for shareholder employees? Shareholder employees naturally want to avoid double taxation, and the profits paid as salary to the management/stockholder must be "reasonable." If not, the "unreasonable" portion is treated as a dividend and is not deductible by the corporation. The corporate form of business entity should not be used without legal and accounting advice.

S Corporation An S corporation provides for a remarkable use of the corporation: It permits the business entity to operate as a corporation but allows it to avoid paying corporation taxes. It also avoids a double tax upon liquidation due to built-in gains from appreciation of assets.

If the corporation owners do not want to accumulate after-tax income in the corporation or if its shareholders are in low tax brackets or have personal tax losses, an S corporation is ideal. In addition to passing income to their shareholders, such corporations can pass through operating losses that can be reported pro rata by the owners and deducted up to the cost or adjusted basis of their stock and loans. This is an excellent arrangement for the first years of the company's existence, if it experiences losses. Once the company begins to operate at a profit, the S corporation election can be ended and the corporation can be taxed at regular corporate rates. The S corporation election is extremely useful in a family restaurant. If there are dependent children or parents, an S corporation offers a tax advantage. Gifts of the restaurant's stock can be made to these dependents who, when they receive the dividends, are taxed according to their income bracket. Corporation taxes are avoided and profits from the restaurant are taxed at the low rates experienced by the dependents.

The IRS requires that corporate officers draw a fair salary so that the company's earnings are not overstated; thereafter, the net income is allocated in proportion to the stock ownership. One disadvantage of an S corporation is that shareholders of the corporation may not deduct benefits, such as medical disability and life insurance premiums, of more than 2 percent of their annual salary. A comparison of the various forms of corporate structures is given in Figure 14.1.

Corporate Structure	Ownership Rules	Tax Treatment	Liability	Pros and Cons
Sole Proprietorship	One owner	Pass-through federal tax entity[a]	Unlimited personal liability for business debts	Is easy to set up but leaves your personal finances at risk. Plus, you miss out on all kinds of business deductions
S Corporation	Up to 75 shareholders; only one basic class stock; slight flexibility on voting rights	Pass-through federal tax entity[a]	Limited	Is easy to set up but limits your financing options later on
Corporation	Unlimited number of shareholders; no limits on stock classes or voting arrangements	Dividend income gets taxed at corporate and shareholder levels; losses and deductions stay at corporate level	Limited	Can be costly from a tax perspective but is investor friendly
Limited Liability Company	Unlimited number of members; flexible membership arrangements, with voting rights and income divided as desired	Pass-through federal tax entity[a]	Limited	Has lots of advantages but makes investors leery, which could make financing the deal dicey; cost of switching forms from S or C corporation status is generally prohibitive
Partnership	Two or more owners	Pass-through federal tax entity[a]; flexibility about profit-and-loss allocations among partners	Personal assets of any operating partner at risk from business creditors[b]	Allows lots of room to play with tax benefits, but in a general partnership, that personal liability can be scary
Limited Liability Partnership	Two or more owners	Pass-through federal tax entity[a]; some flexibility about ownership arrangements	Limited	Has many advantages as an alternative to traditional partnerships; is easy to switch to but is a new form and hasn't gained acceptance in all states

[a] In a pass-through tax entity, income and losses "pass through" to owners and are taxed by the IRS at the personal level.
[b] In a limited partnership variation, limited partners' liability can be restricted to the amount of the original investment.

FIGURE 14.1 Comparison of corporate forms.

Buy–Sell Agreement with Partners

In the sale of a business, a buy–sell agreement preserves continuity of ownership in the business. It also ensures that the buyer as well as the seller is treated fairly. A buy–sell agreement is made up of several legal clauses in a business that can control these business decisions:

- Who can buy a departing partner's or shareholder's share of the business
- What events will trigger a buyout
- What price will be paid for a partner's share

In closely held corporations and with partnerships, it is wise to arrange a buy–sell agreement with the co-stockholders or partners. Such agreements specify a price or a way of arriving at a price if a sale becomes necessary. This situation arises when owners die or, for some reason, want out. The buy–sell deal sets the tax value that the IRS will accept, even though the fair market value of the stock at the valuation date is actually higher. A buy–sell agreement can be funded by life insurance on the partners or stockholders. This means that the business carries the cost of the life insurance and collects the proceeds if the owner dies.

Setting an agreed-on price or an agreed-on way of pricing removes much of the potential for conflict among the owners when the time comes that one or more of the owners wants to sell or when an estate owning part of the restaurant must be settled.

Legal Aspects of Doing Business

Many legal requirements must be addressed when setting up a restaurant business. In California, for example, these are the required steps:

I. Form a business entity.
  A. Sole proprietorship
  B. General partnership
  C. Limited partnership
  D. Subchapter S Corporation
  E. Corporation
II. Identify necessary permits and licenses.
  A. Local requirements
    1. Business licenses: county clerk's office
    2. Tax registration (county or city)
    3. Police, health, and fire department permits
  B. State requirements: check with your state. (For example, in California, the Department of Economic and Business Development has a book titled *California License Handbook,* available from 1120 N. Street, Sacramento, CA 95814.)
    1. Liquor license
    2. Any other state requirements

C. Federal requirements

III. Identify local restrictions on proposed business licenses.
   A. Zoning requirements (City Planning Commission)
   B. Building inspections

IV. Obtain environmental or similar permit (new for coastal areas, shorelines, floodways, and wildlife habitats) as needed.

V. Obtain state sales tax permit. Obtain from Board of Equalization Publication BT-741-1 ("Your Privileges and Obligations as a Seller") and related regulations, including 1698–1700.

VI. Determine applicability of employer registrations.
   A. Obtain federal employer identification number (complete Form SS-4 at Social Security or IRS office).
   B. Register with the State Employment Development Department (relates to unemployment insurance).

VII. Get insurance.
   A. Obtain mandatory workers' compensation insurance.
   B. Join employers' reciprocal exchange plans. Buy insurance policy from broker or state comprehensive insurance fund.
   C. If self-insured, you need consent. Write to Director of Industrial Relations, Self-Insurance Plans, Room 5043, 107 S. Broadway, Los Angeles, CA 90012.
   D. Dram shop insurance
   E. Real property insurance
   F. Auto insurance

VIII. Comply with relevant statutes and regulations with respect to employees' wages.
   A. Comply with State Industrial Welfare Commission orders with respect to employee wages, hours, and working conditions (post required posters).

IX. Fulfill occupational and health requirements.
   A. Federal OSHA replaced some state regulations with comprehensive bottom-line regulations.

X. Assess applicability of other antidiscrimination laws.
   A. Title VII if 15 or more employees comply (no discrimination in employment)
   B. Executive Order 11246: If you will have government contracts, then they must comply; affirmative action program required.
   C. Federal Equal Pay Act
   D. Federal Age Discrimination Act
   E. State Fair Employment Practices Act

XI. Check for eligibility for government assistance.
   A. Small Business Administration—special loans
   B. Minority Business Development Agency—assistance with obtaining loans
   C. Others: Purchase *A Survey of Small Business Programs* from US Government Printing Office.

   D. State programs: Purchase *A Guide to Starting a Business* in a local bookstore.

XII. File fictitious business name.

   A. File with county clerk in your county within 40 days of purchase of business.

   B. Publish in paper on county.

   C. Sign Affidavit of Publishing.

XIII. Meet posting requirements.

   A. Sales tax permit—conspicuous place

   B. Employment Development Department—re: unemployment (from EDD office)

   C. Payday and right to vote

   D. State OSHA notice—from Department of Industrial Affairs

   E. Wage and Hour poster—from Department of Industrial Relations, Division of Labor Standard Enforcement

   F. State Fair Employment Law poster—from Department of Fair Employment and Housing

   G. US Equal Opportunity Commission and Age Disclosure Law posters from Public Information Assistance, Equal Employment Opportunity Commission (EEOC) as required by your state

XIV. Obtain and arrange tax return filings.

   A. Sales and use taxes

      1. Collect or obtain exemption or resale certificate with each sale.

      2. File quarterly returns.

      3. Keep required records—see Regulation 1698.

   B. Federal and state employment taxes (Read Circular E.)

      1. Federal income tax, FICA, and FUTA (Federal Unemployment Tax Act) withhold, file records

      2. Federal self-employment tax, if appropriate

      3. State employment tax and contribution includes income tax, SDI, and unemployment insurance tax

   C. Corporate income tax

   D. Local property taxes

   E. Excise, license, or privilege taxes probably not applicable

XV. Learn reporting and notice procedure in event of employee injury or exposure to toxic substances. (Read "Recordkeeping and Reporting Requirements under [your state] OSHA" from Department of Industrial Relations, Division of Labor Statistics and Research.)

It is essential to obtain these licenses and permits before opening a restaurant. Without them, costly delays in opening will occur. Protect yourself by making your lease contingent on these licenses and permits being granted. This is particularly important when taking over an existing restaurant, because although the previous owner may have had the necessary licenses and permits, the authorities seize the opportunity of change of ownership to enforce codes. This can be costly. We suggest you consult with the requisite authorities in your area.

STATE REGISTRATION

Plans to open a new business should be discussed with the secretary of state's office—each state has its own regulations. This office can explain the state's legal requirements and give information about possible further local and county offices for additional registration. There is a fee of about $100 for registering a new business. This normally includes an investigation to ensure that your business name is not currently in use. In addition, it may be necessary to file and publish a fictitious name statement in a general circulation newspaper. Periodic updates are necessary to legally protect the name.

Most states have income tax on wages; therefore, all necessary information should be obtained, such as tax guides and tables. The State Department of Employee Compensation must also be contacted for information on regulations and filing procedures. Cities generally require a permit to operate a business. These permits must be obtained from the city's business department.

SALES TAX

Congratulations, you get to be a tax collector. You need to register the new business with the state revenue or taxation agency and find out the collection procedures for your state—of course, they are all different. Most states require an advance deposit or bond posted against future taxes to be collected. Sales tax is collected on the retail price paid by the guest. Fortunately, you don't have to pay tax when purchasing raw food products from wholesalers. However, you must give your tax permit number when ordering and sign a tax release card for the wholesaler's records.

THE PATIENT PROTECTION AND AFFORDABLE HEALTH CARE ACT (PPACA), AND OTHER REGULATIONS

The restaurateur has always had to deal with government regulation and laws. There have been numerous laws written to protect the guest from unscrupulous inn and tavern owners. Back in the 1800s, some inn and tavern owners were known to collude with robbers and thieves.[5] Although times have changed drastically, state and federal governments are still creating lists of laws and regulations every year for hospitality owners to adhere to. "Many states delegate the responsibility of regulating inns and restaurants to administrative bodies or agencies such as a state hotel and restaurant commission, or a state board of health."[6] What has often been missed by government is that the small business owner makes up about 90 percent of the entire hospitality industry. Most small business owners have admitted that many of these changing laws are hard to keep up with and can be extremely cumbersome on their day-to-day activities.

Perhaps the most important topic affecting restaurants is The Patient Protection and Affordable Health Care Act (PPACA), which takes effect January 2014. Large restaurant chains are affected more than small independent restaurants. Darden said staffing changes are "just one of the many things we are evaluating, to help us address the cost implications of health care reform will have on our business. There are still many unanswered questions regarding the health care regulations, and we simply do not have enough information to make any decisions at this time."[7]

Analysts say many other companies, including some quick service chains, are considering employing fewer full-timers because of key features of the Affordable Care

Act scheduled to go into effect in January of 2014. Under that law, companies employing more than 50 people must provide affordable health insurance to employees working an average of at least 30 hours per week or face thousands of dollars in fines.

Smaller operators are likely to implement similar hourly programs, so no new jobs will be created and the ones that are created will come with no health-care benefits.[8]

These health-care requirements for hospitality businesses can be very costly. Fortunately for the small business owner, the business will not have to adhere to this new health-care mandate if it has fewer than 50 employees.[9] But, employers with more than 50 employees who work more than 30 hours per week will be required to provide health coverage or pay a fine. Darden Restaurants, with 45,000 employees, tried cutting back on full-time staffing at some restaurants but, after a public outcry, Darden decided not to change staffing in 2014 when PPACA begins.[10]

Health plan requirements are likely to include more benefits than those currently offered by restaurants. The employees' share of insurance premiums cannot be more than 9.5 percent of their income. Many companies are still trying to deal with several unknowns, such as the number of people who decide to take health care insurance versus going into the exchanges at the state level. Also, several states have yet to decide if they will accept federal government money or opt out.[11]

Restaurants and hotels may also have to deal with other regulations and laws:

- Paid sick leave requirements
- Nutrition labeling requirements
- Smoking laws
- Depreciation of restaurant improvements
- Drink taxes
- Special event permits

State and federal laws have created very strict drunk-driving laws that have affected the liquor sales The National Transportation Safety Board recommends that all states require breathalyzer ignition locks, called ignition interlock devices, for convicted drunk drivers. Many states already require the device. The American Beverage Institute opposes such measures, even though many hospitality professionals believe this would be a public relations disaster.[12]

Other watchdogs of the government's overzealous nature include John Penrose, formerly England's Ministry of Tourism. He challenged many of England's existing and proposed laws that inhibit the hospitality and tourism industry. His "red tape challenge," for example, successfully reduced labeling laws from 34 to 14. His easy-to-access website encouraged many hospitality and tourism professionals to report any regulations that they believe need to be scrapped.[13] Penrose's main focus was to try to bring to light the problems that ". . . can be solved without intrusive government regulations."[14]

Business Plan

Gathering information and writing up a good business plan take time. However, as already stated, the more effort that goes into the business plan, the more likely you are to be successful. Following the headings as a guide, begin to fill in the information specific to your restaurant. As we progress through the book, you will learn more and should find it easier to complete your own plan. Remember, it's okay to ask for advice.

A good business plan will not only improve the chances of operational success, but also assist in obtaining financing, in communicating to potential investors, and in serving operational purposes.

Today, sustainability is a key ingredient in a restaurants business plan. More and more restaurant guests are not only interested in but expecting sustainable restaurants. Joining the National Restaurant Association's Conserve program and the Green Restaurant Association's certification programs shows a commitment to sustainable restaurant operations, although restaurants should be careful to avoid *greenwashing*—that is, engaging in public relations tactics (such as joining programs) in order to portray the company as being more engaged in environmentally friendly practices than it really is.

Business plans begin with an executive summary, which outlines the elements of the plan. A sample outline of headings for a business plan follows. The cover sheet also should have the name of the business, the logo or trademark (if any), the current or proposed address of the restaurant, the restaurant telephone number, the owner's name and associates' names, and their qualifications. In addition, it should list the name of the company, the addresses and telephone numbers of the executives, and an introductory statement. Each of the elements needs to be fully written up, and that takes research and critical thinking. Logically, the plan expects the operator to assess where the business is now and where it should be in 5 to 10 years—and of course, how it is going to get there. The headings for a business plan are as follows:

Cover Sheet:
  Executive summary
  Statement of purpose
  Table of contents
  Name and legal structure
Description of the Business:
  Management philosophy:
    vision, mission, goals,
    strategies
  Type of organization
  Management qualifica-
    tions, experience, and
    capabilities
  Business insurance
Description of the Concept, Li-
censes, and Lease:
  Concept
  Menu
  Menu pricing
  Liquor license, health and fire
    permits
  Business license
  Lease

Market Analysis and Strategy:
  Description of target market
  Demographics, psychograph-
    ics, lifestyles
  Market potential (size, rate of
    growth)
Competitive Analysis:
  Number of competitors
  Strengths, weaknesses,
    opportunities, and threats
    (SWOT) analysis
  Location, ease of access and
    parking
  Sales and market share
  Nature of competition
  Potential new restaurant
    competition
Pricing Strategy:
  Menu and beverage list
    pricing
  Location analysis
  Description of the area

Commercial/residential
profile
Traffic flows
Accessibility
Advertising and Promotional
Campaign:
Objectives
Techniques
Target audience, means of
communication schedule
Other Information:
Schedule for growth
Financing schedule
Schedule for return on
investment
Financial Data:
Sales figures
Sources of funding
Capital equipment
Proposed restaurant balance
sheet
Projected income statements
First year—detail by month
Second year—detail by
quarter
Third year—detail by quarter
Existing restaurant balance sheet

Previous three years' income
statements
Previous three years' cash
flow statements
Previous three years' tax
returns
Breakeven analysis
Appendices:
Sales projections
Organization chart
Copies of resources, tax re-
turns (last five years), and
financial statements of all
principles
Job descriptions
Résumés of management
team
Legal documents
Leases
Licenses
Firm price quotations
Insurance contracts
Sample menu
Furniture, fixtures, and equip-
ment (FF&E)
Floor plan, letters of intent
Anything else that is
relevant[15]

Peter
Drucker,
the highly
regarded management
scholar and author,
stated, "The only valid
definition of business
purpose is to create a
customer." In the restau-
rant business, we should
add, "and to keep a cus-
tomer returning."

It is important
to remember that the
guest pays the bills and
determines the level of
profit—not the owner,
manager, accountant,
banker, or controller.

People do not purchase features, they purchase benefits, and each person purchases only those that specifically satisfy his or her personal or professional needs,
wants, desires, hopes, aspirations, and dreams. We are really in the business of
motivating people to purchase those benefits that satisfy their specific, and often
changing, needs and wants.

Peter Drucker said we must frequently ask ourselves, "What business am I in?"
Are we in the service business, the production business, the business of making
incredible memories, or the entertainment business? For restaurants, the answer is
yes to all of the above. The food and service aspect predominates, however, so we
need to determine our guests' needs and wants.

A business plan will help to shed light on areas you will need to research
further. Some questions you may want to ask yourself while developing a business
plan include:

- What is the forecast outlook for the restaurant sector and market?
- Who will your guests be, and how many of them are there?
- What kind of people are they?

- Where do they live?
- Will you be offering what they want and when they want it?
- What type of insurance will you need?
- What is a ballpark figure of your overhead expenses?
- How will your restaurant compare with your competitors?
- What type of promotional tools will you use?

Answering these questions and more helps reduce business risks.

We know we're in the restaurant business, so the next step is to come up with a mission statement (discussed in Chapter 3). The mission generally does not change. The *goals*, however, are reviewed as often as necessary. Goals should be established for each key operational area (e.g., sales, food, service, beverage, labor costs, and so on).

Strategies or action plans typically include deciding who is going to do what and by when and in what order for the organization to reach its strategic goals.[16] They are more specific than goals and are generally short term. Strategies are specific as to the date by which they are to be achieved and how much should be achieved. Based on strategies, a detailed action plan with individual responsibilities should be implemented.

A large factor in restaurant failure is the naive belief that if food, service, price, and atmosphere are good, guests are certain to appear and will return in the future. It is assumed that potential guests will want what is offered and are waiting. Marketing makes no such assumption.

This chapter explores the meaning and ramifications of the restaurant business and marketing plans. It also delineates marketing practices that, if followed, can help ensure success and avoid the financial costs and heartaches of failure.

Restaurant marketing is based on a *marketing philosophy* that patterns the way management and ownership have decided to relate to guests, employees, purveyors, and the general public in terms of fairness, honesty, and moral conduct, needed in part because of greater importance being placed on the ethical and moral conduct of business. Building on the marketing philosophy, the techniques and practices of marketing include the efforts by managements to match what a particular group of people (the target market) wants in terms of restaurant food, service, price, and atmosphere.

Marketing is finding out what guests want and providing it at a fair price that leaves a reasonable profit. Marketing asks would-be operators to ask themselves, "Who will be my guests? Why will they choose my restaurant? Where will they come from, and why will they come back?"

Marketing assumes that guests change, that they will want new menu items, new atmospheres, and, sometimes, new service. Just look at McDonald's. Its new restaurant designs look almost like a Starbucks, and menu items like Asian salad and premium coffee are beating all sales expectations.

> The old joke sums it up well. "Do you know how to make a small fortune in the restaurant business? Start with a large fortune!" To be successful, a restaurant needs great food, service, and atmosphere. Some restaurants get by with mediocre service and atmosphere. Few survive with inferior food.

Courtesy of Childs Restaurant Group

A marketing director prepares a section of the marketing plan.

Marketing asks operators to expect change in the marketplace and to position or reposition the restaurant to meet those changes.

Many of us have been tempted to open a restaurant at one time or another. Perhaps Grandma passed down some good recipes and a desire to cook. Whatever the reason, the restaurant business is easy to get into because, apart from finances, there are no real barriers to entry.

Yet the restaurant business is complex. There are few businesses in which customers rely on all their senses to experience the product. In the restaurant business, our customers see, smell, touch, taste, and hear our offerings.

The Difference between Marketing and Sales

It is important to distinguish among the terms *marketing, sales*, and *merchandising*. *Marketing* is the broad concept that includes the other two. Marketing implies determining who will patronize a restaurant (the market or markets) and what they want in it—its design, atmosphere, menu, and service. Marketing implies constant review of patrons and the identification of possible others. It is an ongoing effort that matches patron with restaurant, matches patrons' desires with what the restaurant has to offer, and identifies people who would like the same thing. Marketing gets into the psyche of current and potential patrons. Once it is known what patrons want and what the restaurant has to offer, the two can be brought together.

Marketing is about solving guest problems. Identifying and solving problems is not easy. Changing lifestyles lead to different wants and needs of guests, which vary from location to location. Increasingly, people are looking for more casual and convenient eating options.

The ideal restaurant experience is different for everyone; some diners look for elegance, some for convenience, all for value. Despite these differing expectations, surveys indicate that the quality of food is of primary importance to customers when selecting a restaurant.

All restaurant guests, however, have one basic urge: hunger. In addition, they may also want entertainment, and they will seek a restaurant with a stimulating environment. Some may want recognition, so they will go to a restaurant that provides the feeling of importance that comes with recognition.

Happy guests result in free marketing known as word-of-mouth advertising, but you may have to ask them to spread the word. There is nothing wrong with responding to praise with something like, "I really appreciate hearing that and I hope you will tell others." One way to kick-start word-of-mouth marketing is to become an active member in your community. Get out there and meet the people in your location. Use social media, discussed later in this chapter, to your advantage. The more people that get to know you, the better.

Marketing focuses on the needs of the buyer; sales focuses on the needs of the seller. This distinction is important because restaurants often approach marketing with a sales mentality, which is a mistake.

Sales is part of marketing. Sales efforts are the activities that stimulate the patron to want what the restaurant offers. Selling is often thought of as the actions of restaurant employees that influence patrons after they have arrived at the restaurant.

The sales mentality exists when the seller thinks only of her or his needs—that is, pushing a menu item on the guest. With this mentality, few guests would return to the restaurant.

Closely related to sales are advertising, promotion, and public relations. The three have similar objectives. Advertising is purchased in newspapers, radio, TV, websites, or similar businesses. Public relations is not. Public relations are efforts to make the public favor the restaurant without resorting to paid advertising. Promotion is further elaborated on later in this chapter.

Marketing Planning and Strategy

Every *marketing plan* must have realistic *goals* for guest satisfaction, market share, sales, and costs while leaving a reasonable profit margin. A marketing plan is a "written document that describes your advertising and marketing efforts for the coming year; it includes a statement of the marketing situation, a discussion of target markets and company positioning, and a description of the marketing mix you intend to use to reach your marketing goals."[17]

Goals for *market share* and sales:

It's hard to calculate a restaurant's market share, yet we need to have a good idea of the market size and opportunities before investing our time and resources. It works like this: If you think that a market has room for your concept—let's say, casual Italian—you must have checked that there are few, if any, restaurants of a similar type in your location, so logically you would get 100 percent (or close to that) of the market looking for that type of restaurant. However, we all know that there are few markets with no competition of one sort or another. To determine the fair market share (the average number of guests who would, if all other things were equal, eat at any of the competing restaurants), we must divide the number of potential guests in a catchment area by the number of competing restaurants. Figure 14.2 shows 5,000 potential guests. If they all decided to eat Italian, we'd all be in trouble! But let's say that there were 10 Italian restaurants in the catchment area; we would expect a fair market share of 500 guests.

In reality, we know this does not happen. For various reasons, one restaurant becomes more popular. The number of guests at this and the other restaurants is called the actual market share. Figure 14.3 shows an example of the actual market share that competing restaurants receive.

Restaurant sales goals are the most important thing. Everything depends on sales, as all the costs are deducted from the sales to leave a profit, one hopes.

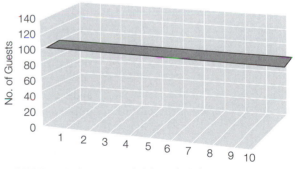

FIGURE 14.2 A restaurant's fair market share.

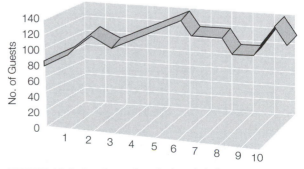

FIGURE 14.3 A restaurant's actual market share.

For start-up restaurants, sales goals are set, as realistically as possible, based on anticipated guest counts and average guest checks; these are discussed and sample forms are available in Chapter 14. Please take a moment to look at the "Budgeting" section, which includes forecasting sales.

Back to goals for *market share* and sales. After careful consideration, we set a market share goal of being the leader in the market segment with an actual market share average of 540 guests, meaning that each of the other competitive restaurants will have fewer guests (an average of 460 guests). After all the weekly and monthly periods are added, a final total is arrived at, and sales goals are set at $1 million. Other goals are set for each of the key operating areas: cleanliness, product quality, service, guest satisfaction, key ratios, and price.

We all realize that it is critical not only to set goals but also to develop strategies regarding how the goals will be met. For each goal there may be several strategies. For example:

> **Goal:** To improve guest satisfaction score from 78 percent to 85 percent by December 1, 20XX.

Realistically, managers would examine the scores to determine the areas of weakness and develop a plan. If service scored lower than acceptable, for example, these strategies would be in order:

Strategies:
1. Managers to determine that all staff members know the service levels expected of them. If not, managers will inform staff, show them by example, and then have them do the task.
2. Training: Managers and supervisors to hold 5- to 10-minute training sessions prior to each shift.
3. Managers and supervisors observe the service levels given by serving staff and later bring to the attention of the staff member any examples of service improvements needed.

Another goal might be to increase the average check by $2 at dinner. The strategy to reach this goal is to improve suggestive sales training.

Goals and strategies are set for all areas of the restaurant; the menu and the quality of each food item along with the service and ambience are all part of the marketing of a restaurant.

Another marketing technique is *SWOT analysis*, which stands for *strengths*, *weaknesses*, *opportunities*, and *threats*. A SWOT analysis is a simple framework for generating strategic alternatives from a situational analysis.[18] Strengths and weaknesses focus on internal factors and can, over time, be controlled by management. Opportunities and threats are external factors. Obviously, strengths and opportunities are issues that affect a company in a positive way, while weaknesses and threats have a negative impact. Remember the old song "Accentuate the positive and eliminate the negative"? Well, that's exactly what marketing managers seek to do. Figure 14.4 illustrates SWOT analysis.

	Internal	External
Positive	Strengths	Opportunities
Negative	Weaknesses	Threats

FIGURE 14.4 SWOT analysis.

Marketing strategy will also position the restaurant in relation to competition regarding price, the food and service offered, atmosphere, and convenience. The marketing strategy needs to conform to the circumstances of the restaurant. For example, a specific market entry strategy is appropriate for a new restaurant concept entering an existing market. We would need to find a competitive advantage based on the four Ps: price, product, place, and promotion.

In taking over an existing restaurant, the goal could be market share. Any one or a combination of tactics could do this. For example, price reduction and heavy local advertising might achieve the strategy's goal.

Marketing strategy is the way the restaurateur accomplishes the goals set for the restaurant. One of the goals could be to increase the number of guests by 10 percent; this would be achieved by means of targeted flyers of the restaurant menu featuring certain dishes. The flyer could be distributed in selected postal ZIP codes.

The strategy is the game plan for attaining determined goals. The key ingredient in any marketing initiative is the marketing plan, which helps focus the marketing and directs it toward the target market. The marketing plan analyzes the marketplace, the competition, and the strengths and weaknesses of the existing or proposed restaurant. See Figure 14.5 for an illustration of the planning process.

FIGURE 14.5 Marketing planning sequence.

Market Assessment, Demand, Potential, and Competition Analysis

MARKET ASSESSMENT AND MARKET DEMAND

By assessing the characteristics of the marketplace, we gain perspective on the operation being planned. The assessment provides initial information that is helpful in planning the success of the restaurant and hopefully avoids the loss of one's shirt! By scanning the horizon and anticipating changes, the odds against failure are raised.

Most restaurateurs have the streetwise smarts to realize that if there are several restaurants of one type in a market, they must either look for another market or come up with a different concept.

A market assessment analyzes the community, the potential guests, and the competition and helps answer the all-important question: Is there a need for a restaurant?

- ▪ Potential guests:
  - ▪ How old are they?
    - ▪ What are their incomes?
    - ▪ What is their sex?
    - ▪ What is their ethnic origin or religion?
- ▪ What are guests' wants and needs?
- ▪ Why would people become guests?
- ▪ What will they like or dislike about the proposed restaurant?
- ▪ What do they like or dislike about existing restaurants?

Courtesy of Damien Few

Mr. and Mrs. Damien Few review their marketing assessment.

The demand for a restaurant is not easy to quantify. At best, one arrives at a guesstimate—a calculated guess. The calculated part is derived from two factors:

1. The population in the catchment area (the area around the restaurant from which people would normally be drawn to the restaurant)
2. The demographic split of this population by nationality, race, age, sex, religion, employment, education, and income

These data indicate the total number of people who might be guests. In recent years, demographic information has lost some of its relevance. One reason is the increasingly multicultural nature of our society. Another is the changing characteristics of lifestyle. The blurring of demographic lines is evident when top executives eat at McDonald's. Using effective marketing techniques over the years, McDonald's has found the answer to that important question: "What do the people need and want, and what price are they willing to pay?" Following the formula of founder

Ray Kroc—quality, service, cleanliness, and value—billions of hamburgers have been sold. McDonald's Corporation sales are greater than those of its three nearest competitors combined.[19]

How does this relate to sound marketing prices? In the early 1960s, Ray Kroc realized that as families moved into the suburbs and adopted a more mobile lifestyle, they had less time in which to prepare meals. The fast-food hamburger was the answer, and it soon became an American favorite.

MARKET POTENTIAL

How many people in the market area are potential customers? What is the potential for breakfast, for lunch, for dinner? Will your restaurant attract guests from outside the immediate market area? Is your market the tourist, the businessperson, the highway traveler, the person in the neighborhood, or some combination of these? Ask these questions to figure out your market potential, which is defined as the "estimated maximum total sales revenue of all suppliers of a product in a market during a certain period."[20] Breakfast and luncheon markets need convenient locations. Rapid service is prized, except in luxury restaurants. Dinner customers are something else. Customers will drive miles to a restaurant they like or one that has developed a reputation for food quality, atmosphere, service, or price.

MARKET SEGMENTATION, TARGET MARKET, AND POSITIONING

The *market*—that is, the total of all actual and potential guests—is generally *segmented* into groups of buyers with similar characteristics. The purpose for market segmentation is to "allow your marketing/sales program to focus on the subset of prospects that are 'most likely' to purchase your offering."[21] Within these groups are target markets, which are groups identified as the best ones for the restaurant to serve. The reason for segmenting the market and establishing target markets is to focus limited marketing resources for maximum effectiveness. Three of the typical segmentations include:

- *Geographic*: country, state/province, county, city, neighborhood
- *Demographic*: age, sex, family life cycle, income and occupation, education, religion, race
- *Behavior*: occasions, benefits sought, user status, usage rates, loyalty status, buyer readiness stage

Figure 14.6 shows a target market segmentation for a restaurant.

Once the target market is identified, it is important to *position* the restaurant to stand out from the competition and to focus on advertising and promotional messages to guests. The key to *positioning* is understanding how guests perceive the restaurant. It involves tailoring an entire marketing program—including product attributes, image, price, packaging, distribution, and service—to best meet the needs of guests within a particular market segment.[22]

Wendy's advertises that its meat is never frozen and is hot off the grill. Burger King promotes and is well known for its flame-broiled food. Subway built a

FIGURE 14.6 Target market segmentation.

Potential Benefits	Own Restaurant	Competition A	Competition B	Competition C	Competition D
Location					
Convenience					
Parking					
Food Quality					
Food Service					
Price					
Beverage Quality					
Beverage Service					
Restrooms					
Decor/Ambience					
Curbside Appeal/Exterior					

FIGURE 14.7 Comparison benefit matrix.

marketing campaign on the weight-loss success of one customer, Jared Fogle. In commercials, he is just Jared, the guy with the wisdom to eat healthy at Subway. Subway has since expanded Jared's role to public relations and community outreach. He has launched the "Jared's School Tour," a program aimed at childhood obesity that stresses the importance of exercise and eating healthy.

COMPETITION ANALYSIS

Analyzing the competition's strengths and weaknesses helps in formulating marketing goals and strategies to use in the *marketing action plan*. The action plan may include goals, strategies, tactics, who's responsible, measurable outcomes (metrics), and methods for tracking progress.[23] All restaurants have competitors; they may be across the street or across town.

When analyzing the competition, it makes sense to do a *comparison benefit matrix* showing how your restaurant compares to the competition. You compare name recognition, ease of access, parking, curbside appeal, greeting, holding area, seating, ambience, food, service, cleanliness, value, and similar characteristics. Figure 14.7 shows an example of a comparison benefit matrix.

Doing a competitive benefit analysis will help you to determine the strengths and weaknesses of your restaurant compared to the competition. The important thing is to put yourself in the mind of a guest and go through the thought process of why the guest should choose your restaurant. What does your restaurant offer, and how is that different and better than the competition?

Marketing Mix—The Four *P*s

Every marketing plan must have realistic goals for sales and costs while leaving a reasonable profit margin. Marketing plans are based on the four *P*s, known as the cornerstone of marketing: place (location), product, price, and promotion.

PLACE/LOCATION

The place or location of a restaurant is one of the most crucial factors in a restaurant's success. Good visibility, easy access, convenience, curbside appeal, and parking are the ingredients of a location's success.

Visibility is necessary so that, as people approach the restaurant, they are able to easily identify it. Often a prominently placed sign catches potential customers' attention; directions, if necessary, can be featured on the sign.

Restaurants are found in freestanding buildings on a lot with parking spaces, in city blocks with no parking, in shopping malls, in office buildings, and in airports, train stations, and bus depots. The University of California at San Diego has a Wendy's in the University Center, and the Marine Corps Air Station at Miramar, California, has a McDonald's on the base. These restaurants are fortunate in that they have a built-in clientele.

A restaurant grouping, sometimes known as a restaurant row, is quite common. The approaches may attract people because of the wide choice of restaurants available. If two French restaurants are already on the block, it would be unwise to compete by opening another.

Most restaurants have little or no problem with Fridays, Saturdays, and Sundays. The big problem is how to fill up on Monday through Thursday and for both lunch and dinner. This feat requires a magician who provides good location, conjures up an exciting atmosphere, and serves great food well.

Several established restaurant chains attempt to cluster their restaurants. Some franchise by territory. Proponents of this idea argue that economies of scale occur in purchasing, preparation, advertising, and management. Opponents of this view suggest that new stores simply take away business from existing stores. Clustering is, however, a tremendous advantage when there is positive customer awareness in the market for a particular restaurant chain.

A word of warning! If a restaurateur opts for the higher-rent district and spends heavily on lavish decor, the food and service should be excellent because customer expectations will be high. Would-be restaurateurs who find themselves in hot water due to spending a lot of money on the lease and alterations may cut corners with the menu and service. This often leads to the restaurant's demise.

The concept of adjacent complementary restaurants is catching on. For example, one finds KFC or Pizza Hut next to Taco Bell (all are companies within Yum Brands Inc.). Other quick-service companies are experimenting with sharing sites with other retailers. For example, Wendy's, Hardee's, McDonald's, and Starbucks have leased space in department and convenience stores. Today there are also fast-food chains inside amusement parks.

Occasionally a restaurant is successful in an odd location, but the norm is to have high visibility, curbside appeal, easy access, and parking, all of which cost money. The better the location, the higher the rent, so there may have to be some compromise.

We have all seen restaurants whose prices are exorbitant. We may have gone

Courtesy of Maggiano's Little Italy
Maggiano's Little Italy, in Chicago. Celebrity visitors definitely boost marketing and promotional efforts.

there for dinner and cocktails once, but because our expectations were not met, we felt robbed and never returned. All too often, interior design consultants talk owners into spending lots of money on decor. Design is important, and many smart restaurateurs have created expensive Italian, movie-theme, or nostalgia-theme restaurants, such as the Hard Rock Cafe. It is unnecessary, however, to spend a lot of money on the decor of a Greek restaurant close to a university campus, because students—the target market—want a good price–value relationship. By contrast, patrons of an elegant New York restaurant—most of whom are probably on a company expense account—expect to pay for, and receive, excellent food, service, and decor.

PRODUCT

The product of restaurants is experiential; the complete package of food, beverages, service, atmosphere, and convenience goes into satisfying the guests' needs and wants and making for a memorable experience, one that guests will want to repeat.

The main ingredient is *excellent food*. People will always seek out a restaurant offering excellent food, especially when good *service*, *value*, and *ambience* accompany it.

Once the target market is selected, it is important to offer the total package in accordance with the wishes of the guests in this market. Menu items should reflect the selections of guests within this group. In other words, if a restaurant is trying to attract a college crowd, it needs menu items popular with this group.

Food service and atmosphere are largely intangible. The purchase of a restaurant product is not like the purchase of an automobile, which can be inspected and driven prior to purchase. With restaurants, guests pay for the total dining experience rather than just the food. Restaurant product can be described as having three *product levels*: the core product, the formal product, and the augmented product (see Figure 14.8).

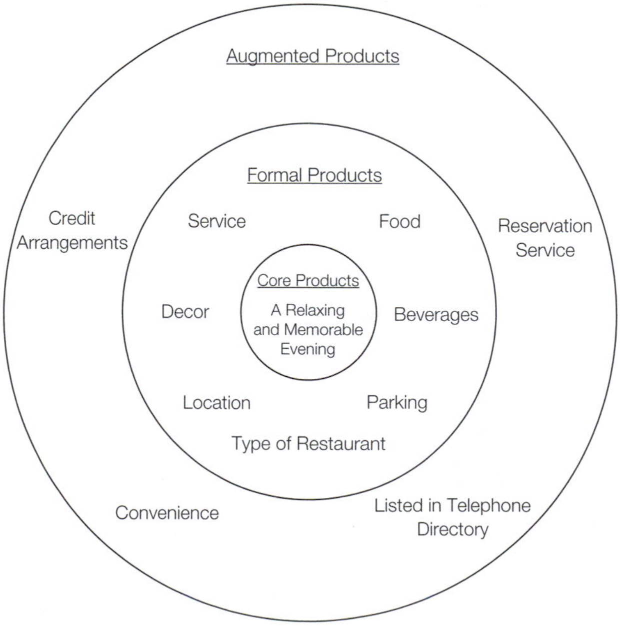

FIGURE 14.8 Three levels of product concept for restaurants.

- The core product is the function part of the product server for the customer. Thus, a gourmet restaurant offers a relaxing and memorable evening.
- The formal product is the tangible part of the product. This includes the physical aspects of the restaurant and its decor. In addition, a certain level of service is also expected. When guests choose a family restaurant, they anticipate a level of service appropriate for the type of restaurant.
- The augmented product includes the other services, such as automatic acceptance of certain credit cards, valet parking, and table reservation service.

Product analysis covers the quality, pricing, and service of the product offered. How will the product—menu, atmosphere, location, convenience, price—differ from the competition? Will it include signature menu items—those that are unusual in some way or that convey the stamp of uniqueness that customers will remember and associate with the restaurant? Will the decor and atmosphere be discernibly different from the competition? Is the service superior in some way, faster or more concerned, more professional or more elaborate? Is the value greater for the price than the competition's? Is the location more convenient, parking easier or more spacious?

Atmospherics Restaurateurs are placing greater emphasis on *atmospherics*, the design used to create a special atmosphere. Years ago, the majority of restaurants were quite plain. Today, they are built with the intent to have an atmospheric impact on guests.

The most noticeable atmospherics are found in theme restaurants. The theme employs color, sound, lighting, decor, texture, and visual preparation to create special effects for patrons. Sporting themes are definitely in with many people, as is the Hard Rock Cafe's rock-and-roll nostalgia. Some McDonald's restaurants rely on atmospherics. They have play areas for kids. The restaurants are decorated with bright colors, bright lights, and hard seats, all of which are designed to persuade patrons to vacate in less than 20 minutes. Care should be taken when creating theme restaurants, because the life of the theme may be only a few years. The atmosphere must be appropriate for the target market.

Product Development Innovative menu items are added to maintain or boost sales. By keeping consumer interest stimulated, restaurants may increase market share and profit. The new items replace those with which the public has become bored. Dining menus have come alive in recent years. Gone are the heavy meat items with their calorific sauces. In their place is fresh pasta, fish, chicken, or other lighter dishes with a more wholesome sauce.

Most of the large chain restaurants test their new product in selected markets. If the new product is accepted, it is launched systemwide. This was the case with the value menu that a number of restaurant chains introduced in recent years. It is interesting to note that as soon as one company rolled out a new value menu, the competition felt compelled to follow suit. In some cases, this was done with too much haste, leading to an inferior product and consequent guest dissatisfaction.

Product Positioning Restaurant guests generally have a perception or image of the restaurant, its food, service, atmosphere, convenience, prices, and how it differs from other restaurants in the area. Positioning conveys to the guest the best face or image of the restaurant, what people like most about it, or how it stands out from the competition. If value is the best feature of the restaurant, it should be emphasized in the positioning statement and reinforced in advertising. Wendy's approach in underscoring the freshness of its product is an excellent way of positioning it.

Restaurant Differentiation Restaurant owners usually want their restaurant to be different in one or more ways, to call attention to the food or ambience.

Courtesy of Panificio
Diners at Panificio Café.

How does a burger restaurant differentiate itself from the competition? An early example happened by chance in 1937, before quick-service restaurants became widespread. In that year, Bob Wian, who four years earlier, as a high school student, had been voted most unlikely to succeed, sold his old DeSoto car for $350 and used the money as a down payment on a 10-stool lunch stand in Glendale, California.

One day, a Los Angeles musician asked Wian for something different from a regular hamburger. Wian thought for a moment, then took a standard hamburger bun and sliced it into three horizontal pieces instead of two. He then placed two cooked hamburger patties on the bun and wrapped the whole thing in paper to keep it warm.

Later, the double-pattied hamburger acquired a name when Wian wanted to call a boy who did odd jobs around the restaurant. Not remembering the boy's name, he called out, "Hey, big boy." On reflection, Wian thought, "What a name for my two-patty hamburger!"

One day a regular customer, an animator, sketched the little boy on a napkin. It became the logo for the Big Boy chain, which grew to include hundreds of franchised restaurants. Wian, who had a knack for promotion, described his milkshake as "so thick you can eat it with a spoon." In the late 1960s, Wian sold the Big Boy chain to the Marriott Corporation.

Product Life Cycle Restaurants, like all businesses, go through a *product life cycle* from introduction to decline. The product life cycle is shown in Figure 14.9, illustrating that sales volume is highest during the maturity and saturation stages. The trick is to extend these stages.

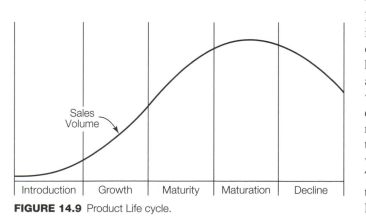

FIGURE 14.9 Product Life cycle.

PRICE

Price is the only revenue-generating variable in the marketing mix. Price is affected by the other mix variables; for instance, if a restaurant has a costly location, then the prices charged are likely to be higher—unless the volume is very high. Price is also an important consideration in the selection of a restaurant. Today, restaurant guests want value and will patronize those restaurants that they perceive offer good value. One restaurant in Chicago was called Take Five; all entrées were, yes, $5 each—this restaurant is no longer in business, which leaves us wondering why?

In restaurant marketing, several factors affect price:

- The relationship between demand and supply
- Shrinking guest loyalty
- Sales mix
- The competitions' prices
- Overhead costs
- The psychological aspects of price setting
- The need for profit

The objective of a pricing policy is to find a balance between guests' perceptions of value and a reasonable contribution to profit. Different strategies may be employed according to the objectives of the restaurant. For example, if an increase in market share is the objective, an extremely aggressive pricing policy would likely bring improved results, all other aspects being equal.

Cost-based Pricing Many industry practitioners advocate a cost-based pricing strategy. This conventional-wisdom method calculates the cost of the ingredients and multiplies by a factor of 3 to obtain a food cost percentage of 33. The price is rounded up or down a few cents, based on the operator's pricing strategy. For example, if the cost of ingredients for a dish on the menu was $3.24, then the selling price would be $9.75 ($3.24 × 3 = $9.72, rounded up to $9.75). Figure 14.10 shows an example of contribution pricing.

Competitive Pricing A restaurant operator may use cost-based pricing to determine the menu price of an item and then check with the competition to see what they are charging for the same item. If there is a significant difference in favor of the competition, then the operator must either choose another item or alter the ingredients of the existing item to bring its price in line.

Contribution Pricing Most operators do not price more expensive items using the cost-based method because it would make them appear too expensive. An expensive meat or fish item, for example, might cost $7 per plate, but there would not be many takers at $21; therefore, the price is adjusted down to an acceptable level. Remember that the contribution of the dish will be greater than one of the lower-priced menu items. Contribution pricing is "a method of computing a product's selling price so that the price, at the least, contributes to the gross income even if a contribution to net income is not possible."[24]

Another important aspect of pricing is the amount of labor cost involved with the preparation and service of the menu items. Food and labor costs, when added

	Food Cost	Selling Price	Food-Cost Percentage	Contribution
Pasta (fettuccini)	$2.15	$ 6.25	34.40	$4.10
Fresh fish	$4.50	$12.75	35.29	$8.25

FIGURE 14.10 Contribution pricing.

together, are known as *prime costs*. Combined, they should not go above 55 to 60 percent of sales.

■ *The relationship of demand and supply is crucial to the pricing equation.* This basic factor controls all pricing policies. If demand is high and supply is limited, prices may be increased. Regrettably, as most restaurateurs know, the opposite is generally the case. In many markets, a saturation point has been achieved, with more and more restaurants opening. They mostly split up the available market just as a hostess divides up an apple pie when an unexpected guest arrives for dinner. Each restaurant receives a smaller market share, assuming equal distribution.

■ *Declining guest loyalty has an effect on pricing.* At one time, it was possible to increase guest loyalty, repeat business, and brand loyalty by dropping prices. Now, however, customers are more inclined to shop around for the best deal in order to make their dollar go further. One strategy that major chains in the airline and hotel business have adopted is to identify heavy users and reward them for their loyalty with frequent-flyer programs and reduced accommodation rates. This concept, while good in theory, has, in a number of instances, run into serious difficulties and contributed to shrinking profits.

■ *The price–value relationship is extremely important, especially in difficult economic times, when guests pay more attention to the value they receive for their dollar.* If a guest is charged $10.95 for a soup, pasta, and salad bar with no service, he or she may think twice about returning if the restaurant across the street is offering a cooked entrée with a soup or salad starter with full table service for the same price. This is why many pizza, Mexican, Chinese, and Italian restaurants are successful. Due largely to low food costs, they appear to offer greater value to customers.

■ *Sales mix is an important aspect in setting pricing levels.* Restaurants have a variety of items on the menu, some of which sell more frequently than others. The trick is to have a sufficient volume of popular items. Although these items might have a smaller contribution margin, they are able to offset the less-frequent sellers, which may have a higher per-item contribution. Because they sell less frequently, they do not produce as great a contribution toward overhead and profit.

Price and Quality There is a direct correlation between price and quality. If high-quality ingredients are used, an appropriate price is charged. Ruth's Chris Steakhouse uses only USDA prime aged beef and charges more than Outback Steakhouse. Both restaurants are successful and balance price and quality. Price is also discussed in Chapter 4.

PROMOTION

Promotion is the activity by which restaurateurs seek to persuade customers to become not only first-time buyers but also repeat customers. Promotion, which includes communication, seeks to inform and persuade customers. A promotional campaign may have these eight goals:

1. To increase consumer awareness of the restaurant
2. To improve consumer perceptions of the restaurant

3. To entice first-time buyers to try the restaurant
4. To gain a higher percentage of repeat guests
5. To create brand loyalty (regular guests)
6. To increase the average check
7. To increase sales at a particular meal or time of day
8. To introduce new menu items

Notice how this paradigm becomes a funnel. The large number of people at the top are the target market, guests we need to first make aware of the restaurant. Other activities are undertaken until the customers become brand-loyal, regular guests. Promotions are conducted to increase sales in several ways:

- To increase guest awareness of the restaurant or a particular menu item. Advertising often does this.
- To introduce new menu items, such as Domino's Dots and Subway's wraps.
- To increase customer traffic, perhaps by advertising a menu special to act as a bring-them-in or a better deal than the competition
- To increase existing guests' spending by building check average. This is often accomplished by personal selling and promotions
- To increase demand during slow periods that are unproductive in that little or no contribution is made to overhead. Examples of efforts to boost sales during nonpeak periods are McDonald's McBreakfast and early-bird dinners for seniors that fill restaurant seats in the early evening—seats that would otherwise be empty.

Promotional programs take a variety of forms. When the economy weakens, some restaurants reduce their prices by finding innovative ways to promote their restaurants, like substituting a three-course, $38 prix-fixe menu for a $52 dinner. The art of downscaling is to create exciting food from lower-cost ingredients.

Of the many promotional ideas for restaurants, some work and some do not. The degree of success varies and often depends on the relevance and value of the promotion as perceived by the target market. McDonald's does a great job not only of getting the attention of kids but also of enticing them to persuade their parents to take them to McDonald's.

A plan would be to ask the town's movers and shakers to come up with a list of foods that they would like to see on the menu. The owners can then select their menu from the list.

Another idea would be to have a soft opening, meaning to open without a big announcement and spend a month working out the finer details. Then have a grand opening, with media in attendance, and enjoy rave reviews. Some restaurants have a camera handy to take photos of guests and then send them along with a thank-you-for-your-patronage note. The next examples are from the American Express booklet titled *50 More Promotions that Work for Restaurants*:

- In order to speed up lunch service, allow guests to text, email, fax, and deliver orders. In some restaurants, this has boosted delivery and take-out by 20 to 25 percent.
- If your restaurant is in an area where you are likely to receive guests from other countries, have menus available in the relevant languages.

Joyce and Evan Goldstein of Square One, San Francisco, say that the relationship between a restaurateur and his or her customers is "like marriage or a relationship—the trick is keeping things fresh and interesting even after the passion period is over."

- Have reading glasses or menus with large print available for those who left their glasses at home.
- Create promotions around the many occasion days of the year. Example: Assistants/Secretaries' Day.
- Create a dinner club to fill the slow nights. Focus around a theme and inform potential guests of the club night by mailings.
- Encourage guests to leave their business cards for a prize drawing. This creates a mailing list.
- One quiet night, say a Monday or Tuesday, announce to the restaurant and the media that one table's bill will be on the house, and that every Monday or Tuesday you plan to "comp" one table. The restaurant will likely fill up on those otherwise quiet nights.
- Give people something to tell their friends about or something to take home as a remembrance of their visit to your restaurant.
- Offer special birthday promotions.
- Send your menu and any relevant information to your catchment area. For example, if you have an Italian restaurant and decide to feature food from various regions of Italy, perhaps with a featured chef, mail an announcement to all addresses in the target market in the catchment area.
- Arrange a cook-off with a prize for the best pie (or whatever). Inform the local media and ask them to be the judges. That should ensure plenty of free coverage.
- Use coupons to build traffic and, once the goal is reached, phase them out. One of the difficulties is reaching the target market. The *Penny Saver* crowd may not be your market.
- Send postcard photos of your menu items to your guests.
- Invite guests to complete an application for dinner for two in another city. Purchase an open ticket and give a $500 spending allowance.[25]

Many restaurants use coupons to promote their restaurants. Coupons may be a mixed blessing. They come in a variety of offerings and are generally distributed in the vicinity of the restaurant. Their purpose is to build awareness and traffic in off-peak periods, such as weeknights and early evenings, and to entice new guests into trying the restaurant. Some offer a price reduction, while others promote a two-for-one deal or other form of discounting.

Corporations like Taco Bell would not promote a discount value strategy with popular menu items already reduced to 99 cents if they did not feel this was sound common sense in the prevailing economic climate. Taco Bell's success in recent years is the envy of the restaurant industry.

Some promotions involve a tie-in to cartoon characters popular with children. Off-hour dinner discounts are a means of capturing higher frequency from regular diners and more patronage from first-time guests. Entrée prices are chopped during nonpeak hours. This trades food costs for occupancy, which is good old-fashioned advertising, according to Mike Hurst, former president of the National Restaurant Association and a pioneer in early-bird discounting at the 15th Street Fisheries, his high-volume waterfront dinner house in Fort Lauderdale, Florida. The early-bird strategy has worked for Hurst, who discounts the entire menu. In fact, his restaurant does one and a half turns before 7:00 P.M., because, he says, early-bird patrons are so impressed with value that they insist on either sending or bringing their friends to dine. This appeals to retired individuals on fixed incomes.

Paul Dobson, a prominent San Diego restaurateur, has not only realized the benefit of early-bird pricing but also appeals to night owls. His restaurants build on the Latin custom of later dining, offered after midevening patrons have finished.

Advertising The extent to which a restaurant needs to advertise depends on several variables. If the restaurant is part of a national chain, a percentage of sales is automatically taken for national advertising. A strictly enforced budget for local advertising is normally a percentage of sales.

Most independent restaurants rely heavily on local guests, so advertisements are placed in city, town, and neighborhood newspapers. It is difficult to determine precisely the degree of success that advertisements have. Operators generally try an advertisement and check the response. The advertisements are coded to a particular telephone number or a person's name for tracking. Coupons are easy to track because people cut them out and bring them in themselves.

Many restaurateurs engage the professional help of an advertising agency. The agency can offer expertise in media services such as artwork, copy (wording), and media relations. The cost of these services can add up, so it is advisable to be well organized by having the key points of the message conveyed in order to achieve the maximum benefit from the advertising budget.

The advertising budget should be carefully planned and not limited to a percentage of sales, because if sales were to drop—as they do periodically—so would the amount spent on advertising, and this may be the time you need more advertising to help increase sales.

Some restaurants refuse to spend money on advertising. They would rather give every guest a $5 bill under every entrée plate, while others give coupons to encourage repeat visits.

Whatever method is chosen, care is required to ensure that the advertisement is appropriate to the target market and will induce the guest to come into the restaurant again and again.

Some restaurants deliberately take a low-key approach to marketing. Instead of expensive television, radio, and media advertising, they concentrate on producing the finest food, service, ambience, and value. Reliance on word-of-mouth advertising has worked for Chart House, which attributes its success to a combination of location, food, and service. This is interesting because their locations often buck conventional wisdom. Many of the Chart House restaurants are in outstanding ocean locations in California, Hawaii, Florida, Puerto Rico, the US Virgin Islands, and New England. Many restaurateurs would not touch a location where half the catchment area is in the ocean! Chart House locations are in "destination locations," most of which are close to major markets.

The first Chart House was opened in 1961 in Aspen, Colorado, with two cocktail tables and four dining tables. On the first night, four customers were served. In 1991, one opening in Scottsdale, Arizona, had sales of over $250,000 in the first month and a healthy operating profit. Patience has been a virtue for Chart House.

This was underlined by the five-year wait to secure its prime Philadelphia location and seven years for the one in Indianapolis. The sites are not always successful, however. The restaurant in San Francisco struggled for several years because it was two blocks from the hub of the Embarcadero.

Another contributing factor to the success of the Chart House chain is that the restaurants are not faddish or "themeish." Tastefully and timelessly decorated, they feature a lot of wood and glass to harmonize with natural surroundings.

In-house Advertising Some innovative restaurant operators embrace in-house advertising by other businesses by letting vacant space be used for advertising media. This either generates additional revenue or decreases costs such as menu printing, which may be as much as $20,000 per year. In-house advertising goes as far as bathroom stall doors and paper cups! Other restaurants have gone to a magazine-type menu advertising a variety of products and services, which guests can read while they wait for their meal. Fast-food chains often do movie tie-ins with their kids' meals. By doing so, they share promotional costs with the movie.

Filling in the Periods of Low Demand Sales curves for restaurants vary by day of the week and time of the year. Sales for the typical restaurant start off the year at the lowest point in January and gradually increase until June or July, when sales reach their maximum. After that, sales decline through December. Weekly sales also follow a typical curve that is lowest on Monday and Tuesday and reaches a peak on Friday and Saturday. Sales usually drop off a little on Sunday, then the weekly cycle repeats. Each restaurant, moreover, has individual sales curves.

Marketing efforts are most needed during the low periods early in the week and the year. Fixed costs remain the same during the slow periods, and efforts are needed to reach and exceed the break-even point during these times.

Tie-ins and Two-for-Ones Downtown restaurants often provide tie-ins with department stores, movies, and the theater. Dinner at the restaurant and tickets to the play or movie provide the buyer with a substantial discount.

Two-for-one promotions are an effective way of getting people into a restaurant for the first time, people who otherwise might not have been aware of the restaurant. Some restaurants give a 50 percent discount on the total food check for two persons. The usual two-for-one is made available by a newspaper advertisement or by sales of dining discount books. On certain days of the week during certain hours, two persons can dine for the price of one. The problem is that regular guests, who would come anyway, also take advantage of the promotion.

Loss-Leader Meals While a restaurant is not likely to price a food item at cost, as is done sometimes at supermarkets, it may offer one or several items at a price that produces much less profit than normal. Some quick-service restaurants offer a free hamburger when one is bought. Discount coupons offer reduced prices for dinner houses, perhaps on selected days, usually on the slow first days of the week. The purposes are to gain market penetration, to attract new guests to the restaurant, and to get people into the restaurant so that they will buy more profitable items as well.

Some restaurants find such loss-leader advertising highly profitable because of the liquor sales generated. The operators reason that any such sales are likely to be above the break-even point and, even though the food cost may be high, fixed costs are already covered. Serving personnel are happy because they are busy and making more tips.

There are literally hundreds of innovative promotional ideas for bringing in new guests, building repeat business, building during slow periods, increasing average checks, and enhancing community relations.

Advertising Appeals The reasons for going to a restaurant vary all the way from plain necessity (the only restaurant around) to great adventure (a trip to a three-star restaurant in Provence). Several motivational forces may operate simultaneously: a respected friend has praised a restaurant, an anniversary is being celebrated, and time is limited.

Generally there are six benefit appeals used in restaurant advertising: food quality, service, menu variety, price, atmosphere, and convenience.

Quality of food is the most important factor in choosing a restaurant. Each of the other factors is important and is featured with greater prominence according to the type of restaurant and the target market for the advertisement.

Social Media Twitter is like a "mini blog"—it's a series of posts limited to only 140 characters—perfect for any busy restaurateur, bar manager, or chef. Twitter is a free social networking and micro-blogging service that allows its users to send and read others updates—known as tweets—which are text-based posts. Updates are displayed on the user's profile page and delivered to other users who have signed up to receive them. The sender can restrict delivery to those in his or her circle of friends—delivery to everyone is the default.[26]

Restaurants are increasingly using Twitter as a low-cost way to connect with patrons and ultimately improve profits. Consider this Twitter success story: Four months before the opening of Tupelo in Cambridge, Massachusetts, the wife of the chef began tweeting about the opening, from getting inspected to planning the menu and picking the paint—so that for opening night the restaurant was packed and at least half the guests were there because of Twitter. A lot of restaurants are discovering Twitter and posting everything from daily specials to luring followers with offers of free appetizers to offering a glimpse of kitchen life.[27]

Sahana Mysore writes in her excellent article:[28] "Restaurants are leveraging Facebook to win new patrons by creating a Facebook page. It's definitely worth your time and it will take you less than one hour to display some basic information about your restaurant."

Facebook has over a billion users. It builds a custom web page every time you visit. It "pores over all the actions your friends have taken—their photos, their friends, the songs they listen to, the products they like." Facebook processes billions of updates a day.[29] Sahana Mysore suggests making your page engaging with applications—show your restaurant's great ratings by displaying the Zagat application or add a reservations widget through Open Table on your main page; display a video of the chefs making the house's special; allow users to click through an interactive menu. "The possibilities are endless—create and promote events online and offline. Let people know about a special Mother's Day brunch or a regular Friday happy hour by sending invitations and asking people to RSVP on Facebook." Your message can "go viral," as information travels from your network of friends and family to their connections and beyond.[30]

Pinterest in another social media format that has potential for attracting customers. Dan Kim, founder of Dallas-based Red Mango and a self-described Pinterest addict, said, "Pinterest is a perfect fit for any brand that can establish an emotional connection with its target consumers using pictures." You can post pictures of highlighted menu items, build a community of people who talk about your restaurant, and share tips. Tender Greens, based in Los-Angeles, uses Pinterest to convey the company's overall brand and philosophy.[31]

Other options include Tumblr, Instagram, and an ever-increasing array of smartphone apps. In the realm of public relations, social networking can be your best friend or your worst enemy, so be aware of what's out there and how you can best use it.

Travel Guides for Free Advertising A listing in one of the major travel guides can be worth thousands of dollars in extra sales at no cost to the restaurant operator. The National Restaurant Association states that travelers and visitors account for 50 percent of all table-service restaurant sales with average checks of $25 or more The *Mobil Travel Guide* lists thousands of hotel/motels and restaurants located in more than 4,000 cities, and can be viewed at www.exxonmobiltravel.com. Some 750,000 copies are sold each year. Solicitations from restaurant operators who wish to be rated are accepted.

By far the largest distribution of travel guides is that of the *AAA Tour Book,* which reaches more than 40 million AAA members. Those near major tourist attractions are preferred. Solicitations from restaurant operators are welcome.

Yellow Pages Advertising Probably the most widely used advertising medium in North America is found in the local telephone directory—the Yellow Pages, a medium that the restaurant operator is almost forced to use because it is available to everyone who has a land-line telephone.

The operator opening a new restaurant must apply for a listing in the Yellow Pages several weeks in advance of publication—which could mean several months, because most directories are published yearly. The restaurant that opens without a published phone number and without a listing in the Yellow Pages is at a disadvantage. A small ad in the Yellow Pages can tell something of the character and menu of the restaurant—that the place serves vegetarian dishes, is "the most romantic dining spot," serves Cajun cuisine, has mesquite-broiled steaks, cooks fish using live oakwood, has fresh seafood, and so on.

Developing a Mailing List Restaurants that appeal to a fairly stable market—some coffee shops, some dinner houses, and luxury restaurants—develop guest loyalty and increase sales by regular mailings. The mailings can be newsy and informational. Photos of guests, receptions held at the restaurant, descriptions of a new wine, or the announcement of specials can be sent to patrons on a mailing list. Restaurant party announcements, such as Halloween and New Year's parties, are examples of events that can be covered in a mailing.

Mailing lists can be purchased, but it is usually better to develop a list of people who are known or potential guests.

Charity affairs attended by the affluent are occasions to collect addresses. Attendants can be asked to sign a register and give addresses. Persons calling for reservations can be asked their addresses. If the caller asks the reason for the address request, the reservation taker can explain that regular guests are mailed information about special events and seasonal affairs offered by the restaurant.

Review Figure 14.7, which shows a comparison benefit matrix that can be used to assess one restaurant's benefits or drawbacks in comparison with other restaurants.

Summary

No restaurant can reach its potential without an understanding of the principles of a good business plan and marketing. Some streetwise owner-managers do not possess formal marketing skills; however, their informal skills are often as savvy as those of any marketing expert. Marketing focuses on the needs and wants of guests, whereas sales focuses on the needs and wants of the restaurant operator. Once the potential market is identified, planning can take place.

The business and marketing plan is completed after an assessment of the marketplace, the competition, and the restaurant's strengths, weakness, threats, and opportunities. The marketing plan, if properly completed and executed, will greatly assist in ensuring that the restaurant's goals are met. The main components of the marketing plan are known as the four *P*s: place, product, price, and promotion.

Key Terms and Concepts

Actual market share	Goals	Product analysis
Ambience	Market	Product levels
Atmospherics	Marketing	Product life cycle
Business plan	Marketing action plan	Segmented
Comparison benefit	Marketing philosophy	Service
matrix	Marketing plan	Strategies or action plans
Competition analysis	Market share	SWOT analysis
Excellent food	Position/positioning	Value
Fair market share	Prime costs	

Review Questions

1. Describe restaurant marketing.
2. What is the difference between marketing and sales?
3. Discuss marketing philosophy in the restaurant business.
4. Give examples of how marketing solves customer problems.
5. In your restaurant project, which will be your principal target market?
6. What is meant by market positioning?
7. In what way does market assessment aid the marketing process?
8. Some restaurant owners question the necessity of developing marketing plans. What is your response?
9. Develop an outline for your restaurant's marketing and business plan.
10. What are the differentiating characteristics of your restaurant?
    a. Product
    b. Atmospherics/decor
    c. Service
    d. Place/location
    e. Price

11. How will you advertise your restaurant? What percentage of total sales will be allocated to advertising?
12. Discuss which restaurant promotions are the most effective.
13. How will you determine your restaurant's pricing policy?
14. How will contribution pricing affect your restaurant's pricing policy?
15. Discuss how the four *P*s of marketing are utilized in your restaurant.

CASE STUDY: Old Salty Dog

Old and Salty

The Old Salty Dog opened in 1986 at the original location of Siesta Key Village, in Sarasota, Florida. The owners, Philip Needs and Judy Fryer, created a concept that combined traditional English fare from their heritage with casual Florida cuisine. In 1990, a second location was opened on City Island, Florida, which serves as a casual and family-oriented waterfront restaurant featuring an array of surf-n-turf themed items. The City Island location opened as a snack bar with a very limited menu featuring burgers, sandwiches, fish-n-chips, and the famous quarter pound hot dog dipped in batter and fried to a golden brown, which coined the name "Salty Dog." The restaurant has since grown immensely, and now offers a much wider variety of items, including the steamer and raw bar, Hawaiian-themed Maui Wow-Wee Burger, and Smoked Salmon BLT, along with an array of entrees.

The Market and Marketing

The two locations have similar, but different, menus based on the fact that they attract different crowds of customers. While both locations cater to families, the Siesta Key location has a more active dinner presence, a late night bar crowd, and an atmosphere that caters to sporting events on the weekends. Additionally, there is more competition in Siesta Key, whereas City Island has an advantage of being one of the only restaurants on the water. For a long time, the Salty Dog properties stayed with their same concept, food, and atmosphere, but over time, the owners listened to the customer's changing wants and needs and the goal became to match the food with the location. The owners wanted to provide a wider variety of reasons for people to frequently patronize

the restaurants. This was accomplished by bringing in fresh ideas to give the restaurant the necessary perspective to adapt to ever-changing trends with consumers demands and the environment.

The Old Salty Dog relies on three staples for success, all of which amount to letting the customer know that you truly care. These staples include the friendliness of the staff, the quality of the food, and always providing good service, which is accomplished by welcoming, assisting and thanking customers for their patronage. Some emphasis has been placed on marketing and advertising over the years. The managers of the restaurant recently started a Facebook page, which is kept up to date with daily specials, promotions, and events. The Old Salty Dog has also been fortunate to have *Man Vs Food, The New York Times* and *Coastal Living* magazine acknowledge the restaurant, which has allowed it to benefit greatly from free advertising. The Old Salty Dog also participates in an array of charity events in and around the Sarasota area to remain active in the community. Recent proceedings include participating in a Humane Society event, a fish fry for the sea bird sanctuary event, and constantly donating gift certificates to charities and fundraisers around town.

The Environment

Creating a positive environment and retaining employees is of high priority. The general manager of the City Island property, Amy Blair, has been with the company from the beginning. Amy encourages employees to put forth effort through techniques of motivation, praise, and accountability. She believes in acknowledging employees for the little things they do that matter so much, by frequently thanking them from their efforts. She seeks to motivate employees by providing both monetary and nonmonetary incentives for them to do their best. Sales contests promoting specials and upselling menu items are rewarded with incentives such as bonuses, gift certificates, or a special shift meal.

Then, Now, and Later

Although the restaurants have successfully operated for more than 20 years, there are many challenges faced on a daily basis. The managers are constantly dealing with elements of the environment, such as weather, climate, and seasonal business. For this reason, they are always tuned into the weather channel, because it affects business so much with half of the seating being outdoors. They must find ways to fight the setbacks of operating in a seasonal climate and draw business during slower periods. Also, continuously growing with the business and keeping up with the times is a challenge that must constantly be overcome. For a long time, the restaurants did not accept credit cards. Over time they have had to adapt to an electronic point-of-sale system for the purposes of processing transactions. They have even begun integrating handheld computers into their daily operations.

The Old Salty Dog is always looking for ways to gain an advantage in the market. One of the future goals includes purchasing a food/catering truck to travel around the Sarasota area for charitable and catering events. The vehicle will be fully equipped with cooking equipment, along with everything else needed to prepare all the food and beverages for these events. This will be a more efficient way of doing things, saving on time and money by having everything ready to go in one location. The owners also want to add a second story over the main dining room area in order to provide Sunday brunch. Finally, they want to create a more uniform training program and set of standard operating procedures. Over the years, they have adapted from a traditional learn-as-you-go approach to a more progressive training system, which has proven to be more developmental. The theory according to the managers is that "if you take time to do things correctly and more efficiently, you will ultimately save more time in the end."

QUESTIONS

1. What are the differences between the City Island and Siesta Key locations? Why does the City Island location have an advantage over other restaurants in the area?
2. How has the Old Salty Dog adapted to the changing environment over the years?
3. How has marketing helped the Old Salty Dog succeed? What are some additional marketing strategies that they could implement moving forward?
4. What are some things the Old Salty Dog can do to fight the setbacks of operating in a seasonal climate and draw business during slower periods?

Endnotes

1. Chekitan S. Dev and Elizabeth Blau, "Crisis Creates Common-Sense Opportunities for Operators," *Nation's Restaurant News, 43* (9) (March 9, 2009), pp. 21–23.
2. *A Guide to Preparing a Restaurant Business Plan,* (Washington, D.C.: The National Restaurant Association, 1992), p. 9.
3. Ibid.
4. National Conference of Commissioners on Uniform State Laws, Uniform Partnership Act (1997), Annual Conference Meeting in Its One-Hundred-and-Fifth Year, San Antonio, Texas, July 12–July 19, 1996, p. 17. Copyright 1994, 1996, 1997 by National Conference of Commissioners on Uniform State Laws. http://www.uniformlaws.org/shared/docs/partnership/upa_final_97.pdf
5. "Hotels and Restaurant Law: An Overview," Legal Information Institute, Cornell University Law School, http://www.law.cornell.edu/wex/hotels_and_restaurants. Retrieved May 22, 2013.

6. Ibid.

7. T. J. Jacobberger, "The Impact of Restaurant Employee Insurance Coverage," *Inside Scoop* (October 12, 2012). http://insidescoopsf.sfgate.com/blog/2012/10/12/the-impact-of-restaurant-employee-insurance-coverage/. Retrieved November 27, 2012.

8. "Summary of Benefits and Coverage (SBC) and Uniform Glossary," http://www.healthcare.gov/law/features/rights/sbc/index.html. Retrieved on November 24, 2012.

9. Ibid.

10. Bertha Coombs, "Drop Coverage or Cut Hours? Big Companies Grapple with Obamacare," CNBC (February 13, 2013), http://www.cnbc.com/id/100456557. Retrieved on May 22, 2013.

11. Ibid.

12. "Drunk Drivers: Congress Gets Behind Breath-test Ignition Devices," *Los Angeles Times* (January 31, 2012), http://latimesblogs.latimes.com/nationnow/2012/01/bill-to-target-drunk-drivers-gains-support-but-other-battles-lay-ahead-over-next-roads-measure-.html.

13. "Red Tape Challenge Turns Spotlight on Recreation Sector," Inside Government (April 24, 2012), https://www.gov.uk/government/news/red-tape-challenge-turns-spotlight-on-recreation-sector. Retrieved November 28, 2012.

14. Ibid.

15. *A Guide to Preparing a Restaurant Business Plan* (Washington, DC: The National Restaurant Association, 1992), p. 9.

16. "Basics of Action Planning." Management Library. http://managementhelp.org/plan_dec/str_plan/actions.htm. Retrieved June 2009.

17. "Marketing Plan." *Entrepreneur Encyclopedia.* www.entrepreneur.com/encyclopedia/term/82450.html. Retrieved November 28, 2012.

18. "SWOT Analysis." Net MBA Business Knowledge Center. www.netmba.com/strategy/swot. June, 2009.

19. Alaina McConnell and Kim Bhasin, "Ranked: The Most Popular Fast Food Restaurants in America," *Business Insider* (July 12, 2012)), http://www.businessinsider.com/the-most-popular-fast-food-restaurants-in-america-2012-7?op=1. Retrieved May 23, 2013.

20. "Market Potential." *Business Directory.* www.businessdictionary.com/definition/market-potential.html. Retrieved November 29, 2012.

21. "Market Segmentation." Center for Business Planning. www.businessplans.org/Segment.html. Retrieved November 29, 2012.

22. "Product Positioning." *Encyclopedia of Small Business.* www.enotes.com/small-business-encyclopedia/product-positioning. Retrieved November 29, 2012.

23. "Creating and Implementing the Action Plan." *Public Affairs.* http://publicaffairs.illinois.edu/marketing/action_plan.html. Retrieved November 29, 2012.

24. "Contribution Pricing," *Business Dictionary.* www.businessdictionary.com/definition/contribution-pricing.html. Retrieved November 29, 2012.

25. American Express Establishment Services, *50 More Promotions that Work for Restaurants.* Ed. Leslie Ann Hogg (New York: Walter Mathews Associates, 1989), 18. www.boston.com/ae/food/restaurants/articles/2009/06/29/restaurants_finding_twitter_a_cheap_effective_marketing_tool/.

26. "Restaurants Using Twitter," *Online Marketing for Restaurants* (October 9, 2008). http://onlinerestaurantmarketing.wordpress.com/2008/10/09/restaurants-using-twitter/.

27. Yoon S. Byun, "Restaurants on Twitter" (June 29, 2009). http://blog.twitter.com/2009/06/restaurants-on-twitter.html. Retrieved December 8, 2012.

28. Sahana Mysore. "3 Things All Restaurants and Bars Should Do to Market More Effectively on Facebook." *Inside Facebook* (February 19, 2009). www.insidefacebook.com/2009/02/19/3-things-all-restaurants-and-bars-should-do-to-market-more-effectively-on-facebook/. Retrieved December 10, 2012.

29. Ashlee Vance, "Facebook: The Making of a Billion Users," *Bloomberg Businessweek* (October 4, 2012). http://www.businessweek.com/articles/2012-10-04/facebook-the-making-of-1-billion-users#p2. Retrieved May 8, 2013.

30. Mysore.

31. Ron Ruggless, "How Restaurants Can Success with Pinterest," Nation's Restaurant News (February 27, 2012), http://nrn.com/social-media/how-restaurants-can-succeed-pinterest. Retrieved May 8, 2013.

Financing and Leasing

LEARNING OBJECTIVES

After reading and studying this chapter, you should be able to:

- Forecast restaurant sales.

- Prepare an income statement and a financial budget.

- Identify requirements for obtaining a loan in order to start a restaurant.

- Discuss the strengths and weaknesses of the various types of loans available to restaurant operators.

- List questions and the types of changes a lessee should consider before signing a lease.

- Discuss the strengths and weaknesses of the various types of loans available to restaurant operators.

- Describe the various forms of business ownership.

- Recognize the legal aspects of doing business.

- Discuss the various types of government regulations.

Courtesy of Sysco

Financing

Once the concept, location, and menu are chosen, the next step is financing the restaurant. Where does the money come from? Many restaurants have been started by borrowing money on property, including the family home. Others have been started with a loan from a relative, a friend, or a group of friends. An experienced restaurant operator may have a lawyer put together a partnership with the operator as managing partner and investors as limited partners. Still other restaurants are financed by groups of investors who form a corporation to buy or build and operate a place. Forming a corporation is simple and can be done quickly and at relatively low cost. The corporation becomes a legal entity that can take on debts and guarantee loans. To do so, however, a corporation must be creditworthy, just as an individual must. It must pay taxes, just as any individual with income must do, which can mean double taxation for the owner. The corporation pays a corporation tax, and the individual owners receiving income from the corporation pay individual income tax as well. But there are ways to avoid double taxation, as we shall see in this chapter.

Sufficient Capital

Many would-be restaurateurs try to start restaurants with only a few thousand dollars in *capital*. Such ventures usually fail. Although the number-one factor in restaurant failure is said to be lack of management, lack of finance and working capital is a close second. No one knows the real rate of failure in the restaurant business because so many restaurants merely fade away, the owners taking severe losses and selling for what they can get. Dun & Bradstreet, the major firm that reports business failures, has no way of assessing the number of fadeaways. After a restaurant opens, owners often lack the working capital needed to keep it alive more than a few months. It is best to have the money in place about six months before you need it, including enough cash to carry you through two months of business.[1] You can always bargain for four to six months of rent free to get the business up and running.

In this fragile economic recovery, restaurant financing has slowed to a trickle as lenders reevaluate loan portfolios amid the financial uncertainty. Lenders are being "much more selective" and there are higher costs of capital, less available leverage, and tighter lending structures for operators that need funding.[2] You're better off borrowing from friends and relatives; or do like the savvy restaurateurs Paul Fleming of P.F. Chang's and Cincinnati restaurateur Jeff Ruby did to create their fund-raising success stories. Fleming raised start-up money from his guest list, and Ruby actually sold $400,000 of food shares.[3]

In financing any business, astute businesspeople are concerned with risking someone else's money rather than their own. Some people have a knack for interesting others in putting up their money for a venture that the promoter controls. Few people entering the restaurant business have the total capital necessary to enter as a complete owner, debt free. Such a course of action would mean owning the land, the restaurant building, and its equipment and furnishings, plus having working

Ruth Fertel, founder of the Ruth's Chris Steakhouse chain, mortgaged her house in 1965 to raise the money to start her first restaurant. This was against the will and wisdom of her brother, lawyer, and banker. She was warned that she would not be able to handle the hard work and that she would lose her home because she didn't have any experience in the business.

capital—that is, a standby amount of cash to open the restaurant and to get through possibly several unprofitable months of operation.

Experienced businesspeople seek to rent or lease the building and land and to search for a loan for the furnishings, equipment, and necessary start-up expenses. Ownership of the land on which the restaurant sits is usually left to a long-term investor. The same may be true for the restaurant building. Rather than using capital for the ownership of the real property, restaurant operators believe their expertise is their investment. They usually want to conserve capital or use it in the most productive way possible. Also, they want to face limited personal risk, should the business fail.

Where does one get the money for a restaurant? Commercial banks are a common source of funds, but the borrower must remember that the lending officers in the banks are only paid employees, not owners, and are also limiting their risks. They take minimal risks because their performance is largely judged by good loans. Lending officers tend to be ultraconservative.

They will ask questions and want proof of income, debt, employment, and credit history. In order to obtain a bank loan, often you will need to prove that you have the funds to pay mortgage insurance, taxes, the required down payment, and closing costs. You may also need to demonstrate that you have the cash equivalent to X amount of months to cover principal, interest, taxes, and insurance payments.

Ordinarily, unless the individual has established a line of credit, the bank wants at least 40 percent (and usually more) of the total needs to be invested by the individual or corporation. This can be a considerable amount. The bank also wants *collateral* (assets that the bank can take should the loan not be repaid) to be pledged. Loans are made for varying periods of time:

 To accumulate enough assets to start a restaurant without borrowing is difficult. To borrow money wisely and to know how to get loans is a major part of a businessperson's acumen.

 In buying or selling a restaurant, there is a simple rule to follow, say the experts: When selling, get as much cash as possible. When buying, put as little cash down as possible.

- A *term loan* is one repaid in installments, usually over a period longer than a year.
- *Intermediate loans* are made for up to five years.
- *Single-use real estate loans* typically run less than 20 years.

A *construction loan* is made in segments during the course of construction and is usually a term loan. The borrower should be clear as to when segments of a construction loan will be available—that is, before or after each phase of construction is completed. Borrowers often ask for a construction loan larger than the actual amount required, and, if granted, use the balance as working capital. (Never pay a contractor all of the money required up front.)

Preparing for the Loan Application

Obtaining the necessary amount of money to get into a restaurant is never easy—unless your friends or relatives are loaded and prepared to back you. Aspiring restaurateurs have bought the furniture and fixtures of an existing restaurant for $30,000. This money is paid to the previous person leasing the property, for the work that had been done to set up a restaurant, including the kitchen, storeroom, toilets, dining area, plumbing, and electrical.

Personal Financial Statement

_____, 20_____

ASSETS

Cash on hand _____

Savings account _____

Stocks, bonds, securities _____

Accounts/notes receivable _____

Real estate _____

Life insurance (cash value) _____

Automobile/other vehicles _____

Other liquid assets _____

TOTAL ASSETS _____

LIABILITIES

Accounts payable _____

Notes payable _____

Contracts payable _____

Taxes _____

Real estate loans _____

Other liabilities _____

Source: Adapted from SBA Online (www.sbaonline.sba.gov/starting/checklist.html)

FIGURE 15.1 Personal financial statement.

Start up Cost Estimates

Decorating, remodeling _____

Fixtures, equipment _____

Installing fixtures, equipment _____

Services, supplies _____

Beginning inventory cost _____

Legal, professional fees _____

Licenses, permits _____

Telephone utility deposits _____

Insurance _____

Signs _____

Advertising for opening _____

Unanticipated expenses _____

TOTAL START UP COSTS _____

Source: Adapted from SBA Online (www.sbaonline.sba.gov/starting/checklist.html)

FIGURE 15.2 Start-up cost estimates.

This $30,000 was paid after a due diligence—that is, a thorough check to ensure that everything works and that the health department or some other agency isn't about to shut the place down for some infringement of their regulations. The kitchen and all its equipment—stoves, ovens, grills, broilers, fryers, refrigerators, mixers, tables, shelves, storerooms—and the tables, chairs, booths, and bar out front are all part of the FF&E—furnishings, fixtures, and equipment. Obviously, it would cost considerably more to make alterations to a building to accommodate a restaurant.

Larger restaurants will naturally cost more to get into, and it's just a matter of finding a location and price that are right for you. Likewise, better locations cost more. For example, you might pay $65,000 for a run-down restaurant in a good location. Danny Meyer got into Union Square Cafe in 1985 for $75,000; he was smart enough to start a restaurant in an area that was on the upswing.

Given that one of the main reasons for restaurant failure is a lack of funds, it is critical to address three important financial questions from the get-go:

1. How much money do you have?
2. How much money will you need to get the restaurant up and running?
3. How much money will it take to stay in business?

A personal financial statement can answer the first question. Figure 15.1 shows the headings for the various assets and liabilities of a personal financial statement.

Figure 15.2 addresses how much money will be needed. The start-up costs need to be accurately assessed, because they must be paid for out of revenues once the restaurant is open. From the signing of the lease until opening day there is often a gap of a few weeks or months. You will need money to live on, and there will also be expenses for the restaurant. Figure 15.3 will help allocate costs for those weeks/months from lease signing to opening. Hopefully, there will be no delays and the opening will be on time. These expenses continue once the restaurant is open but will then be on the income statement.

Logically, the next step in planning the restaurant is to do a budget.

BUDGETING

The purpose of budgeting is to "do the numbers" and, more accurately, forecast if the restaurant will be viable. Sales must cover all costs, including interest on loans, and allow for reasonable profit, greater than if the money were successfully invested in stocks, bonds, or real estate. Financial lenders require budget forecasts as a part of the overall business plan. The first step in the budget process is to forecast sales. The next is to allocate costs to the forecasted sales, allowing for a fair profit margin. This must all be done in relation to the competitive price-value-quality equation.

In establishing an accounting format to project sales and operational costs of a restaurant, these basic categories are useful:

- Sales
- Cost of sales
- Gross profit
- Budgeted costs
- Labor costs
- Operating costs
- Fixed costs

Expenses for One Month

Your living costs _____

Employee wages _____

Rent/lease _____

Advertising _____

Supplies _____

Utilities _____

Insurance _____

Taxes _____

Maintenance _____

Delivery/transportation _____

Miscellaneous _____

Source: Adapted from SBA Online (www.sbaonline.sba.gov/starting/checklist.html)

FIGURE 15.3 Expenses for one month.

FORECASTING SALES

Sales forecasting for a restaurant is, at best, calculated guesswork. Many factors beyond the control of the restaurant, such as unexpected economic factors and weather, influence the eventual outcome. Without a fairly accurate forecast of sales, however, it is impossible to predict the success or failure of the restaurant because all expenses, fixed and variable, are dependent on sales for payment.

Predicting sales volume, while not easy, can be done with a high degree of accuracy if a budget forecast is completed.

Sales volume has two components: the average guest check and guest counts. The average guest check is the total sales divided by the number of guests. Menu prices plus beverage sales partly determine the amount of the average check. The guest count is simply the total number of guests patronizing the restaurant over a particular period.

The first step is to estimate the year's projected guest count. This is done by dividing the year into one 29-day and twelve 28-day accounting periods, then breaking these down into four 7-day weeks. It is better to keep separate records for each meal, because the sales and therefore staffing levels will need to be compatible. Keeping a sales history from day one is recommended (see Figure 15.4 for a budget forecast of restaurant sales for one week).

After the four weekly forecasts are complete, they are totaled on the period-one sheet. The remaining 12 accounting period sheets are then completed, giving the total sales forecast for the year (see Figure 15.5).

Budget Forecast of Restaurant Sales, Period 7 Days, Date _____ 20XX

Period	Forecast No. of Guests	Actual No. of Guests	% + or (−)	Forecast Amount of Average Check	Actual Amount of Average Check	% + or (−)	Forecast Amount of Food Sales	Actual Amount of Food Sales	% + or (−)	Forecast Amount of Beverage Sales	Actual Amount of Beverage Sales	% + or (−)	B	L	D	Total Forecast Sales	Total Actual Sales	% + or (−)
1																		
2																		
3																		
4																		
5																		
6																		
7																		
Annual Total																		

Note: B = Breakfast; L = Lunch; D = Dinner.

FIGURE 15.4 Budget forecast of restaurant sales for one week.

Budget Forecast of Restaurant Sales, Period _____ – 28 Days, Date _____ 20XX

Period	Forecast No. of Guests	Actual No. of Guests	% + or (−)	Forecast Amount of Average Check	Actual Amount of Average Check	% + or (−)	Forecast Amount of Food Sales	Actual Amount of Food Sales	% + or (−)	Forecast Amount of Beverage Sales	Actual Amount of Beverage Sales	% + or (−)	B	L	D	Total Forecast Sales	Total Actual Sales	% + or (−)
1																		
2																		
3																		
4																		
5																		
6																		
7																		
8																		
9																		
10																		
11																		
12																		
13																		
Annual Total																		

Note: B = Breakfast; L = Lunch; D = Dinner.

FIGURE 15.5 Sales forecast for the year.

The totals from each of the accounting periods add up to a yearly total sales forecast. The results may be checked by discussing with other restaurant personnel and credit card representatives to gain an estimate of sales at a similar restaurant. With experience, the margin of error in estimating a restaurant's total sales generally decreases.

The sales forecast for the first few months should take into consideration the facts that it takes time for people to realize that the restaurant is open and that usually a large number of people are attracted to a new restaurant.

Once weekly, monthly, and yearly sales figures are estimated, the cost of sales is determined. It is then possible to allocate fixed and variable costs to reveal a predicted profit (or loss) figure.

INCOME STATEMENT

The purpose of the income statement (see Figure 15.6) is to provide information to management and ownership about the financial performance (profitability) of the restaurant over a given period of time. Information on sales and costs is provided in a systematic way that allows for analysis and comparison. The net income (or loss) is shown after expenses are deducted from sales. Notice that percentages are used in the right-hand column, making it easier to compare one statement with another or one restaurant with another.

The income statement begins with sales of food, beverage, and other sales (which could be take-out, catering, cigars, cigarettes, tobacco, telephone, etc.). The cost of goods sold is deducted from total sales. This leaves a gross profit, which is sales minus cost of goods sold.

From the gross profit, the remaining controllable variable and fixed costs must be deducted before taxes are paid and profits distributed.

BUDGETING COSTS

Costs may be budgeted according to two main categories: fixed and variable.

Fixed costs are normally unaffected by changes in sales volume—that is, they do not change significantly with changes in business performance. Whereas fixed costs may change over time, such changes are not normally related to business volume. Examples of fixed costs are real estate taxes, depreciation on equipment, and insurance premiums.

Variable costs, by contrast, change proportionately according to sales. Food and beverage costs belong to this category. Thus, a restaurant that incurs a $30,000 food and beverage cost when sales are at $100,000 is expected to register a $45,000 food and beverage cost when sales rise to $150,000.

The following simple income statement illustrates the point:

	Week 1	Week 2
Sales	100,000	150,000
Cost of food	30,000	45,000
Gross profit	70,000	105,000

	Amount	Percentage
Revenues		
Food		
Beverage		
Others		
Total Revenues	_____	100.00
Cost of Sales		
Food		
Beverage		
Others		
Total Cost of Sales	_____	
Gross Profit		
Food		
Beverage		
Others revenue		
Total Gross Profit	_____	
Controllable Operating Expenses		
Salaries and wages		
Employee benefits		
Direct operating expenses[a]		
Music and entertainment		
Marketing		
Energy and utility		
Administrative and general		
Repairs and maintenance		
Total Controllable Expenses	_____	
Operating Income		
Rent and other occupation costs		
Income before interest, depreciation, and taxes		
Interest		
Depreciation		
Net income before taxes	_____	
Income taxes		
Net Income	_____	

[a]Telephone, insurance, accounting/legal office supplies, paper, china, glass, silver, menus, landscaping, detergent/cleaning supplies, and so on.

Source: Adapted from Agnes L. DeFranco and Thomas W. Latin, Hospitality Financial Management *(Hoboken, NJ: John Wiley & Sons, 2007), p. 24.*

FIGURE 15.6 Projected income statement showing controllable expenses.

GROSS PROFIT

Sales minus cost of sales equals gross profit is a standard accounting entry. Although it may be standard for the accountant, the concept is not always clearly understood by the restaurant manager. Gross profit is the amount of money left from sales after subtracting the cost of sales, and it must provide for all other operating costs and still leave enough dollars for a satisfactory profit. Some of those operating costs are fixed. Some are variable, meaning that management has some control over them and they vary according to sales volume. All costs must be covered by gross profit dollars. When gross profit is insufficient to cover the remaining operating costs and provide a satisfactory profit, the sales and cost mix must be replanned. If this cannot be accomplished, the business venture is not viable.

CONTROLLABLE EXPENSES

The term *controllable expenses* is used to describe those expenses that can be changed in the short term. Variable costs are normally controllable. Other controllable costs include salaries and wages (payroll) and related benefits; direct operating expenses, such as music and entertainment; marketing (including sales, advertising, public relations, and promotions); heat, light, and power; administration; and general repairs and maintenance. Payroll is the largest controllable operating expense at most restaurants, including full-service operations with average checks of $25 or more, according to the National Restaurant Association analysis.[4] The total of all controllable expenses is deducted from the gross profit. Rent and other occupation costs are then deducted to arrive at the income before interest, depreciation, and taxes. Once these are deducted, the net profit remains.

Uniform System of Accounts for Restaurants

The income statement recommended for commercial food service operations is prescribed in the Uniform System of Accounts for Restaurants (USAR) published by the National Restaurant Association. USAR has several benefits:

- It outlines a uniform classification and presentation of operating results.
- It allows for easier comparisons with foodservice industry statistics.
- It provides a turnkey accounting system.
- It is a time-tested system.[5]

Accounting principles advocate the use of an income statement that clearly shows sales and costs for a specific accounting period, which is normally one month or one year. Figure 15.7 presents a balance sheet prepared in accordance with USAR.

BALANCE SHEET

The balance sheet is an important document in the restaurant or any other business. It is used to determine a sole proprietor's or company's worth, which is done by listing all the assets and liabilities. The balance sheet is a photo of the restaurant's financial standing at a given moment in time—usually at the end of a financial period or at the end of a financial year. The title will read: Balance Sheet of ABC Restaurant as of December 31, 20XX. The balance sheet shows the restaurant's assets (what it owns) and liabilities (what it owes). A balance sheet must always balance (that is, Assets = Liabilities + Net worth).

When balance sheets are analyzed over time, it is possible to see the business trends and owner's strategies—for example, how assets and liabilities, return on investment, and inventory are managed. Assets are divided into two categories: current and fixed. Current assets are assets that will mature in less than one year. They are the accumulation of cash, accounts receivable, inventory, notes receivable, prepaid expenses, and other current assets. Fixed assets are the physical assets whose life expectancy is more than one year and include land, buildings, machinery and equipment, furniture and fixtures, and leasehold improvements.

The balance sheet shown in Figure 15.7 uses the USAR. All restaurants using the USAR method of doing balance sheets will follow this format, which was developed under the guidance of the National Restaurant Association.

> Learn from the mistake that a friend of one of the authors made. Jim successfully opened one restaurant with a term loan from a bank. He was negotiating with another bank to obtain financial backing to open a second when the first bank found out about it and decided to call in his loan. Jim had to borrow from relatives he hardly knew in order to pay off the first bank before continuing on to successfully open several more units with the second bank.

BALANCE SHEET FORMAT
ANNA MARIA RESTAURANT AS OF 12-31-20XX

CURRENT ASSETS		
Cash on hand	$20,000	
Cash in banks	15,000	
		35,000
Accounts Receivable:		
Trade	10,000	
Employees	1,500	
Other	1,500	
	13,000	
Deduct: Allowance for doubtful accounts	(1,000)	
		12,000
Inventories:		
Food	7,500	
Beverages	1,500	
Gift and sundry shop	300	
Supplies	1,200	
		10,500
Prepaid expenses		8,000
TOTAL CURRENT ASSETS	65,500	
FIXED ASSETS		
Land	100,000	
Buildings	200,000	
Furniture, fixtures, and equipment	12,000	
Uniforms, linens, china, glass, utensils	3,000	
Deduct accumulated depn./amortization	(58,000)	
Net book value of fixed assets		257,000
DEFERRED EXPENSES		
Preopening expenses	5,000	
Loan initiation fees	5,000	
		10,000
OTHER ASSETS		
Amount paid for goodwill	7,500	
Cost of bar license	15,000	
Cash surrender life insurance	3,000	
		25,500
TOTAL ASSETS		$358,000

FIGURE 15.7 Example of a restaurant balance sheet.

Source: Adapted from Raymond Schmidgall, David K. Hayes, and Jack D. Ninemeier, Restaurant Financial Basics *(Hoboken, NJ: John Wiley & Sons, 2002), p. 75.*

LIABILITIES AND NET WORTH		
CURRENT LIABILITIES		
Accounts Payable:		
Trade	$125,000	
Others	2,000	
		127,000
Notes payable banks		18,000
Taxes collected		4,500
Accrued Expenses:		
Salaries and wages	4,000	
Payroll taxes	2,500	
Real estate/personal taxes	8,000	
Interest	1,000	
Utilities	2,000	
Other	1,500	
		19,000
Deposits on banquets		700
Income taxes—Federal (no state in FL)		5,000
Current portion of long-term debt		12,000
TOTAL CURRENT LIABILITIES		186,200
Long-term debt, net of current portion		60,000
Deferred income taxes		2,000
Other noncurrent liabilities		1,000
TOTAL LIABILITIES		249,000
NET WORTH (FOR INDIVIDUAL PROPRIETOR)		
Proprietor's Account	108,800	
TOTAL LIABILITIES and CAPITAL		$358,000

FIGURE 15.7 (*continued*)

PREOPENING EXPENSES

A new facility must consider preopening expenses. Although these are not present in an ongoing facility and probably not in the purchase of an existing facility, they are a consideration in the construction and opening of a new facility. One encounters the costs of preopening offices; the initial purchase of all equipment, including china, cutlery, and glassware; the hiring and training of personnel; and preopening advertising. A budget forecast should be allocated for this classification.

Fixed Costs (if restaurant building is owned)
- Depreciation
- Insurance
- Property taxes
- Debt service

Variable costs change in direct proportion to the level of sales: food, beverage, labor, heat, light, power, telephone, and other supply costs.

CASH FLOW BUDGETING[6]

Any business needs available cash. If McDonald's, with all its potential for profit, had no cash with which to purchase necessary food and beverage items, it, like any other restaurant business, would be in trouble. In fact, the bigger the business, the

	Month 1		Month 2		Month 3		Month 4		Month 5		Month 6	
	Budget	Actual	Budget	Actual	Budget	Actual	Budget	Actual	Budget	Actual	Budget	Actual
Cash Opening Balance												
Cash Sales												
Credit Sales												
0–30 Days												
31–60 Days												
Total Cash Receipts												
Cash Disbursement												
Purchase Cash												
Purchase Credit												
0–30 Days												
31–60 Days												
Payroll												
Benefits												
Payroll Tax												
Benefits												
Advertising												
Telephone												
Insurance												
Accounting/ Legal												
Repairs/ Maintenance												
Office Supplies												
Utilities												
Taxes												
Miscellaneous												
Total Cash Disbursements												
Net Cash Surplus (Deficit)												

FIGURE 15.8 Six-month cash flow budget for a hypothetical restaurant.

greater the need for cash. Net income means nothing if bills can't be paid. Managing cash is crucial to a restaurant, especially during the first few months of operation. It is unwise to spend all your time managing the restaurant to the exclusion of maintaining an efficient cash management system. Figure 15.8 shows a six-month cash flow budget for a hypothetical restaurant.

Positive cash flow is enhanced either by increasing sales while containing costs or by decreasing costs while maintaining sales. To manage a restaurant's cash flow, the Bank of America recommends "a cash management system that can speed up the availability of incoming funds, slow down the disbursement of outgoing funds, and accurately monitor the amount of funds going in either direction."[7]

This can be achieved by:

- Keeping a cash receipts journal and a cash disbursements journal for day-to-day transactions
- Preparing period cash flow budgets to track cash flows and balance books
- Collecting cash and accounts receivable as quickly as possible
- Disbursing cash and paying accounts as slowly as possible
- Improving inventory turnover
- Consolidating cash reserves to use the money more efficiently and profitably

Fortunately, nearly all restaurant guests pay by cash or credit card, and some credit card companies have a direct debit from the guest's account to the restaurant in two days. Otherwise, the average time for credit card companies to pay restaurants for the charges that cardholders incur is about two weeks. These days, unless a credit arrangement is made in advance, many suppliers insist that restaurants that are just starting out pay on delivery. Good inventory management can assist positive cash flow. Restaurants generally turn over their inventory between four and eight times a month.

PRODUCTIVITY ANALYSIS AND COST CONTROL

Various measures of productivity have been developed: meals produced per employee per day, meals produced per employee per hour, guests served per waitperson per shift, labor costs per meal based on sales. Probably the simplest employee productivity measure is sales generated per employee per year (divide the number of full-time equivalent employees into the gross sales for the year). An easy and meaningful measure is to divide the number of employees into income per hour. Some restaurants achieve a $70-per-hour productivity rate. When labor costs get out of line, the manager can analyze costs per shift or even productivity per hour to pinpoint the problem.

Without knowing what each expense item should be as a ratio of gross sales, the manager is at a distinct disadvantage. He or she should know, for example, that utilities ordinarily do not run more than 4 percent of sales in most restaurants, that the cost of beverages for a dinner house ordinarily should not exceed 25 percent of sales and could be much less, and that occupancy cost should not exceed 8 percent of gross sales in most cases. The rising cost of energy is giving restaurant managers and owners the incentive to cut back on energy costs whenever and wherever possible. Not surprisingly, about three in five operators said in an association study last fall that they were taking specific actions to combat rising energy prices, such as cutting back on unnecessary equipment use or switching to more efficient equipment.[8] Ratio analysis must be in terms of what is appropriate for a particular style of restaurant: coffee shop, fast-food place, or dinner house (see Figure 15.9).

Moreover, the ratios must be appropriate for the region. Restaurant labor costs, for example, are usually low in the South compared with the North.

SEAT TURNOVER

Some restaurant operators consider the number of times a seat turns over in an hour the most critical number in the entire operation. This number roughly indicates volume of sales and is also an index of efficiency for the entire operation.

	Percent
Sales	100
Cost of sales	33.0–43.0
Gross profit	57.0–67.0
Operating expenses	
Controllable Expenses	
Payroll (including manager)	23.0–33.0
Employee benefits	3.0–5.0
Direct operating expenses	3.5–9.0
Music and entertainment	0.1–1.3
Advertising and promotion	0.8–3.0
Utilities	3.0–5.0
Administrative and general	3.0–6.0
Repairs and maintenance	1.0–2.0
Occupation Expenses	
Rent, property tax, and insurance	6.0–11.0
Interest	0.3–1.0
Franchise royalties (if any)	3.0–7.0
Income before depreciation	12.0–19.0
Depreciation	0.7–5.0
Net profit before income tax	5.0–15.0

FIGURE 15.9 Operating ratios.

Source: Figures were developed by the Small Business Reporter *in California.*

What should seat turnover be per hour? This figure varies with the style of operation and what the operator is trying to accomplish. Restaurants featuring bar sales may wish to slow down seat turnover, making it possible for the patron to indulge in several drinks rather than none or a few. At the other end of the spectrum, the restaurant where people line up to wait for lunch is concerned with as rapid a turnover as possible.

Some restaurants have set a turnover rate as high as seven in an hour; others have one turnover every two hours. The rapid-turnover style of restaurant generally has a low check average, which produces high sales volume. The fast-turnover restaurant features rapid-production menu items—those that are already prepared or those that can be prepared quickly.

A dinner house on Friday or Saturday night—the busy periods—may want to feature roast beef, which is already prepared. The cooks merely slice it and place it on the plate. The concept is known as stored labor, preparing as much as possible during slow periods for use during rush periods.

Restaurants that depend on fast turnover have a number of techniques for speeding service. Servers are instructed to clear the tableware as soon as possible. One technique is to ask the guests if they would care for anything else. Guests who are due back at work may not mind such rush treatment, whereas those eating in a dinner house would resent it.

Servers and the entire staff can be tuned to rapid service. A clumsy or slow waitperson is a *liability* in an operation that depends on turnover for sales volume. The rush period may last only an hour or an hour and a half. Maximum sales must be achieved in that period. Rapid seat turnover may be critical not only for the operator but also for the patron who needs and wants fast service. The menu, the kitchen production, the service, and the style of operation all affect seat turnover and help determine the appropriate target figure for seat turnover.

Seating guests who cannot be served quickly can be a problem. The guests expect service that does not appear and might be happier sitting at the bar. Yet operators have been known to ask patrons to wait in the bar in order merely to increase bar sales. The guest, however, seeing empty tables, may become infuriated and leave.

Any new restaurant that relies heavily on a lunch business must do it right, from the start. Guests will expect that lunch can be completed within about 45 minutes.

Securing a Loan

The best-laid plans go nowhere without funding. Only people who are independently wealthy (or have rich backers) can ignore the funding issue. Everyone else will need to secure a loan.

COMPARE INTEREST RATES

When operators or would-be restaurateurs have a choice of lenders, they should, by all means, compare *interest rates*. A difference of 1 percent over a period of years is big money. Lenders often ask for *points*, dollars added to the interest rate. If possible, these should be avoided.

Over the past years, interest rates have gone up and down like a yo-yo. In the late 1970s and early 1980s, Prime interest rates were in the 11 percent range. They then went down to 8 percent, then as low as 3.5 percent. For and SBA loan, banks usually add 2 to 3 percent. If at all possible, delay borrowing during the very high range, even though it might mean delay in starting a restaurant or expanding it. For the past few years, the Small Business Association (SBA) loan interest rate has hovered around 5.25 to 6.26 percent, depending on the amount being borrowed and the collateral pledged.

Beware of bankers who demand interest discounted in advance or a *compensating balance*. Borrowers are often pleased to receive a loan no matter what the cost, and they may overlook conditions placed on the loan. One such condition is when interest on a loan is discounted in advance. The borrower pays interest on a lower amount than was actually received.

Another condition that may be placed on a loan is the requirement of a compensating balance. Here the banker requires a certain amount to remain in the bank at all times. In effect, the borrower is not borrowing the full amount, but rather the amount minus the compensating balance.

LOAN SOURCES

In seeking funds for financing a restaurant, a number of possible sources can be approached.

- *Local banks.* Usually the banker wants at least one-third to one-half more collateral against the loan as a lien against the loan. In other words, if an individual wants to borrow $50,000, she must have collateral of perhaps

$80,000 to $100,000. Banks are very reluctant lenders for restaurant ventures.

■ *Local savings and loan associations.* Local savings and loan associations usually insist on similar security against any loans.

■ *Friends, relatives, silent partners, syndicates.* Funds secured from these sources often have no security other than a lien against the property to be purchased or built. Individual arrangements vary considerably, from noninterest loans to active participation and ownership in the project.

■ *Limited partnerships.* A limited partnership, where the managing partner calls the shots, is a good way for some restaurants to start debt-free. The partners invest; the managing partner—often the one with the expertise but little or no money—makes the decisions and the other partners receive a percentage of any profits. The advantage of this method of financing is that the restaurateur may start up a restaurant using very little of his or her own money. The downside risk is that a piece of the business is given away in the form of profits. However, creative limited partnership agreements include clauses for buyouts, payback, and, possibly, a percentage of profit as rent for the first few months.

SMALL BUSINESS ADMINISTRATION

The Small Business Administration (SBA) is user friendly and has an excellent success record in lending money to restaurants. In fact, there is a 65 percent success rate of the SBA loans to restaurants, compared to the often-quoted failure rate of restaurants. Over the years, the SBA guaranteed loan program has helped launch some of the nation's biggest entrepreneurial success stories—companies such as Apple computer, Federal Express, and Intel—that had no place to go for financing when they got started.[9] In the past few years, thousands of restaurant owners have utilized the SBA loan guaranty program to start, acquire, or expand their business.

The SBA now guarantees loans up to 90 percent. The maximum guarantee on loans exceeding $150,000 is 85 percent and up to 75 percent on loans greater than $150,000.[10] The SBA can generally guarantee up to $750,000 of a private-sector loan. It works like this: If you can borrow money from the banks, Uncle Sam cosigns the loan.

🍷 BEFORE SIGNING A LEASE

Bruce Barteldt, of Little and Associates Architects, offers these tips:

■ *Don't guess about the size and shape of the building.* Do a feasibility study; all 2,500-foot retail spaces are not created equal. Depending on the shape of the space, you may be able to fit in 80 seats or only 50 seats. The difference could have a major impact on the restaurant's bottom line.

■ *Don't let sunlight wash out your profit.* Harsh sunlight streaming in will annoy diners and wash out the effect of accent lighting and artwork. Window blinds or tinting will control the glare but, unless designed properly, create a less than welcoming atmosphere.

■ *Negotiate for extra HVAC.* In most leases, the landlord will provide heating, ventilating, and

(continued)

air conditioning, or HVAC, or give a tenant an improvement allowance to cover HVAC costs. But as a result of new energy codes adopted around the country, restaurants are required to increase the rate of outside air coming in, which in turn increases the required HVAC capacity.

■ *Know how the kitchen hood will exhaust.* Codes governing kitchens are strict and complicated. Before you sign a lease, inspect where the hood exhaust ducting will be located. That exhaust must run through the roof and be at least 10 feet from any door, window, or fresh-air intake. In a multistory building, this may mean constructing a shaft through each tenant space above; that can be costly

and should be negotiated into the lease.

■ *Get the power supply plugged in.* Typical retail spaces are provided with 200 amps of electrical service, but even a small restaurant requires approximately 400 amps for running the appliances, coolers, and lights. Who pays if the retail space isn't equipped to handle such a heavy power load?

■ *Preserve the roof warranty.* Restaurants require a large number of roof penetrations for hood, gas, and bathroom exhausts, fresh-air intakes, and HVAC ducting. The more times the roof is punctured, the more it is likely to leak. Always employ the roofer who installed the building's original roof to make the penetrations and holes.

Often the best option is to ask the landlord to coordinate the roofing work. Yielding it to the landlord and his or her roofing contractor will keep the roof's warranty intact and prevent you and your contractors from being blamed if a leak occurs.

■ *Strive for perfect timing.* A retail store can be designed, given a permit, and become operational within 90 days, so most developers give retailers 60 to 90 days after the lease is signed before rent is due. But restaurants take longer to design, permit, and construct. Negotiate for a longer grace period before rent must be paid, or work into the budget the cash needed to pay the rent before the restaurant is opened.[11]

Never sign a restaurant lease until you have conducted thorough due diligence. Due diligence is a legal term, borrowed from the securities industry, that means, essentially, to make sure that all the facts and figures are available and have been independently verified. In some

respects, it is similar to an audit. All the documents of the firm are assembled and reviewed, and a team of financial experts, lawyers, and accountants interviews the management. The health department, fire department, and Liquor Control Board are contacted to ensure that

the restaurant is in compliance with all regulations, because the one-time licensing authorities can step in and require extensive alterations to bring a restaurant up to code when there is a change of ownership. So make any lease contingent on gaining all necessary licenses.

There are three principal parties to an SBA-guaranteed loan: the SBA, the small business borrower, and the private lender. The lender plays the central role. The small business submits a loan application to the lender for initial review. If the lender finds the application acceptable, it forwards the application and its credit analysis to the nearest SBA office. After SBA approval, the lender closes the loan and dispenses the funds. The borrower then makes loan payments to the lender.

Loans cannot be made at more than 2.75 percent interest over the prime lending rate,[12] so if the prime rate is 3.25 percent, the total loan interest would be

6.00 percent. However, if banks are eager to lend money, they may drop that rate by up to 1 percent. There are no points involved, and the borrower has to pay only out-of-pocket expenses. The bad news is that there is a 2 percent fee for the guarantee.

The best part about an SBA loan is that the government cosigns the loan by guaranteeing it. When applying for an SBA loan, the borrower must have 33 to 50 percent of the project cost, and this must be debt-free; you cannot borrow $10,000 on your credit cards.

There are only three forms to complete in order to fulfill the SBA requirements: an application, a disclosure, and a personal disclosure. The SBA cites poorly presented financial information as the number-one reason why loans are rejected. Loan applications to the bank and the SBA must contain accounts that are prepared in accordance with generally accepted accounting principles.

SBA loans have four basic requirements:

1. The right type of business
2. A clear idea of which loan program is best for you
3. Knowing how to fill out the application properly
4. Willingness to provide the detailed financial and market data required[13]

SBICs *Small business investment companies (SBICs)* are licensed by the SBA. They are independently owned and managed companies set up to provide debt and equity capital to small businesses. They are permitted to leverage their private capital by using federal funds.

Courtesy of the author and Jon Kingsbury

Talking with an SBA loan officer: Being prepared for a meeting with a loan officer makes it easier to obtain a loan. Banks that participate in the SBA's Low Doc Program do not have to submit all of the usually required financial data to the SBA for analysis and review. Rather, the borrower completes a one-page application form and the bank completes a one-page analysis. The SBA processes these loan applications quickly—usually in 48 to 72 hours. Most traditional SBA loans can be processed under this program as long as the amount of the loan is under $100,000. The approval process focuses on the lender, as well as certain income tax returns.[14]

A variation of SBICs, *minorities enterprise SBICs (MESBICs)*, specialize in loans to minority-owned firms. Amounts loaned range from $20,000 to $1 million or more. A free directory of SBICs can be obtained from the National Association of SBICs, 618 Washington Building, Washington, DC 20005.

Soliciting an SBA Loan The SBA was established for the purpose of getting small businesses like restaurants going. The federal government encourages small business, especially those owned by minority groups. Funded by the federal government, the SBA, headquartered in Washington, DC, has dozens of field officers spread over the country. The term *small business* is defined to include almost every independently owned and operated or even contemplated restaurant.

The SBA can help in a number of ways, but primarily through guaranteeing loans to start or expand a business and through providing expert consulting and counseling service via an auxiliary organization called the *Service Corps of Retired Executives (SCORE)*. This organization is made up of successful retired businesspeople who work on a volunteer basis to help businesses with specific problems. In some areas, SCORE executives are among the most knowledgeable in the business and are available to consult with any restaurant operator, whether fledgling or veteran.

As no one can know everything about the restaurant business, SCORE executives who are expert in disciplines such as accounting, layout, food purchasing, menu planning, and so on can be requested, and their services are provided at no charge.

The SBA is in business to make business loans, not outright grants, and the loan applicant must meet certain qualifications:

- Be of good character.
- Show ability to operate a business successfully.
- Have enough capital in an existing firm so that, with an SBA loan, the person can operate on a sound financial basis.
- Show that the proposed loan is of such sound value or so secured as reasonably to assure repayment.
- *If the request is to cover an existing business:* Show that the past earnings record and future prospects of the firm indicate ability to repay the loan and other fixed debts, if any, out of profits.
- *If a new business:* Be able to provide from the person's own resources sufficient funds to withstand possible losses, particularly during the early stages.

Like any other lender, the SBA, when guaranteeing a loan or making money available otherwise, wants collateral, which may take the form of mortgages on land, liens on equipment, guarantees, or personal endorsements. The SBA also wants, in writing, a great deal of information concerning the proposed or current business. For a restaurant, the information desired by the SBA encompasses:

- A detailed description of the proposed restaurant
- A description of the experience and management capabilities of the applicant
- An estimate of the applicant's worth and how much he or she and others will invest in the business and how much will be borrowed
- A financial statement (balance sheet) listing the personal assets and liabilities of the owner(s)
- A detailed projection of earnings for the first year of the restaurant's operation
- Collateral offered as security for the loan, with an estimate of the present market value of each item listed

WHERE TO FIND THE SBA POT OF GOLD

If you're eligible for an SBA-backed loan, the money may be in your own backyard, according to Mike Stampler, public relations officer in the SBA's office of Public Communications. All SBA loan paperwork is initiated at the local level, so Stampler recommends talking with your banker first to determine if an SBA guarantee would help you obtain the financing you need. If your banker doesn't handle SBA loans, call the SBA district office in your area to locate banks in your state that are approved SBA lending sources. To find the district office's telephone number, consult the Small Business Administration listings under United States Government in the telephone book, or call (800) 8ASK-SBA or 827–5772. You can access the SBA home page at www.sbaonline.sba.gov.[15]

Sequence for Securing an SBA Loan The SBA guaranteed loan-application process consists of four stages. First, the applicant requests a list of participating banks in the area from the SBA. Second, the applicant completes the SBA's six- to eight-page loan application (available at most commercial banks) and submits it to a lender for review. The form might take only about an hour to complete but the supporting documents can take time to track down, and no one can ever predict what the SBA will request. A restaurant owner, for example, must provide a copy of the lease and liquor license. Third, on completion of the loan request, the lending bank sends the application to the local SBA for approval. Fourth, if the SBA approves the loan, the borrower is requested to visit the bank to sign the loan documents. Keep in mind that the SBA also wants to see these six items for all loans it guarantees:

1. A current business balance sheet listing the company's assets, liabilities, and net worth
2. Income statements for the current period and the three most recent fiscal years, if available
3. A current personal financial statement of the proprietor or each partner or stockholder owning 20 percent or more of the corporate stock
4. A list of collateral to be offered as security for the loan, along with an estimate of the current market value of each item, as well as the outstanding balance of any existing liens
5. A statement noting the total amount of the financing you are trying to raise and the specific purpose of the loan
6. Tax returns for the most recent three years, which may be your personal returns or your company's returns, depending on how long you've been in business[16]

The applicant first approaches the SBA for a list of participating banks, then selects five banks to ask for a loan under SBA's Loan Guarantee Plan. If a banker finds the application acceptable, he or she will contact the SBA. The SBA approves 50 percent of loans in three days and a further 35 percent in 10 days.

The details for making a loan application can be extensive. The loan application can be a number of pages or it can be rather brief, depending on the relationship

You submit loan application and other documents to a lender (SBA-approved bank).

If lender approves loan (subject to SBA guaranty), a copy of the application and a credit analysis are forwarded to SBA office.

After SBA approval the bank closes the loan and gives you the money.

You make monthly loan payments and are responsible for repaying the full amount of the loan.

Repayment is usually 5 to 10 years for working capital and up to 25 years for fixed assets.

FIGURE 15.10 Sequence for obtaining an SBA loan.

between the lender and the loan applicant and the amount of the loan requested. A detailed business plan, including a statement of resources, abilities, and experience of the applicant and a forecast for the business, tends to support the application. Figure 15.10 shows the sequence of obtaining an SBA loan.

STOCKPILING CREDIT

The borrower should not wait to request a loan until just before it is needed. Processing a loan may take time. Much of the required information can be put together in draft form, ready to be updated when a loan is needed. You can make the process smoother by assembling this information and keeping it current:

1. A personal financial statement:
   a. Education and work history
   b. Credit references
   c. Copies of federal income tax statements for the previous three years
   d. Financial statement listing assets and liabilities and life insurance
2. If in business:
   a. Business history
   b. Current balance sheet
   c. Current profit-and-loss statement
   d. Cash flow statement for last year
   e. Copies of federal income tax returns for past three to five years
   f. Life and casualty insurance in force
   g. Lease
   h. Liquor license
   i. Health department permit

SELLING THE PROPOSAL

Borrowing money involves selling the lending officer on the belief that the borrower will be successful. To do this, the borrower must be able to convince the officer that a carefully thought-out business plan is ready and can be put into effect once the funds are available. The business plan not only presents what is proposed but also includes a financial and work history of the applicant—information necessary to support the view that the applicant will be successful in the restaurant. The business plan is evidence, to some extent, of the applicant's ability to think logically and project plans into the future. The manner of presentation can be impressive and has an effect similar to a well-conceived resume. (Applicants sometimes turn to specialists who develop business plans for a fee.)

Any lending bank will check your credit history. So, before going to the bank, you should check your credit rating. First, get your personal credit report. You can obtain a copy by calling Trans Union, TRW, or any credit bureau. Remember, personal credit may have errors or be out of date. People often find that they paid off a bill but that it was not recorded on the credit report. It can take three to four weeks to correct this kind of error, and it's up to you to do the double-checking. On the credit report you will see a list of all the credit you have obtained in the past—credit cards, mortgages, and, yes, student loans. Each credit is listed along with how you paid. Any credit where you had a problem in paying appears near the top and may make it difficult to get a loan.

The Bank of America provides an outline (see Figure 15.11) for a business plan that can be followed in drawing up a loan proposal package.

The SBA places emphasis on the business plan required of the borrower as part of the loan application. The SBA suggests the plan be written in seven sections:

1. Cover letter, including the amount of the loan being requested, the terms, and the repayment period
2. Business summary with the restaurant's name, location, menu, target market, competition analysis, and business goals, and profiles of the management
3. Market analysis explaining the kind of restaurant and where it fits into the overall industry
4. Menu analysis, including a copy of the proposed menu, the signature (special) items that will be offered, and a comparison of the menu with those of the competition
5. Marketing strategy, including promotion and advertising plans for reaching the target markets
6. Management plan, including the organization chart, job descriptions, and résumés for the officers
7. Financial data, including a financial history of the borrower(s) and financial projections month by month for the first year, by quarter for the second year, and for the third year as a whole, including projections of the key ratios such as food, labor, and beverage costs as a percentage of sales and how the projections compare with industry averages and those of competitors

Quite correctly, the SBA would like loan applicants to have had at least three years of experience working in a restaurant similar to the one being proposed. The SBA also wants the loan applicant to personally invest at least 20 percent of the total cost of opening the restaurant.

OTHER SOURCES OF MONEY

Several other loan sources are often overlooked. These sources include:

- *Borrowing from the landlord.* Often the landlord is as interested in the restaurant as the operator. He or she may help in financing the restaurant with start-up costs and allow the loan to be paid back in higher rent.
- *Borrowing from the landlord's bank.* The landlord may have more credit than the operator and may even be prevailed upon to endorse a loan.
- *Borrowing from the local government.* Many municipalities have raised large sums of money by selling industrial revenue bonds. That money is usually available at rates lower than the going rate. A number of quick-service chains have tapped this source of money and saved large sums ordinarily paid in interest charges.

I. Summary
    A. Nature of business
    B. Amount and purpose of loan
    C. Repayment terms
    D. Equity share of borrower (equity/debt ratio after loan)
    E. Security or collateral (listed with market value estimates and quotes on cost of equipment to be purchased with the loan proceeds)
II. Personal information (on persons owning more than 20 percent of the business)
    A. Educational and work history
    B. Credit references
    C. Income tax statements (last three years)
    D. Financial statement (no older than 60 days)
III. Firm information (whichever is applicable—A, B, or C)
    A. New business
        1. Business plan
        2. Life and casualty insurance coverage
        3. Lease agreement
    B. Business acquisition (buyout)
        1. Information on acquisition
            a. Business history (include seller's name, reasons for sale)
            b. Current balance sheet (not older than 60 days)
            c. Current profit and loss statements (less than 60 days old)
            d. Business's federal income tax statements (past three to five years)
            e. Cash flow statements for last year
            f. Copy of sales agreement with breakdown of investors, fixtures, equipment, licenses, goodwill, and other costs
            g. Description and dates of permits already acquired
        2. Business plan
        3. Life and casualty insurance
    C. Existing business expansion
        1. Information on existing business
            a. Business history
            b. Current balance sheet (not more than 60 days old)
            c. Current profit and loss statements (not more than 60 days old)
            d. Cash flow statements for last year
            e. Federal income tax returns for past three to five years
            f. Lease agreement and permit data
        2. Business plan
        3. Life and casualty insurance
IV. Projections
    A. Profit and loss projections (monthly, for one year) and explanation
    B. Cash flow projection (monthly, for one year) and explanation
    C. Projected balance sheet (one year after loan) and explanation

Source: Adapted from Bank of America "Financing Small Business," Small Business Reporter, 2001.

FIGURE 15.11 Sample loan package outline.

- *If the restaurant owns the land or restaurant building, selling it and leasing it back.* Several restaurant chains have been built on the sale-and-leaseback plan. Investors who buy the restaurant are promised a good yield on their money plus depreciation on the building and, sometimes, on the equipment as well.
- *Borrowing from the public.* Sell stock in the restaurant company to the public. Stock offerings of less than $1.5 million can be done simply with the help of good legal advisors.
- *Selling bonds or convertible bonds.* Bonds are debts, taken on by a company, that pay the bondholder a certain rate of interest and must be repaid in full by a fixed date. Convertible bonds are the same but can be converted into common stock of the issuer according to fixed terms.
- *Getting a bank loan guaranteed by the Farmer's Home Administration.* These loans are made to businesses in rural areas and cities with fewer than 50,000 people. The loan must be used to create jobs or add to the tax base of the community.
- *Borrowing from the Economic Development Administration (EDA).* The loans are made for businesses that can create jobs or add to the tax base of a community.
- *Borrowing from a city with the help of the Urban Development Action Grant (UDAG) program.* The UDAG was created to help 320 large cities and more than 2,000 small cities defined as "distressed." The borrower goes to such a city or town government with a proposal for an investment that will benefit the town or city. The government then applies for the grant.

COLLATERAL

What security does the borrower offer in return for the loan? Collateral, security for the lender, is the personal property or other possessions the borrower assigns to the lender as a pledge of debt repayment. If the debt is not repaid, the lender becomes the owner of the collateral. The most important collateral is the character of the applicant. How does the lender determine character?

- By personal observation—knowing the borrower over a period of time.
- By references—provided by the borrower and records of previous borrowings and payments.
- By credit reputation—established in previous credit transactions. Lenders, especially banks, refer to credit rating firms for credit reputation.

Unless the borrower has already established a line of credit with the lender (for example, a bank), the lender wants collateral (any asset acceptable to the lender). Banks customarily accept these forms of collateral:

- *Real estate (homes, other buildings of value, land).* The lender determines the value of the property and the amount of insurance carried on it.
- *Stocks and bonds.* Banks use loan securities; stocks and bonds are often discounted by as much as 50 percent to allow for decline in value.
- *Chattel mortgages.* Liens (legal claims) on specified physical assets, such as automobiles or machinery, are used.

- *Life insurance.* Insurance companies commonly lend money against paid-up insurance policies, usually at interest rates below bank rates. Banks will lend up to cash value of a life insurance policy provided the policy is assigned to the bank.
- *Assignment of lease.* Commonly, a bank lends money on a restaurant building and takes a mortgage. A lease is worked out between the operator and the franchiser such that the bank automatically receives rent payment. In this manner, the bank is guaranteed repayment.
- *Savings accounts.* Sometimes a loan can be made on a personal savings account. In this case, the account is signed over to the bank, which keeps the savings account passbook.
- *Endorsers, co-makers, and guarantors.* Closely related to other forms of collateral are loans guaranteed by others who must prove themselves capable of repaying the loan and who are liable for the debt if the borrower does not pay.

An endorser is contingently liable for the loan. If the borrower does not pay, the lender expects the endorser to do so. An endorser may be asked to pledge collateral in the same way as the borrower.

A co-maker joins the borrower on equal terms of obligation to the lender. The lender can collect directly from either the maker or the co-maker of the loan. A guarantor signs the note and guarantees payment.

Private and government lenders often require corporate officers to sign as guarantors, which makes them personally liable for repayment.

KEEPING THE LOAN LINES OPEN

In seeking a plan, it is important to keep in mind that one loan may lead to another. The development of a line of credit is a valuable asset, one that is nurtured by businesspeople. Friendship with a lending officer can help, but more important is a series of loans that have been repaid as scheduled. In other words, try to borrow money under circumstances where you may go back for more when necessary.

AVOIDING PERSONAL LIABILITY

Large corporate chains usually have sufficient credit standing to command loans without the necessity of personal guarantees. The shrewd individual who guarantees a sizable loan sees to it that very few personal assets can be claimed in case of default. Ownership of automobiles, homes, land, and other personal assets is transferred to a spouse or other relative with the thought that, should the business fail, the creditor has little to claim. Giving one's assets to another, however, may be hazardous. For example, the spouse may end up with the assets after an estrangement or divorce.

Leasing

Restaurant buildings and equipment are more likely to be leased than purchased by the beginner because less capital is required for *leasing* than for building or buying. The beginner reduces the investment and, should the venture fail, reduces loss.

Keep in mind, however, that signing a lease obligates the signer to come up with the lease payments for the entire period of the lease. This means that if a building is leased for five years and the restaurant fails in the first year, the lessee has to find someone suitable to sublet or make the lease payments for the entire five-year period, or try to get the landlord to terminate the lease. If the lessee is truly in desperate financial straits, he or she can declare bankruptcy.

A restaurant lease should be good for both parties—the landlord (lessor) and the tenant (lessee). Established restaurant companies often sign 20-year leases. Beginners probably should try for a five-year lease with an option to renew for several additional five-year periods. If the beginning restaurateur is apprehensive about failing, a shorter lease period with options to renew, or even a month-to-month lease, might be desirable.

The option to renew can be a large financial factor if it permits a renewal at the same dollar amount as the original lease. If this is possible and inflation is high during the period of the original lease, the restaurateur can be a big gainer. Most leases, however, are in terms of a fixed dollar amount per month plus a percentage of gross sales. The percentage reflects the effects of inflation.

Be aware of the normal leasing terms of 60 to 90 days to get set up before rent is paid. Remember, it often takes much longer to get all the permits and construction done. Get a head start with the design and negotiate for a longer grace period before beginning to pay rent.

Beginning restaurateurs who are short of cash often lease restaurant equipment as well as the building. The building and equipment are sometimes available as a package lease. The beginner may also lease individual pieces of equipment. For example, a coffeemaker may be leased from a coffee supplier. A dishwashing machine can be leased. Ice cream cabinets are frequently loaned, provided the ice cream is purchased from the lender.

Beyond location and square footage, there is more to consider when selecting restaurant space within a retail center. For example, do not let sunlight wash out profits. Sunlight and glare streaming in through south-facing windows will annoy diners.[17] The sunlight will play havoc with the restaurants lighting and ambiance plus add to air-conditioning costs. Window blinds will detract from the appearance of the restaurant.

Negotiate for extra heating ventilation and air conditioning (HVAC). As a result of energy codes, restaurants are required to increase their outside air ventilation rate, which, in turn, increases the required HVAC capacity. In the southeast, restaurants now require one ton of HVAC per approximately 150 square feet, which is almost twice as much as required in a typical retail space.[18]

♓ CAUTION WHEN TAKING OVER AN EXISTING RESTAURANT LOCATION

Just as you think you've found the perfect location for your restaurant, think again! The transfer of restaurant ownership is the one time when licensing authorities may demand costly modifications to bring the restaurant up to code. Be sure to hire a lawyer skilled in restaurant leases and build in conditional clauses that say the lease is contingent on all necessary licenses and permits being obtained.

LEASE COSTS

The amount of a lease is dependent on the length and type of lease negotiated. Depending on location, leases are generally approximate 5 to 8 percent of sales, but in exceptional circumstances they may go as high as 12 percent. Leases are normally triple net leases (meaning that any alterations made to the property come out of your pocket). Lease costs are calculated on a square-foot basis, with charges ranging from $2 to $50 per square foot per month, depending on the location. A suburban strip mall will be around the $2 range; Main Street USA will be around $14 to $18; and yes, you guessed it, New York City will be in the $50 range. That's why the tables in New York are so close to each other. The restaurant operator forecasts the amount of sales to determine if the lease cost is fair. A choice location could be suitable for one restaurant concept, much too expensive for another.

Sales per square foot or per seat depend on the average customer check amount and the speed of seat turnover. California Pizza Kitchen, which has very high sales per square foot, has an average table turnover of 10 or 11 times on weekends. High seat turnover, an average check of about $10, and relatively small kitchens help account for the high per-square-foot sales. With high sales and relatively low labor cost, the California Pizza Kitchen can afford to lease in affluent malls and neighborhoods where rents are high.

DRAWING UP A LEASE

Ask these questions before agreeing on a lease:

1. Why is the building up for rent? Will an airport locate nearby? Is the highway being expanded? Is it a high crime area? Is there sufficient parking? Is the building in bad repair? Is it a bad location—for example, near a fertilizer plant? Are there rodents? fire hazards? Check with the fire department, police, and health department for information.
2. Who was the last tenant? Why did the tenant leave?

A lessee of a restaurant would want to consider including these and other clauses in the lease:

- Names and addresses of the parties—landlord and tenant; period of time the lease is in effect.
- Amount of lease payment.
- How paid. Rent is payable on the last day of the month, unless there is a clause in the lease saying, "Pay in advance."
- Occupancy (how many people are allowed to occupy the space?); facilities available and time of availability.
- Parking (exact amount of space to be available).
- Appliances and equipment included as a part of the lease.
- Specification of party responsible for repair or replacement of appliances.
- Security deposit to be returned at the end of the lease, provided tenant has not damaged property.

- An assignment or sublet clause—for example, "The tenant has the right to obtain a new tenant with the landlord's permission" (and this permission must not be unreasonably withheld) and the new tenant pays the rent directly to the landlord. The original tenant is released from further liability for the balance of the lease. In the sublet arrangement, "The new tenant pays the rent to the old tenant, who continues to pay the landlord. The old tenant remains liable to the landlord for the balance of the lease."
- A clause stating, "The landlord agrees not to withhold unreasonably his consent for the tenant to assign or sublet."
- Common area maintenance (CAMs) costs, yes or no. Landlords often try to pass on to tenants the tax, insurance, and maintenance expenses of operating the property, usually in proportion to the amount of occupied space. If you are paying CAMs, then the landlord has no incentive to control costs. If there are CAMs at the location you want, one suggestion is to insist on a cap—for example, 10 percent of minimum rents. Thus, if rent is $3 per square foot, CAMs would be 30 cents or less.[19]
- A condemnation clause. A successful business housed in leased property may find that the leased property is condemned. A clause in the lease protects the tenant.

In the lease, include statements that you have:

- The right to operate a restaurant.
- Permission to alter the building.
- Permission to erect a sign (a sign can be a risk that forces the landlord to pay higher insurance).
- Permission to landscape and put up outside lighting.
- An exact amount of parking (describe it).
- The right to paint the building the color you wish (interior and exterior).
- A wine and liquor license, health permit, business permit, fire department permit. Include a conditional clause stating, "This lease will have no effect if any of the above permits are denied. The lease is conditional on obtaining the necessary licenses and permits."
- An option to renew the lease and the method of computing the rent at that time.
- The right to remove equipment that you have installed provided you put the building back in its original shape.
- An exclusive provision—a clause saying that the landlord will not rent to another restaurant within a certain radius.
- A clause protecting the tenant in case of death or insanity, such as, "Wife or partner may terminate the lease."
- A clause stating that unpleasant odors that cannot be eradicated easily will terminate the lease.
- The broadest clause possible to eliminate restrictions. You do not want to limit the products you are able to sell. One day you may want to sell subs, and after a while you may want to include pizza. Also, a more broadly defined use is more attractive to potential buyers.

■ A co-tenancy clause. If you move to a shopping center and three months later the anchor tenant moves out—along with most of the foot traffic—you could lose a lot of money. Include a clause that says if there are major losses of occupancy in the center—to, say, 65 percent—you have the option, after a certain period of time, to move out with 30 days' notice. An alternative is to specify that rent will be reduced during times of low occupancy. Normally landlords are permitted a reasonable period of time (say, six months) to fill the vacancy before you can exercise your option.

LEASE TERMINOLOGY AND LENGTH

In making a lease, both parties should consult a lawyer versed in real estate terminology to avoid misunderstandings. An example of lease language that has a specialized meaning is *triple net lease*. In short, the term refers to a lease in which the landlord, the lessor, passes on to the lessee the responsibility for building leasehold improvements and paying for increases in taxes and insurance. This guarantees that the landlord incurs no expense beyond the investment made at the time the lease is signed. In other words, the restaurant operator who has a triple net lease assumes the burden of upkeep, taxes, and insurance on the building. Clearly agreeing on who is responsible for what avoids confusion and ill will.

Operators have different opinions about the length and details of an ideal lease. Some specialists recommend obtaining a renewable lease for as long a period as possible—normally, a long lease is about 20 years (30, if you can get it). The option to renew for periods up to 20 years appeals to some. There is a security in knowing that the restaurant may be around for some time.

Others prefer a five-year term plus three five-year renewal options. The shorter the lease time lock-in, the better, they say. Be sure to lock in the renewal and a fair method of computing the rent at renewal time. The rationale for this option is that circumstances can and do change quickly in the restaurant business, and you might not want to tie yourself into a business that you can't get out of. An additional option is to use a short-term lease that includes a clause that says at the end of the X-year lease, the operator may leave without penalty, providing a one-year notice is given.

A big point to remember in leasing anything: If the business does not survive, you, the lessee, are still liable for the payment if you have signed a personal guarantee. You can be burdened with the debt for the rest of your life if it is not paid off.

SPECIFICS OF MOST RESTAURANT LEASES

The annual rent for lease space is calculated per square foot per month and is known as the base rate. Chez Ralph, a hypothetical restaurant, is a space of 4,000 square feet leased at $5 per square foot.

The annual rent would be:

$$4,000 \text{ square feet} \times \$5/\text{square foot} = \$20,000 \text{ per month}$$

The annual rent would be:

$$\$20,000 \text{ (monthly rent)} \times 12 = \$240,000$$

On average, total rent cost should be about 7.3 percent of yearly gross sales. If the rent costs go as high as, say, 10 percent, then other costs must be proportionately lower, in order to maintain suitable profit margins.

Term of Lease Most foodservice business leases are for five years, with two more five-year options, for a total of 15 years. In addition to rent and percentage factors, it is not unusual to have an escalation clause in the lease detailing a "reasonable rent hike after the first five-year term." The increase may be based on the Consumer Price Index (CPI) or the prevailing market rate (what similar spaces are being rented for at the time the lease is negotiated). Make sure the lease agreement clearly spells out the basis for any rent hike.

Power Supply Typical retail spaces are provided with 200 amps of electrical service. But even a small restaurant requires approximately 400 amps to run the appliances, coolers, and lights. Who pays if the space isn't equipped to handle such a heavy power load? Be prepared to negotiate with the landlord for the cost of repair to the site and to run lines from the main panel to the tenant space.[20]

Financial Responsibility Early in the lease negotiations, you should cover the touchy topic of who will be responsible for paying off the lease in case, for any reason, the restaurant must close its doors. If an individual signs the lease, that person is responsible for covering these costs with his or her personal assets. If the lease is signed as a corporation, then the corporation is legally liable. As you can see, it makes sense to pay the state fees to incorporate before signing a lease.

Within your corporation, multiple partners must have specific agreements about their individual roles in running the business. You should probably also outline how a split would be handled if any partner decides to leave the company. Your peace of mind will be well worth the attorney and accountant fees when you have these important contractual agreements written and reviewed.

Preserve the Roof Warranty Restaurants require a number of roof penetrations for hoods, gas and bathroom exhausts, fresh-air intakes, and HVAC ducting. The more times you puncture a roof, the more likely it will leak. Always employ the roofer who installed the buildings original roof and ask the landlord to coordinate the roofing work because the roofing warranty will be kept intact. The restaurant owner can either pay the landlord or decrease the tenant improvement allowance.[21]

Maintenance Agreement Another important part of a lease is the complete rundown of who is responsible for repairs to the building. Some leases give the tenant full responsibility for upkeep. Others give the landlord responsibility for structural and exterior repairs, such as roofing and foundation work, while tenants handle interior maintenance, such as pest control or plumbing and electrical repairs. These items are easy to gloss over if you have your heart set on a particular site. Remember, however, that all buildings need maintenance, and costs can really add up. How much are you willing to do—and pay for?

Real Estate Taxes Each city and county decides on the value of land and buildings, and taxes an address based on its assessed value. These taxes are typically due once a year, in a lump sum, but most landlords ask that the taxes be prorated and paid monthly, along with rent and insurance. A triple net lease is the term for a lease that includes rent, taxes, and insurance in one monthly payment.

Municipal Approval Just because you sign a lease does not mean you will ever serve a meal at this site. Cover your bases by insisting, in writing, that this lease is void if city or county authorities do not approve the location to operate as a restaurant (or bar, or cafeteria, or whatever you're planning). Potential roadblocks: Do you intend to serve alcohol? Is your concept somewhat controversial—scantily clad waitstaff, for instance? You will save yourself a lot of time and money if your lease allows these items in writing and if you also obtain permission from the county or city first. Politely inquire about all the necessary licenses and permits before you begin work on the site.

Leasing and Insurance Generally, the tenant is responsible for obtaining insurance against fire, flooding, and other natural disasters as well as general liability insurance for accidents or injuries on the premises. The lease must specify how the policy should be paid—monthly or yearly are the most common stipulations—and also the amount of coverage required. Both tenant and landlord are listed as the insurance parties, so the landlord should be given copies of all insurance policies for his or her records.

RESTAURANT INSURANCE

Restaurant owners must also consider a variety of insurance policies including (but not limited to) these types:

- *Property/building insurance.* This type of insurance generally covers holders for a variety of unforeseen losses, such as fire, vandalism, and so on. Additional coverage can be added for other possible losses due to floods, earthquakes, and hurricanes.
- *General liability insurance.* Liability insurance covers the business in the event of a lawsuit if someone is injured or if property is damaged. It is crucial for a restaurant to carry extensive liability insurance. By nature, restaurants are fast paced and have a lot of consumer traffic. Accidents such as slips and falls happen. It is best to be safer now than sorry later. Liability insurance can also be added to protect the business against disgruntled employees who may claim wrongful termination, sexual harassment, discrimination, and the like.
- *Business income insurance.* If a business is interrupted and normal operations are suspended, business operation insurance takes over and provides the income that the business would have generated under normal circumstances.
- *Workers' compensation and employers' liability insurance.* In most states, this insurance is mandatory if the business employs more than three individuals. It covers on-the-job injuries and illnesses. It generally pays medical and rehabilitation bills, income in the event of a disability, and death benefits.
- *Employee benefit liability insurance.* Employee benefit liability is optional. It may include benefits such as dental plans and health plans.

- *Liquor liability insurance*. In a number of states laws are in effect that make the person who serves liquor liable for crimes, as well as accidents, that happen as a result of the patrons' intoxication.
- *Equipment breakdown insurance*. This insurance provides coverage for equipment, such as computer systems, air conditioning, heating equipment, and telephone systems. As restaurants have become more dependent on computer systems (and the Internet), this insurance is increasing in value.
- *Food contamination/spoilage insurance*. As the name implies, this insurance provides coverage in the event of food becoming contaminated or spoiled. For example, this coverage would take effect if there was a long-term power outage or unsanitary food handling.
- *Crime/employee dishonesty insurance*. This insurances covers the expenses if business is lost due to dishonest acts committed by employees.
- *Auto/valet liability insurance*. If the restaurant uses a car to make deliveries, cater events, or valet parking, this insurance protects the automobile in the event of an accident or damage. In addition, it protects the driver in the event that he or she is injured.
- *Umbrella/excess liability insurance*. Once a policy has reached its limits, this type of policy provides additional coverage for the specifics that would not be ordinarily covered by the other insurance plans.
- *Fire insurance*. There is no need to point out the necessity of carrying fire insurance on a restaurant. However, we offer a few suggestions:
  - If you are leasing or renting the building, it must be very clear who carries the fire insurance—the operator or the landlord.
  - Is the restaurant insured by business interruption insurance—insurance that is paid over a definite period of time in case the restaurant is closed because of fire or other reasons? (Because of its expense, many—probably most—operators do not carry this insurance.)
  - Is insurance carried on inventory as well as on the building?
  - Is current insurance coverage sufficient to replace losses? Inflation and new equipment make it necessary to update insurance coverage periodically to reflect replacement costs.
  - Is a sprinkler system in place and operative? Sprinkler systems reduce insurance costs. Insurance rates also reflect construction material, alarm systems, cooking hood protection, fire extinguisher protection, exit signs, and housekeeping practices.

What Is a Restaurant Worth?

What is a fair price to pay for a restaurant building? A restaurant has two potential values: its real estate value and its value as a profit generator. The two values should be considered separately. A restaurant building may actually detract from the real estate value, especially if the building has failed as a restaurant one or several times or is unattractive. The real estate value may be greater than the operational value.

A restaurant buyer is very concerned with the real estate value, a potential lessee less so. However, even the person wanting to lease a restaurant must consider the real estate value (or potential value) because, if the value increases, the owner will increase the rent (unless the lease agreement is written to prevent such an increase).

What is the real estate value? The value is usually determined by competitive values in the community. The market value of real estate tends to follow the value set by similar properties in the area. Is the asking price above or below the market value for the area? Potential changes in property zoning by local or state zoning boards affect market value. Will highway or other changes be made in the near future that will affect the value of the property? Is the area going downhill or being revitalized? Is the area getting better or worse for a particular kind of restaurant? As an area changes, the kind of restaurant that will be supported also changes. A declining area may need a lower-check-average restaurant, fast-food place, or coffee shop. As affluence grows, more dinner houses can be introduced.

A final note: Just because a sweet financial deal has been put together, the success of the restaurant is not assured. Too often, a group of businesspeople are afflicted with the restaurant-ownership bug. They figure all of the angles, find a cheap source of money, contemplate the benefits of investment tax credits and depreciation, and can hardly wait to become restaurant owners. They fantasize about all of those wonderful meals they will provide clients in their restaurant, all tax deductible. What they overlook is the need for concept development, menu development, location, and other planning. They may also lack a qualified general manager and chef. Financial planning is only one aspect of the success or failure of a restaurant.

Going through all the steps to open a restaurant takes time and perseverance; ask Korianne Hoffman and her partner, well-known and respected chef Dudley, who, when setting up a great upscale casual Mexican restaurant in Chicago, at first looked for a suitable location in the upcoming and trendy South Loop warehouse area. There were a couple of funky restaurants already there. Unfortunately, there were no decent restaurants to take over, and the cost of conversion of a warehouse-type building was $1.5 million. The lease costs ranged from $18 to $35 per square foot per month. They planned to make money by "making the turns" (restaurant lingo for turning the tables, meaning you eat dinner and then vacate the table and then someone else uses the table, that's a turn), but they hadn't planned on that many!

Their real estate broker advised them of a location in the suburbs—this was a new twist, because Korianne and Dudley were used to the city, not the suburb of Oakbrook. However, an existing 30-year-old French restaurant was for sale, and the price included the building. The good news was that the SBA had a special loan interest rate of 3 percent for the first six months, after which it would be prime plus 2 percent—or, then, 8 percent. More good news was that the amount they would be paying in mortgage costs would be less that the lease costs in the South Loop area. Just think of the upside potential for equity appreciation in the value of the building.

Physically, the restaurant was on the ground floor of an eight-unit condominium building. The restaurant was about 6,000 square feet, plus basement. Since it had been a French restaurant, there were plenty of burners but no grills, so they had to purchase a grill or two. Luckily, all the other kitchen equipment was good to go. The French restaurant had 115 seats, but that was a more formal layout, so the new owners considered stretching that to 125. They anticipated an average check of $15 for lunch and $31 for dinner. The area is upscale, with average household incomes of $187,000. There are several nearby office buildings that draw about 40,000 people to the area during the week. The restaurant has virtually unlimited parking plus 40 valet spots.

Korianne and Dudley had a friend who is an architect. He took care of the plans for modification, and they are shopping for a designer—several friends who know the area are advising on the peculiarities of the likely clientele. They are also clipping design ideas from books and magazines. They are talking with local area bartenders to find out which one would be the most suitable to make the move and bring some of his regulars with him. The servers will all be experienced and will either have worked with them before in other restaurants or be from local restaurants. Korianne is working on press releases and public relations to give the chef-driven restaurant an opening boost. They expect to break even in two months, and with a glowing restaurant review, they will. Good luck, Korianne and Dudley and partners.

Summary

Careful evaluation of the advantages and disadvantages of the various forms of legal entities under which a restaurant may operate will help the operator select the best one. The time and effort invested will be rewarded by fewer problems as the business matures. Depreciation, tax issues, and benefits are also important considerations for the restaurateur. Setting up a business entails considerable time and effort and involves meeting a number of legal requirements with which the average person will require help. This fact reinforces the value of experience in the restaurant business before operating as an owner.

Each step in the process of the restaurant evolution, from concept to operation, is important. Finance and leasing are of equal importance to the overall success of the restaurant. The amount of capital required, how much to keep in reserve for the first few months of operation, where the capital is obtained, and how much it will cost to borrow the money are all critical issues. Soliciting a Small Business Administration loan is a lengthy and complex process. Other sources of loans are discussed.

Leases are also a complex commitment. Generally, leases are for a fixed dollar amount per square foot per month plus a percentage of gross sales, depending on the negotiated terms of the lease. With triple net leases, the restaurant operator assumes the burden of upkeep, taxes, and insurance on the building.

Key Terms and Concepts

Capital	Intermediate loan
Collateral	Leasing
Compensating balance	Liability
Construction loan	Minorities enterprise SBICs
Interest rates	(MESBICs)

Small business investment companies (SBICs)

Service Corps of Retired Executives (SCORE)

Single-use real estate loan

Stockpiling credit

Term loan

Review Questions

1. In drawing up a sales budget for a casual Italian restaurant, what percentage of weekly sales should be forecasted for Friday and Saturday evenings?
2. A casual restaurant with $1 million sales volume should have how many full-time equivalent employees?
3. What labor, food, beverage, and occupancy costs should the above restaurant have? Express your answer as both a percentage of sales and as a dollar figure.
4. Aside from its value in planning, why is it essential to do a budget forecast of sales, costs, and profit?
5. Suppose that after forecasting sales and deducting expenses, you are left with 3 percent operating profit before interest charges and taxes. What would you do?
6. List, in order of priority, four sources of financing you would approach in seeking funds for your restaurant.
7. In seeking a construction loan, would you expect to have the entire amount of the loan given to you in a lump sum? Explain.
8. The procedure in seeking a loan from the Small Business Administration is fairly elaborate. What is the usual sequence for this process?
9. The recommendation is made to "stockpile your credit." What does this mean?
10. Is it possible (not probable) to start a restaurant without any cash of your own? Explain.

CASE STUDY: Hopleaf

Introduction

Michael and Louise's Hopleaf is a Brasserie-style pub in Chicago, Illinois, that was founded in 1992 by Michael Roper, a long-time bar owner and restaurateur who had recently moved to the Chicago area in search of a new business venture. While searching for a desirable location for the business, Roper came upon a building that was used as a liquor store business with a taproom connected. Roper purchased the business for a moderate $77,000; however, until Roper was able to purchase the building itself, Hopleaf functioned solely as a bar without the ability to offer food, as there was no kitchen in the venue. During this time, Roper's business brought in $420,000 annual revenue on beverage sales alone. Once the building was purchased, Roper installed a kitchen and made other necessary renovations, which resulted in annual revenue jumping to $1.5 million and continuing to grow until eventually topping out at $3.2 million.

The Challenge

Originally, when the kitchen was installed, food service was not expected to be a large revenue builder, and the restaurant was only open for dinner. As it turned out, food business was a large part of

Hopleaf's growth and success, and it became a part of the overall concept. As business continued to increase each year, the restaurant began to reach full capacity. At this point, the kitchen was too small and there were not enough seats to handle the level of business demand. Currently, Hopleaf is at full capacity every day of the week, and the only way to grow is to add more space, seats, and hours of operation. The biggest challenge is finding the space necessary to provide customers with extraordinary guest service and the desired overall experience at Hopleaf.

Expansion Proposal

In late 2007, Roper was approached by the owners of the struggling restaurant business in the connecting building, who offered him the chance to purchase their building for $2 million. However, none of the commercial buildings in the area had yet approached selling for that amount of money, and these same owners had just sold a larger three-story building across the street for $1,075,000. Roper knew that purchasing this building would require him to take out a large construction loan to renovate the building and create one Hopleaf business, which would cost an additional $1.5 million on top of the building purchase. Also, in order to fund this expansion, Roper would need to find a bank that would be willing to back a large construction loan during a time when the economy was struggling, and most banks were not willing to fund a project of this caliber.

A second option would be to take on investors or limited partners to help fund the expansion. However, this would compromise the independence of being the sole proprietor of a business, which meant that business decisions and the way the restaurant was run would include those partners or investors. Ultimately, Roper expects that the addition of the new building would provide a much larger kitchen, an extra 113 restaurant seats, and an additional 20 draft beer lines. Annual revenue is expected to increase from $3.2 million to $5 million, and hopefully top off at $6 million to $7 million, but this is not for certain.

QUESTIONS

1. Do you think the return on investment merits purchasing the building for $2 million?
2. Are there any alternatives to providing extraordinary guest service at the current level of business demand without expanding the physical building? What should the restaurants seat turnover be?
3. If the building is purchased, is it more feasible to wait for a bank that is willing to back the construction loan, or should Roper take on investors or limited partners to get the project moving faster?
4. What are examples of different sources of money the owners could use to fund the building?

Endnotes

1. "Financing Your Restaurant." All Food Business. www.allfoodbusiness.com/financing_business. php. Retrieved June 2009.
2. Sarah E. Lockyer, "GE Tightens Reigns Amid Credit Crunch," *Nation's Restaurant News* (October 6, 2008).
3. Brad Saltz, "Capital Quest," *Restaurant Hospitality* (September 2001), p. 50.
4. "Checking on Profits." National Restaurant Association. www.restaurant.org/rusa/magArticle. cfm?ArticleID=417. Retrieved June 2009.
5. Raymond S. Schmidgall, *Hospitality Industry Managerial Accounting,* 7th ed., (East Lansing, MI: Educational Institute of the American Hotel and Lodging Association, 2011).
6. This section draws from *Small Business Reporter* (San Francisco: Bank of America, 2001).
7. Ibid., p14.

8. James Scarpa, "Energy Costs Can Be Managed with Demand Ventilation Control." *Nation's Restaurant News* (April 20, 2009), http://nrn.com/archive/energy-costs-can-be-managed-demand-ventilation-control. Retrieved May 17, 2013.

9. Joseph R. Mancuso, "The ABCs of Getting Money from the SBA," *Your Company* 6 (4) (June/July 1996).

10. U.S. Small Business Administration, "Quick Reference to SBA Loan Guaranty Programs" (June 2012), http://www.sba.gov/sites/default/files/files/Loan%20Chart%20Baltimore%20June%202012%20Version%202.pdf. Retrieved May 9, 2013.

11. Bruce A. Barteldt, "Strategies for Negotiating the Best Restaurant Lease," *Nations Restaurant News* 31 (28) (July 21, 1997).

12. "The 7(A) Loan Guaranty Program." www.cftech.com/BrainBank/GOVERNMENT/7ALoanGuarPrgm.html. Retrieved June 2009.

13. Mancuso.

14. Jenny Hedden, "The Bucks Start Here," *Restaurant USA* 10 (November 16, 1996), p. 13.

15. Ibid.

16. Mancuso.

17. Bruce A. Barteldt Jr., "7 Strategies for Negotiation a Lease," *Restaurant Hospitality,* 81 (8) (August 1997), pp. 97–99.

18. Ibid.

19. Ibid.

20. Ibid.

21. Ibid.

Glossary

Accommodation: Refers to accommodating persons with a disability by making the restaurant accessible.

Accuracy in menu: Ensuring that the menu is accurate in describing the dishes.

Action plan: Dictates how the marketing plan will be carried out. It assigns specific responsibilities to individuals and dates for accomplishment. An action plan is a detailed list of the steps necessary for carrying out the strategies and tactics designed for reaching each objective.

Actual market share: The actual market share that a business has.

AIDS: Acquired Immune Deficiency Syndrome.

Alcoholic beverage license: A license to serve alcoholic beverages

Alternative dispute resolution: To problem-solve and resolve differences by offering employees and employers an alternative to courts with a fair and private forum to settle disputes.

Age Discrimination: It is illegal to discriminate against a person on the basis of their age.

Ambiance: The atmosphere or mood created by the restaurant.

American's with Disabilities Act (ADA): Prohibits discrimination against employees who are disabled.

Amortize: To gradually repay a debt through scheduled periodic payments.

Appreciation: The increase in property value over time.

Aromatized wines: Aromatic wines fortified and flavored with herbs, roots, flowers, and barks.

ASP: Application service provider.

Atmospherics: The design used to create a special atmosphere.

Availability: To ascertain whether a product is available.

Avoidance: When both parties in a conflict avoid actions to resolve the situation.

Back bar: The shelf or counter space along the back of a bar or counter area.

Back of the house: Refers to the areas that the guest does not usually see—includes the kitchen, dishwashing area, stores, and receiving area.

Back-of-the-house technology: Technology related to the back of the house, including inventory, payroll, food and beverage costing and menu software, and manager's station.

Bain-marie: Double boiler or steam table.

Bakery-café: A café that is also a bakery serving a variety of freshly baked goods.

Balloon payment: The bulk payment that retires a loan when minimal previous payments have not fully amortized.

Bay: Specific area assigned for workers to cover.

Behavior modeling: A method of showing how to behave with an emphasis on interpersonal skills.

Beverage cost percentage: The cost of beverages expressed as a percentage of beverage sales.

Biodynamic alcohol: A traditional way of making wine with as little interfearance by the wine makes as possible.

Booster heater: Supplies 180°F water for dishwashing machines.

Brandy: A distilled wine sometimes aged in wooden barrels.

Brazier: Heavy-duty stewing pan with tightly fitting cover.

Breading machine: Manual or machine-driven device for rapid application of coating to raw foods such as chicken and fish.

Breakeven point: The point at which neither a profit nor a loss is made in operating a restaurant.

Broiler: Equipment with heating elements above a rack on which food cooks.

Bourbon: An American type of whisky that is a barrel aged distilled spirit.

Business plan: A detailed plan for starting a business.

Butcher's test: A test to see the portion and yield of a piece of meat.

Buyout: The outright purchase, usually with borrowed funds, of a business, as by its employees or management; the acquisition of a controlling interest of a company's stock.

Cabernet Sauvignon: A very popular full-bodied red wine grape grown in most wine producing areas.

California menu: The name given to menus at many restaurants in which guests can order any item from the menu at any time of the day.

Capability/consistency: The ability of a cook to produce the food required. Consistency is aided by the use of standardized recipes.

Capital: Net worth of the individual or business; combination of fixed and liquid assets after the deduction of liabilities; the funds used to start up or capitalize a business.

Cash flow position: The presence or absence of surplus cash for recycling into business operations (sometimes known as positive or negative cash flow).

Casual restaurant: An informal restaurant.

Categories of kitchen equipment: Different types of kitchen equipment.

Centralization: Reduces the costs of order taking, food preparation, and accounting.

Chafing dish: A pan for preparing foods at tableside using portable or canned heating device.

Chain restaurant: Several restaurants belonging to a person or company.

Chardonnay: A green skinned grape that originated in the Burgundy region of France that makes fine white wines.

Cheese melter: Similar to a salamander and used for melting cheese, browning, toasting, glazing, plate warming, and finish-heating items such as onion soup and Mexican specialties.

Chef-owned restaurant: A restaurant owned by a chef.

Civil Rights Law: A law stating that employers may not discriminate in employment on the basis of an individual's race, religion, color, sex, national origin, marital status, age, family relationship, mental or physical handicaps, or juvenile records that have been expunged.

Clarified: Wine is clarified by adding either egg white or bentonite which removes impurities.

Cognac: A twice distilled brandy made with Saint-Emilion grapes and matured in wooden casks in the Cognac region of France.

Collaboration: In conflict management, collaboration occurs when both parties in a dispute resolve to work together to find a solution.

Collateral (security): Personal or business possessions that the borrower assigns to the lender as a pledge of debt repayment. If the borrower does not repay the loan, the lender assumes ownership of the collateral.

Combination convection oven and microwave: A convection and microwave oven combined.

Commercial kitchen equipment: Any piece of heavy-duty equipment sized and built to cook for as few as 50 or as many as 5,000 people.

Commissary: A large kitchen where foods are prepared to be served in quantity at another location or group of locations.

Communication mix: The variety of methods used to tell consumers about a product, including advertising, merchandising, promotions, public relations, and direct selling.

Communications: The exchange of information and the transfer of meaning.

Compactor: Machine for crushing and compacting refuse; some crush bottles and cans as well.

Comparison benefit matrix: A matrix to compare the benefits of both the competition and one's own restaurant.

Compartment steamer: A piece of kitchen equipment with cavities in which pans can be placed; food is cooked by steam.

Compensating balance: A banking industry term referring to a balance to at least partially compensate for the loan amount.

Competition analysis: The analysis of a company's strengths and weaknesses within the market by comparing with competitors and environment.

Compromise: In conflict management, a compromise is when both parties find a resolution that partially satisfies both groups.

Conflict management: The management of conflicts.

Considerations in menu planning: Factors to consider when planning a menu.

Consistency: Consistency in food production is aided by standardized recipies

Construction loan: Loan made in segments during a term loan.

Contribution margin (CM): The difference between the sales price and the cost of the item.

Control: To verify, or regulate, restrain, or influence the outcome or to take corrective action if results are different from those expected.

Controllable expenses: Expenses that can be changed in the short term.

Convection oven/convection steam cooking: An oven that has fans inside to move hot air all around containers of food being baked, decreasing the baking time. Cooking with steam in a convection oven.

Convenience food: Food that comes in a form that makes possible storage in a minimal amount of space.

Conveyor: Moving belt that takes dishes or other items from one area to another; it can slant, turn corners, and go from room to room.

Cook-chill: Cook-chill enables chefs to cook large quantities of food for long-term storage in a refrigerated environment.

Cooking line: Known as "the line," it is the line of stations in the kitchen: broiler, grill, sauté, fry, and so on.

Co-op: A nonprofit institution that provides restaurants with food and supplies at lower cost than do the profit-oriented purveyors.

Creel: Rack with a handle for carrying dishes.

Culinary heritage: The heritage of a country's cuisine.

Current assets: Cash or such assets as accounts receivable and inventory that are converted to cash in normal business operations.

Customer relationship management (CRM): Programs for managing the guest relationship.

Decision-making process: The process of developing and analyzing alternatives and choosing from among them.

Deep fryer: A temperature controlled fryer that allows for food to be immersed in the frying oil.

Degree of service: The level or amount of service that a restaurant offers.

Degustation menu: Menu featuring the chef's best dishes.

Demographics: The characteristics of the market population in terms of age, income, education, sex, and occupation.

Department of Alcoholic Beverage Control (ABC): The Department of Alcoholic Beverage Control is responsible for matters concerning the sale and consumption of alcoholic beverages.

Depreciation: The process of writing off against expenses the cost of an asset over its useful life.

Development: Progressing towards a personal or corporate growth goal.

Difference between marketing and sales: Marketing focuses on the needs and satisfaction of customers; sales focus on the distribution of products to customers.

Different and Better (D&B): How one restaurant is different and better than others.

Difficult guest: A guest who, for whatever reason, is being difficult to handle.

Dishwasher: A machine for washing dishes.

Disposal: A machine to grind and flush food waste into drain lines.

Diversify: To broaden the product offerings.

Diversity: Different cultural and physical dimensions which separate and distinguish us as individuals and groups.

Dolly: A small cart or wheeled platform used to move or transport heavy objects.

Dough divider: A machine used to cut rolls into uniform sizes from a piece of raw dough.

Dumbwaiter: A small elevator for transporting food between floors.

E-learning: Learning that incorporates the Internet and other technologies.

Fair market share: An equal share of the market.

Employer of choice: A restaurant that prospective employees apply to ahead of others.

Environmental analysis: The analysis of environmental factors that influence the organization and the market. The factors are grouped under headings: political, economic, social, and technological.

Equal employment opportunity (EEO): The legal right of all individuals to be considered for employment and promotion on the basis of their ability and merit.

Equal Employment Opportunity Commission (EEOC): The organization to which employees or job applicants may appeal if they feel they have been discriminated against.

Equity: The value of a business or piece of property that is owned free and clear. The money—equity dollars or investment—that purchases ownership.

Ethnic restaurant: A restaurant of a particular ethnicity.

Excellent food: Food that is excellent.

Eye contact: To make eye contact by looking at a person in the eyes.

Fabricate: To build in equipment in kitchens, as opposed to installing separate pieces of stock equipment.

Family restaurant: A family-style restaurant either run by a family or appealing to families as guests.

Federal Equal Pay Act: The Equal Pay Act requires that men and women be paid the same rate for the same work.

Federal Wage and Hour Law (Fair Labor Standards Act): The Fair Labor Standards Act of 1933 was designed to increase wages and increase employment by reducing the number of hours of the average work week. Today it applies to restaurants with sales of more than $500,000. The Wage and Hour Division requires that restaurants pay at least the Federal Minimum Wage.

Fermentation: A process of the yeasts converting the sugar in the grapes into ethyl alcohol.

Filter: A strainer made of paper, cloth, or metal.

Fine-dining restaurant: A restaurant that is finely decorated and has outstanding food and service.

Fining: The filtering of wine to remove the solid particles.

Fixed assets: Permanent business properties, such as land, buildings, machinery, and equipment, that are not resold or converted to cash in normal business operations.

Fixed costs: Expenses normally unaffected by changes in sales volume.

Floor machines: Powered kitchen equipment, as compared to separately installed pieces of stock equipment.

Food checker stand: Place where food checker is located.

Food-cost percentage: The cost of food sold expressed as a percentage of food sales.

Food purchasing system: A system for purchasing food.

Food specification standards: Standards that specify the quality of foods and other items being purchased.

Forced-air convection oven: An oven with a fan that forces air around the oven for quicker heating.

Forecasting: Predicting the future—in a restaurant setting, the number of guests and sales figures are forecast.

Fortified wines: Wines that have brandy or wine alcohol added.

Formality or informality: To be either formal or informal

Franchise: (1) The authorization given by one company to another to sell its unique products and services; and (2) the name of the business format or product being franchised.

Franchisee: Person who purchases the right to use or sell the products and services of the franchiser.

Franchiser: An individual or company that licenses others to sell its products or services.

Freezer: A large walk-in container/small room used for the storage of frozen items like meats and fish.

Freezing unit: Place where frozen foods are stored, often a part of a walk-in refrigerator.

Fringe benefits: Benefits other than salary or wages.

Front bar: Both the place where guests belly up to the bar and where the bartender prepares the drinks.

Front of the house: The operations and people who interface with guests in the dining and bar areas of a restaurant.

Fusion: A blending of techniques and ingredients of two cuisines.

Gin: A spirit with a predominant juniper berry flavor.

Glass washer: Machine with rotating brushes for washing glasses; most often used under bars.

Goals: Specific results to be achieved; the end results of a plan.

Grade standards: A set of standards for fruits and vegetables.

Griddle: Large square or rectangle of heavy metal that can be heated to cook foods poured or placed directly on it, as pancakes or hamburgers.

Gross profit: Sales minus cost of sales in a standard accounting entry.

Groupthink: Thinking done by a group.

Guest count: The number of guests.

Handling complaints: To handle guest complaints.

Hard sell/soft sell: To sell an item forcefully or the opposite.

Hearth: Heated baking surface or floor.

Holding area: The area used to "hold" guests before seating them.

Host/Hostess: A person who greets and seats the guests at a restaurant.

Hot plate: Counter-model electric heating unit, usually with two heating coils, used for heating, pan-frying, and sautéing.

Ice machine: Equipment that makes ice in cubes, chips, or flakes; may also store ice after it is made.

Immigration Reform and Control Act of 1986: Makes it illegal for employers to hire undocumented aliens.

Independent restaurant: A restaurant that is independent and not belonging to a chain or franchise.

Individual Retirement Annuity: An individual tax-deferred savings plan.

Infrared warmer: Overhead warmer with quartz tubes that produce infrared waves; keeps food warm at or near point of service.

Interviewing: A conversation with two or more people with questions being asked to determine if the candidate and the company are a good fit for each other.

Institutional Meat Purchase Specifications (IMPS): Meat purchasing specifications for restaurants and institutional purchasers.

Interest rates: Rates the banks charge for loans.

Intermediate loan: Loan made for up to five years.

Inventory: Stock on hand.

Job: A series of related responsibilities.

Job description: A description of the duties and responsibilities involved in a particular job.

Job instruction: Step-by-step details needed for training.

Job specification: Qualifications and skills needed to perform a job; also, the education and technical/conceptual skills a person needs to perform the requirements of the job satisfactorily.

Kitchen display systems: A system that displays guests food orders in the kitchen.

Key result area (KRA): Areas of the operation where the results are key to the success of the restaurant—including labor, food and beverage costs, guest satisfaction, staff turnover, profit, and so on.

Kitchen equipment: Equipment used in the kitchen.

Kitchen floor coverings: Surfaces usually made of quarry tile, marble, terrazzo, asphalt tile, or sealed concrete materials that are nonabsorbent, easy to clean, and resistant to cleaning chemicals.

Kitchen manager: Some restaurants call the chef a kitchen manager.

Labor-cost percentage: The cost of labor expressed as a percentage of sales.

Labor management: A software program that helps operators manage labor scheduling and costs.

Leader: A person who leads—influencing the behavior of others in a desired way.

Leadership: The art of leading—the influence of one person over another to work willingly toward a predetermined goal.

Leadership by walking around: Leadership by being close to guests and employees rather than working in an office.

Learner-controlled instruction (LCI): A program in which employees are given job standards to achieve and asked to reach the standards at their own pace.

Leasing: Paying for the use of the building and equipment for a specified time.

Leverage: (1) The extent to which a business is financed by debt; and (2) to boost a business's available funds by the injection of loan dollars.

Leveraged buyout (LBO): The use of a target company's asset value to finance the debt incurred in acquiring the company; a buyout using mostly borrowed money and in which the principals put up little or no money of their own.

Liability: To be liable for something—to insure against a liability.

Liquidate: To convert assets into cash.

Liquidity: The degree to which individual or business assets are in cash form or can quickly be converted to cash.

Liquor control: Control of liquor—part of an overall system of beverage controls. Liquor is controlled from ordering, delivery/receiving, storage, issuing, pouring, and cash receipts.

Loading dock: A platform outside an establishment, usually at the rear, where deliveries of food and supplies are unloaded.

Loan principal: The original amount borrowed or the unpaid loan balance, not including interest charges.

Magic phrases: Phrases used by the host or hostess to welcome or part with the guest.

Market: The total number of potential guests.

Management: Management is the process of planning, organizing, leading, assessing and controlling resource use to reach given goals.

Manager as coach: Managers act as a coach.

Market assessment: An assessment that provides initial information helpful in planning the success and reducing the loss of the organization.

Marketing: The activities involved in developing product, price, distribution, and promotional mixes that meet and satisfy the needs of customers.

Marketing action plan: An plan of action to achieve the goals of the marketing plan.

Marketing mix: The combination of the four *P*s of marketing: product, price, place, and promotion.

Marketing philosophy: The belief and approach to marketing is to give guests what they want— the way owners have decided to relate to guests, staff, and suppliers, in terms of fairness, honesty, and ethical and moral conduct.

Marketing planning: The establishment of marketing goals and the design of marketing programs expected to be implemented in the future.

Market positioning: The placement in the general market that distinguishes a restaurant from others in terms of price and service.

Market segment: Population group with similar characteristics (needs, wants, income, background, buying habits, and so on). A restaurant aims to address the wants and needs of specific market segments. When the product matches the desired segment's wants and needs, a successful marketing relationship is formed. Groups that respond in a similar way must be identifiable, measurable, and of appropriate size. In addition, they must be reachable by advertising media.

Market share: The share of the market that a business has.

Meat buyers guide: A guide for purchasing meat.

Mentor: A person who advises a mentee.

Menu engineering: Menu engineering is a tool for maximizing revenue from restaurant menus. It focuses on the dollar contribution of items not the cost percentage.

Menu items: The choices offered on a menu.

Menu management: Managing the menu to maximize guest satisfaction and profitability.

Menu pricing strategies: The strategy of pricing menus.

Menu types: The various types of menus.

Merlot: A popular red wine grape that produces wonderful red wines that are softer than Cabernet Sauvignon.

Microwave: An electronic high-speed oven.

Minorities enterprise SBICs (MESBICs): Loans for minority owned firms.

Mission statement: A statement of purpose.

Mise en place: The precise assembly of ingredients and equipment required for the preparation of a recipe.

Mixer: Mechanical equipment that revolves to mix ingredients; comes in a variety of sizes with several speeds of operation; can be either on a counter or installed.

Mobile: Describes portable equipment on wheels.

Mobile payment: The ability to pay a restaurant bill via a mobile phone.

Module: A unit of measurement selected for equipment or furniture, such as modular pans to fit racks or refrigerator spaces, or chairs matching in size and shape.

Mother/Leading sauce: One of five sauces from which many others are derived: béchamel, velouté, brown, tomato, hollandaise.

Motivation: Refers to what makes people tick: the needs and desires and fears and aspirations within people that make them behave as they do. Motivation is the energizer that makes people take action; it is the *why* of human behavior.

National Restaurant Association: A national association representing restaurants.

Nappy: A shallow, open serving dish, sometimes having one handle.

Net worth: The book or on-paper dollar value of an individual or business when liabilities have been subtracted from assets.

Nonprogrammed decision: A one-off decision that requires more thought as the situation is a unique one. The opposite of a programmed decision.

Nouvelle cuisine: New cuisine—lighter with fewer calories.

Nutritional value: The value of nutrients in food.

Off-sale beer and wine: Authorizes the sale of all types of beer, wines, and malt beverages for consumption off the premises in original containers.

Off-sale general: Authorizes the sale of all types of alcoholic beverages for consumption off the premises in original, sealed containers.

On-sale beer: Authorizes the sale on the licensed premises of beer and other malt beverages with an alcoholic content of 4 percent or less by weight.

On-sale beer and wine: Authorizes the sale on the premises of all types of beer, wine, and malt liquor.

On-sale general: Authorizes the sale of all types of alcoholic beverages—namely, beer, wine, and distilled spirits—for consumption on the premises.

Operating ratios: Important ratios that indicate performance in the key operating areas.

Organizing: To get a job done efficiently and effectively by completing certain tasks.

Orientation: Explaining to new employees all information that will be helpful about the company and the job, policies and procedures, culture and values, that will help ensure their success with the company.

Oven: A piece of equipment designed to bake; a chamber for baking, heating, or drying, especially in a stove; may be in a range or separate, as in deck or stack ovens, or constructed with moving belts, as in revolving ovens; also see "Convection oven."

Paddle: A long metal implement used for stirring or mixing ingredients in a steam kettle.

Pan tree: Treelike device for holding pans, usually overhead.

Pantry: A room for storage of food or china; also an area for finishing off foods, assembling foods on trays, garnishing.

Par stock: Level of an inventory item that must be maintained at all times. If the stock on hand falls below this point, a computerized reorder system automatically orders a predetermined quantity of the item.

Partnership: Legally defined under the Uniform Partnership Act as any venture where two or more persons endeavor to make a profit.

Pass: The area where the food is passed from the kitchen cooks to the servers.

Pass-through: A hot or cold compartment with doors on both sides where prepared food is placed to be picked up for service.

Pastry bag: Cone-shaped bag with a metal tip at the small end; used to decorate cakes, prepare fancy toppings, or insert fillings.

Pastry cart: Cart holding a selection of dessert pastries to be served at tables from the cart.

Payment Card Industry Data Security Standard (PCIDSS): The standard for data security payments.

Pay-at-the-table: Making a restaurant bill payment whilst at the table.

PDA: Personal digital assistant.

Pellet: A small heated metal disc placed under a dish to keep it warm; sometimes the disc is frozen and placed under dishes to keep them cold.

Performance management: The setting of work standards and assessing the work outcomes to the standards and taking corrective actions when necessary; managing the performance of an organization.

Petit Syrah: Petit Syrah is a variety of red wine grape mostly grown in Australia, California, France and Israel.

Pickup counter: Place where kitchen workers place prepared food for pickup and serving.

Piece of the action: A term used by some restaurants in encouraging unit managers to acquire, through purchase, 20 percent of the store they manage.

Pinot Grigio: A popular white wine grape from Italy.

Pinot Noir: A black grape that makes wonderful wine in the Burgundy region of france and beyond.

Placement: Placing a person in a certain position.

Planning: The process of defining the organization's goals and establishing an overall strategy for achieving those goals.

Plus-minus-plus model: Disciplinary technique that starts with praise followed by criticism, then ends with praise.

Point-of-sale (POS) system: Software that records the data of each guest order and can be programmed to provide a variety of data on demand.

Portion cut: A piece of meat cut to its portion size.

Positioning: Positioning the restaurant so that it stands out as a restaurant of choice in the minds of its target market.

Pre-employment testing: Testing before employment.

Premium brand liquors: High-quality brands of liquor.

Price: Price is a major factor in guest menu selection.

Prime costs: The combined costs of food and labor, usually expressed as a percentage of sales; it should not go above 55 to 60 percent of sales.

Prime rate: The interest rate set by individual banks for their lowest-risk loans; usually short-term credit unsecured to their biggest, most creditworthy customers within a particular geographic area.

Product analysis: Analyzing a product—example: comparing the features and benefits of one restaurant compared to another.

Product development: The marketing functions associated with the generation of new products and their introduction to the marketplace.

Product differentiation: The marketing strategy of calling the attention of buyers to those aspects of a product that set it apart from its competitors.

Production sheet: A sheet used by the chef/kitchen manager to plan the shift's food production.

Product levels: There are three levels of product concept for restaurants: the core, the formal and the augmented.

Product life cycle: A marketing management concept providing a graphic description of a product's sales history. It is depicted as having four stages: introduction, growth, maturity, and decline.

Product management: A system to streamline a restaurant's daily processes for ordering, receiving and inventory.

Product/service mix: Combination of product and services, whether free or for sale, aimed at satisfying the needs of the target market.

Profitability: The amount left over after all expenses have been paid.

Programmed decision: A decision-situation that reoccurs and so can have a programmed response.

Promotion: The activities by which restaurateurs seek to persuade not only first-time buyers but also repeat customers.

Proof cabinet: Container for proofing dough in preparation for baking or for holding prepared food. Some models have a built-in water reservoir.

Protecting: Protecting the restaurant name is important and is done by registering the name.

Pull handle: A handle for drawing draft beer which usually has the name of the beer on it.

Purchasing: Buying the food and sundry items to run a restaurant.

Quality control: The control of quality.

Quick casual restaurant: A restaurant that is both quick and casual in nature.

Quick-service restaurant: A more politically correct way of saying fast food.

Rack: Open shelving designed to hold pots and pans, baked goods, and so on.

Ramekin: Shallow baking china or dish.

Range: A cook stove, usually a heated top; it may also contain an oven.

Raw fare: Uncooked foods.

Receiving room: The point at which incoming supplies are checked in, weighed, and routed to destinations within the operation.

Recruitment: The process by which prospective employees are attracted to a restaurant for employment.

Refrigerator: Reach-in and walk-in cooling units for cold storage of foods.

Reorder point: The point at which more of an item is required to be ordered.

Responsible alcoholic beverage service: Serving alcoholic beverages responsibly.

Restaurant concepts: Various styles and themes of restaurants.

Retarder: Equipment used to slow down rising of bakery products.

Riesling: A white wine grape originally from Germany.

Rotisserie: A cooking appliance fitted with a spit on which food is rotated before or over a source of heat.

Rule of 72: A simple method of calculating the number of years required to double money at a particular rate of interest. Divide the rate of return into 72 to obtain the result.

Salamander: A broilerlike stove with heat from above and a shelf below; it has an open front so that dishes can be put on the lower shelf for glazing.

Sauvignon Blanc: A green skinned grape from the Bordeaux region of France that makes good white wines.

S corporation: A type of business that permits the business entity to operate as a corporation but allows it to avoid paying corporation taxes.

Scullery: A place where culinary utensils and tableware are cleaned and kept.

Segmented: Segmenting the market up into segments of like minds and behaviors.

Selected cuts of meat: Cuts of meat that have been selected for use in the restaurant.

Selection: The process of selecting an applicant.

Self-leveling dispenser: Equipment that dispenses dishes, automatically keeping them at counter level.

Service: Refers to serving restaurant guests and internal staff—cooks, servers, dishwashers.

Service Corps of Retired Executives (SCORE): Retired executives who offer assistance and advice to startup and operating restaurants.

Service encounter: The encounter between a guest and a server or other restaurant employee.

Sexual harassment: Unwelcome advances, requests for sexual favors, and other verbal or physical conduct of a sexual nature.

Side of beef: Half a beef carcass.

Single-use real estate loan: A loan that, typically, runs for less than 20 years.

Slicing machine: Motor-driven machine for slicing meats and other foods.

Slip and fall: The action when a guest or employee slips on a wet floor or something on the floor, causing a fall and injury.

Slow cooking: Cooking slowly.

Small Business Investment Companies (SBIC): SBIC's may provide some investment opportunities for startup restaurants.

Social distance: In a restaurant, booths and other decor separate tables/guests by giving a territory space to each.

Soft sell: Selling in a low-key manner.

Sole proprietorship: When one person operates a restaurant.

Soufflé cup: Cup used to cook souffléd ingredients; soufflés are made with enough egg whites to make them puff during cooking.

Sous vide: A technique of preparing food during slack times then individually vacuum packing items to be refrigerated for future use.

Speed gun: A dispenser for serving popular sodas and mixes for making up drink orders.

Speed rack: The rack where a bar's well brands are stored for speedy service.

Standards for food: Food specifications.

Steakhouse restaurant: A restaurant specializing in steaks.

Steam cooker (steamer): Equipment with steam-heated compartments in which pans of food are cooked. Some include a forced convection feature, with steam constantly moved by fan.

Steam-jacketed kettle: A kettle with a double jacket that steam enters; the steam is used to heat the contents of the kettle.

Steam table: A table having openings to hold containers of cooked food over steam or hot water circulating beneath them.

Stockpiling credit: Accruing good credit by taking positive financial measures.

Stockpot: A large pot in which stock, as for soup or gravy, is prepared.

Stored labor: The technique of preparing food during slow periods for use during rush periods.

Strategic plans: Plans devised to steer the organization toward its vision and mission.

SWOT assessment/analysis: SWOT assessment is done by comparing the organization to its competitors and the general business environment.

Table management: A software program that facilitates the efficient and effective management of restaurant tables.

Tact: Be appropriate.

Target market: The market segment that a restaurant identifies as having the greatest potential for customers.

Task and job analysis: Analyzing the related sequence of tasks that makes up a job.

Team: A special kind of group.

Term loan: A loan that requires only interest payments until the last day of its term, at which time the full payment is due; an intermediate or long-term secured loan granted to a business by a commercial bank, insurance company, or commercial finance company, usually to finance capital equipment or provide working capital.

Theme restaurant: A restaurant having a particular theme.

Tequila: Tequila is a spirit distilled from the agave plant.

Thermostat: An automatic device for regulating the temperature of cooking, heating, or cooling equipment.

Third-party liability: Liability that extends to owners, managers, bartenders, and servers if they serve alcohol to persons who are intoxicated.

Tilting skillets: Large skillets that are used for cooking quantities of various foods: meats, sauces, and pastas.

Tourist menu: Menu designed to attract tourists' attention to a particular restaurant or for acceptability to guests from foreign countries.

Training schedule: A schedule for training.

Tureen: A deep, footed vessel with a cover from which cooked foods (as soup, sauce, or eggs) are served at table.

Two-and-a-half-times (2½) rule: Measure the contact with each patron and party in the restaurant during the course of a meal. A hello when they come in equals ½ contact. A contact during the meal to obtain feedback equals 1 contact. A contact when the meal is over equals 1 contact. Adding them gives you a total of 2½ contacts.

Under bar: The part of the bar under the front counter where the bartender prepares drinks.

Underliner: A doily or blotting circle placed under a dish or cup to absorb drops of moisture from condensation or spills.

Urn: A closed vessel, usually with a spout, for serving beverages, such as tea and coffee.

USDA wholesale produce grades: USDA grades for wholesale produce.

Utensil: Tableware or kitchenware used in the storage, preparation, conveying, or serving of food (includes such items as scoops, scrapers, measures, knives, hand peelers, cooks' spoons, whisks, pots, and pans).

Value: An amount considered to be a suitable equivalent for something else. In a restaurant setting value relates to the price paid for the meal experience.

Variable costs: Expenses that change proportionately to fluctuations in sales.

Vegan: A strict vegetarian who does not eat any animal or dairy products at all.

Vegetable cutter: A device that cuts, slices, grates, and shreds vegetables; it may include plates for cutting potatoes into french-fry and julienne sizes.

Vegetarian: A person who eats no meat or fish.

Vendor: Seller; supplier.

Vintage: A fine wine of a specific year that is generally kept for a few years to mature.

Vision: What a person or company aspires to be.

Vodka: A clear and odorless distilled spirit that often comes with various flavors.

Walk-in refrigerator: A refrigerated area with doors through which people and carts carrying merchandise may enter.

Waterless cooker: A cooking utensil of heavy metal in which foods are cooked in their own juices.

Well or pouring brand: The brand kept in the well for pouring regular—non called for—drinks.

White Zinfandel: A pinkish color blush wine made from the red Zinfandel grape.

Wholesale cut: A specific cut of meat sold wholesale.

Wine: The fermented juice of freshly gathered grapes.

Whisky: A distilled spirit from malt of grain known as Scotch, when it comes from Scotland and is otherwise called Whisky. In Ireland is spelled—whiskey.

Work centers: A creation of Dr. Arthur Avery where work centers are part of a food system from storage to service.

Working capital: The excess of current assets over current liabilities, or the pool of resources readily available to maintain normal business operations.

Zinfandel: A red grape that is planted in about 10 percent of the California vinyards.

Index

A

ABC (Department of Alcoholic Beverage Control), 190, 215
ABT (Alcohol Beverage and Tobacco), 190
Accessibility
    Americans with Disabilities Act (ADA), 319
    criteria, 96–97
Access to streets, 90
Accommodation, 295, 300
Accuracy in menus, 120–122, 137
Acquired Immune Deficiency Syndrome. *See* AIDS
Action plans, 401, 408, 421
Active listening, 288
Actual market share, 403, 404, 421
Adams, John, 7
Adaptation of restaurant concepts, 72–74
ADR (alternative dispute resolution), 297–299, 300
Advertising, 81, 417–418, 419
African American influences, 248
Age discrimination, 317, 318, 326
Age Discrimination Act (1967), 318
AIDS (Acquired Immune Deficiency Syndrome), 319–320, 326
Alcohol Beverage and Tobacco. *See* ABT
Alcoholic beverages
    licenses, 190–192, 215
    responsible alcoholic beverage service, 190, 211–212, 215
Aliens, employment of undocumented, 316
Allergies, food, 116–117
Almandine, 249
Alternative dispute resolution. *See* ADR
Ambiance, 18, 410, 421
American Gas Association, 144
American Revolution, 7
American-style restaurants, 9–11
Americans with Disabilities Act (ADA), 318, 320, 326
Analysis
    competition, 408
    conflict, 295

job, 326
productivity, 242–243, 436
products, 421
SWOT (strengths, weaknesses, opportunities, and threats), 404, 421
Anderson, Erik, 62
Anonymous shoppers, 223–227
Antioxidants, 170
AP (as purchased), 178
Appeals, advertising, 419
Appetizers
    menus, 124
    serving process, 222
Applebee's, 15, 34
Applications
    loans, 427–432
    questions to avoid on job, 320–324
Applying for alcohol licenses, 191–192
Arbitration, 298
Aromatic wines, 205, 215
Asian restaurants, 42–43
As purchased (AP), 178
Assessment, market, 406–407
Associates, 281–282
Atkin's diet, 118
Atlanta Bread Company, 32
Atmospherics, 411, 421
Au Bon Pain, 32
Auto/valet liability insurance, 455
Availability of ingredients, 108–109, 137
Avoidance, 295, 300
Awards, 51

B

Bacillus cereus, 264
Back bar, 193, 215
Back-office, 362
Back of the house, 220, 227–228, 243, 362–364, 381
Back-of-the-house green, 146–147

C